U.S. Department of Agriculture

SHOPPER'S GUIDE

How to get the most for your money

U.S. Department of Agriculture

SHOPPER'S GUIDE

How to get the most for your money

BARRON'S EDUCATIONAL SERIES / WOODBURY, N.Y.

The publisher gratefully acknowledges the kindness of all organizations concerned with granting us permission to reprint their photographs, sketches, and diagrams. Because this list is so extensive, we have included them all in the section "Sources of Photography" located on page 351.

Published in 1975 by
Barron's Educational Series, Inc.
113 Crossways Park Drive
Woodbury, N.Y. 11797

International Standard Book No. 0-8120-0607-0
Library of Congress Catalog No. 74-600137

PRINTED IN THE UNITED STATES OF AMERICA

2 3 4 5 6 7 8 9 10 11 M 7 6 5

CONTENTS

HOW TO BE A SMART FOOD SHOPPER

The RDA's–Daily Dietary Allowances 2
Combining Foods to Your Own Best Advantage 5
Food for the Family at Different Costs 18
How Much Food Should You Buy 21
Food Cost Tables to Help Stretch Your Dollars 27
Can's and Can'ts for Canners 41
The Cold Facts about Freezing 44
USDA Grades Can Help Out Food Shoppers 51
Behind the Label: Federal Food Standards 55
Nutrient Labeling and Guidelines 62
Organic, Inorganic: What They Mean 70
How the Shopper Benefits from Nutrition Labeling 73
Guides to Buying–Open Dating and Price Per Unit 76
Food Shopper Language 78
Always Play It Safe in Food Buying, Handling, Cooking 87

HOW TO IMPROVE YOUR HOME

Home Improvements Using Concrete 90
All about Brick and the 10,000 Ways It Comes 93
Concrete Block–A Wide Choice for Different Jobs 98
Framing Lumber, Board Selection 102
Plywood for Jobs around the Home 108
Panel Products to Choose from 112
Airing the Facts about Ventilation 115
Floor Coverings–Resilient, Wood, Tiles and Clay 118
Your Own Pool to Get in the Swim 122
Electrical Wiring: Homeowner Tips 125
Picking the Right Types of Pipe 130
Insulating to Save Energy in Heating, Cooling a Home 133
Selecting Doors and Windows 137
Keeping a Roof over Your Head 142
Exterior, Interior Wall Materials 146
Adding Carports, Garages, Storage 149
Heating and Cooling Systems and Fuels 154

HOW TO CHOOSE HOUSEHOLD EQUIPMENT TO FIT YOUR NEEDS

Kitchen Appliances, Including Freezers and Range Hoods 164
Washers, Dryers, Related Equipment 168
Imaginative Ways with Bathrooms 170
Cozy Fireplaces, Franklin Stoves, Other Heaters 175
Lighting Fixtures and Equipment 179
How to Avoid Those Tumble Out Closets 183
Window Treatments: Curtains, Shades, Shutters, Drapes 186
New Furniture—Getting Value for Your Investment 190
Furnishings Tips for Your Outdoor Living Areas 195
The A, B, C's of Cleaning Materials 198
Tools You Need for Repair Jobs 202

HOW TO MAKE YOUR GARDEN BLOOM

Buying Seeds—Pellets, Tapes and Blankets 206
Seedlings Guide: Grow Your Own or Buy Them 208
Buying and Caring for Cut Flowers; Arrangements 219
Potted Plants to Brighten Your Life 222
Those Fascinating Cacti, and Other Succulent Plants 226
Tips on Interior Landscaping 230
Trees and Shrubs for the Landscape 233
A Rose Is a Rose, but Roses Come by the Thousands 236
Ground Covers and the Vines 241
Nursery Stock—What to Buy and What to Expect 246
Home Gardening with Small Fruits 250
Apples, Cherries, Pears, Plums and Other Tree Fruits 253
Subtropical Fruits for Warm Climates or Tub Growing 256
The Why and How of Garden Design 261
Botanic Gardens and Arboretums 266

HOW TO SHOP WISELY FOR SERVICES

When You Move—Do's and Don'ts 272
Where You Shop Is as Important as What You Buy 277
The Steps to Take when a Purchase Doesn't Satisfy 282
Ways to Shop the Educational Marketplace 286
The Federal-State Food Programs—A Helping Hand 290
Toward a Network of Service for Older Americans 295
Shopping for Credit Can Save You Cash 298
Having Appliances Repaired for a Minimum Cost 302
Servicing Your Car without Anguish 306
Putting Your Finger on Green Thumb Garden Helpers 310

HOW TO MAKE THE MOST OF YOUR LEISURE TIME

Vacation Planning, with Tips for Trips to Save Your Gas 314
From the Horse's Mouth—How Not to Ride for a Fall 321
Wheeling Along with a Bicycle 324
Backpacking Gear: Shoes and Packs to Sleeping Bags 327

Keeping Afloat with a Boat 332
Basic Equipment for Fishermen 335
Bring It All Back Alive—on Film 339
Don't Rush Out for a Ski Outfit: Make Sure It's Your Snowflake 344
Bow and Arrow Hunting Gear 348

SOURCES OF PHOTOGRAPHY 351

INDEX 352

PREFACE

U.S. Department of Agriculture Shopper's Guide is essentially the *1974 Yearbook of Agriculture.* Most of the authors are from the U.S. Department of Agriculture (USDA) and the state land grant universities and colleges; they have drawn heavily on federal and state research. Other authors are affiliated with federal agencies outside the USDA, with associations, and with magazines. Combined, their expertise in a wide variety of consumer affairs makes this book extremely valuable for the shopper.

In addition to the authors, many other individuals have contributed to this book. Paul W. Wertz, Chief of the Printing Branch, Office of Communication, USDA, served as production coordinator. Members of the Yearbook staff include Jack Hayes, Yearbook editor; Mary Vest; and Denver Browning. Ruth Leverton, formerly at the Agricultural Research Service, was chairwoman of the 1974 Yearbook Committee that planned this book. Helen Souders, a member of the Agricultural Research Service, was vice chairwoman. Nineteen other committee members represented a variety of federal agencies and associations: Agricultural Marketing Service, Agricultural Research Service, American Association of Nurserymen, Animal and Plant Health Inspection Service, Cooperative State Research Service, Economic Research Service, Extension Service, Farmers Home Administration, Food and Nutrition Service, Forest Service, and National Park Service.

INTRODUCTION

As PRICES rise and purchasing power dwindles, getting the most for one's money has become an essential concern of all but the very wealthiest of American consumers. No longer are comparison shopping, careful study of available purchase options, and protests against consumer "rip-offs" confined to the home economist or the consumer advocate. Simply stated, the great majority of Americans have become, or would like to become, their own "home economists" and "consumer advocates." *U.S. Department of Agriculture Shopper's Guide* is designed to show you how to shop wisely for a sizeable number of the major purchases you are likely to make—food, home improvements, household equipment, garden supplies, services, and leisure-time activities.

"HOW TO BE A SMART FOOD SHOPPER" explains daily dietary allowances, federal food grading, nutrient labeling, food dating, unit pricing, organic and inorganic foods, and home freezing and canning. It also provides you with guidelines on how much food to buy and how to stretch your food dollars without sacrificing your family's nutrition or taste buds.

"HOW TO IMPROVE YOUR HOME" tells homeowners how they can "do it themselves" with such materials as concrete, brick, lumber, plywood, floor covering, pipe, electrical wiring, and insulation. The section explains the uses of each material, how to select the proper material, how to get the job done, and how to recognize a job that is beyond the skills of an amateur.

"HOW TO CHOOSE HOUSEHOLD EQUIPMENT TO FIT YOUR NEEDS" is a boon to anyone who has ever faced a smooth-talking salesman and his assurances that this washing machine or that outdoor furniture set is "just what you need." Kitchen appliances, washers and dryers, lighting fixtures, new furniture, and household tools are some of the items discussed in this section.

"HOW TO MAKE YOUR GARDEN BLOOM" will convince you that green thumbs are made, not born. This section includes a broad survey of gardening, including buying seeds, trees and shrubs, rose bushes, nursery stock, fruit trees, garden design, and cut flowers. The indoor gardener has not been neglected—tips are included on growing potted plants and on interior landscaping.

"HOW TO SHOP WISELY FOR SERVICES" can prevent you from developing post-purchase headaches. This section tells you how to choose where to shop, how to pick a moving company, what to do when you are not satisfied with a purchase, how to shop for credit, and how to have your appliances and car repaired without losing either sleep or your bank account. How to take advantage of government food programs and what services are available to senior citizens are also included.

"HOW TO MAKE THE MOST OF YOUR LEISURE TIME" explores some of the most popular forms of recreation available today: horsemanship, bicycling, backpacking, boating, fishing, photography, skiing, and archery. These articles are especially helpful for the novice who is about to buy recreational equipment, but they can prove just as timely to the experienced sportsman. This section also gives tips on planning a gas-saving vacation.

The huge variety of goods and services available in the marketplace need not overwhelm and confuse you. *U.S. Department of Agriculture Shopper's Guide* can supply you with the essentials you need to purchase the best product at the best price.

FOOD

The RDA's—Daily Dietary Allowances

FOOD SHOPPERS are now seeing new labels on some foods showing the percentage of the U.S. Recommended Daily Allowances (U.S. RDA) of protein, vitamins and minerals in a serving of the food. The U. S. RDA were established by the Food and Drug Administration (FDA) to implement regulations for showing the nutrient content of foods on labels.

A single value for each nutrient was derived by the FDA from the Recommended Daily Dietary Allowances (RDA) for different age and sex groups. The RDA are developed by the Food and Nutrition Board of the National Academy of Sciences, National Research Council (NAS-NRC).

A clear differentiation between the terms and purposes of the RDA and the U.S. RDA is important for shoppers who are concerned with planning nutritious diets for themselves and others. In this chapter you will learn about the evolution of the RDA and how the U. S. RDA are derived from them.

The Food and Nutrition Board was first established in 1940 as a Committee on Food and Nutrition within the NAS-NRC to advise on nutrition problems in connection with national defense. One of its first concerns was to define in accordance with the latest information the recommended daily allowances for the various dietary essentials for people of different ages.

In May 1941 Dr. Russell M. Wilder, Chairman of the Committee on Food and Nutrition, presented the first RDA to the public via radio. The first published issue of the RDA was in 1943. Seven revisions have subsequently been made: 1945, 1948, 1953, 1958, 1964, 1968 and 1973 (published in 1974).

The periodic changes in the RDA made by the Food and Nutrition Board reflect the fact that knowledge about human nutrition is being expanded continuously by research. As more precise knowledge of the range of known nutrient requirements of different age groups becomes available, this information is reviewed and evaluated by scientists with the Food and Nutrition Board.

RDA represent the judgment of the Food and Nutrition Board about levels of intake of essential nutrients considered adequate to meet the known nutritional needs of almost any healthy person.

All editions of RDA have consisted of a tabulation of the daily amounts of kilocalories (1,000 calories) and selected nutrients for different age and sex groups, a text discussion of the basis for the tabulated allowances, and a consideration of nutrients not tabulated.

AUTHOR *Helen J. Souders* is Staff Specialist on the National Program Staff of the Agricultural Research Service.

Children enjoy good food. Wisely chosen food for school lunches, snacks, and meals at home all contribute their share of nutrients for good health.

Tabulations in the first six editions included kilocalories, protein, calcium, iron, vitamin A, thiamin, riboflavin, niacin, ascorbic acid and vitamin D.

The number of age categories of groups as well as the daily allowances for some nutrients have been changed from time to time.

In 1968 seven nutrients not previously tabulated were given specific recommended allowances: vitamin E, folacin, vitamin B_6, vitamin B_{12}, phosphorus, magnesium and iodine. Some changes were also made in the age categories and in the amounts of nutrients recommended in previous editions.

In the 1973 revision, zinc was added to the tabulated nutrients and the number of age categories was decreased. Major reductions were made in the RDA for protein, ascorbic acid, vitamin E and vitamin B_{12}. The vitamin A allowance for adult females was reduced, but no change was made for adult males. Changes in age-sex groups necessitated minor adjustments for folacin, niacin, riboflavin, thiamin and vitamin B_6. Only minor adjustments were made in the RDA for calcium, phosphorus and magnesium.

The U.S. RDA, except for calcium and phosphorus, were derived from the highest value for each nutrient in the 1968 RDA of NAS-NRC for males and females four or more years of age, excluding pregnant and lactating females. RDA for calcium and phosphorus were each set at 1.0 gram. In addition the FDA established specific U.S. RDA for four nutrients not tabulated in the 1968 RDA of the NAS-NRC—biotin, pantothenic acid, copper and zinc.

The U.S. RDA for protein was set at 45 grams if the Protein Efficiency Ratio (PER) of the total protein in the food is equal to or greater than that of casein, and 65 grams if the PER is less than that of casein. PER is a measure of the quality of protein for growth. Casein, the chief protein of milk, is used as the comparative protein in standardized tests of PER.

The U.S. RDA for minerals and vitamins are shown in tabular form.

In the rules and regulations for nutrition labeling FDA stated: "It is anticipated that the U.S. RDA values will be amended periodically to concur with major changes that may be made in the

Recommended Daily Dietary Allowances,[1] Revised 1973

Designed for the maintenance of good nutrition of practically all healthy people in the U.S.A.

(Years) From Up to	Weight (kg)	Weight (lbs)	Height (in)	Energy (kcal)	Protein (g)	Fat-Soluble Vitamins: Vitamin A Activity (IU)	Vitamin D (IU)	Vitamin E Activity (IU)	Water-Soluble Vitamins: Ascorbic Acid (mg)	Folacin (mg)	Niacin (mg)	Riboflavin (mg)	Thiamin (mg)	Vitamin B_6 (mg)	Vitamin B_{12} (mg)	Minerals: Calcium (mg)	Phosphorus (mg)	Iodine (mg)	Iron (mg)	Magnesium (mg)	Zinc
INFANTS																					
0.0-0.5	6	14	24	kg x 117	kg x 2.2	1400	400	4	35	50	5	0.4	0.3	0.3	0.3	360	240	35	10	60	3
0.5-1.0	9	20	28	kg x 108	kg x 2.0	2000	400	5	35	50	8	0.6	0.5	0.4	0.3	540	400	45	15	70	5
CHILDREN																					
1-3		28	34	1300	23	2000	400	7	40	100	9	0.8	0.7	0.6	1.0	800	800	60	15	150	10
4-6		44	44	1800	30	2500	400	9	40	200	12	1.1	0.9	0.9	1.5	800	800	80	10	200	10
7-10		66	54	2400	36	3300	400	10	40	300	16	1.2	1.2	1.2	2.0	800	800	110	10	250	10
MALES																					
11-14		97	63	2800	44	5000	400	12	45	400	18	1.5	1.4	1.6	3.0	1200	1200	130	18	350	15
15-18		134	69	3000	54	5000	400	15	45	400	20	1.8	1.5	2.0	3.0	1200	1200	150	18	400	15
19-22		147	69	3000	54	5000	400	15	45	400	20	1.8	1.5	2.0	3.0	800	800	140	10	350	15
23-50		154	69	2700	56	5000	—	15	45	400	18	1.6	1.4	2.0	3.0	800	800	130	10	350	15
51+		154	69	2400	56	5000	—	15	45	400	16	1.5	1.2	2.0	3.0	800	800	110	10	350	15
FEMALES																					
11-14		97	62	2400	44	4000	400	12	45	400	16	1.3	1.2	1.6	3.0	1200	1200	115	18	300	15
15-18		119	65	2100	48	4000	400	12	45	400	14	1.4	1.1	2.0	3.0	1200	1200	115	18	300	15
19-22		128	65	2100	46	4000	400	12	45	400	14	1.4	1.1	2.0	3.0	800	800	100	18	300	15
23-50		128	65	2000	46	4000	—	12	45	400	13	1.2	1.0	2.0	3.0	800	800	100	18	300	15
51+		128	65	1800	46	4000	—	12	45	400	12	1.1	1.0	2.0	3.0	800	800	80	10	300	15
PREGNANT																					
				+300	+30	5000	400	15	60	800	+2	+0.3	+0.3	2.5	4.0	1200	1200	125	18+[2]	450	20
LACTATING																					
				+500	+20	6000	400	15	80	600	+4	+0.5	+0.3	2.5	4.0	1200	1200	150	18	450	25

IU stands for International Unit.
1 kilogram (kg) = 2.2 pounds (lbs)
1 kilogram (kg) = 1,000 grams (g)

1 kilocalorie (kcal) = 1,000 calories
1 gram (g) = 1,000 milligrams (mg)
1 milligram (mg) = 1,000 micrograms (mcg)

[1] Slightly abridged.
[2] This increased requirement cannot be met by ordinary diets; therefore, the use of supplemental iron is recommended.

National Academy of Sciences—National Research Council RDA values."

You can expect that in due time the FDA will decrease U.S. RDA values for protein, ascorbic acid, vitamin E, and vitamin B_{12} to reflect the 1973 revision of the RDA. The rules and regulations for applying the U.S. RDA in nutrition labeling are discussed in another chapter in this section of the yearbook.

VITAMINS AND MINERALS
U.S. RECOMMENDED DAILY ALLOWANCES
(U.S. RDA)

NUTRIENT	U.S. RDA
Vitamin A	5,000 I.U.
Vitamin C (ascorbic acid)	60.0 mg.
Thiamin (vitamin B_1)	1.5 mg.
Riboflavin (vitamin B_2)	1.7 mg.
Niacin	20.0 mg.
Calcium	1.0 g
Iron	18.0 mg.
Vitamin D	400 I.U.
Vitamin E	30 I.U.
Vitamin B_6	2.0 mg.
Folacin (folic acid)	0.4 mg.
Vitamin B_{12}	6.0 mcg.
Phosphorus	1.0 g.
Iodine	150 mcg.
Magnesium	400 mg.
Zinc	15 mg.
Copper	2.0 mg.
Biotin	0.3 mg.
Pantothenic acid	10.0 mg.

NOTE: The first seven nutrients require label listing; others may be included on labels. (See earlier table for explanation of abbreviations).

You should bear in mind that U.S. RDA are being used to give you information about the nutrient content of foods. Hints on how consumers can use this information are given in the chapter beginning on page 73.

FOR FURTHER READING:

Food and Nutrition Board. *Recommended Dietary Allowances,* eighth revised edition, for sale by National Academy of Sciences, 2101 Constitution Ave., N.W., Washington, D.C. 20418.

Food and Drug Administration. *Food Labeling,* Federal Register, Vol. 38, No. 13, Jan. 19, 1973.

Combining Foods To Your Own Best Advantage

YOU CAN EAT any food you like if you know how to combine it with other foods to provide yourself a desirable diet. And it is easy to learn to do this.

Furthermore, it is to your advantage to learn to select and eat a diet that you enjoy and that at the same time promotes nutritional health. Good nutrition not only adds to the joy of living but makes a difference in how you look, how you feel, and how well you can work and play.

It is not necessary that everyone make the same food choices. Lifestyles, national origins, religious beliefs, individual tastes, prices, and shopping and preparation time all influence the choices we make. We are fortunate to have a wonderfully abundant and varied food supply made up of foods at many price levels.

We can buy foods fresh, frozen, canned, dried, partially prepared, completely prepared, fortified with nutrients, and even fabricated foods such as fruit-flavored beverages with vitamin C added. All these foods are temptingly displayed and lavishly recommended. It is no wonder, then, that some people make better choices than others as far as meeting individual nutrient and energy needs is concerned.

Scientists have established human requirements and made recommendations for amounts of a number of nutrients and for calories for people of all ages. Nutritionists have translated these recommendations into kinds and amounts

AUTHOR *Mary M. Hill* is a nutritionist in the Consumer and Food Economics Institute, Agricultural Research Service.

of food needed for a good nutritional foundation. These translations are known as food guides. If followed, they provide an easy way to make desirable food choices.

Food for Fitness—a Daily Food Guide (Leaflet 424) is a reliable one. It was developed by U.S. Department of Agriculture nutritionists and is for sale by the Superintendent of Documents, Washington, D.C. 20402. It groups foods into four broad categories and allows for innumerable choices within the groups. They are as follows:

Milk and milk products

Foods included:

Milk—fluid whole, evaporated, skim, skim dry, buttermilk

Cheese—cottage, cream, Cheddar type (natural or processed)

Ice cream

Amount recommended:

Some milk every day for everyone

Recommended amounts are given below in terms of whole fluid milk:

	8-ounce cups
Children under 9	2 to 3
Children 9 to 12	3 or more
Teenagers	4 or more
Adults	2 or more
Pregnant women	3 or more
Nursing mothers	4 or more

Part or all of the milk may be fluid skim milk, buttermilk, evaporated milk, or dry milk.

Cheese and ice cream may replace part of the milk. The amount required to replace a given quantity of milk is figured on the basis of calcium content. Common portions of various kinds of cheese and of ice cream and their milk equivalents in calcium are:

1-inch cube Cheddar-type cheese = ½ cup milk

½ cup cottage cheese = 1/3 cup milk

2 tablespoons cream cheese = 1 tablespoon milk

½ cup ice cream or ice milk = 1/3 cup milk

Contribution to diet:

Milk is our leading source of calcium, which is needed for bones and teeth. It also provides high-quality protein, riboflavin, vitamin A, and many other nutrients.

Calcium:

Calcium is the most abundant mineral element in the body. Teamed up with phosphorus, it is largely responsible for the hardness of bones and teeth. About 99 percent of the calcium in the body is found in these two tissues.

The small amount of calcium in other body tissues and fluids aids in the proper functioning of the heart, muscles, and nerves, and helps the blood coagulate during bleeding.

- Calcium is not absorbed into the body completely.
- The extent of absorption varies with individuals and conditions.
- Human adults can be expected to absorb from 20 to 50 percent of calcium in a mixed diet.

Milk is outstanding as a source of calcium. Appreciable amounts are contributed by cheese (especially the Cheddar types), ice cream, certain dark-green leafy vegetables (collards, kale, mustard greens, turnip greens), and canned sardines (if the bones are eaten).

Riboflavin—one of the B vitamins:

- Helps cells use oxygen to release energy from food.
- Helps keep eyes healthy.
- Helps keep skin around mouth and nose smooth.

Fruits and vegetables

Foods included:

All vegetables and fruit. This guide emphasizes those that are valuable as sources of vitamin C and vitamin A.

Amount recommended:

Choose four or more servings every day, including:

One serving of a good source of vitamin C, or two servings of a fair source.

One serving, at least every other day,

(Top) fruits and vegetables, one of the basic food groups. (Above) bread and cereals, another of the basic food groups.

of a good source of vitamin A. If the food chosen for vitamin C is also a good source of vitamin A, the additional serving of a vitamin A food may be omitted.

The remaining one to three or more servings may be of any vegetable or fruit, including those that are valuable for vitamin C and vitamin A.

Count as one serving: ½ cup of vegetable or fruit, or a portion as ordinarily served, such as one medium apple, banana, orange, or potato; half a medium grapefruit or cantaloupe; or the juice of one lemon.

Contribution to diet:

Fruits and vegetables are valuable, chiefly because of the vitamins and minerals that they contain. In this plan, these foods are relied on to supply nearly all the vitamin C needed and over one-half of the vitamin A.

Vitamin C is needed for healthy gums and body tissues. Vitamin A is needed for growth, normal vision, and healthy condition of skin and other body surfaces. Vitamin C:

• Helps hold body cells together and strengthens walls of blood cells.
• Helps build bones and teeth.
• Helps in healing wounds.
• Helps resist infection.

Sources of vitamin C:

Good sources—Grapefruit or grapefruit juice, oranges or orange juice, cantaloupes, guava, mangoes, papaya, raw strawberries, broccoli, brussels sprouts, green peppers, and sweet red peppers.

Fair sources—Honeydew melons, lemons, tangerines or tangerine juice, watermelons, asparagus tips, raw cabbage, cauliflower, collards, garden cress, kale, kohlrabi, mustard greens, potatoes and sweet potatoes cooked in the jacket, rutabagas, spinach, tomatoes or tomato juice, and turnip greens.

Vitamin A:

• Helps eyes adjust to dim light.
• Helps keep lining of mouth, nose, throat, and digestive tract healthy and resistant to infection.
• Keeps skin healthy.
• Promotes growth.

Vitamin A occurs only in foods of animal origin. However, many vegetables and fruits—particularly the green and yellow ones—contain a substance called carotene that the body can change into vitamin A.

Liver is outstanding for vitamin A. Important amounts are found also in eggs, butter, margarine, whole milk, and cheese made with whole milk. Carotene is found in largest amounts in dark-green and deep-yellow vegetables and in deep-yellow fruits.

Fiber:

Fiber provides bulk in diets and promotes motility and health of the gastrointestinal tract.

Foods that are bulky, coarse, or watery crisp are sources of fiber. Sometimes, foods as we know them are fine or smooth, but are also sources of fiber. Examples are cocoa and chocolate that have been ground. Other good fiber sources include fruits and vegetables such as apples, plums, pineapples, carrots, celery, and cabbage; legumes, such as dried peas and beans; and whole-grain cereals.

Bread and Cereals

Foods included:

All breads and cereals that are whole grain, enriched, or restored; check labels to be sure.

Specifically, this group includes: breads, cooked cereals, ready-to-eat cereals, cornmeal, crackers, flour and grits, macaroni and spaghetti, noodles, rice, rolled oats, and quick breads and other baked goods, if made with whole-grain or enriched flour. Parboiled rice and wheat may also be included in this group.

Amounts recommended:

Choose four servings or more daily; or if no cereals are chosen, have an extra serving of breads or baked goods. This will make at least five servings from this group daily.

Count as one serving: One slice of bread; 1 ounce ready-to-eat cereal; ½ to ¾ cup cooked cereal, cornmeal, grits, macaroni, noodles, rice, or spaghetti.

Contribution to diet:

Foods in this group furnish worthwhile amounts of protein, iron, several of the B vitamins, and food energy. Small amounts of many other nutrients may also be present.

Food energy:

• Energy is needed to support the many functions of the body at work or play.

• Energy comes from fats, carbohydrates, and proteins in the food you eat.

• Fat is the most concentrated source of energy—it supplies more than twice as much energy for a given weight as protein or carbohydrate.

• Energy is measured in calories.

• Alcohol also supplies energy and ranks next to fat as a source—providing about three-fourths as much energy as an equal weight of fat.

All foods furnish calories, some much less in a given serving than others. Foods that contain appreciable amounts of water are relatively low in calories, because water has no caloric value and thus dilutes the energy-yielding nutrients. Many fresh fruits and vegetables are in this category. However, when sugar, fats, or cream are added to them, calories increase.

Foods rich in fat, starch, or sugar, and beverages high in alcohol, are rich in calories.

Meat or alternates

Foods included:

Beef, veal, lamb, pork, variety meats such as liver, heart, and kidneys.

Poultry and eggs.

Fish and shellfish.

As alternates—dry beans, dry peas, lentils, nuts, peanuts, peanut butter.

Amounts recommended:

Choose two or more servings every day.

Count as a serving: 2 to 3 ounces (not including bone weight) cooked lean meat, poultry, or fish.

Count as alternates for ½ serving meat or fish: one egg; ½ cup cooked dry beans, dry peas, or lentils; or 2 tablespoons peanut butter.

Contribution to diet:

Foods in this group are valued for their protein, which is needed for growth and repair of body tissues—muscle, organs, blood, skin, and hair. These foods also provide iron, thiamin, riboflavin, and niacin and other nutrients.

Protein:

- Builds and repairs all tissues.
- Helps form antibodies to fight infection.
- Supplies food energy.
- Helps to make hemoglobin, the blood protein that carries oxygen to the cells and carries carbon dioxide away from the cells.
- To have daily meals rank well in protein quality, only part of the protein must come from animal sources. Combining cereal and vegetable foods with a little meat or with another source of animal protein will improve the protein value of the meal. Examples of nourishing combinations are cereal with milk, rice with fish, spaghetti with meat sauce, and vegetable stew with meat. You could simply have milk as a beverage along with foods of plant origin. It is a good idea to have some food from animal sources at each meal.
- You need protein all through life for the maintenance and repair of body tissues. Children urgently need protein for normal growth.

Courtesy of Better Homes and Gardens

Important amounts of protein are found in meat, poultry, fish, milk, cheese, eggs, dry beans, dry peas, and nuts.

Bread, cereals, vegetables, and fruits contain relatively smaller amounts of protein. However, the quantity of bread—and perhaps of cereal—eaten daily may be large enough to make these foods important protein sources.

Iron:

Iron combines with protein to make hemoglobin, the red substance of blood that carries oxygen from the lungs to muscle, brain, and other parts of the body.

Only a few foods contain much iron. Liver is a particularly good source. Lean meats, hearts, kidneys, shellfish, dry beans, dry peas, dark-green vegetables, dried fruit, egg yolks, and molasses also count as good sources. Whole-grain and enriched bread and cereals contain smaller amounts of iron, but when eaten frequently become important sources.

Frequent use of foods that provide important amounts of iron is particularly encouraged for young children, preteen and teenage girls, and for women of child-bearing age. Research shows that these are the groups whose diets are most likely to be low in iron.

B vitamins—thiamin, niacin, and riboflavin:

• Play a central role in release of energy from food.

• Help with proper functioning of nerves, normal appetite, good digestion, and healthy skin.

Generally, foods in the meat group are leading sources of these vitamins. Whole-grain and enriched bread and cereals supply smaller but important amounts. A few foods are outstanding sources—milk for riboflavin, lean pork for thiamin, and organ meats for all three.

Getting enough niacin is not a problem if a good amount of protein is included in daily meals. An essential amino acid—tryptophan—present in protein can be changed by the body into niacin.

Other foods

Most people want and need more food than the minimum servings suggested from the four food groups. To round out meals and satisfy appetites, you can include additional foods from the four groups, as well as other foods not listed in these groups. Such foods include unenriched, refined breads; cereals; flours; sugars; butter; margarine; and other fats. These are often ingredients in a recipe, or are added to other foods during preparation or at the table. Fabricated foods can also be included in this group.

Try to include some vegetable oil among the fats used.

Fats:

Fats are concentrated sources of energy. Weight for weight, they give more than twice as much energy, or calories, as either carbohydrates or protein.

Everyone needs some fat. Primarily, the fats supply energy, but they also carry the fat-soluble vitamins A, D, E, and K.

Fats also

• Make up part of the structure of cells.

• Form a protective cushion around vital organs.

• Spare protein for body building and repair by providing energy.

• Supply an essential fatty acid, linoleic acid.

The body does not manufacture linoleic acid, so it must be provided by food. It is found in valuable amounts in many oils that come from plants—particularly corn, cottonseed, safflower, sesame, soybean, and wheat germ. These are referred to as "polyunsaturated" fats or oils. Margarines, salad dressings, mayonnaise, and cooking oils are usually made from one or more of these oils. Nuts contain less linoleic acid than do most vegetable oils. Poultry and fish oils have more linoleic acid than do other animal fats, which rank fairly low as sources.

In choosing daily meals, it is well to keep the total amount of fat at a moderate level and to include some foods that contain polyunsaturated fats.

Common sources of fats are: Butter, margarine, shortening, cooking and salad oils, cream, most cheeses, mayonnaise, salad dressings, nuts, and bacon and other fatty meats. Meats, whole milk, eggs, and chocolate contain some fat naturally. Many popular snacks, baked goods, pastries, and other desserts are made with fat or cooked in it.

The task is to combine foods into meals to meet nutrient and energy needs of various family members, taking into account food preferences of family members, cost, and shopping and preparation time. This is how to use the guide—and it makes no difference whether you eat at home or away from home. (See menu plan on page 11.)

Some people make their choices consistent with their religious beliefs. For example, the selections on page 12 might be made by a Jewish homemaker using the specified amounts per serving as listed in the guide.

Then there are those who enjoy the foods associated with their national origins. Perhaps an Italian would make the choices on page 13, using the food guide to help him select the kinds and amounts of food to meet his nutrient and energy needs.

A Day's Food Intake for an Adult Based on Specific Amounts as Listed in the Food Guide

EARLY MORNING
Fruit-flavored beverage—vitamin C added
Cooked whole wheat cereal with milk
Toast—jam
Coffee

MIDDAY MEAL
Cream of asparagus soup
Tuna salad sandwich   Iced tea
Ice cream

SNACK
Pear

EVENING MEAL
Broiled chicken
Parslied potatoes   Spinach
Lettuce-tomato salad   French dressing
Apricot-tapioca cream pudding
Coffee

EVENING SNACK
Toast with jam
Milk

Nutrional Foundation of This Day's Food

Milk Group 2 cups	Fruit-Veg. Group 4 servings	Meat or Alternate 2 servings	Bread-Cereal—4 servings (enriched or whole grain)
½ cup—on cereal ½ cup—in tapioca 1 cup—as beverage	1 serving pear 1 serving potato 1 serving spinach 1 serving salad	1 serving tuna—in sandwich 1 serving chicken	1 serving cooked whole wheat cereal 2 servings in sandwich 1 slice toast

Foods That Provide Additional Nutrients and Food Energy to Meet Individual Needs

From the 4 Food Groups	From Other Foods
Milk and asparagus in soup Lettuce in sandwich Apricots and other ingredients in the pudding Toast in evening snack	Fruit-flavored beverage—vitamin C added Jam Sugar in iced tea and coffee French dressing on salad Butter on toast and hot vegetables

A Jewish homemaker's plans for a day's meals:

EARLY MORNING

Orange juice

Poached egg   Bagel with butter

Coffee

MIDDAY MEAL

Chopped chicken liver sandwich—rye bread

Perfection salad (mixed vegetables in gelatine)

Watermelon

Hot tea

EVENING MEAL

Broiled halibut

Baked potato   Glazed carrots

Pickled beets   Roll and butter

Cheesecake

Skim milk

EVENING SNACK

Graham crackers   Skim milk

Nutritional Foundation of This Day's Food

Milk Group 2 cups	Fruit-Veg. Group 4 servings	Meat or Alternate 2 servings	Bread-Cereal—4 servings (enriched or whole grain)
2 cups as beverage	Orange juice Watermelon Baked potato Carrots	Chicken liver Halibut	1 bagel 2 slices bread 1 roll

Foods That Provide Additional Nutrients and Food Energy to Meet Individual Needs

From the 4 Food Groups	From Other Foods
Poached egg Hard-cooked egg and onion in chicken liver spread Perfection salad Pickled beets Cheesecake—enriched Graham crackers—enriched	Butter on roll and bagel Sugar for coffee and tea Dressing on salad

An Italian selection from the four food groups:

EARLY MORNING

Banana

Sweet sausage   Scrambled egg

Italian bread (enriched)

Coffee

MIDDAY MEAL

Minestrone   Italian bread

Mixed vegetable salad (lettuce, tomato, green pepper, carrot, onion)—French dressing

Ice cream

Milk

EVENING MEAL

Veal Parmesan   Spaghetti—tomato sauce

Kale   Italian bread

Zabaglione (soft custard flavored with wine)

Coffee

Nutritional Foundation of This Day's Food

Milk Group 2 cups	Fruit-Veg. Group 4 servings	Meat or Alternate 2 servings	Bread-Cereal—4 servings (enriched or whole grain)
1 cup as beverage ½ cup equivalent in ice cream ½ cup in zabaglione	1 serving—banana 1 serving in salad 1 serving—kale 1 serving in minestrone	1 serving—sausage 1 serving—veal	3 servings—Italian bread 1 serving—enriched spaghetti

Foods That Provide Additional Nutrients and Food Energy to Meet Individual Needs

From the 4 Food Groups	From Other Foods
Scrambled egg Milk in coffee Remaining ingredients in minestrone Tomato sauce	Butter or margarine on bread Sugar in coffee French dressing

A day's food intake for a "snacker" might look like this:

7:30 a.m.	**Instant breakfast (instant breakfast powder+1 cup milk)**
10:00 a.m.	**Two doughnuts (enriched) Milk**
11:00 a.m.	**Apple**
12:30 p.m.	**Hamburger (onion, relish, tomato slice), French fries, Cola**
3:00 p.m.	**Plain Danish (enriched) Milk**
4:30 p.m.	**Hard-boiled egg Saltines**
6:00 p.m.	**Lasagna, Coleslaw, Iced tea**
8:30 p.m.	**Cheese dip with assorted raw vegetables (carrot strips, tomato wedges, cauliflower flowerets, broccoli flowerets)**

Nutritional Foundation of This Day's Food

Milk Group 2 cups	Fruit-Veg. Group 4 servings	Meat or Alternate 2 servings	Bread-Cereal—4 servings (enriched or whole grain)
1 cup in instant breakfast **1 cup as beverage**	**Apple—1 serving** **French fries—1 serving** **Coleslaw—1 serving** **Raw veg.—1 serving**	**Hamburger—1 serving** **Lasagna—1 serving (meat in it)**	**2 doughnuts—2 servings** **Hamburger roll—1 serving** **Danish—1 serving**

Foods That Provide Additional Nutrients and Food Energy to Meet Individual Needs

From the 4 Food Groups	From Other Foods
Onion, relish, tomato Served on hamburger **Hard-boiled egg** **Saltines—enriched** **Lasagna noodles (enriched) and sauce** **Cheese dip** **Milk in coffee**	**Instant breakfast powder** **Sugar in coffee** **Cola** **Dressing on coleslaw**

Ovo-lacto vegetarian diet (text page 17):

EARLY MORNING MEAL
Pineapple juice
Wheat flakes with milk
Doughnut (enriched)
Coffee

MID-MORNING
Peach

MIDDAY MEAL
Hard-cooked eggs—cream sauce
Whole-wheat bread—butter or margarine
Brussels sprouts
Molasses cookies Milk

EVENING MEAL
Vegetarian baked beans
Green pepper stuffed with rice and tomato sauce
Tossed green salad French dressing
Raisin pie
Milk

Nutritional Foundation of This Day's Food

Milk Group 2 cups	Fruit-Veg. Group 4 servings	Meat or Alternate 2 servings	Bread-Cereal—4 servings (enriched or whole grain)
1 cup as beverage ½ cup with cereal ½ cup in cream sauce	1 serving—pineapple juice 1 serving—peach 1 serving—brussels sprouts 1 serving—green pepper	1 serving—2 eggs 1 serving—vegetarian baked beans	1 serving wheat flakes 1 serving doughnut 1 serving whole-wheat bread 1 serving rice

Foods That Provide Additional Nutrients and Food Energy to Meet Individual Needs

From the 4 Food Groups	From Other Foods
Milk as beverage and in coffee Remaining ingredients in cream sauce Molasses cookies—enriched Tomato sauce Tossed green salad Raisin pie	Butter or margarine with bread Sugar in coffee French dressing

Meal plan for a strict vegetarian (text page 17):

EARLY MORNING

Orange	1 medium
Bulgur	1 cup
with brewer's yeast	1 tablespoon
Toasted wheat-soy bread	1 slice
with honey	1 tablespoon

MID-MORNING SNACK

Shelled almonds	¼ cup

MIDDAY MEAL

Split pea soup	2 cups
Peanut butter sandwich:	
Peanut butter	2 tablespoons
Whole wheat bread	2 slices
Honey	1 tablespoon
Fruit-sunflower seed salad:	
Apple	½ medium
Banana	½ medium
Sunflower seeds	¼ cup
Lettuce	1 leaf

SNACK

Peach	1 medium

EVENING MEAL

Soybeans	1 cup
Brown rice cooked	1 cup
fried in oil	2 tablespoons
with chestnuts	2 tablespoons
with sesame seeds	2 tablespoons
Collards	1 cup
Pear	1 medium

EVENING SNACK

Raisins	¼ cup

An increasing number of people seem to be cutting down on the size of meals and satisfying appetites with snacks of various types and nutritional qualities. Many are shortchanging themselves on nutrients. With a little record-keeping or a good memory, these individuals can eat well when and where they choose with the help of the food guide. (See plan on page 14.)

In recent years, there has been an increase in the number of individuals who subscribe to vegetarian diets, particularly among young adults.

To many people, a vegetarian diet is one that does not contain meat, poultry, or fish. However, vegetarian diets differ in the kinds of foods that they contain. They usually include some or all of the following foods—vegetables, fruits, enriched or whole-grain breads and cereals, dry beans and peas, lentils, nuts and nut-like seeds, peanuts, and peanut butter. They may also include other foods, but some diets are more strict than others in the foods permitted. For example:

• A pure or strict vegetarian diet. This diet excludes all foods of animal origin—meat, poultry, fish, eggs, all dairy products such as milk, cheese, and ice cream.

• An ovo-lacto-vegetarian diet. This diet includes eggs and dairy products, but excludes meat, poultry, and fish.

• A lacto-vegetarian diet. This diet includes dairy products, but excludes meat, poultry, fish, and eggs.

The ovo-lacto and the lacto-vegetarians can select a good diet using the four food groups plus other foods as a guide. On page 15 is an example of an ovo-lacto-vegetarian diet which provides a good nutritional foundation plus other foods to meet individual needs.

The strict vegetarian must choose from only three of the four groups—that is, fruits and vegetables, breads and cereals, and meat group alternates such as dry beans, peas, lentils, and nuts. Foods from the milk group are omitted altogether. In order to have a desirable diet, a strict vegetarian must have more knowledge of food composition than the average person has plus great skill in applying that knowledge. Nutritionist Nancy Raper (USDA) gives the following example and caution:

"The volume of food required to meet energy and nutrient needs may be greater with a vegetarian diet than with a traditional diet. This is because many foods of animal origin are more concentrated sources of energy and certain nutrients than are foods of vegetable origin; and when these are omitted from the diet, a larger quantity of food is needed to replace them.

"Eating large quantities of food may be particularly difficult for young children. This is another reason for including milk and other foods of animal origin in a child's diet, if at all possible.

"Although foods such as fats, oils, sugars, and sweeteners are good sources of energy, their use in a vegetarian diet may need to be curtailed in order to achieve a well-balanced diet. Their nutritional contribution in relation to number of calories supplied is often quite small."

Vitamin B_{12} is not believed to occur in foods of vegetable origin. This means that a person eating a pure vegetarian diet will need to take a vitamin preparation containing this vitamin or to include vitamin B_{12} fortified foods in his diet—for example, some breakfast cereals have this vitamin added.

With the coming of nutritional labeling, nutrition educators will have a new tool with which to help people gain a depth of understanding of the nutrient and energy value of the foods they eat. Nutritional labeling and its use are discussed in two other chapters in this section of the Yearbook.

However, a good food guide such as the one discussed earlier is sufficient at this time to help you choose a good diet that you can enjoy. Make your choices good ones. Bon appetit!

FOR FURTHER READING:

U.S. Department of Agriculture, *Food For Fitness*, Pamphlet 424, for sale by Superintendent of Documents, Washington, D. C. 20402.

Food for the Family At Different Costs

TODAY'S WELL-STOCKED markets and ever-changing food prices cause many shoppers to wonder if they make the best use of their food money. How much should they spend? What foods should they buy?

To help you know how much you might reasonably expect to spend, the U.S. Department of Agriculture has developed three basic food plans for providing nutritious meals and snacks. The costs of these plans—low-cost, moderate-cost, and liberal—reflect buying practices of low, middle, and high income families respectively.

A fourth plan, an economy food plan, is a guide for families with little money for food—such as those eligible for Food Stamps. This plan provides for nutritious eating, like the other plans, but relies more heavily on dry beans, bread, cereals, and potatoes. It includes smaller amounts of meat, poultry, fish, fruits and vegetables than most families ordinarily use. This plan requires more time and skill to buy and prepare food than the other plans.

Here's a general idea of what these plans cost in March 1974. Weekly food bills for a family of four with elementary school children would be about $43.70 for the low-cost, $55.10 for the moderate-cost, and $66.90 for the liberal plan. Their bill for the economy plan would be about $34.80 per week.

You can estimate how much a family like yours might reasonably spend for a nutritionally good diet using information in the two tables.

AUTHORS *Richard Kerr*, an Economist, and *Cynthia Cromwell*, a Home Economist, are with the Consumer and Food Economics Institute, Agricultural Research Service.

Some shoppers budget their food money by food groups.

Locate the food plan in the first table suitable for your family's size and income. If you spend the way urban families similar to yours do, you can probably afford this food plan.

Use the second table to figure the cost of the food plan for a family like yours as follows:

- For those eating all meals at home (or carrying some meals from home), list the cost shown opposite the sex and age of the family member.
- For those eating some meals out, list the cost shown minus 5 percent for each meal eaten away from home. Thus, for a person eating five meals away from home in a week, subtract 25 percent from the cost shown in the table.

Food plans that families of different sizes and incomes can usually afford, 1974

Family income (after taxes)	2-person family	3-person family	4-person family	5-person family	6-person family
$2,000 to $4,000	Economy or low cost	Economy [1]	Economy [1]	Economy [1]	Economy [1]
$4,000 to $6,000	Moderate-cost	Low-cost	Economy [1]	Economy [1]	Economy [1]
$6,000 to $8.000	Moderate-cost or liberal	Low-cost or moderate-cost	Low-cost	Economy or low cost	Economy [1]
$8,000 to $10,000	Liberal	Moderate-cost	Low-cost or moderate-cost	Low-cost	Economy or low cost
$10,000 to $15,000	Liberal	Liberal	Moderate-cost	Moderate-cost	Low-cost or moderate-cost
$15,000 and over	Liberal	Liberal	Liberal	Moderate-cost or liberal	Moderate-cost or liberal

1 Many families of this size and income are eligible for assistance through the Food Stamp Program.

- For each meal a guest eats at your home, list 5 percent of the cost shown for a person of the guest's age and sex.

Next, total the costs listed. Adjust this amount—as shown in the next paragraph—if more or fewer than four persons usually eat at your family table. Adjustments are necessary because larger families tend to buy and use food more economically than smaller ones.

Thus, if yours is a family of—

1 person	add 20 percent
2 persons	add 10 percent
3 persons	add 5 percent
4 persons	use as is
5 persons	subtract 5 percent
6 or more persons	subtract 10 percent

Now compare the adjusted total to the amount you actually spend for food eaten at home during a week. Be certain to include the cost of all food eaten

Cost of food for a week, all meals and snacks prepared at home (U.S. average, March 1974)

Individual	Economy plan	Low-cost plan	Moderate-cost plan	Liberal plan
WOMEN:				
20–54 years	$ 8.50	$10.60	$13.40	$16.00
55 years and over	7.00	8.80	11.30	13.40
Pregnant	10.20	12.80	16.00	18.70
Nursing	12.00	14.90	18.40	21.40
MEN:				
20–54 years	9.80	12.20	15.40	18.70
55 years and over	8.30	10.40	13.30	15.90
CHILDREN:				
1–2 years	5.10	6.30	7.90	9.40
3–5 years	6.00	7.50	9.60	11.40
6–8 years	7.40	9.30	11.70	14.50
9–11 years	8.50	10.60	13.60	16.00
Girls 12–19 years	9.30	11.70	14.80	17.60
Boys 12–19 years	10.90	13.60	17.50	20.70

Costs are estimated quarterly by the Consumer and Food Economics Institute, Agricultural Research Service, U.S. Department of Agriculture, Hyattsville, Md. 20782. Current cost figures are available from the above address on request.

at home, whether it comes from a supermarket, a specialty shop, or from milk delivery. Do not include the amount you spend at the grocery store for nonfood items such as cigarettes, soap, paper goods or pet foods.

Costs of the USDA food plans are only rough guides to your spending. The amount you spend may be more or less depending on factors such as—

- What foods you select
- Where you live
- How much food you prepare yourself
- Whether you raise some of your own food
- How carefully you plan and buy
- The importance you place on food in relation to other family needs

If you spend considerably more for food than the cost of the plan you selected, you may want some help in pushing food costs down. If you spend a great deal less, you may not be providing the assortment of food your family needs. If you spend about the same amount weekly for food, your spending is in line with the spending of families similar to yours in size and income. Additionally, this amount is sufficient to provide a nutritious diet.

However, spending any given amount for food does not necessarily assure well-balanced meals or adequate diets. Only a variety of foods can accomplish this. Food and nutrition scientists in USDA have developed a flexible, four food group guide to help you determine your family's food needs. (See the second chapter in this section of the Yearbook.) This guide can help you plan interesting, varied, and nutritious meals.

One set of well-balanced meals may cost much more than another. Well-balanced meals at low-cost usually include:

—Less expensive kinds of foods from each of the four food groups—milk and milk products; meat and meat alternates (poultry, fish, eggs, dry beans and dry peas, peanut butter); vegetables and fruit; and whole grain and enriched breads and cereals. For example, nonfat dry milk instead of fresh whole milk; chicken instead of beef rib roast; frozen orange juice instead of strawberries; and enriched white bread instead of specialty bread.

Courtesy of Better Homes and Gardens

—Less expensive kinds and possibly fewer "other foods" (cookies and other bakery products, spreads for breads, sweets and beverages).

—More dry beans, peas, and peanut butter replacing some of the meat, poultry, and fish.

—More home-prepared foods and fewer ready-to-heat or ready-to-eat foods.

Some shoppers like to budget their food money by food groups. The share that goes to a food group is a personal preference. You may be willing to use economical choices from one food group so you can splurge on another. For example, replace some of your fresh whole milk with reconstituted nonfat dry milk and then spend the amount you save on a favorite bakery product.

The share of each food dollar that U.S. families across the country spend for major food groups is shown in the first column below. The way these families would have divided their dollars if they had followed the low-cost food plan for getting a good diet is shown in the second column.

	Family practices	*Low-cost plan*
Milk, cheese, ice cream	$0.13	$0.18
Meat, poultry, fish, eggs, legumes	.40	.30
Vegetables and fruit	.20	.25
Cereals, bakery products	.13	.16
Other foods	.14	.11
	$1.00	$1.00

The shopper who budgets food money like the average family in the United States could get a good diet at a lower cost by using a larger share of each dollar for:
—milk and milk products
—vegetables and fruit
—cereals and bakery products
and less of each dollar for:
—foods in the meat group, and
—other foods such as fats, oils, sugar, sweets, coffee, tea, and soft drinks.

Stretching food dollars in today's well-stocked markets is a challenge to most shoppers, regardless of income. You should spend enough to give your family nutritious meals they enjoy eating. But many combinations of foods—at various levels of cost—can provide the nutrients for a well-balanced diet.

FOR FURTHER READING:
U.S. Department of Agriculture, Office of Communication, *Your Money's Worth in Foods*, G183, Washington, D.C. 20250.
________. *Family Food Budgeting . . . for Good Meals and Good Nutrition*, G94, Washington, D.C. 20250.
________. *Money-Saving Main Dishes*, G43, Washington, D.C. 20250.

How Much Food Should You Buy

WISE SHOPPERS buy only the amounts of food needed to feed their families. You too can learn to be a wise shopper.

This guide will help you know how many servings you can expect from a package of food and how many of those packages you will require. It will also help you compare costs of food in various forms—fresh, frozen, or canned.

The serving size for various foods defined in this guide may differ from that you customarily use. Therefore, you may first have to make adjustments to suit your family needs.

More of your food dollar is spent on meat, poultry, and fish than on other foods. You can make that dollar go further if you know how many servings you can expect from your meat purchase.

The guide shows the number of servings obtained from various meat cuts with average amounts of fat and/or bone, cooked at moderate temperatures.

A serving of meat, poultry, or fish in this guide is the cooked lean meat that you eat—and does not include the drippings, bone, or fat you trimmed off and left on your plate. Neither does a serving of poultry or fish contain skin.

Boneless cuts of meat may be better buys than the same cuts with bone when both cost per pound and yield are compared. Roasts with bone yield ½ to 1 serving less cooked meat per pound than boneless roasts. Two pounds of beef rib roast with bone are required to obtain the same four 3-ounce servings of cooked lean as 1½ pounds of boneless rib roast.

Certain chicken parts may be a better buy than whole chickens when cost of the amounts needed is compared. For instance, for four 3-ounce servings of cooked meat, chicken wings are a better buy if three pounds cost less than a 2¼-pound whole chicken. Chicken breasts will probably cost more for the same amount of cooked meat.

How many people will a pound of fresh vegetable or fruit serve? It varies with loss in preparation and how much the volume decreases in cooking. Keep preparation losses at a minimum by using good quality produce. The less you have to throw away the more you have to eat. The servings per pound given in this guide are based on good quality produce.

A serving of vegetable or fruit for the average person is considered in this guide to be about ½ cup. One cup of salad greens is specified as a serving because the dressing you add to the greens will reduce the volume considerably.

AUTHORS *Olive M. Batcher* and *Lois H. Fulton* are food technologists with the Consumer and Food Economics Institute, Agricultural Research Service.

Description of food as purchased	Size of market unit	Size of serving or measure of food as used	Servings or measures per market unit	Amount-to-buy factor per serving
MEAT				
Fresh or frozen:				
Roasts, boneless	**Pound**	**3 ounces cooked lean**	**2 to 2½**	**.40**
Pork shoulder, beef rib roasts		**1 cup cooked diced lean**	**1⅓ to 1½**	**.66**
Fresh pork (leg, loin, and Boston butt), cured pork shoulder, cook-before-eating ham	**Pound**	**3 ounces cooked lean**	**2½ to 2¾**	**.35**
		1 cup cooked diced lean	**1⅔**	**.60**
Beef (rump, round, shoulder, sirloin), veal chuck, lamb leg and shoulder, fully cooked ham, cured Boston butt	**Pound**	**3 ounces cooked lean**	**3 to 3½**	**.32**
		1 cup cooked diced lean	**1¾ to 2**	**.53**
Beef chuck, veal leg	**Pound**	**3 ounces cooked lean**	**3¾**	**.29**
		1 cup cooked diced lean	**2⅓**	**.49**
Other cuts				
Short ribs, spareribs, lamb or pork loin chops, steaks (T-bone, porterhouse, club)	**Pound**	**3 ounces cooked lean**	**2 to 2½**	**.51**
Veal loin chops, beef or pork cubes (stew meat)	**Pound**	**3 ounces cooked lean**	**2½**	**.40**
Steaks (round, flank)	**Pound**	**3 ounces cooked lean**	**3 to 3½**	**.34**
Beef or calf liver, lamb or veal cubes (stew meat), ground meat, steaks (cubed, minute), veal cutlets	**Pound**	**3 ounces cooked lean**	**3½ to 4**	**.30**
Canned:				
Corned beef	**12 ounces**	**3 ounces heated lean**	**4**	**.25**
Ham	**Pound**	**3 ounces heated lean**	**3½**	**.28**
		1 cup heated diced lean	**2**	**.49**
POULTRY				
Fresh or frozen:				
Chicken				
Backs	**Pound**	**3 ounces cooked meat only**	**1 to 1¼**	**.89**
Wings	**Pound**	**3 ounces cooked meat only**	**1¼ to 1½**	**.74**
Drumsticks, thighs, whole	**Pound**	**3 ounces cooked meat only**	**1¾ to 2**	**.53**
		1 cup cooked diced meat	**1¼**	**.81**

Description of food as purchased	Size of market unit	Size of serving or measure of food as used	Servings or measures per market unit	Amount-to-buy factor per serving
POULTRY				
Breasts	**Pound**	**3 ounces cooked meat only**	**2½**	**.39**
Turkey				
Backs	**Pound**	**3 ounces cooked meat only**	**1½ to 1¾**	**.61**
Drumsticks, wings, whole	**Pound**	**3 ounces cooked meat only**	**2 to 2¼**	**.51**
		1 cup cooked diced meat	**1⅓**	**.75**
Necks, thighs	**Pound**	**3 ounces cooked meat only**	**2¼ to 2½**	**.41**
Breasts	**Pound**	**3 ounces cooked meat only**	**2¾**	**.37**
Boneless roasts	**Pound**	**3 ounces cooked meat**	**3¾**	**.27**
		1 cup cooked diced meat	**2⅓**	**.43**
Canned:				
Chicken or turkey, boned	**6 ounces**	**3 ounces**	**2**	**.50**
SEAFOOD				
Fresh or frozen:				
Whole fish (dressed)	**Pound**	**3 ounces cooked flesh**	**1½**	**.69**
Oysters (shucked)	**Pound**	**3 ounces cooked oysters**	**2 to 2½**	**.47**
Breaded fish (sticks, portions), clams	**Pound**	**3 ounces cooked seafood**	**2½ to 3**	**.39**
Shrimp in shell	**Pound**	**3 ounces cooked without shell**	**2½ to 3**	**.39**
Scallops, fish (unbreaded portions, fillets, cakes)	**Pound**	**3 ounces cooked seafood**	**3¼ to 3½**	**.30**
Canned:				
Mackerel	**15 ounces**	**3 ounces, drained**	**4 to 4¼**	**.24**
Salmon	**16 ounces**	**3 ounces, drained**	**4¼ to 4½**	**.23**
Tuna	**6 to 7 ounces**	**3 ounces, drained**	**2**	**.50**
VEGETABLES				
Fresh:				
Vegetables served raw				
Lettuce (head or leaf), cabbage	**Head**	**1 cup shredded or pieces**	**5 to 6**	**.19**
Carrots, celery, onions	**Pound**	**1 cup chopped**	**2½**	**.36**
Tomatoes	**Pound**	**½ cup sliced**	**5½**	**.20**
Vegetables served cooked				
Asparagus, beets, broccoli, cauliflower, onions, summer squash	**Pound**	**½ cup cooked cut-up**	**3 to 3½**	**.30**

Description of food as purchased	Size of market unit	Size of serving or measure of food as used	Servings or measures per market unit	Amount-to-buy factor per serving
VEGETABLES				
Brussels sprouts, cabbage, carrots, green beans, potatoes	Pound	½ cup cooked whole or cut up	4½ to 5	.22
Potatoes for mashing	Pound	½ cup cooked mashed	3½	.29
Collards, kale, spinach	Pound	½ cup cooked pieces	4 to 5	.23
Canned:				
Bean sprouts, beets, carrots, whole kernel corn, beans (green, kidney, lima), okra, peas, potatoes	15 to 16 ounces	½ cup heated, drained	3½	.29
Asparagus, greens	14 to 15 ounces	½ cup heated, drained	2¾	.37
Tomatoes	28 ounces	½ cup heated	6¾	.15
Frozen:				
Asparagus, kale, okra, spinach	10 ounces	½ cup cooked, drained	2½	.41
Broccoli, brussels sprouts, carrots, cauliflower, whole kernel corn, beans (green, lima), peas, summer squash	9 to 10 ounces	½ cup cooked, drained	2¾ to 3¼	.33
French fried potatoes	9 to 10 ounces	½ cup cooked	2¾ to 3¼	.33
FRUIT				
Fresh:				
Apples, apricots, plums	Pound	½ cup slices, halves, or whole	5 to 5½	.19
Berries (black-, blue-, straw-, red raspberries)	Pint	½ cup	4½ to 5	.21
Cherries	Pound	½ cup	5 to 5½	.19
Melons (honeydew, Cantaloupe)	Melon (medium)	½ cup cubes	4¼ to 4¾	.21
Oranges, grapefruit	Pound	½ cup sections	2¼	.45
Peaches, pears	Pound	½ cup slices or cubes	3½ to 4	.27
Canned:				
Apricots, fruit cocktail, fruits for salad, grapefruit sections, peach (slices, halves), pear halves, purple plums	16 ounces	½ cup fruit and juice	3½ to 3¾	.28
		1 cup fruit	1¼	.78
	29 to 30 ounces	½ cup fruit and juice	6½ to 7	.15
		1 cup fruit	2 to 2¼	.53
Berries (black-, blue-,	15 to 16	½ cup fruit	3½	.28

Description of food as purchased	Size of market unit	Size of serving or measure of food as used	Servings or measures per market unit	Amount-to-buy factor per serving
Canned:				
boysen-, red raspberries)	ounces	and juice		
		1 cup fruit	¾ to 1¼	1.12
Pineapple (chunks, crushed)	20 ounces	½ cup fruit and juice	4½	.23
		1 cup fruit	1¾	.56
Juice	32 fluid ounces	½ cup	8	.12
	46 fluid ounces	½ cup	11½	.09
Frozen:				
Fruit, sweetened	10 ounces	½ cup fruit and juice	2¼	.43
	12 ounces	½ cup fruit and juice	3	.34
	16 ounces	½ cup fruit and juice	3¾	.27
Juice concentrate	6 fluid ounces	½ cup, reconstituted	6	.17
MISCELLANEOUS				
Beans, dry	Pound	1 cup uncooked	2¼ to 2½	
		½ cup cooked	22½	.04
Bread (white, wheat)				
Regular sliced	Pound	1 slice	15	
Thin sliced	Pound	1 slice	18	
Cereals, ready-to-eat				
Flakes	12 ounces	1 cup	11	
Puffed	6 ounces	1 cup	13½	
Cheese	Pound	1 cup shredded	4	
Flour, wheat				
All-purpose	5 pounds	1 cup	18	
Cake	32 ounces	1 cup sifted	9¼	
Macaroni	Pound	1 cup uncooked	3¾	
		½ cup cooked	17	.06
Milk, evaporated	13 fluid ounces	1 cup, undiluted	1¾	
Noodles	Pound	1 cup uncooked	10¼	
		½ cup cooked	14¾	.07
Nuts (almonds, cashews, pecans, walnuts), shelled	Pound	1 cup chopped	3½	
Oats, rolled	18 ounces	1 cup uncooked	7¼	
		1 cup cooked	13	.08
Rice	Pound	1 cup uncooked	2¼	
		½ cup cooked	17¼	.06
Shortening, hydrogenated	48 ounces	1 cup	7	
Soups, condensed	10½ ounces	1 cup, reconstituted	2½	.40
Spaghetti	Pound	½ cup cooked	14	.07
Sugar				
Brown	Pound	1 cup packed	2¼	
Confectioner's	Pound	1 cup sifted	4¾	
Granulated	5 pounds	1 cup	11¼	

Cooking also decreases the volume of some vegetables. A pound of fresh spinach looks like plenty for a crowd, yet will yield only four to five ½-cup servings when cooked.

Do you need the same amount of potatoes for serving mashed as parsley-buttered pieces? No, mashed potatoes require almost 1¼ pounds for four ½-cup servings while parsley-buttered potatoes require less than a pound.

Canned and frozen vegetables and fruits have little preparation loss. Liquid from canned vegetables not included in the serving can be used in gravies and soups. Cooking may cause a small decrease in volume of frozen vegetables.

Canned fruit may be served with juice or used without juice as a salad ingredient. Amounts for both measures are given in the guide. Frozen fruit is most often used with its juice.

Many dry foods, like beans and cereals, increase in volume when cooked. For instance, one cup of raw rice will yield over three cups after cooking.

Will you need to buy more sugar for that batch of jelly? The guide shows the number of cups of sugar in the five-pound bag in your cupboard.

Use the amount-to-buy factor shown in the guide to determine how much to buy for your family and to compare cost per serving of different forms of food.

To determine how much to buy, first decide how many servings you need. Remember your teenage son may eat two servings of the size shown in the guide, while your small daughter may only eat one-half a serving. Multiply the number of servings needed by the factor for the food to be served. For five ½-cup servings of mashed potatoes, multiply 5 by 0.29 (factor) and get 1.45 or about 1½ pounds of fresh potatoes.

Is fresh or frozen spinach a better buy for cooking? To compare, multiply the cost of each form by the factor. Frozen spinach, at 25 cents per package, costs about 10 cents for a ½-cup serving and fresh spinach, at 50 cents a pound, costs about 12 cents. In this case, frozen spinach would be a better buy. Season of the year will affect cost and new comparisons should be made as cost of food changes.

Buying fresh produce.

Using this guide, you can now plan your food purchases to more closely match your food needs, thus making better use of your food dollars by eliminating costly leftovers and food waste.

FOR FURTHER READING:

Dawson, Elsie H., Gladys L. Gilpin, and Lois H. Fulton. *Food Buying: A Guide for Calculating Amounts to Buy and Comparing Costs,* Home Economics Research Report No. 37. For sale by Superintendent of Documents, Washington, D. C. 20402.

Food Cost Tables To Help Stretch Your Dollars

STRETCHING your food dollar to provide nutritious meals your family will enjoy presents a continuing challenge. A part of the job is comparing costs of foods you might use to replace each other in meals. The tables in this chapter have been prepared to help you.

Milk and milk products provide 60 percent of the mineral calcium in U.S. diets. To get the calcium you need without using milk in some form is very difficult. The "cost of milk and milk products" table shows the cost of a cup of milk and of amounts of cheese, ice cream, yogurt and other milk products with approximately the same amount of calcium as a cup of milk.

For example, 1½ cups of ice cream, costing 18 cents in Washington, D.C. in January 1974, provided the calcium equivalent to that in a cup of whole milk costing 10 cents. As a source of calcium, ice cream was about twice as expensive as whole milk.

You can use local prices to bring the costs up to date. First, in the column headed "price per market unit," insert the prices for the market units listed in the second column. Then, divide the local price by the number of portions listed in the fourth column, to find the cost of a calcium-equivalent portion for any of these foods.

Suppose a pound of natural Cheddar cheese costs $1.56 or 156 cents. A calcium-equivalent portion costs 156 ÷ 12.0, or 13 cents.

Meat, poultry and fish items in meals usually cost more than other foods. But the range in prices of different types and cuts of meats is great, so careful selection can result in worthwhile savings. When you plan, consider the price per pound and how much meat the pound provides after it is cooked and after you discard the parts you do not eat, such as bones and fat.

The "cost of 3 ounces of cooked lean" table will help you compare costs of equal-size servings of cooked lean meat from different types and cuts of meat, poultry and fish. To use it, locate the kind and cut you plan to buy, and follow the line on which it appears across to the column headed by the price most like the current price at your market. The figure at this point is the approximate cost of a 3-ounce serving of cooked lean. (Table, pages 30–33.)

As examples, a 3-ounce serving from a chuck roast (bone in) priced at 130 cents a pound would cost 58 cents; from ground beef, at 110 cents a pound, the cost would be 29 cents.

Poultry remains one of the best buys at the meat counter. However, not all packages of chicken or turkey are equally good buys. The chicken and

---

AUTHORS *Judy P. Chassy* and *Jennie B. Nichols* are with the Food and Diet Appraisal Research Group, Consumer and Food Economics Institute, Agricultural Research Service.

Cost of milk and milk products as sources of calcium

Milk product	Market unit	Portion that provides as much calcium as 1 cup whole fluid milk	Calcium-equivalent portions per market unit	Price per market unit [1]	Cost of a calcium-equivalent portion
			(number)	(dollars)	
Nonfat dry milk	38.4 ounces (makes 12 quarts)	⅓ cup dry (1 cup reconstituted)	48.0	2.03	.04
Evaporated milk	large can (1⅔ cup)	½ cup	3.7	.25	.07
Cheese spread	2 pounds	1⅞ ounces	17.1	1.22	.07
Grated Parmesan cheese	8 ounces	¾ ounce (2½ tablespoons, packed)	10.7	.98	.09
Fresh skim milk	½ gallon	1 cup	8.0	.75	.09
Whole fluid milk	½ gallon	1 cup	8.0	.77	.10
Buttermilk	1 quart	1 cup	4.0	.42	.11
Natural Cheddar cheese	1 pound	1⅓ ounces	12.0	1.40	.12
Process American cheese	1 pound	1½ ounces	10.7	1.32	.12
Natural Swiss cheese	1 pound	1¼ ounces	12.8	1.59	.12
Ice milk	½ gallon	1½ cups	5.3	.79	.15
Ice cream	½ gallon	1½ cups	5.3	.97	.18
Cheese food	8 ounces	1⅞ ounces	4.3	.84	.20
Plain yogurt	8 ounces	9½ ounces (1 cup)	.8	.24	.30
Cottage cheese, creamed	2 pounds	10¾ ounces (1⅓ cups)	3.0	.98	.33
Natural blue cheese	4 ounces	3¼ ounces	1.2	.50	.42
Fruit-flavored yogurt, 75% plain yogurt	8 ounces	12⅔ ounces (1⅓ cups)	.6	.26	.43
Table cream	1 cup	1¼ cups	.8	.40	.50
Cream cheese	8 ounces	17 ounces	.5	.44	.88

[1] Prices from three Washington, D.C. supermarkets, January 1974, store brand or least costly brand.

turkey tables can be used to estimate the added cost, if any, of using chicken or turkey parts or turkey products rather than the whole chicken or whole turkey. Each line of the chicken table shows prices at which ready-to-cook whole chicken and different chicken parts are equally good buys. The turkey table allows similar comparisons for ready-to-cook whole turkey and turkey parts and turkey products. (Tables, pages 34–35.)

For example, the chicken table shows that breast halves without ribs at 80 cents a pound, breast halves with ribs at 78 cents a pound, thighs at 66 cents a pound, thighs and drumsticks at 63 cents a pound, drumsticks at 61 cents a pound, and wings at 48 cents a pound all provide as much meat for the money as ready-to-cook whole chicken at 59 cents a pound. Any amount above these prices for parts—when ready-to-cook whole chicken is 59 cents per pound—pays for the convenience of having the parts of chicken.

Another way to cut food costs is to replace some of the meat in meals with alternates such as dry beans, dry peas, peanut butter and eggs. These foods provide the protein and many other nutrients for which meat, poultry and fish are valued. The table on protein from meats and meat alternates allows you to compare the costs of amounts of selected foods that each provide approximately 20 grams of protein. (Table, page 40.)

To figure costs of these foods using local prices, enter in the fifth column your new price per market unit (specified in the third column). To obtain the cost of 20 grams of protein, multiply the price by the decimal part of the market unit needed to furnish 20 grams of protein (see center column).

For example, the price of tuna in a 6½-ounce can is 50 cents. That means, 20 grams of protein costs 50 cents x .44, or 22 cents.

Egg sizes most often found in stores are small, medium, large and extra large. By the dozen, larger sizes usually cost more than smaller sizes of the same grade. By weight this is not always the case.

To find the better buy between two egg sizes by weight, you need to know first the price of large eggs and then the price difference between the two sizes you are considering:

When the price of a dozen "large" eggs is—	Buy the larger of two sizes if the price difference per dozen between any size and the next larger size is less than—
(cents)	(cents)
41–48	6
49–56	7
57–64	8
65–72	9
73–80	10
81–88	11
89–96	12
97–104	13
105–112	14
113–120	15

For example, the price of large eggs is 79 cents a dozen. The price of the next larger size, extra large eggs, is 85 cents. The difference is 6 cents. Since 6 cents is less than 10 cents (the difference listed in the table), and because extra large is the next larger size, the extra large eggs are the better buy.

Vegetables and fruits are an important part of each day's food, as Mary Hill's chapter in this section of the Yearbook points out. To find the least expensive ones, you can compare costs of ½-cup servings of various vegetables and fruits using the tables for these products, pages 36–37 and 38–39.

Find the vegetable or fruit you plan to serve in the first column, and the appropriate market form and unit in the second and third columns. Follow that line of numbers to the right to the column headed by the price of the market unit. The number located there is the approximate cost of a ½-cup serving. Similarly, find the cost of a serving of other vegetables or fruits that might be served. To cut costs, use the one with the lowest cost for a serving.

For example, when fresh carrots cost 20 cents per pound, ½ cup of cooked

Cost of 3 ounces of cooked lean from selected kinds and cuts of meat, poultry and fish at specified retail prices

Kind and cut	Price per pound[1] (dollars)																
	.30	.40	.50	.60	.70	.80	.90	1.00	1.10	1.20	1.30	1.40	1.50	1.60	1.70	1.80	1.90
	Cost of 3 ounces (dollars)																
Beef: Brisket, bone out	.12	.16	.20	.24	.28	.33	.37	.41	.45	.49	.53	.57	.61	.65	.69	.73	.78
Chuck, bone in	.13	.18	.22	.27	.31	.36	.40	.45	.49	.54	.58	.62	.67	.71	.76	.80	.85
Chuck, bone out	.10	.14	.17	.21	.24	.28	.31	.35	.38	.42	.45	.48	.52	.56	.59	.62	.66
Ground lean	.08	.10	.13	.16	.18	.21	.23	.26	.29	.31	.34	.36	.39	.42	.44	.47	.49
Porterhouse steak, bone in	.16	.21	.26	.31	.36	.42	.47	.52	.57	.62	.68	.73	.78	.83	.88	.94	.99
Rib roast, bone in	.13	.18	.22	.27	.31	.36	.40	.45	.49	.54	.58	.62	.67	.71	.76	.80	.85
Round, bone in	.10	.13	.17	.20	.23	.27	.30	.34	.37	.40	.44	.47	.50	.54	.57	.60	.64
Round, bone out	.09	.12	.16	.19	.22	.25	.28	.31	.34	.37	.40	.44	.47	.50	.53	.56	.59
Rump roast, bone out	.10	.14	.17	.20	.24	.27	.31	.34	.38	.41	.44	.48	.51	.54	.58	.61	.65
Short ribs	.18	.23	.29	.35	.41	.47	.53	.59	.64	.70	.76	.82	.88	.94	1.00	1.05	1.11
Sirloin steak, bone in	.13	.17	.21	.26	.30	.34	.38	.43	.47	.51	.55	.60	.64	.68	.72	.77	.81
Sirloin steak, bone out	.12	.16	.20	.23	.27	.31	.35	.39	.43	.47	.51	.55	.59	.62	.66	.70	.74
T-bone steak, bone in	.17	.22	.28	.33	.38	.44	.50	.55	.61	.66	.72	.77	.83	.88	.94	.99	1.05
Fish: Fillets, fresh or frozen	.09	.12	.15	.18	.20	.23	.26	.29	.32	.35	.38	.41	.44	.47	.50	.53	.56
Steaks, fresh or frozen, backbone in	.10	.13	.16	.19	.23	.26	.29	.32	.36	.39	.42	.45	.48	.52	.55	.58	.61
Tuna, canned[1]	.08	.11	.14	.16	.19	.22	.24	.27	.30	.33	.35	.38	.41	.44	.46	.49	.52

Lamb: Leg roast, bone in	.13	.17	.21	.25	.29	.33	.38	.42	.46	.50	.54	.58	.62	.67	.71	.75	.79
Loin chop, bone in	.14	.18	.23	.27	.32	.36	.41	.46	.50	.55	.59	.64	.68	.73	.78	.82	.87
Rib chop, bone in	.17	.22	.28	.33	.38	.44	.50	.55	.61	.66	.72	.77	.83	.88	.94	.99	1.05
Shoulder roast, bone in	.14	.18	.23	.27	.32	.36	.41	.46	.50	.55	.59	.64	.68	.73	.78	.82	.87
Liver: Beef	.08	.11	.14	.16	.19	.22	.24	.27	.30	.33	.35	.38	.41	.44	.46	.49	.52
Chicken	.09	.12	.14	.17	.20	.23	.26	.29	.32	.34	.37	.40	.43	.46	.49	.52	.55
Pork: Butt, cured, bone in	.11	.14	.18	.22	.25	.29	.32	.36	.40	.43	.47	.50	.54	.58	.61	.65	.68
Ham, cured: whole, bone in	.10	.14	.17	.21	.24	.28	.31	.35	.38	.42	.45	.48	.52	.56	.59	.62	.66
whole, bone out	.08	.10	.13	.16	.18	.21	.23	.26	.29	.31	.34	.36	.39	.42	.44	.47	.49
slices	.09	.12	.16	.19	.22	.25	.28	.31	.34	.37	.40	.44	.47	.50	.53	.56	.59
canned	.08	.10	.12	.15	.18	.20	.22	.25	.28	.30	.32	.35	.38	.40	.42	.45	.48
Loin, fresh: chops, bone in	.13	.18	.22	.27	.31	.36	.40	.45	.49	.54	.58	.62	.67	.71	.76	.80	.85
roast, bone in	.15	.20	.25	.30	.35	.40	.46	.51	.56	.61	.66	.71	.76	.81	.86	.91	.96
roast, bone out	.10	.14	.17	.21	.24	.28	.31	.35	.38	.42	.45	.48	.52	.56	.59	.62	.66
Picnics: cured, bone in	.14	.18	.23	.27	.32	.36	.41	.46	.50	.55	.59	.64	.68	.73	.78	.82	.87
cured, bone out	.11	.14	.18	.21	.25	.28	.32	.35	.39	.42	.46	.50	.53	.57	.60	.64	.67
fresh, bone in	.16	.21	.27	.32	.38	.43	.48	.54	.59	.64	.70	.75	.80	.86	.91	.96	1.02
Rib chops, fresh, bone in	.15	.20	.25	.30	.35	.40	.46	.51	.56	.61	.66	.71	.76	.81	.86	.91	.96
Poultry: Chicken, whole, ready-to-cook	.14	.19	.23	.28	.32	.37	.42	.46	.51	.56	.60	.65	.70	.74	.79	.84	.88
Turkey, whole, ready-to-cook	.14	.19	.23	.28	.33	.38	.42	.47	.52	.56	.61	.66	.70	.75	.80	.84	.89
Veal: Chuck roast, bone in	.14	.19	.23	.28	.33	.38	.42	.47	.52	.56	.61	.66	.70	.75	.80	.84	.89
Leg roast, bone in	.16	.21	.26	.31	.36	.42	.47	.52	.57	.62	.68	.73	.78	.83	.88	.94	.99
Loin chop, bone in	.12	.16	.20	.24	.28	.32	.36	.40	.44	.48	.52	.56	.60	.64	.68	.72	.76
Rib chop, bone in	.15	.20	.25	.30	.34	.39	.44	.49	.54	.59	.64	.69	.74	.79	.84	.89	.94

[1] For tuna fish, use price for 13-ounce can.

Cost of 3 ounces of cooked lean from selected kinds and cuts of meat, poultry and fish at specified retail prices—continued

Kind and cut	Price per pound[1] (dollars)												
	2.00	2.10	2.20	2.30	2.40	2.50	2.60	2.70	2.80	2.90	3.00	3.10	3.20
	Cost of 3 ounces (dollars)												
Beef: Brisket, bone out	.82	.86	.90	.94	.98	1.02	1.06	1.10	1.14	1.18	1.22	1.26	1.31
Chuck, bone in	.89	.94	.98	1.02	1.07	1.12	1.16	1.20	1.25	1.29	1.34	1.38	1.43
Chuck, bone out	.69	.73	.76	.80	.83	.87	.90	.94	.97	1.01	1.04	1.08	1.11
Ground lean	.52	.55	.57	.60	.62	.65	.68	.70	.73	.75	.78	.81	.83
Porterhouse steak, bone in	1.04	1.09	1.15	1.20	1.25	1.30	1.35	1.41	1.46	1.51	1.56	1.62	1.67
Rib roast, bone in	.89	.94	.98	1.02	1.07	1.12	1.16	1.20	1.25	1.29	1.34	1.38	1.43
Round, bone in	.67	.70	.74	.77	.80	.84	.87	.90	.94	.97	1.00	1.04	1.07
Round, bone out	.62	.66	.69	.72	.75	.78	.81	.84	.87	.90	.94	.97	1.00
Rump roast, bone out	.68	.72	.75	.78	.82	.85	.89	.92	.95	.99	1.02	1.06	1.09
Short ribs	1.17	1.23	1.29	1.35	1.41	1.46	1.52	1.58	1.64	1.70	1.76	1.82	1.88
Sirloin steak, bone in	.85	.89	.94	.98	1.02	1.06	1.11	1.15	1.19	1.24	1.28	1.32	1.36
Sirloin steak, bone out	.78	.82	.86	.90	.94	.98	1.02	1.06	1.09	1.13	1.17	1.21	1.25
T-bone steak, bone in	1.10	1.16	1.21	1.27	1.32	1.38	1.43	1.49	1.54	1.60	1.65	1.71	1.76
Fish: Fillets, fresh or frozen	.59	.62	.64	.67	.70	.73	.76	.79	.82	.85	.88	.91	.94
Steaks, fresh or frozen, backbone in	.65	.68	.71	.74	.78	.81	.84	.87	.90	.94	.97	1.00	1.03
Tuna, canned[1]	.55	.57	.60	.63	.66	.68	.71	.74	.76	.79	.82	.85	.87

Lamb: Leg roast, bone in	.83	.88	.92	.96	1.00	1.04	1.08	1.12	1.17	1.21	1.25	1.29	1.33
Loin chop, bone in	.91	.96	1.00	1.05	1.10	1.14	1.19	1.23	1.28	1.32	1.37	1.42	1.46
Rib chop, bone in	1.10	1.16	1.21	1.27	1.32	1.38	1.43	1.49	1.54	1.60	1.65	1.71	1.76
Shoulder roast, bone in	.91	.96	1.00	1.05	1.10	1.14	1.19	1.23	1.28	1.32	1.37	1.42	1.46
Liver: Beef	.54	.57	.60	.62	.65	.68	.71	.73	.76	.79	.82	.84	.87
Chicken	.58	.60	.63	.66	.69	.72	.75	.78	.81	.84	.86	.89	.92
Pork: Butt, cured, bone in	.72	.76	.79	.83	.87	.90	.94	.97	1.01	1.05	1.08	1.12	1.16
Ham, cured: whole, bone in	.69	.73	.76	.80	.83	.87	.90	.94	.97	1.01	1.04	1.08	1.11
whole, bone out	.52	.55	.57	.60	.62	.65	.68	.70	.73	.75	.78	.81	.83
slices	.62	.66	.69	.72	.75	.78	.81	.84	.87	.90	.94	.97	1.00
canned	.50	.52	.55	.58	.60	.62	.65	.68	.70	.72	.75	.78	.80
Loin, fresh: chops, bone in	.89	.94	.98	1.02	1.07	1.12	1.16	1.20	1.25	1.29	1.34	1.38	1.43
roast, bone in	1.01	1.06	1.12	1.17	1.22	1.27	1.32	1.37	1.42	1.47	1.52	1.57	1.62
roast, bone out	.69	.73	.76	.80	.83	.87	.90	.94	.97	1.01	1.04	1.08	1.11
Picnics: cured, bone in	.91	.96	1.00	1.05	1.10	1.14	1.19	1.23	1.28	1.32	1.37	1.42	1.46
cured, bone out	.71	.74	.78	.81	.85	.88	.92	.96	.99	1.03	1.06	1.10	1.13
fresh, bone in	1.07	1.12	1.18	1.23	1.29	1.34	1.39	1.45	1.50	1.55	1.61	1.66	1.72
Rib chops, fresh, bone in	1.01	1.06	1.12	1.17	1.22	1.27	1.32	1.37	1.42	1.47	1.52	1.57	1.62
Poultry: Chicken, whole, ready-to-cook	.93	.98	1.02	1.07	1.12	1.16	1.21	1.26	1.30	1.35	1.40	1.44	1.49
Turkey, whole, ready-to-cook	.94	.98	1.03	1.08	1.12	1.17	1.22	1.27	1.31	1.36	1.41	1.45	1.50
Veal: Chuck roast, bone in	.94	.98	1.03	1.08	1.12	1.17	1.22	1.27	1.31	1.36	1.41	1.45	1.50
Leg roast, bone in	1.04	1.09	1.15	1.20	1.25	1.30	1.35	1.41	1.46	1.51	1.56	1.62	1.67
Loin chop, bone in	.80	.84	.88	.92	.96	1.00	1.04	1.08	1.12	1.16	1.20	1.24	1.28
Rib chop, bone in	.99	1.04	1.08	1.13	1.18	1.23	1.28	1.33	1.38	1.43	1.48	1.53	1.58

[1] For tuna fish, use price for 13-ounce can.

Prices per pound at which ready-to-cook whole chicken and chicken parts provide equal amounts of cooked chicken meat for the money [1]

If the price per pound of whole fryers, ready to cook, is—	Chicken parts are an equally good buy if the price per pound is—					
	Breast half: Without rib	Breast half: With rib	Thigh	Thigh and drumstick	Drumstick	Wing
Dollars	Dollars	Dollars	Dollars	Dollars	Dollars	Dollars
.31	.42	.41	.35	.33	.32	.25
.33	.45	.44	.37	.35	.34	.27
.35	.48	.46	.39	.38	.36	.28
.37	.50	.49	.41	.40	.38	.30
.39	.53	.52	.43	.42	.40	.31
.41	.56	.54	.46	.44	.42	.33
.43	.59	.57	.48	.46	.44	.35
.45	.61	.59	.50	.48	.46	.36
.47	.64	.62	.52	.50	.48	.38
.49	.67	.65	.55	.53	.50	.39
.51	.70	.67	.57	.55	.53	.41
.53	.72	.70	.59	.57	.55	.43
.55	.75	.73	.61	.59	.57	.44
.57	.78	.75	.63	.61	.59	.46
.59	.80	.78	.66	.63	.61	.48
.61	.83	.81	.68	.66	.63	.49
.63	.86	.83	.70	.68	.65	.51
.65	.89	.86	.72	.70	.67	.52
.67	.91	.89	.75	.72	.69	.54
.69	.94	.91	.77	.74	.71	.56
.71	.97	.94	.79	.76	.73	.57
.73	1.00	.97	.81	.78	.75	.59
.75	1.02	.99	.84	.81	.77	.60
.77	1.05	1.02	.86	.83	.79	.62
.79	1.08	1.04	.88	.85	.81	.64
.81	1.10	1.07	.90	.87	.83	.65
.83	1.13	1.10	.92	.89	.85	.67
.85	1.16	1.12	.95	.91	.88	.69
.87	1.19	1.15	.97	.93	.90	.70
.89	1.21	1.18	.99	.96	.92	.72

[1] Based on yields of cooked chicken meat with skin (only ½ skin on wings and backs included), from frying chickens, ready to cook, that weighed about 2¾ pounds.

sliced carrots cost 5 cents. The same size serving of carrots from a 16-ounce can priced at 35 cents would cost 10 cents. The fresh carrots would be the better buy.

Another example: A ½-cup serving of orange juice from a 16-ounce can of frozen concentrate priced at 60 cents would cost 4 cents.

From a 46-fluid-ounce can at 45 cents, orange juice costs 4 cents per ½ cup. From fresh oranges at 90 cents a

Prices per pound at which ready-to-cook whole turkey and turkey parts and turkey products provide equal amounts of cooked turkey meat for the money [1]

If the price per pound of whole turkey, ready-to-cook is—	Turkey parts and products are an equally good buy if the price per pound is—										
	Breast quarter	Leg quarter	Breast, whole or half	Drum-stick	Thigh	Wing	Turkey roasts: Ready-to-cook [2]	Turkey roasts: Cooked [3]	Boned turkey, canned	Turkey with gravy,[4] canned or frozen	Gravy with turkey,[5] canned or frozen
Dollars	Dollars		Dollars		Dollars		Dollars		Dollars		
.51	.57	.55	.65	.52	.62	.47	.89	1.17	1.15	.45	.19
.53	.60	.57	.68	.54	.65	.49	.93	1.22	1.19	.46	.20
.55	.62	.59	.70	.56	.67	.51	.96	1.26	1.24	.48	.21
.57	.64	.61	.73	.58	.70	.53	1.00	1.31	1.28	.50	.21
.59	.66	.63	.75	.60	.72	.55	1.03	1.36	1.33	.52	.22
.61	.69	.66	.78	.63	.75	.56	1.07	1.40	1.37	.53	.23
.63	.71	.68	.80	.65	.77	.58	1.10	1.45	1.42	.55	.24
.65	.73	.70	.83	.67	.80	.60	1.14	1.50	1.46	.57	.24
.67	.75	.72	.85	.69	.82	.62	1.17	1.54	1.51	.59	.25
.69	.78	.74	.88	.71	.85	.64	1.21	1.59	1.55	.60	.26
.71	.80	.76	.91	.73	.87	.66	1.24	1.63	1.60	.62	.27
.73	.82	.78	.93	.75	.89	.68	1.28	1.68	1.64	.64	.27
.75	.84	.81	.96	.77	.92	.69	1.31	1.72	1.69	.66	.28
.77	.87	.83	.98	.79	.94	.71	1.35	1.77	1.73	.67	.29
.79	.89	.85	1.01	.81	.97	.73	1.38	1.82	1.78	.69	.30
.81	.91	.87	1.03	.83	.99	.75	1.42	1.86	1.82	.71	.30
.83	.93	.89	1.06	.85	1.02	.77	1.45	1.91	1.87	.73	.31
.85	.96	.91	1.08	.87	1.04	.79	1.49	1.96	1.91	.74	.32
.87	.98	.94	1.11	.89	1.07	.80	1.52	2.00	1.96	.76	.33
.89	1.00	.96	1.13	.91	1.09	.82	1.56	2.05	2.00	.78	.33
.91	1.02	.98	1.16	.93	1.11	.84	1.59	2.09	2.05	.80	.34
.93	1.05	1.00	1.19	.95	1.14	.86	1.63	2.14	2.09	.81	.35
.95	1.07	1.02	1.21	.97	1.15	.88	1.66	2.18	2.14	.83	.36
.97	1.09	1.04	1.24	.99	1.19	.90	1.70	2.23	2.18	.85	.36
.99	1.11	1.06	1.26	1.01	1.21	.92	1.73	2.28	2.23	.87	.37

[1] Based on yields of cooked turkey meat excluding skin, medium to large birds.
[2] Roast, as purchased, includes 15 percent skin or fat.
[3] Roast, as purchased, has no more than one-fourth inch skin and fat on any part of surface.
[4] Assumes 35 percent cooked boned turkey, minimum required for product labeled "Turkey with Gravy."
[5] Assumes 15 percent cooked boned turkey, minimum required for product labeled "Gravy with Turkey."

dozen, ½ cup of juice costs 8 cents. Juice made from frozen concentrate costs the same as canned juice—about half as much per serving as fresh squeezed juice.

Food in large containers frequently costs less than the same amount bought in small containers. If you can store the food conveniently and use it without waste or monotony in meals, buying the large size may save trips to the store as well as money.

Cost of a ½-cup serving of selected vegetables purchased at specified prices per market unit—canned, fresh and frozen

Vegetable, as served (cooked and drained unless specified)	Market form	Market unit	Price per market unit .10	.20	.30	.40	.50	.60	.70	.80	.90	1.00
			Cost of ½-cup serving									
Asparagus, cuts and tips	canned	14 oz	.04	.08	.11	.15	.19	.23	.27	.30	.34	.38
	fresh	pound	.03	.06	.08	.11	.14	.17	.20	.22	.25	.28
	frozen	10 oz	.04	.08	.12	.16	.20	.24	.28	.32	.36	.40
Beans, green or wax	canned	15½ oz	.03	.06	.08	.11	.14	.17	.20	.22	.25	.28
	fresh	pound	.02	.04	.05	.07	.09	.11	.13	.14	.16	.18
	frozen	9 oz	.03	.06	.09	.12	.15	.18	.21	.24	.27	.30
Beans, lima	canned	16 oz	.03	.05	.08	.11	.14	.16	.19	.22	.24	.27
	fresh, in pod	pound	.05	.09	.14	.19	.24	.28	.33	.38	.42	.47
	frozen	10 oz	.03	.06	.09	.12	.15	.18	.21	.24	.27	.30
Beets	canned	16 oz	.03	.06	.09	.12	.14	.17	.20	.23	.26	.29
	fresh, no tops	pound	.03	.05	.08	.11	.14	.16	.19	.22	.24	.27
Broccoli, chopped	fresh	pound	.03	.06	.09	.12	.16	.19	.22	.25	.28	.31
	frozen	10 oz	.04	.07	.11	.14	.18	.22	.25	.29	.32	.36
Brussels sprouts	fresh	1 qt (16 oz)	.02	.05	.07	.09	.12	.14	.16	.18	.21	.23
	frozen	10 oz	.03	.07	.10	.13	.16	.20	.23	.26	.30	.33
Cabbage, shredded	fresh	pound	.02	.04	.07	.09	.11	.13	.15	.18	.20	.22
raw	fresh	pound	.01	.02	.03	.04	.06	.07	.08	.09	.10	.11
sauerkraut	canned	16 oz	.02	.05	.08	.10	.12	.15	.18	.20	.22	.25
Carrots, diced or sliced	canned	16 oz	.03	.06	.08	.11	.14	.17	.20	.22	.25	.28
	fresh	pound	.02	.05	.07	.09	.12	.14	.16	.18	.21	.23
	frozen	10 oz	.03	.06	.09	.12	.15	.18	.21	.24	.27	.30
raw	fresh	pound	.02	.04	.06	.08	.10	.11	.13	.15	.17	.19
Celery, chopped or diced	fresh	24-oz bunch	.02	.03	.05	.06	.08	.10	.11	.13	.14	.16
raw	fresh	24-oz bunch	.01	.02	.04	.05	.06	.07	.08	.10	.11	.12
Corn, cream-style	canned	16 oz	.03	.06	.08	.11	.14	.17	.20	.22	.25	.28
Corn, whole kernels	canned (vacuum)	12 oz	.03	.06	.08	.11	.14	.17	.20	.22	.25	.28
	canned (liquid)	16 oz	.03	.06	.09	.12	.15	.18	.21	.24	.27	.30
	fresh	1 medium ear	.06	.12	.18	.24	.30	.35	.41	.47	.53	.59
	frozen	10 oz	.03	.07	.10	.13	.16	.20	.23	.26	.30	.33

Cucumbers, sliced, raw	fresh	10-oz cucumber	.04	.07	.11	.15	.18	.22	.26	.30	.33	.37
Greens:												
All types	canned	15 oz	.04	.08	.11	.15	.19	.23	.27	.30	.34	.38
Collards	fresh	pound	.02	.05	.07	.10	.12	.14	.17	.19	.22	.24
Collards	frozen	10 oz	.03	.07	.10	.14	.17	.20	.24	.27	.31	.34
Kale	fresh	pound	.02	.04	.06	.08	.10	.11	.13	.15	.17	.19
Kale or spinach	frozen	10 oz	.04	.08	.13	.17	.21	.25	.29	.34	.38	.42
Mustard greens	fresh [1]	10 oz	.06	.13	.20	.26	.32	.39	.46	.52	.58	.65
Mustard or turnip greens	frozen	10 oz	.04	.09	.14	.18	.22	.27	.32	.36	.40	.45
Spinach	fresh [2]	10 oz	.04	.08	.12	.16	.20	.25	.29	.33	.37	.41
Turnip greens	fresh [2]	10 oz	.08	.15	.22	.30	.38	.45	.52	.60	.68	.75
Lettuce pieces, raw	fresh	16 oz head	.01	.02	.02	.03	.04	.05	.06	.06	.07	.08
Onions, green, raw chopped	fresh	pound	.02	.03	.05	.07	.08	.10	.12	.14	.15	.17
Onions, mature	fresh	pound	.03	.06	.08	.11	.14	.17	.20	.22	.25	.28
raw	fresh	pound	.01	.03	.04	.06	.07	.08	.10	.11	.12	.14
Peas, green	canned	16 oz	.03	.06	.09	.12	.14	.17	.20	.23	.26	.29
	fresh, in pod	pound	.05	.10	.15	.20	.26	.31	.36	.41	.46	.51
	frozen	10 oz	.03	.06	.09	.12	.15	.18	.21	.24	.27	.30
Potatoes, cooked (whole)	canned	15 oz	.03	.07	.10	.13	.16	.20	.23	.26	.30	.33
diced	fresh	pound	.02	.04	.07	.09	.11	.13	.15	.18	.20	.22
mashed	dehydrated	7 oz	.01	.02	.03	.04	.05	.06	.07	.08	.09	.10
mashed	fresh	pound	.03	.06	.09	.12	.14	.17	.20	.23	.26	.29
French fries	frozen	9 oz	.03	.06	.09	.12	.16	.19	.22	.25	.28	.31
Sweetpotatoes	canned (syrup)	29 oz	.02	.04	.06	.08	.10	.11	.13	.15	.17	.19
	canned (vacuum)	18 oz	.02	.04	.06	.08	.10	.12	.14	.16	.18	.20
	fresh	pound	.03	.05	.08	.11	.14	.16	.19	.22	.24	.27
Tomatoes	canned	16 oz	.03	.05	.08	.10	.13	.16	.18	.21	.23	.26
raw	fresh	pound	.02	.04	.06	.08	.10	.12	.14	.16	.18	.20

SOURCE: Yields from "Family Food Buying: A Guide for Calculating Amounts to Buy and Comparing Costs," USDA HERR 37.

[1] Trimmed.
[2] Partly trimmed.

Cost of a ½-cup serving of selected fruits purchased at specified prices per market unit—canned, dried, fresh or frozen

Fruit or juice as served[1]	Market form	Market unit	Price per market unit									
			.10	.20	.30	.40	.50	.60	.70	.80	.90	1.00
			Cost of ½-cup serving									
Apples, sliced	canned	18 oz	.02	.05	.07	.09	.12	.14	.16	.18	.21	.23
cooked	fresh	pound	.04	.08	.11	.15	.19	.23	.27	.30	.34	.38
raw	fresh	pound	.02	.04	.05	.07	.09	.11	.13	.14	.16	.18
Applesauce	canned	17 oz	.03	.05	.08	.10	.13	.16	.18	.21	.23	.26
Apricot halves	canned	30 oz	.02	.05	.07	.10	.12	.14	.17	.19	.22	.24
cooked	dried	11 oz	.02	.04	.05	.07	.09	.11	.13	.14	.16	.18
uncooked	dried	11 oz	.02	.05	.07	.09	.12	.14	.16	.18	.21	.23
	fresh	pound	.02	.04	.05	.07	.09	.11	.13	.14	.16	.18
Bananas, sliced	fresh	pound	.02	.05	.07	.09	.12	.14	.16	.18	.21	.23
Cantaloup, diced	fresh	18-oz melon	.02	.05	.07	.10	.12	.14	.17	.19	.22	.24
Cherries:												
All varieties, pitted	fresh	pound	.02	.04	.06	.08	.10	.11	.13	.15	.17	.19
Sweet, unpitted	canned	16 oz	.03	.07	.10	.13	.16	.20	.23	.26	.30	.33
Tart red, pitted	canned	16 oz	.03	.07	.10	.14	.17	.20	.24	.27	.31	.34
	frozen	20 oz	.03	.05	.08	.11	.14	.16	.19	.22	.24	.27
Grapefruit sections	canned	16 oz	.04	.07	.11	.15	.18	.22	.26	.30	.33	.37
	fresh	20-oz fruit	.05	.09	.14	.18	.23	.28	.32	.37	.41	.46
	frozen	13½ oz	.05	.09	.14	.18	.23	.28	.32	.37	.41	.46
Juice:												
Any fruit (or vegetable)	canned or bottled	46 fl oz	.01	.02	.03	.04	.04	.05	.06	.07	.08	.09
	canned or bottled	32 fl oz	.01	.02	.04	.05	.06	.07	.08	.10	.11	.12
	frozen concentrated	16 fl oz	.01	.01	.02	.02	.03	.04	.04	.05	.05	.06
	frozen concentrated	12 fl oz	.01	.02	.02	.03	.04	.05	.06	.06	.07	.08
	frozen concentrated	6 fl oz	.02	.03	.05	.07	.08	.10	.12	.14	.15	.17
Grapefruit	fresh	20-oz fruit	.05	.10	.15	.20	.25	.30	.35	.40	.45	.50
Orange	fresh	dozen medium	.01	.02	.03	.04	.04	.05	.06	.07	.08	.09

Mixed fruit	canned	30 oz	.02	.05	.07	.09	.12	.14	.16	.18	.21	.23
Orange sections	fresh	dozen medium	.01	.01	.02	.03	.04	.04	.05	.06	.06	.07
Orange sections, mandarin	canned	11 oz	.05	.09	.14	.18	.23	.28	.32	.37	.41	.46
Peach slices or halves	canned	30 oz	.02	.05	.07	.10	.12	.14	.17	.19	.22	.24
cooked	dried	11 oz	.02	.03	.04	.06	.08	.09	.10	.12	.14	.15
uncooked	dried	11 oz	.02	.05	.08	.10	.12	.15	.18	.20	.22	.25
	fresh	pound	.03	.05	.08	.10	.13	.16	.18	.21	.23	.26
	frozen	10 oz	.07	.13	.20	.26	.33	.40	.46	.53	.59	.66
Pears: halves	canned	30 oz	.02	.05	.07	.09	.12	.14	.16	.18	.21	.23
diced	fresh	pound	.03	.05	.08	.11	.14	.16	.19	.22	.24	.27
Pineapple chunks	canned	20 oz	.03	.06	.08	.11	.14	.17	.20	.22	.25	.28
	fresh	2½-lb fruit	.01	.03	.04	.06	.07	.08	.10	.11	.13	.14
	frozen	13½ oz	.04	.09	.13	.18	.22	.26	.31	.35	.40	.44
Plums, whole	canned	30 oz	.02	.05	.07	.09	.12	.14	.16	.18	.21	.23
	fresh	pound	.02	.05	.08	.10	.12	.15	.18	.20	.22	.25
Prunes	canned	16 oz	.03	.05	.08	.11	.14	.16	.19	.22	.24	.27
cooked	dried	16 oz	.02	.03	.05	.06	.08	.10	.11	.13	.14	.16
uncooked	dried	16 oz	.02	.04	.06	.08	.10	.11	.13	.15	.17	.19
Raisins (cooked)	dried	15 oz	.01	.02	.04	.05	.06	.07	.08	.10	.11	.12
uncooked	dried	15 oz	.02	.03	.05	.07	.08	.10	.12	.14	.15	.17
Rhubarb, cooked with sugar	fresh	pound	.04	.08	.12	.16	.20	.23	.27	.31	.35	.39
	frozen	12 oz	.06	.12	.19	.25	.31	.37	.43	.50	.56	.62
Strawberries	canned	16 oz	.08	.15	.23	.30	.38	.46	.53	.61	.68	.76
whole	fresh	1 qt (24 oz)	.01	.02	.04	.05	.06	.07	.08	.10	.11	.12
whole	frozen	16 oz	.05	.09	.14	.19	.24	.28	.33	.38	.42	.47
sliced	frozen	10 oz	.10	.20	.30	.40	.50	.59	.69	.79	.89	.99
Tangerine sections	fresh	dozen (3 lb)	.01	.02	.03	.04	.04	.05	.06	.07	.08	.09
Watermelon, diced	fresh	pound	.04	.08	.11	.15	.19	.23	.27	.30	.34	.38

SOURCE: Yields from "Family Food Buying: A Guide for Calculating Amounts to Buy and Comparing Costs," USDA HERR 37.

[1] Fruit is served without juice or syrup.

Cost of 20 grams of protein from specified meats and meat alternates

Food	Amount, ready-to-eat, to give 20 grams protein [1]	Market unit	Part of market unit to give 20 grams of protein	Price per market unit [2]	Cost of 20 grams of protein
				(dollars)	
Peanut butter	4½ tbsp	12 oz	.23	.58	.13
Bread, white enriched [3]	9 slices	pound	.51	.34	.17
Dry beans	1⅓ cups	pound	.24	.78	.19
Eggs, large	3	dozen	.25	.78	.20
Chicken, ready-to-cook	3 oz	pound	.37	.56	.21
Bean soup, canned	2½ cups	11½ oz	.96	.22	.21
Milk, whole, fluid [4]	2⅓ cups	½ gal	.29	.80	.23
Ground beef	3 oz	pound	.24	1.01	.25
Chicken breast halves	¾	pound	.25	.98	.25
Beef liver	2⅔ oz	pound	.24	1.05	.25
Tuna, canned	2½ oz, drained	6½ oz	.44	.57	.25
Turkey, ready-to-cook	2¼ oz	pound	.35	.76	.27
Process American cheese	3 oz	8 oz	.38	.76	.29
Cured ham	3⅓ oz	pound	.29	1.09	.31
Round beefsteak, bone in	2¼ oz, lean	pound	.22	1.79	.39
Ocean perch fillet, frozen	3⅔ oz	pound	.36	1.10	.40
Frankfurters	3½	8 oz	.36	1.20	.43
Chuck roast of beef, bone in	2½ oz, lean	pound	.35	1.25	.44
Rump roast of beef, boned	2½ oz, lean	pound	.26	1.75	.45
Pork chops, center	2⅓ oz	pound	.35	1.50	.52
Bologna	6 1-oz slices	pound	.73	.77	.56
Bacon, sliced	10 slices	pound	.52	1.25	.66
Porterhouse beefsteak	2⅓ oz, lean	pound	.34	2.06	.69

[1] Approximately one-third of the daily amount recommended for a man.
[2] Average retail prices in U.S. cities, April 1974, Bureau of Labor Statistics, U.S. Department of Labor.
[3] Bread and other grain products, such as pasta and rice, are frequently used with a small amount of meat, poultry, fish or cheese as main dishes in economy meals. In this way the high quality protein in meat and cheese enhances the lower quality of protein in cereal products.
[4] Although milk is not used to replace meat in meals, it is an economical source of good quality protein. Protein from nonfat dry milk costs less than half as much as from whole fluid milk.

To find out if you can save by buying the large size, compare the cost per unit of food from different size containers.

Some stores show prices per unit—ounce, pound, pint or quart—that you can use to compare prices right in the store.

If unit prices are not posted in your store, you can figure them out yourself for foods you want to compare. On the label of the container, find the statement of contents—in ounces or pounds of net weight or in fluid ounces, pints or quarts for foods sold by volume. Then divide the price by the number of units in the container to find the cost per unit.

Example: For crackers in a 7-ounce box at 42 cents, 42 ÷ 7 = 6 cents per ounce. For a 16-ounce box at 48 cents, 48 ÷ 16 = 3 cents per ounce. The larger box is a better buy.

FOR FURTHER READING:

U.S. Department of Agriculture, Office of Communication, *Money-Saving Main Dishes*, G43, Washington, D.C. 20250.

———. *Your Money's Worth in Foods*, G183, Washington, D.C. 20250.

Can's and Can'ts For Canners

FOOD PRESERVATION has evolved through continuous research until it has revolutionized man's eating habits and thus his diet. Research continues to make canned food nutritious, convenient, safe—and sometimes more economical than its counterpart in other forms. Whether home canned or commercially prepared, canned foods continue to be a popular money saver in the food budget.

Before the canning season, make a food conservation plan. The daily food guide, size of your family, its food likes and dislikes, the number of non-productive months, and your food budget should be considered in the plan. Numerous studies indicate that families who produce and conserve their food supply are better fed than those who do not, regardless of income.

Check your canning equipment and supplies early. Money may be saved by comparing prices on canners, jars and supplies from various sources—and often by buying them "out of season."

Jars are usually purchased in one-half pint, pint, and quart size. Although one-half gallon jars may be purchased, we have no directions for their use in home canning. Inspect used jars for nicks and cracks. Since lids will seal only once, always use new ones.

Test pressure canners periodically (how often depends on use and care) for accuracy. The gauge is a vital part since this registers the internal pressure and thus temperature. If the gauge is off two pounds or less, you should be aware of it and make adjustments accordingly. If the inaccuracy is more than two pounds, you need a new gauge if proper internal temperature is to be maintained. Accuracy in time and temperature should be your canning watchword.

Variety, maturity, method of canning and storage affect the quality of the product. Canned foods will be no better than the raw products you begin with and the procedures used. If canned foods are defined broadly as those foods treated with heat in hermetically sealed containers, three methods are used today in home canning. The method recommended is determined by the pH of the food plus the treatment prior to canning.

Foods in their natural state are classified as acid or low-acid. Tomatoes (generally) and fruits, except figs, are acid foods with a pH ranging from 3.0 to 4.4. Because of their acidity, or low pH, these may be safely processed by the boiling water bath method. A temperature above the boiling point is excessive and unnecessary. No foods can be safely processed by this method if the pH is above 4.5 (see chart).

Meats and vegetables, except tomatoes, are low-acid foods with a pH ranging from 4.6 to 6.3. These must be processed at a temperature higher than can be obtained in boiling water. Therefore, need for using the pressure canner or retort is evident.

In home canning of meats and vegetables, a pressure of ten pounds yielding a temperature of 240° F is recommended because of the safety factor. Commercially, under controlled conditions, a higher temperature—shorter time process is often used. The amount of time the food must be processed depends on such factors as pH of the food, heat penetration rate, size of the jar, and type pack. Under no conditions should you either lower the processing temperature or shorten the time that has been established through reliable research.

A pressure saucepan may be used for home canning if it (1) has a false bottom; (2) is tall enough so steam can circulate around and over jars; (3) has a gauge that will maintain ten pounds

---

AUTHOR *Iola Pritchard* was Specialist in Food Conservation and Marketing, Agricultural Extension Service, North Carolina State University, Raleigh. She is now retired.

Average pH Values for Some Common Foods

pH	Food	
0		ACID
.		
2.9	Vinegar	
3.0	Gooseberries	
.		
3.2	Rhubarb, dill pickles	
3.3	Apricots, blackberries	
3.4	Strawberries	
3.5	Peaches	
3.6	Raspberries, sauerkraut	
3.7	Blueberries	
3.8	Sweet cherries	
3.9	Pears	
.		
4.2	Tomatoes	
4.4	Lowest acidity for processing at 212° F	

pH	Food	
4.6	Figs, pimentos	LOW ACID
.		Process at 240° F
5.0	Pumpkins, carrots	
5.1	Cucumbers	
5.2	Turnips, cabbage, squash	
5.3	Parsnips, beets, snap beans	
5.4	Sweet potatoes	
5.5	Spinach	
5.6	Asparagus, cauliflower	
5.8	Mushrooms, meat, ripened	
6.0	Tuna, carrots	
6.1	Potatoes	
6.2	Peas	
6.3	Corn	
.		
.		
7.0	Meat, unripened	NEUTRAL
.		ALKALINITY
.		
.		
14.0		

pressure; and if (4) 20 minutes are added to the processing time.

All low-acid foods are potential carriers of *Clostridium botulinum*, a type bacterium that exists in both a vegetative and heat resistant spore form. The vegetative form is easily killed by moist heat at 212° F; however, some spores may survive that temperature for five to six hours.

Clostridium botulinum is a rod shaped bacterium found in some dust and common to soil all over the world. Some plants grown in soil containing this organism could carry the bacterium. In addition, meat from animals that have eaten contaminated plant life could be a carrier.

This bacterium is harmless under aerobic conditions (the presence of oxygen); however, it multiplies under anaerobic conditions (absence of oxygen) producing a toxin extremely lethal to man. Anaerobic conditions suitable for growth and multiplication of this bacterium prevail in vacuum sealed jars or cans. Thus, a can or jar of low acid food improperly processed could provide these conditions.

It is true that low-acid foods, even though contaminated with *Clostridium botulinum* toxin, may be made safe by boiling them in a container at least ten minutes before eating. But the risks are too great in terms of time, money, and safety. Consider the homemakers who "just taste" to be sure the food is good; or the ones who decide to make a cold bean salad.

In home canning, one-half inch headspace should be left for most fruits and vegetables. Very starchy foods, such as corn, require one inch. Generally, the jar is filled with solids and liquid added to fill spaces and cover the product.

Most fruits and vegetables may be canned either hot or raw pack, depending on individual preference. There is a tendency for some foods, especially fruits, to float when the raw pack method is used. This floating does not indicate spoilage, but the product may be low in esthetic value. The hot pack method of canning vegetables generally insures a better fill. This is because air and moisture are released from the plant cells during heating.

The third method of canning is a pasteurization process. Pickes, relishes, preserves, jams, conserves and marmalades are packed hot in hot sterilized jars, sealed, and processed in a hot water bath at simmering temperature (about 200° F) for ten minutes. Since they are naturally acid foods or have vinegar added, this mild treatment is effective. The procedure sterilizes headspace and expels air from the jar. If the vacuum seal is retained, growth of aerobic microorganisms such as molds is prevented.

Jellies are not generally pasteurized in the home, but a thin coat of paraffin is added. (Paraffin may be reused). This does not prevent mold, but retards its growth. Should mold appear because of long and/or damp storage, discard the product in its entirety.

Foods properly canned require no preservatives, although some may be used. When sugar is added to fruits and salt to vegetables, they serve to improve flavor, but in nominal amounts they are not regarded as preservatives. If these ingredients are used in large quantities as in some pickles and preserves, sugar and salt may then become preservatives.

It is not recommended that combinations of foods, such as vegetable stew, be canned. Usually they contain a mixture of meats, corn, tomatoes and some other vegetables. If safe to eat, the product would have to be processed at 240° F for 85 minutes, the highest temperature and longest time required for any ingredient. Texture and flavor would be altered for ingredients requiring less time and/or lower temperatures for processing. Foods, properly canned and combined at the time of use, give a superior quality product.

Economic conditions and decreased availability of food are among the factors causing an upsurge of interest in home canning. As this interest broadened, community canneries opened similar to those in operation during World War II. Success or failure of such operations appears to be in direct proportion to the educational programs conducted by cooperating agencies and cannery management.

Equipment at these operations varies from commercial type retorts for canning in tin or glass, to the regular home type pressure and water bath canners. It is suspected that some of these canneries are not operating at peak efficiency.

Before canned foods are stored, they should be checked carefully. When a jar is properly vacuum sealed, the top is slightly concave. Any lids that bulge out indicate a gas has formed inside the can and this suggests spoilage.

Canned foods, whether commercially done or prepared at home, should be stored in a cool, dark, dry place. Color, flavor, texture and some nutrients are preserved best under these conditions.

Freezing canned foods may cause physical damage to the container—even breakage in glass. However, if the seal is not broken, or in the case of glass, the container is not cracked, the texture of the product may be slightly inferior, but the food should be safe to eat. If storage temperature is maintained at excessively high levels, the nutritive value declines and the texture becomes less desirable.

It is not recommended that most canned foods be kept more than a year or two because of possible deterioration of texture and flavor. However, it is true that they should still be safe from microbiological growth if they were properly prepared and stored and if there is no damage to the container (such as rust).

Canning crosscut pickle slices.

Few other convenience foods on the market today are used more than canned ones—and convenience foods do not have to be purchased as such. Almost any home kitchen can be turned into a miniature processing plant for preparing your own convenience foods.

We are told the energy crisis will be a limiting factor in our lives for some time. When feasible, this could be used to our advantage by producing a portion of our own food supply. A change in family patterns from the "highway to a garden" could also mean ready access to your own pantry of home canned goodness.

The Cold Facts About Freezing

YOUR FAVORITE supermarket has a beef sale, and a special on orange juice. Besides, your garden seems to be setting a production record. Should you freeze or not freeze?

Freezing may be the answer—if you have freezer space. It can be the key to varied family meals, an easy and excellent way to preserve many of today's surpluses for tomorrow. But selecting a freezer to fit your needs and filling that freezer with high quality food takes time, energy, money, and know-how.

First, let's tackle the question of freezer space. The amount of space you need depends on the kinds and quantities of food you'll store at one time. If freezing is just one of the ways you preserve food, 3 cubic feet per person may be adequate. However, you may use as much as 10 cubic feet per person if most of the food you consume is stored in the freezer.

Home freezers are available in sizes ranging from less than 3 to more than 30 cubic feet of storage space. If you need more than 10 cubic feet of freezing space and have room for it, a separate freezer may be the best choice. But if your freezer requirement is limited and floor space is not one of your luxuries, a refrigerator-freezer combination may meet your needs. Refrigerator-freezer combinations which maintain 0° F in the freezer cabinet will keep food as long as a separate freezer appliance.

Costs of owning and operating a freezer vary widely. However, you can

---

AUTHOR *Marcile Allen* is an Extension specialist in foods and nutrition at Purdue University, West Lafayette, Ind.

CO-AUTHOR *Mardel L. Crandall* is an information specialist, Indiana Cooperative Extension Service, Purdue University.

make an estimate of operating expenses by adding the cost of electricity, packaging, and probable repairs.

Cost of electricity depends upon amount used and local rates. You may soon find electrical energy requirements listed on the name plate of new equipment. In the meantime, your local utility representative and your appliance dealer can probably give you the information.

Energy required to maintain an empty freezer cabinet at a desired temperature is related mainly to the temperature at which the freezer is kept, the effectiveness of its insulation, and the size and design of the freezer. With equally good design and operation, larger size freezers tend to be more efficient. For example, the energy required to maintain 0° F in a 6-cubic-foot freezer for one day is about 0.3 kilowatt-hour (kwh) per cubic foot, while an 18-cubic-foot size requires about 0.2 kwh per cubic foot per day.

The amount and kind of food you freeze influence the operating cost. Each food must be lowered to its freezing point, frozen at that point, and lowered to the freezer storage temperature. The freezer uses more energy to freeze some foods than others. On the average, freezing a pound of food and lowering its temperature to 0° F requires about 0.1 kwh.

Seasonal operation of one freezer can cut costs for families who operate two or more units. You'll also save by reducing the number of times you open and close the freezer door. Such frugal management cuts operating costs and saves energy.

Packaging materials vary in cost from less than 1 to more than 3 cents per pound of frozen food. Estimated annual freezer repairs may run about 2 percent of the initial cost of your freezer.

To complete your cost estimate, figure yearly depreciation of the freezer (purchase price divided by expected years of operation). Also figure the loss of interest on your freezer money which could have been otherwise invested (generally estimated at 5 percent a year).

But does a freezer lower food costs enough to make these operating costs worthwhile? That depends on freezer use. If you have large quantities of high quality, home-produced foods that you

APPROXIMATE YIELD OF FROZEN FRUITS FROM FRESH

FRUIT	FRESH, AS PURCHASED OR PICKED	FROZEN NUMBER OF PINTS
Apples	$1\frac{1}{4}$ to $1\frac{1}{2}$ lb.	1
Apricots	$\frac{2}{3}$ to $\frac{4}{5}$ lb.	1
Berries except raspberries	1 crate (24 qt.)	32 to 36
and strawberries	$1\frac{1}{3}$ to $1\frac{1}{2}$ pt.	1
Cantaloupe	1 dozen (28 lb.)	22
Cherries, sweet or sour	$1\frac{1}{4}$ to $1\frac{1}{2}$ lb.	1
Cranberries	$\frac{1}{2}$ lb.	1
Currants	2 qt. (3 lb.)	4
	$\frac{3}{4}$ lb.	1
Peaches and pears	1 to $1\frac{1}{2}$ lb.	1
Pineapple	5 lb.	4
Plums and prunes	1 to $1\frac{1}{2}$ lb.	1
Raspberries	1 crate (24 pt.)	24
	1 pt.	1
Rhubarb	$\frac{2}{3}$ to 1 lb.	1
Strawberries	1 crate (24 qt.)	38
	1 lb.	1

APPROXIMATE YIELD OF FROZEN VEGETABLES FROM FRESH

VEGETABLE	FRESH, AS PURCHASED OR PICKED	FROZEN, NUMBER OF PINTS
Asparagus	1 to 1½ lb.	1
Beans, Lima (in pods)	2 to 2½ lb.	1
Beans, snap, green and wax	⅔ to 1 lb.	1
Beets (without tops)	1¼ to 1½ lb.	1
Broccoli and Brussels sprouts	1 lb.	1
Carrots (without tops)	1¼ to 1½ lb.	1
Cauliflower	4 lb. (2 medium heads)	3
Corn, sweet (in husks)	2 to 2½ lb. (3 large ears)	1
Peas	2 to 2½ lb.	1
Peppers, sweet	⅔ lb. (3 peppers)	1
Pumpkin and winter squash	3 lb.	2
Spinach and other greens	1 to 1½ lb.	1
Squash, summer	1 to 1½ lb.	1
Sweet potatoes	⅔ lb.	1

can't use during the growing season—and if you will seek and preserve good quality, low cost food—a freezer may help lower your food bill.

At the peak of production, foods produced or processed locally may be good buys for your freezer. Consider buying fresh fruits and vegetables in season from roadside stands or farms. A "pick your own" operation can help you save money in many communities. And, of course, grocery stores offer "specials" on fresh or frozen products throughout the year.

Packaged food plans may be still another possibility—but BEWARE! Although such plans offer the convenience of home delivery, the quality, type, or even quantity of offered foods may not be what you would choose. Often, too, such plans involve purchase of a freezer in addition to frozen food. Some consumers complain about overall costs of the plan, irregularity of food delivery, and differences between expected quality and quality delivered. So, consider alternatives before you obligate yourself to such a plan.

To stock your freezer, select foods that freeze well, foods your family will enjoy. If time is limited, freeze foods you can serve with little added preparation. If your food budget is limited, choose foods that will help you save money.

You probably will use most of your freezer space for such basic foods as meats, vegetables, and fruits. As packages of basic foods are used, you may fill empty spaces with prepared foods or other seasonal foods.

Because meats take a sizable hunk of your food dollar, you may wonder if you can save money by buying a side of beef, pork, or lamb. To answer your question, carefully compare the costs of buying a whole carcass, side, or quarter; buying wholesale cuts; or buying retail cuts.

A carcass, side, or quarter is normally sold by its "hanging" weight, the weight before cutting and trimming. For a beef carcass, cutting losses vary from 20 to 30 percent or more.

You also need to know the yield grade of meats when buying by the carcass. Yield Grade I is the highest yield, and Yield Grade V, the lowest. Yield Grade I means the carcass will yield 79.8 percent or more in retail cuts; Yield Grade V, 65.9 percent or less.

If you don't want some of the cuts that come from a side or quarter, or if your freezer space is limited, consider buying wholesale cuts. Wholesale cuts can often be purchased from those who sell meat by the side or quarter. Or you may save by watching for specials on retail cuts. Remember, retail cuts usually need to be rewrapped for long-term freezer storage, and this wrapping cost must be considered.

Whether you buy a carcass, wholesale cuts, or retail cuts, take special note of quality when buying beef. Beef varies more in quality than any other meat. The grade of beef most widely sold in supermarkets today is USDA Choice. Most consumers like this level of quality.

For more details on buying meats for your freezer see *Food for Us All,* the 1969 Yearbook of Agriculture, and Home and Garden Bulletin No. 166, *How to Buy Meat for Your Freezer.*

Chickens, ducks, geese, and turkey are good buys for your freezer if you take advantage of specials. Poultry can go into the freezer in a variety of forms. To save space when freezing cut-up poultry, freeze only fleshy pieces; cook the bony pieces such as wings and backs for immediate use or store as cooked meat picked off the bone. Recommended storage time for cooked poultry is shorter than for uncooked poultry.

You will want to make room in your freezer for your fisherman's catch and good buys in fish. Small fish are often dressed and frozen whole; large ones are usually cut into steaks or fillets.

Fresh eggs can be frozen when they are plentiful. Egg whites freeze well "as is" with no additions. To freeze whole eggs or egg yolks, break the yolk and blend with syrup, sugar, or salt. Blending before and after freezing reduces the undesirable thickening of frozen fresh yolks.

A home freezer lets you preserve fruits and vegetables with little time between harvest and freezing. You'll have the highest quality possible if you use good methods and quickly freeze freshly harvested, sound fruits and vegetables at their best maturity. If you wonder how well a particular fruit or vegetable will freeze, test freeze a few packages.

The quantity of frozen food you get from a given amount of fresh fruits or vegetables depends on the quality, condition, maturity, and variety of the item and how it is prepared.

If you plan to grow some of your own fruits and vegetables for freezing, you may want some information about recommended varieties which grow well in your locality. For such information contact your County or State Extension Service.

For information on how to select and freeze fresh fruits and vegetables see *Food for Us All,* the 1969 Yearbook of Agriculture, and also Home and Garden Bulletins No. 141, *How to Buy Fresh Fruits;* No. 143, *How to Buy Fresh Vegetables,* and No. 10, *Home Freezing of Fruits and Vegetables.*

Once you have obtained fruits and vegetables for the freezer, there's no time to waste. Most vegetables lose flavor quickly—some more quickly than others. Hence the rule, one hour from garden to freezer.

In general, prepare fruits and vegetables—and other foods, too—for freezing in about the same way as for cooking or table use. However, some fruits require special treatment to make them more pleasing in color, texture, or flavor. Fruits that tend to darken may be given anti-darkening treatment to prevent browning by oxidation.

Most fruits have better texture and flavor if packed in sugar or syrup. But, if sugar is limited in the diet of any family member, you may pack prepared fruit into containers without added sweetening.

An important step in preparing vegetables for freezing is blanching, a heating process which slows or stops the action of enzymes. Otherwise, enzyme activity would cause deterioration of flavor, color, and nutritive value of the vegetable during storage. Cooling is the final step of preparation.

Freezing is a good method of preserving nearly all baked products. However, baked products tend to be bulky and may take too much of your valuable freezer space. And even if you have space, don't freeze cakes with seven minute or boiled frostings. These icings do not freeze well. For more information on buying and storing bread and cereal products, see *Food for Us All*, the 1969 Yearbook of Agriculture.

Frozen milk desserts are the main dairy product stored in the freezer. Butter and margarine will keep well for two months in the freezer. Heavy cream and whipped cream may be frozen. However, freezing is not recommended for most cheeses.

Wise use of frozen prepared foods can offer convenience and variety to your meals. But don't fill your freezer with *just any* prepared food! Concentrate on dishes that your family especially likes or dishes that require many or seasonal foods, special preparation skills, or much time or work to prepare.

After foods are selected and prepared, cool them promptly and package in amounts suitable for your family meals.

Experience will show you what amount your family needs.

Don't take packaging lightly; proper packaging helps control the quality of your freezer foods. Cost should not be your only guide. Look for packaging that: effectively protects food during freezer storage, is strong at freezer temperature, and is convenient for both packaging and removing frozen foods with or without thawing.

To retain highest quality in frozen food, packaging materials should be moisture-vapor-proof. Glass, metal, and rigid plastic containers are examples of this type. Most bags, wrapping materials, and waxed cartons made especially for freezing are moisture-vapor-resistant enough to retain satisfactory quality. Unacceptable packaging for freezer storage includes ordinary waxed papers, lightweight household aluminum foil, and unwaxed or lightly waxed cartons.

Label each package with product name and date, including other specific information needed. It's also a good idea to keep a record of the foods you freeze. Without a record, you can easily forget what's hidden in your freezer. When you take a food out, cross off the entry for it. You'll find the freezer record a handy reference for meal planning.

Freeze food quickly to 0° F or lower. Limit the amount of food to be frozen at one time. Freeze no more than 2 or 3 pounds per cubic foot of your freezer capacity. Otherwise, the food will require more than 24 hours to freeze—a real no-no for high quality frozen foods.

Once foods are frozen, stack like foods together. Place the most recently frozen foods at the bottom or back of your freezer, and move foods that have been frozen longer toward the top or front.

Keep the freezer at 0° F or lower at all times. At this temperature the nutritive value of properly prepared and frozen food, stored for the recommended time, nearly equals that of fresh food. At temperatures above 0° F, more of the vitamins, flavor, color, and texture will be lost during the same storage time than at 0° F or lower. The higher the temperature, the faster the loss of quality.

Some loss of water-soluble vitamins and minerals occurs during blanching and water chilling of vegetables. And additional nutrient losses can be attributed to trimming and cutting food during preparation. These losses will be similar to those resulting from preparing fresh fruits and vegetables for the table.

SUGGESTED HOME STORAGE PERIODS TO MAINTAIN HIGH QUALITY FROZEN FOODS STORED AT 0° F OR LOWER

Food	*Months*
FRESH MEATS	
Beef and lamb roasts and steaks	8 to 12
Veal and pork roasts	4 to 8
Chops, cutlets	3 to 6
Variety meats	3 to 4
Ground beef, veal or lamb and stew meats	3 to 4
Ground pork	1 to 3
Sausage	1 to 2
CURED, SMOKED AND READY-TO-SERVE MEATS	
Ham—whole, half or sliced	1 to 2
Bacon, corned beef, frankfurters and wieners	Less than 1
Ready-to-eat luncheon meats	Freezing not recommended
COOKED MEAT	
Cooked meat and meat dishes	2 to 3
FRESH POULTRY	
Chicken and turkey	12
Duck and goose	6
Giblets	3
COOKED POULTRY	
Cooked poultry dishes and cooked poultry slices or pieces covered with gravy or broth	6
Fried chicken	4
Sandwiches of poultry meat and cooked slices or pieces not covered with gravy or broth	1
FRESH FISH	6 to 9
COMMERCIALLY FROZEN FISH	
Shrimp and fillets of lean type fish	3 to 4
Clams, shucked, and cooked fish	3
Fillets of fatty type fish and crab meat	2 to 3
Oysters, shucked	1
FRUITS AND VEGETABLES, most	8 to 12
Home-frozen citrus fruits and juices	4 to 6
MILK PRODUCTS	
Cheddar type cheese—one pound or less, not more than one inch thick	6 or less
Butter and margarine	2
Frozen milk desserts, commercial	1
PREPARED FOODS	
Cookies	6
Cakes, prebaked	4 to 9
Combination main dishes and fruit pies	3 to 6
Breads, prebaked and cake batters	3
Yeast bread dough and pie shells	1 to 2

Once food is tucked away in the freezer, don't forget it. The longer the storage period, the greater the loss of quality. Recommended maximum storage periods have been established and are discussed throughout *Food for Us All,* the 1969 Yearbook of Agriculture.

When you take food out of the freezer, be cautious about thawing. Although illness-causing bacteria don't grow while frozen, they can multiply upon thawing. To avoid food spoilage, thaw foods in the refrigerator or cook frozen foods without thawing. If you thaw food rapidly—or in the refrigerator—and use it promptly, you'll have little trouble with spoilage.

Some special management is required if your freezer stops. To conserve the cold, do not open the freezer door except to check on the temperature after you suspect it has risen. A fully loaded freezer will generally keep food frozen for several days. When only half full, it may not keep food frozen longer than a day.

If the freezer will not be operating for several days and dry ice is available, you may use it to keep the food cold. Or transfer food to an operating freezer or a locker plant.

But what if the food has already started to thaw? Is it safe to refreeze? It is usually safe to refreeze if the food still contains ice crystals and no portion of the food is warm.

Preparing to wrap a whole bird for the freezer.

If thawing is complete, you can refreeze fruits that smell and taste good. Beef, veal, and lamb which show no sign of spoilage may be refrozen, too. However, if the color or odor of any thawed food is poor or questionable, get rid of it. And don't refreeze melted ice cream and completely thawed vegetables, sea foods, and prepared dishes.

What it all boils down to is this: a well managed freezer offers convenience, variety, personal satisfaction, and sometimes even a savings on your food bill. But it won't work by itself. You need to put some effort into selecting, preparing, and packaging freezer food. And you have to be a manager extraordinaire.

FOR FURTHER READING:

U.S. Department of Agriculture, *Food for Us All,* 1969 Yearbook of Agriculture, for sale by Superintendent of Documents, Washington, D.C. 20402.

———, Office of Communication, *Home Freezing of Fruits and Vegetables,* G10, Washington, D.C. 20250, 1971.

———. *Freezing Meat and Fish in the Home,* G93, Washington, D.C. 20250, 1973.

———. *Home Freezing of Poultry,* G70, Washington, D.C. 20250, 1970.

———. *Freezing Combination Main Dishes,* G40, Washington, D.C. 20250, 1973.

———. *Home Care of Purchased Frozen Foods,* G69, Washington, D.C. 20250, 1973.

———. *What to Do When Your Home Freezer Stops,* Leaflet 321, Washington, D.C. 20250, 1967.

———. *How to Buy Meat for Your Freezer,* G166, Washington, D.C. 20250.

———. *How to Buy Beef Roasts,* G146, Washington, D.C. 20250, 1968.

———. *How to Buy Beef Steaks,* G145, Washington, D.C. 20250, 1968.

———. *How to Buy Fresh Fruits,* G141, Washington, D.C. 20250, 1967.

———. *How to Buy Canned and Frozen Fruits,* G191, Washington, D.C. 20250, 1971.

———. *How to Buy Fresh Vegetables,* G143, Washington, D.C. 20250, 1967.

———. *How to Buy Canned and Frozen Vegetables,* G167, Washington, D.C. 20250, 1969.

USDA Grades Can Help Out Food Shoppers

SHOPPERS IN TODAY'S supermarkets face a bewildering array of products. But there is an increasing amount of information to help them make a rational choice.

Nutritional labeling will soon be used on many products. Open dating, showing the expected shelf life of a product, is being used on more and more products. Unit pricing—showing the cost per ounce, per pint, or other common measure—is also featured by many stores. These subjects are explained in other chapters of this book.

USDA (U.S. Department of Agriculture) grade shields on certain products can also be useful guides to the shopper who understands their meaning.

You are most likely to find this shield on beef, lamb, turkey, chicken, duck, eggs, and butter. The shield is used less often on canned and frozen fruits and vegetables, veal, calf, Cheddar cheese, instant nonfat dry milk, and—rarely—on fresh fruits and vegetables.

The USDA grade shield is used only on foods that have been officially graded according to the Federal quality grade standards which define exactly what each grade means.

Further, the U.S. Department of Agriculture—and the state departments of agriculture which cooperate in providing the services—will grant grading services only to packers and processors who meet strict requirements for cleanliness and sanitary processing. In the case of meat and poultry, grading may be done only on products which have passed inspection for wholesomeness.

The grading services are voluntary, not required by Federal law. Packers and processors who want their products to carry the USDA grade shield must apply for the service, meet the requirements, and pay a fee to cover the cost. The service and use of the grade shield are withdrawn if the packer or processor fails to meet sanitation and other requirements (for example, accurate net weights).

Federal grading services began well over 50 years ago. They were originally established as an aid in wholesale trading, to enable the producer to get a price for his product in line with its quality and to let sellers and buyers communicate about quality with a common language.

Today most grading is still done for this purpose, and the consumer is usually the indirect, instead of the direct, beneficiary. However, where the grade shield is used—and carried on the retail package or product—the consumer can use the USDA grades as a direct guide to quality. To do so, he should understand something about the nature of the grades and their limitations.

Grades for each product cover the entire range of quality, so there are more grades for some products than for others. For example, since beef varies widely in quality, it takes eight grades—from USDA Prime to USDA Canner—to span the range. But for broiler-fryers, which are quite uniform in quality, only three grades are needed, USDA Grades A, B, and C.

In most cases, retail stores carry only one or two grades of a product, so it is not necessary for consumers to learn the whole range.

There is some variation in the grade names used because most of the grade names are simply carryovers from many years' use in the food industry. However, with the exception of those used for meat—USDA Prime, Choice, Good, Standard, and Commercial—the most common grades are USDA Grades A and B. In the case of eggs and butter, there is a higher grade, USDA Grade

---

AUTHOR *Eleanor Ferris* is chief of the Marketing Services Branch, Information Division, Agricultural Marketing Service.

AA, which is a premium quality, above that normally considered a very good quality.

Packers of canned and frozen fruits and vegetables may use either of alternative grade terms—U.S. Grade A or U.S. Fancy; U.S. Grade B or U.S. Choice or Extra Standard; U.S. Grade C or U.S. Standard. If you see one of these terms on canned or frozen fruits or vegetables, whether or not used within the grade shield, then the product has been officially graded.

Packers of canned and frozen fruits and vegetables sometimes use those terms without the prefix "U.S." In other words, they may label the product simply "Grade A" or "Fancy." In that case, the product is not required to have been officially graded, but *is* required to measure up to the quality stated as if it had been. Otherwise, the product is considered misbranded under Federal labeling laws.

Here is a brief summary of the USDA grades for each of the foods which may carry an official grade shield:

MEAT

This mark on the outer fat covering of a meat cut means it has been officially graded for quality. This is the grade (Choice) you are most likely to see. Several kinds of meat—beef, lamb, veal, and calf—are graded and the same mark is used on each. There are no quality grades for pork at present.

Beef

Two things are important in buying and cooking beef—the quality grade and the cut. Some cuts, like steaks and roasts from the rib and loin (including porterhouse, T-bone, club, tenderloin, and sirloin) are fairly tender in any grade you will find in retail stores and can be cooked with dry heat (roasted or broiled). Other cuts, like round steaks and chuck roasts, are less tender and usually should be pot-roasted, braised, or pan-fried.

The beef grades are a guide to how tender and flavorful most cuts will be:

- USDA Prime is the best—the ultimate in tenderness, juiciness, and flavor.
- USDA Choice is very high quality. Steaks and roasts of this grade will be quite tender, juicy, and flavorful.
- USDA Good is somewhat leaner and not as juicy and flavorful as Prime and Choice. It is fairly tender, however, and may be an economical buy.
- USDA Standard has a high proportion of lean and very little fat. It is not as flavorful as higher grades and will be somewhat dry unless cooked with moist heat. But it is fairly tender since, like the above grades, it comes from young animals.
- USDA Commercial has abundant marbling (like Prime) and is very tasty, but since it comes from mature animals it requires long, slow cooking with moist heat to make it tender.

Lamb, Veal, Calf

Most cuts of Prime and Choice lamb are tender and can be roasted in the oven or broiled. Lower grade lamb is seldom sold at retail. To be called lamb, the meat must come from animals less than a year old. Meat from older sheep is called yearling mutton or mutton, and if it is graded these words will appear with the grade mark.

Prime and Choice grade veal is juicier and more flavorful than lower grades, but most veal is not tender enough to be broiled. Roasts in the higher grades, however, can be oven-roasted. Lower grades should be cooked with moist heat.

Most of the above comments on beef grades apply to the grades of calf, but you cannot expect calf meat to be as savory as more mature beef.

POULTRY

This grade shield may be found on the package or wing tag on fresh or frozen poultry—chickens, turkeys, ducks, geese, guineas, squab. USDA Grade A is the only grade you are likely to see—the lower grades, B and C, are practically never printed on a poultry label. Grade A birds have more meat and a better appearance than those of the lower grades. Class of poultry is important, too; look for the word "young" (or words indicating a young bird, such as broiler, fryer) if you want to broil, fry, or roast the bird.

EGGS

This is the grade shield used on eggs. It may show both the quality grade—USDA Grade AA, A, or B—and the size. Or the size may be printed separately on the carton. Consider both size and grade in buying eggs—they are not related, but both affect the price.

Size means the minimum weight per dozen, not the size of each egg. The sizes sold most frequently are Extra Large—at least 27 ounces per dozen; Large—24 ounces per dozen; Medium—21 ounces per dozen; and Small—18 ounces per dozen.

USDA Grade AA and A eggs have a high, rounded yolk and upstanding, thick white that does not spread out widely. They are the best to use for poaching and frying. USDA Grade B eggs may have a flatter yolk and thinner white, so are appropriate for use in baked goods and other dishes where appearance is not a factor.

DAIRY PRODUCTS

You'll find this grade mark on many butter packages. USDA Grade AA butter is the best, with highly pleasing sweet flavor and aroma, smooth texture, and good keeping ability. USDA Grade A is almost as good. USDA Grade B butter may have a slightly acid flavor.

These same grades, and the same grade shield, are used for Cheddar cheese. USDA Grade AA Cheddar cheese has highly consistent good flavor—appropriate for its type (mild, mellow, or sharp), smooth texture, uniform color, and attractive appearance. USDA Grade A Cheddar is also very good, but may vary slightly in flavor and texture from package to package.

NONFAT DRY MILK

To earn this "USDA Extra Grade" shield, instant nonfat dry milk must have a sweet and pleasing flavor, natural color, and must dissolve instantly when mixed with water. Instant nonfat dry milk may be labeled with the grade shield only if it is manufactured in an officially approved plant, in a sanitary manner, under the continuous inspection of a USDA grader.

PACKED UNDER CONTINUOUS INSPECTION OF THE U. S. DEPT. OF AGRICULTURE

U. S. GRADE A FANCY

CANNED AND FROZEN FRUITS AND VEGETABLES

Either or both of these shields may be found on canned and frozen fruits and vegetables. The "continuous inspection" shield, if used alone, means what it says—that the product was packed in a plant operating under the constant supervision of a USDA grader. It may be used only on products meeting at least minimum quality requirements.

The U.S. Grade A shield may be used only on products which meet the USDA standards for the grade and which have been officially graded.

Grade A fruits and vegetables are the most tender, succulent, and uniform in size, shape, and color. Grade B is a very good quality, but requirements are less strict for uniformity, size, and color—and there may be a few blemishes. Grade C products are fairly good quality, just as wholesome and nutritious as the higher grades, and often a thrifty buy.

FRESH FRUITS AND VEGETABLES

Although most fresh fruits and vegetables are sold at wholesale on the basis of U.S. grades, not many are marked with the grade when sold at retail. Packers may mark the grade on products that have not been officially graded, so long as they meet requirements for the grade.

The typical range of grades for fresh fruits and vegetables includes U.S. Fancy, U.S. No. 1, and U.S. No. 2. For some products there are grades above and below this span. For apples, as an example, the grades are U.S. Extra Fancy, U.S. Fancy, U.S. No. 1, and U.S. Utility.

The grades are based on the product's color, size, shape, maturity, and number of defects. Check for these qualities yourself. Look for color that is typical for the product—especially where it is an indication of maturity or ripeness. Watch for produce that *looks* fresh; avoid any that is wilted or has spots of decay—there may be more inside.

FOR FURTHER READING:

U.S. Department of Agriculture, Office of Communication, *How to Buy Beef Roasts,* G146, Washington, D.C. 20250, 1968.

________. *How to Buy Beef Steaks,* G145, Washington, D.C. 20250, 1968.

________. *How to Buy Canned and Frozen Fruits,* G191, Washington, D.C. 20250, 1971.

________. *How to Buy Canned and Frozen Vegetables,* G167, Washington, D.C. 20250, 1969.

________. *How to Buy Cheese,* G193, Washington, D.C. 20250, 1971.

________. *How to Buy Dairy Products,* G201, Washington, D.C. 20250, 1972.

________. *How to Buy Dry Beans, Peas, and Lentils,* G177, Washington, D.C. 20250, 1970.

________. *How to Buy Eggs,* G144, Washington, D.C. 20250, 1968.

________. *How to Buy Fresh Fruits,* G141, Washington, D.C. 20250, 1967.

________. *How to Buy Fresh Vegetables,* G143, Washington, D.C. 20250, 1967.

________. *How to Buy Lamb,* G195, Washington, D.C. 20250, 1971.

________. *How to Buy Meat for Your Freezer,* G166, Washington, D.C. 20250, 1969.

________. *How to Buy Potatoes,* G198, Washington, D.C. 20250, 1972.

________. *How to Buy Poultry,* G157, Washington, D.C. 20250, 1968.

________. *Food for Us All,* 1969 Yearbook of Agriculture, for sale by Superintendent of Documents, Washington, D.C. 20402.

Behind the Label: Federal Food Standards

ALL OVER the United States, if you buy evaporated milk, you can be sure you're getting essentially the same product. And if you buy USDA Choice beef, you can be sure it's the same quality.

The various kinds of food standards set by the Federal Government make this possible.

Just as Federal standards for weights and measures established by the National Bureau of Standards define how long a foot is (so measurements of distance are the same from coast to coast), standards of identity set by the Food and Drug Administration (FDA) define what certain food products are, and U.S. Department of Agriculture (USDA) grade standards define levels of quality for various foods.

Egg cartons usually show the grade and size of eggs.

FDA food standards of identity are mandatory or regulatory. They set requirements which products must meet if they move in interstate commerce. They protect against deception, because they define what a food product must consist of to be legally labeled "mayonnaise," for example.

USDA grade standards for food are voluntary. Federal law does not require that a food processor or distributor use the grade standards. The standards are widely used, however, as an aid in wholesale trading, because the quality of a product affects its price. The grade (quality level) also is often shown on food products in retail stores, so consumers can choose the grade that best fits their needs.

Food standards established by the Federal Government usually fall into these two general classes—voluntary or mandatory.

In addition to USDA's voluntary grade standards for various food products, similar standards for fishery products have been established by the U.S. Department of Commerce.

FDA's standards of identity for food products have their counterpart in standards of identity and composition established by USDA for meat and poultry products. FDA has also set standards of minimum quality and fill of container.

A third class of Federal standards consists of those recommended for adoption by State and local governments. The most familiar of these food standards is for "Grade A" milk. In contrast to USDA quality grade standards for food, the standard for Grade A milk, developed under the U.S. Public Health Service Act, is largely a standard of wholesomeness.

AUTHOR *Tom Bellis,* now retired, is former chief, Food Standards Branch, Food and Drug Administration.

CO-AUTHOR *Harry C. Mussman* is deputy administrator, Animal and Plant Health Inspection Service.

CO-AUTHOR *Charlene Olsson* is a public information officer in the Agricultural Marketing Service.

All of the various kinds of Federal food standards have some effect on what a food may be legally labeled—its name, contents, grade or quality, or other factors. Here's some information to help you figure out what those listings on the label actually mean.

Under authority of the Agricultural Marketing Act of 1946 and related statutes, USDA has issued grade standards for some 300 food and farm products.

Food products for which grade standards have been established are: beef, veal and calf, lamb and mutton; poultry, including turkey, chicken, duck, goose, guinea, and squab; eggs; manufactured dairy products, including butter, cheddar cheese, and instant nonfat dry milk; fresh fruits, vegetables, and nuts; canned, frozen, and dried fruits and vegetables and related products such as preserves; and rice, dry beans, and peas. U.S. grade standards are also available for grains, but not for the food products, such as flour or cereal, into which grain is processed.

USDA provides official grading services, often in cooperation with State departments of agriculture, for a fee, to packers, processors, distributors, or others who wish official certification of the grade of a product. The grade standards also are often used by packers and processors as a quality control tool.

Products which have been officially graded may carry the USDA grade name or grade shield, such as the familiar "USDA Choice" shield seen on cuts of beef or the "U.S. Grade A" on cartons of eggs. Grade labeling, however, is not required by Federal law, even though a product has been officially graded. On the other hand, a packer or processor may not label his product with an official grade name such as Grade A (even without the "U.S." prefix) unless it actually measures up to the Federal standard for that grade. Mislabeling of this sort would be deemed a violation of the Federal Food, Drug, and Cosmetics Act.

USDA grade standards define the requirements of each grade of a product—they separate USDA Prime from USDA Choice beef and U.S. Grade A from U.S. Grade B canned peas.

To develop these standards, standardization specialists study a product to determine the quality factors involved and the range of quality produced. Nature doesn't stamp out plastic balls with the same size, shape, and bounce as can be done in a manufacturing plant. As anyone who's climbed an apple tree can testify, apples on the same branch vary in size, shape, color, and number or size of blemishes.

But any one product generally can be divided into two or three grades, and that is what the standards do—they set the requirements and limits for each grade. As the chapter on USDA Grades explains, the quality factors for different foods—meat, eggs, canned or frozen vegetables, poultry—may differ, because what is considered "quality" in a food depends on the product itself.

The National Marine Fisheries Service of the U.S. Department of Commerce (USDC) has established grade standards for such products as fish fillets and fillet blocks; raw fish portions and fish steaks; raw breaded and precooked fish portions and fish sticks; raw headless and raw breaded shrimp; raw and precooked breaded scallops; and raw headless whiting. A total of 18 grade standards are in effect. The fishery product standards are also established under authority of the Agricultural Marketing Act.

Many of the USDC grade standards also specify the amount of fish component required in the product. For example, raw breaded fish portions and precooked fish sticks must contain 75 percent and 60 percent fish flesh respectively in order to be identified as U.S. Grade A.

USDC's grade standards, like USDA's, are for voluntary use. In fact, the fishery product standards originated in USDA years ago. USDC also provides a voluntary inspection and grading service for fishery products. The grading service is similar to USDA's, and fishery products that have been officially graded may be labeled U.S. Grade A, B, or C.

Products that consumers are most likely to find the U.S. grade name on are frozen fish sticks, breaded shrimp, fish portions, and fish fillets.

The Commerce grading program also provides for official inspection for edibility and wholesomeness of fishery products. If an official U.S. grade name or grade shield is used on a fishery product, that product must have been officially inspected and graded. If the fishery product bears a Federal inspection mark, but no grade designation, it means that the product was produced under official inspection and may also have been graded. Any fishery product, whether it has official grade standards or not, may be inspected for wholesomeness under the Commerce program.

Under the Federal Meat Inspection Act and the Poultry Products Inspection Act, USDA establishes minimum content requirements for many meat and poultry products (usually canned or frozen) and regulates the labeling of all meat and poultry products.

All labels on Federally inspected meat and poultry products must be truthful and accurate and must be approved by USDA before they can be used. To be labeled with a particular name—"Beef with gravy," for example—a Federally inspected meat or poultry product must be approved by USDA as meeting specific product requirements. USDA sets the standards for such products. These standards or requirements describe what is to be in the product—such as the minimum amount of meat, maximum amount of water, and what other ingredients are allowed.

In USDA test kitchens, home economists and food technologists examine similar products processed by various manufacturers to learn what current practices are and acquire information on ways used to prepare foods. Cookbooks and other reference sources reveal information about the standard definition of a product.

Consumer feedback is especially important. Taste panels are used. Technical work is done in laboratories to establish how much fat or moisture may be in a product. If a manufacturer markets a product which is similar to one for which requirements are set, but which does not comply exactly with the standard, then he must call his product by another name.

The standards assure that you're getting what the label says. They do not, however, keep different companies from following distinctive recipes. For instance, to be labeled "Brunswick Stew," a product must contain at least 25 percent of at least two kinds of meat and/or poultry and corn as one of the vegetables.

Knowing USDA's standards can help you in your menu planning, not to mention making comparisons between products.

To be labeled "Beef with gravy," the product must contain at least 50 percent cooked beef. On the other hand, a product labeled "Gravy with beef" must contain at least 35 percent cooked beef.

To set these standards for meat and poultry products, and to be sure that a label is appropriate for a product, USDA requires processors to submit the label, container, formula, method of manufacture, and frequently a sample of the product. Technical personnel check the contents and cooking instructions to make sure they conform to the label.

Labels of meat and poultry products must have an accurate name and description of the product. If an ingredient is not traditionally expected to be found in the product, it must be shown as part of the product name.

If a picture is used, it must accurately represent the product. For instance, if six slices of meat are shown on the label, there must be at least six slices of meat inside the package. If the picture shows the product with a garnish or in a serving dish, it must be marked "Suggested Serving" or "Serving Suggestion."

Each label must contain a list of ingredients, beginning with the item weighing the most, and continuing to the item weighing the least.

Labels must also show the net weight

of the contents, not including the packaging; the packer's or distributor's name and address; and the round mark of inspection. If the product is imported, the name of the country of origin must be on the label. All imported products must be inspected for wholesomeness.

Moreover, a minimum amount of meat or poultry must be in a product before it can be called a beef or chicken product. Chicken Noodle Soup, for example, must contain at least 2 percent chicken on a "ready-to-eat" basis. A soup which contains less must be called something like Chicken-Flavored Noodle Soup, and would not be considered a poultry product.

USDA regulations for meat and poultry products also require that additives—ingredients aimed at improving physical qualities such as flavor, color, and shelf-life of a product—must be approved by USDA before they are used in inspected meat and poultry products. USDA sees that additives used are approved by the Food and Drug Administration and are limited to specified amounts; meet a specific, justifiable need in the product; do not promote deception as to product freshness, quality, weight, or size; and are truthfully and properly listed on the product label.

In January 1974, USDA proposed prohibiting use of terms such as "all," "pure," and "100 percent" on labels of meat and poultry products containing more than one ingredient. In the past, USDA has approved labels for products such as "Pure Pork Sausage," "Pure Pork Luncheon Meat," "All White Meat Turkey Roll," and others, in which small amounts of seasoning or curing ingredients, or both, were included in the formula.

USDA made the proposal in view of a court order against use of such terms on frankfurter labels. In the court's opinion, "all" means "wholly, com-

Some meat product labels.

pletely, exclusively, and solely." Most processed meat and poultry products contain small amounts of seasoning and curing agents, so they do not comply with the court's interpretation of the descriptive term.

The Food and Drug Administration establishes food standards for the promotion of honesty and fair dealing in the interest of consumers.

From a consumer protection point of view, FDA food standards fit in well with USDA standards. They tend to supplement each other. The law that authorizes FDA food standards exempts from FDA jurisdiction meat and meat food products to the extent that the meat and poultry inspection Acts are applicable.

Also, by the significant choice of the article "a" in the phrase granting authority to establish "*a* reasonable standard of quality," the law limits FDA standards of quality to a single level of quality below which the food is substandard in quality and is required by law and regulations to be conspicuously labeled "Below Standard in Quality."

USDA standards of identity for those articles of food exempted from FDA food standards, and the USDA standards for multiple grades for many food products, extend consumer protection to areas not reached by FDA food standards.

Perhaps one of the most significant features of FDA standards is that they are mandatory. If a manufacturer's food product purports to be or if it is represented as being one for which an FDA food standard has been established, he must make certain, before he introduces it into interstate commerce, that it complies with the compositional and labeling requirements of the applicable standard. If it fails to comply, it will be deemed to be misbranded and subject to seizure. Moreover, he will make himself subject to criminal penalities. In the terminology of lawyers, FDA food standards have the force and effect of law.

There are three categories of FDA food standards. They are standards of quality, standards of fill of container, and standards of identity. The designations fairly well explain the differences. However, it is not invariably obvious into which kind of standard a given attribute of a food will have been placed.

You might suppose that the use of artificial color in canned peas would be an identity factor, but the standard of quality prescribes that the use of artificial coloring in canned peas is a factor of quality and requires the label declaration "Below Standard in Quality—Artificially Colored."

In the case of raw shucked oysters, you might anticipate that the attribute of size, whether the oysters are "standards," or "selects," or "very small," would be considered a quality factor, but actually each separate size classification is covered by a separate standard of identity. (This may have been done to circumvent the legal limitation of a single standard of quality.)

But instances such as treating artificial coloring in canned peas as a quality factor and the size of shucked oysters as an identity factor are unusual. Most compositional attributes appear in standards of identity, and factors such as blemishes and lack of uniformity of units are in standards of quality.

As an example of a quality standard, let us examine the one for canned tomatoes. This standard sets out four factors of quality: 1. The weight of the tomato units, when the contents of a can are drained on a one-half inch mesh screen, is not less than 50 percent. 2. Redness of color is not less than that measured by a prescribed testing procedure. 3. Amount of peel per pound is not more than one square inch. 4. The total blemishes per pound are not more than one-fourth square inch.

The label declaration prescribed for canned tomatoes failing to meet the standard of quality is "Below Standard in Quality," coupled with one or more of the statements: "Excessively Broken Up," "Poor Color," "Excessive Peel," or "Excessive Blemishes," as appropriate.

Tomato canners strive to avoid producing any packs that will require the below-standard label declaration. This is equally true for producers of other food products for which FDA quality standards or fill of container standards have been established. You may rarely encounter food with a label saying "Below Standard in Quality" in your food store. The incentive that the quality standard exerts on packers to avoid the necessity for such labeling is beneficial to consumers.

Only a limited number of fill of container standards have been established, and some of them are not particularly effective. For example, the fill standard for canned cherries states that it "is the maximum quantity of the optional cherry ingredient that can be sealed in the container and processed by heat to prevent spoilage, without crushing such ingredient." The fill of container standards for canned peaches, apricots, and pears are analogous.

A fill of container standard that can be better enforced for the benefit of consumers is the one for canned fruit cocktail. It prescribes that "the total weight of the drained fruit is not less than 65 percent of the water capacity of the container . . ." and it prescribes in detail the procedure for ascertaining compliance.

The label declaration for showing substandard fill is quite comparable to the one for showing substandard quality. It is worded "Below Standard in Fill." You may never encounter a product in your store so labeled, but the fact that there is a standard of fill of container for the product will have promoted your interests by stimulating packers to avoid permitting the fill to fall below the requirements in the standard.

Aside from the provisions in the law concerning standards of fill of container, there is a general provision, applicable equally to standardized and nonstandardized foods, which deems foods in package form to be misbranded unless labels bear an accurate statement of their quantity of contents.

Questions have arisen about this provision in the law. Let us consider our instance of canned fruit cocktail again. Some have urged that the statement of quantity of contents should be the drained weight of the fruit. But you do not ordinarily drain off and throw away the liquid in a can of fruit cocktail. You regard it as part of the food you bought and you use it. On the other hand, when you buy a can of wet pack shrimp you drain off and discard the brine packing medium.

These examples illustrate the way FDA construes the quantity of contents label requirement. In the case of the canned fruit cocktail, the statement includes both the fruit and liquid. In the case of canned shrimp, the statement is for the drained weight of the shrimp and excludes the brine packing medium.

Most FDA food standards are standards of identity. It is difficult to set a precise number on the foods for which identity standards have been established. For example, the single section for fruit jelly lists 27 fruit jellies, and this does not count the permitted combinations. Rather than undertaking to name all foods covered by standards of identity, it is more feasible to list them by categories.

The categories of foods with standards are:

Cacao (cocoa bean) products
Wheat flour and related products
Corn flour and related products
Rice and related products
Macaroni and noodle products
Bakery products
Milk and cream products
Cheeses, processed cheeses, cheese foods, cheese spreads, and related foods
Frozen desserts
Food flavorings
Dressings for food
Nutritive sweeteners
Canned fruits and fruit juices
Fruit pies
Fruit butters, fruit jellies, fruit preserves and related products
Nonalcoholic beverages
Shellfish
Fish
Eggs and egg products
Oleomargarine
Nut products
Canned vegetables
Tomato products

No doubt the compositional requirements in identity standards are the most significant characteristic of such standards, but the labeling requirements are also important to consumers.

The law furnishes a basis for considering the ingredients specified in identity standards as falling into two classes, mandatory ingredients and optional ingredients.

Perhaps the standard for mayonnaise will serve to illustrate our point. This standard requires that mayonnaise must contain not less than 65 percent of edible vegetable oil and a sufficient quantity of egg yolks to produce a stable emulsion. It permits salt, sweetening ingredients, spices (with some exceptions), and non-imitation seasonings and flavorings, except ingredients that impart to the mayonnaise the yellow color of egg yolks. The vegetable oil and egg yolks are mandatory; all the others are optional ingredients.

This distinction is important because the law furnishes no authorization for requiring in standards that labels shall name *mandatory* ingredients. It does authorize designating *optional* ingredients to be named on labels where making such a requirement promotes honesty and fair dealing in the interest of consumers.

Those optional ingredients that are spices, flavorings, or colorings may be declared as such, but all other optional ingredients designated in the standard for label declaration must be named on labels by their common names.

Some of the standards of identity that were first proposed many years ago do not include extensive requirements for ingredient label declaration. However, those standards more recently established fully exercise the authority to designate optional ingredients for label declaration. Quite recently the Commissioner of Food and Drugs has urged that food packers voluntarily name mandatory ingredients on the labels of their foods covered by identity standards.

As standards come to require all optional ingredients to be named on labels and packers are agreeable to listing mandatory ingredients, there will be no difference as regards ingredient labeling between foods covered by FDA identity standards and those not standardized.

Some of you may wish to send for copies of the standards for certain foods to learn what ingredients are required and what are optional. You may address your request to: U.S. Food and Drug Administration, Office of Consumer Information, Washington, D. C. 20204. You should specify by food category, from those listed in this chapter, the foods for which you wish standards.

A general provision in the law administered by FDA states, "A food shall be deemed to be misbranded if it is an imitation of another food unless its label bears . . . the word 'imitation' and, immediately thereafter, the name of the food imitated." Another provision holds a food to be misbranded if it purports to be one for which a standard of identity has been prescribed unless it conforms to such standard.

An identity standard was established for fruit preserves. This standard required strawberry jam to contain not less than 45 percent strawberries. A preserver shipped a product labeled "Imitation Strawberry Jam" that contained significantly less than 45 percent fruit. The FDA initiated a seizure charging the jam to be misbranded because it purported to be a food for which there was a standard of identity but that it did not conform to the fruit requirement in the standard.

Litigation ensued and the case was ultimately decided in the Supreme Court. In effect the Supreme Court decision held that a food that purports to be one for which there is an identity standard is not required to conform to the compositional requirements of the standard provided it is labeled "imitation."

Following this ruling we began seeing more and more foods in our grocery stores labeled "imitation."

Some of these products were nutritionally inferior to the foods imitated. Others were nutritionally equivalent to foods conforming to standards, and it is possible that some may have been superior. However, including the word "imitation" in the names for these variant foods has not aided consumers in choosing between the foods that are inferior and those that are at least nutritionally equivalent to the foods imitated.

A White House Conference on Food, Nutrition and Health recommended that "oversimplified and inaccurate terms such as 'imitation' should be abandoned as uninformative to the public." To implement this recommendation, FDA has proposed that the word "imitation" be used only on foods nutritionally inferior to an imitated food.

For variant products that are not less than nutritionally equivalent to an imitated food, it was proposed that different common or usual names, names fully descriptive and informative to consumers, be established.

As a starter, FDA proposed to rescind its 1955 statement of policy calling for labeling frozen desserts made in semblance of ice cream, but containing vegetable fats in substitution for milk fat, with the name "Imitation Ice Cream." Instead, FDA proposes that an identity standard should be established for vegetable fat frozen desserts under the name Mellorine.

Mellorine is not a new name. Some 25 states have sanctioned distribution of vegetable fat frozen desserts labeled Mellorine in their intrastate commerce. A new standard was also proposed under the name Parevine for frozen desserts made in semblance of ice cream but containing no milk, meat, or ingredients derived from milk or meat.

The proposals for Mellorine and Parevine remind us of the identity standard for oleomargarine. As is well known, oleomargarine originated in France in 1870 as a butter substitute. It was first marketed in our country in 1874. Here dairymen and food regulatory officials were diligent in preventing the word butter from appearing on the labels of oleomargarine.

When the standard was established in 1941, it was declared that the common and usual name for this food was oleomargarine. Corporations engaged in marketing butter challenged the standard in court. They argued that the standard should have prescribed the name "Imitation Butter."

The court rejected this argument, saying "Oleomargarine is a well-known food product with an identity of its own . . ."

Congress recognized that consumers are interested in being dealt with honestly and fairly in their purchases of food. The FDA proposals for more complete ingredient declarations and more informative labeling on standardized foods are intended to promote these consumer interests.

FOR FURTHER READING:

U.S. Department of Agriculture, Office of Communication, *Standards for Meat and Poultry Products—A Consumer Reference List,* unnumbered publication, Washington, D.C. 20250, 1973.

________. *USDA Grade Standards for Food—How They are Developed and Used,* PA-1027, for sale by Superintendent of Documents, Washington, D.C. 20402.

U.S. Department of Commerce. *Federal Inspection Marks for Fishery Products,* Food Fish Facts 50, 100 E. Ohio St., Chicago, Ill. 60611.

________. *U.S. Grade Standards for Fishery Products,* Food Fish Facts 51, 100 E. Ohio St., Chicago, Ill. 60611.

Nutrient Labeling And Guidelines

THE FOOD AND DRUG Administration has completed a major rearrangement of regulations dealing with food labeling. "Nutrition Labeling," the most important of these regulations, involves a whole new concept—the direct listing of nutrient contents of a food on the label.

Formerly, when vitamins were added to foods the products carried "Special Dietary" labels. Now, common foods, including most of those that contain added nutrients, can be labeled under *Nutrition Labeling.*

The *Special Dietary Foods* label will be restricted to foods that really are special, such as those used for sole items of the diet or under the supervision of a physician.

Nutrition labeling is voluntary, with a few major exceptions. The exceptions are foods to which nutrients are added or about which nutrition claims have been made. Enriched bread, breakfast cereals, and enriched milk products are among the foods to which nutrients have been added and for which *Nutrition Labeling* is mandatory.

Another change brought about by nutrition labeling is that the Minimum Daily Requirement (MDR) values that were listed by the Food and Drug Administration starting in 1941 have been replaced by "U.S. Recommended Daily Allowance" (U.S. RDA) values, a new set of labeling standards. The U.S. RDA standards were derived from the "Recommended Dietary Allowances" published by the National Academy of Sciences-National Research Council (see the first chapter in this Yearbook) and are subject to amendment from time to time as more information on human nutrition becomes available. Values to be used on most foods are listed in a table with the first chapter.

During development of the Nutrition Labeling regulation, nutrition educators and spokesmen stressed the advantages of a standard format for the consumer and as an aid in consumer education. An example of the standard format required by the regulation is illustrated in the sample label for Green Beans.

The explicit statement "per serving" is required under (or following) the heading "Nutrition Information." To avoid confusion about the basis for the various values, all values on the table refer to the amount provided per serving. Size of a serving must be listed in common household units (such as "cup") or as a recognizable portion (slice).

The number of servings that are in a container must be listed.

Caloric content is the next item in the format. Calories are listed in two-calorie increments below 20 calories and in five-calorie increments up to 50 calories.

Above 50 calories, 10-calorie increments are used.

Contents of protein, carbohydrate and fat are listed to the nearest gram, for the purpose of simplifying consumer understanding and use. Information on fat composition or cholesterol content may also be provided, as discussed below. The listing of the protein content provides information to aid in comparative shopping for complex food products such as potpies. Calorie and fat content probably will be of the greatest overall use—to those interested in weight-reduction and fat-modified diets.

The amounts of eight nutrients—protein, vitamin A, vitamin C, thiamine, riboflavin, niacin, calcium and iron—are shown as "Percentage of U.S. Recommended Daily Allowances (U.S. RDA)." These seven vitamins and minerals plus protein form the lower portion of the standard format and must always be listed.

Many manufacturers did not think it reasonable to list the "zeroes" which products lacking in some of these nutrients would require. Many nutritionists and educators believe it is time consumers learn that every food does not necessarily contain all nutrients.

Two modifications of the standard format are permissible. Both provide the same basic information but in a simplified format. In the first, the zeroes that might be listed opposite some of the nutrients can be replaced by an asterisk which relates to a footnote at the bottom stating: "Contains less than 2% of the U.S. RDA of these nutrients." According to the second modification, if a food contains three or less of the eight nutrients in the standard format at more than 2 percent of the U.S. RDA, these may be listed as a footnote, indicated by an asterisk, that would read, "Contains less than 2% of the U.S. RDA of ———, ———, ———, ———, and ———, listing whichever of the eight nutrients are missing.

For example, nutrients present at less than 2 percent of the U.S. RDA might be protein, vitamin A, riboflavin, niacin and calcium. This alteration of the standard format was an effort to

---

AUTHOR *H. Neal Dunning* is with the Bureau of Foods, Food and Drug Administration (FDA).

CO-AUTHOR *Ogden C. Johnson,* formerly with the Bureau of Foods, FDA, is now with the Hershey Food Co., Hershey, Pa.

NUTRITION INFORMATION
(per serving)
SERVING SIZE = 1 CUP
SERVINGS PER CONTAINER = 2

CALORIES	40
PROTEIN	2 grams
CARBOHYDRATE	7 grams
FAT	0 grams

PERCENTAGE OF U.S. RECOMMENDED DAILY ALLOWANCES (U.S. RDA)

PROTEIN	2%
VITAMIN A	10%
VITAMIN C	8%
THIAMINE	2%
RIBOFLAVIN	4%
NIACIN	2%
CALCIUM	6%
IRON	10%

Sample Nutrition Label for Green Beans

Checking a label.

achieve some reality while providing full nutrition information.

Final regulations also have been issued for the "Labeling of Foods in Relation to Fat, Fatty Acid, and Cholesterol." A manufacturer may indicate on the label of his product the composition of the fat and/or the amount of cholesterol that are in the product. The use of cholesterol or fat labeling invokes full nutrition labeling. For that reason, fat composition labeling may be conveniently considered together with nutrition labeling. A Frozen Main Dish label illustrates this combination.

Besides a statement of the total grams of fat, fat labeling requires a statement of the percent of calories provided by fat. Below this are listed the grams of polyunsaturated fat and grams of saturated fat.

The sum of "saturated" and "polyunsaturated" does not equal the grams of fat (total). Unsaturated fats, short chain fats, and some others are not included in either "saturated" or "unsaturated." However, the data on the label provide the ratio of polyunsaturated-to-saturated fats and also gives the actual amount of polyunsaturated fat. These were the two figures that most dietitians and nutritionists wanted. In addition, a conditional statement must be made as follows: "Information on fat and cholesterol content is provided for individuals who, on the advice

NUTRITION INFORMATION
(per serving)
SERVING SIZE=8 OZ.
SERVINGS PER CONTAINER=1

CALORIES	560	FAT (percent of calories 53%)	33 g
PROTEIN	23 g	*Polyunsaturated	2 g
CARBOHYDRATE	43 g	Saturated	9 g
		*CHOLESTEROL (20 mg/100 g)	45 mg
		SODIUM (300 mg/100 g)	680 mg

PERCENTAGE OF U.S. RECOMMENDED DAILY ALLOWANCES (U.S. RDA)

PROTEIN	35%	RIBOFLAVIN (VITAMIN B_2)	15%
VITAMIN A	35%	NIACIN	25%
VITAMIN C (ASCORBIC ACID)	10%	CALCIUM	2%
THIAMINE (VITAMIN B_1)	15%	IRON	25%

*Information on fat and cholesterol content is provided for individuals who, on the advice of a physician, are modifying their total dietary intake of fat and cholesterol.

Sample Nutrition Label for Frozen Main Dish

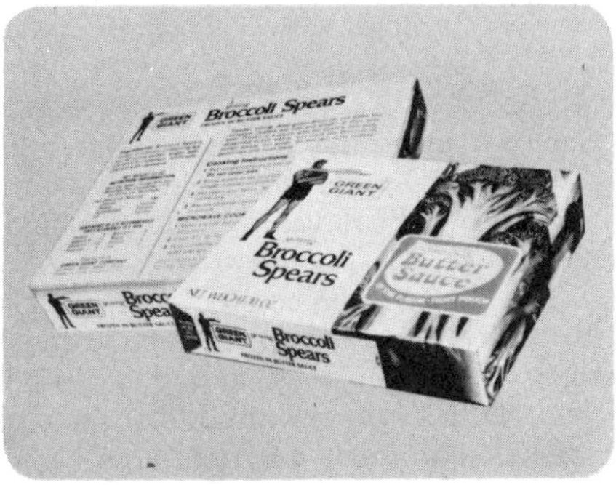

(Top) Part of a carton of frozen broccoli spears. (Above) Milk carton labeling allows nutritive comparison between regular milk and 2% low fat milk.

of a physician, are modifying their total dietary intake of fat and cholesterol."

It is permissible to list sodium content without using nutrition labeling. However, sodium content also may appear on a nutrition label as shown in the frozen main dish label. In both cases, it also is listed in milligrams per 100 grams, each declared to the nearest multiple of 5 milligrams.

Nutrition labeling contains another new concept—details of testing compliance are specified, including the statistical guidelines. The compliance section provides ample range of nutrient content for indigenous nutrients in recognition of natural variations. However, it has a solid statistical base to assure that the consumer obtains the amounts of nutrients listed on the label. Tolerances for added nutrients are considerably more strict, but still provide room for reasonable variation consistent with good manufacturing practices.

Nutrition labeling also takes into account the quality of protein in the food.

NUTRITION INFORMATION
(per serving)
SERVING SIZE=8 FL. OZ. (1 CUP)
SERVINGS PER CONTAINER=4

	Per Serving (8 fl. oz.)	Per Day (1 quart)
CALORIES	160	640
PROTEIN	8 grams	32 grams
CARBOHYDRATE	12 grams	48 grams
FAT	9 grams	36 grams

PERCENTAGE OF U.S. RECOMMENDED DAILY ALLOWANCES (U.S. RDA)

PROTEIN	15%	60%
VITAMIN A	6%	25%
VITAMIN C	4%	15%
THIAMINE	4%	15%
RIBOFLAVIN	20%	80%
NIACIN	0%	4%
CALCIUM	25%	100%
IRON	0%	4%
VITAMIN D	25%	100%

Sample Nutrition Label for Whole Milk

Protein quality is commonly described scientifically by an expression, "Protein Efficiency Ratio" or "PER." PER is defined as the gain in weight of a young rat divided by the weight of protein consumed during a period of rapid growth, usually of three-week duration. A control is run with as nearly identical rats as possible in which casein is the protein.

The ratio for the casein-containing diet commonly is about 2.5. If it differs from 2.5, both ratios are corrected so that the ratio for casein becomes 2.5 and the other PER is adjusted accordingly.

Two adult U.S. RDA values for protein have been set. The U.S. RDA values for adults are listed as 65 grams if the PER of the protein is less than that of casein, and 45 grams if the PER is equal to or better than that of casein.

This means that when a "better than casein" protein is consumed, less protein is needed for a person to obtain the U.S. RDA value than when a protein with a PER value below casein is consumed.

The "better than casein" group would be the traditional high quality proteins from meat, fish, eggs and dairy products. Other protein products such as vegetable proteins and mixtures of cereal and animal proteins would be expected to fit the 65 gram value.

The regulation is also written so that protein that has a value less than 20 percent of the PER of casein cannot be counted as contributing protein at all. Basically, this would include a protein like gelatin which is of little value as a protein contributor. Generally speaking, the common vegetable proteins such as those present in soy, lentils, wheat and the like would have a U.S. RDA of 65 grams. Actually, the penalty is not large and recognizes the large contribution such vegetable sources make to the daily protein supply.

Nutrition labeling has had a very beneficial effect on the amount of information on nutrient content that is being determined for foods. Major food producers had programs to analyze most of their products even before the regulations were final. Groups of smaller producers combined, with the help of their trade associations, to obtain analytical results on their foods.

The milk industry formed a task group to develop a working plan and accumulated detailed data. Their efforts were aimed toward complete updating of the information on the nutrient content by seasons of the year, by geographic location, by species and other factors. They also provided a logical way of using nutrition labels on most dairy products. An example is shown in the Whole Milk label.

One of the major stimuli for establishment of nutrition labeling was consumer groups who desired more information on what is in foods they buy and eat. These groups wanted up-to-date information on nutrient content of each brand, and not just representative nutrient values based upon years of survey averages. Consumers emphasized that they were not only interested in learning whether products were appetizing and attractive, but wanted to know whether or not food products contained vitamin A, vitamin C or other nutrients.

A few kinds of foods with added nutrients are exempted from "Nutrition Labeling." These include infant formulas which are regulated under foods for "Special Dietary Use."

Other baby and junior-type foods marketed and promoted for infants or very young children are being labeled in accordance with "Nutrition Labeling." For such foods, the "serving" means a reasonable quantity for an infant or a child and the nutrient content information is based on one of two special sets of U.S. RDA's for infants and children under four, instead of the adult allowances.

Other exemptions are foods that are represented for use as the sole item of a diet—not the sole item of a meal, and a food product that is represented for use under medical supervision for the dietary management of specific diseases.

Use of iodized salt does not require nutrition labeling as long as neither iodine nor iodized salt is otherwise referred to on the label or in labeling.

A nutrient included in a food solely for technological purposes may be declared simply on the ingredient statement without the invoking of nutrition labeling. Also, a standardized food containing an added nutrient—for example, enriched flour—may be included in another food as a component and may be listed simply in the ingredient statement by its standardized name without invoking nutrition labeling, provided no other claims are made.

Food products shipped in bulk form also do not require "Nutrition Labeling." Foods containing an added vitamin, mineral or protein or for which a nutritional claim is made require "Nutrition Labeling" *unless* the product is supplied only for institutional purposes. in addition, the manufacturer must supply the nutrition information required by this section directly to the institution on a current basis.

Vitamin and/or mineral supplements in the form of a food (for example, a breakfast cereal) must conform to labeling established in both "Nutrition Labeling" and that governing dietary supplements, which are classified as "Foods for Special Dietary Use."

The regulations covering "Foods for Special Dietary Use" have been changed markedly. As we mentioned above, common foods which contain added nutrients formerly were labeled using requirements for "Special Dietary Foods"; they now will be labeled under "Nutrition Labeling."

These regulations establish the U.S. Recommended Daily Allowances (U.S. RDA) as a replacement for the "Minimum Daily Requirement" (MDR) as the official measurement of nutrient content. Four sets of U.S. RDA values are now established. These include values for infants, children under four years of age, adults and children over four years of age, and pregnant and lactating women (see table in first chapter). Also published for the first time is a table of chemically identifiable "reference forms" of vitamins.

A standard of identity has been finalized for dietary supplements of vitamins limit is 150 percent of this value for each nutrient. Dietary supplements are classified as foods, but at nutrient levels above 150 percent of the U.S. RDA they are classed as over-the-counter drugs.

Two exceptions are vitamin A and D

Meat and Poultry Products

J. C. deHOLL *

FEDERAL Meat and Poultry Inspection laws outline U.S. Department of Agriculture (USDA) responsibilities to control the processing and labeling of meat and poultry or their products.

Regulations require that labels for these products be approved before they are used. Thus, everything which appears on the label must be reviewed and approved by a representative of the Secretary of Agriculture whether the information be voluntary or mandatory.

Nutritional labeling of meat and poultry products is voluntary. However, those who elect to nutritionally label their products must follow specific labeling requirements providing for uniform format and ease of consumer evaluation.

Label approval is granted only after it is determined that the required information is presented in the proper manner, that declared values are supported by adequate analytical data, and that the processor has a control program to ensure that products comply with their label claims. The consumer can be confident, after such critical review by both processor and the USDA, that nutrition information on the label is factual and reliable.

All products nutritionally labeled must contain label information which declares the nutrition information on an "as purchased" basis. Products requiring cooking before they are eaten, and which are nutritionally labeled, are required to declare the nutrition information on an "as purchased" and "as prepared" basis. A specific method of cooking must be shown in a statement adjacent to the nutrition information.

This proviso that certain meat and poultry products be labeled on an "as prepared" basis is required because in many instances cooking results in significant nutritional changes, especially in fat and caloric values, which are of such widespread consumer interest and concern.

Raw poultry, uncooked red meats, and bacon are examples of products which will be required to present the nutrition information on the "as purchased" and "as prepared" basis with preparation instructions.

Nutrition labeling on an "as purchased" basis aids the consumer in making value comparisons prior to purchase. Nutrition labeling on an "as prepared" basis aids the consumer in making value comparisons of the product as it may be consumed. Presentation of nutrition information in this manner will assist the consumer in making

* With Meat and Poultry Inspection Program, Animal and Plant Health Inspection Service, USDA.

and minerals, under the "Special Dietary Foods" regulations. Upper and lower limits for the vitamin and mineral contents of dietary supplements are specified in terms of U.S. RDA levels. Generally the lower limit is 50 percent of the U.S. RDA value and the upper that are classed as prescription drugs at 200 percent and 100 percent of their respective U.S. RDA values. This distinction is made because of the proven toxicity of these two vitamins at high dosage levels.

Certain kinds and combinations of

vitamins and minerals are specified. A dietary supplement may consist of:

1. All vitamins and minerals.
2. All vitamins.
3. All minerals.
4. All vitamins and iron.
5. Any single vitamin or mineral.

Thus, the standard provides that a wide variety of vitamin and mineral supplements will be available.

Besides establishing nutritional labeling rules for foods and dietary supplements, the Food and Drug Administration has also issued Nutritional Quality Guidelines for several food products.

The purpose of a guideline is to prescribe a basic level of nutrient composition for a class of food.

When the nutrient composition of a product complies with the prescribed guideline, the product's label may make the statement, "This product provides nutrients in amounts appropriate for this class of food as determined by the U.S. Government."

The product must carry the common or usual name provided for in the guideline, present nutrition labeling on the product, and make no special claim for nutrients that were added to permit the product to meet the prescribed guideline. Any nutrients added, however, are to be included in the ingredient statement and on the "Nutrition Label."

The first of the nutritional quality guidelines to be published is for "Frozen 'heat-and-serve' dinners." To qualify as a dinner, the product must consist of three parts which include: 1. One or more protein sources from meat, poultry, fish, cheese or eggs; 2. One or more vegetables or vegetable mixtures other than potatoes, rice or cereal products; and 3. Potatoes, rice or cereal products or another vegetable or vegetable mixtures. Other items of food that may be included, such as soup, bread, beverage or dessert, are not counted as fulfilling any part of the basic nutrient requirements of the components specified, but must be included in "Nutrition Labeling."

This first regulation on "Frozen 'heat and serve' dinners" also prescribes the use of iodized salt, if technologically feasible. It provides for maintaining a calcium-to-phosphorus ratio of 1 to 1, and suggests that wherever possible calcium should be added and phosphates should be minimized within technological restrictions.

Although there is still much more to do in providing information on the nutrient content of foods, the first major steps have been taken with the advent of nutritional labeling of conventional foods, updating labeling of foods for special dietary purposes, including die-

the best selection of products to meet particular needs.

USDA also requires that companies which nutritionally label products must maintain a USDA approved, plant operated quality control program ensuring that all products being shipped will meet all label claims. Intent of this control program is to ensure that mislabeled products do not reach the market place.

It is USDA's belief that nutrient composition can be controlled through effective ingredient, processing, and distribution control programs carried out by the companies involved.

Nutrition labeling is a program under which consumers will be able to learn more about the quality and character of meat and poultry products. Consumers are encouraged to read and study the information available on nutritionally labeled products. Increased understanding of the nutritional quality of foods will be of inestimable value to the consumer in evaluating new foods for family feeding.

USDA believes the nutritional character of meat and poultry products will become a more significant factor in the marketing and purchasing of foods in the future.

Growing shortages in the world supply of animal protein will focus more and more attention on the nutritional character and importance of meat and poultry products. Nutrition labeling will be a key aid in providing the consumer with this vital information.

tary supplements, and the development of guidelines for different classes of foods or meals.

"Nutrition Labeling" resulted from consumer interest in nutrition and has led to an unprecedented opportunity for nutrition education. Nutrition has become of major interest in food marketing as shown by the various approaches used by food manufacturers and distributors. It is vital that these efforts be conservative, correct and coordinated with several operating programs of governmental and academic organizations. It is also essential that these programs be brought up to date with rapidly expanding nutritional knowledge and awareness.

Organic, Inorganic: What They Mean

The words "organic", "chemicals", "natural", and "health" are among the most misunderstood, misused, and maligned in our vocabulary, especially when they are applied to our food.

All organic materials are complex combinations of chemicals and contain one chemical element in common. That element is carbon. But not all chemicals occur in the form of organic material. All of our usual food supply is in organic form because it has come from animal or plant sources. Most man-made foods are also in the organic form.

Today our chief concern about things organic and chemical relates to how foods are grown and processed. There are no precise, official definitions for these but some have been proposed for legal use and can be useful here:

"The term 'organically grown food' means food which has not been subjected to pesticides or artificial fertilizers and which has been grown in soil whose humus content has been increased by the addition of organic matter."

"The term 'organically processed food' means organically grown food which in its processing has not been treated with preservatives, hormones, antibiotics, or synthetic additives of any kind."

Organic material or humus used in growing the plants which we eat directly, or which are fed to the animals that furnish our meat, includes manures, plant composts, and other plant residues such as peat moss and aged sawdust.

These are all made by the living cells in animal or plant tissues. They contain the nutrients, nitrogen, phosphorus, potassium, sulfur, magnesium, and other essential minerals in complex combinations with carbon, hydrogen, and usually oxygen.

Inorganic or commercial fertilizers contain the same chemical nutrients but in simpler forms and not always in combination with carbon. It is not accurate to refer to inorganic fertilizers as "artificial" just because they have not been made by living cells.

A plant is not aware of the type of fertilizer, organic or inorganic, that is furnishing the chemicals for its growth. It does demand that these building blocks for its nutrients be in the inorganic form. Cells of the plant itself synthesize the complex materials needed for growth rather than absorbing them ready-made from the soil.

When organic fertilizers are used, they are first decomposed by the microorganisms in the soil. This converts nutrient materials to the inorganic form which can be used by the plant.

Organically raised animals are fed on organically grown pasture and feed. They are given no growth stimulants, antibiotics, or synthetic materials. But it is not likely that an animal's cells are aware of whether the many essentials for their growth and repair are being furnished by feed in the organic or inorganic form.

AUTHOR *Ruth M. Leverton* is a Science Advisor, Agricultural Research Service.

IS IT ORGANIC
OR INORGANIC ?

All good gardening and farming practices call for the addition of organic matter or humus to the soil. Soils rich in humus absorb and hold water better and are easier to till then soils with little organic content. Using organic materials is also a practical way of recycling naturally occurring materials that are valuable for plant growth.

Using only organic fertilizers, however, will perpetuate any soil deficiencies that may have been caused by nutrient deficiencies in the organic material. Soil deficiencies can seriously reduce crop yields. Yields are dramatically increased when the specific chemicals that are missing or in short supply are added to the soil in inorganic form.

Adding iron to the soil in the Western United States and phosphorus in the Southeastern Seaboard States are examples of increasing yields and quality by eliminating soil deficiencies. But the food would not meet the definition proposed for "organically grown."

Foods claimed to be organically grown must not have been treated with pesticides. Thus, one of the benefits of organic farming would be to reduce pollution of our environment.

Unfortunately, organically grown food is not necessarily free of pesticides. Chemical residues from pesticides may remain in the soil for years after their use is discontinued. Also, pesticides sprayed on one field or crop may drift through the air onto another field.

Foods and feeds grown by usual commercial practices may contain no more chemical residues than those grown organically. In one State laboratory, 55 foods labeled as being organically grown were tested for pesticide residues. Seventeen, or 30 percent, of them contained residues. This was in contrast to only 20 percent of the foods grown by the usual commercial methods.

Foods referred to as "natural" are those in the same form as they were harvested. They come from their place of growth to the consumer without having any man-made alterations or treatments. They are unprocessed.

Fresh fruits and vegetables are natural, but canned or frozen are processed. Natural foods may or may not be grown organically. Experience indicates that many natural foods claimed to be organically grown, and thus sold at premium prices, actually come from large commercial producing operations.

The term "health foods" is particularly confusing because every food that offers the body something it needs, contributes to health. The term is used chiefly by untrained health enthusiasts to refer to foods that are claimed to have some special virtues in preventing, treating, and curing disease or providing superior health.

Food and Drug Administration regulations do not permit such claims to be stated on the labels. Therefore, most of the claims are made in special articles or pamphlets used to advertise the "health" food.

Appearance and flavor of the food we buy or that we produce for ourselves depend on its variety, the nutrients supplied to it through the soil and air, how it is tended, the temperature, light, and moisture available to it, and the care used in harvesting, transporting, storing, and retailing it. These factors have much more influence on appearance and flavor than just the kind of fertilizer or processing that are used.

Organically grown produce can rate high in appearance and flavor. On the other hand, it is not unknown to find it undersized, shrivelled, harboring insects, rapidly deteriorating, and yet costing more than regular food.

There is no scientific evidence that plants grown with only organic fertilizers, or meat from animals raised on only organically fertilized feed, have greater nutritive value than our regular food produced by the usual agricultural methods.

Organic foods are likely to cost considerably more than the same items produced and marketed by regular commercial methods. Producing organically grown and processed foods and natural foods does not lend itself to the mass production methods used to supply most of our food. Also organic and natural foods cannot be stored as long as regular foods. Often their packaging materials and methods are inferior to those used for regular foods.

To compare prices, 55 common food items were priced at a chain supermarket and at a "natural" food store on the same day. The processed foods in the "natural" food store averaged 190 percent of the cost of the same items in the supermarket, almost twice as much. Cost of the unprocessed "natural" foods averaged 164 percent of their cost in the supermarket, or two-thirds more.

When a market basket was made up of a unit (a pound or quart) of each of these foods, it cost $55.42 in the "natural" food store and $33.31 at the supermarket.

These organic foods cost at least twice as much in the "natural" food store as regular foods cost in the supermarket:

Processed:

- Canned applesauce, tomatoes, tomato juice, and grape jelly
- Dried apples and raisins
- Frozen corn
- Cream of rice, whole wheat bread

Unprocessed:

- Beef liver, chicken breast with rib, and chicken leg
- Fresh grapefruit and oranges, green cabbage, celery, cucumbers, and white potatoes

Cooperative health food stores may have somewhat lower prices because the members volunteer to help and thus cut labor costs. Some of the co-op groups reduce costs by buying foods in large quantities and repackaging them in household amounts. Unless great care is taken in the handling and with the repackaging and storing, the foods may become contaminated and unsafe to eat. In some localities, repackaging food for sale is against food sanitation regulations.

Before their recent popularity you had to hunt for places where you could buy organically grown and processed and natural foods. You found them in out-of-the-way places and usually in a small store that was a one-man or one-family operation.

Today you can find these foods in almost every kind of store. Huge supermarket chains and mail order houses have complete departments devoted to such foods. Specialty stores are often in the center of shopping areas and farmers' markets. Their decor ranges from handsome and sophisticated to earthy and primitive.

There are many indications that much more food is being sold as organic or natural than is being produced. This means that some unscrupulous marketers are deceiving the consumer and making large profits.

At present there is no way to distinguish between organic and natural foods and those produced by modern agricultural practices. The conscientious, ethical producers and handlers of organic and natural foods are as distressed as anyone about the possibility for fraud and deceit. It threatens their reputation for honesty and responsibility in dealing with their customers.

To prevent fraud and deceit, Federal legislation has been proposed that would set standards and regulations for certifying foods that are claimed to be organic or natural.

The Food and Drug Administration prohibits false labeling of any product whether organic, natural, or from the general food supply. Therefore, if a label states "no preservatives or synthetic additives," the food must not have such ingredients. A person can be prosecuted for falsely labeling a product.

Different people have different reasons for choosing to eat organic, natural, and health foods. Some enjoy using foods in their more natural state as part of a return to nature idea. Some are finding that foods, such as whole grain products, have delightful flavors that are not present in the highly milled products. (It is a mistake, however, to attribute the improved flavor to the organic method of production.)

Still others are bored or dissatisfied with their way of life and go to extremes in focusing on their food as a means to a new and better life style. A number of young people, especially, have focused on different food ways as one means of revolting against established patterns of culture, the capitalistic system, waste of natural resources, and contamination of the environment.

Extremists have convinced some people that foods produced in certain ways have special values in preventing or in curing diseases.

Anyone who chooses to use organic, natural, or health foods should be aware that:

—He must find markets where he can feel sure that the foods come from ethical suppliers and are what they claim to be.

—He must be able and willing to pay more for this food than if he was buying regular foods in usual markets.

—He must not expect the higher cost to buy additional nutritive value.

—He must not neglect his total nutritional needs for good health by restricting his food choices to only a limited variety of organic foods.

FOR FURTHER READING:

Cooperative Extension Service. *Let's Take a Look at Organic Gardening,* Bulletin 555, The Ohio State University, Columbus, Ohio 43210. 35 cents.

Darling, Mary. *Natural, Organic, and Health Foods,* Ext. Folder 280, Agricultural Extension Service, University of Minnesota, St. Paul, Minn. 55101. 15 cents.

Topoleski, Leonard. *Growing Vegetables Organically,* Inf. Bul. 39, Cooperative Extension Service, New York State College of Agriculture and Life Sciences, Ithaca, N. Y. 14850. 20 cents.

Bernarde, Melvin A. *The Chemicals We Eat,* American Heritage Press, McGraw-Hill, Inc., 330 West 42nd Street, New York, N. Y. 10036, $6.95.

Institute of Food Technology. *Organic Foods,* 221 N. LaSalle Street, Chicago, Ill. 60601. 50 cents.

Margolius, Sidney. *Health Foods: Facts and Fakes,* Public Affairs Pamphlet, 498, Public Affairs Committee, 381 Park Avenue S., New York, N. Y. 10016.

How the Shopper Benefits From Nutrition Labeling

NUTRITION LABELING acknowledges the shopper's right to know about the nutritional qualities of foods. Facts about the nutrients in foods now appear on nutrition information panels on many foods in the supermarket. How can these facts help you?

You are likely to receive some benefits even if you ignore nutrition information on labels. Because of labeling, food companies are expected to consider the nutritive value of food increasingly in producing and selecting agricultural commodities, and in processing and handling products they market. This may result in a more nutritious food supply for you to select from.

Also, food companies analyze their

products to determine nutritive values for labeling. These values, pooled and used by scientists, can help lead to a better understanding of how food relates to health.

If you learn to use facts on the nutrition information panels of food labels, you may benefit in the following ways as well.

You may become more knowledgeable about nutrients your body needs and which foods provide them. You can see from the list of nutrients and the percent of the U.S. Recommended Daily Allowance (U.S. RDA) furnished by a specified serving that:

—Foods vary in the kinds and amounts of nutrients they contain.

—No one food provides recommended amounts of all nutrients listed on the label. Exceptions may be a few foods that have vitamins and minerals added.

—Certain foods are worthwhile sources of specific nutrients on the label. For example: Milk is a leading source of calcium. It also provides protein, riboflavin, and vitamin A, among other nutrients.

Fruits and vegetables furnish some minerals and vitamins. Citrus fruits are especially valued for their vitamin C; dark green vegetables and deep yellow ones, for their vitamin A.

Meat, poultry, fish and eggs are important sources of protein and also provide iron, thiamin, riboflavin, and niacin.

Dry beans and dry peas, nuts and peanut butter provide most of these nutrients too.

Breads and cereals, especially whole grain or enriched ones, furnish worthwhile amounts of protein, iron, thiamin, riboflavin, and niacin.

—A variety of foods is usually required to supply the U.S. RDA for the nutrients shown on the label. This is one reason for eating foods of different types, such as those specified in *Food for Fitness—A Daily Food Guide* described in the second chapter in this section of the Yearbook. Another reason is that a variety of foods is needed to provide nutrients other than those on labels that are known to be important to health and well-being.

If you are trying to lose or gain a few pounds, the calories per serving on the label will be helpful. To reduce, choose foods with fewer calories; to gain weight, choose foods with more calories. But be sure to include foods that provide needed protein, vitamins and minerals. If you have more than a few pounds to lose, check with your physician before going on a reducing diet.

If you are on a special diet, your physician or dietitian may tell you how to use the protein, carbohydrate and fat content of foods shown on labels, or the label information about fatty acids and cholesterol or sodium, in selecting your food.

You can use information on labels to compare the protein, vitamin and mineral content of foods you might substitute for each other in meals or snacks. For example, you might compare the percentages of the U.S. RDA for various nutrients from fresh whole milk with the percentages from chocolate drink; from a food of one brand with those of another brand; from a frozen plate dinner or entree with those from similar food combinations that you prepare.

The foods with the highest percents on their labels are not always the best selections.

The notion that any food with a high percent on its label is especially good for you may result in a diet abundant in some nutrients and short in others.

You can get the U.S. RDA for some nutrients from a serving of a single food; but for others, only from several servings of a number of foods—each providing a small percent of the U.S. RDA.

For example, many foods marketed can boast over 50 percent of the U.S. RDA for vitamin C on their labels, but almost none have this high a percent for iron or riboflavin. If in selecting foods you favor those showing over 50 per-

---

AUTHOR *Betty Peterkin* is a home economist in the Consumer and Food Economics Institute, Agricultural Research Service.

cent of a U.S. RDA on the label, you may get plenty of vitamin C, but shortchange yourself on foods for iron and riboflavin.

It's important to remember that a food with a high percent improves your diet only if your diet is short in that nutrient.

If you regularly select one or a few foods to meet the U.S. RDA, your diet may be short in energy (calories), bulk, and some of the nutrients not shown on labels. For example, a serving of a breakfast cereal with 100 percent of the U.S. RDA for all nutrients on the label does not by itself provide enough calories or satisfy your appetite for the day, and probably does not furnish important nutrients not listed.

On the other hand, a food may provide more calories than you need. For example, you select a potpie because it provides slightly more of some vitamins and minerals than a hearty vegetable soup. The pie furnishes 520 calories; the soup, 200.

Depending on the adequacy of the day's food with regard to calories and nutrients, the soup may be the better choice. Its selection, instead of potpie, would free 320 calories for foods that might provide additional nutrients needed.

Meals may be less acceptable to family members and no better for them if food selections are limited to those with highest percents on labels. For example, you choose stewed tomatoes instead of applesauce—a family favorite—for dinner, because labels show that tomatoes provide more vitamin A and vitamin C. The U.S. RDA for these vitamins was already met by orange juice at breakfast and carrots at lunch.

The food budget suffers unnecessarily if expensive foods with high nutritive values are selected instead of less expensive ones with lower values that would, with other foods used during the day, provide recommended amounts of nutrients. For example, you select sliced ham for lunch instead of bean soup, which has a lower protein value and a lower price. Either the ham or the soup, along with other foods eaten, would provide allowances for the day.

Almost everyone uses some foods that do not show up well in relation to the U.S. RDA to round out meals and to meet energy needs. Some of these foods may be important sources of certain nutrients not listed on labels.

In addition, you will want to continue to use many foods not labeled with nutrition information. Nutrition labeling is a voluntary program, and many nutritious foods are not labeled.

You may be able to use nutritive values on labels to help plan food for a day that will provide recommended amounts of nutrients. To handle this admittedly difficult job efficiently, however, you will need this information not on labels:

—A meal pattern or food guide to help identify a variety of foods that is likely to meet nutritional goals.

—A table of nutritive values, expressed as percentages of the U.S. RDA, for foods you use that are not labeled with nutrition information.

—Information about the U.S. RDA and how it compares with the amounts of nutrients recommended for persons of your sex and age (see the first chapter in this section of the Yearbook.)

For some people—young children or elderly women, for example, a diet that provides 100 percent of the U.S. RDA is unnecessarily high in some nutrients. Thus the use of the U.S. RDA in meal planning for these persons may result in unnecessary dietary changes and food expenditures as well as unwarranted concern about nutrient shortages.

—Lists of foods that are good sources of certain nutrients to show what foods might be added or substituted to improve the diet.

Nutrition labeling does not offer the shopper a simple approach to selecting nutritious meals. It does, however, offer a wealth of information about nutritional qualities of foods available. With supplemental tools and guidance from nutrition educators, nutrition information on labels can be used by interested shoppers to help evaluate and improve their diets.

Guides to Buying—Open Dating and Price Per Unit

GROCERY SHOPPERS who would like to have all the help they can get in coping with family food buying may have overlooked two important shopping guides now available in many retail food stores.

Value for the food dollar is always an important concern for the food shopper, but recent price increases have encouraged many consumers to look for new ways to compare value and be sure of quality. A combination of voluntary food industry programs and some local legislative efforts have made two helpful shopping aids—unit pricing and open dating—available in grocery stores throughout the United States.

As every family food shopper knows, many factors have to be considered when it comes to buying the weekly groceries. Total dollars available, family tastes, storage and preparation facilities, end use, and item cost all affect a buying decision. Unit pricing can help by taking the guesswork out of the price factor and simplifying cost comparisons.

Unit pricing is just what its name implies—the price per unit. To be more specific, it gives you the cost per ounce or per pound or per 100 or per square foot. This price per unit enables you to readily find the best buy, dollar wise, among several items in different size packages with different total prices.

Thousands of retail food chain stores now have unit pricing programs. In several areas such programs are required by local laws; but generally the programs are voluntary. Today unit pricing is available in most major population areas to the shopper who is interested in using it.

Stores that offer unit pricing generally use a shelf tag system—a label on the shelf edge below the item gives the name of the item, the size, the total price, and the unit price. You may also find some other numbers which are store inventory numbers.

When unit pricing was first introduced there were some problems with the shelf tag system—just keeping the tags on the shelves, in the right location, can be difficult. In addition, some machine printed tags are not easy to read. But as unit pricing has gained acceptance, some of these mechanical problems have been overcome and the label information has become more usable from the shoppers' standpoint.

Value for your food dollar involves quality as well as price, and open dating offers a guide to one aspect of quality—freshness. Open dating—a date on a food package that can be read and understood by shoppers—has been introduced on a wide variety of products.

What the date means and where you will find it on the package varies, but the purpose of the open date—telling something about the freshness of the product—remains the same. While some products have been open dated for years, many food processors and retail food chains have begun open dating programs within the last five years.

Interest in open dating grew out of consumer interest in codes used on most food packages. While the codes primarily include production identification information, some also have a production date or shelf life estimate. Just translating the codes would not necessarily give the consumer useful information, but many companies have begun open dating programs that will give shoppers a guide to freshness.

Four types of dates are often suggested for use on food packages:

- Pack date—date of processing or final packaging; "Packed Dec. 1974"

AUTHOR *Eileen F. Taylor* is a Social Science Analyst in the National Economic Analysis Division, Economic Research Service, at Albany, Calif.

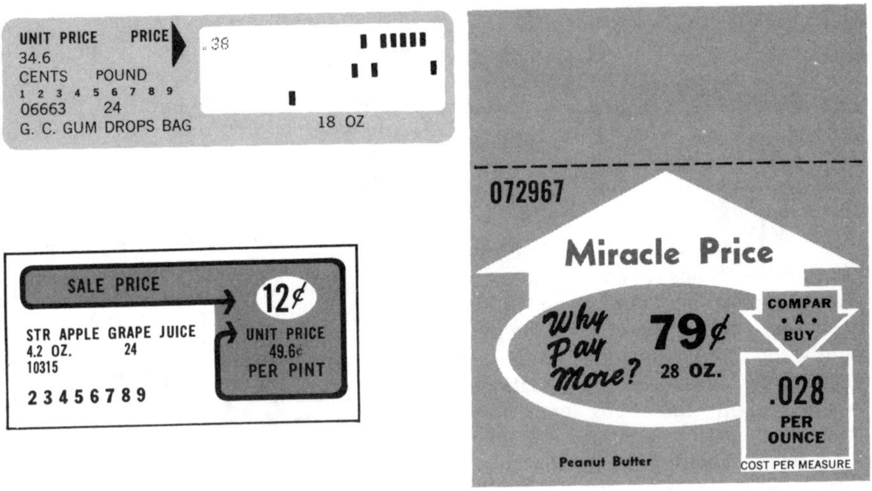

Examples of unit price labels.

• Pull date—the last day of retail sale as fresh; "Sell by Jan. 16"

• Quality assurance or freshness date —date recommended for obtaining optimum product quality; "Better if used before May 75"

• Expiration date—final date of recommended use; "Do not use after Jun. 30, 1975"

The pull date—the last day of fresh sale—is by far the most commonly used type of date, although there is some variation among different product groups. As a shopper you should keep in mind that the pull date method allows sufficient time for you to store and use the product at home, even if you buy it on the last day it is offered for sale.

If you see a freshness date—a recommended use date—on a food package, remember that the processor is suggesting when you should use the item so that you will enjoy it while it is still at peak quality. Sometime after that date, with a cushion of time allowed, the product will begin to lose quality, although it should still be usable.

Expiration date—the last day of use —is rarely seen because it is nearly impossible to predict solely on the basis of time, when a product will no longer be usable. And, again, the processor would like you to use his product while it is at its peak, not as it approaches the end of its acceptable life.

Pack date seems to have limited use, on products like fresh and frozen meat and poultry and fresh produce, and it does represent a known date in the past. From a consumer's standpoint, however, the pack date may not be too helpful because the consumer could not be expected to have the technical expertise to predict the shelf life of thousands of different products.

While open dating is helpful—to store personnel in rotating stock, to you when you select an item to buy and when you rotate items at home—it has its limitations. The quality of the food, its freshness, is more dependent on the storage and handling it has received than on just elapsed time.

In other words, if an item has not been kept at the proper temperature before or after you buy it, the chances are it won't measure up to your expectations, regardless of the date on the package.

Have you thought of using unit pricing to help you make a choice? Have you noticed open dates on the foods you buy, especially perishable and semiperishables? Each time we shop for groceries, we make hundreds of decisions—sometimes without even realizing that we are doing it. Let's not overlook the information available to help make those decisions.

Food Shopper Language

WE SPEND A LOT of time shopping for the things we eat. To do a good job satisfying our family's nutritional needs and at the same time keep the family food budget to a minimum, we need to have as much information as possible about the items available on grocery shelves. Knowing the language used in the food trade should help us in making the best selections.

Here are some familiar and, perhaps, some not so familiar terms used in the meat, dairy and cereal sections of the grocery store—which is where a good part of our food dollars go. Also included are a few cooking terms.

MEAT PRODUCTS *

Kinds of Meat

Meat is the flesh of animals, usually the "red meats" produced from cattle, sheep, and swine as distinguished from fish and poultry. Poultry is from domesticated birds such as chickens, turkeys, ducks, geese and guineas.

Beef—Meat from mature cattle, usually older than 9 months of age.

Broiler—(or fryer)—A young chicken (usually 7 to 10 weeks of age) of either sex, that is tender-meated and has a smooth-textured skin.

Bullock Beef—Meat from young male cattle under about 24 months of age. When such beef is federally graded, "bullock" will appear in the grade stamp.

Calf—Meat from young cattle, usually between 3 and 8 months of age.

Capon—A surgically unsexed male chicken (usually under 8 months of age) that is tender-meated with soft smooth-textured skin.

Fowl—(or hen or stewing chicken) —A mature female chicken (usually more than 10 months of age) with meat less tender than that of a roaster.

Lamb—Meat from young sheep, usually less than one year old.

Mutton—Meat from mature sheep usually more than two years old.

Pork—Meat from swine.

Roaster—A young chicken (usually 3 to 5 months of age) of either sex, that is tender-meated with a soft, smooth-textured skin.

Rock Cornish Game Hen—A young immature chicken (usually 5 to 7 weeks of age) that is tender-meated with soft, smooth-textured skin. Weighs not more than 2 pounds ready-to-cook. A chicken of the Cornish breed or crossed with that breed.

Veal—Meat from very young cattle, usually less than 3 months of age.

Yearling Mutton—Meat from sheep usually between 1 and 2 years old.

Seven Basic Cuts of Meat

Muscle and bone structures of the different kinds of meat are very similar. Therefore, cuts from all kinds can be classified into seven basic groups based on the portions of the carcass where they originate.

Shoulder or Chuck Blade Cuts—These cuts from the upper part of the shoulder usually include a portion of the shoulder blade. The cuts contain several muscles which make carving and serving somewhat difficult. These muscles also differ considerably in tenderness so braising usually is the preferred cooking method.

Shoulder Arm Cuts—Cuts are from the lower, more muscular part of the shoulder. They are round in shape and usually include a small round bone with a close-by round muscle that is darker in color than the other muscles. Cuts from the leg or round do not have this muscle. These cuts also may have portions of up to five ribs.

* AUTHOR *W. Edmund Tyler* is Chief of the Standardization Branch, Livestock Division, Agricultural Marketing Service.

THE SEVEN BASIC RETAIL CUTS OF MEAT*

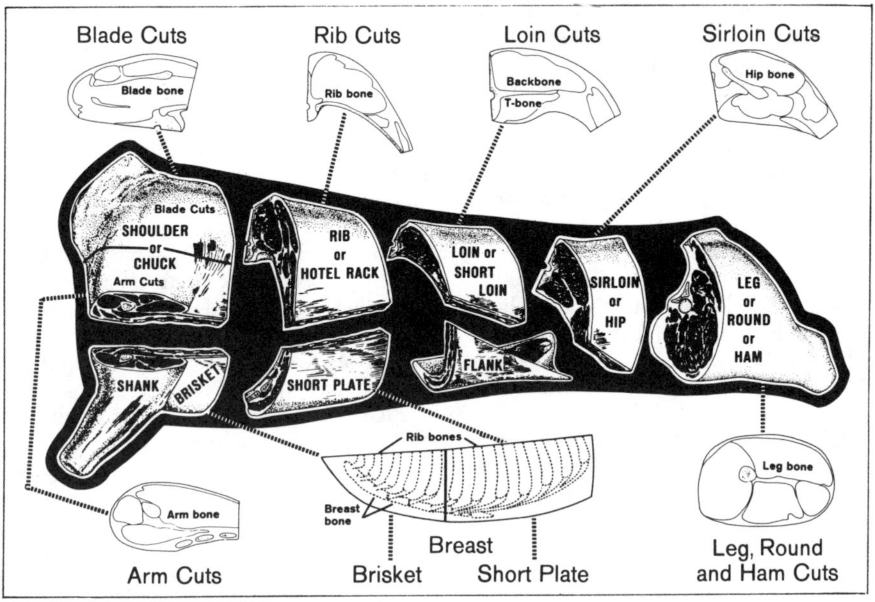

* *A side of beef appears in the chart above as an example. It could just as well have been veal, pork or lamb, for comparison purposes.*

Breast Cuts—Cut from the chest portion of the animal, they include brisket, short rib, and riblet cuts. Most of the cuts consist of several thin muscles with alternate layers of fat. These cuts are generally "less-tender" and are best prepared by braising.

Rib Cuts—Cut from the rib area along the back of the animal, they usually include portions of the back bone and rib bones. The "ribeye" is the main muscle in these cuts. In the higher grades this is a very tender muscle so the cuts are usually prepared by roasting or other dry-heat methods. Rib cuts are attractive and easily carved.

Loin or Short Loin Cuts—The cuts are from the animal's back between the ribs and the hip and usually include a T-shaped bone and two major muscles. The larger muscle is the loineye and the smaller one is the tenderloin. In the higher grades the cuts are very tender, juicy, and flavorful.

Sirloin Cuts—These are from the hip portion of the animal. In addition to the hip bone, the cuts may contain portions of the back bone. These cuts are also naturally tender in the higher grades and are best when cooked by dry-heat methods.

Leg, Round, or Ham Cuts—Cut from the back leg of the animal, they often include a round bone. In the beef round, the sections—inside, outside, and sirloin tip—frequently are sold separately.

General Meat Terms

American Leg—Leg of lamb with shank bone removed, shank meat folded back into a pocket and fastened with skewers.

Boston Butt—Upper part of a pork shoulder. The major boneless inside portion of this cut is often cured and smoked.

Canadian Style Bacon—Boneless eye muscle of a pork loin that has been cured and smoked.

Club Steak—Bone-in beef steak from the rib end of the loin section. It does not contain any of the tenderloin muscle. Bone-in rib steaks are also often sold as club steaks.

Country or Country Style Ham—Dry cured ham with a distinctive flavor. Saltier and firmer than smoked hams, it does not need refrigeration.

Country Style Spareribs—A blade or rib end of a pork loin split lengthwise.

Crown Roast—An elegant cut made with at least two rib (rack) roasts of lamb, pork, or veal, with back bone removed, shaped into a crown, and secured with twine.

"Cured and Smoked" Pork—Hams, picnics, and loins which have been cured and smoked but which require additional heating to complete cooking and to fully develop flavor. Should be refrigerated.

Delmonico Steak—A name sometimes used for a boneless beef steak which consists primarily of the "ribeye" muscle.

Filet Mignon—A boneless steak cut from the tenderloin muscle. Generally considered the most tender beef cut.

French-Style Leg—Leg of lamb with a small amount of meat trimmed from the end of the shank. After roasting, the exposed bone is sometimes decorated with a paper frill.

"Fully-Cooked" Pork—Cured and smoked pork which was cooked during the smoking process. While these cuts can be served without further cooking, heating will develop flavor. Should be refrigerated.

Ground Beef—Ground beef usually is made from lean trimmings and the less tender and less popular cuts of beef. If prepared under Federal inspection, the fat content may not exceed 30 percent and straight fat may not be included. When terms such as ground chuck, ground round, and chopped sirloin are used, the ground beef should be prepared from that specific cut.

Hamburger—Ground beef to which straight fat may have been added. Like "ground beef", it may not contain more than 30 percent fat if prepared under Federal inspection.

Ham Cuts—

Ham—Cut taken from the hind leg of a pig. It may be sold fresh or cured and smoked.

Halves—Shank or butt halves that have none of the "center" section removed.

Portions or ends—The remaining shank or butt portions of halves after the "center" section has been removed.

Center—The thick, nearly round, meaty section which contains only a small round bone.

London Broil—No specific cut but usually a beef flank steak. It generally is broiled and served in thin diagonal slices. Other less tender cuts also may be sold as London Broil to be prepared in a similar manner.

Picnic Shoulder—The lower or shank part of a pork shoulder. A picnic shoulder is sometimes confused with a ham. It is sold as fresh pork or may be cured and smoked.

Pike's Peak—Heel of round. A less tender, boneless beef roast from the lower portion of the round section.

Pork Loin Cuts—

Halves—The rib half should contain at least 10 ribs. The loin half should contain one or two ribs.

Ends—The blade or rib end contains only five to seven ribs, a section of the shoulder blade, and several different muscles. The loin end includes the hip or sirloin section.

Center—The middle portion after removal of the blade and sirloin ends. The ribeye and the tenderloin are the major muscles.

Porterhouse Steak—Usually sold interchangeably with T-Bone steaks but it contains a larger portion of the tenderloin muscle. Porterhouse and T-Bone steaks may be recognized by the T-shaped bone with the large "eye" muscle on one side and the smaller tenderloin muscle on the other.

Pot Roast—Any of a number of meaty, less-tender beef roasts. These should be braised or cooked in liquid to increase their tenderness.

Prime Rib—A name sometimes used for a beef rib roast. In that context, it does not mean the grade is U.S. Prime —it could be any grade.

Rack—Rib section of lamb or veal usually containing seven ribs.

Saratoga Chop—Boneless lamb chop from the inside shoulder muscles.

Sirloin Tip—Boneless steak or roast from the round (not the sirloin) section, in most beef cutting methods. This cut is usually less tender than "sirloin" steaks.

Spring Lamb—Meat from young lambs born in late winter or early spring and slaughtered between March 1 and the end of the week that contains the first Monday in October.

Strip—The beef short loin portion with the tenderloin muscle removed. A strip steak is the same as Porterhouse or T-Bone steak without the tenderloin muscle. If the bone is removed it is called a boneless strip steak or roast.

Swiss Steak—Not a specific cut but a method of preparation. Usually applied to less tender beef steaks which should be prepared by moist heat cookery. Such cuts frequently are mechanically tenderized.

"Water-Added" Pork—Cured and smoked pork which weighs up to 10 percent more than the fresh cut due to added water.

Meat Cookery Terms

Braise—To cook in a covered pan, usually with a small amount of added liquid. Braising is frequently preceded by browning in fat.

Broil—To cook steaks or chops by exposure to direct, intense heat.

Panbroil—To cook steaks or chops uncovered in a pan while removing fat as it accumulates.

Panfry—To cook steaks or chops with fat in an open pan.

Roast—To cook large cuts of meat in an oven with dry heat, uncovered.

FOR FURTHER READING:

U.S. Department of Agriculture, Office of Communication. *How to Buy Beef*, G 146, Washington, D.C. 20250, 1968.

________. *How to Buy Beef Steaks*, G 145, Washington, D.C. 20250, 1968.

________. *How to Buy Lamb*, G 195, Washington, D.C. 20250, 1971.

________. *How to Buy Meat for Your Freezer*, G 166, Washington, D.C. 20250, 1969.

________. *Beef and Veal in Family Meals*, G 118, Washington, D.C. 20250, 1970.

________. *Lamb in Family Meals*, G 124, Washington, D.C. 20250, 1971.

________. *Pork in Family Meals*, G 160, Washington, D.C. 20250, 1973.

________. *How to Buy Poultry*, G 157, Washington, D.C. 20250, 1968.

National Live Stock and Meat Board. *Lessons on Meat*, 36 S. Wabash Ave., Chicago, Ill. 60603, $1, 1973.

________. *Uniform Retail Meat Identity Standards*, 36 S. Wabash Ave., Chicago, Ill. 60603, $6.95.

MILK AND MILK PRODUCTS **

General Terms

Grade A Milk or Cream Products must comply with the U.S. Public Health Service's recommended *"Grade A Pasteurized Milk Ordinance."* The milk must come from healthy cows, produced and processed under sanitary conditions, and be pasteurized to kill harmful bacteria.

Homogenized. Processed to break milkfat into small particles that remain uniformly distributed throughout the product.

Vitamin D Added. Vitamin D increased to at least 400 international units per quart.

Vitamin A Added. Vitamin A increased to at least 2,000 international units per quart.

Skimmed Milk. Processed to remove most of the fat, which also removes most of the vitamin A and D of fluid whole milk.

Cultured Milk. Specially selected bacterial cultures added to milk and milk products to produce characteristic flavors and body textures.

Fresh Fluid Milk

Whole Milk. At least 3.25 percent milkfat and 8.25 percent nonfat milk

---

** AUTHOR *Joseph A. Rubis* is Chief, Standardization Branch, Dairy Division, Agricultural Marketing Service.

solids. (A minimum of 3 percent milkfat and 8 percent nonfat milk solids has been set by some States.)

Skim Milk (nonfat milk). Less than 0.5 percent milkfat and at least 8.25 percent nonfat milk solids. Addition of vitamin A is required, vitamin D is optional.

Lowfat Milk contains between 0.5 and 2 percent milkfat, and 8.25 percent nonfat milk solids. The label must show milkfat as 0.5, 1.0, 1.5, or 2.0 percent. Addition of vitamin A is required, vitamin D is optional.

Chocolate Milk. Whole milk with added chocolate and sweetener.

Chocolate-flavored Milk. Whole milk with added cocoa and sweetener.

Chocolate Drink (chocolate lowfat milk). Skim or lowfat milk with added chocolate and sweetener. Nonfat milk solids may be added.

Chocolate-flavored Drink. Skim or lowfat milk with added cocoa and sweetener. Nonfat milk solids may be added.

Cream

Light Cream (coffee or table cream) contains at least 18 percent milkfat.

Light Whipping Cream has at least 30 percent milkfat.

Heavy Whipping Cream contains at least 36 percent milkfat.

Whipped Cream in Aerosol Can. Any of the above types of cream with added sugar, stabilizer and emulsifier packaged in an aerosol can.

Imitation Cream (Coffee Whitener). Either liquid or dry product made in semblance of and used as a substitute for cream. It is made from any safe and suitable substance which may include but is not limited to substances derived from milk.

Half and Half is a mixture of milk and cream. It contains at least 10.5 percent milkfat.

Cultured Milk and Cream

Cultured Buttermilk is made by adding bacterial culture to skim milk or lowfat milk to obtain a thick, smooth body and characteristic acid flavor. It contains at least 8.25 percent nonfat milk solids.

Yogurt is made from whole or skim milk with a specific bacterial culture added to obtain semi-solid body and characteristic flavor. It may be plain or with added fruits or flavoring.

Sour Cream is made by adding a bacterial culture to fresh cream to obtain a semi-fluid to semi-solid body with characteristic acid flavor. It is at least 18 percent milkfat.

Sour Half and Half is made by adding a bacterial culture to a mixture of milk and cream to obtain a semi-fluid to semi-solid body with characteristic acid flavor. It is at least 10.5 percent milkfat.

Acidified Sour Cream. Instead of using a bacterial culture to develop the characteristic body and acid flavor, special food grade acids are added to the cream.

Canned Milk

Evaporated Milk. Whole milk concentrated by removing part of the water is homogenized, sealed in a container, and processed by heat to prevent spoilage. It has at least 7.5 percent milkfat and 25.5 percent total milk solids, with vitamin D added.

Sweetened Condensed Milk. Whole milk concentrated by removing part of the water and adding sugar to help preserve the milk. It has at least 8.5 percent milkfat and 28 percent total milk solids.

Eggnog is made from milk and cream of at least 6 percent milkfat. It contains at least 1.0 percent egg yolk solids, added sweetener, flavoring, emulsifier, and stabilizer.

Dry Milk

Nonfat Dry Milk is made by removing most of the water from skim milk. It contains not over 5 percent moisture and 1.5 percent milkfat.

Instant Nonfat Dry Milk. Nonfat dry

milk is processed to result in larger particles which are easily dissolved in water.

Whole Dry Milk is made by removing most of the water from whole milk. It has at least 26 percent milkfat.

Butter and Milkfat Products

Butter is made by churning cream, and may have added salt and coloring. It contains not less than 80 percent milkfat. Unsalted butter is sometimes called "sweet" butter.

Whipped Butter. Butter is whipped to improve spreadability by incorporating approximately 50 percent air or an inert gas. It contains not less than 80 percent milkfat and may be salted or unsalted.

Cheese

Natural Cheese is made directly from milk with no further processing. The cheeses are classed as unripened, soft ripened, semisoft ripened, firm ripened, very hard ripened and mold ripened.

Pasteurized Process Cheese is a blend of fresh and aged natural cheeses which have been shredded and mixed with emulsifiers and heated (pasteurized). It melts easily when reheated. The blend may consist of one or two or more varieties of natural cheeses, and may contain pimentos, fruits, vegetables or meats and/or smoke flavor may be added.

Pasteurized Process Cheese Food is prepared in the same way as process cheese, except it contains less cheese with nonfat dry milk, or whey solids and water added. This results in a lower milkfat content and more moisture than process cheese.

Pasteurized Process Cheese Spread is prepared in the same way as process cheese food, but generally contains more moisture and less milkfat.

Cold Pack or Club Cheese is a blend of fresh and aged natural cheese, as in process cheese, except the cheese is mixed into a uniform product without heating.

Cold Pack Cheese Food is prepared the same way as Cold Pack Cheese, but includes other dairy ingredients as used in process cheese food.

Grating Cheese. Any ripened hard-type cheese, usually the hard Italian types—Parmesan, Romano, Asiago, and Provolone. The cheese is ground, grated or shredded and dried. It is used as a condiment in cooking.

American Cheese. Descriptive term often used to identify the varieties of cheeses which include Cheddar (made in the U.S.), Colby, Granular or Stirred-curd and Washed-curd cheeses. Sometimes Monterey or Jack cheese is included in this group.

Longhorn Cheese. A style or shape of cheese, sold at retail. May be any one of the American cheese varieties, usually a mild flavor.

Mild or Current Aged, Mellow or Medium Aged, Sharp or Aged. Terms used to describe the increasing degree of flavor development in certain varieties of cheese, such as Cheddar.

Cottage Cheese

Dry Curd Cottage Cheese is a soft, uncured cheese made from skim milk with the addition of a special bacterial culture, and with or without a milk-clotting enzyme. It contains less than 0.5 percent milkfat and not over 80 percent moisture.

Cottage Cheese is made the same way as dry curd cottage cheese with cream added. It contains not less than 4 percent milkfat and not over 80 percent moisture. The percent of milkfat should be shown on the label.

Lowfat Cottage Cheese is made the same way as dry curd cottage cheese and may have some cream added. It contains between 0.5 and 4 percent milkfat, and not over 82.5 percent moisture. The percent of milkfat should be shown on the label.

Direct Set or Curd Set by Direct Acidification. Terms used to identify cottage cheese made by adding special food grade acids, instead of a bacterial culture, to skim milk to develop acidity and coagulate the milk to form the cheese curd. Such cheeses must include on the label the statement "Direct Set" or "Curd Set by Direct Acidification".

Frozen Desserts

Ice Cream is made by freezing while stirring a pasteurized mix of cream, milk, sweeteners and stabilizers. It contains at least 10 percent milkfat and 20 percent total milk solids. It may be vanilla flavor or with added fruits, nuts or other flavorings.

Frozen Custard (French or New York Ice Cream) is made by freezing while stirring a pasteurized mix of cream, milk, sweeteners and stabilizers plus added egg yolks. It contains at least 10 percent milkfat and 20 percent total milk solids.

Ice Milk is made by freezing while stirring a pasteurized mix of milk, sweeteners and stabilizers. It contains between 2 and 7 percent milkfat, and at least 11 percent total milk solids.

Fruit Sherbet is made by freezing while stirring a pasturized mix of milk, fruit or fruit juice, stabilizers and sweeteners. It contains between 1 and 2 percent milkfat and 2 and 5 percent total milk solids.

Nonfruit Sherbet. The same as fruit sherbet, except the fruit or fruit juice is replaced with spices, infusion of coffee or tea, chocolate, candies, liqueurs, wines or other natural or artificial flavorings.

Water Ices are made by freezing while stirring a mix of water, fruit or fruit juice, sweeteners, and stabilizers. It is similar to sherbet but has no milk solids.

FOR FURTHER READING:

U.S. Department of Agriculture, Office of Communication. *How to Buy Dairy Products,* G201, Washington, D.C. 20250.

———. *How to Buy Cheese,* G193, Washington, D.C. 20250.

*** AUTHOR *Edith A. Christensen* is Head of Testing Section, Commodity Inspection Branch, Grain Division, Agricultural Marketing Service.

GRAIN PRODUCTS ***

Wheat Products

White flour is the food prepared by grinding and bolting cleaned wheat with removal of up to 28 percent of the outer branny layers.

Bleached flour is flour with one or a combination of optional ingredients in a quantity not more than sufficient for bleaching and/or to produce an aging effect. Bleaching agents are oxides of nitrogen, chlorine, nitrosyl chloride, chloride dioxide, acetone peroxides, or azodicarbonamide. Some of these have maximum limitations prescribed by the Food and Drug Administration. A flour so treated must always be marked "Bleached" on the label.

All Purpose Flour is white flour prepared for home use to make a complete range of satisfactory products as yeast breads, quick breads, cakes, cookies, and pastries.

Family flour is another name for all purpose flour.

Cake flour is flour milled from low protein soft wheat or from low protein fraction derived from the milling process. It is especially suitable for baking cakes and pastries which require light, fluffy flour, but not high protein flour. It is not suitable for baking yeast-raised products.

Hard wheat or bread flour is flour milled from hard, high protein wheat. High protein (strong gluten) is required for bread baking. This type of flour is used chiefly in commercial bread production where doughs must withstand the rigors of machine handling.

Enriched flour is flour to which vitamins and iron have been added. This addition is, in part, to replace what is lost in milling. The branny layer removed in milling is higher in these nutrients than the floury center of the wheat kernel.

Self rising flour is all purpose flour to which leavening agents and salt have been added. The leavening agents are sodium bicarbonate and one or more acid reacting substances. Salt is added for seasoning. Self rising flour is not recommended for baking yeast-raised products.

Whole wheat flour is prepared by grinding cleaned wheat so that natural constituents of the flour are unchanged from those of the wheat from which it is milled. It includes the bran and germ.

Graham flour is another name for whole wheat flour.

Instantized flour or granular flour is made by special processes of grinding and bolting (sifting), or from regular flour subjected to a controlled amount of atomized moisture which causes the flour to clump or agglomerate. It is dried to a normal moisture level and processed for uniformity. It is free pouring and dust free compared to regular flour. It instantly disperses in cold water and does not pack down in the package. It may be used in almost all recipes in place of regular flour, but tends to be more expensive.

Gluten flour is wheat flour especially milled to have high gluten (protein) and a low starch content. It is used primarily by bakers as an ingredient for special products or to mix with other flour of lower protein content. It is also used as an ingredient in breakfast cereals.

Semolina is prepared by grinding and bolting cleaned durum wheat to a granular consistency with removal of the bran. It has a natural yellow color and is used to prepare pasta products like macaroni and spaghetti. It imparts a desirable yellow to pasta products.

Durum flour is prepared by grinding and bolting cleaned durum wheat with removal of the bran coat and germ, and reducing to the consistency of flour. It has a natural yellow color and is used in the manufacture of pasta products like macaroni and spaghetti.

Macaroni is prepared by drying formed units of dough made from semolina, durum flour, farina, flour or any combination of two or more of these, with water. Macaroni units are tube shaped.

Spaghetti is a product of similar ingredients and processing to macaroni, but formed in cord shapes (not tubular).

Vermicelli is a product of similar ingredients and processing to macaroni, but formed in cord shapes smaller than spaghetti.

Enriched macaroni, spaghetti and vermicelli contain added vitamins and iron in the following amounts per pound: Thiamine (vitamin B_1) 4–5 mg, Riboflavin (vitamin B_2) 1.7–2.2 mg, Niacin or Niacinamide 27–34 mg. and Iron 13–16.5 mg.

Farina is prepared by grinding and bolting cleaned wheat, other than durum wheat, to a granular consistency with removal of the bran coat and germ. It is used directly as a cereal and as an ingredient in pasta products.

Enriched farina is farina to which the following vitamins and mineral have been added per pound: Thiamine (B_1) 2.0–2.5 mg, Riboflavin (B_2) 1.2–1.5 mg, Niacin or Niacinamide 16.0–20.0 mg, and Iron minimum 13.0 mg.

Wheat cereals, uncooked cover a variety of products, all made by processing wheat by cutting, rolling, or fine grinding. Crushed wheat is one product, another is cracked wheat, where cleaned wheat is cut into angular fragments. Rolled wheat is another. Finer wheat cereal products are whole wheat meal and farina. They may contain added vitamin and mineral enrichment.

Wheat cereals, ready-to-eat are a variety of wheat products precooked and shaped and formed into products ready to serve. Bran flakes and wheat flakes are formed from precooked or toasted mixtures of bran and wheat.

Corn Products

Degermed cornmeal is the food prepared by grinding cleaned white or yellow corn with removal of the bran and the germ so that the fat content does not exceed 2.25 percent. Corn products are lower in protein content than wheat products.

Whole or regular cornmeal is prepared by grinding cleaned white or yellow corn including the germ, so that fat in the product does not differ by more than .3 percent from that of the corn. The fat content is usually over 3.0 percent.

Corn grits are prepared by grinding and sifting white or yellow corn—with removal of the corn bran and germ—to a granular size, larger than cornmeal. *Hominy grits* is another name for corn grits.

Corn flour is prepared by grinding and bolting white or yellow cleaned corn similar to cornmeal, but to a finer, flour consistency.

Enriched cornmeal and grits are products to which the following amounts of vitamins and minerals have been added per pound: Thiamine (B_1) 2.0–3.0 mg, Riboflavin (B_2) 1.2–1.8 mg, Niacin or Niacinamide 16–24 mg, and Iron 13–26 mg.

Rice Products

Milled white rice is made by removing the hull in a mechanical hulling device, producing rice without the hull, but with bran (brown rice). The brown rice is further processed in a pearler to remove the bran.

Enriched white rice is milled white rice to which nutrients have been added in a harmless carrier. The level of nutrients per pound are: Thiamine (B_1) 2.0–4.0 mg, Niacin or Niacinamide 16–32 mg, and Iron 13–26 mg.

Brown rice is the product which results as removal of the rice hull. It contains the brown branny layer. Removal of the bran layer yields milled white rice.

Parboiled rice is milled rice specially processed by steam or hot water. The rough rice is treated before removal of the hulls to cause a migration of the vitamins from the hull to the center of the kernel. When the hull is removed in milling, most of the vitamins are not removed but retained in the final milled product. This is especially effective for increasing the nutrition of milled rice, as up to 75 percent of the Thiamine (vitamin B_1) is retained in the parboiled milled kernel, whereas up to 90 percent may be lost if not parboiled. Enrichment of rice will make up for this loss on nonparboiled rice.

Converted rice is another name for parboiled rice.

Quick cooking rice is milled rice precooked to some degree before packaging and sale. The cooked or partially cooked rice is dried in such a way as to retain the grains in a porous and open-structured condition. The purpose is to provide consumer convenience by reducing cooking time. Consumer products vary from a partially precooked rice product requiring up to 15 minutes cooking to a minute rice product which cooks in 2 minutes.

Rice flour is a ground product made from milled rice from the broken kernels. Production is small because the demand is small. It is generally not available as a consumer product, but to food processors and formulators. You may see it listed as an ingredient in cereal and baby food formulas.

Rice cereals, uncooked are farina-like products made from granulated white milled rice, as Cream of Rice. They are often enriched with vitamins and minerals to enhance their nutritional value. Protein content of rice and its cereals is lower than wheat and oat cereals.

Rice cereals, ready-to-eat appear in many forms—as rice flakes, puffed rice, oven-puffed rice, shredded rice, and rice blended into a multigrain cereal using wheat, corn, oats, or soybeans in the mixture. They are all made by processing milled white rice in a variety of ways or by using rice flour.

Oat Products

Oatmeal or rolled oats is a cereal made from the kernel of the oat called groat. In processing, the tough, inedible husk is removed from the groat. The groat then may be cut, steamed and flaked to prepare this consumer product. Groat is higher in protein than whole oat grain, so needed nutrition is not discarded. Fat and protein contents of oat cereal are generally higher than wheat, corn, and rice cereals.

Quick cooking oatmeal is prepared from oat groats, by cutting them into smaller pieces, sometimes steaming, then flaking to a thinner flake than regular oatmeal.

Always Play It Safe In Food Buying, Handling, Cooking

SAFE FOOD must be planned and not left to chance. For the consumer, food safety begins in the marketplace. All cooperative efforts made by the U.S. and State Departments of Agriculture to make available a clean, safe, wholesome food supply will be in vain unless the consumer takes certain precautions to keep it that way. These precautions include care in buying, storing, handling and cooking food.

Damaged cans at meat counter.

Shop for groceries last after all other errands have been run. Take foods home immediately and don't leave them unattended for a long period of time. Purchase foods from stores that meet strict requirements for cleanliness. Sufficient light in grocery stores is necessary to enable you to adequately view foods for proper selection. Store personnel should make sure that foods are replaced frequently in order to keep them as fresh as possible.

Make sure the foods you pick are in good condition. If the store is running a special on certain foods, be sure those bargain foods are in no way less safe.

Under no circumstances buy swollen or leaking cans. Call them to the attention of the store manager and suggest he remove them from the shelf. The food in a swollen or leaking can may be dangerous to eat, or even to taste.

Select refrigerated and frozen foods last before going to the checkout counter so they'll have less time to warm up. Make sure frozen foods are hard-frozen and are kept below the frostline in the freezer. The temperature of the freezer should be 0° F or below.

If food has softened, chances are it has already lost quality. An ice coating on the outside of packages is an indication of some previous thawing.

Make sure refrigerated foods are cold and came from the refrigerated case. The temperature of the refrigerated case should be 40° F or below.

Ask the checkout clerk to bag cold foods together so that they keep cold longer; interspersed with room temperature foods they may warm up quickly. Ice cream and frozen juices will keep better on the way home if placed in insulated bags at the checkout counter. Take perishable items home and refrigerate or freeze them immediately.

Chances of maintaining good quality in foods during storage are increased if the initial food quality is high.

Keep hot foods hot (above 140° F) and cold foods cold (below 40° F). Food may not be safe to eat if held more than two hours at temperatures between 40 and 140° F. Remember that this includes all the time of preparation, storage and serving.

Because cooking temperatures are especially important for meats, a meat thermometer should be used. Although beef may be eaten rare, 140° F, always cook pork and poultry thoroughly. The meat thermometer should indicate 170° F for pork and 180—190° F for poultry.

Your hands or any equipment or utensils used in preparing or handling

---

AUTHOR *Sara Beck* is Consumer Specialist, Animal and Plant Health Inspection Service.

Select refrigerated food last at store. Clean cutting board and utensils after contact with raw meat or poultry. Use meat thermometer in cooking poultry. Ask store clerk to bag refrigerated items together. Store freezer should be 0° F or below. Clean hands help keep food safe.

raw foods such as meat, poultry or eggs, should be thoroughly cleaned before handling other foods. Hot sudsy water followed by a rinse, then a chlorine solution is good for thorough cleaning of utensils and work surfaces. Prepare the chlorine solution from sodium hypochlorite bleach, as directed on the label.

Poor food-handling practices in the home often cause illness in the family, even though the foods were safe to eat when purchased or first prepared. Lack of sanitation, insufficient cooking, and improper storage can allow bacteria in food to increase to dangerous levels.

You can help protect your family from foodborne illness by: stressing personal hygiene for all members of your household; making sure all dishes, utensils, kitchen equipment, and work surfaces are clean; and taking simple precautions in buying, storing, preparing and cooking all foods.

MATERIALS

Home Improvements Using Concrete

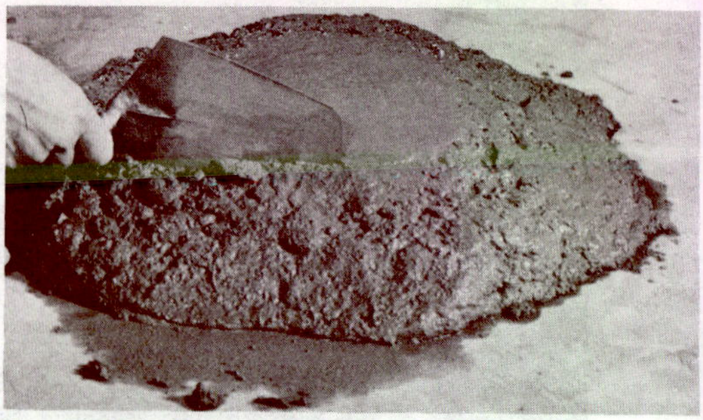

(Above) Small batches of concrete can be mixed by hand on a smooth flat surface such as a concrete floor. (Top right) A wood float may be used to compact and level the surface. It leaves a gritty texture.

CONCRETE HOME IMPROVEMENTS can enhance the beauty and the value of your property. They can also make your routine lawn maintenance easier, your outdoor entertaining more enjoyable, and your housecleaning chores less burdensome from tracked-in dirt.

Ordinary tools and easily obtained materials are all that are needed for concrete work. You will usually have three options for obtaining concrete:

- buy ready mixed concrete;
- buy portland cement, sand and coarse aggregate, and mix your own concrete; or
- buy commercially dry-mixed concrete by the bag and merely mix with water.

Your choice depends on the size of the job and the amount of labor you wish to provide. In general, the more of your own labor, the less will be your out-of-pocket cost.

Forms for the concrete can be built with materials available from the local building materials dealer. Dimension lumber like 2x4's or 2x6's is used for most jobs. If large surfaces must be formed, like the sides of concrete steps, plywood is the most commonly used forming material. You should use either forming grade or exterior grade plywood that is undamaged by moisture. A light coat of oil on the forms will permit easier removal and help preserve the wood for possible reuse.

Reinforcing steel may or may not be needed. In general, flatwork such as sidewalks, patios, stepping stones, and driveways requires no reinforcement if proper attention is paid to jointing. However, retaining walls and items subject to heavy loading will need to be reinforced.

Tools for doing concrete work consist of a strike-off board, a float of wood or light metal, a metal trowel, and edging tools.

When planning the job, first calculate roughly the amount of concrete you'll need. Calculate the volume by multiplying length by width by thickness, all expressed in feet:

V (cu. ft.) = L (ft.) x W (ft.) x T (ft.)

Divide cubic feet by 27 to secure cubic yards. For flatwork, a simple rule for estimating the amount of concrete needed is: One cubic yard of concrete will cover about 300 sq. ft. one inch thick, allowing for some waste. If the slab is 4 in. thick, a cubic yard will cover $\frac{300}{4}$, or about 75 sq. ft.

Example: How much concrete will be needed to place a 2-ft. 6-in. x 7-ft. sidewalk 4-in. thick?

$2\frac{1}{2} \times 7 = 17\frac{1}{2}$ sq. ft.

One cubic yard 4-in. thick will place

$\frac{300}{4} = 75$ sq. ft.

$\frac{17\frac{1}{2}}{75}$ = less than ¼. Thus, ¼ cu. yd. is needed.

Most ready mix producers specify a minimum volume that they will deliver. This may be as little as one cubic yard (27 cu. ft.) If your job requires an amount smaller than the minimum order, you may wish to investigate the

---

AUTHOR *Maurice L. Burgener* is vice president, U.S. regional promotion, Portland Cement Association, Skokie, Ill.

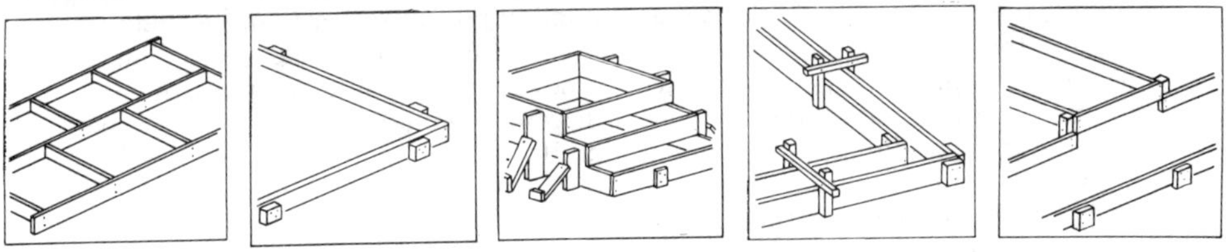

Forming for common concrete jobs. (Left) Precast work only.

other options described below. However, on larger jobs such as patios and driveways, ready mixed concrete usually is the best choice.

When you order ready mixed concrete, a good rule to follow is to ask for a mix that contains 550 lbs. of cement (about six bags) to the cubic yard. Experience has shown this to be a durable mix for outdoor exposure. Also ask that the concrete be air entrained. Air entrainment gives hardened concrete increased resistance to salt action and cycles of freezing and thawing. It is good practice to tell the ready mix producer what you expect to build so that he can furnish the mix best suited to your job.

On jobs that you intend doing a piece at a time or where the quantity of concrete is less than the ready mix producer's minimum order, you may wish to mix your own. If you do so, remember that variations in proportions between batches will result in minor color differences in hardened concrete. Therefore, if the job is all one piece, such as a patio, try to do it in a continuous operation rather than spreading it over several days.

Hand-mixing in a mortar box or wheelbarrow is satisfactory only for very small jobs. It is difficult to get continuous-volume production by hand-mixing. Renting a small mixer will save back-breaking labor and make the job move more smoothly.

To mix one cubic yard of concrete you'll need:

- 6 bags of portland cement
- 1,250 lbs. of concrete sand
- 1,900 lbs. of gravel or crushed stone
- About 30 gallons of water

Sand and gravel vary, but a good mix to try for a starter is 1 part cement, $2\frac{1}{4}$ parts sand, and 3 parts gravel or crushed stone. The key to quality concrete is the proportion of water to cement. Plan to use about 5 gallons of water for each bag of cement and keep this proportion constant. The amount of sand and gravel can be adjusted in later batches to get the workability desired.

Example: Determine the amount of materials to order for the 2-ft. 6-in. x 7-ft. x 4-in. sidewalk. You previously found that $\frac{1}{4}$ cu. yd. of concrete was required, so you'll need:

$6/4 = 1\frac{1}{2}$	Say 2 bags of cement
$\frac{1,250}{4} = 315$	Say 325 lbs. of sand
$\frac{1,900}{4} = 475$	Say 500 lbs. of gravel or crushed stone

For jobs too small to order sand, gravel, and cement separately, you can buy bagged dry-mixed concrete at hardware stores and building materials dealers. Calculate the quantity of concrete needed; then find out the volume contained in each bag and determine the number of bags needed. Dry-mixed concrete needs only to be mixed with water, having been accurately proportioned in the factory.

The drawings show methods of forming for common jobs around the home. While 1-in. thick lumber can be used for forming, 2-in. lumber requires less bracing and is easier to keep in true alignment. A hint: Always err on the side of overbracing the forms. Once forms begin to bow from concrete pressure, it is virtually impossible to restore true alignment.

Two simple rules for placing concrete will help you get a quality job:

1. Place the concrete as near its final position as possible. This will save the labor of moving it and will prevent segregation of the mix. Compact or spade the concrete into the forms as it is being placed.
2. Work the surface as little as possible in the early stages. Overworking of concrete draws fine material to the surface and results in less durability. Strike the surface off to the desired level, moving the strike-off board across the surface as many times as needed. Smooth out irregularities with a float. Run an edger along the form boards. Cut dummy groove joints wherever needed. Then wait.

When the watery sheen has left the concrete surface, it is ready for final finishing. The first step is to use a wood or light metal float. On sidewalks, driveways, and steps this is often the final finish since it leaves a gritty slip-resistant finish. For smooth surfaces, use a steel trowel after the float. This finish is not commonly used on outdoor work since a troweled surface tends to be slippery when wet.

Here's a helpful hint: A gritty wood float finish hides irregularities better than a smooth surface. A beginner will often be better pleased with his work when the final finish is done with a wood float or a light brush drawn across the surface.

Concrete needs to be kept moist for several days after it has set. An economical way of curing is to cover the new concrete with a waterproof material such as polyethylene. This traps moisture in the concrete. Setting a sprinkler to keep the concrete continuously wet, or covering concrete with moist sand or burlap, also provides good curing. Hardness of the surface is greatly influenced by the length of time of moist curing.

Wherever possible, divide concrete into sections that are nearly square. Do this by cutting dummy groove joints in the fresh concrete to about one-fourth the concrete thickness. Then any cracks that form will tend to follow the straight dummy groove rather than be irregular. A 3-ft. sidewalk would have dummy grooves at 3- to 4-ft. intervals. A 10-ft. driveway would have dummy grooves at 10- to 12-ft. intervals.

A concrete slab should be separated from a foundation by putting expansion joint material along the foundation. This permits slight movement and avoids unsightly cracks along the wall.

Most concrete slabs are made at least 4 in. thick. This is thick enough for driveways that carry only autos and an occasional truck. Delivery trucks require a 6-in. thickness.

Stepping stones can be cast to any shape desired (like footprints) by removing sod, then carving the earth to the shape desired. Concrete is placed in the hole and finished. After concrete has hardened, the sod can be replaced.

With a little experience you can make concrete with an attractive decorative surface. The easiest way is to work colored stone into the surface of the fresh concrete. After the concrete is firm but not fully set, wash the surface with water, using a stiff bristle brush. This will expose the colored aggregate.

You can precast flagstones, splash blocks, or other small items on any flat surface such as a garage floor. Place a layer of building paper, polyethylene, cardboard, or other bond breaker on the floor. Then build forms and place them over the bond breaker. Fill the forms with concrete and finish in the usual way. Precast items are usually made at least 2½ in. thick.

Precast flagstones are most easily set on a sand bed. One part portland cement mixed with 3 to 5 parts sand will result in a firmer bed than will sand alone. After the stones are set, washing the patio with water provides moisture that will permit the sand-cement bed to harden into a firm base.

A wide range of precast items for the home, lawn, and garden is available at local precast plants. These items are often available in a variety of colors that are impossible for the individual homeowner to produce. The precaster also can provide artistic designs more economically since his forms will be reused several times. Suggestions on how to handle and set the precast items can usually be obtained from the seller.

Publications on a number of uses of concrete and recommendations for proper construction practices are available from the Portland Cement Association, Old Orchard Road, Skokie, Ill. 60076. A list of publications, with prices, will be sent free on request.

All About Brick And the 10,000 Ways It Comes

Brick can be used in a wide variety of ways in and around the home. These uses include fireplaces, floors, decorative walls, dividers and planters inside the home, and barbecues, patios, screen walls, retainer walls and tree wells outside the home. Choosing the right brick and using proper construction techniques are key factors in the success of any brick project.

A brick is defined as a small building unit, solid or cored not in excess of 25 percent, commonly in the form of a rectangular prism formed from clay or shale and fused by heat. The cores in some units have been introduced as an aid to uniform drying and burning of the clay and as a means of reducing the weight.

Other brick-like materials on the market today include concrete brick, plastic brick, fly ash brick, glass brick, sawdust brick and even cow dung brick. All of these materials have different engineering properties than the real clay brick. These different properties may or may not suit the need for which they are intended.

The Federal Trade Commission requires the manufacturer of any product sold as a brick but produced from a material other than clay to specifically preface it as concrete brick, plastic brick or whatever. Only a clay brick can be referred to generically as "brick."

If other than clay brick is used, the purchaser should be thoroughly aware of the limitations of its use and not expect the same results that would be achieved by the use of clay units. Unless otherwise stated, I will be referring to clay brick when I use the term "brick" in this chapter.

Two principal types of manufacturing techniques are used in the production of brick.

- Molded brick is produced either by machine or hand molding techniques. A handmade appearance is achieved through the use of soft mud in the manufacturing process.
- Extruded brick is produced by forcing stiff mud through a die. These bricks are usually cored and have a more machine-perfect appearance. Various textures are applied to the sides of the unit.

Both molded and extruded brick can be used in most applications in and around the house. Molded brick is usually more expensive than extruded brick, but many feel the handmade look is worth the additional cost.

Brick is available in over 10,000 different sizes, shapes, textures and colors. The final choice of the brick unit having the right combination of these qualities

---

AUTHOR *G. William Detty* is the Chief of Federal Liaison for the Brick Institute of America, McLean, Va.

is usually an esthetic consideration of the purchaser. Certain qualities, however, may be more desirable for some applications than for others.

Brick sizes are quoted as either a "nominal" or "actual" size. The nominal size is equal to the manufactured or actual size plus the thickness of the mortar joint for which the unit is designed.

For example, the standard modular brick has these actual dimensions: 3⅝″ thick, 2¼″ high, and 7⅝″ long. Corresponding nominal dimensions for the same brick would be 4″, 2 2/3″ and 8″. In this case a ⅜″ mortar joint accounts for the difference.

All brick used in outdoor structures should be of an SW Grade. Used or salvaged brick should not be used unless they have been tested and meet SW Grade requirements. Type M or Type S mortar should be used.

Composition of these mortars by volume is as follows:

Type M	*Type S*
1 part portland cement	1 part portland cement
¼ part hydrated lime	½ part hydrated lime
3 parts sand	4½ parts sand

All joints should be completely filled with mortar. This is particularly important since outdoor structures will be exposed to extreme weather.

Another common brick used around the home is the paving brick. This brick unit does not have any coring and is available in various sizes. Typical patio or walkway paving brick is 3⅝″ thick by 7⅝″ long and 2¼″ in height. A 4″ by 8″ unit is generally used when mortarless paving is desired. The bricks are tightly abutted to each other over a firm base. The 3⅝″ by 7⅝″ by 2¼″ unit is more easily utilized if mortar joints are desired.

If mortarless paving is desired, brick units that are twice as long as they are wide permit the selection of a wider range of design patterns. Mortared paving should be placed on a rigid base such as a concrete slab.

A few patterns available with the use of brick paving.

I would recommend a membrane layer of roofing felt or polyethylene plastic directly beneath mortarless paving. This reduces the tendency toward staining, and prevents grass and weed growth in the joint between the units.

Mortarless paving can be done with semi-skilled labor or by the handyman around the house. This may result in significant cost savings.

A brick fireplace or barbecue in conjunction with a patio will greatly enhance the livability of a back yard area.

For small yards a very simple barbecue grill can be constructed. To insure proper disposition of smoke, care should be taken in selection of the outdoor fireplace location. The fireplace should be planned to face the prevailing breezes so that the smoke will blow away and the best draft will be provided. Fire brick should be selected for the firebox of an outdoor fireplace.

While the simplest form of the barbecue grill might be built with brick by a handyman, I would suggest hiring an experienced mason for construction of a fireplace. Natural earth tones of brick make it ideal for these and other outdoor applications.

Other applications of brick outside the home include brick screen walls, planting boxes, edging, concealment

Some ways that brick can be used outside the home.

structures, fences and retaining walls. Pierced brick screens offer beauty as well as privacy without loss of light or air. They can provide a handsome separation between a children's play area and the adults' terrace.

Planters can be constructed of a wide variety of designs. Care should be taken to provide drainage in the form of weep holes through the brick or a drain at the bottom. The inside face of the walls should be waterproofed with an asphalt coating to prevent efflorescence or staining on the outside face.

Brick edging may be used to define a lawn area. Small brick enclosures may be used to conceal undesirable items. These structures may either be pierced walls to provide ventilation as

required in the case of an air conditioning unit, or solid walls which may be desirable in the case of trash cans. Brick fences can provide privacy and create a courtyard effect. This is particularly true for small lots such as townhouse lots.

One of the most frequent uses of brick in landscaping is in retaining walls. Applications of retaining walls are almost endless. A word of caution about retaining walls—they will function properly only if properly designed and constructed. They will be subject to the most severe conditions and, consequently, more care should be taken in their construction than for other brick structures. Professional advice should be sought.

Inside the home, brick has traditionally been used in fireplaces and in kitchens. Other interior applications in recent years include brick flooring, dividers and planters, and as exposed walls. Most interior applications require the skill of an experienced mason. Fireplaces, brick flooring and exposed walls are usually installed during construction of the home. Because brick is a heavy material, care should be taken to insure structural soundness when brick work is undertaken inside existing homes.

A fireplace has been called the "heart of the home." Literally hundreds of designs are possible, from colonial to contemporary. Choice of the design and style of brick will set the atmosphere of the room, whether it be a living room, family room, recreation room or even a bedroom. Fire brick should always be used around the firebox and special care should be taken to insure proper flue construction.

A brick fireplace wall is often expanded to include an entire wall in one room. An exposed interior brick wall such as this can be very decorative and provide a real contrast to paneling or other wall coverings.

Brick floors in entrance halls, family rooms and kitchens can be laid in a variety of patterns. Brick can be laid on concrete slabs or, with structural adjustments, over basements and crawl slabs. Interior brick flooring, if properly sealed, is easy to keep clean and will not show wear.

Brick dividers and planters are an inexpensive way to divide a large space or to create an attractive area for live plants.

Although brick used inside the home will be subject to virtually no deterioration, the texture of the face of the brick may be of concern in certain areas. Texture will vary from very smooth to very rough and include sand faced units and glazed brick.

A sand faced brick may not be desirable in areas where it will often be touched or rubbed. The sand will readily be rubbed off and may present a cleaning problem at floor level. Sand faced brick should never be used for flooring application.

A very rough textured brick will tend to snag clothes when the two come into contact. This type of texture, however, can produce an attractive wall if properly constructed.

Glazed brick can form a very striking wall. The typical glazed brick of the single-glaze type will cost about twice as much as an unglazed unit. Brilliant colors can be produced with a double glazed unit but this type of brick is seldom used, principally due to its cost—usually four to five times that of regular brick. Special ordering will probably be necessary.

Brick performs its functions of beauty and durability most noticeably when used on the exterior walls of the home. Brick is fire resistant and virtually maintenance free. It will not corrode, rot, split or warp. It can't be dented and it never has to be painted.

A unique characteristic of brick is its design flexibility. No other material can offer the designer the wide variety of colors, textures and patterns that can be incorporated into a house design as can brick. With proper design it can be used to bring out the stateliness of a traditional home as well as the natural look of a contemporary home.

Brick inside the home.

Brick walls will usually cost a little more than walls of other materials. The walls, however, are only a small portion (between 5 and 10 percent) of the price of a house. The cost differential between brick and other wall types is, therefore, modest. This initial cost difference will be recovered by the owner in the form of lower maintenance cost and through a higher resale value if the house is ever sold.

Bricks that have their exposed face sealed with some type of sealer are not recommended for exterior use. Glazed brick would fall in this category. Sealed brick does not allow the wall to "breathe" and may result in spalling or flaking away of the face of the brick. The painting of brick is not recommended for this same reason.

In summary, brick can be used to form a structure that is durable, esthetically pleasing, and virtually maintenance free. The variety of colors, textures and patterns available with brick give it a design flexibility unsurpassed by other materials. The success of a project, however, often requires the skill of an experienced mason.

Concrete Block— A Wide Choice for Different Jobs

VERSATILITY of concrete masonry is vividly demonstrated by the range of sizes and shapes of units being manufactured today. Forty years ago, inventory of a typical block manufacturing plant consisted of less than 30 different sizes. Today, this figure exceeds 100 and the total number of different sizes, shapes and types manufactured across the country is well over 700.

Units are made in sizes which range from one inch in thickness and in lengths up to 24 inches; they are solid or hollow and are made with dense and lightweight aggregates (materials).

The name designating various units has been fairly well standardized, and usually relates to the function in the wall. Illustrated with this chapter are several such units where the configuration implies the use for which the block is intended.

Size of a concrete masonry unit is usually described by listing its thickness, or width first, followed by its height and then its length. Thus, a 4 x 8 x 16 block has a nominal width of 4″, height of 8″ and length of 16″.

The nominal dimension includes ⅜″ allowed for the thickness of a standard mortar joint, so the actual dimensions of the well known 8″ x 8″ x 16″ unit are manufactured as 7⅝″ x 7⅝″ x 15⅝″.

American Society for Testing and Materials (ASTM) specifications permit a maximum variation in overall dimensions (length, width and height) of plus or minus ⅛″ from the actual dimensions specified by the manufacturer. It is the usual practice, however, to manufacture the units within a tolerance of plus or minus 1/16″.

Although the industry has standardized on exterior dimensions of modular units, differences in thickness of face shells and webs, and size and number of cores for the same size hollow unit may exist between manufacturers. As an example, the 8 x 8 x 16 hollow unit may range from about 50 percent to 63 percent solid, depending upon the size and number of cores. These variations may result from the need to obtain properties such as fire resistance, sound insulations, and the like.

Concrete masonry units offer a vast array of choices of natural faces and finishes for walls. These range from a wide variety that come at no extra cost to highly unusual, more expensive block for developing luxurious effects. Concrete masonry units may be classified with respect to wall finishes according to the headings described herein.

AUTHOR *Kevin D. Callahan* is Senior Design Engineer, National Concrete Association, Arlington, Va.

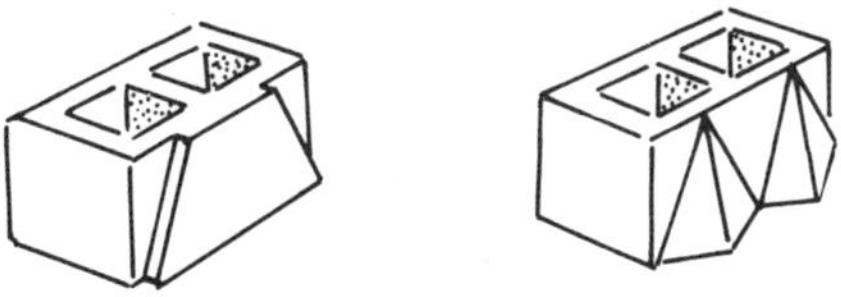

Some patterned blocks.

Concrete masonry may be used as veneer to produce a nonstructural masonry facing on a backing of wood, concrete, or masonry. The purpose may be protection, insulation or ornamentation. Units with tile-like faces, ground surfaces, or sculptured or other finished faces are often used. The veneer is ordinarily supported at its base and may be held to the wall with mortar, grout or steel anchors.

With skill in laying, block may be used to produce walls in which the block surface is left exposed on both sides, a practice that may introduce

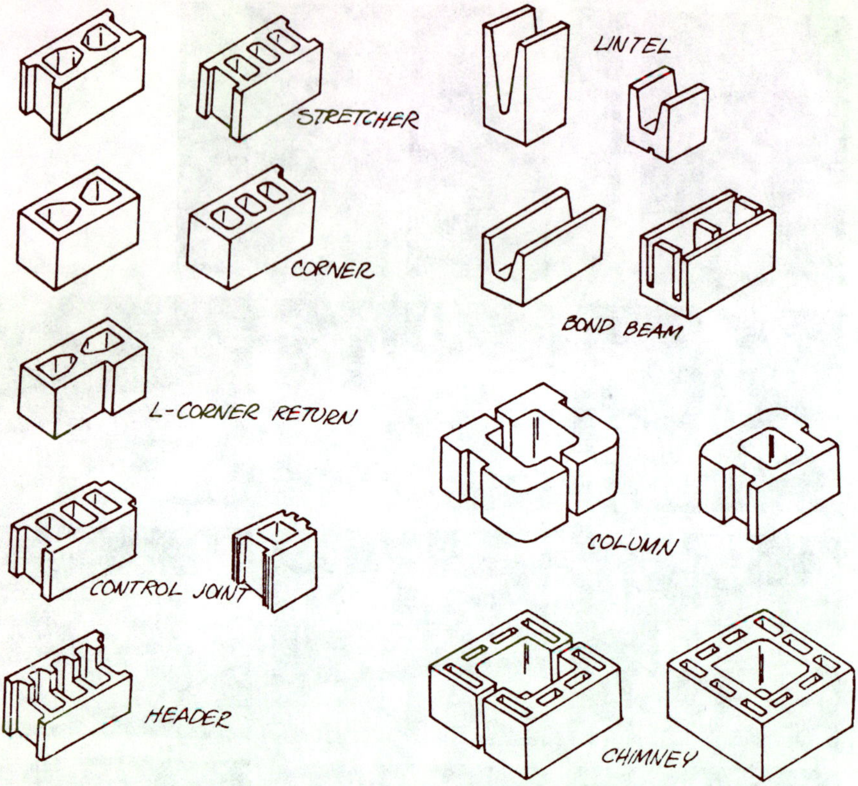

The name usually relates to function.

significant economy. It is often possible to make use of tile-faces or other decorative units to provide a special finish on one side of the wall and yet to leave the plain face exposed as an attractive finished surface on the other.

Nominal thicknesses of as little as 4 inches in interior walls may be used when necessary, provided the block meets all necessary requirements such as strength and sound resistance. Exterior walls may be exposed on both sides where thermal transmission requirements permit.

Texture in block is of interest in relation to its appearance, its sound absorption, and the ease with which the block may be painted or waterproofed.

Coarse textures provide better sound absorption than smooth textures. To satisfy the demand for coarse textured units the block manufacturer may use large coarse aggregate, a harsh aggregate grading, an angular aggregate, a dry or lean mix, or any combination of these which is needed to produce a quality product.

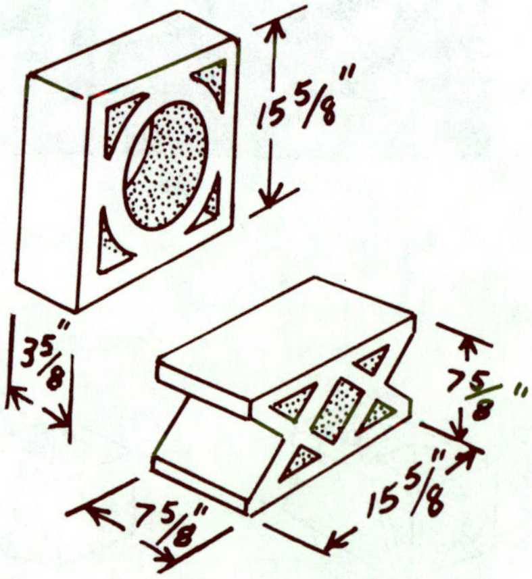

Typical screen block.

Fine textures also have decorative

appeal. A mix containing mainly fine natural sand may give an appearance much like that of quarried limestone. Various degrees of smoothness can be achieved with any aggregate by changes in mix proportions. Fine textures may be less absorptive of sound but are also less absorptive of paint than coarse textures.

With some aggregates—whether normal weight or lightweight—surface grinding brings out great color and variety from units that would otherwise be nondecorative. Ground surfaces are also more accurately planed than molded surfaces, an advantage in the ease of making the wall plumb.

"Customized," or the "Architectural Facing" concrete masonry units, are designed and manufactured to provide the finished surface of a wall without the addition of opaque coatings or treatments which would appreciably change its appearance.

Using these units, a wall may be built as an exterior or interior bearing or non-loadbearing wall. It may be designed of "through-wall" units where only one masonry unit comprises the wall section. The wall section may consist of architectural facing concrete masonry units as a veneer, backed up with concrete masonry or other materials. Or the units may be the facing portion of the structural composite or cavity wall.

The same variables that influence the performance of any masonry wall—units, mortar, workmanship, and construction details—must be given more thorough attention in the design and construction of a wall using architectural facing units. This is particularly true for exterior walls which will not receive painting or coating.

Fluted and scored, or ribbed, units provide the architect with raised striations that can be developed into many kinds of patterns. The accuracy that is achieved in machine production of these units makes it possible to produce the effect of long, continuous vertical straight lines, even when the block are laid in running bond.

Shadowall block, developed and introduced by the National Concrete Masonry Association, are units with recessed corners that may be put together in such limitless variety of patterns that this product has been called the "block of 1,000 faces." Hi-Lite block, another type of raised pattern, may be used similarly. Interesting changing shadow effects can be obtained with such units when used on exteriors.

Irregular, slumped or overhanging surfaces can be used to produce rugged or rustic effects. Such block are made from mixes that are slightly wetter than normal so that they can be deformed, or slumped immediately after they have come out of the mold box of the machine.

Units with many of the characteristics of rough quarried stone are produced by lengthwise mechanical splitting of solid concrete block. A variety of sizes are available and special hollow block may also be used for splitting. Ribbed units, previously described, can be split to produce unusual effects.

Each individual block acquires its own distinctive texture in the splitting operation. By changes in aggregate, pigment and block size many different colors, textures and shapes become possible.

Split block is useful for entire walls on either the exterior or interior, as well as for fireplace facings, chimneys and planters. It has the same high durability and low maintenance cost as other concrete masonry units.

Open-faced block of many patterns is available for decorative uses, or for partially screening walls or yards from either the sun or outside viewers. This screen block is made in a wide variety of patterns and is useful, both indoors and out, for fences and carport walls, sun screens, curtain walls, room dividers, and veneers and friezes. Only a limited number of patterns may be available in a single locality.

Due to the fragile nature of screen walls, the use of steel reinforcement is recommended wherever it can be embedded in mortar joints, in bond beam courses, or grouted into continuous vertical or horizontal cells. Horizontal joint reinforcement, two No. 9 gauge wires or equivalent, placed 12 or 16 inches apart is recommended when screen wall units are laid in stack bond.

Block with colorful, hard, glossy, mar-resistant surfaces that resemble ceramic tile in appearance, durability, and ease of cleaning are produced by some manufacturers. Surfaces may be made of epoxy or polyester resins and may contain fine sand or other fillers. Ceramic or porcelainized glazes, mineral glazes and cement-like finishes have also been used.

Most of the variations discussed so far depend on the shape, size, configuration or texture of the block. The designer can achieve still further finished wall effects simply by varying the pattern in which the block are laid. Basically the patterns group themselves into several main classifications: running bond, stacked bond, coursed or patterned ashlar (various repeating patterns), diagonal bond, basket weave, and diagonal basket weave. Each classification includes various kinds of arrangements and the number can be enlarged by the use of various sizes of block, alone or in combinations.

In addition to its many other uses, concrete masonry can serve for such applications as retaining walls, swimming pool walls, patios, planters, and fences. Whenever a masonry wall is to be exposed to substantial lateral loads, such as from earth pressure, earthquakes or high winds, it should be properly reinforced with steel reinforcement and grout. Detailed information is available from the National Concrete Masonry Association or the local block manufacturer.

A number of rapid assembly systems have come into use in the past 20 years. These are systems designed for assembly by the unskilled or partially skilled. They include: 1. Tongue-and-groove interlocking systems that are assembled dry and then bonded together by grout that flows through horizontal and vertical channels. 2. Wedge shaped blocks that interlock and are self-aligning and self-plumbing. 3. Surface bonding application which involves stacking the block up without mortar and then trowelling both sides with a plaster containing strands of fiberglass, providing a waterproof wall with good lateral strength.

Framing Lumber, Board Selection

THE HOMEOWNER or hobbyist who hasn't browsed through his local lumber yard, selected an appropriate grade and species of lumber, and brought a construction project or repair project to successful completion has a creative experience awaiting him.

The day of the skilled cabinet maker is said to be rapidly passing. Competent carpentry tradesmen are costly to employ. As a result, many of the amenities which make the older home or the custom home more attractive and more livable are beyond the means of the average home buyer.

Fortunately, most of the features that distinguish the custom home from one having only the bare essentials are well within the capabilities of the home craftsman. Lumber, the oldest yet in many respects the most modern and most readily workable building material, makes this possible.

Lumber was a more familiar item to our parents and grandparents when locally grown species were used and when grades and species selections were minimal. Softwood lumber of several species and from a number of regions is currently available in many communities, and dimension lumber grades have been developed on a more precise engineering basis.

For these reasons, any complete listing of all the grades and species of softwood lumber available throughout the nation tends to appear somewhat confusing at first. Not all the listed grades and species of lumber are available in every locality, however. Just as the builder must do, the home craftsman will quickly become familiar with the most commonly marketed species and grades in his community.

At the retail level, lumber is classified primarily by use and by size. It is also differentiated by the extent to which it has been manufactured, that is, rough sawn, dressed and worked (tongued and grooved, shiplapped or patterned.)

Types of lumber by use are *Yard, Factory and Shop,* and *Structural.*

Yard lumber consists of those grades, sizes and patterns used in ordinary construction. It is broken down into *Select* and *Common* grades.

Select grades of yard lumber have the best appearance and are used where a clear or high grade of finishing is desired. Grade names such as "B and Btr" (Better), C" and "D" are used for most species.

Common grades of lumber are suitable for general construction. The home craftsman will find even the lower common grades of boards yield many clearcuttings which can be used for furniture, cabinetry and other household projects. Common grades of lumber are "No. 1," "No. 2," "No. 3," and "No. 4." Alternate names for common lumber, such as "Sel Merch" (Select Merchantable), "Merch", "Const." (Construction), "Std" (Standard), and "Util" (Utility), may also be encountered.

The common grades will frequently be found at the retail level as combination grades where the grade requirements for many uses make it practical to inventory and sell a "No. 2 and Btr" ("No. 1" and "No. 2" grades, combined), or "No. 3 and Btr" ("No. 3" and "No. 2" and possibly "No. 1", combined). The home craftsman can check the suitability of such combined grades for his purposes by inspecting several pieces of the material which is inventoried this way at the lumber yard.

Structural lumber is 2 inches or more in nominal thickness (1½″ actual dressed thickness). It is also called stress graded lumber because each grade is assigned working stress values to permit its use in engineered structures.

Factory and Shop lumber is produced primarily for industrial purposes such as the manufacture of windows and doors. It will not ordinarily be encountered by the home craftsman at the retail yard.

Lumber is separated by size into *boards, dimension,* and *timbers.*

Lumber sizes are usually referenced for convenience and tally as nominal sizes, such as 1″ x 2″, 2″ x 4″, 4″ x 10″, etc. Actual surfaced sizes are smaller in thickness and width. Lengths are actual lengths as specified or slightly longer. A table with this chapter contains some common nominal sizes and corresponding surfaced sizes.

Boards are less than 2 inches in nominal thickness and are 1 inch and larger in width. Boards less than 6 inches in nominal width may be called strips. Boards are used for fencing, sheathing, subflooring, roofing, concrete forms, box material and as a source of many smaller cuttings.

Dimension is from 2 inches to, but not including, 5 inches in nominal thickness and 2 inches or more in width. Such lumber, depending upon use, may be called framing, studs, joists and planks, rafters, and the like.

Timbers are 5 inches or more in their least dimension. According to use in construction, they are classified as beams and stringers, girders, purlins and posts.

If the home craftsman buys what the trade calls a 2 x 4 and measures it, the dimensions will be found to be significantly less. Actually, the 2 x 4 surfaced size at 19 maximum percent moisture content is 1½″ x 3½″.

Nominal sizes (2 x 4, etc.) are widely used in lumber tallying and, for simplicity, by the construction trades. Board and dimension lumber is generally sold by the *board foot.* This is a

---

AUTHOR *Gerald F. Prange* is Vice President—Technical Services, National Forest Products Association, Washington, D.C.

Nominal and minimum-dressed sizes of finish, boards, dimension, and timbers
(The thicknesses apply to all widths and all widths to all thicknesses)

ITEM	THICKNESSES			FACE WIDTHS		
	NOMINAL	MINIMUM DRESSED		NOMINAL	MINIMUM DRESSED	
		Inches			Inches	
Select or Finish (19 per cent moisture content)	3/8 1/2 5/8 3/4 1 1-1/4 1-1/2 1-3/4 2 2-1/2 3 3-1/2 4	5/16 7/16 9/16 5/8 3/4 1 1-1/4 1-3/8 1-1/2 2 2-1/2 3 3-1/2		2 3 4 5 6 7 8 9 10 11 12 14 16	1-1/2 2-1/2 3-1/2 4-1/2 5-1/2 6-1/2 7-1/4 8-1/4 9-1/4 10-1/4 11-1/4 13-1/4 15-1/4	
		Dry Inches	Green Inches		Dry Inches	Green Inches
Boards	1 1-1/4 1-1/2	3/4 1 1-1/4	25/32 1-1/32 1-9/32	2 3 4 5 6 7 8 9 10 11 12 14 16	1-1/2 2-1/2 3-1/2 4-1/2 5-1/2 6-1/2 7-1/4 8-1/4 9-1/4 10-1/4 11-1/4 13-1/4 15-1/4	1-9/16 2-9/16 3-9/16 4-5/8 5-5/8 6-5/8 7-1/2 8-1/2 9-1/2 10-1/2 11-1/2 13-1/2 15-1/2
Dimension	2 2-1/2 3 3-1/2	1-1/2 2 2-1/2 3	1-9/16 2-1/16 2-9/16 3-1/16	2 3 4 5 6 8 10 12 14 16	1-1/2 2-1/2 3-1/2 4-1/2 5-1/2 7-1/4 9-1/4 11-1/4 13-1/4 15-1/4	1-9/16 2-9/16 3-9/16 4-5/8 5-5/8 7-1/2 9-1/2 11-1/2 13-1/2 15-1/2
Dimension	4 4-1/2	3-1/2 4	3-9/16 4-1/16	2 3 4 5 6 8 10 12 14 16	1-1/2 2-1/2 3-1/2 4-1/2 5-1/2 7-1/4 9-1/4 11-1/4	1-9/16 2-9/16 3-9/16 4-5/8 5-5/8 7-1/2 9-1/2 11-1/2 13-1/2 15-1/2
Timbers	5 & Thicker		1/2 Off	5 & Wider		1/2 Off

Source, PS 20-70 American Softwood Lumber Standard

Nominal and minimum-dressed dry sizes of siding at 19 percent maximum-moisture content

(The thicknesses apply to all widths and all widths to all thicknesses)

ITEM	THICKNESSES		FACE WIDTHS	
	NOMINAL [1]	MINIMUM DRESSED	NOMINAL	MINIMUM DRESSED
		Inches		Inches
Bevel Siding	½ 9/16 5/8 ¾ 1	7/16 butt, 3/16 tip 15/32 butt, 3/16 tip 9/16 butt, 3/16 tip 11/16 butt, 3/16 tip ¾ butt, 3/16 tip	4 5 6 8 10 12	3½ 4½ 5½ 7¼ 9¼ 11¼
Bungalow Siding	¾	11/16 butt, 3/16 tip	8 10 12	7¼ 9¼ 11¼
Rustic and Drop Siding (shiplapped, 3/8-in. lap)	5/8 1	9/16 23/32	4 5 6	3 4 5
Rustic and Drop Siding (shiplapped, ½-in. lap)	5/8 1	9/16 23/32	4 5 6 8 10 12	2⅞ 3⅞ 4⅞ 6⅝ 8⅝ 10⅝
Rustic and Drop Siding (dressed and matched)	5/8 1	9/16 23/32	4 5 6 8 10	3⅛ 4⅛ 5⅛ 6⅞ 8⅞

[1] For nominal thicknesses under 1 inch, the board measure count is based on the nominal surface dimensions (width by length). With the exception of nominal thicknesses under 1 inch, the nominal thicknesses and widths in this table are the same as the board measure or count sizes.

volume unit 1″ in thickness, by one foot in length and one foot in width. To determine the number of board feet in a piece of lumber, multiply the thickness (in inches) by the width (in feet), by the length (in feet). For example, a 2″ x 4″ twelve feet long contains 2″ x 4″/12″ x 12′ = 8 bd. ft.

The exception to the rule occurs where the nominal thickness is less than 1 inch. In this case it is only necessary to multiply the width in feet by the length in feet to obtain the board foot tally of the piece.

Select or finish lumber sizes apply at 19 or lower percent moisture content. Most finish lumber is manufactured at a maximum moisture content of 15 percent.

Board and dimension lumber may be surfaced "dry" at 19 percent maximum moisture content (marked S-DRY), at 15 percent maximum moisture content (marked MC15 or KD), or at the green

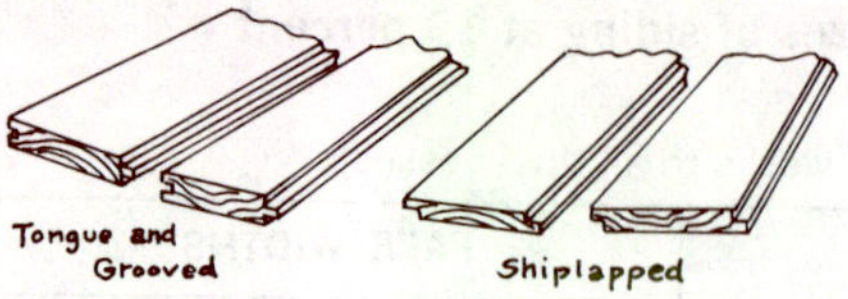

condition (S-GRN). Dressed sizes for such lumber at the dry and green conditions are given in a table with this chapter. Timbers (over 4 inches in thickness) are produced at the green condition, permitting them to season in service.

Lumber may be manufactured *rough, dressed,* and *worked* (matched, shiplapped or patterned). *Rough* lumber has been sawed, edged and trimmed but not surfaced. *Dressed* lumber has been surfaced on one or more sides to remove saw marks and surface blemishes. The most common dressed lumber is surfaced on all sides or S4S.

Worked lumber has been tongued and grooved (T&G), shiplapped or patterned, in addition to being surfaced. Examples of nominal and finished sizes for various items of standard worked lumber are shown in a second table.

With the issuance of the American Softwood Lumber Standard, PS 20–70, in September 1970, development of a National Grading Rule for dimension lumber became a reality.

Prior to development of the standard published by the U.S. Department of Commerce, each regional grade writing agency developed structural grades for dimension lumber based upon regional species or species groups. These grades took into consideration the characteristics of the species i.e., knot size, size of timber, non-dimension uses of the species, etc. As a result, a great many different engineering stress levels were developed and an even greater number of allowable spans for joists and rafters were tabulated.

To simplify the multitude of structural grades and working stresses available to the designer and the user, the Softwood Lumber Standard PS 20–70 published in 1970 provided that a National Grading Rule Committee be established, "To maintain and make fully and fairly available grade strength ratios, nomenclature and descriptions of grades for dimension lumber". These grades and grade requirements, as developed, are now used by all regional grade writing agencies.

Since development of the National Grading Rule and the adherence of all regional and species rules to its requirements, a great deal more uniformity has resulted and use of dimension lumber by the architect and engineer has been materially simplified.

All softwood grade writing agencies which publish grading rules, certified by the American Lumber Standards Committee, adhere to this rule for dimension lumber. The rule provides for uniform grade names for all species and grades of structural lumber.

The National Grading Rule separates dimension lumber into two *width* categories. Pieces up to 4 inches wide are graded as "Structural Light Framing," "Light Framing," and "Studs." Pieces 6 inches and wider are graded as "Structural Joists and Planks." (See dimension lumber table). For special uses where a fine appearance and high bending strength are required, the national rule also provides a single "Appearance Framing" grade.

"Structural Light Framing" grades are available for those engineered uses where the higher bending strengths are required.

The four grades included in this category are "Sel Str" (Select Structural), "No. 1," "No. 2," and "No. 3."

"Light Framing" grades are available for those uses where good appearance at lower design level is satisfactory. Grades in this category are called "Const" (Construction), "Std" (Standard), and "Util" (Utility).

A single "Stud" grade is also provided under the National Grading Rule. It is intended specifically for use as a vertical bearing member in walls and partitions and is produced to a maximum length of 10 feet.

"Structural Joists and Plank" grades are available in widths 6 inches and wider for use as joists, rafters, headers,

Dimension Lumber Grades
(National Grading Rule)

	Grade
2"–4" Thick, 2"–4" Wide	
Structural Light Framing	Sel Str (Select Structural) No. 1 No. 2 No. 3
Studs	Stud
Light Framing	Const (Construction) Std (Standard) Util (Utility)
2"–4" Thick, 6" and Wider	
Structural Joists and Planks	Sel Str (Select Structural) No. 1 No. 2 No. 3
2"–4" Thick, 2" and Wider	
Appearance Framing	A (appearance)

built-up beams, etc. Grades in this category are "Sel-Str" (Select Structural), "No. 1," "No. 2," and "No. 3."

Not all grades described under the National Grading Rule and listed in the last table will be available in all species or regions. The "Sel-Str" and "No. 1" grades are frequently used for truss construction and other engineered uses where high strength is required. For general construction, the grades normally encountered at the retail yard are "No. 2," or "No. 2 and Btr," or "Std and Btr." The "No. 3" and "Util" grades are also available and provide important economies where less demanding strength requirements are involved.

In selecting dimension lumber for load bearing purposes, it is prudent to have engineering assistance and, where required, a building permit.

Span Tables for Joists and Rafters are available from the National Forest Products Association and the other lumber organizations.

Careful use of such tables and the assigned working stress for the various grades permits selection of the species and minimum grade to satisfy requirements of span and floor loadings.

Where severe use conditions require lumber to be frequently wet or exposed to damp soil, naturally durable species and pressure-treated lumber are available.

Lumber used for sleepers or sills resting on a concrete slab which is in direct contact with the earth, or joists closer than 18 inches to the ground, should be of naturally durable species or pressure-treated lumber. Where lumber is imbedded in the ground to support permanent structures, pressure-treated lumber should be used.

Naturally durable species most frequently encountered at the retail yard are California redwood, Western red cedar and tidewater red cypress. The Foundation grades of redwood and red cedar should be selected for ground contact. In cypress, a heart Structural grade should be selected for similar exposure.

Assume you have decided upon the species and grade of lumber required for a project, as well as the appropriate number of board feet you will need. Make a simple sketch showing the layout of framing members, furring strips, paneling, etc., and include it with the list of materials you will take to the lumber yard. At the yard, request the assistance of a clerk who can check your sketch, quantity and grade selections.

If at all possible, follow your order through the yard. Look at the types of material in stock, the grade marks and other identification. Inspect other wood items, such as windows, doors, moulding and trim. This is a part of the education process which will be most helpful in planning the next project and in providing a mental picture of the appearance of the various lumber grades and species.

Plywood for Jobs Around the Home

FOR EVERYTHING from subfloors to roof decks to siding and built-ins, plywood is an all-round building material. But before employing plywood to do a task around the house, you should know the product, its capabilities and its limitations.

Plywood is a real wood. Although it is an engineered product, the natural wood is changed very little in the manufacturing process.

When a log arrives at a plywood mill, it is peeled, placed in a giant lathe, and turned against a lathe knife. The veneer (thin sheet of wood) that flows from the lathe in a continuous ribbon is clipped into pieces of a convenient size for kiln drying and assembly into plywood panels.

Every plywood panel is a built-up board made of kiln dried layers of veneer. An odd number of layers is used for every panel so that the grain direction on the face and back run in the same direction.

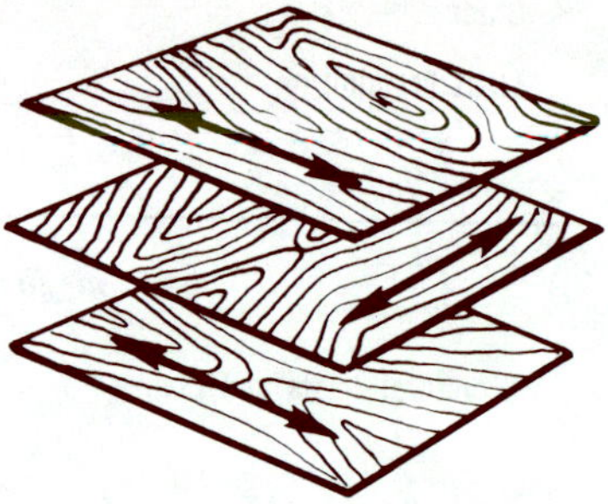

The veneer layers are assembled at right angles to each other and united under high pressure with an adhesive. The resulting glue-bonds become as strong or stronger than the wood itself.

Since wood is stronger along the grain, this cross-lamination distributes wood's strength in both directions.

Peeling veneers from a log and reassembling them also provides a means for making panels much larger than those that could be produced by sawing. (Standard plywood panels are 4 x 8 feet, though wider and longer panels are also produced.)

Whether you're building, remodeling, adding on, or making furniture in your home workshop, plywood may be the material you need.

In residential construction, plywood's structural role extends to floor, wall, and roof systems. You can also use it for interior paneling, exterior siding, furniture, cabinets, shelving, fences, wind screens, patio decking, outdoor storage units, and hundreds of do-it-yourself projects.

One basic thing to remember in selecting plywood is to look for the grade-trademark which identifies the product, subject to the quality inspection of an approved testing agency.

The grade and type of a panel should also be considered in the selection of plywood. Type refers to the durability of the glueline or the degree of exposure the panel should be subjected to. Letter grades N, A, B, C, D, refer to the quality of the face and back veneers. N represents the highest veneer quality.

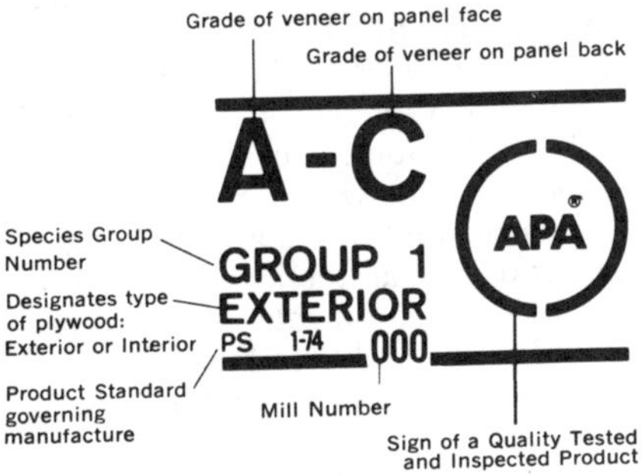

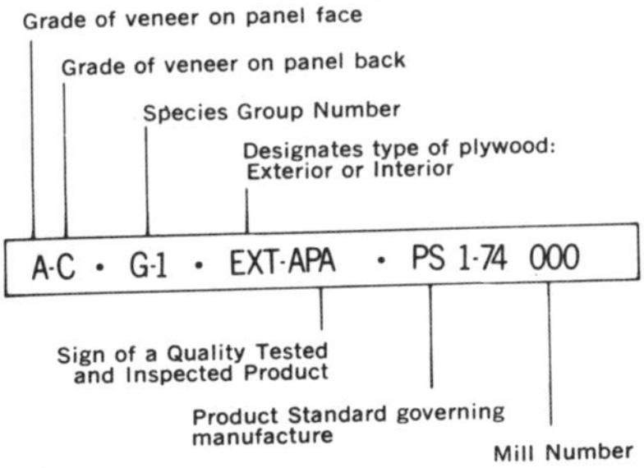

A two letter combination, for example, A-C, is used to indicate the quality of the panel face and back. "A" indicates the face quality and "C" describes the back.

Grades A-A, A-B, or A-D Interior type sanded plywood are recommended for cabinet doors, furniture, built-ins, and other projects to be painted. B-D may also be painted.

If you prefer a waxed, sealed, or varnished natural finish, select fine grain panels in A-A, A-B, or A-D grades.

For exterior siding, interior paneling and ceilings, textured plywood panels are available in many different species, surfaces, and patterns. Textured plywood sidings are best finished with stains, although some species may be left to weather naturally.

Good results for painted surfaces, interior or exterior, can also be achieved with Medium Density Overlaid (MDO) plywood. This grade has a smooth resin-treated fiber surface bonded to the panel face. It takes and holds paint well.

Plywood is available in both appearance and in engineered grades. Appearance grades are normally sanded. Engineered grades which are left unsanded are generally applied where a high degree of strength and rigidity are required.

You'll notice that the approved grade-trademark on appearance grades includes a group number. That number stands for one of the more than 70 wood species from which plywood is manufactured.

Since species vary in strength and stiffness, they have been classified into five groups under PS 1 (Product Standard 1). The strongest woods are found in Group 1.

Unsanded engineered grades of plywood bearing a grade-trademark carry an Identification Index which tells you the maximum support spacing to which the plywood can be applied in conventional construction.

The Identification Index appears as two number designations separated by a diagonal such as 24/0, 32/16, etc. The number to the left of the diagonal indicates the maximum spacing of supports in inches which should be used when the panel is applied as roof deck-

---

AUTHOR *Mary Ann Warwick* is with the Public Relations Department, American Plywood Association (APA).

CO-AUTHOR *M. T. Fast* is Manager, Distribution/Agriculture Markets, APA.

ing. The number designation to the right provides the same information for subflooring applications.

Unsanded grades designated as STRUCTURAL I and STRUCTURAL II are recommended for heavy load applications, where plywood's strength properties are of maximum importance.

Now that you've become a little better acquainted with plywood, we can move on to its role in residential construction.

Starting with the basics, let's look at the part it plays in the area of flooring.

In a double layer system, your floor will be made up of plywood subflooring and a separate layer of underlayment. The underlayment plywood offers a high degree of dimensional stability that eliminates swelling and buckling. The result is a smooth, solid, stable base for any kind of finish flooring you desire.

One good way to save money and time is to use one layer of plywood as a combination subflooring and underlayment material. The plywood serves both as a structural subfloor and as an excellent base for resilient floorings, carpeting, and for other nonstructual floorings.

Plywood bearing the registered grade-trademark 2.4.1 can be used to provide both subflooring and an underlayment surface in a single 1⅛ inch thick plywood panel. It's best to use 2 x joists spaced 32 inches on center or 4 x girders spaced 48 inches as the support system.

One excellent construction system you can use in building a floor is the APA Glued Floor System in which glue and nails are used to secure the structural underlayment to wood joists. This system was designed to produce floors that would be stronger and less apt to squeak.

The glues needed for this system are elastomeric adhesives meeting performance specification AFG-01. These glues, which may be applied even in below freezing weather, are available in cartridges designed for conventional caulking guns.

Specific recommendations on the APA Glued Floor System may be obtained from the American Plywood Association.

Plywood is also a key word in any discussion of wall construction. Performing structurally as wall sheathing, it covers large areas rapidly and supplies strength and rigidity. Neither let-in bracing nor building paper is required with it.

Plywood wall sheathing may be installed either vertically or horizontally. Horizontal application of panels will give you greater stiffness under loads perpendicular to the surface. So, if you're going to be nailing siding such as shingles directly into your wall sheathing, it would be wise to apply the sheathing horizontally.

The availability of many siding textures adds an aesthetic dimension to plywood's structural role as a wall material. Textured plywood can be used for interior paneling as well as exterior siding.

Although many builders and handymen still apply plywood siding in a two layer system, more and more are turning to the APA Single Wall System in which plywood siding is applied directly to studs.

Accepted by the Federal Housing Administration, the Farmers Home Administration, and most local building codes, the single wall system is designed to offer tight wall construction. All horizontal and vertical joints are backed with lumber framing members. Nails around the edges secure panels to the framing and provide draft stops at all points.

To insure weather tightness, single wall joints are shiplapped, battened, or backed with building paper.

When you're using the APA Single Wall System, you may apply plywood panel siding, or lap, or beveled siding. Specify ⅜, ½, or ⅝ inch, depending on your stud spacing.

Be sure to seal plywood edges. If you're going to paint the surface, the prime coat can serve as your sealer. If the plywood is to be stained, seal it first with a water-repellent preservative that's compatible with the finish.

Although plywood sidings are normally installed vertically, you may place panels horizontally with the face grain across supports.

Determining what is the allowable support spacing for the construction of single walls is a simple matter. Panels for single wall construction which are identified as 303 sidings have their maximum support spacing listed in their grade-trademark.

A 303 siding, for example, bearing a "303–24 in. o.c." may be applied vertically to studs 16 or 24 inches on center, while panels marked "303–16 in. o.c." may be applied vertically over studs spaced no more than 16 inches apart.

Texture 1–11, a ⅝ inch thick exterior siding panel with a ⅜ inch wide vertical grooving spaced 2, 4, 6, or 8 inches on center may be used vertically over studs spaced 16 inches on center.

All edges of panel siding should be backed with framing or blocking. And to keep from staining siding with nails, use hot dip galvanized, aluminum, or other nonstaining nails. No extra corner bracing is needed with plywood panel siding.

Moving along to roof construction, you'll find that plywood roof sheathing gives you the strength and rigidity you need while it makes a solid base for roofing material.

Plywood sheathing bears an Identification Index which tells you the recommended rafter spacing for a specific plywood thickness. For example, for roof systems with a 24 inch span (distance between rafters), plywood with a marking of 24/0 will do the job.

These Identification Index panels are available in thicknesses ranging from 5/16 through ⅞ inch.

Plywood roof sheathing has superior nail holding capabilities. Extensive laboratory and field tests have proven that even 5/16 inch plywood will hold shingle nails securely and permanently in place, in the face of hurricane force winds.

Your house plan will show either "open soffits" or "closed soffits". For a roof deck over closed soffits, you can use C-D Interior grade sheathing. To enclose the soffits, Medium Density Overlaid plywood is preferable because it has a superior painting surface.

With open soffits, panels will be exposed at the overhang. Thus, you'll want to select an Exterior type plywood. In addition to being an Exterior type plywood, the plywood you choose for an open soffit application should be a high enough appearance grade to permit painting or staining.

Textured plywood with the textured side down can be used for exposed soffits and ceiling applications. Staining is the only finishing required.

In this chapter we've sketched a brief outline of plywood's role in residential construction. A broad assortment of publications available from the American Plywood Association will offer you in-depth coverage of each of the areas mentioned here.

Detailed information for everything from laying out a foundation to framing a ceiling are presented in a new set of "How To" sheets. Used with APA's "How To" book, this series acquaints you with the terms you'll need to know and it offers 360 degree coverage of efficient house construction techniques.

For more information on APA publications, write the American Plywood Association, 1119 A Street, Tacoma, Wash. 98401.

Panel Products To Choose from

Besides softwood plywood, the homeowner has several choices of panel products for that new or remodeling job. Some provide needed strength and stiffness while others are primarily for finish, sound reduction, insulation, or other characteristics. Take time to look them over and select the materials that best fit your need and pocketbook.

Most of these products are partly or entirely of wood-based material—hardwood plywood, insulation board, hardboard, laminated paperboard, particleboard, and gypsum board. Manufacturing and finishing methods vary greatly to provide materials with specific desirable properties. The materials don't look or feel alike and vary widely in properties but all are manufactured in panel form. Thus they can cover large areas quickly and easily.

Panel sizes are commonly 4 by 8 feet and can be handled by one man. While some panels are larger, others may be appreciably smaller—for instance, decorative and acoustical ceiling tile. Additionally, there are other special products such as insulating roof deck, but here we discuss only the most common panel products.

Most easily recognizable is hardwood plywood. Veneers have been "unrolled" from the tree and the layers glued together to form a product that finds particular use as decorative paneling for walls. Manufacturers often prefinish the panels.

Most other panel products involve breaking the wood down to small portions and then reassembling the elements into boards. For such common materials as insulation board, hardboard, and laminated paperboard, the material is broken essentially into fibers, which are interfelted into panels. With particleboard, the wood is broken into particles that are bonded together with resin, heat, and pressure. Processes vary until sometimes the distinctions are blurred.

The other main member of the panel group is gypsum board, which has a noncombustible gypsum core between faces of paper.

The insulation board-hardboard-paperboard group is customarily known as building fiberboard and may be called by such proprietary names as "Celotex," "Insulite," "Masonite," "Beaverboard," and "Homasote" without regard to the actual manufacturer.

Oldest of the boards is insulation board, made in two categories—semirigid and rigid. Semirigid consists of the low-density products used as insulation and cushioning. The rigid type includes both the interior board used for walls and ceilings, as well as the exterior board used for wall sheathing.

Hardboard is a grainless, smooth, hard product. It is used for siding, underlayment and as prefinished wall paneling.

Laminated paperboard serves as sheathing and other covering but is not used as much as the other building fiberboards.

Particleboards are often known by the kinds of particle used in their makeup, such as flakeboard, chipboard, chipcore, or shavings board. New products have greater strength, stiffness, and durability than those made a few years ago. Some higher quality products have recently been approved for subfloors and sheathing. Underlayment, however, is still the principal use of particleboard in houses even though more and more is going into shelving.

Gypsum board is used principally for interior covering. Builders like it because, unlike plaster, it is a dry-wall material. Edges along the length are usually tapered to allow for a filled and taped joint. It may be obtained with a

---

AUTHOR *Fred Werren* is Research Project Leader, Engineered Wood Products, Forest Products Laboratory, Madison, Wis. 53705.

foiled back which serves as a vapor barrier on the exterior walls and is also available with vinyl or other prefinished interior surface.

Each product will serve well if used as intended. Panels must be properly fastened to framing members and used in the right places under conditions for which they were designed. Manufacturers have found most instances of unsatisfactory performance directly related to improper application. Therefore, they usually include application and use instructions on each package or bundle of their material.

With this much background, let's talk about the job you have in mind. Assume you are going to build an addition to your house. Construction starts with the foundation and subflooring, proceeds to the wall and roof structure, and ends with the interior finish of the room. We'll talk about materials in that order—beginning at the wall covering stage.

Wall sheathing covers the outside wall framework of studs, plates, and headers and ties them into a structural unit. It forms a flat base upon which the exterior finish can be applied. Many kinds of panel sheathing provide good strength and stiffness when properly fastened and thereby eliminate the need for corner bracing. Sheathing also serves to minimize air infiltration and, in certain forms, it will provide good insulation.

Insulation board has been and continues to be used extensively for this purpose, reportedly more than any other sheathing material for residential construction in the United States. It is inexpensive and it combines bracing strength, insulation, and a degree of noise control through walls.

Insulation board sheathing is available in three types—nail-base, intermediate density, and regular density—in order of decreasing density and strength. Thickness is ½ inch in the first two types and ½ or 25/32 inch in the latter. Wood and asbestos shingles can be applied directly to nail-base with annular-grooved nails. Regular density, as the least dense, is the best insulator.

The Federal Housing Administration recommends that all types be applied vertically on the wall. The boards provide adequate racking resistance without corner bracing except that some specifying agencies require corner bracing with half-inch regular-density board.

Insulation board and gypsum board sheathing are also available in 2- by 8-foot panels. They are applied horizontally and require corner bracing of the walls.

A special type of exterior particleboard sheathing panel, 4 feet wide, has been approved by some building codes. It must be not less than ⅜ inch thick and the studs must not be more than 16 inches on center. A ⅜-inch-thick sheathing grade of laminated paperboard is also approved. Corner bracing is not required for either.

Roof sheathing provides the strength and stiffness needed for expected loads, racking resistance to keep components square, and a base for attaching roofing. Panels have several advantages over lumber, particularly in ease and speed of application and resistance to racking.

Softwood plywood is now used most extensively for roof sheathing, but other panel materials are satisfactory if they meet performance requirements. Special structural particleboards are under development for such purposes and the Federal Housing Administration has approved specific ones for some areas. Some insulation boards also meet the requirements.

With wall sheathing in place, rough wiring and plumbing done, and insulation and vapor barriers installed as needed, you are ready to apply the inside ceiling and walls. Inside covering materials are generally considered as nonstructural. Usually, however, they contribute to the strength and stiffness of the ceiling or wall. Additionally, all must be capable of performing satisfactorily under the normal conditions to which they are subjected. Ceilings must not sag; walls must remain flat in use and withstand mild knocks and bumps.

Panel products are available in a wide variety of forms and finishes for interior coverings, and the homeowner generally finds these far easier to apply than lath and plaster. The thin sheet materials, however, require that studs and ceiling joists have good alinement to provide a smooth appearance.

Finishes in bathrooms and kitchens have more rigid stain and moisture requirements than those for other living spaces. Be a bit more careful when selecting materials for these areas.

For ceilings, gypsum board is perhaps the most common sheet material, but large sheets of insulation board are also used. The panels are generally nailed or screwed in place and then joints and fasteners are suitably covered or trimmed. Insulation board in the form of acoustical and decorative ceiling tile is popular, especially for dens and recreation rooms.

Interior wall coverings of many types are available and these are discussed further in the chapter on wall coverings. Panel materials most frequently applied are gypsum board, hardwood plywood, and prefinished hardboard that may be embossed or wood-grain printed.

Panels are typically 4 by 8 feet and applied vertically as single sheets so that the vertical joints butt at the stud. But there are many alternatives. For example, builders in some areas apply gypsum board horizontally in sheet sizes 4 feet wide and up to 16 feet long; or they may use more than one layer.

After ceiling and wall covering is complete, you need prepare for and install the "finish flooring"—the final wearing surface applied to a floor. Unless you apply wood strip or wood tile over the subfloor, you will usually need an underlayment. Underlayment is supplied in 4-foot-wide panels and provides a smooth, uniformly thick base ideal for resilient flooring, carpeting, and other finish flooring. Panels are installed just before applying the finish flooring.

Hardboard and particleboard join plywood as the principal panel products used for floor underlayment. Hardboard comes in 3′ by 4′ or 4′ by 4′ panels a little less than ¼″ thick. It is often used in remodeling because of the floor thicknesses involved. Particleboard comes in a 4′ by 8′ size in a variety of thicknesses from ¼″ to ¾″. Special insulation boards are also used as underlayment for carpeting as a resilient, noise-deadening material.

Before buying the underlayment, find out what is recommended for your specific covering and the techniques for installing it. You need to know about conditioning the underlayment, preparing the surface, panel arrangement, edge clearances to allow for shrinking and swelling, nailing, stapling or gluing, and possibly filling and sanding. Do it right and avoid future problems.

Sound insulation, or minimizing unwanted noise, is accomplished to some extent in conventional construction. With increasing emphasis on the "quiet" home, it may be that you want to plan for better-than-normal sound barriers. Unwanted sounds, whether from a crying baby, a noisy party, or the flushing of a toilet can be reduced by special construction.

Airborne noises inside the house create sound waves that radiate outward until they strike a surface such as a wall, floor, or ceiling. Insulation board, especially with holes in it (acoustical tile), absorbs these waves and reduces room reverberation. Draperies and carpeting do too. The sound waves set the room surfaces in vibration and how much sound is transmitted to the next room depends on the construction.

If sound barriers are to be better than conventional walls and ceilings, they require extra thought and care in construction. They usually include "decouplers" to reduce transfer of sound waves.

For a wall, the covering can be decoupled from the stud by resilient channels, ½″ sound-deadening insulation board, or ¼″ hardboard. Improved walls can be made with double-row-of-stud construction. The wall must, of course, also be suitably sealed against leaks through or around it. Information on sound control is available without charge from industry associations.

How do you finish interior surfaces? Prefinished materials—such as acoustical and decorative ceiling tiles, hardwood plywood and hardboard wall panels, and overlaid panels require no further work.

A clear natural finish is usually applied to unfinished plywood. Gypsum board and the denser insulation boards are readily painted or papered. Particleboard should be protected by paint or clear finishes.

Now that you've read this far, what next? Talk with your building supply dealer and paint supplier. Ask questions. Read the literature he gives you. Don't overlook writing to various industry associations. They have good information (free) on their members' products—what they are, what they will do, how to apply them, etc. Explain what you would like. These associations include:

-Acoustical and Insulating Materials Association, 205 W. Touhy Ave., Park Ridge, Ill. 60068.

-American Hardboard Association, 20 N. Wacker Drive, Chicago, Ill. 60606.

-Gypsum Association, 201 N. Wells St., Chicago, Ill. 60606.

-Hardwood Plywood Manufacturers Association, P. O. Box 6246, Arlington, Va. 22206.

-National Particleboard Association, 2306 Perkins Place, Silver Spring, Md. 20910.

Plan ahead, select your materials, apply them correctly, and take pride in a job well done.

Airing the Facts About Ventilation

YOUR HOME needs ventilation in its living spaces, its attic, and crawl spaces (if you have any) for a number of reasons. Most of the time natural air movement can provide the needed ventilation but there are times and places when it is desirable and even necessary to use mechanical ventilation.

In living spaces, ventilation is needed to—

1. Provide fresh air for the people living there.
2. Remove excess moisture that comes from cooking, bathing, laundry and from people.
3. Remove odors that are produced throughout the house.
4. Cool in the summer.
5. Provide combustion air for heating systems during the winter.

We normally think of ventilation requirements for the living spaces of a house (including the basement). In addition, however, the attic will need ventilation for cooling during the summer and removing moisture during the winter.

Crawl spaces under houses which are common in many places will need special attention to remove moisture that could collect there.

Moisture in crawl spaces migrates from the ground below or it condenses when outside temperatures drop suddenly, causing the air to reach its dewpoint and condense on floor framing or foundation wall.

To control this potential condition, ventilation air is needed to carry the moisture out of the crawl space.

If your house has a crawl space, the control of any moisture problems there

AUTHOR *Theodore J. Brevik* is a Professor and Extension Agricultural Engineer, Agricultural Engineering Department, University of Wisconsin-Madison and University of Wisconsin-Extension.

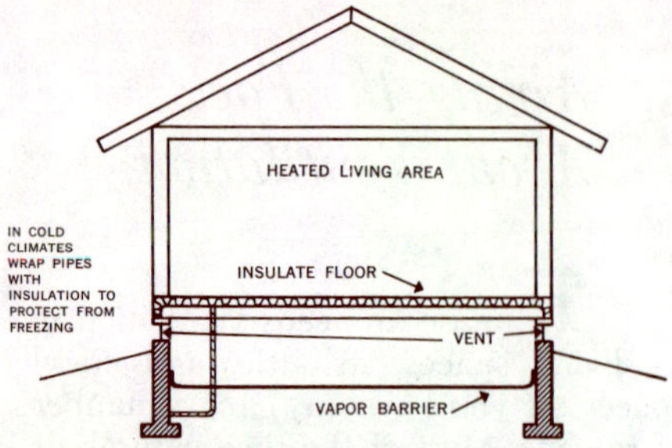

VENTILATE UNHEATED CRAWL SPACES

can usually be handled by natural air movement. A screened opening at each corner properly sized will normally provide all the ventilation needed.

If the ground in the crawl space is not covered with a vapor barrier, the total opening should equal 1 square foot for each 200 square feet of crawl space. Better still, cover the ground with a 4 mill polyethylene plastic film and provide adjustable ventilation openings which can be reduced to about 1 square foot of opening for each 1,500 square feet of crawl space. The vents should be open all the time.

The floor of a house which is over a crawl space should be well insulated since the temperatures within the crawl space will be near outdoor temperatures. In cold climates any pipes that pass through the crawl space will need to be insulated.

Attics are ventilated so heat can escape in the summer, and any moisture that finds its way in during the winter can escape. A "cool" attic will also mean that the living quarters below will be cooler during hot weather.

Ventilation openings equal to 1 square foot of opening for each 300 square feet of attic floor space is recommended. One-half of this should be at the eaves and one-half at the peak to insure air movement through the attic, especially with a low-sloped roof lower than a 4-foot rise in 12 feet of horizontal run.

For summer cooling, larger openings should be provided or the attic should be equipped with an exhaust fan that can be switched on to discharge the heated air to the outside. The ceiling, of course, should be well insulated in a properly ventilated attic space as described above.

Living spaces of most homes are generally well enough ventilated by infiltration or by opening doors and windows. This is especially true during the winter.

In milder weather and at other times supplementary ventilation may be needed in spaces such as the kitchen, laundry and bathroom. There are times when moisture and odors may be produced at such a high rate that normal air change will not provide proper control, and mechanical ventilation will be needed.

If you are providing fan ventilation in spaces such as the kitchen, bath or laundry, you will want to: 1) locate the fan where it will do the most good, 2) size it properly, 3) make sure that it has an acceptable noise level, and 4) discharge the air to the outdoors—not to the attic.

The Home Ventilating Institute, an organization whose membership consists of manufacturers of residential ventilation equipment, has developed ventilation guidelines and has certified ratings of home ventilation equipment. Range hoods and exhaust fans which bear their labels show how much air they will move, and have a number which tells their relative noise level. The guidelines also tell how much capacity is needed for each room needing ventilation.

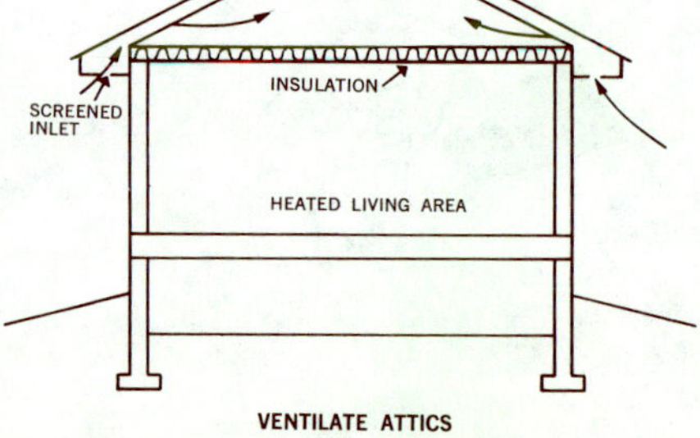

VENTILATE ATTICS

A range hood with a fan is a popular method of ventilating a kitchen. The hood is normally located over the range to collect the moisture, grease and odors at their source so the fan located in the hood can discharge to the outside.

The Home Ventilating Institute recommends that a minimum fan capacity of 40 cubic feet per minute (cfm) per lineal foot of hood be provided for wall mounted hoods. A range hood over a cooking island should have a capacity of 50 cfm per foot of length. A 36 inch wide hood then would have a minimum capacity of 120 cfm if on the wall or 150 cfm if over an island or a peninsula.

You should consider a hood fan with a larger capacity than this to handle ventilation when extensive cooking is underway. There are times when the minimum capacity will not be enough.

Since multi-speed fans are usually installed in range hoods, it's a good idea to select a fan that provides the minimum capacity at low speed and extra capacity at higher speeds.

If you select a range hood with the minimum capacity it may not meet minimum air change recommendations for a kitchen, which is 15 air changes per hour. For example, if you have a 10′ x 12′ kitchen (120 square feet) with an 8′ ceiling you should have a fan capacity of at least 240 cfm. This amounts to 2 cfm per square feet of kitchen floor area.

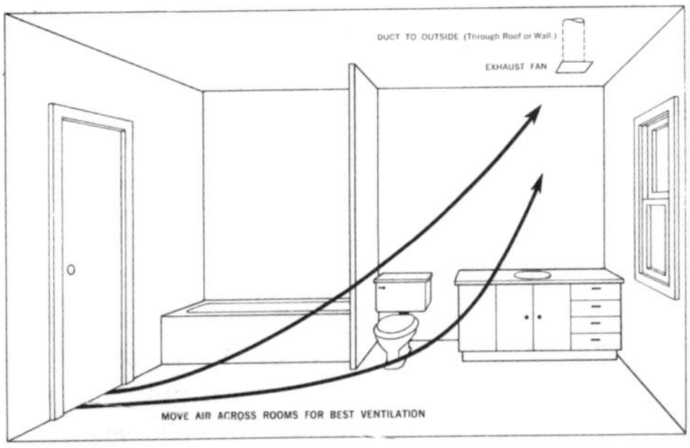

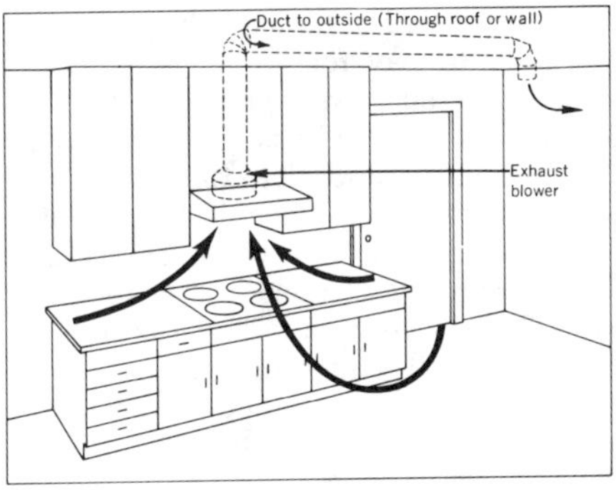

If this capacity was built into the minimum capacity of the fan at low speed, the speed control switch can increase the air discharged when more is needed.

Most range hoods have two or three motor speeds so that you can select a speed to more nearly fit a particular need. More recently, variable speed controls have been made available with range hoods which will give you a choice of air movement from 0 up to the maximum for the fan when it is operating at high speed.

The Home Ventilating Institute rates fan noise level in sones. A sone is a unit of loudness which provides a way for you to compare the noise of one fan with another. A fan that has a sone rating of six would be twice as noisy as one that has a rating of three sones. By way of comparison, one sone is equivalent to the sound of a modern refrigerator in a quiet kitchen.

The institute rates the noise level of home ventilating fans that are manufactured by various companies. The centrifugal fan "squirrel cage" type is generally quieter and should be considered when fan capacities are above 200 cfm. These generally cost more and are more efficient if long exhaust ducts are needed in your house.

Upper limits of nine sones for kitchen fans and 6.5 sones for bathroom fans have been set as the maximum acceptable by the institute. You can decide when buying a fan how much quietness you want to pay for.

Hoods often have lights and filters. Be sure that the light is bright enough for your range and that the bulb can be easily replaced when it burns out. The filter should be easy to remove so that it can be cleaned on a regular basis. This is very important because a dirty filter will reduce the air flow. If it is allowed to collect enough dirt and grease, it may cause odors and even become a fire hazard.

Hoods should be firm to the grasp and constructed with seams that are easily cleaned. A flimsy hood is apt to be a noisy one.

Bathrooms and laundry areas are often equipped with ceiling or wall mounted fans. All that is exposed in the room is a grill. Fans are sized to provide eight air changes (about 1.1 cfm per square feet of floor area) per hour in a bathroom, and six air changes (about .8 cfm per square feet of floor area) per hour in a laundry room. Other rooms equipped with ventilating fans should use a minimum of six air changes per hour.

Fans in bathrooms and laundry rooms should be installed opposite the side of the room where the air enters so there will be air flow across the room.

Control switches of various types are available for fan operation. These vary from a standard on/off wall switch to a timer control and a variable speed control. The degree of control desired should be carefully studied so that your needs will be met.

Check local building or other codes that may apply to house construction when installing ventilating equipment in your home.

Duct work should be planned with the shortest run and with the fewest elbows to reach the outside. Quality galvanized or aluminum sheet metal is recommended for ducts. Be sure they are sized according to the manufacturer's recommendation.

Duct work which extends through unheated areas should be insulated to prevent condensation that may form and drip back into the house.

Floor Coverings—Resilient, Wood, Tiles, and Clay

TRADITIONALLY, PEOPLE have used linoleum in areas such as the kitchen, ceramic tile in the bathroom, and wood floors throughout the rest of the house. With the variety of flooring materials available today—approximately 30 types and hundreds of varieties—there is little reason to be bound by tradition.

In making a choice, livability, esthetics, durability, maintenance, and cost should be considered. Remember, no one material is ideally suited to the requirements of every room in your home.

The principal kinds of floor coverings used as wearing or "finished" surfaces are: Resilient, Wood, Ceramic Tile, Clay, and Carpet. The first four will be considered here.

Resilient surfaces refer to a number of different types of water-resistant materials that range from the traditional linoleum available in rolls to thin sheets or tile materials differentiated according to their ingredients: asphalt, vinyl, vinyl asbestos, rubber, and cork.

They are dense and have non-absorbent surfaces. Their resilience aids in sound control and provides resistance to indentation. Density of the material usually provides long life and ease of maintenance. The most expensive material will usually give the most beauty and highest wear resistance. The lowest cost materials give the least wear and should be used only as a short term covering.

The sheet materials are more difficult to install than tile; however, in comparable materials, sheet usually costs less than tile. Most resilient surfaces are secured to the subfloor with an adhesive: linoleum paste, asphalt emulsion, latex, or epoxy. What you use is dictated by the flooring manufacturer's specifications.

Linoleum is a blend of linseed oil, pigments, fillers, and resin binders bonded to a backing of asphalt-saturated felt. It is available in solid colors or with inlaid, embossed, or textured patterns, simulating stone, wood, or tile. It is available in rolls eight feet or wider and tiles either 9″ X 9″ or 12″ X 12″ square with thicknesses of 1/16″, .090″, and ⅛″.

Linoleum provides fair wear resistance, and its color extends completely through to the backing material.

Inlaid linoleum has a hard durable surface, is greaseproof, and easy to clean; however it is damaged by cleaning products containing alkali solutions.

It should not be installed on a concrete slab on grade (the ground), since moisture permeating through the concrete from below will cause the material to rot.

Asphalt tile is a combination of asbestos fibers, ground limestone, and mineral pigments with an asphalt binder. It is the least expensive and most commonly used tile. Its price depends on the color; dark colors are the least expensive, light colors and special patterns are the most expensive.

Asphalt tiles are manufactured with the pattern through the total thickness. Some tile patterns simulate other materials. In this case, the pattern does not penetrate its thickness and it will wear rapidly under heavy use.

Normal tile size is ⅛″ thick and 9″ X 9″ square.

Asphalt tile will stain and break down if it contacts animal fats and mineral oils. It is brittle and breaks easily. Its recovery from indentation is negligible. It can, however, be used on concrete slabs on grade and where there may be a moisture problem.

Vinyl floor covering's chief ingredient is polyvinyl chloride (PVC). It also contains resin binders, with mineral filters, stabilizers, plasticizers, and pigments. The vinyl may be filled or clear.

Clear vinyl consists of a layer of opaque particles or pigments covered with a wearing surface of clear vinyl bonded to a vinyl or polymer-impregnated asbestos fiber or resin-saturated felt. The clear vinyl surface provides high resistance to wear.

Filled vinyl is made of chips of vinyl of varied color and shape immersed in a clear vinyl base and bonded by heat and pressure. When used in a basement, a vapor barrier or an epoxy adhesive should be used to install it.

Vinyl tile is the most costly, but also the most wear resistant and easily maintained of the various tiles. It is produced in standard size squares, 9″ X 9″ and 12″ X 12″, in standard thicknesses of 1/16″, .080″, 3/32″, and ⅛″.

Sheet vinyl may be produced with a layer of vinyl foam bonded to the backing or between the finish surface and the backing. The result is a resilient flooring with good walking comfort and an effective sound absorbent quality.

The vinyl is produced in rolls eight feet wide or wider and can be installed over most subsurfaces. While the material has high resistance to grease, stains, and alkali, its surface is easily damaged by abrasion and indentation since it is, generally, a soft product.

Vinyl-Asbestos tile consists of blended compositions of asbestos fibers, vinyls, plasticizers, color pigments, and fillers. The tiles, without backing, are 9″ X 9″ or 12″ X 12″ square and 1/16″, 3/32″, and ⅛″ thick.

The tile may be obtained in marbleized patterns, or textured to simulate stone, marble, travertine, and wood.

It is semiflexible and requires a rigid subfloor for support. The tile has high resistance to grease, oils, alkaline substances, and some acids. It is quiet underfoot and many forms can go without waxing for extended periods of time. It can be used almost anywhere, and can be obtained with a peel-and-stick backing.

Rubber tile is based on natural or synthetic rubber. Mineral fillers and

---

AUTHOR *Walter H. Hill* is Extension Housing Specialist in the Washington State University Cooperative Extension Service, Pullman.

nonfading organic pigments are used to produce a narrow range of colors and patterns.

The standard sizes are 9″ X 9″ and 12″ X 12″. Larger sizes are available at higher cost. The thicknesses are 0.080″, ⅛″, and 3/16″.

Rubber tile is resilient and has high resistance to indentation. The material is softened by petroleum products and its resistance to grease and kitchen oils depends on its method of manufacture. Waxing and buffing are necessary to maintain a high gloss. The surface becomes slippery when wet.

Use of a vapor barrier or epoxy adhesive for a slab on grade installation is required.

Cork tile consists of granulated cork bark combined with a synthetic resin as a binder. The best tile has a clear film of vinyl applied to improve its durability, water resistance, and ease of maintenance. Tile sizes are 6″ X 6″ and 12″ X 12″ with a range of thicknesses from ⅛″ to ½″.

Cork floors are great for foot comfort and sound control. They wear rapidly and do not resist impact loads well. Maintenance is difficult since the material is broken down by grease and alkalies.

Wood floorings. Many varieties of both hard and soft woods are available for flooring.

Certain hardwoods, because of their high resistance to wear, are more often used than others. Two are oak and maple.

Wood flooring is finished with a combination of coatings such as a sealer and varnish, or a liquid plastic.

Wood flooring may be simply nailed to the subfloor or, when used over a concrete slab, nailed to wood "sleepers" fastened to the slab. In either case, the floor is sanded smooth, and finished with stain and sealer.

The most commonly used hardwood flooring is oak because of its beauty, warmth, and durability. Maple flooring is produced from the sugar, or rock, maple. It is smooth, strong, and hard. The grain of maple does not have as much contrast as oak; however, where a smooth polished surface is necessary, maple makes a superior floor.

Beech, birch, hickory, and several other hardwoods are also used.

Hardwood strip flooring is hollowed or has "V" slots cut into its back surface to minimize warping. It is produced in thicknesses of ⅜″, ½″, or 25/32″ and widths varying from 1½″ to 3¼″, with the most popular width being 2¼″, and is tongue and grooved to provide tight joints.

Hardwood flooring is graded on its appearance according to the number of defects, variations of color, and surface characteristics. Strength and wear are not dependent on grading since all grades are comparable in these respects.

Strip flooring is available prefinished. The finish is applied at the factory and the floor can be used right after installation. It comes as imitation peg style, random width, and simulated plank.

Softwood Flooring—The softwood most used is southern yellow pine; Douglas fir is next, with western hemlock and larch following. Some woods such as redwood, cedar, cypress, and eastern white pine are used in areas where they are common and available.

Softwood flooring is available in several sizes and thicknesses; the most common is 25/32″ thick and 4½″ wide. The long edges of the flooring are tongue and groove or side matched in order to give tight joints. Similar to hardwood, the underside is hollowed or V-grooved to minimize warping.

Hardwood squares 9″ X 9″ or 12″ X 12″ by 5/16″ or ½″ thick can be purchased to produce a parquet floor. These squares are available in several types of wood such as oak, maple, mahogany, cherry, and teak.

Thin block flooring is normally produced in prefinished form. The blocks may be nailed to the subfloor or secured with a mastic. These materials, while costing more than strip flooring, require no finishing and are competitive in completed cost.

Non-Resilient Flooring.—These include brick "pavers", ceramic, and clay tile, stone, and terrazzo. These materials are more difficult to install than other

MATERIAL	CHARACTERISTICS	DIFFICULTY OF INSTALLATION	WHERE TO USE	COST PER SQUARE FOOT
Wood Strip Flooring	Long Wear Life Moderate Resiliency Moderate Care Required	Moderate	All areas except bath and utility	$ .70–$1.50
Wood Block Flooring	Moderate Long Wear Life Moderate Resiliency Moderate Care Required	Moderate	All areas except bath and utility	$ .75–$1.30
Linoleum	Moderate Wear Life Resilient Moderate Care Required	Moderate—Low	All areas	$ .40–$1.00
Sheet Vinyl	Long Wear Life High Resiliency Low Care Required	Moderate—Low	All areas	$ .35–$4.00
Vinyl Tile	Long Wear Life High Resiliency Low Care Required	Low	All areas	$ .40–$4.00
Vinyl Asbestos Tile	Long Wear Life Resilient Moderate Low Care Required	Low	All areas	$ .20–$ .70
Asphalt Tile	Moderate Wear Life Moderate Resiliency Moderate High Care	Low	Avoid areas where grease is used	$ .20–$ .30
Ceramic Tile	Long Wear Life No Resiliency Easy Care	Moderate—Difficult	Bathrooms, entrance areas, kitchens, halls	$ .60–$1.75
Clay Tile	Long Wear Life No Resiliency Easy Care	Moderate—Difficult	Bathrooms, entrance areas, kitchens, halls, utility rooms	$1.00–$1.50

flooring materials and usually are the most expensive. However, they have a long life.

They may be installed using a special "thin-set" cement, or in the traditional ¾″ bed of mortar. They require a "grout" (cement fill) between the tiles.

Glazed ceramic tile and terra cotta are relatively non-porous and as a result resist staining. These glazed tiles are, however, susceptible to scratching and crazing (formation of minute cracks) with age. Ceramic tiles range in size from what is called "mosaic" tile of ⅜″ X ⅜″ to a large 16″ X 18″ size.

Mosaic tiles commonly are sold on a backing sheet, making possible the installation of larger areas at one time. It is necessary to grout the joints between each tile after they are set in place.

Unglazed ceramic tile, slate, and flagstone are porous unless treated with special stain-resistant sealants.

Clay or quarry tile, usually unglazed, is produced from clays that result in a strong, long-wearing surface. It is relatively easy to maintain and withstands impact well.

The color range is reds, buffs, blacks, browns, greys, and gold. A semiglazed type is produced in greys, browns, and greens. The product is available with a variety of surface patterns.

The tiles come in several thicknesses from ¼″, ½″, and up to 1½″ depending on their width and length. They may be square, rectangular, or some geometric shape.

Terrazzo is made of marble chips in combination with portland cement mortar and is ground and polished to a smooth finish. It is very resistant to moisture and therefore relatively easy to maintain. It is very noisy and is a tiring walking and work surface.

Most non-resilient flooring is installed using a masonry mortar. This demands a higher degree of skill than other types of flooring and adds to the installed cost.

Cost of each type of flooring will vary depending on its quality and the manufacturer. As an example, asphalt tile may cost as little as 20¢ a square foot while high quality vinyl may reach $4 per square foot. If you consider that an oak floor may cost only 75¢ per square foot, it is obvious that a wide variety of options is available.

Your Own Pool to Get in the Swim

THERE ARE now over a million in-ground residential swimming pools in the United States and the figure is growing at a rate of some 85,000 per year. In addition, another three million American families own above-ground pools large enough to swim in.

Both above and in-ground pools are now within the range of the average family's budget, although pool prices vary throughout the country. Generally, in-ground pools are least expensive in the Northeast and most expensive in the Rocky Mountain area.

The average 1974 cost of a middle size, in-ground pool is around $6,500. Most in-ground backyard pools are 15′ x 30′ to 20′ x 40′ and have three or four feet of surrounding decking. Bank financing is usually available at reasonable rates and terms for homeowners.

Check the effect of the pool on property taxes with the local taxing authority. Usually an in-ground pool is a home improvement taxed on the basis of half its cost. Premiums for liability are already included in the homeowner's policy, but check with your agent to insure maximum coverage which costs just a few dollars more than a basic policy.

Estimates on installation—of which there should be several from reputable dealers—should include labor, construction materials, and basic equipment such as the filter, pump, vacuum cleaner, surface skimmer and ladder. Be sure all bids are for comparable construction and equipment.

Installation costs of an in-ground pool will be the major expense and will vary

Water sports participants and a backyard pool.

according to type of pool selected (concrete, fiberglass, vinyl-liner), but operating costs should also be computed beforehand. These will include costs of water, electricity, chemicals and, if a heater is to be installed, the utility service (natural gas, oil or electricity) to operate it.

In above-ground pools, a pool large enough for family splashing can be purchased in 1974 for $150 to $400, depending upon size and shape. For a pool large enough for swimming laps and equipped with a pump and filter, prices start around $600 but can go as high as $5,000 or more for luxury models which include a large deck, railing and other accessories.

Installation of above-ground pools ranges from inexpensive up to $600 to $700, depending upon size, shape and site preparation requirements. Most homeowners can install the less expensive models themselves. A building permit is rarely required.

Popular and widely available sizes range from 12 to 28 feet in diameter. Usual shapes are round, oval, rectangular, hexagonal or octagonal. A good quality above-ground pool will remain serviceable for at least seven to ten years if properly cared for.

Reasons for the popularity of above-ground pools are that they are relatively low cost, usually don't add to the real estate tax property assessment, are portable, and have the built-in safety feature of being about four feet higher than ground level.

Choice of a pool should depend upon budget, site, and family use plans. For example, sub-surface rock may make an above-ground pool more practical and much less expensive. A pool built primarily for exercise rather than entertainment should be rectangular to facilitate the swimming of laps.

Families with children will want the pool where it can be watched from the house at all times while in use. The advice of a landscape architect can help save your trees while positioning the pool to receive maximum sun during periods of greatest use.

Given America's current energy shortage, the choice of a swimming pool for family recreation is a wise investment. Once installed, the backyard pool requires little energy to operate and no gasoline to get there.

In addition to equipment such as ladders and diving boards, the swimming

---

AUTHOR *William P. Markert* is Director of Communications, National Swimming Pool Institute, Washington, D.C.

pool has "work equipment": the skimmer, the filtration system and, as an option, an automatic cleaning system.

Allow two or three hours a week minimum if intending to clean the pool yourself. A built-in fully automatic cleaning system will save you time, but will add 10 to 15 percent to total construction cost of the pool. However, portable cleaning systems are also available and may be installed on already constructed pools.

Both automatic and portable (operated by a garden hose) cleaning systems work on the principle that the agitation of water keeps dirt and algae from adhering to the walls and bottom of the pool, thus making it easier for the filter to process them out.

The following types of filters are most generally used: sand, diatomaceous earth (DE), and cartridge.

The sand filter is a simple vat through which the water passes, leaving behind dirt particles.

The DE filter uses inexpensive minute diatomes (microscopic sea creatures) spread over a membrane inside the filter tank. As the water passes through, these "creatures" trap the equally microscopic dirt particles.

The cartridge filter contains fibrous material which traps the dirt particles as water passes through it.

Algaecides and chemicals, usually chlorine or bromine, are used in swimming pools to kill algae, retard the growth of bacteria, and oxidize tiny dirt particles not processed out by the filter.

Heavy traffic in the pool requires careful attention to the pool's pH or acid/alkalinity count. The ideal pH range for a pool is 7.2 to 7.6.

Muriatic acid or soda may be used to restore the desired balance if the pool becomes too acidic or alkaline. Follow directions carefully in both use and storage of chemicals.

Pool water increases in acidity due to acids used in chlorine to help it maintain stability. There is also natural chemical decomposition. To maintain the correct balance, chemicals should usually be added daily. Inexpensive and simple test kits are available to determine how much chemical to add each time.

The chore of daily chemical additions may be avoided by purchase of an automatic chemical dispenser. Safe and easy to use, it may be timed to dispense chemicals when the pool is not in use.

An in-ground swimming pool built with quality materials costs the average American pool owner between $100 and $200 per year for regular maintenance, far less than the upkeep expenses on a house or car.

A simple check list to follow when cleaning your pool is:

- Skim the pool's surface with a standard leaf skimmer
- Brush down pool walls and tile with a stiff-bristled brush
- Clean the skimmer's basket and hair-lint strainer
- Vacuum the pool bottom
- Clean the filter (when sufficient dirt has accumulated and the recirculation flow has decreased)
- Hose clean the pool deck

A heavy duty vinyl pool cover (at an average cost of $350 for a medium size residential pool) cuts down on maintenance time and expenses.

The pool owner will also want—or be required by law to provide—adequate fencing around the pool to prevent accidents. Proper attention to pool safety rules and checks on equipment will prevent poolside accidents; however, it is a good idea to keep a first aid kit on hand.

Both family members and guests should adhere to a posted set of "pool rules." Simple reminders of "no running" and "no swimming alone" are needed by everyone.

Two precautions—the fence to keep out toddlers and pets, and a clean pool deck, free of slippery substances—will prevent many accidents. If yours is an above-ground pool, keep the ladder up when the pool is not in use.

A pool cover is recommended whenever the pool is not in use for long periods of time.

Pool alarms, triggered by introduction of objects into the water, are available as an extra precaution. A spotlight which turns on automatically at night may also be advisable, particularly if your pool is any distance from the house.

Diving boards and water slides are potentially dangerous, and are not places for horseplay. Don't try out for Olympic diving competition in a small backyard pool. For water slides, a feet-first seated position is recommended, or, if head-first, then face down with arms well extended. Never slide or dive onto other swimmers.

If planning to install a diving board on an already installed pool, check with the National Swimming Pool Institute or a reputable builder to be sure you aren't inviting disaster by buying a board too big for your pool.

Underwater lights and other pool area wiring should be checked at least annually. Equipment should conform to local regulations or to the National Electric Code. Keep all radios and appliances well away from the pool area.

A home swimming pool, carefully selected to suit your needs and pocketbook, with the proper equipment and maintenance, can give you many hours of family fun and healthful exercise at reasonable cost.

Electrical Wiring: Homeowner Tips

MANY ELECTRICAL maintenance and repair jobs around a home do not justify calling an electrician, but can be done by the homeowner if care is taken to understand what is involved.

Probably the most baffling part of the wiring system to many people is the fusebox, and it is likely that the fusebox will need attention sooner or later in most homes.

Electric current enters the home through the main fuses (or circuit breakers), then goes through the individual circuit fuses or breakers to the circuits. The purpose of fuses or breakers is to limit the current flow, in case of a fault, to prevent overheating of the wiring.

To save time when you have trouble, it is a good idea to label all the circuits in a fusebox as to what they serve. This can be determined by disconnecting circuits one at a time (by removing the fuse or switching the circuit breaker off), and checking to see what doesn't work by operating the switches and plugging in a portable lamp around the house.

If there isn't room to label directly on the box, you can place a number by each fuse and fasten a listing on a sheet of paper inside the door of the fusebox. Then, when power is off in part of the wiring system, you can quickly find which fuse or circuit breaker is involved.

The circuit protection you find in the fusebox may be cartridge fuses, screw-in fuses, or circuit breakers. Fuses must be replaced when they blow, but when a circuit breaker trips you need only push it all the way to the off position, then back "on" to restore service.

It is wise to disconnect all appliances from the circuit before doing this, or it will probably trip the breaker or blow the fuse again. If all equipment is disconnected, and it happens again, the trouble is likely in the wiring, and you probably should call an electrician.

There are several kinds of screw-in fuses. Besides the ordinary screw-in fuse with brass threads, there is the "non-tamperable" fuse (usually labeled "fustat") which has porcelain threads, and must be replaced with one of the same ampere rating (the wrong size will not fit). Besides the amperage stamped on the top of the fustat, different sizes are color-coded so that if you replace with the same color fustat, it should work.

When the fustat is missing, you can look into the bottom of the hole, and read the amperage needed. If you read "SA20" this means it uses a 20–amp fustat.

AUTHOR *William H. Peterson* is Extension Agricultural Engineer, South Dakota State University, Brookings.

Fustats give better performance on circuits that serve electric motors since they will carry several times their rated current for a few seconds, and will handle the high starting current of motors. A fustat will also tell you what caused it to blow.

Inside a fustat are two elements. One element is like an ordinary fuse link, and another, called a thermal element, looks like a drop of solder. There is a small spring pulling against the top of the conductor where it enters the thermal element.

If the fuse link is partly missing, or if the transparent window is black, this tells you that a short-circuit caused it to blow. If the spring has contracted, separating at the thermal element, it means that the cause was an overload. Usually information and instructions are printed on the box in which you buy fustats.

To determine the cause of fuse-blowing or tripping of breakers, it is helpful to know how much load a circuit will carry. Use this formula:

Volts times amps equals watts. For instance, in the case of a 115 volt small appliance circuit rated 20 amperes: 115 volts times 20 amps equals 2,300 watts.

This means that if the total wattage of all appliances plugged into this circuit exceeds 2,300 watts, the fuse will blow. Most appliances have the watts stamped on them somewhere. Motors may be labeled with amps. In the case of our 20–amp circuit, it would work like this:

Coffee maker	600 watts
Toaster	1,000 watts
Frypan	1,100 watts
TOTAL	2,700 watts

If the three appliances are all operated at the same time, you can expect the fuse to blow. To operate all three of these at one time, you will need two circuits.

Probably more electrical problems originate in plugs and cords than anywhere else.

Cords should be checked periodically to be sure they are in good condition. To check a cord, after disconnecting it, pull the length of the cord around your finger, watching for cracks, worn spots, or a point where it bends too easily, indicating a broken wire.

Cords that have part of the insulation worn off can be restored by wrapping with plastic electrician's tape, but cords that are broken or cut should not be spliced. A good splice takes quite a bit of time and too few people will do it right. Rather, put a plug on one cord and a cord-end receptacle on the other. Check carefully that you do not get a plug on both ends of a section of cord!

When replacing cords, be sure you get the type of cord that is suitable for the intended use, and of the correct wire size. Here are the allowable current-carrying capacities and wattages on 115 volts for different wire sizes:

Wire Size	*Amps*	*Watts Load on 115 Volts*	*Approximate Thickness*
No. 18	5 amps	575 watts	
No. 26	7 amps	805 watts	
No. 14	15 amps	1,725 watts	One Penny
No. 12	20 amps	2,300 watts	One nickel
No. 10	30 amps	3,450 watts	Two dimes

The above capacities are for ordinary rubber-covered cords. For special heater cords, capacities are higher. Wire sizes are usually stamped on the cord itself or on the reel on which it is purchased by the store.

There are a number of types of cords, and a replacement cord should be of the type it is replacing, if the original was correct. Here are some cord types and uses:

Parallel cord—types SP and SPT—is used on lamps, radios, and other light loads. Junior hard service cord—type SJ, SJT, and SJO—is a round, jacketed cord, used on appliances such as washing machines, drills, and trouble lamps. The SJ has a rubber jacket, SJT a thermoplastic jacket, and SJO an oil-resistant jacket material. Another type, Hard-service cord, types S, ST, and SO has similar uses, but for rougher service.

Heater cords—type HPN and HSJ—are used on heating appliances. Type HPN has a neoprene insulation, type

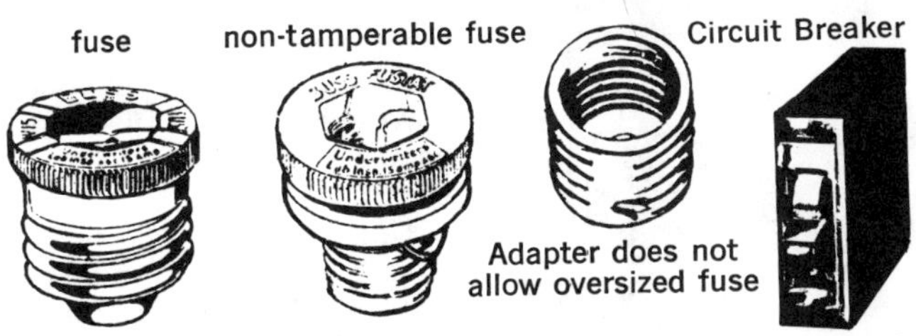

Fuses and circuit breakers protect electric wires from overloads and short circuits. Never replace a fuse with one of a larger size.

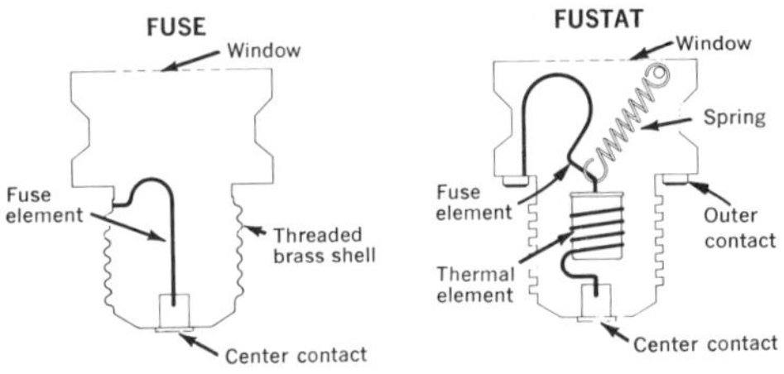

Parts of an ordinary fuse and the newer fustat fuse (also called Type S fuse). The fustat will carry temporary overloads (such as motor starting currents) better than an ordinary fuse. It cannot be replaced by one of higher amp rating.

HSJ has asbestos insulation with a rubber outer jacket. Asbestos-insulated cord with a cloth outer braid is also used. The type with the gold thread will stand the most flexing, the one with red thread, less flexing, and the white thread, the least flexing.

There are also special cords, such as for a range or dryer, usually made with a molded cap to fit the proper receptacle.

Christmas tree lighting strings and cords are made for either indoor or outdoor use. Outdoor lights can be used inside, but inside lights must not be used outside, because of the moisture.

When replacing the cord in a plug, be sure to run the wires around the prongs and clockwise under the screws. Wires stay under the screws better for tightening, and running wires around the prongs helps relieve the stress on the individual strands where they are held down by the screw. Heavy-duty plugs, which clamp to the cord and will stand more pulling, are available.

If the plug or cord you are replacing is of the three-wire grounding type, you must be very careful to replace with a three-wire cord and plug, and put the green-insulated wire under the green colored screw in the plug. The other end of the green-insulated wire fastens to the frame of the appliance, so it is very important that it be connected correctly.

If connected wrong, it could energize the appliance and produce a serious shock. Conventional color coding calls for connecting the red or black wire to the brass-colored screw and the white wire to the silver-colored screw.

When purchasing appliance cords, remember that it may not be necessary to have a full-length cord where the appliance is used on the kitchen counter. You can buy coiled cords that will retract like a telephone cord, and short cords only about two feet long. This avoids cord clutter on the kitchen counter.

Switches wear out eventually, and these can be replaced if care is given to put things together the same as they came apart. Switches are available that have a pilot light so they can be found in the dark, and you can get switches that operate silently. Also available are "dimmer" switches that allow turning lights up and down as you wish. These fit in a standard switch box, and are efficient in that they are solid-state devices that do not waste any power, as would a rheostat.

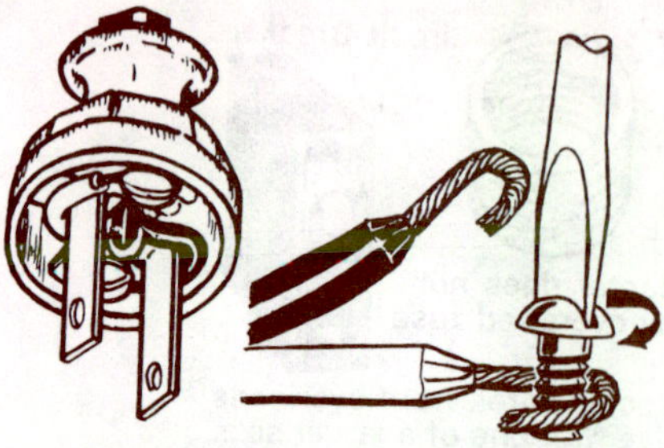

In wiring a plug, the wires should be run around the prongs to the screw. The end of the wire is twisted and run clockwise around the screw. A protective disc (not shown) slips over the prongs and conceals the connections.

Receptacles also wear out, though this is not always realized. Bending the prongs of a loose-fitting plug is only a temporary solution at best, and on a heating device could cause overheating of the plug. What usually has happened is that the contacts inside the receptacle no longer exert pressure on both sides of the prong. A new receptacle is the answer.

If the receptacle is the three-prong grounding type, be sure the bare or green grounding wire is connected under the green, hexagon-shaped screw. The white wire goes to the silver screw, and the black or red wire to the brass-colored screw.

When purchasing electrical parts, be sure they carry the label of Underwriters' Laboratories. The UL label means that the cord or device has met minimum safety requirements for the purpose intended. It could still be unsafe if improperly used. For instance, a brass-shelled socket is acceptable for a lamp for use only in dry places, not for use in a basement or outdoors. The cardboard separator can become wet and conduct electricity to the shell.

The most common receptacle is the parallel-blade type, which is intended for use on 115 volts. There are several types of receptacles for 230–volt use, depending on the size of the electrical load, ranging from 15 amps up to 50 amps.

Should you try to do your own electrical wiring? Wiring is a trade that takes several years to learn, and this author advises that if your wiring involves more than just adding a receptacle, switch or light, you get an electrician to do it.

Unfortunately, in many homes more circuits are needed. Adding a receptacle may increase the convenience of using electricity, but it will not add anything to the capacity of that circuit.

If you do wish to do some wiring, get a good wiring handbook, study it thoroughly, and follow it carefully. Such handbooks are available from major mailorder catalog houses who sell wiring supplies.

Check with your electric power supplier on your legal status in doing wiring. In most states you can do your own, but the law may require that you have wiring inspected.

Safe wiring depends on good design, proper materials, and good workmanship, so don't go about it casually.

Several types of wire may be used around a home. The most common is type NM (non-metallic) cable, usually referred to as "romex", which is for dry locations. Type NMC is non-metallic cable for corrosive or damp locations.

Type AC (armored cable) has a metal armor spiralled around the wires, and is required for home wiring in some areas. Type UF (underground feeder) is meant for burial underground, and usually is also labeled for NMC use.

Cable comes stamped with the type number, number of wires, and size of wire stamped on the outside every foot or two. For instance, "NM 12/2 w.g." would mean type NM cable, wire size 12, two insulated wires with one bare wire for grounding. Sometimes wiring is

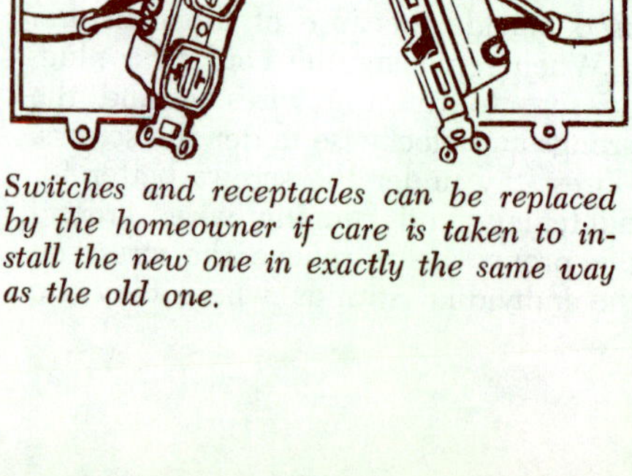

Switches and receptacles can be replaced by the homeowner if care is taken to install the new one in exactly the same way as the old one.

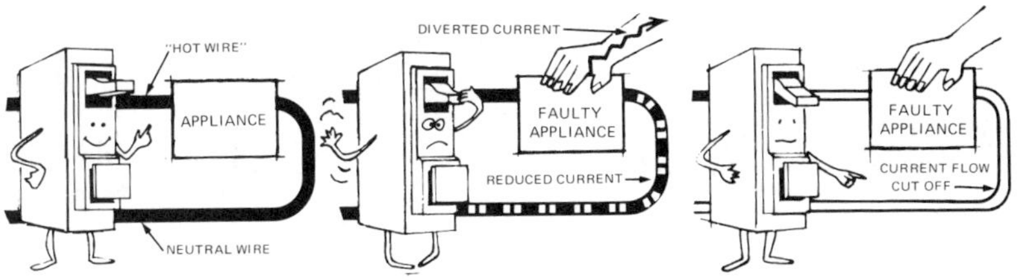

How a Ground-Fault Interrupter works.

run inside electrical conduit (pipe) where mechanical protection is needed.

Receptacles on the outside of buildings require a weatherproof box and cover. They usually have spring loaded covers with rubber gaskets to keep moisture out.

A recent requirement of the National Electrical Code for new outdoor receptacles in residential locations requires that a "Ground-Fault Interrupter" (referred to as "GFI") be used. (The National Electric Code is a voluntary standard by the electrical and insurance industries which has been made compulsory in many states.)

The GFI is a device which will sense the fact that current is going to ground (such as through a person receiving a shock) and shut off the power before the person is injured. These are available as portable, plug-in units, as separate devices in a metal box, and as part of a circuit breaker for mounting in a breaker box.

It must be mentioned that a GFI does not protect from all kinds of shock, such as from grasping one wire in each hand, but since shocks usually involve current flow to ground, it will protect against most of them.

Each GFI has a test button. When pressed, it simulates a current flow to ground, so you can check periodically to be sure the GFI is working.

Electrical cords and fittings used outdoors should be of the non-metallic type, or weatherproofed and properly grounded. Generally, outdoor lights require porcelain-base sockets, and cords should be heavy duty rubber. Permanent, outdoor weatherproof receptacles can be installed for plugging in outdoor lighting. If fixtures are intended for outdoor use they will carry the UL label and a statement as to their purpose.

A great variety of light bulbs and fluorescent tubes is available for replacement. Fluorescent lamps are available in color ranges from "cool-white" to "warm-white." The "warmer" the lamp, the more pleasing are the colors from skin and food. The "cool" lamp, though efficient, makes people and food look less attractive. For most home uses, a "warm white" or "Deluxe Warm White" lamp is advised.

Light bulbs may be clear, inside-frosted, or all-white. For enclosing in a diffuser, the clear bulb is acceptable. Where the bulb will be visible, the all-white is preferred, since its "hot spot" brightness is less. Also, the all-white bulb does not darken as it is used.

Most light bulbs are designed to burn from 750 to 1,000 hours. It is possible to build a bulb to last longer, by operating the filament at a cooler temperature, but doubling the life of the bulb means reducing the light output about 15 percent for the same wattage. An exception to this is the bulb filled with Krypton gas, which has a longer life without sacrificing light output.

You can compare light bulbs by looking at the information on the carton. You will find there the watts (rate of power consumption), the lumen output (quantity of light), and the expected burning life in hours. A bulb which has a lower light output, but longer life, may be a logical choice for a hard-to-reach place, such as a yard light.

FOR FURTHER READING:

Sears Roebuck and Company. *Simplified Electrical Wiring Handbook,* Minneapolis, Minn. 55407.

Picking the Right Types of Pipe

MANY MATERIALS are used for plumbing but let's consider only those that are generally acceptable and available. Local plumbing codes determine piping which may be used. The demands of professional plumbers along with wholesale and retail outlets generally dictate the availability of particular materials in a community.

The choice of pipes to use depends upon several decisions you should make. First, is this a do-it-yourself job or will it be turned over to a professional plumber?

In case it's a job for the plumber, you should be interested in the total cost, local code requirements, expected life, freedom from maintenance and failure, friction loss, and corrosion resistance. Other factors are safe working pressure, resistance to deposits in pipe, effect on water flavor, and ease of installing additional fixtures and lines.

If you are a do-it-yourself fan, consider several additional factors. Among these are ease of installation, availability of plumbing tools, time limitations, and availability of pipes, fittings and supplies. Also, some plumbing codes limit the work that can be done by anyone except licensed plumbers.

Pipes generally available for potable water supply and distribution lines include galvanized iron or steel, copper, and plastics. Each has several types and grades.

Galvanized steel has been extensively used for home and out-of-doors distribution lines and in individual water wells. It resists mechanical damage, thus making it the best pipe for installing under roadways or to faucets subject to abuse.

Galvanized steel pipe should last 30 years or more buried in most soils and much longer if no inside corrosion occurs. It will easily withstand the pressures found in most homeowner water systems.

Main drawbacks to galvanized piping are inside deposits from hard water and corrosion due to acid, alkaline or hard water. Because of this the flow is reduced, often requiring the next larger size pipe as compared to copper or plastic. Also, acid water will cause iron staining on bathroom fixtures.

Present cost of steel pipe and fittings is less than copper but considerably more than plastic. However, the cost of installation, if done by a plumber, may make it comparable to copper.

The initial cost of copper pipe is the highest of commonly used plumbing materials. However, several advantages make it a much sought-after potable water distribution material.

Copper is very resistant to corrosion except when carrying water containing free CO_2 (carbon dioxide). Acceptable types will withstand burial in most soils for long periods of time. One caution: don't bury it in cinders or soil with high sulfide conditions. Acid water or water containing free CO_2 will remove enough copper to cause blue-green stain on fixtures. Some off flavor of water may also occur.

Copper pipe or tubing is generally available in type L (standard), type K (heavy duty), and type M (thin walled). Types L and K come in soft or hard temper while type M is hard temper only. Type K is primarily used for water service or other lines buried underground. Soft temper copper tubing comes in coils, while hard temper pipes come in 12 and 20 foot lengths.

Hard temper copper pipe is difficult to bend and requires fittings where turns in direction are needed. Soft temper tubing bends easily, eliminating the need for many fittings. Its ease in being pulled through wall openings makes it an excellent material for use by the do-

---

AUTHOR *E. B. Hale* is Extension Specialist, Agricultural Engineering, Cooperative Extension Service, at the Virginia Polytechnic Institute and State University, Blacksburg.

it-yourself homeowner. Hard temper copper pipe should be used in exposed locations because it makes a much neater installation.

Solder-type copper fittings provide an easy and secure means of making plumbing connections. Few tools are needed by the homeowner in making repairs or additions to copper plumbing.

A word of caution here. Don't connect copper piping directly to steel, as electrolysis may cause corrosion and eventually leakage at the joint. Non-conducting adapters should be used for these connections. Also, nails will penetrate copper pipes, so be careful when nailing into walls containing them.

Plastics are the newcomer to plumbing. Polyethylene (PE) pipe was introduced to the general market shortly after World War II. Since then a whole array of thermoplastics has been developed for handling water and waste. The main problem with plastics has been their loss of strength as temperatures increase.

Recent developments in some plastics have made them usable in hot as well as cold water lines.

Polyethylene (PE) comes in pressure ratings of 80 to 160 pounds per square inch at 73° F. It is used extensively for lawn sprinkler systems, in water wells, and supply lines to homes and outbuildings. PE is not recommended for use where high temperatures occur. Extended exposure to direct sunlight will cause deterioration of PE.

PE's low cost and ease of installation make it a desirable material for the homeowner to install outside. It withstands some freezing but should be buried below the frost line or drained before freezing occurs when used for lawn sprinkling.

The nationally recognized BOCA (Building Officials and Code Administrators International, Inc.) Plumbing Code has included plastic pipe as an acceptable material for cold water plumbing. In 1972, for the first time, the Code included a plastic hot water pipe, CPVC (Chlorinated Polyvinyl Chloride) as being an acceptable water distribution material.

Check your local plumbing code before planning to use plastics.

Plastic pipe and fittings available for cold water distribution include PE, PVC (Polyvinyl Chloride), ABS (Acrylonitrile-Butadiene-Styrene), PB (Polybutalene) and CPVC cold water pipe. PE, PVC and ABS have been on the market for many years. PB and CPVC are relative newcomers.

PVC and ABS are rigid plastic pipes and have been widely used for underground water service lines. Indoors, they are acceptable only for cold water, drain, waste or vent lines. Both are available in different types and pressure ratings. PVC is manufactured in sizes as small as ½ inch.

Both PVC and ABS are relatively inexpensive plumbing materials, although at this writing the cost is climbing rapidly due to the shortage of oil from which they are a derivative.

Rigid plastic pipes are generally connected to fittings by solvent welding. The solvent dissolves portions of the pipe and fitting, allowing them to fuse together as one homogeneous material. An excellent connection results providing the joints are cleaned and the proper solvent is correctly applied. Once joined, only a few seconds are required for the pipe and fitting to fuse together permanently. Therein lies one of the problems with using these pipes. In case of a mistake in measuring the pipe or positioning of a fitting, the pipe must be cut off, new fittings secured, and a new installation made.

Water hammer, the knocking often heard in pipes, is a serious threat to rigid plastic pipe. A remedy can be approved water hammer arrestors installed at critical points in the line. Commonly used metal pipes can withstand more water hammer but they also fail in severe cases.

CPVC hot water pipe as well as the cold water version is now an acceptable plumbing material. It will withstand normal hot water temperatures but should not be exposed to temperatures in excess of 180° F. CPVC cold water pipe is not designed for hot water use, so don't use it interchangeably.

The present cost of CPVC pipe and fittings is two to four times that of other common plastics but remains only about a third of the cost of copper.

Because of its smooth interior and resistance to corrosion, plastic pipe has less friction than other commonly used materials.

All plastic pipe should be clearly marked with the pressure rating, manufacturer's name or trademark, and nSf (National Sanitation Foundation) insignia.

Drain, waste and vent (DWV) pipe must carry solids and chemically active materials, and provide for the free flow of water. Because DWV pipe doesn't function under pressure, it must be larger than water lines.

There is a large choice of materials for DWV piping not installed in the ground. You may use cast iron, galvanized wrought iron or steel, copper, lead, ABS plastic, or PVC plastic pipe.

Drain pipe underground must be cast iron, hard temper copper, or plastic DWV piping. Lines going to sewers or other waste disposal areas and not in the same trench with water lines may be cast iron, concrete, vitrified clay tile, bituminized fiber, plastic, asbestos cement or copper. In case of burial in the same trench with water lines, only cast iron, hard temper copper or plastic (PVC or ABS) are acceptable.

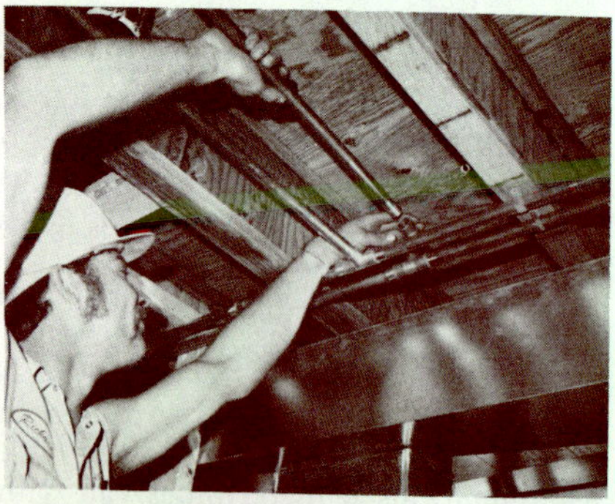

Cast iron (CI) has been used extensively as DWV pipe and is still the premium material. It is in demand for the soil stack, underground drain and soil pipe to the water closet. Conventionally, a hub type joint, which is sealed with oakum and lead or a neoprene ring, has been used. A new development is the hubless CI pipe which uses a sleeve and clamp to connect pipes and fittings. The cost of CI pipe and its installation is greater than plastic but less than copper.

Galvanized iron or steel is used primarily in fixture branch lines and in sizes 3 inch and smaller.

Plastic pipe can be used for the entire DWV plumbing system and is probably the least expensive of the available materials. It is easy to work with, but be careful about positioning fittings when making the solvent weld connection. Plastic pipe is subject to mechanical damage such as puncture.

Copper DWV pipe is very satisfactory but its cost makes it too expensive for most homeowners.

No matter what types of pipe are selected, make sure the size is adequate. Remember that local plumbing codes specify the minimum size as well as the type that may be installed for particular uses.

A local plumbing contractor, plumbing supply outlet, or code enforcement agency can be of much assistance in selecting pipes, fittings and fixtures.

There are several do-it-yourself books and magazines on the market that provide information on selecting and installing plumbing.

FOR FURTHER READING:

U.S. Department of Agriculture. *Plumbing for the Home and Farmstead,* F 2213, for sale by Superintendent of Documents, Washington, D.C. 20402.

Henderson, G. E. *Planning For an Individual Water System,* American Association for Vocational Instructional Materials, Agricultural Engineering Center, Athens, Ga. 30602, $6.95.

Insulating to Save Energy in Heating, Cooling a Home

CONSERVING ENERGY used in home heating and cooling is of paramount importance to every homeowner and potential homeowner in America, since we are depleting our present sources of energy, primarily fossil fuels, at an alarming rate.

Proper use of insulation is the most positive and efficient means of conserving home conditioning energy.

This chapter is designed to give, in basic terms, information which will help you make better decisions on whether to insulate, and on choosing and installing insulation materials. But first off, let's briefly review some fundamental facts and terms from physics.

Heat energy always flows from a warm material, body, or space to a relatively cooler material, body, or space. In winter, heat energy flows from the warm interior of a house to the cooler exterior. This is referred to as "heat loss" when discussing heating systems. In summer, heat flows from the warmer exterior to the relatively cooler interior of a house. This is referred to as "heat gain" when considering air conditioning.

Heat is transferred in three basic ways:

By Conduction, heat passes through a dense material such as an iron skillet sitting on a hot stove or a steel rod held in a hot fire.

By Convection, heat is transferred by movement of air over a heated panel or radiator surface.

By Radiation, heat is radiated in the form of infra-red rays from one place to another, such as from the sun to the earth.

The term insulation used in this chapter refers to thermal insulation, not electrical insulation. Some very good electrical insulators, such as glass, are poor thermal insulators.

Thermal insulation materials are those developed specifically to reduce heat transfer materially. Insulation materials are generally very light in weight and are produced in four common forms. These are batts or blankets, loose fill or granulated, rigid boards, and reflective.

Batt and blanket insulation is made of matted mineral, glass, or cellulose fibers.

Insulation batts or blankets are usually encased in paper, one face of which is made to serve as a vapor barrier. This may be an asphalt paper or a paper with a reflective metal foil backing. Proper installation of this vapor barrier is very important.

Blankets and batts range in thickness from 1″ to 6″ and in widths to fit between joists, rafters, and studs spaced 12″, 16″ and 24″ on center. Blanket insulation may come in lengths of 50′ or more. Batts generally are between 2′ and 8′ in length. The batt and blanket type insulation is normally used during initial construction when it can be easily placed between structural members of the sidewall, ceiling and floor.

Loose fill or granulated insulation generally consists of mineral wool, vermiculite, treated cellulose fiber, granulated polyurethane and other material. It is usually sold in bags for easy storing and handling. Depending on the particular job, it can either be poured directly from the bag or blown in place by mechanical means.

Loose fill insulation is especially convenient for insulating the ceilings of existing houses where there is access to the attic. Granulated forms such as vermiculite are well adapted for placing in the cores of masonry blocks, thereby reducing heat loss through masonry walls considerably.

AUTHOR *Cecil D. Wheary* is Extension Specialist, Agricultural Engineering, Virginia Polytechnic Institute and State University, Blacksburg.

Placing loose fill insulation into sidewalls and ceilings of existing houses by special blowers is about the only method of insulating when the spaces are inaccessible otherwise, but this can create moisture problems from a lack of proper vapor barriers. Please read the chapter on "Preventing Moisture Damage in Houses" by H. O. Fleischer—page 170 in *Handbook for the Home,* the 1973 Yearbook of Agriculture.

Rigid type insulation, commonly referred to as insulation boards, has many special uses. Its rigidity and strength give it advantages which other types of insulation do not have.

Rigid insulation boards are used on the outside of wall studs as sheathing or inside as a wall finish. Insulation board is relatively dense, and therefore less effective as an insulator than batt or blanket types of the same thickness.

Rigid insulation boards 1′ to 2′ wide and 1″ to 4″ thick are used as perimeter insulation around the outside edges of houses built with concrete slab floors. This insulation must be moisture resistant so it is generally made of foamed glass, or foamed plastic such as polyurethane.

Reflective insulation is made from reflective foils such as aluminum, or polished metallic flake adhered to a reinforced paper. It retards the flow of infra-red heat rays passing across an air space. To be effective the foil surface must face an air space of ¾″ or more. Reflective insulation is available in single sheets, strips formed to create 3 or 4 separated air spaces of ¾″, and as a combination vapor barrier and reflective surface attached to batts or blankets.

The critical factor to insure efficiency of reflective insulation is installing it so the reflective surface always faces an air space of ¾″ or more. Once the reflective surface touches surrounding materials it is ineffective as an insulator because it does not retard conducted heat or heat of convection.

Many types and forms of materials are used in manufacturing building insulation. Also, there are many building materials which are mistakenly assumed by the uninformed to have much more insulating value than they really have.

Because of these variations and misunderstandings, it is unrealistic to compare insulating values of materials by thickness in inches. For example many people are shocked when told that 1″ of mineral wool insulation has more insulating value than an 18″ masonry wall of common brick.

Fortunately for consumers, reliable standard rating methods have been developed to help you rate various insulations. Although the rating method is quite reliable, some of the terms used to explain it may be new and somewhat confusing to you at first. I will try to omit most of the technical details and present some guidelines in simple terms.

Effectiveness of insulation is specified in two ways. One is stated as the resistance offered by a material or materials to the flow of heat under known conditions. This "Resistance" is generally designated by the letter "R". The second specification is stated as the amount of heat that will pass through a material or materials under known conditions. This is designated by the letters "C" or "U".

Most manufacturers of insulation have adopted the "R" rating and stamp it on their product for easy evaluation by the purchaser. For example, a 3″ thick batt of one insulation might have an R10 rating, whereas a 3″ batt of another type might have an R12 rating. On the other hand a 2″ thick rigid foam material might have an R10 rating stamped on it.

In all cases when you are given the "R" rating it is a simple matter to evaluate and make comparisons.

When you are building a wall containing several materials and have the "R" values for each, you can determine the total "R" value or insulating value by simply adding them directly. For example: R4 + R10 + R5 = R19 total. Another example of how the rating can be used is in determining values of various thicknesses of materials. If 2″ of insulation "A" has a rating of R8 then 4″ would have a rating of R16, for all practical purposes.

You cannot add the "C" and "U"

INSULATING VALUES OF VARIOUS MATERIALS

Material	"R" per inch thickness
BATT OR BLANKET	
Wood or cellulose fiber with paper backing and facing	4.00
Mineral wool (rock, slag or glass)	3.80
LOOSE FILL	
Mineral wool (rock, slag or glass)	3.30
Vermiculite, expanded	2.08
BOARD OR RIGID	
Expanded Urethane, foamed in place, sprayed or preformed	5.88
Polystyrene foam, extruded or expanded	4.50
Glass fiberboard	4.34
CONSTRUCTION MATERIALS	
Wood fiberboard, laminated sheathing	2.90
Plywoods and Softwoods	1.25
Plaster, stucco, brick	0.20
DOORS	
Solid wood, 1"	1.56
Solid wood, 2"	2.33
WINDOW (Glass area only)	
Single glazing	0.88
Double glazing with ¼" air space	1.64
Single glazing with storm window	1.89

values directly. When you can only find the "C" or the "U" rating you change them to "R" before adding. Simply stated the procedure is this: when you know the "C" or "U" value, you divide one (1) by this value to get "R". Example: a "C" or "U" value is .5, then "R" = 1 ÷ .5 = 2.

Do not let these conversions confuse you. There are many tables in insulation publications which give the "C" value, the "U" value and the "R" value for various materials.

The most important thing for you to remember about the factor "R" and factors "C" or "U" is the simple fact that the *larger* the "R" the better the insulating qualities of the material, and the *smaller* the "C" or "U" the better the insulating quality.

These simple rating designations also make it easy to compare costs of insulations. If one insulation rated R13 meets your job requirements and costs 10 cents per square foot, and another is identical in every way except cost, your choice is positive. Also, you can easily determine the amount of insulation required for a desired "R" value for any type of construction.

Now you have to make the important decision on where to insulate and how much insulation to use.

To determine the location for insulation, imagine the insulation as a blanket completely surrounding the living area of your home. This means all areas which are to be heated in winter and cooled in summer. For a complete job, insulation should be placed in the sidewalls, ceiling, and floors over unheated spaces.

Windows and doors are insulated by weather stripping, storm doors and windows, or double glazing. More details on these are given in another chapter of this 1974 Yearbook.

In answer to the question of how much insulation to use under present conditions of critical shortages and high costs of energy for heating and cooling, it is safe to say that you need not worry about over-insulating from an economic standpoint. Some general recommendations have been prepared which may be used as guidelines.

The standards most recommended now are those in the "All Weather Comfort Standard" prepared by electric power suppliers with the cooperation of material and equipment manufactures. This standard specifies these insulation "R" values: *Ceiling–R19, Walls–R11,* and *Floors–R13.*

Initially these values were specified for electrically heated and air conditioned homes. However, because of the present and projected energy situation,

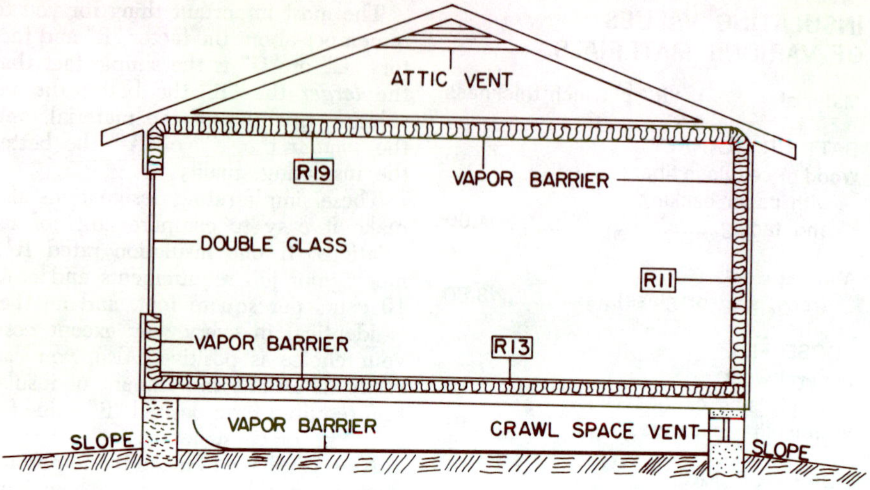

I recommend that you use the "All Weather Comfort Standard" in any case if possible.

Another standard for insulation is The Department of Housing and Urban Development (HUD) Minimum Property Standards. In some areas the insulation requirements are higher than the "All Weather Comfort Standard." The HUD requirements are based on the number of winter degree days in an area.

Any amount of insulation used will generally pay for itself in a few years, not only by the savings from using less high cost fuel, but also because you can use smaller and less costly heating and cooling equipment.

Some characteristics or features of insulation materials besides "R" values and cost could influence your choice of materials used for particular conditions. A few of these are:

-Structural requirements, which must be considered when you want to use rigid insulation for such things as sheathing, plaster base, interior ceiling or wall finish, and roof decks.

-Fire resistance of any insulating material should be considered regardless of where it is used in the house.

-Effects of moisture on an insulation material sometimes determine whether or not it can be used for some jobs such as perimeter insulation under concrete slabs. When any insulation material becomes saturated, the insulating value decreases to practically nothing.

-Vermin resistance is an important consideration, but you must make relative evaluations. No material is absolutely vermin proof.

Here are a few summary guidelines on insulation:

Before you buy, know the insulation value of any material being considered, and make cost comparisons on the basis of cost per unit of resistance (Divide cost per sq. ft. by "R" value).

Follow manufacturers' directions for proper installation.

Adequate ventilation of the attic and crawl space is necessary for best results from use of insulation in these areas.

Following these simple recommendations will help you and your family save money and energy and have a more comfortable year-round home to enjoy.

FOR FURTHER READING:

Forest Products Laboratory. *Condensation Problems: Their Prevention and Solution,* FPL 132, Madison, Wisc. 53203, 1972.

Selecting Doors and Windows

TODAY'S WINDOWS are picked more for the view and the light they let in than for the amount of ventilation they give. Even doors are stressing views, such as the wide sliding patio doors.

Ventilation, of course, has taken a back seat due to the more sophisticated heating and cooling systems of today's homes. But with the concerns for energy conservation, ventilation may come back as a substitute for air conditioning.

So how do you choose? What should be of prime importance in selecting doors and windows?

Both sides of the glass can be washed from the inside when casement windows are hinged this way.

With windows, you can narrow down the field by asking yourself these four questions: What kind of viewing will it give? How easy is it to clean? Will it be easy to open and close where it's located? And, if important, will it give good ventilation?

You have only three basic types of windows to look at: 1) fixed, 2) sliding, and 3) swinging. Of course, there are many variations in design and style under these categories. See the accompanying guide for window shoppers.

Choosing the type of window you wish is only one part of window selecting. You need also to pay attention to materials used in the makeup of that window. What's the glass area made of? How about the frame around it? And what about the quality of hardware?

Of course, cost is always a major factor in making any purchasing decision. To get a true picture, be sure you're comparing total costs.

Find the cost of the window unit itself. Then add to it the extras such as hardware and screens, plus installation and finishing costs. In general, it's usually wise to buy the best quality windows you can afford.

The same can be said of doors—especially the exterior ones exposed to weather. Buy the best you can afford.

If you're looking at wood doors, the solid door is the highest quality—and the highest priced. The solid-core door is next with a wood-filled core between two slabs of high quality wood veneer such as birch, oak or mahogany. Exterior door construction requires that the veneers and their attachment to the core be made with waterproof glue. These are known as Type I doors. Type II doors use a non-waterproof glue.

Hollow-core doors may have high quality veneer faces, but the lower-priced ones are covered with less durable wood or composition board.

AUTHOR *Fred W. Roth* is Extension Agricultural Engineer, Iowa State University, Ames.

CO-AUTHOR *Virginia L. Harding* is Associate Extension Editor, Information Service, Iowa State.

GUIDE FOR WINDOW SHOPPERS

WINDOW TYPE	HOW DOES IT OPERATE?	IS IT EASY TO CLEAN?	HOW IS IT FOR VIEWING?	HOW IS IT FOR VENTILATION?
FIXED	Does not open, so requires no screens or hardware	Outside job for exterior of window	No obstruction to views or light	No ventilation Minimum air leakage
SLIDING				
Double-Hung	Sash pushes up and down. Easy to operate except over sink or counter	Inside job if sash is removable	Horizontal divisions can cut view	Only half can be open
Horizontal-Sliding	Sash pushes sideways in metal or plastic tracks	Inside job if sash is removable	Vertical divisions cut view less than horizontal divisions	Only half can be open
SWINGING				
Casement (Side Hinged)	Swings out with push-bar or crank Latch locks sash tightly	Inside job if there is arm space on hinged side	Vertical divisions cut view less than horizontal	Opens fully. Can scoop air into house
Awning (Top Hinged)	Usually swings out with push-bar or crank. May swing inward when used high in wall	Usually an inside job unless hinges prevent access to outside of glass	Single units offer clear view. Stacked units have horizontal divisions which cut view	Open fully. Upward airflow if open outward; downward flow when open inward
(Bottom Hinged)	Swings inward, operated by a lock handle at top of sash	Easily cleaned from inside	Not a viewing window, usually set low in wall	Airflow is directed upward
Jalousie	A series of horizontal glass slats open outward with crank	Inside job, but many small sections to clean	Multiple glass divisions cutting horizontally across view	Airflow can be adjusted in amount and direction

GUIDE FOR WINDOW MATERIALS

GLASS AREA	
Single-strength glass	Suitable for small glass panes. Longest dimension—about 40 inches
Double-strength glass	Thicker, stronger glass suitable for larger panes. Longest dimension—about 60 inches
Plate glass	Thicker and stronger for still larger panes. Also more free of distortion. Longest dimension—about 10 feet
Insulating glass	Two layers of glass separated by a dead air space and sealed at edges. Desirable for all windows in cold climates to reduce heating costs. Noise transmission is also reduced
Safety glass	Acrylic or plexiglass panels eliminate the hazard of accidental breakage. Panels scratch more easily than glass. Laminated glass as used in automobiles also reduces breakage hazard
FRAME	
Wood	Preferable in cold climates as there is less problem with moisture condensation. Should be treated to resist decay and moisture absorption. Painting needed on outside unless frame is covered with factory-applied vinyl shield or other good coating.
Aluminum	Painting not needed unless color change is desired. Condensation a problem in cold climates unless frame is specially constructed to reduce heat transfer. Often less tight than wood frames.
Steel	Painting necessary to prevent rusting unless it is *stainless* steel. Condensation a problem in cold climates
Plastic	Lightweight and corrosion-free. Painting not needed except to change color
HARDWARE	Best handles, hinges, latches, locks, etc. usually are steel or brass. Aluminum satisfactory for some items but often less durable. Some plastics and pot metal are often disappointing.

In colder climates, modern insulated steel doors are gaining favor for exterior use. They do not warp, shrink or swell with weather changes. And they need painting less often.

Like wood doors, the steel doors come in designed styles and can be fitted with glass openings for viewing. Those with magnetic gaskets that grip like a refrigerator door give the tightest seal against the weather. They are usually pre-hung, so the frame and hinges are included. Costwise, steel is quite comparable with the commonly used wood doors.

Glass is used in exterior doors primarily where a view is desired, such as of a landscaped backyard. In cold climates, insulating glass should be se-

Upper left, standard solid-core wood door. Upper right, hollow space of this steel door is filled with insulation. Above, wood-frame patio doors. Some patio doors have a vinyl-covered wood frame for minimum maintenance.

Left and center, bi-fold doors for closets. Right, pocket doors that slide into the wall.

lected as well as wood frames. Condensation poses a problem with either metal frames or single-layer glass.

Whether you buy wood, steel or glass, give the width of the doorway careful consideration. To move major pieces of furniture in and out, at least one door in the house needs to be a minimum of 36 inches wide. This generally is the front door. But width may be a factor in interior doorways as well.

Interior doors are usually either wood or metal. And some plastic is used.

In wood doors used inside, hollow-core construction is most commonly found. However, solid wood is also available. Thickness of an interior door is less than that of doors made for exterior use, since this thinner construction is not meant to stand outside use.

Most wood doors are sold unfinished. However, factory-finished doors are

GUIDE FOR INTERIOR DOORS

TYPE OF DOOR	
Hinged	The most common type for openings 18 to 36 inches wide. Use wherever there is no objection to a swinging door.
Bi-fold	A special type of hinged door. Panels fold against each other to reduce swing-out space. Gives access to full width of closets. Use in openings 3 to 8 feet wide.
Glide-by	Two or more door panels slide by each other. Main use is on closets where door projection is not permissible. Gives access to only half the opening at once.
Pocket	Door which slides into wall. Use where a hinged door would interfere with traffic or other doors.
Folding	A special type of sliding door with *accordion-fold* sections. It can substitute for the other types, but door width is reduced unless a stacking pocket is provided.

available. Metal doors, on the other hand, are usually factory-primed. Then finish painting is done on the job.

Most metal doors are made of steel. Compared to wood, they are generally noisier.

Whether metal or wood, interior doors are found in five basic styles. The style you select generally depends on the purpose intended and the conflicts involved with both traffic patterns and construction details.

Before you choose either windows or doors, make yourself a checklist like the one with this chapter.

CHECKLIST

What's really most important to you in the climate you live in?

To have windows that:

——Capture a view outside?

——Let plenty of daylight stream in?

——Ventilate the house adequately?

——Make your house weathertight?

——Open and close easily?

——Clean easily from inside?

——Enhance the appearance of your house?

And to have doors that:

——Won't interfere with each other?

——Insulate well against cold?

——Won't interfere with trafficways?

——Require the least upkeep?

——Are wide enough to meet needs?

FOR FURTHER READING:

Small Homes Council. *Selecting Windows,* F 11.1, University of Illinois, Urbana, Ill., 25 cents.

——. *Window Planning Principles,* F 11.0, University of Illinois, Urbana, Ill., 25 cents.

Keeping a Roof Over Your Head

DRIP! DRIP! DRIP! Isn't it horrifying to think that you may be listening to a hole in your roof? Well, it was only the bathtub faucet, but maybe you should give the roof a second thought. How old is it and for how long was it guaranteed?

Most of us clean up, fix up and paint those parts of a house which show the most apparent need, but the roof gets little attention as long as it sheds water. The life of your roof and the kind of maintenance that it will need depends mostly on the materials from which it is made.

Some roofing materials, such as asphalt, wear away as they are attacked by wind, water and other elements. These roofs must be re-covered when the remaining material becomes thin. Steel roofs are structurally strong and thin, but if they are not coated, painted and otherwise protected, moisture and oxygen will cause them to deteriorate rapidly.

Nearly all types of roofs can be coated or painted to extend their life. Coatings have even been developed to extend the life of asphalt and aluminum. If roofs are painted or recoated at proper intervals, the base materials will not deteriorate or wear away and the life of the roof can be extended almost indefinitely.

When some materials like aluminum begin to deteriorate, a durable weather-resistant compound forms on their surface, protecting them from the oxygen and moisture in the air. If this compound is scratched or worn away, new compound is quickly formed and the material is again protected.

With normal wear, aluminum may last the life of the structure. Aluminum may be given additional protection by a process called anodization. A relative-

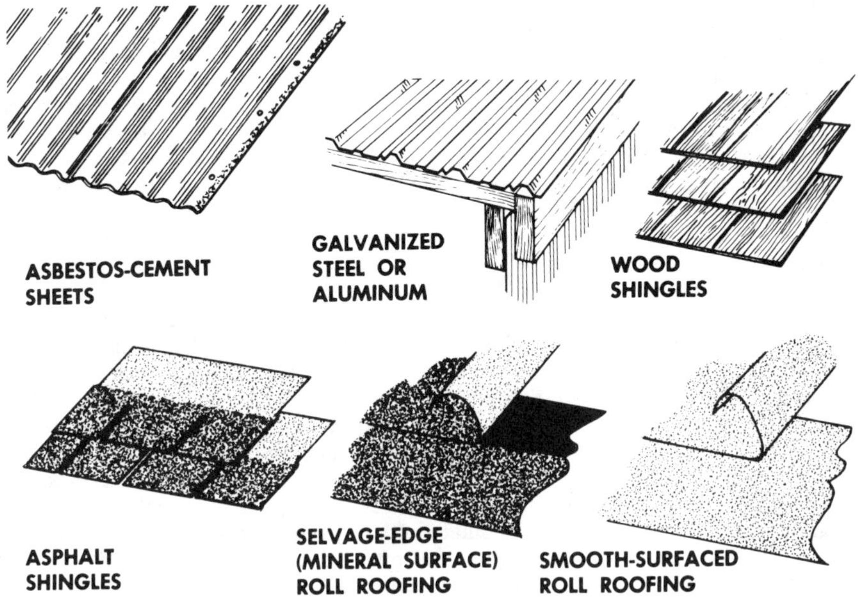

ly inert compound is fused into the surface of aluminum sheets, providing an almost permanent coating.

Other coatings or means of protection like galvanizing, where zinc protects steel by an electrical-chemical process, have been widely used.

Several roofing materials such as slate, asbestos and copper are relatively stable. Barring structural damage, deteriorating nails or failure of the supporting frame, they will outlive most houses.

If you live near a chemical or other plant which emits gaseous compounds, you should check with your local building officials before using these common roofing materials or coatings which may react chemically with such gases to cause deterioration.

The most common roofing material is asphalt. It is low in cost, resilient and a good noise insulator. You can buy it in several forms. In rolls, it may be found in several weights; for example, 15, 30, 60 or 90 pounds per 100 square feet. It may be either plain or surfaced with mineral granules.

Flint or mineral coatings reduce erosion by slowing the flow of water across the shingles, and they shield the asphalt from direct rays of the sun by reflection. Direct sun rays cause the asphalt to become brittle and easily damaged or eroded.

In shingles, the asphalt is overlapped to give a total roofing weight of about 235 pounds per 100 square feet and the mineral surface is applied almost without exception. Asphalt shingled roofs allow moisture to escape from attics in vapor form, and the mineral surface permits a variety of decorative colors to be used.

Breakage and erosion are the major contributors to asphalt shingle failure. Breakage can be held to a minimum by secure fastening and by keeping the roof free from traffic and debris. Self-sealing or interlocking shingles are effective in insuring secure fastening.

The normal life of asphalt shingles without coatings or special treatment is about 20 years; then they must be re-

---

AUTHOR *Jerry O. Newman* is an agricultural engineer in the Rural Housing Research Unit, Agricultural Research Service, at Clemson, S.C.

newed. At replacement time the old shingles may be removed or left in place. If they are left in place, don't forget to use nails which are long enough to reach through the extra roofing thickness.

Although the cost of asphalt roofing is relatively low, its strength is not sufficient to span even short spaces and an expensive solid deck is needed to support it.

A special kind of asphalt roof is the built-up roof which is used on flat or low pitched roofs of up to 1½ feet in height to 12 feet of horizontal span. The built-up roof is formed by several layers of 15 to 30 pound building paper which are cemented together with cold asphalt or hot pitch on a solid roof deck.

Built-up roofs are usually three to six layers thick and they are protected from the sun by a covering of small rocks. In some cases the built-up roof catches the water which falls on it, forming a shallow pool which provides evaporative cooling during the summer. Built-up roofs are easily renewed by recoating with asphalt and adding layers of felt paper.

Since asphalt roofs have an organic base, they are sometimes attacked by fungi which discolors and deteriorates the roof. If you live in the warm, moist southeastern United States, you have probably noticed asphalt roofs with ugly dark spots on them.

Metal roofing is more expensive than asphalt, but aluminum and steel are stronger and capable of spanning relatively long distances without support. You don't need a solid deck under metal. Thus, overall cost of the roof plus the sheathing may be less than asphalt. Perlins spaced 2′ on center are common and some steel roofs can span as much as 6′.

Aluminum reflects sun rays, providing a cool attic.

Be careful to use special nails with aluminum. Steel nails in contact with aluminum will cause rapid deterioration.

Copper is quite expensive, but some builders use it for decorative effect. Copper roofing is generally thin and a relatively solid deck is needed to support it.

Ternemetal is another metal roofing material which was widely used in the past. It is a soft steel coated with a lead and tin alloy which can be crimped and bent easily. It has wide use for irregular roof shapes, but has decreased in popularity because of its high labor requirement and special tools needed.

Ternemetal roofs are not so strong and a relatively solid sheathing should be used under them.

Many roofs, like asphalt, come in several different thicknesses. All metal roofs are fireproof, but remember that they melt at relatively low temperatures and are easily damaged in the presence of a fire. Metal roofs are also poor insulators and if their surface is dark they make good heat collectors. Therefore, as mentioned before a new appropriate coating for the type metal used may be applied to lengthen life and reflect the sun's rays to provide a much cooler attic.

Wood shingles or shakes are quite popular in the hot or humid climates where satisfactory species of wood are available.

Shakes may be made from a variety of weather durable wood species. They are light in weight, attractive, and provide a well insulated roof. Their economy will vary in relation to the cost of timber and labor. They may be laid on slopes as gentle as 1 in 4, but they perform best on steeper slopes.

Wood shingled roofs will crack and curl as they dry out, but their life can be extended by specially prepared shake paints or stains which contain creosote and other preservatives. For long lived roofs, they should be renewed every four to five years with such a paint or stain.

Wood shingles may be used with a solid deck or with slats. In colder climates the solid deck is preferred, but in the warmer, more moist climates, wood shingles over slats allow air to flow from the attic space and reduce the high temperature and high moisture problems.

Asbestos and slate shingles are long

lived, but they are also heavy, hard and brittle. Nails cannot be driven through these materials unless holes are prepunched; therefore, a special hole punching tool or machine is needed to install or repair them. Perlins or batten boards must be placed precisely, especially if the holes are prepunched.

Both slate and asbestos require a minimum of maintenance, with only pulled nails and other physical damage being the main concern. These roofs are fireproof; therefore, fire insurance rates will generally be lower. One should remember that such roofs will not be so fireproof if they are painted or coated with a flammable material.

Once you have selected roofing, a change in the type of material may be quite expensive. If your present roofing system uses a solid deck, most any type of roof can be placed over it. But if you try to put an asphalt type roof in place of a roof which does not have a solid deck, you'll probably need to install an entirely new roof deck.

Color is an extremely important part of your roofing system. With proper planning you can make maximum use of a dark roof as a heat collector and a part of your heating system in the winter, but in the summer when cooling is required, the excess heat is not needed or wanted.

A light colored roof which will reflect the sun's rays would be most favorable during summer, but obviously a biannual roof color change would be too expensive. Attic ventilation to divert the excess summer heat will be more realistic if you choose the dark colored roof for its winter benefits. With light colored roofs, excessive winter heat loss may be controlled by extra layers of overhead insulation.

The greatest need for gutters and downspouts is in those areas which have high rainfall, and especially where cold temperatures accompany high rainfall. Such diversionary equipment will reduce erosion and protect walkways and stairs from unwanted drips.

In cold climates, gutters can effectively reduce the problems of frozen stairs and walkways.

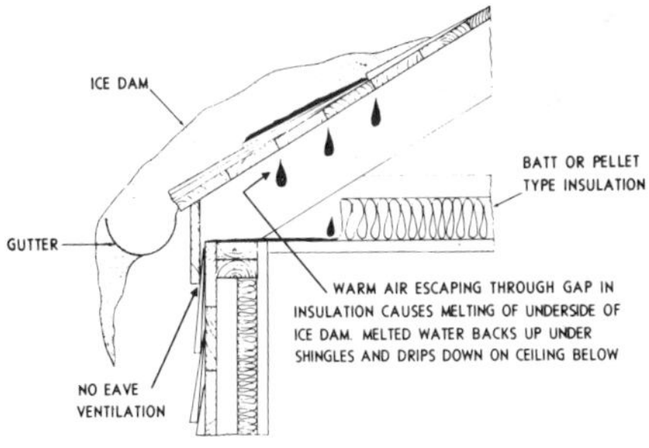

Snow guards should be used on steep roofs in cold climates to prevent sheets of accumulated ice from sliding. Sliding ice can cause considerable damage to your gutters and the roofing in general. Shrubs and bushes around the house may also be broken and even destroyed by an uncontrolled sheet of ice.

Also, in cold climates, care must be taken to prevent ice dams which can cause water to back up under the shingles and leak into the attic.

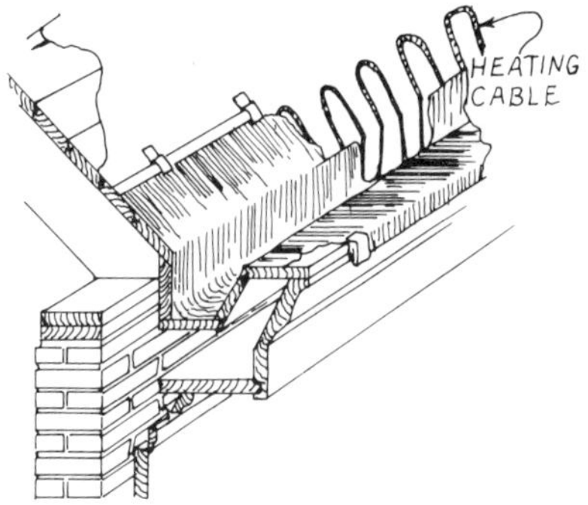

Such ice dams are caused by the colder roof temperatures near the edge of the eaves. Ice or snow melts over the heated part of the house, and flows to the overhanging eaves where it refreezes and builds up. An electric heating cable can be installed in a zigzag pattern along the eaves to prevent such refreezing and a build-up of ice.

FOR FURTHER READING:

U.S. Department of Agriculture, Office of Communication. *Roofing Farm Buildings,* F 2170, Washington, D.C. 20250.

Exterior, Interior Wall Materials

EXTERIOR *

MANY people are surprised to learn that walls ordinarily represent a minor portion (usually 5 to 10 percent) of the cost of a house. Most of us think that the exterior walls of a house are more costly, if not more important.

In buying or building a house, probably the single most important element is its walls. For one thing, walls tell us what kind of house we are looking at—a brick house, a wood house, a stone house, etc. Also, they tell us something about the owner. They indicate his taste, ideas of quality, and intentions toward permanent residence.

Let's look, then, at the types of exterior walls most commonly built in today's market and the pros and cons of each. No one wall is right for all possible circumstances. Walls differ in quality, ease of installation, cost, permanence and recyclability.

Brick and stone require virtually no maintenance, will not corrode or dent or rot, are fireproof, termite-proof, and —when properly installed—last longer than other building materials. They carry a quality image unmatched by other materials. Finally, brick and stone are just about totally recyclable. In an energy-conscious society, this feature will become more and more important.

Disadvantages of brick and stone primarily center on initial cost and the skilled workmanship (bricklayer—stonemason) needed.

Concrete block shares many advantages of brick and stone. One plus that it has over brick and stone is lower initial cost. Disadvantages include a relatively limited selection for residential use, an unfinished look which may not be esthetically pleasing in all applications, and possible need for painting.

Wood walls include cedar, plywood, redwood, lap siding, shingles and shakes. Advantages are that wood is a natural material and an excellent insulator. Additionally, it is easy to work with and is erected by a carpenter.

Wood siding is available in most parts of the country and its in-place cost is generally lower than that of masonry. Disadvantages lie primarily in the need for painting or staining every few years, higher fire insurance rates, and susceptibility to termites and weather.

Advantages of hardboard siding lie in its generally reasonable cost and availability. It is relatively easy to work with and, like wood siding, is often installed by a carpenter.

Disadvantages closely follow those of wood siding. They include the need for paint, and susceptibility to termites and weather.

Hardboard siding may require more maintenance through the years than most other materials. Some homeowners feel this is offset by the modest initial cost.

Aluminum siding is often less expensive than wood sidings, and aluminum is fire resistant, rot-proof, termite-proof and has a number of textures and colors readily available to builders. It is often sold and erected in packages which include aluminum gutters, downspouts and soffits.

Disadvantages include the possibility of fading, denting, and the need for grounding in case of an electrical storm. Also, some people feel that aluminum lacks the quality image of masonry or wood siding.

Advantages of vinyl siding are somewhat similar to aluminum. However, vinyl siding won't fade or rust and tends to resist dents.

Disadvantages are the possibility of cracking in low temperatures, and difficulty of installation. Also, the fire re-

---

*AUTHOR *Kenneth S. Dash* is Director of Marketing, Brick Institute of America, McLean, Va.

sistance of vinyl siding is less than that of aluminum or masonry.

Nevertheless, this is a relatively new material which is constantly being improved. At a distance, it is a dead ringer for aluminum siding.

Builders and buyers have a choice of a number of other finished sidings including steel, asphalt, and asbestos-cement. They are not nearly as widely used as masonry, wood and the major finished sidings. Their advantages primarily lie in the area of durability, while disadvantages include selection and esthetics.

Stucco is a cement-lime material that may be applied over masonry (concrete block) or over a metal lathe. Advantages are that the material is readily available, since it is generally prepared on site, and has a unique appearance.

Stucco can have a rugged Mediterranean textured look or appear to be smooth as glass. And it can be prepared in a wide range of colors.

Disadvantages of stucco are sensitivity to climatic changes, tendency to crack, and need for skilled craftsmen.

All materials mentioned herein can be painted. Several materials—brick, wood, aluminum, stucco, vinyl and stone—may be left unpainted, depending on their finish.

Advantages of choosing a material that requires painting solely lies in color. Disadvantages are the need to repaint or restain every few years. A table in *Exterior Painting,* G–155, a booklet published by the U.S. Department of Agriculture, shows what type of paint to use on wall materials.

At the outset, it was said that the walls of a house not only tell a visitor something about the house, but also something about its owner. By careful selection and consideration of initial cost, ease of installation, permanence and recyclability, the homeowner will have the opportunity to choose the right wall for his budget today and for his investment tomorrow.

FOR FURTHER READING:

U.S. Department of Agriculture. *Exterior Painting,* G 155, Washington, D.C. 20250.

*Interior***

COLOR, TEXTURE, and design play an important role in selection of interior wall coverings. Some wall coverings can be both decorative and functional. They may serve as backgrounds for furniture and furnishings or to provide beauty and decorative effects. They may also provide color where needed and help to add light or contrast to a room.

Some coverings may serve as noise barriers, or help to further insulate rooms. Some may have fire or flame-resistant qualities.

Gypsum board or sheet rock, paint, regular or vinyl wallpapers, paneling, tiles of ceramic or mirror, laminates or plastic wallboard, plaster, glass, and bricks are among the many choices of materials that can be used on walls. Other materials such as plygrill, carpet, fabrics, and cork may also be used as wall coverings.

Walls are of two types from a construction standpoint—wet wall and dry wall. They are also classified into rigid materials and flexible materials.

Dry wall construction includes gypsum board or sheet rock, paneling and wood finishes, wallpapers, fabrics, and plastic type coverings. Wet wall construction includes plaster, masonry and brick.

Rigid materials include sheet rock, paneling, ceramic tiles, glass tiles, and laminated plastic sheeting. Flexible materials include wallpapers, plastic materials, cork, linoleum, fabrics, and leather.

Paint is used as a finish over walls. One gallon will cover 450 to 500 square feet. Some paints require one coat and some may require two coats. Quality paint will range from $7 to $12 per gallon. A wide range of colors are avail-

**AUTHOR *Sarah F. Fountain* is Specialist in Home Furnishings, Mississippi Cooperative Extension Service, Mississippi State University, Starkville.

able already mixed or by mixing. Many stores can mix about any color you desire.

Paints are generally classified into water-based (latex paint) or oil-based (alkyd) paint. They are very easy to apply. You have the choice in alkyd paints of either a flat, semi-gloss, or high gloss finish. These finishes may be washed.

For better quality latex paint, make sure at least 50 percent of the pigment binder consists of latex solids. The main ingredient in the pigment should be titanium dioxide, which has a covering up or hiding ability. The ingredients should be specified by weight and not by volume.

A few pieces of small equipment are needed for painting, including a 3″ brush and a 1″ or 1½″ brush. Rollers are available with short and long handles for walls and ceilings. Have several cloths for spot cleaning.

Gypsum board or sheet rock is the leading material used or applied to interior walls. It runs relatively inexpensive, as a 4′ x 8′ panel costs about $2. You have to tape and apply sheet rock compound to the edges or joints. Finishes such as paint, wallpaper, or fabric may be used over sheet rock. The most common sheet rock thickness is ½″. New flame-resistant finishes are available in sheet rock.

Paneling can be applied directly to framing materials but is much more substantial if applied over sheet rock. A wide variety is available.

Most paneling today is of plywood or pressed wood. True plywood makes the best paneling for use in the home. Pressed wood is used more for commercial walls. The difference between true wood and wood grained is that a simulated wood grain is reproduced either directly on the panel, or vinyl film is laminated to the panel. Paneling requires few tools to do a good job. An electric saw, measuring instruments, and special adhesive are the major equipment needed.

Paneling comes in different thicknesses, colors, and textures—usually 3/16″ to ¼″. Cost will vary according to the thickness, height, and finish. It will range from $5 to $20 per panel. Panels are 4′ x 8′ for sheet rock and paneling. Taller panels can be bought.

Wallpapers are classified as water sensitive and water resistant. Water-sensitive wallpaper includes roller prints, and screen or hand prints.

Roller prints are made by machine and range from $4 to $12 per single roll. Colors are applied simultaneously from one, two, or as many as 12 rollers. Prices of roller prints vary depending on the weight and quality of paper used, complexity of the design, and number of yards manufactured.

Screen or hand prints are colored manually by using a separate screen for each color of the design. Since the hand process takes time and skill, these papers are expensive. They range from $10 to $20 per single roll.

Water resistant wallpaper includes part vinyl and all vinyl wall coverings. Vinyl wall coverings are available as plain acrylic, vinyl, foil, or flock. They range in price from $5 to $20 per roll.

The term vinyl refers to a whole family of chemical compounds. They are durable, rough, cleanable, and should last longer than regular wallpaper.

Those with plastic latex over ordinary wallpaper—the plastic-coated ones—are fragile and not true vinyl. Latex-impregnated materials have paper laminated to lightweight fabric and are vinyl coated. Besides the vinyl coating, a vinyl latex is used in the decorative coating or ink, making the coverings more stain resistant and scrubbable.

A true all vinyl wall covering is made of polyvinyl chloride. The vinyl is laminated to lightweight fabric. Vinyl chloride resin used as a binder provides durability. Thickness of the resin-bonded surface varies. The thicker the surface, the more expensive it is.

Wallpaper requires few tools to do a good job. The main things to have on hand are wallpaper paste, a bucket, some heavy brushes, and tools for measuring and cutting.

Ceramic tile comes in different qualities, sizes and designs. Cost is around

$2 per square foot. Decorative tiles will run higher. Usually a professional installation is needed.

Plastic wallboard comes in both enamel and plastic finishes. The cost range is about $1 per square foot for enamel and $2 per square foot for formica or plastic finish. This type wall covering is used mostly in bathrooms and kitchens.

Plaster is seldom used except in commercial buildings. Cost will run higher than most wall coverings because of labor involved. This requires special skills and facilities. Plaster is generally painted.

Brick or stone is used mostly for decorative walls and fireplace walls. The price runs higher for this material as brick and stone are used for structural purposes too. Brick and stone work should be done by a professional.

Wall mouldings of both wood and plastic are available for trimmings and decorating rooms. They are available in different sizes with simple or elaborate decorative effects.

Plastic moulding is cheaper in most cases than wood moulding.

An approximate comparative cost analysis of sheet rock, wallpaper, and paneling for a 12'x14' room might be made. This analysis does not include labor, tools, or equipment required to do a skillful job.

A room with sheet rock @ $2 per panel and enough paint to finish walls and the trim would cost about $100.

A room with wallpaper @ $10.00 per roll over sheet rock and enough paint for trim and woodwork would run about $260.

A room of true wood paneling @ $10 per panel and sheet rock ceiling and enough paint or stain woodwork would run about $230.

Walls and wall coverings generally require skilled workmen to do a good job. Labor may cost as much as materials for most walls and wall coverings. Be sure you secure skilled workmen and quality materials to get the most for your money. Painting and papering may be done by the do-it-yourselfer; follow the manufacturer's directions.

Adding Carports, Garages, Storage

ADDING A GARAGE or carport to your home may be your first experience with building of any kind. Whether it results in a pleasant or unpleasant experience depends somewhat on the amount of time and preparation you and your family are willing to make.

It takes time to investigate the conditions that will influence many of your decisions concerning the location, size and design of your garage. It will take time to consider your family's space needs for storage, work, play, etc., before deciding to build a garage, carport, or storage building. And if you do not expect to build your own garage or carport, you will need time to communicate your thoughts to an architect and/or builder.

In this chapter, the overall procedure will be discussed so that the "do-it-yourselfer" will have some idea of what is involved and the person hiring the services of an architect, engineer or builder can communicate more effectively when discussing anything from what he wants or needs to how he expects it to be done.

To begin with, a scale drawing of your lot showing the location of your house, property lines, the setback and clearances required by local zoning ordinances, trees, walkways, etc., will prove an invaluable source of information concerning existing conditions.

If you have the information needed to locate your property lines exactly, you may wish to make your own drawing. If you don't have the information, you may need to have your property sur-

---

AUTHOR *Anne Nickerson* is Extension Housing Specialist, University of New Hampshire, Durham.

CO-AUTHOR *Francis E. Gilman* is Extension Engineer at the University.

PLAN NO. 6086

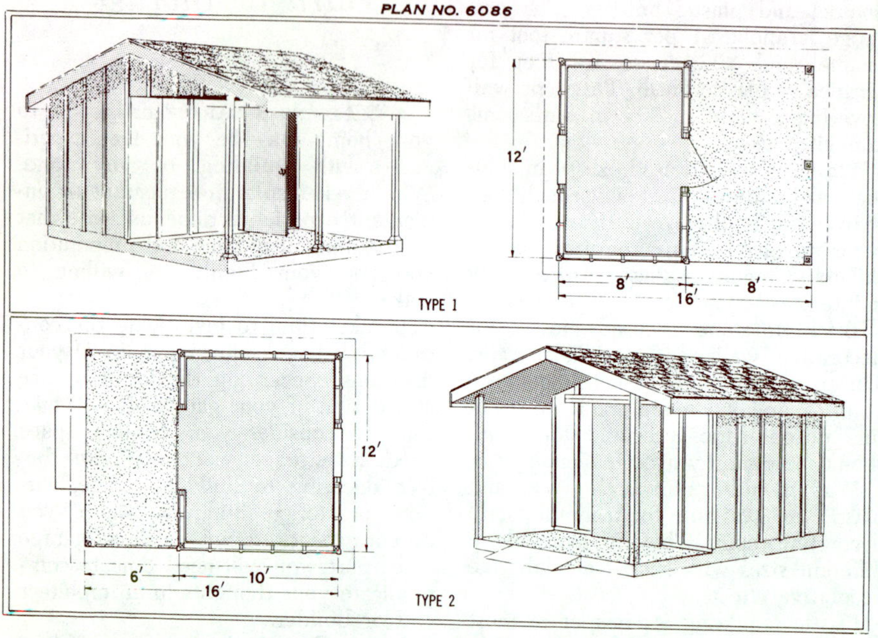

veyed. In this case, an engineer can provide you with a scale drawing of your lot, locating any additional features on it that you request.

These features would include any and all things that would prevent you from locating your garage in any position you might choose. Besides those noted previously, you would need to indicate the location of your septic tank, leaching field and/or well. Also, it would be wise to note the location of any moderate or steep slopes.

Although the information will not be shown on the plan, you need to collect information about the type of soil on which you are building, the existence and location of ledges, and the height of the water table. Most of this information can be found on a soil survey map of your county which is available through your local office of the Soil Conservation Service.

Now is the time to consider your family's space needs. The following questions may prove helpful:

1. Do you need space for one___ or two___ cars?

2. Do you need space for play or recreation? For a laundry? A greenhouse? A workshop?

3. Do you need to store any of the following items:

Garden tools	Window screens
Freezer	Storm sash
Building materials	Lawn furniture
Snowblower	Firewood
Bicycles	Snowmobiles
Boats	Travel trailer
Carpentry tools	Motor bikes

4. Do you need complete protection from the wind, rain, snow and sun?

5. Do you need partial protection from the weather for living space, play area recreation?

6. Are you trying to save money?

If you need space for storing an average car, a 12′ x 22′ structure will

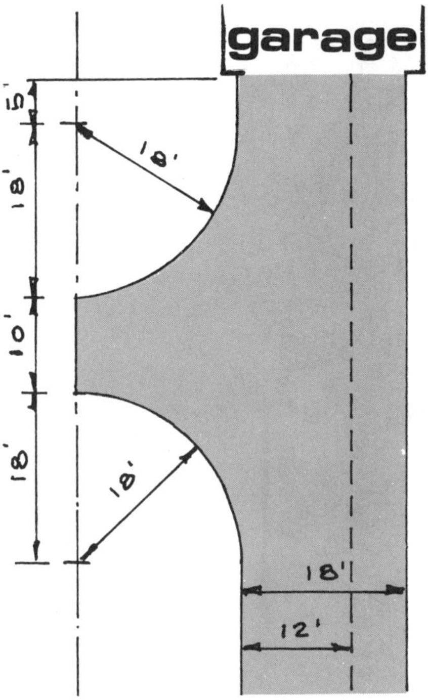

Turning "Y"

be adequate for a single car and a 24′ x 22′ structure for two cars.

For those considering a separate area for laundry, small greenhouse or workshop addition at the side or end of the garage, a minimum 5′ is suggested. A 12′-long work space would be adequate for a small greenhouse or laundry, and probably more than adequate for a work bench.

If you do not need a wall, you can use some of the garage for work space and reduce the addition to 3′.

Many of the items listed in Question #3 can be stored in an additional two feet of depth. Other items like lawn mowers, garden tractors, bicycles and snowblowers which vary greatly in dimensions may need to be stored separately.

Once you have answered the questions relating to your space needs and determined the amount of space available for placing the garage or carport in the location you and your family consider most desirable, you can probably decide whether a carport or garage would be most suitable.

If you are trying to save money and need only partial protection from the weather for your activities and storage a carport will probably provide the best solution for your family's needs.

Where you will locate your garage or carport may be determined initially by the amount of space available between the house and the edge of your property which is unrestricted by zoning or other existing conditions on the lot.

One item not previously discussed is the orientation of the garage. If the garage will block light and air from entering the house where needed, you must consider either changing its location or building a carport instead.

Another factor is the location of your driveway and turning space. For a straight driveway with a "Y" for turning and backing you will need a minimum of 15′ and a maximum of 20′ between the edge of your garage and the property line. The 18′ shown on the driveway illustration is for backing and turning a car of average length.

Other points to consider when designing driveways are ease of access and safety. A safe driveway avoids the dangers of backing into the street, steep grades, and areas that will collect water or be covered with ice in winter.

Where to locate the garage or carport in the plan is frequently easier than designing the exterior so that it looks as if it belongs there instead of being an afterthought. This can be done by adding a single car garage directly to the end of a building the same width, continuing the same roof and eave lines, and using the same exterior material and finish. Such a solution is particularly suitable when making additions to small homes 32′ to 48′ in length.

Where steep grades are encountered it is usually wise to detach the garage or carport from the house. It may not be as convenient but it avoids difficult roofing, foundation and design problems. Frequently the family is grateful for the semi-secluded space created when this is done.

If you are unsure about how your

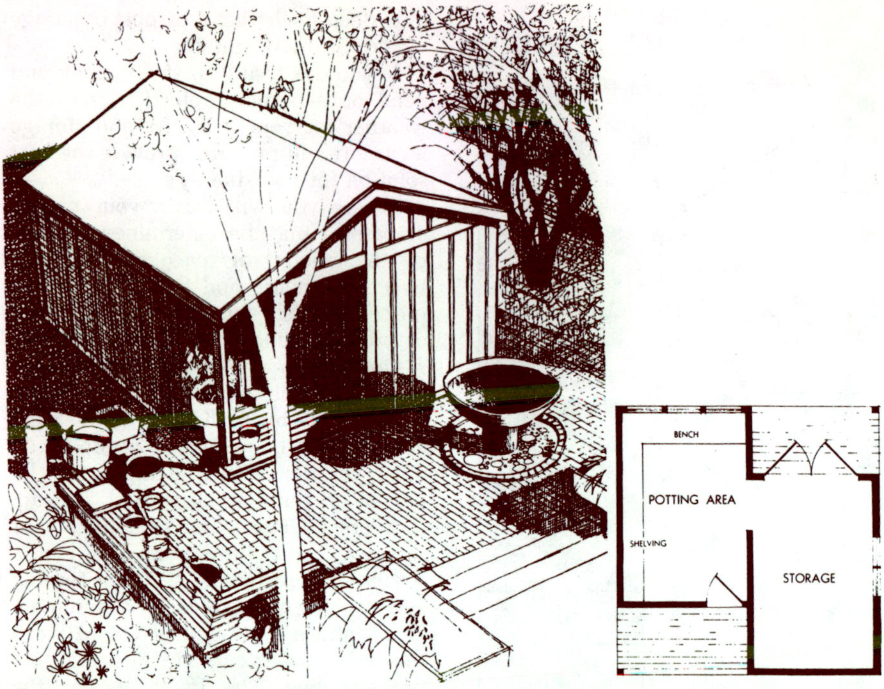

This storage and potting shed illustrates a multi-use building in which lawn and garden equipment can be stored on one side and the other side used for a potting area.

home may appear when you add a garage or carport, do not hesitate to consult an architect, house designer or specialist at your state university extension service.

It will be helpful to the person you consult if you send him the drawing you have made showing lot conditions as well as photographs of the house and a clear statement of your problem. If you have planning or construction difficulties he will be able to help you with these, too.

Having chosen the location for your garage, carport or storage building, be sure construction plans comply with any local building codes. Such codes primarily specify construction standards designed to meet the basic safety and health requirements. Proper selection and use of materials or overall prefabricated unit design, not building codes, generally determine the structure's durability and appearance.

Grading for good drainage is absolutely essential to satisfactory performance. Roofs collect water. This must be considered. So must the runoff onto the surrounding land. Structures added to existing buildings can cause problems if connections are poorly planned.

The bottom of all foundation footings should be placed below the prevailing frost penetration. Detached structures can, however, be satisfactorily built on floating slab foundations if there is good drainage under and away from this slab.

Masonry is not the only alternative for use as a permanent foundation material. Do not overlook pressure-treated wooden posts or poles. Wood treated with penetrating preservatives under pressure can be very durable. In fact, treated wood pilings driven deep into the ground support many large buildings and some major highways.

Carport and garage floor drains seem to be a perennial problem. A simple but effective way to drain a floor is to slope the whole floor toward the driveway opening. Three inches of slope in 24 feet is often recommended. But constructing this slope is easier said than done, and mistakes made laying concrete are hard to correct.

Plan #5930, prepared by the U.S. Department of Agriculture, is available from the Cooperative Extension Service at your State University. It shows how to construct a 24′ x 24′ two-car garage using pressure-treated posts. Plan #5929 is for construction of the same garage but with a conventional masonry foundation. Both are "idea" plans which can be modified to suit your specific needs.

Roof and wall design varies in different parts of the country according to what is known as live load. Live load is usually determined by the prevailing winds and snow. Unfortunately, many small buildings are structurally unsound and require much maintenance or they may be subject to total failure.

Avoid false economy. Try to be sure that the builder has the knowledge and the experience to adapt plans for your location.

Doors in new, single-car garages should be at least 9′ wide. Two-car garages might have two 9′ doors or a single large door 16′ to 18′ wide. Wide doors are helpful when the approach to a garage cannot be straight. Interior posts should be avoided whenever possible.

Well-made large or small doors are readily available with hardware permitting easy opening. Automatic or remote-controlled door-openers may be worth considering, depending on your needs. Garages used for storage should also have a pedestrian door.

Small, portable storage buildings are popular. Durability of prefabricated units varies mostly with price. Proposed use and location may determine whether or not one of these structures will suit your needs. Light construction which makes structures easily transported and low in cost may lead to poor serviceability. Failure due to wind and snow is not uncommon.

The U.S.D.A. Cooperative Plan Exchange has several good designs available from the Cooperative Extension Service at your State University. Plan #6093 is for a 10′ x 12′ storage building in the style of a traditional, gambrel-roofed barn. Plan #6086 has four designs, 12′ x 16′, 10′ x 8′, 12′ x 10′ and 12′ x 16′. Three of these plans have a gable roof and a single-slope shed roof. Plan #6100 is an expandable-shed type that may be 8′ x 8′ or 8′ x 16′.

When considering additional storage space in a garage or carport, it may be possible to add loft space around perimeter walls or directly overhead in an attic under roof slopes which are steep enough. This type of storage is good for seldom-used items and out-of-season articles.

After all plans are completed, it is only human to hope for an instant building. But you must consider your builder's schedule and the availability of materials. Substantial savings may also be possible during periods of slow construction demand.

Heavy rains or deep snows can cause costly slowdowns and should be avoided. It might be helpful to put in the foundation during good weather and build above grade whenever conditions are favorable.

FOR FURTHER READING:

U.S. Department of Agriculture. *Wood-Frame House Construction,* AH 73, for sale by Superintendent of Documents, Washington, D.C. 20402.

Midwest Plan Service, *Family Housing Handbook,* Iowa State University, Ames, Iowa.

Ramsey, Charles G. and Sleeper, Harold R. *Architectural Graphic Standards,* John Wiley & Sons, Inc., New York, N.Y., 1956.

Heating and Cooling Systems and Fuels

*M*ODERN central heating and cooling systems were rare until after World War II. Many present systems are becoming dilapidated and inefficient and may need to be upgraded or replaced. The energy shortage has focused attention on the need to maximize efficiency to reduce our energy usage.

Today's central heating and cooling systems offer the comfort level most Americans desire all year round, regardless of exterior temperatures.

Central heating systems can be classified by the types of fuel and the kind of transfer medium used to carry the heat throughout the house: The ideal heating systems should supply the amount of heat necessary to keep body heat loss in balance, while preventing drafts, by warming the floors and walls to provide steady temperatures from room to room and floor to ceiling.

The hot air gravity system was one of the first widely popular warm air central heating systems. Despite deficiencies it is still being installed in some small homes today and many furnaces are still in use.

In this system, cold air is heated in the furnace and rises, by natural circulation, through many small pipes from a large furnace that resembles a giant octopus. Air rises and enters the rooms either through floor or side-wall registers.

The air is normally very hot, usually dirty, and moves slowly, resulting in uneven distribution throughout the house. With the exception of some very small homes, this type furnace should be replaced with a modern forced air system, because the major portion of the duct work can be used with the forced air system.

Another gravity type hot air system is the floor furnace, which is normally suspended below the floor so that hot air rises through a large floor grill. There are usually no ducts, and the system is inexpensive to install.

This furnace is unsuitable for large multi-room areas because there is no air circulation through the furnace. The grill can become extremely hot and is especially dangerous to small children because of the chance of being burned. These heaters are rarely satisfactory except in mild climates, in cottages, or for supplemental heat in areas beyond the main heating system.

Forced warm air systems corrected the deficiencies of the gravity system. With this setup, the furnace has a fan or blower that pushes the warmed air through small ducts that may be run horizontally as well as vertically, allowing much more flexibility in their placement.

The system can be installed in homes with or without basements, as the furnace need not be below the area to be heated nor centrally located. The furnace can be located in a utility room, attic or crawl space of a house. The furnace blower circulates heated air to all rooms in the house, and one or more return grills and ducts carry the cool air back to the furnace where it is reheated.

Forced warm air systems heat uniformly and respond rapidly to changes in temperature.

A system in proper working order does not create dirt or dust. It does, however, stir up already existing dust and redistributes it. This may be turned to advantage by the installing throw-away filters which can remove the larger dust particles, or electrostatic air cleaners that electrically charge the dust particles and remove up to 90 percent of them by attaching the particles to metal collector plates.

Electrostatic air cleaners will remove pollen and other irritants that pass

---

AUTHOR *Luther C. Godbey* is Agricultural Engineer, Rural Housing Research Unit, Agricultural Research Service, Clemson, S.C.

GRAVITY HOT AIR SYSTEM

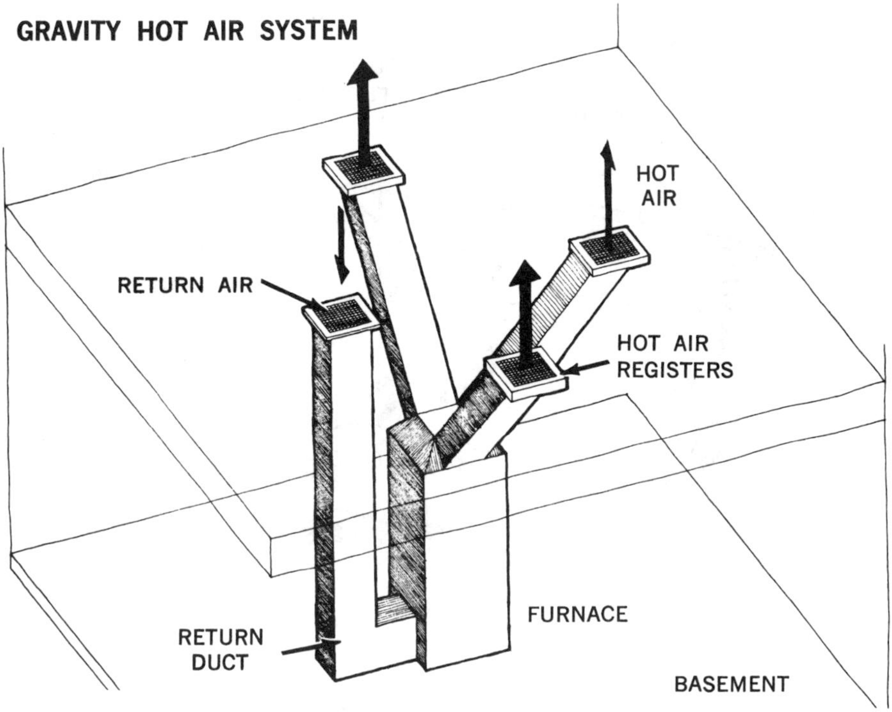

EXTENDED PLENUM WARM AIR SYSTEM

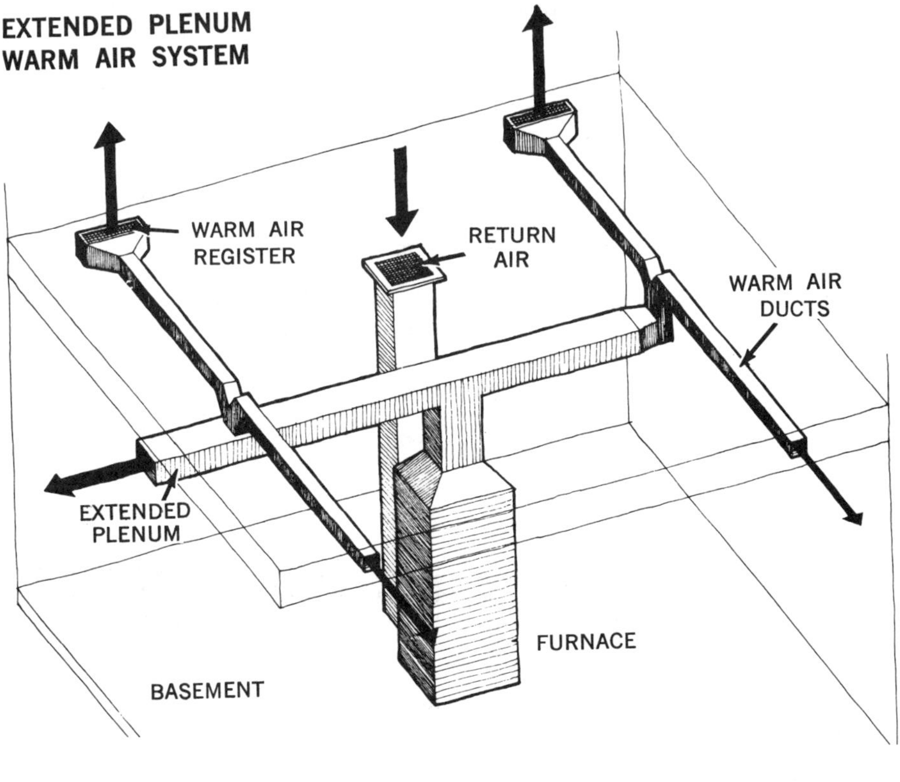

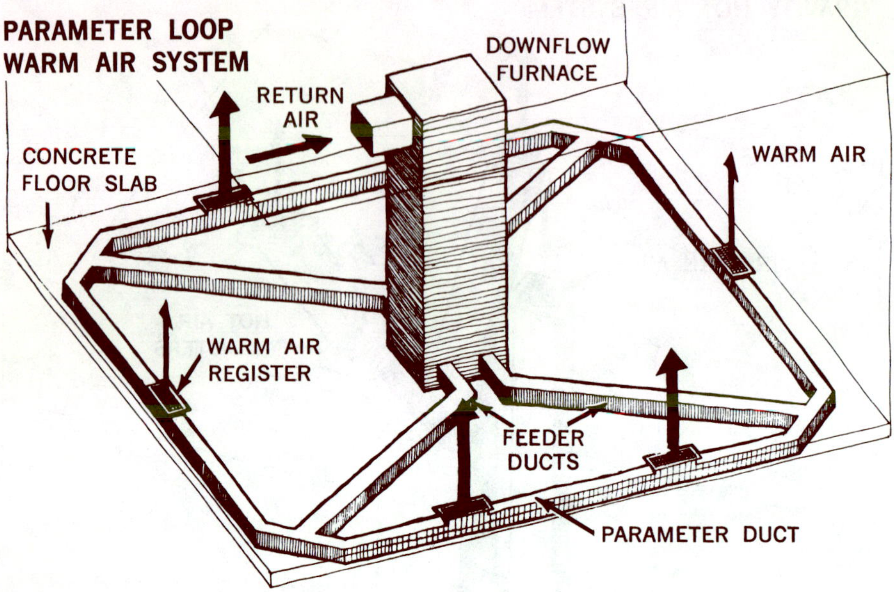

through porous media filters. Some manufacturers now claim that their units will even clear tobacco smoke from the air.

The more expensive units feature automatic washing and drying of the cleaner. This is important because the cleaners are extremely efficient and remove considerable amounts of material; they must be cleaned often. For a person with allergies or other respiratory ailments, these cleaners offer considerable relief, as well as reducing the amount of dusting the homemaker must contend with.

Dry air in the winter can be a problem with all types of heating systems. Humidity added to the air can make you feel warmer so your thermostats can be lowered to save energy and reduce your heating bill.

You can install a humidifying device in a hot air heating system, or add a portable humidifying device to other systems. Often a small vaporizer in the bedroom at night will solve the problem. Two types of humidifiers are available to mount on the plenum system of your furnace for total home humidification.

The first and least expensive is the evaporator plate type that fits in the distribution plenum. Occasionally, these plates must be replaced and the humidifier pan cleaned.

The most expensive type injects small vapor particles into the furnace air system. This is the easiest to control, with a humidistat in the return air supply duct, and is the most problem-free in regard to maintenance. Normally the humidity of a home should be kept below 40 percent because at this point moisture will condense on windows and other cold surfaces. Twenty-five to 30 percent relative humidity is sufficient for comfortable living.

Other types of hot air systems include free standing unit heaters that may be fueled by gas, oil, electricity or a solid fuel such as wood or coal. They are sufficient for use in small areas, but do not provide well-regulated, even distribution of heat throughout the room they are located in and the heat cannot be easily transferred to other rooms.

In a hot water (hydronic) system, water is heated in a boiler made of cast iron or steel and is then pumped by one or more circulators through small pipes

RADIAL DUCT WARM AIR SYSTEM

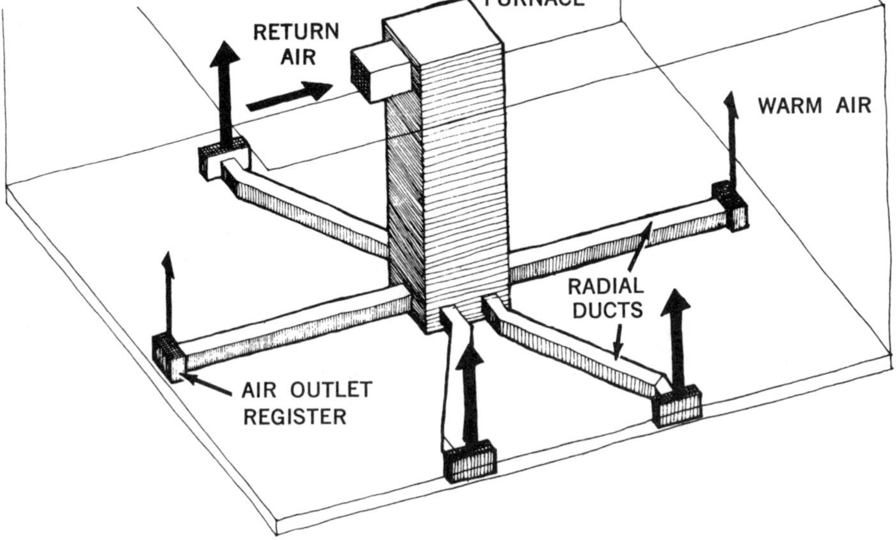

to individual room heating units (radiators or convectors). Heat is added to cool air as it moves through the finned tubing of the convectors; this heat is circulated by natural convection throughout the room.

Water is an excellent heating medium, retaining heat longer than other common media. Three types of hot water piping systems are in widespread use today.

The first and most popular system, because of its relatively low cost, has hot water piped through individual room convectors in series to various rooms and then returned to the boiler. Disadvantage of this system is lack of control over the amount of heat to an individual room or convector. The most heat is liberated at the first convector in the line and the last convector provides the least heat.

A second system is also a one-pipe system. It differs from the first in that the radiators or convectors do not circulate all the water through each convector. The convector takes the hot water from a main supply line and this water can be metered into the convector to regulate the heat.

As water leaves the convectors it reenters the supply lines by means of a special "T", which produces a suction on the return line from the convector by means of a siphoning action of the main line water flow. The water then circulates to the next register.

This system is somewhat improved over the single pipe series system in that each convector can be controlled. The basic problem still exists, though, of the first radiator receiving hotter water than the last.

A third system, and by far the most superior and the most costly, uses separate supply and return pipes. The supply pipe feeds each individual register, which allows each one to receive water of the same temperature. Water is not recirculated through other registers, but is returned to the boiler and reheated to the proper temperature before it is returned to the register.

This system requires larger diameter pipes than the two previous systems, but each individual register can be controlled by a separate thermostat with electric valve or by adjustable metering valves placed in the supply line to the individual register.

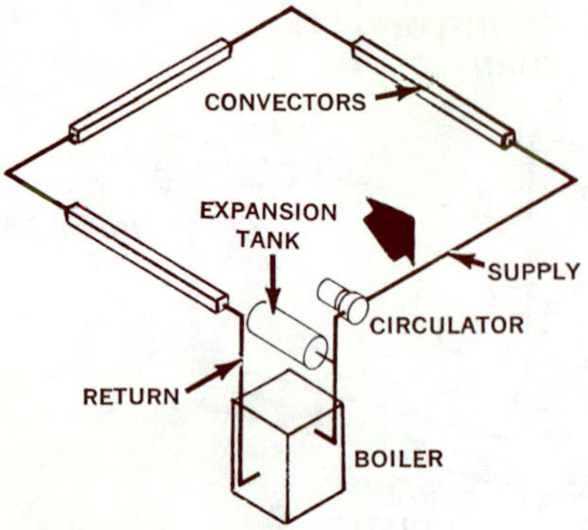

ONE-PIPE SERIES CONNECTED HOT WATER SYSTEM

Hot water systems are very adaptable in that the pipes running to the radiators take up very little space in the head room of a basement compared to the large ducts of a warm air system. A hot water system can be expanded to meet other needs—such as for melting ice and snow on sidewalks and driveways, heating a swimming pool, or heating a green house.

Steam heat is produced by a boiler with a fire box underneath it that is similar to a hot water furnace except it must be stronger. The water in the boiler boils, making steam which is forced by its pressure through pipes into radiators located throughout the house.

There are two systems for radiator piping. One is a single-pipe system in which steam cools, turns into water, and runs back to the furnace to repeat the cycle. In the two-pipe system condensed steam returns by a separate pipe. All steam heating systems have an inherent noise, but the two-pipe system tends to be less noisy than the one pipe system.

These heating systems are extremely difficult to control, especially when only small amounts of heat are needed. Consequently, they are found only in very large and usually older homes. Forced hot water systems are as a rule installed in newer homes rather than steam.

Electricity can be used with any of the heating systems mentioned above in the same way as coal, gas, or oil—it can be thought of as just another fuel. It becomes unique in house heating when used with resistant elements which produce heat in much the same manner as an electric toaster, in the immediate area to be heated.

The most popular form of electric heaters are individual baseboard units controlled by a thermostat in the same room.

Electrical unit heaters can be mounted in the wall, using blowers to force the air out into the room. These can be used advantageously in large areas, or areas with insufficient room to put a baseboard convector.

Electrical resistance cables can be placed in ceilings or floors to provide radiant heat. They are imbedded at the time of construction, or may be installed later and a new topping put over them.

The electric heating system is one of the least expensive to install compared to other fuel systems. It also provides the advantage of individual temperature control for each room.

One of the better uses for electric heat is for bathrooms, hobby rooms or other areas where auxilliary heat is needed for short periods, or when adding new rooms in which it would be difficult to extend the present heating system. Often the present heating system may not have adequate capacity to heat additional room areas.

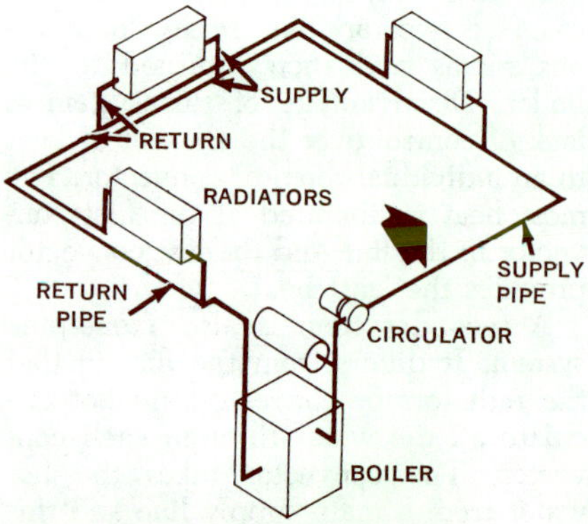

TWO PIPE REVERSE RETURN HOT WATER SYSTEM

Before installing any electric heating units, make certain your wiring service entrance is sufficient. Existing homes generally do not have enough extra capacity for these units. In most cases, a new and larger service entrance will be required.

Another type of electric heating system worth considering is the heat pump. It operates much like a refrigerator, and is actually a reversible air conditioning unit.

In winter, the heat pump absorbs heat from outside air, from the ground, or from well water and distributes it in the house. In summer, the system reverses and extracts heat from the inside of the house like a typical air conditioning unit.

The heat pump's efficiency decreases when it is very cold outside, and it must usually be supplemented with resistance heating.

This modern heating and cooling system is becoming more and more popular in warmer areas of the country, particularly where the home uses electric heat. The heat pump is extremely efficient and will produce approximately twice as many BTU per kilowatt as standard electrical resistant heating.

Today, solar heating is still in the primitive stages of development. The first commercial solar heat units generally have heat collectors that are used to heat water, which in turn can be used for either domestic hot water or pumped throughout the house similar to a hydronic system to provide heat.

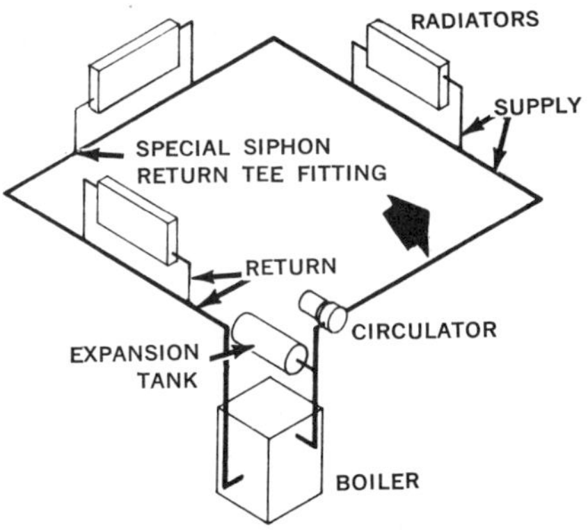

SINGLE PIPE INDIVIDUAL FEED HOT WATER SYSTEM

Fuels

What fuels should you select? This will depend on which heating fuel representative you talk to. Each proclaims the merits of his own product and the disadvantages of the competitors. Each fuel has its own significant advantages and disadvantages and must be considered against your individual needs and preferences and then weighed against the relative cost in your area.

The ideal time to select a heating system and fuel, of course, is before the house is built. It rarely pays to tear out a working system and replace it. If the furnace does need to be replaced, consideration should then be given to changing fuels.

Natural gas, liquid petroleum (LP) gas, fuel oil and electricity are all about equally safe and clean. Coke and coal are definitely dirtier.

With the exception of a few isolated areas of the country, coal and coke are rarely used in new systems for residential heating. In general, systems using them as fuel are fast becoming obsolete—although the energy crisis could bring a change. Where coal and coke are used, the extent of safety and cleanliness is governed by the condition of the heating system itself.

Fuel oil may be the least expensive fuel in the Northeast and Northwest sections of the country, and it may be competitive in many other sections. Fuel oil may be stored in the basement of the house in free standing tanks, not larger in size than 275 gallons (larger tanks or more than two tanks in the basement are considered unsafe).

Most oil companies offer automatic delivery, virtually assuring a continuous supply with a reserve in the event of interrupted service. Automatic delivery is accomplished by using the degree day method of determining the amount of heat required and knowing the size and heat loss characteristics of your home.

In most areas of the country except the Northeast and the Northwest, natural gas is the most economical fuel. Gas, like electricity, is normally sold on a sliding rate scale—the more you use the less it costs per unit.

Therefore, you may be able to obtain a smaller gas rate if you use gas for hot water heating and cooking.

A gas burner and furnace is less complex than an oil furnace and requires less maintenance. Gas needs no on-site storage, but in the event of supply interruption, there is no reserve.

L.P.G. (Liquid Petroleum Gas) is used mainly in rural areas. It requires an on-premise storage tank and is usually more expensive than natural pipeline gas. In other respects, it is similar to natural gas. A minor change is required in gas burning appliances to change from liquid petroleum to natural gas or vice-versa.

L.P.G. is a fuel like gasoline, in that it is heavier than air and the fumes from leaks are likely to accumulate in the lower areas of a house, such as the crawl space or basement. Natural gas is lighter than air and it will rise and be more easily dissipated into the air. Where L.P.G. is used, the location of the equipment and storage tank will be governed by codes in many cases, but regardless the storage and equipment should be located as recommended by the fuel supplier.

Heating the entire house electrically is economical only in communities where rates are low.

Power companies insist on certain minimum insulation values for your home to enable you to obtain what they call an electric heating rate, which is normally lower than the normal rate above a certain minimum power usage. It is highly recommended that you insulate and weatherstrip your home thoroughly no matter which fuel or heating system you select, because of the energy situation and its rapidly rising costs.

Electricity requires no on-site storage and can be used with hot air or hot water heating systems like coal, gas or oil. Electricity is unique when used in unit resistant heaters such as baseboards or wall heaters with or without fans. These units offer convenience, cleanliness and evenness of heat. No chimney is required unless you desire a fireplace.

Electricity is the energy source used for the heat pump, described earlier.

Cooling

There are three main types of cooling that you may use in your home. The one you choose will depend upon how much you are willing to invest, both initially and for operating expenses. The climate in your area and the type heating system you have or will select will be a factor in determining the method of cooling.

You can use room-type fans to produce air movement in a room. This increases moisture evaporation, which has a cooling effect on the body or skin surface.

The most effective fans have large blades that rotate at about 1,000 revolutions per minute (RPM) and are equipped with an oscillating mechanism. The fan may be a large pedestal type floor model or a smaller table model.

Attic and window fans pull cool outside air into the house and exhaust warmer air produced by heat buildup during the warmer part of the day. These fans are effective at night and when the outside air temperature is below the inside temperature. When your house has cooled off at night, close up the house the next day as long as it is cooler inside than outside.

Window fans are easy to install—simply set them in the window and plug them in. Attic fans must be installed and an opening provided in the ceiling. These fans should have louvers that open when the fan is on and close at other times. Permanent wiring is required for an attic fan, and a switch or an elapsed-time timer is needed to control its operation.

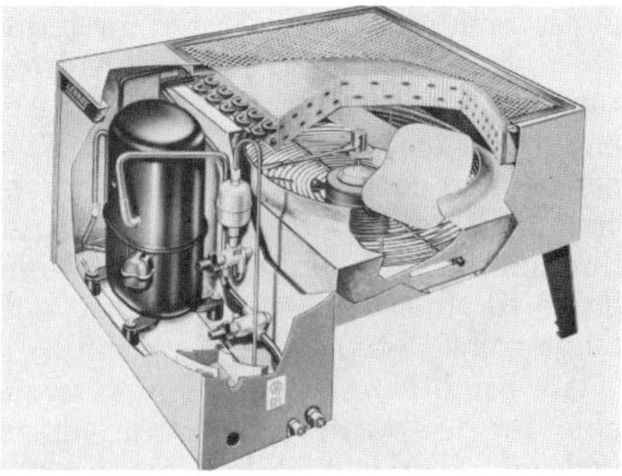

Fans are rated by the amount of air they will move at a certain pressure in cubic feet per minute (c.f.m.). The size fan you select depends on the area you live in and the volume of air you need to move.

Take the length and width of the area you plan to cool, whether it be the room or the complete house, and get the square footage. Then multiply this by the wall heights to obtain the volume you want to cool. This figure will be the same as the c.f.m. rating you will need for the fan except in some mountainous areas, and areas along the northern tier of states, which have cool nights. In these areas, the fan capacity can be reduced by about 33 percent.

Night cooling has some disadvantages. The fan is apt to produce noises in the living quarters and pull dust and humidity into the house.

In some areas of the Southwest and West, the humidity is very low, particularly during periods of high heat. In these areas, evaporative cooling is a useful method. This occurs when air is blown across or through a wet porous media. When the water evaporates, absorbing heat from the air, temperature of the air is reduced.

Package units are made for home installation in windows and duct systems. These are simple machines and are less expensive, both initially and in operating cost, than conventional air conditioning. The water consumption is 5 to 10 gallons per hour for an average size home.

When the comfort desired cannot be obtained solely by house design and night ventilation, use of an air conditioning system is suggested. Insulation, attic ventilation and shading of windows are necessary for efficient, economical operation. During many periods of the year, night cooling using an attic or window fan will reduce considerably the amount of time the air conditioning system must operate.

While it is desirable to select a compatible heating and cooling system at the time of construction, this is not always possible.

For existing homes, central air conditioning equipment is available in many arrangements to suit the location—basement, crawlspace, utility room, attic or roof. Small room and multiroom size self-contained units are available to fit in windows or through an opening in the wall.

Air conditioners are rated in terms of "tons of cooling capacity." A 1-ton capacity is equivalent to the melting of one ton of ice per day, or 12,000 BTU per hour of cooling. Unit air conditioners vary from 1/3 to 2½ tons for large through-the-wall units. Central units designed for home installations will range from 1½-ton to 5-ton capacity.

Air conditioning equipment is available for use with your warm air or hydronic (hot water) heating systems.

The hot water system is used in room units resembling convectors and containing the heating and cooling coils. These units normally contain a small air circulating blower, operated by a room thermostat.

The cooling coils can be placed in ducts and the air from rooms circulated through them. This system can also use hot water for winter heat if desired.

Central air conditioning systems can be separate systems with their own ducts or they can be combined with a forced air heating system.

Cooling requires a greater amount of air flow than heating. If you choose an add-on system, it will probably be necessary to increase the fan capacity of your furnace, and you may need to enlarge or even relocate your distribution ducts. Larger ducts decrease the velocity of the air and the noise resulting from high air speeds.

Central air-conditioning systems tend to be less noisy because they are located away from the living area. The best location for air conditioning registers is in the side wall near the ceiling, or else use diffusers in the ceiling.

Heating grills are best located at lower levels. If economy dictates using only one grill for both heating and cooling, locate the grill near the floor.

The central system is normally a split system with the evaporator coils located downstream of the fan in the duct. The condenser unit sits outside the house and contains the condenser coils, condenser fan, compressor and coils. The two units are connected by a gas tube and a return liquid line.

The cool evaporator coil in the duct cools the air and allows moisture in the circulating air to condense on it and drip off, with the moisture then piped away. Humidity is lowered in the air stream but there is no control over the humidity. In some very humid areas, a dehumidifier may be required to supplement the air conditioning system to help prevent mold and mildew within the house.

Millions of room type air conditioners are manufactured and sold each year. They provide an economical method of cooling a small section of a house.

Major disadvantage is the high noise level produced in the area to be cooled. The units may be unattractive on both the exterior and interior, and are not a good solution for year-round home temperature control.

Smaller units up to one horsepower can be connected to a 115-volt household plug. Larger units are usually 220 volts and require an individual electric circuit.

The heat pump has become more popular in warmer areas of the U.S., as it is both a heating and cooling unit. The cooling cycle is the same as for a standard split system air conditioner. Heating characteristics were described in the heating section of this chapter.

FOR FURTHER READING:

U.S. Department of Agriculture. *Equipment for Cooling Your Home,* G 100, for sale by Superintendent of Documents, Washington, D.C. 20402, 1970.

———. *Home Heating,* F 2235, for sale by Superintendent of Documents, Washington, D.C. 20402, 1968.

EQUIPMENT

Kitchen Appliances, Including Freezers and Range Hoods

TODAY'S HOME has four or five major appliances and a dozen or more smaller ones. Expenses for such household equipment include purchasing, operating, and servicing costs.

Most dealers stock middle-of-the-line models of appliances which meet the needs of most consumers. The bottom-of-the-line appliance will do the basic task for which it is designed but will have no extra conveniences nor will it allow choices for the user. Top-of-the-line appliances may have many extras, programmed cycles, and many choices for the user—all of which add to the initial cost.

The appliance should carry an Underwriters' Laboratories seal which signifies that the product design meets safety requirements for fire, electrical shock, and related accident hazards to the user. Gas appliances should carry the American Gas Association blue star which certifies that the product meets national safety standards.

The Association of Home Appliance Manufacturers seal certifies that the net refrigerated volume and shelf area of refrigerators and freezers are as stated. It also certifies the stated water removal capacity of dehumidifiers and output in gallons of water per day for humidifiers, and the stated BTU/hour cooling capacity, amperes, and watts rating on air conditioners.

The Home Ventilating Institute label assures the consumer that the air movement performance in cubic feet per minute of a range hood fan is accurate, based on independent tests of a recognized authority on air movement engineering.

Principal and interest payments on appliances purchased as part of the home mortgage are made over the entire period of the mortgage. Due to the long period of interest payments, the total cost of the appliance is more than twice the purchase price. A $400 appliance purchased on a 25-year, 8 percent mortgage would cost the buyer more than $900. If the appliance lasts 15 years, the buyer is paying for a "dead horse" for the last 10 years.

With emphasis on conservation of energy, the consumer is interested in the efficiency of appliances. The energy efficiency ratio for room air conditioners is available to the consumer. The higher the EER, the more efficient the air conditioner.

According to the Stanford Research Institute, 19 percent of the energy is consumed by the residential sector. Of this, 57.5 percent is consumed in home heating, 15.1 percent in heating water, 10.9 percent in lighting and operating miscellaneous appliances, 5.7 percent in cooking, 5.7 percent in refrigeration, 3.6 percent in air conditioning, and 1.6 percent in drying clothes.

Brown-outs (voltage reduction) may occur during air conditioning peak usage. Appliance manufacturers design appliances to operate from a minimum of 104 volts to a maximum of 127 volts.

AUTHOR *Jacqueline Anderson* is Assistant Professor in the School of Human Resources and Family Studies, University of Illinois, at Urbana-Champaign.

Brown-outs cause heating appliances such as toasters, coffeemakers, frypans, and ranges to heat more slowly.

Voltage reductions do not cause permanent damage to heating appliances. The effect on motor-driven appliances, especially those with induction motors with a split phase or capacitator start principle, is much more complex. The life of the motor can be dramatically shortened. When the picture on a television shrinks so there is a ½″ to 1″ band around it, motors should be disconnected.

No appliance lasts forever. An idea of the expected life of an appliance can be gained from a USDA study written up in the January 1964 *Journal of Home Economics.*

The Association of Home Appliance Manufacturers has established recommended guidelines for warranties that can be read quickly and easily and be understood. Most manufacturers have rewritten their warranties using those guidelines.

Information should include who is making the guarantee, what the guarantee covers, for how long, and who is going to do the work.

The owner should read and study the instruction booklet that comes with an appliance, and then store it in a convenient place for future reference.

If service is needed, an authorized and reputable serviceman should be contacted. The brand, model number, and a detailed description of the problem should be relayed to the person taking the message. The consumer should expect quality service wherever she may live when she needs it at reasonable costs.

The consumer must realize that service call costs must cover not only the technician's time in the home, but time traveling between jobs, costs of training the service technician, fringe benefits for the technician, tools, trucks, a building with utilities, parts inventory investment, office personnel, and taxes.

The service technician expects the consumer to check for burned-out fuses, disconnected electric plugs, and dust, dirt or soil that would interfere with operation of the appliance. The technician expects an adult to be at home at the time of the service call, or other arrangements to be made in case the consumer may not be at home.

If all attempts for satisfaction from the local dealer and/or repair service and manufacturer fail, the consumer may appeal to the Major Appliance Consumer Action Panel (MACAP) for assistance. MACAP is a panel of members who serve as ombudsmen to make recommendations regarding complaint handling and final disposition of cases to industry.

There are features that energy conscious consumers should be aware of in household equipment.

A dishwasher that dries dishes by natural air convection eliminates the need for fans that move the heated air over the dishes.

A microwave range with a wattage output of at least 600 watts is desirable.

A 46 percent efficiency is considered normal. The wattage output divided by the wattage input gives the efficiency. Microwave cooking is more efficient than oven cooking at 25 percent efficiency, but less efficient than surface cookery at 60 to 80 percent efficiency.

Of the ranges readily available on the market today, the conventional range and the smooth-top range with a thermostat in each unit are more efficient than smooth-top ranges with conventional heating elements.

A few manufacturers put an on-off switch for the resistance heater which prevents condensation around the refrigerator door in humid weather. The heater can be turned off during the heating season or if the house is air conditioned.

The compressor of a manual defrost refrigerator operates approximately 30 percent of the time while the compressor of a frost-free model will operate 40 to 60 percent of the time. Fans must move the cold air throughout the interior of a frost-free model.

A clothes washing machine which uses fewer gallons of hot water can save on fuel used for heating water. One current consumers magazine shows in chart form that the amount of hot water used varies from 15 gallons in the least thirsty brand to 25 gallons in the most thirsty brand.

A water level selector allows the user to correlate water level with the size of load to be washed.

A room air conditioner with an EER of at least 7 is desirable. An EER of 8 to 11 is even better, but consumers should make sure they are selecting the correct size room air conditioner by using the cooling load estimate form that can be obtained from the dealer, *Consumer Reports Buying Guide*, or the Association of Home Appliance Manufacturers.

The following suggestions on selection, use, and care of selected large and small appliances complement the 1973 Yearbook of Agriculture chapters, *Major Appliances for Homemakers* (pages 289 to 295), and *Buying Smaller Appliances* (pages 296 to 302).

Freezers

There are two main styles of food freezers.

Chest freezers are lower in initial cost and operating cost and spread the weight of appliance and food over a larger floor area. Little cold air is lost when the freezer is opened. Items may be more difficult to find and more difficult to remove if they are near the bottom of the freezer.

Uprights take less floor space but concentrate the weight in a smaller area. Food is easier to locate and remove, but cold air has a tendency to spill out when the door is opened.

Freezers may be manual defrost, automatic defrost, or frost-free. Some manual defrost freezers have a control that allows the user to turn on a heater or allow hot refrigerant to flow through the coils to speed up the melting of accumulated frost. A drain for the defrost water is convenient.

Automatic defrost food freezers allow hot refrigerant to flow through the cooling coils at preset time intervals, which melts off accumulated frost.

The frost-free food freezer collects frost on a plate between the walls. Fans continually move the cold air. The constantly moving air tends to dry out food that is not packaged in moisture, vapor-proof materials and containers. The frost-free freezer costs more initially, and operating cost is greater than for the manual or automatic defrost food freezer.

The size of freezer should depend upon the family's use of this appliance. If the freezer is only a supplement to weekly shopping trips, 3 cubic feet per family member should be adequate. Six cubic feet per person might be preferred if the family purchases meat in quantities and produces some of their fruits and vegetables.

In summary, freezing and storing food adds 10¢ to 25¢ per pound to the cost of the food itself. The food freezer becomes a good investment financially only if half or more of the family's food is home produced or purchased at "bargain" prices, and when the family uses the freezer continually and to capacity.

To determine the financial soundness of buying meat by the side, use the form provided in the U.S. Department of Agriculture Home and Garden Bulletin No. 166, *How to Buy Meat for Your Freezer*.

Range Hoods

Odors, grease, smoke, water vapor, and heat in the kitchen may be removed by a range hood.

The vented hood dispels all these contaminants out of doors. The shortest, most direct route with the fewest elbows promotes dispersal. Contaminants may be discharged through a roof cap, wall cap, or eave cap. The motor blower assembly should be easy to remove for cleaning off grease and to oil the motor bearings.

The non-vented range hood's effectiveness is determined by air movement and the efficiency of the filters. A combination of three filters—aluminum mesh, fiberglass, and charcoal—will remove odors, grease and smoke but not water vapor and heat.

Aluminum mesh traps grease and

should be washed every 2 to 4 weeks in hot water with detergent. Fiberglass filters smoke, grease, and odor. Charcoal removes odors and should be replaced every 6 to 12 months.

Types of fan blades used in exhaust fans or hood fans may be propeller or centrifugal blower (squirrel cage). The latter operates more quietly and efficiently than the propeller.

The Home Ventilating Institute recommends a minimum of 40 cubic feet per minute (CFM) of air moved per linear foot of range surface, or a minimum of 120 CFM. Members of the institute provide information certifying the amount of air moved in CFM, and sound-level ratings, on a tag attached to the unit.

Small Appliances

Since there is little difference in overall quality among most frypans, other factors such as size, shape, cooking surface, covered depth, warm-up speed, and handle location and type should be considered.

The temperature control should range from 150° F (keep warm) to 425° (fry). A vent in the lid allows more flexibility in cooking processes.

Electric food warming trays may be used to warm plates or keep foods at serving temperatures. They vary in size from a 6-inch unit to a unit 52 inches long.

Some models are on when they are connected to an electrical source. Some have a high-low setting; and others have adjustable thermostatic controls. Hot spots that are said to hold temperatures about 40° F higher than the rest of the tray may increase the temperature only 10° to 15° and may not be located beneath the designated spot on the surface.

For long holding of food, temperatures above 150° F are desirable to prevent the growth or multiplication of bacteria.

One of the earliest thermostatically controlled appliances was the cooker-fryer. The heating element is housed in the same shell as the container for food.

Electric casserole or slow cooker.

The heat control should allow a wide range of temperature selections to allow low temperatures for the slow cooking of stews, pot roasts and baked beans, and high temperatures for deep-fat frying.

Look for sturdy construction, easy-to-see signal light, and heat resistant handles, legs and knobs.

A probe thermostat allows the entire utensil to be immersed in water for ease of cleaning.

A recent derivative of the cooker-fryer is the electric casserole or slow cooker. The electric unit may be housed in the same shell as the food container, or in a base separate from the food container. This is similar to a hot plate with a utensil. Temperature and time are very similar to those used for oven cookery.

Another variation has heating coils wound around the side of the appliance between the crockery food container and the metal outer shell. There is a high and low setting. One hour on the high setting equals 2 to 2½ hours on the low.

Wattage of the low setting is comparable to the warm setting of a 6″ electric range unit. The high setting is comparable to the low setting of a 6″ electric range unit or the warm setting of the 8″ unit.

The utensil should be at least half full for best results. Temperature of the contents may show a 20° F difference between that near the outside of the appliance and that in the center. Occasional stirring may help overcome this problem with liquid or chunky foods, but not with volume pieces of meat.

Cooking foods at the high setting for the first hour and on low for the remaining time helps bring the temperature of the food to 140° F within the USDA recommended maximum time of 4 hours for protein foods.

FOR FURTHER READING:

U.S. Department of Agriculture. *How to Buy Meat for Your Freezer,* G 166, for sale by Superintendent of Documents, Washington, D.C. 20402.

———. *Handbook for the Home,* 1973 Yearbook of Agriculture, for sale by Superintendent of Documents, Washington, D.C. 20402.

Washers, Dryers, Related Equipment

APPLIANCES and related equipment used to care for clothing may be organized as you plan a specific utility area. Families may prefer to locate centers used to wash, dry, iron, and mend clothing in different areas of the home.

Convenience and good use of space are important as you select and place laundry equipment. To save steps, locate the laundry area on the same floor level as other work areas of the house.

If you do laundry while you work in the kitchen, put the washer and dryer in a utility area or hall near the kitchen. If space allows, put them in a corner of the kitchen. Another good location is in the bathroom or hall near the bedrooms, for most household linens and clothing are used and stored there.

AUTHOR *Jean K. Carlson* is Extension Specialist, Management and Household Equipment, Kansas State University, Manhattan.

Place the washer next to a sink or laundry tub where you can pre-treat clothes before washing. Put the dryer beside the washer for your convenience in handling wet clothes. Wet clothes often weigh twice as much as dry ones. Allow at least 3′ of workspace in front of the laundry equipment.

Appliance manufacturers offer many kinds of laundry equipment. Different models may fit your space or special needs better than others. Selection of laundry equipment is important since this equipment will be used for many years and represents a major portion of the appliance dollar.

As textiles and fabric finishes change you should select equipment to help insure fabric appearance retention. Special appliance features and improvements are designed for this purpose.

Washers are available in many types of models. They may be classified as wringer, portable, or automatic machines.

Wringer washers require considerable hand operation, but are less expensive. They may be preferred by families with specific water problems. Some families may select the non-automatic washer to help them manage large quantities of laundry on a specific wash day. New fabrics may be more difficult to handle in the wringer washer.

Many portable washers are spinner washers. The clothes are washed in one tub and rinsed in another. These have been designed for use with minimum space and perhaps a limited water supply. Some portables are available as smaller automatic machines. They also can be purchased with casters and unicouples for use in varied places.

Automatic washers fill, wash, drain, rinse and extract water with one setting of the controls. Many have special features to perform a variety of specific laundry tasks.

Consider what type of controls and features you want on your machine. Special features usually add costs and many may even complicate service problems. Some machines are completely pre-programmed. These may have an advantage for the person who does not like to make decisions for the details of each wash load. Others may find it better to select a model that lets you program the variables of laundry procedures.

Some may need to consider how many family members are using the laundry appliances as they make selections. Today's laundry loads contain a variety of fibers, fabrics, colors, and construction. They need to be washed in special ways.

Some features related to operation of the automatic washer are: type of fill control, design to remove sediment, kind of rinse, and cycle speed during washing and spinning operations.

The total amount of water and the amount of hot water used varies between models. With special water and energy problems this may be a most important fact to consider before purchase. Many knit cycles use extra amounts of cool water.

Machines in most manufacturers' lines have variable water fill capacities. Some families may prefer to do most of their laundry in large and more economical loads. Others may find it best to use several different load sizes in any week. If you seldom need a large washer, consider the compact washer.

Most manufacturers provide dispensers to add laundry products to the wash at the correct time. These may be especially important to you if your laundry equipment is placed far away from other work areas.

Installation of automatic washers should meet local electrical and plumbing standards. It is suggested that washers be leveled and installed to individual-equipment circuits. Washer manufacturers will specify the correct water pressure needs. Water temperatures and quality may also need to be selection variables.

Automatic dryers reduce the time and effort required for drying. They also help a family have greater flexibility in laundry management. Dryers can help reduce the need for some clothing and storage space.

Dryers are offered in bottom, middle, and top-of-the-line models. The price often depends on number of features, flexibility, size, and construction.

Lower priced models may give you less flexibility of time and temperature controls. Some may have a choice of venting and cool down cycles.

As dryers get more expensive they may become more automatic. The most expensive models require less attention and judgment by the user. A number of manufacturers have added special cycles to their dryers, and convenience options.

Wrinkle prevention or appearance retention is of primary importance as you select a dryer. More and more dryers are doing the ironing for the homemaker. For this reason you may be interested in knit, permanent press, or wrinkle relaxing cycles.

There are two basic types of automatic drying. One is moisture sensing, and the other is a temperature sensing control.

The moisture sensing control system is used in electronic dryers. This is done by setting a particular control. The temperature and degree of dryness can be set for the temperature controlled dryer.

Portable dryers are compact low temperature dryers designed for limited space. These may be sold in combination with washers or individually. They operate on regular household electricity. They usually have half the capacity of a full-size dryer. They may be moved on rollers or even installed above the washer on special wall brackets. Some homes use them as a second dryer.

The venting of a dryer is important when buying or installing this appliance. It is desirable and highly recommended that most clothes dryers be vented to the exterior. This will prevent accumulations of lint and moisture. It will also maintain drying efficiency and save on energy costs. The dryer should also have an adequate air supply to operate at peak efficiency.

Proper installation of a dryer is very critical. Poor leveling can contribute to unsatisfactory tumbling characteristics. A gas or electric dryer should be installed according to local ordinances.

Automatic dryers are available in electric or gas models. There is little difference in performance between the fuels. Generally gas dryers are more expensive to buy and less expensive to operate.

As fuel costs and availability differ, this must be decided on an individual basis.

All home laundry appliances should include a factory warranty. Service costs and availability may be a big factor in the maintenance of automatic equipment. Some washers and dryers are more easily serviced than others. Those with front opening controls are more accessible.

Consider the controls and use and care instructions as you select a washer or dryer. The instruction booklet usually has a part number and is an important tool for the user.

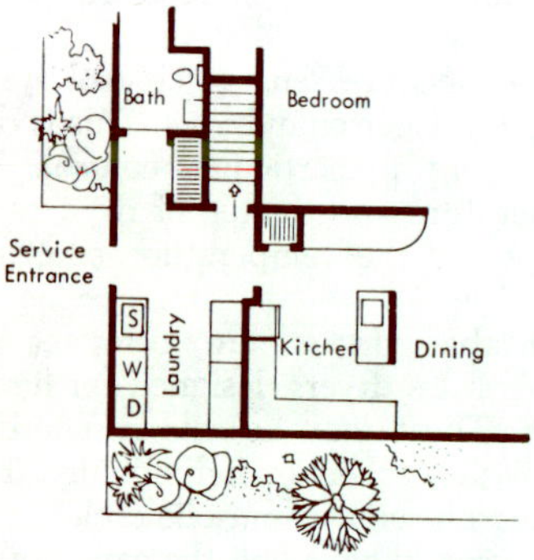

Plan for a sorting area to save effort at laundry time. Use ventilated bins made of perforated hardboard fastened on the wall above the washer and dryer. Or provide clothes baskets placed on wide shelves above the dryer or on pull-out shelves beneath a counter next to the laundry sink.

Fasten a sturdy rod or rack in a well-ventilated place above a laundry tub, sink or floor drain where you can hang knits and permanent press items. This may also be used for dripping clothes.

Plan storage for detergents, bleaches, and other laundry supplies. Keep them out of reach of children. Use sturdy adjustable shelves or a cabinet above the washer, or a locked cabinet near or under the sink.

Imaginative Ways With Bathrooms

TODAY, a bathroom can be anything you want it to be. With a little imagination and an understanding of the possibilities that exist, you can make decisions that will make your daily life more enjoyable. Whether a bathroom is being planned for a new house, or you are just remodeling or improving an existing bathroom, it is important to examine your personal needs, desires, and finances before buying and building. Extra energy spent in thinking before doing will be well worthwhile.

The first consideration to be faced concerns functions of the bathroom. A bathroom need not be just a small, white-tiled room with three fixtures. It might also include a dressing and grooming area, a space for sunbathing and exercising, a sauna, or even an area to relax, read, listen to the radio, or watch television. Free yourself from conventional ideas, and you will probably be happier with the results.

The bathroom, even in its conventional uses, is a very important place. There is no one who can do without a bathroom or would want to. The bathroom is the first place we go in the morning, and the last place at night. We probably use the bathroom more often than any other room in the house. These are good reasons for making it a pleasant and comfortable place to be and use.

In planning for a new house or new bath in an existing house, the size of the family will largely determine the number of bathrooms needed. Particular individual needs and desires must also be taken into account. And of course the financial situation of the family will have an effect on final decisions.

If you can have only one bathroom, it must serve many purposes. Therefore, it should be as large as possible.

Master bath.

If it will be used by guests, it should be accessible through a hallway or other public area, and not through a bedroom, for example. It should be discreetly but centrally located.

If you want and can afford to have more than one bathroom, then each can be more specialized. The standard two-bathroom solution is to have a family bathroom and a guest bath or powder room, perhaps with only a lavatory and toilet.

However, if there are older children in the family, a better solution might be a separate bath for them. It could be compartmented with a personal lavatory for each, connecting to a shared shower and water closet area. If there are small children in the family, a "mud room" by the back door rather than a powder room by the front door might be a good solution.

If you are considering a master bath, it should be thought of as part of an entire suite, related to the bedroom and to dressing and clothes storage areas. You should not have to go through the bedroom itself, however, to get to this bathroom.

A master bath should be a large and comfortable room. Designing it can be an excellent opportunity to make it a very individual place, reflecting your personal tastes and ideas. For example, many plants grow well in the moist, warm bathroom climate and could give the room a distinctive, unusual appeal.

The master bath might also be split into various compartments, or have his

AUTHOR *Alexander Kira* is Professor of Architecture, College of Architecture, Art & Planning, Cornell University, Ithaca, N.Y. CO-AUTHOR *Julia M. Smyth* is Research Assistant in the college.

and her tubs. On the other end of the scale, you might consider having one of the new large tubs for two.

If there is a family bathroom upstairs, it might be sensible to locate the laundering facilities next to it. Then soiled laundry would not have to be taken downstairs for washing, and back upstairs again for storage.

Top, modular shower. Above, combination tub-shower. Left, sink with storage

EQUIPMENT: An enormous variety of bathroom equipment is available, in a wide range of colors, styles, and prices. Careful planning is essential in order to get the best value for your investment, and to give the bathroom the specific character and style you want. In general, a higher price will not only mean better quality and better design, but most importantly, a wider selection.

TUBS AND SHOWERS: The safest rule-of-thumb in deciding whether to buy a shower or a tub is: if in doubt, or if you have only one bathroom, choose a combination tub-shower. Although most tubs are used almost exclusively as shower receptors, a tub is adaptable. If you have more than one bathroom, a shower might serve you well in the second bathroom.

One-piece fiberglass shower modules answer several needs. They are easy to install, clean, and maintain. Because they are integral units, there are no seams to leak. They also solve the question of wall-coverings around the inside of the shower.

The smallest comfortable shower is 42 inches by 30 inches, although models which include a built-in seat are available up to five feet long. A shower stool is a good investment in any case. A built-in ledge or shelf for soap and shampoo is another essential feature.

For safety, a shower with a non-skid floor should be chosen. There should also be a grab bar located at the entry to the shower. The shower controls should *not* be located under the shower head, nor in such a place where they are difficult to reach from outside the shower. If doors are used for closure, by law they must be either plastic or safety glass. Check these requirements with the builder.

If a shower is installed, it is important to provide an exhaust fan. This will protect the walls and ceiling from excess moisture, and provide necessary ventilation.

Cast-iron tubs are available, but enameled steel, acrylic, or molded fiberglass are more common today. Tubs like showers are available with complete wall surrounds.

Because tub baths are generally enjoyed for relaxation and soaking, the tub chosen should be comfortable to lie back in. The slope and height of the back of the tub is therefore an important feature. Try out the tub for comfort before buying. You may also wish to consider a five and one-half or six-foot long tub, rather than the standard five-foot length.

Many convenience features for tubs are available. Hand showers which attach to the tub-filler spout or the shower head can be purchased. These are useful for shampooing, child-bathing, and cleaning the tub after use.

For safety, tub controls should be higher than is customary, and near the entry side of the tub. Forty inches is a good height. The shower head should be at the opposite end of the tub from the controls.

A non-skid surface is necessary on the tub bottom. Grab bars and hand grips should be securely and strategically located for help in stepping into and out of the tub.

A sunken tub may be elegant, but it is also a great safety hazard and exceedingly awkward to clean.

Lavatories: There are several basic kinds of sinks: metal-rimmed, self-rimming, under-counter mounted, and ones which are in one piece with the counter top. They come in a wide range of styles, sizes, colors, materials, and prices. For maximum convenience and adaptability, choose the largest basin built into the largest counter top (set at a height of 34 to 36 inches) that you can accommodate.

Space beneath the sink should be planned as a storage area. Old-fashioned sinks on legs or wall brackets provide no counter space and waste the space underneath—a luxury very few of us can afford today.

Faucet controls should be easily reached, and easily cleaned and maintained. Cartridge-type controls are especially long-lived. The faucet itself should be as long as possible, and should be the mixing type.

Water Closets: There are three types of water closets (toilets). The siphon-jet type is the most efficient, quietest, cleanest, most expensive, and has the largest water-surface area. The reverse-trap type is less expensive and noisier. The washdown type is the cheapest, noisiest, and least efficient.

Wall-mounted toilets are efficient and easy to clean under, but they are more expensive and must be specially mounted. This is not always possible when remodeling.

Toilet seats should be easy to clean. The hinges should be sturdy. Plastic seats are the longest-lasting. Painted wooden seats chip, and become unsightly sooner than the all-plastic type.

Toilets are also available with self-venting exhaust systems which carry off odors.

For safety and convenience, especially for older people, grab bars may be installed on either side of the water closet.

Bidets: If space and money permit, a bidet may be installed. A bidet is useful for both male and female genital hygiene, and is also refreshing. Models are available which match the water closet.

A bidet seat which fits on the water closet and includes a water jet and a drying jet might also be considered, most especially by those who suffer from hemorrhoids.

Storage: The commonest shortcoming of present-day bathrooms is the lack of adequate storage and counter space. Most of us are probably so accustomed to inadequate space that we do not even realize we have less space than we need.

Make a list of all the items that logically could or should be kept in the bathroom, considering personal needs, and plan accordingly.

This list might include the following:

- Electrical grooming aids, such as toothbrushes, water-pics, shaving equipment, hot combs, hairdryers, etc.
- Beauty and grooming materials, such as lotions, powders, perfume, deodorant, brushes and combs
- Medicines, drugs, sick-room and first aid supplies, such as heating pads, hot water bottles, and bandages
- Cleaning supplies and spare paper goods
- Soiled laundry, and clean underwear
- Linens, including towels, face and hand cloths

To this list might be added such amenities as a telephone, radio, or television, a clock, sunlamp, or exercise equipment, for example. Older people and young children will have added storage needs, perhaps for such things as water toys, diapers, scales, lotions and creams.

In planning storage equipment, consider whether it should be open or closed storage. A medicine cabinet should be placed out of reach of small children for safety.

A minimum of two lineal feet per person should ordinarily be planned for towel and washcloth racks. Hooks and rings result in bunched up towels, and inadequate drying. Hooks should be provided for hanging clothes and robes. The bathroom scale might be wall-mounted, but in all cases it should not be left out where it can present a hazard. A full-length mirror is often a useful addition.

LIGHTING: Ample lighting above or around the lavatory mirror is necessary for grooming and shaving. If the bathroom is large, or includes a shower, overhead lighting will also be necessary. For safety, a night light or illuminated switch plate should always be installed at the entrance to the bathroom.

REMODELING TIPS: In less extensive remodeling or improvement jobs, the cautions and advice given above also apply. Because options in remodeling are limited by space, plumbing arrangement, and such, planning in advance is perhaps even more important than when one is building new.

Remodeling could include anything from gutting the entire room or knocking out a wall, to replacing a fixture or installing new wall surfacing. Some ideas about the more common or useful changes that might be made follow.

If carpeting is desired, make sure that scatter rugs have non-skid rubber backing. If wall-to-wall carpeting is used, it should be removable and washable, and have a rubber backing.

Shower heads should be adjustable. The more expensive types, which have self-cleaning plastic parts inside, are preferable because they are more durable and do not become clogged, a common problem in hard water areas.

If grab bars are to be installed, they should be mounted to the wall studs or some similarly secure foundation. This requires forethought. Grab bars should be good quality, approximately one inch in diameter, and sturdy. You should not substitute towel rods for these bars, because a filmsy bar could do more damage by giving way, than having no bar at all.

Plan for ample electrical outlets which should be the grounded, three-pronged variety. They should not be placed in such a way as to pose the danger of electrical accidents. Never use extension cords in a bathroom, nor metal pull cords on lights.

The addition of non-skid decals and strips in the tub or shower is not only a safety aid, but can also be attractive. Otherwise rubber suction-cup bath mats should be used.

When planning additional storage, consider built-in closets or shelves. These not only look better, they are also easier to maintain. Counter space can often be effectively increased by installing a *removable* section over the toilet tank.

A wise rule to follow in choosing new fixtures or accessories for the bathroom is to buy only what you need. Many of the available bathroom gadgets are merely decorative and only add to clutter. If one storage unit can be made to answer several needs, for example, it is preferable to several smaller items.

PLANNING AIDS: Planning is probably the most important part of building, remodeling, or improving a bathroom, or any room. For help in planning and collecting ideas and information, there are numerous home magazines to consult, as well as planning literature put out by all the leading manufacturers.

Bath shops, often associated with plumbing shops, are an excellent place to browse. They can give you a sense of the range of possibilities available and enable you to visualize how various things would fit together.

Department stores also will often have bathroom accessories and aids in stock.

For a wealth of imaginative ideas on what your bathroom could be, consult: Hicks, D., *David Hicks on Bathrooms,* New York: World Pub., 1970; and Gilliatt, M., *Bathrooms,* New York: The Viking Press, 1971.

A useful source of detailed information is Kira, A., *The Bathroom: Criteria for Design,* New York: Viking Press, 1975; also: Schram, J. F., *Modern Bathrooms* (A Sunset Book), Menlo Park, Cal.: Lane Books, 1968.

Cozy Fireplaces, Franklin Stoves, Other Heaters

GATHERING at the fireside for comfort and fellowship is a custom as ancient as the use of fire. When fireplaces were developed, families cooked all of their food there and much fuel was used. Now, the situation is different. Fireplaces, long appreciated for their esthetic value, are being looked to as a source of supplemental heat, for use on chilly fall mornings when the central heating system is turned off, or during emergencies.

If you yearn for a fireplace, you can build one of masonry, with or without a metal lining, or use a prefabricated metal fireplace.

A fireplace consists of a non-combustible firebox in which the fire is built and by which heat is reflected into the room, a chimney to vent products of combustion, a damper which regulates the amount of air drawn to the burning fuel, and a hearth which extends out into the room from the fireplace.

A fire screen across the fireplace opening and a spark arrester on top of the chimney keep sparks from setting the house afire.

The masonry firebox should be at least 8″ thick if the fireplace is on an inside partition, or if at least 2″ of fire brick lines the firebox. Use at least 12″ of masonry if the chimney is on an outside wall.

Fireboxes range from 1′6″ to 6′0″ in width, 1′9″ to 3′0″ in height and 1′4″ to 2′4″ in depth. A small or medium sized fireplace will provide comfort and use only a moderate amount of fuel.

A tight, well-built and well-maintained flue which is smooth inside is essential for your safe use of any fireplace, furnace or heating stove in which wood, coal, liquefied petroleum gas, fuel oil or natural gas is burned.

If you install a fireplace or heating stove, connect it to a new brick or stone chimney which has a clay tile flue liner, use an existing flue which is in good condition, or use a double-walled metal flue filled between walls with asbestos.

Be sure to comply with all building codes which apply to your community when you install a fireplace, heating system, and chimney. Codes provide for your safety and protection. They are enforceable and govern in disputes.

If you live where earthquake construction is required, reinforce and an-

---

AUTHOR *Vera E. Ellithorpe* is Extension Specialist, Family Housing and Safety, Kansas State University Cooperative Extension Service, Manhattan.

chor the chimney as required by the code.

Optimum height of the flue above the roof will vary with the design and height of your house.

The top of the chimney must be at least 4′ above the roof ridge of a house with a pitched roof, and should be at least 6′ above a house of more than one story with a flat roof, and 8′ above a one story house which has a flat roof.

Choose a flue of adequate size, equal to at least one-tenth of the fireplace opening for chimneys more than 15′ tall, and at least one-eighth of the area of the fireplace opening for chimneys less than 15′.

Pipes connecting free-standing stoves and fireplaces to a chimney should be at least No. 24 U.S. Standard gage steel, Underwriters' Laboratories listed, and installed in accordance with the listing. No pipe should be longer than 10′, or more than 75 percent of the vertical height of the chimney, whichever is less.

Each fireplace needs its own flue, but more than one flue may be located in the same chimney.

Wall-hung chimneys and fireplaces are apt to put undue weight on walls and partitions, cause settling of floors and walls, and cause masonry flues to crack. A masonry chimney should rest on its own foundation, below frost line.

The hearth in front of the fireplace should extend into the room at least 16″, and on either side of the fireplace opening at least 8″. Use brick, stone, tile, concrete or other non-combustible heat-resistant material at least 4″ thick for the fireplace hearth.

Protect the floor or sub-floor beneath a factory-built fireplace by a hearth which extends at least 16″ on all sides of the unit and is at least ⅜″ thick.

A conventional masonry fireplace opens on just one side, but you can build a fireplace which opens on more than one side, and build it to harmonize with the architectural style of your house.

A modified fireplace is one with a steel liner at least ¼″ thick, which may replace a firebrick lining in a firebox. Fresh air which enters from the room or from outdoors, is warmed in an air chamber behind the firebox and circulated to adjoining rooms or upstairs through registers.

A modified fireplace equipped with a fan will help to circulate warm air effectively.

The metal lining of a modified fireplace may eventually rust out, and the advantage of circulating heated air through registers may be reduced or lost.

Prefabricated metal fireplaces and chimneys should be labeled as approved by the Underwriters' Laboratories (UL) and installed as specified by the instructions.

Prefabricated fireplaces cost less than masonry fireplaces but they may be less durable.

Metal fireplaces are available in black or colored finishes, and in varying sizes and shapes. A small cone-shaped prefabricated fireplace may be 30″ or 36″ in diameter. If you build in a metal fireplace, be sure to thoroughly insulate it from the surrounding walls, according to the UL instructions.

The Franklin Stove is an ancestor of the coal and wood heating stoves now treasured by their owners. In 1744, Benjamin Franklin promoted the use of a metal fireplace, now known as the Franklin Stove. The stove, which stands out in the room, radiates heat from all sides, and is more efficient than a fireplace. It can be vented through a chimney or a fireplace, when the fireplace opening is closed with just space for the stovepipe to enter.

Doors of a Franklin Stove can be opened when you want to use it as a fireplace, and closed when you use it as a stove.

Experienced architects, builders, and masons in your community can advise you on the design, construction and cost of a fireplace best suited to your needs. Prefabricated fireplaces and accessories are sold by heating and building supply stores and by department stores.

Fuels and their present and predicted

Top, Franklin Stove. Above, prefab metal fireplace.

availability are of importance, as you make a choice of supplemental heating. Plan to use the fuel which is now most readily available and which will probably continue to be available for a long period of time.

Your choice of fuel will determine the type of supplemental heating equipment you will need to have. All fuels which burn require venting of the products of combustion through a chimney.

Wood, coal and natural gas can be burned in fireplaces, Franklin stoves and circulator heaters. These fuels, liquefied petroleum gas, and fuel oil can be burned in circulator heaters.

Fuels vary in their capacity to produce heat, and burn with varying efficiency. One pound of coal has a potential of 12,000 BTUs (British Thermal Units) and burns with 50 percent efficiency. One gallon of fuel oil burns with 70 percent efficiency and has a potential of 140,000 BTUs. One Kilowatt Hour of electricity has 100 percent efficiency in a resistance heating unit in the room in which it is used, with a potential of 3,413 BTUs.

One cubic foot of natural gas has a potential of 1,000 BTUs and burns with an efficiency of 80 percent.

Pound for pound, dry, heavy hardwoods have about half the heating value of coal and a third the heating value of oil.

You can make "logs" of rolled newspapers to burn in your fireplace.

Roll many thicknesses of newspaper tightly around a sturdy broomstick to make a log as thick and long as you need. Fasten a wire or tie a string near each end of the log. Pull the broomstick from the roll. You can then burn the log, or process it further by soaking it in water overnight.

Add a tablespoon of detergent to the water to assist soaking and compaction and to reduce the amount of fly ash produced when the log is burned.

Knead the log with your fingers to make it more compact, when you remove it from the water. Dry the logs in a flat place for several weeks before using them.

Keep flues in good condition at all times. Clean an existing flue before using it and frequently thereafter. Tie a rope to a weighted cloth sack filled with straw and lower and raise the sack in the flue to loosen soot, ashes and any creosote which may have formed in the chimney.

Creosote is formed by a combination of moisture from burning wood and acids given off when wood burns slowly. Green wood contains much more moisture than dry wood. To remove creosote from a flue safely, chip it from the inside of the flue with a blade fastened to a long pipe.

Remove bricks, stone and mortar which may have fallen into the flue.

Build a very small fire in the fireplace and cover the top of the chimney. Use chalk to mark mortar joints where smoke seeps from the chimney. Point up the mortar joints and replace broken, eroded, or porous stones and bricks.

Install a metal spark arrester on the chimney top. Make needed repairs to metal flashings which protect areas where the flue goes through the roof.

You can become an expert fireplace manager, and here's how:

Lay a fire carefully. For kindling, use a few small branches with the bark cut into curls along the sides. Lay medium sized pieces of wood above the kindling and a few larger pieces of wood on top of the fire. Lay the fire toward the center and back of the fireplace, leaving space for air to circulate around and between the wood.

Place a tightly rolled and tied piece of paper in among the kindling and light it. In cold weather, you may want to light one end of a rolled paper and hold it, with extreme care, just below the open damper in the top of the firebox. Hold it there a few seconds to warm the flue so that it will draw well. Then tuck the lighted paper in among the kindling at the base of the fire. Close the firescreen quickly. Fan the blaze gently if necessary, until the wood burns readily.

A fireplace fire requires about five times as much air as is needed for liberal ventilation, in order to keep burning. You may need to open a window slightly to bring in enough fresh air to keep the fire going, if your house is insulated and completely weatherstripped.

To keep smoke from entering the room, turn off kitchen and bathroom exhaust fans and close registers of forced air heating systems which are near the fireplace.

After the fire is well started, adjust the damper to control the draft, so that there is enough to keep the fire burning but that the amount of heat escaping up the chimney is kept at a minimum. Fireplaces are only about 15 percent efficient.

Use only enough fuel to keep the fire as hot as you need. The heated firebox will reflect heat, and glowing coals add comfort.

You may want to use electric heat. You can use portable heaters, add built-in or free-standing units to your present house, or install an electric heating system in a house being built. Electric heat requires no venting.

Look for portable heaters or baseboard units which have automatic thermostats, fans, over-heat safety devices, and tip-over safety switches. In hydronic baseboard units, water is heated electrically.

Thermostatically controlled electric heating units of varying heat capacities, with or without fans, can be recessed in walls, ceilings, or floors.

Heaters can be installed in the ducts of a forced air heating system.

Electric fireplace units have "logs" and motor driven cylinders which create the effect of burning flames. Some of these units have fans and heating units.

Units are available for use with both 110–120 volt and 220–240 volt circuits.

All electrical heating equipment should carry the UL label and be used as recommended.

Natural gas "logs" are also a quite favored means of heating. The "logs" retain and reflect the heat from the fireplace. Look for the AGA (American Gas Association) label. Be sure to install and use the "logs" according to instructions.

FOR FURTHER READING:

U.S. Department of Agriculture, *Fireplaces and Chimneys*, F 1889, Office of Communication, Washington, D.C. 20250, 1971.

Lighting Fixtures and Equipment

FAMILIES talk a lot about light: "It sure is dark in here; we need more light," they say. Or, "turn the light off; it's too bright." But despite all the talk, we generally take good lighting for granted. And that's a shame because a little planning before the lighting system is installed can save lots of frustrations later—such as fuses that blow or plug-ins that are overloaded.

If you are building a home, remodeling your present one, or just updating your electrical system, you can prevent problems by planning ahead.

The first step is to consider how much light you want in each room. Every room needs some general lighting. That's the low level light you need for moving about safely and doing some household chores.

The amount of general light you need depends on the size, shape, and type of your room. Begin by classifying rooms into living areas and utility areas. One lighting fixture or portable lamp might supply enough general light for a living area. But utility areas such as kitchens, laundries, and workshops need more general light because more work goes on there.

Room size makes a big difference. One portable lamp or one lighting fixture may provide enough light in a small room, but a large room will probably need two or more light sources.

In addition to general light, you'll need specific lighting in some rooms. Specific lighting is often called task lighting, and it takes eye strain out of studying, reading, sewing or other tasks which require visual concentration.

Whether your need is for general or specific lighting, all lighting falls into one of three categories: diffused, direct, and indirect. The one you select will depend on the total effect you are trying to create.

Diffused or indirect light is a low level, general light. Diffused light is scattered evenly throughout a room or area. It is not directed at any particular object. Indirect light, on the other hand, is reflected on ceilings or walls. The bulb or tube is hidden from view, but the reflected light is visible.

Direct light is usually specific—directed onto the surface where you are working.

And now for the second step. After you have figured out how much light is needed in each room and whether it should be direct, indirect, or diffused, you're ready to consider the type of light you want.

Two kinds of light are used in the home, incandescent and fluorescent.

An incandescent bulb produces light when electricity passes through a fine tungsten filament in a bulb that contains no air. When you screw a bulb into a socket, electricity causes the wire to become so hot that it glows, producing light. Bulbs are available in many sizes, from small night lights of 10 watts to bulbs of 100, 200, and 300 watts as well as three-way bulbs. The bulbs, which usually burn 750 to 1,000 hours, are made of clear or opaque glass in assorted colors and shapes.

When choosing incandescent bulbs for the home, consider inside frosted and white bulbs first. They win the award for efficiency. And keep in mind that one 100-watt bulb produces at least 50 percent more light than four 25-watt bulbs.

If variety is important, fixtures that use incandescent bulbs are your best bet. You can buy bulbs of various wattages, colors, and shapes to fit the same fixtures as long as the bases of the bulbs are the same size.

Fluorescent fixtures aren't this flexible. Once you have selected a fluorescent fixture, you're stuck with its wattage. For example, if the fluorescent kitchen fixture that you choose doesn't provide enough light, you're out of luck;

AUTHOR *Sandra Westall Shank* is an Extension Specialist, Housing-Home Furnishings, at Purdue University, West Lafayette, Ind.

the larger wattage tube will be too long. So be sure to choose fluorescent fixtures with care.

Fluorescent tubes produce three or four times as much light as an incandescent bulb of the same wattage and last seven to ten times longer. However, fluorescent light is cooler—both in color and temperature—than an incandescent light of the same size. You can avoid this coldness or bluish appearance by selecting warm white or deluxe warm white tubes.

Of course, a light bulb is worthless without a lighting fixture. There are many types of lighting fixtures—from converted antique oil lamps to stark chrome chandeliers. Base your selection on the amount and type of light you need and the atmosphere you want to create in your home.

Selection Guide for Incandescent Bulbs

Activity	Minimum recommended wattage [1]
Reading, writing, sewing:	
Occasional periods	150
Prolonged periods	200 or 300
Grooming:	
Bathroom mirror:	
1 fixture each side of mirror	1–5 or 2–40's
1 cup-type fixture over mirror	100
1 fixture over mirror	150
Bathroom ceiling fixture	150
Vanity table lamps, in pairs (person seated)	100 each
Dresser lamps, in pairs (person standing)	150 each
Kitchen work:	
Ceiling fixture (2 or more in a large area)	150 or 200
Fixture over sink	150
Fixture for eating area (separate from workspace)	150
Shopwork:	
Fixture for workbench (2 or more for long bench)	150

[1] White bulbs preferred.

Fluorescent Tube* Wattage and Size

Wattages	Normal Length
14 watts	15 inches
15 watts	18 inches
20 watts	24 inches
30 watts	36 inches
40 watts	48 inches

Circline Fluorescent tubes designed for use in fixtures used most often in kitchens

Wattages	Outside diameters
22 watts	8½ inches
32 watts	12 inches
40 watts	16 inches

*Available in lengths other than those listed.

Fixtures are permanent or portable. Permanent lighting fixtures are either ceiling fixtures or wall-mounted, architectural fixtures.

If you use a ceiling fixture, it will be a recessed, ceiling-mounted, or pendant fixture. The type you pick depends on the number of fixtures, the amount of light desired, and the amount of money you want to spend.

A recessed fixture is mounted in the ceiling so that only the face of the fixture shows. Recessed lighting can be used for decorative effects or for general lighting. The light is focused downward, either spotlighted on an object or diffused for general lighting.

A ceiling-mounted fixture is entirely visible, but you can't see the light bulb. These fixtures may give off general dif-

Above left, lighting can be made more flexible in a child's room with a hanging fixture. Left, pendant fixture can be hung above eye level to give general light or below eye level for specific light. Top, table lamps with 3-way switches can be used as general light as well as specific light.

fused light or light that shines downward. The general diffused fixture produces a wide pattern of light that illuminates walls and ceilings. However, if the light shines downward but is not diffused, you will need several fixtures for general lighting; otherwise, some corners of the room will be dim.

A pendant or hanging fixture often hangs in a hallway or over a dining table or corner table. These fixtures are suspended on a cord, chain, or stem and may be hung above or below eye level. Hung above eye level, the light will create a formal atmosphere. If you place the light below eye level, the effect will be friendlier. Placement must be carefully planned so the fixtures do not interfere with activity.

Wall-mounted fixtures are an entirely different matter. A wall-mounted fixture is built into the wall. These fixtures allow the light to shine both up and down or just up or down, and they contribute to the general illumination of the room. They may be located over draperies, on one wall, or on all four walls of a room.

The wall-mounted fixture that goes over draperies is called a valance. It is located near the ceiling, and its light shines down over draperies and up toward the ceiling.

Cornice lighting is mounted on the wall at ceiling height, but is closed at the top so that all light shines down. Cove light directs all the light upward, while bracket lighting, located lower on the wall than the others, directs the light downward.

You may decide you do not want ceiling fixtures or wall-mounted fixtures. In that case, you will need to choose table and floor lamps for both general and specific lighting. If so, plan to have some of your plug-ins switched at the wall so that you can flip a switch and have a table lamp light up. And don't forget: a lamp with a three-way switch will enable you to use it for both general and specific lighting.

The design of portable lamps for general lighting should harmonize with your decorating schemes. In addition, look for a hang tag on reading or study lamps that says, "This is a Better Light Better Sight Bureau Study Lamp." These lamps give good glare-free light. However, if you need the lamp to provide specific task lighting as well as general light, there are more considerations: the lampshade, the size of the lamp, and where you are going to place the lamp.

The shade for a lamp that is to be used for reading, study or sewing should be 16 to 18 inches at the bottom, 8 to 17 inches at the top, and 10 to 20 inches deep. The lining of the shade should be white to reflect the light. Your eye level will determine the best height for the lamp. The lower edge of the shade should be slightly below eye level when you're seated so that the glare doesn't blind you.

Indoor lights aren't your only lighting problem. Your yard needs its fair share of light, too. The main reasons for outdoor lighting are convenience, personal safety and to avert vandalism. There should be a light anywhere you have a change in height—for example, on a porch, steps, or a garden path. House numbers and front doors should be lighted, too.

Fixtures for outdoor lighting should be designed to withstand all weather conditions. Convenience outlets should be weatherproof, and the light bulbs you use should be designed for outdoor use unless they are protected in some way. Reflector bulbs, decorative bulbs, and fluorescent tubes must be shielded from the weather.

Household bulbs up to the 25-watt size may be used without protection from the weather. Larger sizes must be shielded or they will break.

Light bulbs that have been made especially for outdoor use are projector or PAR bulbs. They are made of heat and cold resistant glass and come in a variety of wattages and colors.

You might try lighting sidewalks and paths with fixtures that are about 8 to 30 inches tall. These fixtures come in a variety of shapes and may be permanently or temporarily mounted. The light is directed downward on the path. To make a long walk safe, you may need several fixtures. Select fixtures that do not produce glare, especially if they are to light steps.

If you want to illuminate areas larger than a few feet, then look for fixtures that are 30 to 65 inches tall with shade diameters of 15 to 23 inches. These fixtures, often called mushroom units, provide downlighting for areas such as terraces, patios, and driveways.

Trees, shrubbery, walls, and fences can be lighted by fixtures that direct the light upward. Usually functional in form, these fixtures should be placed where they are inconspicuous.

Of course, you may not need permanent outdoor lighting. But you may need outdoor lights every once in a while for a party or other special occasion. That's when you'll wish for a weather-proof plug-in. If you don't have one, you can still light up the outside with a 3-wire (grounded) weatherproof extension cord. Plug the cord into the nearest interior outlet, and start turning on the lights! But be sure your regular circuit can handle the additional load.

And while planning your home lighting, don't forget to plan for flexibility. For example, you can make light more flexible with dimmer switches and timers.

There are two basic types of incandescent dimmer switches. The high-low switch has three positions for controlling light. The upper position is full brightness, the center off, and the lower position for one-third brightness. If you choose a full-range solid state dimmer, you can control the brightness from zero to almost 100 percent. These dimmers have a 400- to 600-watt range and generally fit in the same place as your present light switch.

If you want to dim fluorescent lamps, you must do so when the system is installed. These switches can provide light from zero to full brightness, too.

Have you ever considered dimming portable lamps? There is a table top dimmer that allows you to dim table or floor lamps. Just plug the lamp into the dimmer and the dimmer into the convenience outlet to create your own level of light! This would give you more control over the level of light than a three-way switch.

Timers are another control that can add flexibility to your lighting system. Timers turn lights on and off in a house when the occupant is away. Some timers will vary the on and off times automatically from day to day, making it seem like you really are at home. Timers are also available to control special lighting for plants or to turn the coffee pot on at a set time each morning.

Timers and dimmer switches offer another plus: they can help save electrical energy.

Of course, lighting is not one of the biggest users of energy in the home. But lights do use some energy. So keep energy conservation in mind as you design your lighting system.

Human energy, as well as electrical energy, will be conserved if you have planned the placement of lighting switches. Place light switches strategically so you can switch them on ahead of you as you walk through the house. If you can turn switches on and off without much effort, you'll save energy. And you'll be more likely to turn lights off, too—one way to save on electrical energy!

For additional information about home lighting, check *Handbook for the Home,* the 1973 Yearbook of Agriculture. Your County Extension Office or your electric company also can give you good tips.

So don't just talk about lighting. Do something. There are many decisions to make: Diffused or direct? Incandescent or fluorescent? Portable or permanent? But you'll find it well worth your time to think through the questions. Well planned lighting makes a home comfortable and safe, and a brighter place to be.

How to Avoid Those Tumble Out Closets

EVER OPENED a closet and had last year's Christmas decorations, old galoshes, an extension cord and, a clothes brush fall on top of you? Good storage makes it possible to take better care of your possessions and to do household tasks with minimum effort.

Applying a few basic principles in a new or older home will help to make sure that storage needs are met, space is used effectively, facilities are provided at a reasonable cost, and the results look good.

First, eliminate the unused, unneeded, and unimportant storage items. This step requires courage, but you would be surprised how much it reduces the storage problem.

Now take a look at how efficiently you are using present storage. More fully utilizing space within existing closets and cabinets may go a long way towards the solution of your storage problem.

Allocate prime space for the items used most frequently. Items used infrequently may be stored in less accessible places. Ideally, store items in or near the area where they are used the most. If an item such as a vacuum cleaner, is used in several areas of the house, store it in a central location for greater convenience.

Provide space to store together items used together, such as the iron and the ironing board, or the coffee and the coffee pot.

Items which could be hazardous if handled or ingested by small children should be stored out of their reach or in secured areas.

Some items may require special consideration such as a cool, warm, or dry location. If valuable papers are kept in the home, store them in a fireproof safe.

Since storage needs change with family growth and activities, consider the flexibility that various types of storage facilities will provide.

Choices today for providing storage facilities are built-in, freestanding or stacked units, or wall-hung units suspended from tension poles. Storage units may be purely utilitarian for use in a garage, attic, or basement, or they may be skillfully crafted and arranged so that they become an important decorative feature of a room.

The smaller the living space a family occupies, the more essential it becomes to use space to better advantage.

Now that you have the basic storage planning principles in mind, you can evaluate the way you are using the storage facilities you have. If there is wasted space, the following ideas may be helpful.

Installing additional shelves between shelves in kitchen cabinets will often make it possible to use much wasted space and greatly reduce the need for stacking smaller plates on top of larger plates and smaller pans inside larger pans, etc.

More space can be used and it is more accessible when base cabinets have pullout shelves or drawers. Pullout trays are available in some new cabinets, or they can be custom designed and built, or there are units on the market which may be installed in existing cabinets.

While turn tables may waste space because of their circular design, they do make it easy to bring needed items stored in the back of cabinets to the front where there is easy access.

Storage capacity may be increased in clothes closets by means of both high and low rods, if the need is for additional rod space. Installing an additional closet shelf or two above the one shelf the builder put in will add storage.

Additional storage may be provided inconspicuously by building in a storage wall with doors that closely match the wall surface of the room.

If clothes closets are being planned, a minimum inside finished depth should be at least 24 inches. For easy access to the clothes closet in a bedroom, the ideal location is just inside the door and preferably on the same wall as the entrance door. This location may not be possible in some situations, so alternatives may need to be considered. Avoid locating a closet where it may partially block the entrance into the room.

If a storage wall is being considered in another area of the house such as in the dining area, consider the location for convenient access from the kitchen as well as from the dining table.

A storage unit may serve as a space divider between the dining and living areas or an entry way from the living area. It also can provide some personal space when two children share a bedroom.

An alternative to the built-in storage wall is the possibility of assembling storage units which may appear to be built-in. A simple background treatment can make this arrangement less conspicuous. A more decorative arrangement can make it the focal point in the room.

Some of the wall storage systems offer many options for flexibility, such as

Hall closet with turntables on the lower shelves to provide easy access.

cabinets with doors to conceal what is being stored or glass doors which will permit objects to be seen as well as protected. Cabinets of varying sizes and number of drawers are available.

Shelves of different widths and lengths may serve different needs, such as a shelf wide enough to accommodate a television set or narrower shelves for books or small decorative objects. Also available are magazine shelves which can be adjusted at an angle to provide for easy access to the desired publication.

Wall storage systems are available in a variety of materials—wood, metal, plastic, or combinations of these. They come in a variety of styles so that you can select a style to harmonize with your house and furniture. There is a wide price range depending on the quality of materials and workmanship.

Advantages of the storage wall systems that are freestanding or supported by tension poles are that additions can be made as the need arises. Also, they provide maximum flexibility to accommodate the family that enjoys rearranging furnishings from time to time. Another advantage is that they solve the problem for the tenant who needs additional storage space and may not be permitted to attach units to a wall or to build in storage areas.

Some storage problems may be lessened by careful selection of furniture pieces which provide for storage of some items. For example, an end table with a shelf or two for magazines, or drawers for storing other items, requires no more floor space than one without these features. Taller chests will provide more storage space for the amount of floor space used than the double and triple width dresser units.

Often old or discarded chests, dresser bases, or other furniture pieces can be converted into attractive and functional storage units.

Storage space is needed for lawn care and gardening items, outdoor furniture, grills, recreation equipment, and other things used outside the house.

AUTHOR *Glenda Pifer* is Housing Specialist, Extension Service.

Discarded TV cabinet converted to a storage unit.

This space may be provided in a garage or a storage unit along the side or end of a carport or in a walk-in basement, or in a storage area incorporated into the house structure but accessible from the outside. Frequently in the country, a separate building may be available for storing garden and shop tools.

For the more creative or do-it-yourself people, many sources of information give directions on how to build various storage pieces. Units may also be purchased ready to assemble or ready to finish.

If you have the opportunity to plan a new house, be sure to allocate space for storage areas just as carefully as you do the remainder of the planning. You can also incorporate good storage into your house if you are doing major remodeling. Perhaps the greatest challenge of all is to develop adequate storage space in an existing house with minimum change and limited resources.

Window Treatments: Curtains, Shades, Shutters, Drapes

THIS YEAR's energy crisis points out the importance of the best selection of window treatments. The covering or lack of covering can make a difference in the comfort of a room.

Orientation of the opening is of primary concern when you are deciding what the covering should be. Depending on the amount of roof overhang, shade trees, and other shade, a window opening on the west or south side of the house can permit a great deal of heat to penetrate inside. Likewise, window openings on the north and east side can permit a great deal of coldness to penetrate inside. A good window treatment for these conditions should concern itself with insulating qualities.

There is a window treatment of a heat-producing nature. This consists of two layers of thin flexible vinyl plus a filling of nylon net interwoven with thin resistance wiring. It comes in flexible panels ranging in sizes of 2 ft. 2 in. by 4 ft. 2 in. up to 3 by 12 ft. Since the panels operate at about body temperature they can be painted without destroying the bonding.

A folding screen which has been permanently installed at a window can be covered with these heat-producing panels, painted, and finished with a trim. The trim may be one of the lovely fabric trims now available at your local fabric department or it may be a wood molding painted a matching or contrasting color.

There are many types of roller shades to fit almost any size window opening. They are available in a variety of fabrics, including some which are coated with an insulating material. This coating is usually white but may be silver colored.

Roller shades generally found in most drapery departments are fabric, plastic, or woven wood. Fabric shades may be rough linen weave or smooth cotton scrim-like cloth which has been heavily filled and sized to be more rigid. They may be fabric which matches or complements your wallpaper. These are sometimes available ready made but otherwise must be custom made.

I prefer shades having fabric laminated to a coated backing. The backing protects the fabric from sunlight and dirt which come through the window, and is a good insulator. A shade shop will do this process for you.

A charming effect can be obtained by using matching or companion fabric and wallpaper. This is especially good in the "vanilla type" subdivision house. You can give individuality to this type house without spending a great deal of money if you will use your ingenuity and time.

You can use one of the many available trims or cut the stripe from a fabric you can repeat on upholstery, table cover, or draperies. Or with Elmer's glue, a ball fringe or tassel fringe can be put on the bottom scalloped or straight edge of the shade. The fabric stripe may be glued on the shade about 2 in. from each outer edge, running from top to bottom. You may like more of these vertical stripes if your shade is wide.

How about adding macrame or crochet at the bottom of the roller shade?

Speaking of width of shade, be careful not to try to use a shade which is too wide, because it is too difficult to roll straight. If your window opening is 6 ft. wide use two 36 in. shades and a buckrum, fiberboard, or plywood strip wide enough to hide the space left between the shades. This strip can be covered with felt, fabric, trim, wallpaper, or may be painted. Perhaps some upholstery gimp applied at the edges of the painted wood strip would add interest. The strip used in the middle is nice to use all around the window too.

If you are artistic, try painting designs on a good quality roller shade. I did "life size" figures from a chess set on roller shades in a home study/office of an olympic chess team coach.

Roller shades are particularly good for window openings in small rooms because they are not as bulky as draperies. They allow partial opening of windows for light and air. The amount of light coming into a room can be regulated.

Another method for trimming your heating and air conditioning bill is to cover your window openings with plantation type shutters. Our ancestors used shutters both inside and outside window openings for protection from the elements.

Shutters may have horizontal or vertical moveable slats to deflect direct sun rays and to regulate light and air while maintaining privacy within. These may be stained or painted to match adjacent walls in small rooms, thereby giving the effect of more space. You may want to use bright or contrasting colors to paint the shutters or pick up a color from wallpaper, carpet, or fabrics used in your room.

I have found that fruitwood stained shutters, used over white theatrical gauze shirred on a rod set inside the window frame, are very interesting in a library or a sitting room having glasscloth wallcovering. The theatrical gauze needs to be five fullnesses (five times the width of the opening), to cut down on glare from the glass yet let light in to make the room more pleasant. The shutters can be closed at night for privacy.

You might prefer to use one of the many lovely colors of theatrical gauze available at an interior design studio to use behind your choice of colors on the shutters. It is 100 percent linen which is durable and relatively inexpensive.

Instead of moveable slats in shutters, fill the frames with fabric. Stretch it on rods at each end and fasten it in-

---

AUTHOR *Jaunita Weber* is Assistant Professor of Housing and Interior Design, Florida State University, Tallahassee.

side or on the back side of the frame. Quarter inch adjustable rods and L hooks are easy to obtain and apply. You may have to cut them off some.

The frames may contain solid panel insets which may be stained, painted, or covered with wallpaper or fabric. Try painting an accent colored stripe on the beveled edge between the frame and panel. This stripe may be a metallic gold or silver to give a luxurious look to a library or bedroom.

Add to this a silver or gold colored French design handle and/or latch to complete the effect or to repeat those used on the French style furniture in the room. Sometimes a "look of luxury" can be accomplished at a comparatively small cost. Certainly metallic paint used in such small amounts of stripping is inexpensive.

To complement your patchwork handiwork around the house you might like to paint a stencil design on the panels, fill the frames with gingham or calico, or be a little fancy with lace. If you do not trust your drawing ability you can buy stencil patterns at a hobby shop where you also can buy paint for the stenciling.

Gingham, calico, and lace can be found in fabric departments at varying prices dependent upon quality. Be sure you buy fast colored and washable fabrics. If your fabric permits too much light to penetrate, you may line it with a washable lining.

How about an hour glass curtain stretched over another fabric? Stretch a gingham on rods at either end, set on back side of frame, and then stretch an eyelet embroidered hour glass over it on rods set inside the frames. Tie the hour glass in the middle with a ribbon bow, rickrack, or small silk flowers. Purchase the frames from a drapery department or cabinet shop. You can finish them yourself as well as make the fabric insets.

Shutters may be as tall as the opening, divided in the middle, or other lengths. Design principles being involved here lead me to install them as tall as the opening or divided in the middle, and with the widest margin of the frame at the bottom end of each panel.

Plantation shutters or the adaptations are properly installed inside a window frame. Shutters may sag when the opening is too wide because there is a limit of support from hinges within a given space. It is best to install them as a pair for this reason.

Measure the window opening, subtract ⅝ of an inch, and divide by 4. This will give you the width panel to buy in drapery or housewares departments. Sometimes it is necessary to shave off a small amount of each panel to fit the opening. Never shave it all off one panel.

Fasten two panels together with hinges, leaving ⅛ of an inch between panels. Then hinge one set of two to the window frame on the right side and one set on the left side, leaving ⅛ of an inch between frame and panel.

Be careful that hinges fastening the two panels together are on the window side while the hinges on the window frame are on the room side. This will allow shutter panels to lay back on the wall when folded and not into the room as an obstacle.

Use a Yardstick

A good way to make certain that shutters do not drag on the window sill is to use a yardstick. Lay it on the sill and set shutters on it while marking the screw holes on the window frame. This will allow clearance and not interfere with privacy.

Be different and purchase black H-L hinges and a latch type closer for a Colonial or country-style look. If you are taking advantage of the many arts and crafts materials available in hobby shops, you might like to make enameled metal pulls for your shutters.

It is wise to do all shaving of wood and fitting of shutters into the opening before staining or painting shutters. If the hinges are removed the shutters can be spray finished. I find that lacquer paint works best because it can be thinner and thereby not clog the moveability of the slats. Also, lacquer seems to be more durable as well as easy to clean because of the smooth finish.

Shutters may be painted with a brush while they are still hinged if you are neat with a paint brush. But remember, smeared hinges look ugly!

An exciting contemporary window treatment is woven wood. The use of colorful yarn woven into a variety of widths and shapes of wood slats makes a decorative window covering.

Flat wood slats vary from 1 inch to ¼ inch wide—and sometimes a variety of widths are used together. Round slats vary from match stick size to approximately 1 inch diameter. Round slats sometimes are cut to a half round, and a variety of sizes and shapes are used.

For added interest and individuality, colorful beads are intermixed with wood slats.

Ready-made woven wood window covering can be found in many drapery departments. Cost of these coverings varies according to the size of opening and the complexity of arrangement and amount of yarn and slats involved.

Custom-made woven wood offers a chance for you to choose the colors and kinds of yarn to be woven in a pattern that you design. Add to this a few strings of bright beads and a compatible color on the slats. You might like white slats in variable sizes with a wide band of colored yarn about 2 inches from the outer edges and down the center of the window.

Woven wood is very effective in the small rooms with strange "postage stamp" windows we see in houses today. Unlike heavy draperies, a feeling of airiness and more spaciousness results when woven wood is used on the surrounding area of the window wall to create an illusion of a large expanse of glass.

Double windows may be treated as one window by using only one panel of woven wood. You may want to put a cloth valance and side draperies around the woven wood, thus using it instead of a glass curtain.

Woven wood window covering can be hung to roll up with aid of cord or be pulled up in a pleated fashion. The wood slats also can be hung vertically on a traverse rod in the same manner as draperies. If these are not installed in wood, use toggle bolts to insure a secure installation. Regular screws tend to chew out surrounding sheetrock or plaster with the tugging of pull cords. A hole drilled with a rock bit slightly larger than the screw and filled with steel wool is good in cement or concrete block walls.

Woven wood is great to cut out the bright hot sun. Wood is a natural insulator. Oh, yes, you can install woven wood on the outside of your house and on the sun porch for practical and decorative purposes because most types will withstand weathering.

Draperies can be lined and interlined as an insulating factor. Choice of fabrics is important here. Open woven fabrics would permit the interlining or lining to show through the right side.

Cotton flannel is the best interlining. It comes in 36- and 48-inch widths and a choice of white, cream, and gray colors. Choice of color of interlining will depend on the drapery fabric chosen because you do not want to spoil the appearance of the finished product by having the interlining show through the right side.

A plain white fabric or printed fabric having large areas of white background will permit the color of interlining to penetrate through to the right side. Printed draperies look better when interlined anyway, and especially if they are on windows having extremely bright sunlight. The color and design get lost in that wash of light, thus destroying the effect.

You can make interlined and lined draperies yourself. Handle all fabric gingerly as fabric will become limp and lifeless when over-handled.

Make certain that outer drapery fabric is neither too loose nor too tight over lining and interlining. All three layers should fit together as one. Regardless of how expensive or inexpensive it is, a drapery fabric will look great only if it is neatly constructed and drapes properly. Avoid any pulling or weeping of fabric.

Draperies should be planned around the style of room they are serving. Each style has a design peculiar to itself. The design determines how short or long, how wide, where hung, what hardware is used, what fabric, and sometimes what color or colors.

An Early American room would call for double hung draperies with or without a shirred valance, and may have ruffled tie-back panels at the top half of the window for the cottage look. These draperies can be purchased or custom made.

A wide selection of these draperies is available in good but inexpensive fabrics. For a custom look try the unbleached muslin ones, and add your own choice of colored bias binding or fringe on the edge of the ruffle. Or add a 2-inch band the color of your carpet at the top edge of the bottom hems of the non-ruffled panels.

You can pipe the edges of the band with another color from your room. To be really Early American, make the band blue piped with red on the off white muslin.

It is difficult to add lining or interlining to draperies which have already been pleated, so in many cases they will have to be made when you desire protection from the elements. You can hang pleated insulated lining on a separate traverse rod behind ready-made unlined draperies.

Some drapery fabrics come with insulation backing applied. This is fairly successful. One disadvantage is that the holes from stitching show. Another might be the stiffness of the fabric which drapes nicely when pleated but cannot be used as an Austrian or Roman Shade.

Draperies can fit the window frame exactly but one purpose of a window is to have light and air plus a view or extension of indoors to outside. This being the point, I like to fit draperies so that when they are open there is as much of the window exposed as possible without the adjoining wall showing.

To accomplish this, install drapery hardware 4 inches above the window opening. The back side of pleats or the hardware should never show on the outside of the window. Usually drapery will bunch to a quarter its width. Using this as a guide, place the hardware bracket out on the wall accordingly.

Example: A 36-inch window rod would end about 5 inches beyond the opening on each side, making the rod length needed 46 inches.

Beautiful fabric and furnishings are spoiled by skimpy draperies, so be sure to use three times the width of the space to be covered. This is called triple fullness.

The back side of pleats, raw seams, hemlines, drapery pins and rods, printed fabric, a different color fabric in every window, and sagging rods are incompatible with exterior building materials, beautiful landscaping, and the order of things.

New Furniture—Getting Value for Your Investment

DESIGN, FUNCTION, construction, and price—these are basic to every furniture purchase. To get the best buy for the money you have to invest in new furniture, ask yourself these questions: How long do you expect the furniture to last? How much do you plan to pay? What will go with your other furnishings? Knowing the answers to these and other key questions will insure more lasting value and satisfaction from your furniture.

Select with extreme care the basic pieces for sleeping, dining, seating, and storage. In considering size, think of the room where the furniture will be placed and the other furnishings with which it will be used. Carefully measure the room or space to make certain the new furniture will fit. Take measurements with you when you shop.

Consider flexible furniture—dining room chairs that are harmonious with living room chairs and chests which look well in the living room, dining room, or bedroom. This quality will permit a piece to be moved from one room to another or one house to another.

Before making a purchase, compare prices as well as quality. Buy from a reliable dealer. Ask questions about delivery, installation, and adjustments for unsatisfactory service. Know the store policies for credit. Remember that cash is the least expensive method of payment. Learn to "speak up" if merchandise doesn't "measure up."

Be alert for sales. Watch newspaper ads for warehouse, seasonal, anniversary, and promotional sales. Furniture sales are most likely to be in January, February, July, and August.

Upholstered Furniture

Inspect all outside features and ask questions about the hidden inside features. Check for these good tailoring features:

-Fabric patterns, whether stripes, plaids, or florals, should be centered and carefully placed.

-Cording, welting, seams, and hems should be smooth and straight. Check for straight grain lines.

-Cushions should be snug fitting. Reversible cushions are desirable. Zippers are placed in cushions to make neater and tighter closures. They are not there so that you can remove the covers for cleaning.

Your knowledge of furniture construction can help you "see inside" for the hidden features in upholstered furniture.

Wood frames should be made of seasoned, kiln-dried hardwood, and should have firm, secure joints with reinforcements at all points of strain. Joints of quality wooden frames are usually of double dowel construction. Plastic and metal are also being used for frames. Test the strength of the frame by sitting and leaning on it as well as moving it about.

Coil springs are preferred in certain construction, especially in large pieces, to the less expensive zigzag spring. Zigzag springs are often used in "thin-line" styles or to reduce cost in other constructions. With coil and zigzag construction, padding is applied so the frame retains its shape.

Determine the quality, comfort, and wearability of the materials used for padding and filling. Since the grade or quality of these materials can vary widely, it is impossible to recommend one specific type. Types used frequently are synthetic fiberfill, foam rubber, polyurethane foam, and down. Look for a label to identify padding and filling materials.

For surface durability, choose a tightly woven upholstery fabric. Loosely woven fabrics tend to sag, snag, and stretch. A good test of density is to hold the fabric sample up to the light to check the closeness of weave. Pull the fabric lengthwise and crosswise to test for strength and firmness of weave. Scratch the surface of the fabric to determine if threads will catch or snag easily.

Determine the fabric's fiber content. Labeling laws require fabrics sold by the yard to be labeled according to fiber content, and fibers must be listed in order of predominance and percentage of each fiber. The label must include the name of the manufacturer or a registered identification. This law does not apply to furniture that is already upholstered.

Ask the salesman to get the fiber information for you. Usually a fabric grade is indicated on the label. The lower numbers or first letters of the alphabet often indicate less expensive fabrics. Ask to see several grades of the

---

AUTHOR *Patsy Keller* is Home Furnishings Specialist, and CO-AUTHOR *Ava D. Rodgers* is State Leader—Home Economics, Cooperative Extension Service, University of Arkansas, Little Rock.

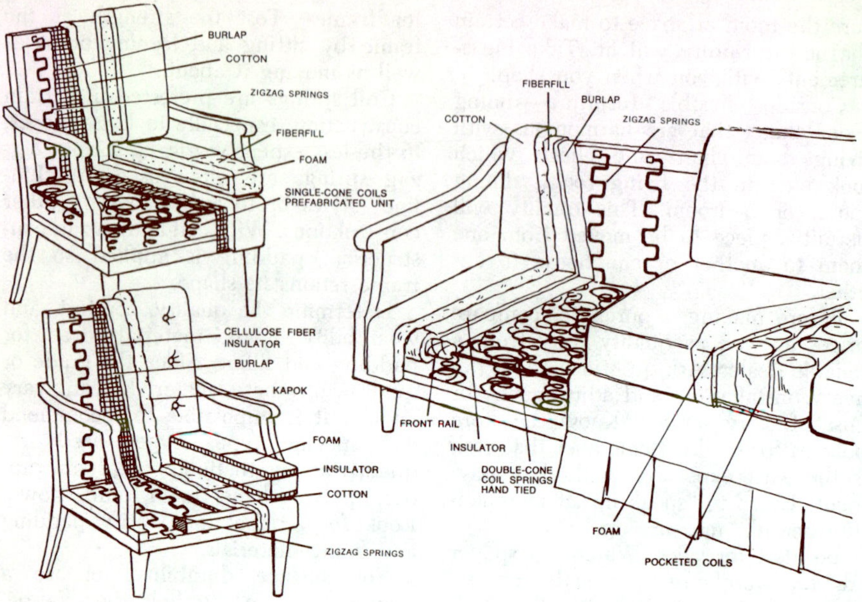

same line of upholstery fabrics in order to compare quality.

Finishes are applied to some fabrics to make them soil and stain resistant. Don't expect the impossible from these "miracle processes." They will cut down on cleaning bills, but they do not last indefinitely. Some manufacturers are including alphabetical symbols on labels to denote recommended cleaning procedures. Look for these symbols and their meanings.

In buying convertible sofas and reclining chairs, work the mechanisms to test strength and mobility. They should operate smoothly, quietly, and without strain. Moving parts must not scratch the floor nor tear bedding.

Consider buying a convertible sofa with a top-quality mattress if it will receive constant use. Convertible sofas are available with standard bedding mattresses in sizes from love seat to queen. Mattressses for convertible sofas are included in the flammability standards established by Federal legislation.

Test each piece of upholstered furniture for comfort. How does it sit? Are the arms comfortable? Check the height, width, and slant of the seat and back for comfort. Remember that convertible sofas must provide comfortable sleeping and sitting space.

Sit on the sofa. Is the depth of the seat uncomfortable? Lie down on the mattress. Is it comfortable?

Case Goods

"Case goods" is the term used for chests, desks, tables, bookcases, bedroom and dining room groupings, and similar pieces. In other words, it is nonupholstered furniture. Wood has been and still is the favorite material for case goods; however, plastics, glass, metals, and other materials are being used more and more.

Test the case goods furniture. Does it wobble? With the base firmly placed, put your hand on top of the surface and try rocking the piece. Does it feel sturdy? Do all movable parts operate? Have you tried to open and close the expandable dining room table? Are all joints tightly fitted? Is the finish durable and smooth?

Drawers and doors should fit snugly and be flush to the furniture surface.

Top above, carefully read all labels and hang tags for information on fiber content, construction, and care instructions. Top right, for durability and suitability of upholstery fabric, consider appearance, fiber, weave, color, pattern, and cost. Above, smart shopper will test for comfort as well as determine if all movable parts operate smoothly. Right, dust panels between drawers and heavy-duty center drawer guides are desirable.

Drawers should slide smoothly on center or side guides. There should be dust-proof panels between drawers.

Are knobs, pulls, and handles attached firmly and easy to grasp? Do they complement the furniture style?

If the furniture is to stand away from the wall, are the sides and back finished the same as the front and top? Have interior surfaces been finished?

Because of new methods and materials used in furniture construction, it is impossible to say there is only one way or one material to use for quality furniture. It is not *what* is done, but *how well* it is done, that is important.

Recognizing quality in wood case goods requires a knowledge of design features, different woods, finishes, workmanship, and care instructions. These factors will, of course, determine the quality and price of the furniture.

Most hardwoods are stronger and more satisfactory for furniture construction than softwoods. Popular hardwoods valued for their beautiful grain and color are mahogany, walnut, maple, cherry, and oak. Other hardwoods may be finished with a painted or stained surface.

Quality furniture is made of solid wood, veneer (plywood), or a combination of both. In solid construction, all wood parts which show are made of solid wood. Plywood or veneered furniture is made of several thin layers of wood bonded together, usually with the top layer or face veneer made of one of the more expensive and beautiful hardwoods.

A majority of the better furniture manufacturers now use a plywood construction in combination with solid wood. Many manufacturers are using molded component plastic for the ornate scrolls and other decorative treatments to replace the more costly solid wood carvings. Such practices allow more people to have durable, attractive furniture at prices they can afford.

Look for descriptive labels. Don't be misled by labels such as "walnut finish." This does not indicate the use of walnut wood. It means the wood used has been finished to resemble walnut.

Many finishes are resistant to stains, scratches, and temperature extremes. Lacquer, oil, varnish, and synthetic finishes are being used. Finishes are good only if properly applied and given proper care.

New Federal Trade Commission guides provide that furniture be labeled with more information on materials used to simulate other materials and veneered construction. Many additional provisions in the guides will give consumers more information about the furniture they buy.

Bedding

Buy the best quality mattress and box springs you can afford. When shopping, test the mattresses by lying down on them, preferably when you are not tired. You can then decide if the bed is too hard, too soft, or just right. Select bedding which will provide proper support.

Since it is impossible for you to see the inside of your purchase, it is important to deal with a reputable firm. Read all labels. Mattresses are included in the government flammability standards established in 1973.

Whether to buy a mattress that is innerspring construction, all foam, or a combination of foam and innerspring construction is a personal choice. All-foam mattresses are often chosen by people who suffer from allergies. Latex rubber and polyurethane foam mattresses are available in varying thickness, firmness, and quality.

When shopping for innerspring mattresses, it is important to consider the number of coils—but it is equally important to consider the gauge or thickness of the wire, the quality and type of construction, the filling and cushioning materials, and the outer covering. Most manufacturers consider that approximately 250 to 300 coils are needed for proper support.

Look for ventilators and handles on the mattress sides. Reinforced supports should be around the edges to prevent sagging.

A box spring, sometimes called a mattress foundation, should be specifically designed for the mattress. It is recommended that a matching box spring be purchased with a new mattress. Usually if a mattress is worn out, so is the supporting spring unit.

The guarantee may depend on the purchase of a matching mattress and spring set. Be sure you know what is covered in the guarantee. Ask for a written copy of the guarantee, and save the sales receipt as proof of purchase.

Size of bedding will depend on personal preference and space. Standard mattress and spring measurements include: twin, 38″ x 75″; twin extra long, 38″ x 80″; full or double, 53″ x 75″; full (double) extra long, 53″ x 80″; queen, 60″ x 80″; king, 76″ x 80″; king extra long, 76″ x 84″. Standard full (double) bed frames can be enlarged with new side rails and width extenders to accommodate long or queen-size mattresses and springs.

If you are shopping on an extremely limited budget, you may wish to complete your bedding by purchasing a sturdy metal bed frame with casters or rollers. At a later date, you can purchase the headboard.

To SUM UP: Learn to be a discriminating shopper. Become familiar with what is available. Be inquisitive and shop all available sources. Look at model rooms and magazines to determine styles and arrangements you like. The simple, well-made piece of furniture can be a better buy for your money than a more elaborate product, because you are buying better construction features rather than fancy finishes and showy hardware.

Take your time—don't rush when you are shopping for furniture. If you really like a piece, wait a week and then decide. You may live with it longer than you plan!

Furnishings Tips for Your Outdoor Living Areas

IT TAKES sharp planning and the right furnishings to make outdoor living areas functional and enjoyable for the entire family. These areas may include patios, terraces, balconies, gardens, decks, lanais or atriums, and they actually extend or enlarge living space.

Composition and age of family members, interests in outdoor activities, size of space, and geographic location should be considered when you select furnishings. A functional outdoor living area not only accommodates comfortable living, but also is furnished to meet the needs of everyone who will use it. Furnishings for outdoor living areas generally include tables, chairs, accessories, cooking equipment, lighting, and perhaps carpeting.

Choose furnishings that are made of durable weather-resistant materials. Heat, sunlight, moisture, and soil cause deterioration. Pick furnishings that are of quality construction. People who make maximum use of outdoor living areas can justify the purchase of better quality furnishings.

If furnishings will be moved frequently to storage or used in other areas, they should be lightweight. However, they ought not to be so lightweight that they have to be retrieved after every gust of wind. Furnishings that fold or collapse into compact shapes are most easily stored.

When furnishings are to be used outside during the summer and brought inside for winter use, it is important they be chosen for that dual role. For example, comfortable, well designed occasional chairs offer serviceability in family rooms, or as additional seating when entertaining. Picnic tables and chairs or benches are also suitable for everyday dining and entertaining.

Outdoor furniture can generally be classified as pieces made of metal, wood, fiberglass, plastic or a combination of those materials.

The metals used include aluminum, wrought iron, molded cast iron, and steel.

Aluminum is lightweight and rustproof. Good quality pieces have an anodized finish to prevent corrosion. Vinyl and various other fabrics and redwood are teamed with aluminum furniture. Look for sturdy locking devices, non-tipping designs, and quality webbing or tubing that is firmly attached and easily replaced. Look also for strong and smooth joints and seams.

Wrought iron furniture is usually quite heavy, making it more suitable for locations where permanence rather than portability is important. It will rust unless a finish such as enamel is used and kept up.

Molded cast iron furniture is brittle, quite heavy and can be broken or cracked. It will rust if the paint is cracked or chipped. It is much heavier than wrought iron, and it generally is uncomfortable due to raised metal designs.

Steel used in outdoor furniture may resemble aluminum or wrought iron. It is available in styles utilizing sheet and wire mesh and may be combined with wood, vinyl, fabric or other materials. Steel furniture is strong, durable and weather resistant. It is unaffected by chemicals and temperature changes. Baked-on enamel finishes provide good service. Pre-enameling treatments such as bonderizing help resist chipping and rusting. Look for strong welds and smooth edges and seams.

Wood furniture is most often made of cedar, cypress and redwood for use outdoors. The wood may be used alone or combined with metal framing for added comfort, increased strength and lighter weight. Wood furniture should be protected with lacquer, varnish, enamel, or a good coat of paste wax. A brush-on wood preservative and water repellant finish can be applied seasonally to wood furniture that receives no protection.

Rattan, wicker and bamboo, often mistaken for wood furniture, are designed only for sun porches and indoor use. They cannot be finished to withstand outdoor conditions for any great period of time.

Fiberglass is among the newer materials used for outdoor furniture. Generally designed to fit the contour of the body, it is lightweight, strong, durable and impervious to weather extremes. Color is added while the material is in a liquid form, eliminating the problems of sun fading, chipping and peeling.

Molded furniture made of plastic, including urethane, is becoming more popular. Polyester and acrylic tops are often combined with plastic bases. Plastic furniture requires minimal maintenance but offers durability. Look for impact resistance, structural strength and smooth surfaces and edges.

For increased comfort, chair and lounge pads are available with covers in various colors, textures and decorative patterns. Unfortunately, mold, mildew and deterioration are major problems.

Pads made of woven or knitted synthetic fibers and filled with weather resistant padding can withstand moisture to a certain extent. However, even these should be protected as much as possible or arranged for maximum water drainage and air circulation when not in use.

Pads made of natural fiber upholstery fabric and filling should not be left outdoors unprotected against rain since they have low resistance to the elements.

Glass, a common material for table tops, should be high quality, impact resistant, and sized to fit securely within the frame or mounting devices.

Additional furnishings such as decorative and functional accessories, cooking equipment, lighting and plants complement an outdoor living area. They add the finishing touch and often set the mood of the living area.

Accessories are divided into two general classifications:

- Decorative—For example, wind chimes, driftwood, sculpture, urns, garden pools, fountains and waterfalls, lighting, etc.
- Utilitarian—For example, cooking equipment, ashtrays, pillows and pads for lounging, mobile carts, lighting, etc. They should be chosen for their beauty as well as their use.

Coordinate the color, pattern and style of the outdoor accessories—from ashtrays to art objects. Considering

---

AUTHORS *Jane Berry, Patricia Anne Bradshaw* and *Anna Marie Gottschalk* are Housing and Home Furnishings Specialists, Texas Agricultural Extension Service of the Texas A&M University System, College Station.

what is needed, where and how it will be used, and establishing a theme will help you choose appropriate outdoor accessories.

Besides furnishing an area for physical and visual pleasure, you need to consider sound effects. Moving, splashing water creates a very pleasing sound and lends interest. Pools, fountains and waterfalls that will fit into the area can be purchased or constructed. Materials selected should relate to other furnishings and the existing space.

Few outdoor areas are considered complete without cooking equipment. Place a portable unit so it does not interfere with the landscape, or store it when not in use. During use locate it to avoid wind and sun, and so the smoke won't run you off.

Installed units may range from simple ones which blend with garden and house, to elaborate free standing structures which serve as the focal point for activities and design of the area. Whether large or small, a well-planned unit can add a touch of luxury. Take care to avoid selecting one that will overwhelm the area. Unless located in precisely the right spot, the installed unit may go unused and prove an expensive eyesore.

Good lighting is both functional and esthetic. It invites you out of doors at night and enhances the view from the house.

Consider your need for the following when planning lighting:

- Functional light for areas requiring light for specific purposes such as badminton, pathways, or eating areas
- Decorative light for special effects such as highlighting a piece of garden sculpture, a prize plant, or sand casting on a concrete wall

Spotlights or floodlights will do the job where more illumination is needed. Fixtures are best situated when not visible. Conceal lights, at or near ground level, behind plants or masonry, on top of the house or under its eaves.

Potted plants, hanging baskets and boxes, or border plantings visually soften outdoor areas. They add color, texture, pattern, fragrance, and sometimes shade. In addition, plants can serve as protection from sun and wind as well as provide privacy. Consider placing plants on steps, in a corner, around porch posts or tree trunks, or against a house.

Choose containers of a suitable size, shape, and material for your plants. Consider also the overall decorative effect of plant containers. For example, natural clay pots offer a pleasing visual effect and relate well to natural surroundings.

A current trend is to furnish outdoor living areas in carpet that is tough, weatherproof, fade resistant, colorful, patterned and textured.

Outdoor carpet must withstand heat, sunlight, moisture, abrasion, insects, soil, and mildew. A good choice is carpeting made from 100 percent synthetic fiber, such as solution-dyed polypropylene olefin, acrylic and nylon fibers.

Construction is as important as fiber content. Several methods may be employed. Needlepunched carpet is made by staple fibers being laid on a backing. The fibers are then forced into the backing with needles. This process results in a felt-like sheet having the appearance of a mat. To secure the fibers, needlepunched carpet may be either heat bonded or have weather-resistant latex or similar material applied to the back.

Tufting is another type of construction used to make outdoor carpeting. In this method yarns are alternately looped above and below the backing and anchored in place with a latex coating. The loops may be cut to create a variety of surfaces. Tufted outdoor carpets look more like traditional pile carpeting than those that are needlepunched.

Non-weather resistant foam or sponge backing which will deteriorate from heat and moisture and are fragile when used on rough surfaces are not acceptable for outdoor use. Outdoor carpet should not have a foam type backing since it would eliminate the possibility of drainage.

Remember, consider the following when selecting outdoor furnishings:

_____Comfort
_____Convenience
_____Durability
_____Portability
_____Storability
_____Quality construction
_____Design
_____Care requirements

Buy furnishings made by reputable manufacturers and sold by reputable dealers. Read hang tags and labels on the furnishings and ask questions about guarantees.

Because of increased standardization, the home has become a refuge. In the home family members can express themselves as individuals. However, the current economic situation has caused consumers to accept less interior space. This has increased the importance of utilizing surrounding exterior space. Increased leisure time has also increased the use of outdoor living spaces. Therefore, a functional, well furnished outdoor living area will complement today's living.

The A, B, C's of Cleaning Materials

CLEANING a modern home is simple with efficient materials and techniques. What is needed is greater knowledge about the composition, finish of the surface to be cleaned, soil, and supplies and equipment that operate most effectively.

Selecting effective cleaning materials for the home can be difficult. Advertising claims of superior cleaning ability, ease, and carefree use of products and equipment for a sparkling clean house often are confusing. How does the consumer know the product best suited for the job from the myriad offerings in the marketplace?

Many cleaning products on the market today are basic ingredients that are premixed, perfumed and packaged in attractive boxes, cans, bottles or jars.

Common basic ingredients are water, alkalies, soaps or detergents, acids, abrasives, bleaches, sanitizers and solvents. Understanding the performance of these ingredients can aid in your selection.

Water is one of the most effective cleaning aids known to man. Soft water, warm or hot with mild soap or detergent, cleans porcelain, painted woodwork and other washable surfaces well. Hard water does not work well with soap because the hardness minerals form curds. Using a water softener can break down these minerals.

Mild detergent is especially effective in cleaning where grease and cooking fumes have collected on walls, woodwork and floors. It can also be used to make an inexpensive shampoo for rugs or upholstery. Whip ¼ cup mild detergent with 1 pint warm water until it makes a stiff foam.

Heavy duty detergent is very alkaline. It is not suitable for cleaning linoleum or painted surfaces, but it is excellent for cleaning the toilet bowl and soaking burner parts of the gas range, and for broiler pans and other greasy or oily surfaces.

Most liquid all-purpose cleaners have soap and/or detergent with water as the main ingredient. Some have ammonia, pine oil, lysol or other cleaning agents. If you study the label carefully, you will find many of the same ingredients as those listed on detergent labels.

Liquid cleaners often come in spray or aerosol containers. In aerosol cans, the product is mixed with a propellant making it foam and bubble.

Most all-purpose cleaners are alkaline and cut grease and dirt easily. They are safe for cleaning porcelain, painted surfaces, ceramic tile and some resilient floors.

Some liquid cleaners may have an acid ingredient to cut hard water spots, soap buildup and rust.

Granular or powdered all-purpose cleaners may list ingredients, such as trisodium phosphate (TSP), and water-softening agents. Trisodium phosphate sometimes is used to clean and rough-up a wooden surface before repainting.

Lye is the main ingredient of many oven cleaners. This highly toxic alkali, often called caustic soda, usually does a good job of removing burned-on grease or soil. Avoid breathing the fumes or getting the lye on chromium and aluminum parts or on the hands. Some oven cleaners contain ammonia, which also loosens burned-on grease and soil. It is toxic in strengths of 5 percent or more.

It's cheaper and safer to clean your range with ammonia and detergent.

Window and glass cleaners with ammonia are good for cleaning greasy cooking fumes that collect on glass surfaces. You can make an effective cleaner with 4 tablespoons of ammonia to 1 quart of warm water.

Cleaners for washing outside windows may have a mild acid base with detergent. Mix 2 tablespoons vinegar to 1 quart of warm water to remove water spots. Add a little detergent if needed.

Selecting the right drain cleaner depends on what is causing the clog and the location of the drain.

For clogged kitchen drains try a non-caustic liquid cleaner first, since it is basically a grease solvent. If it is not effective, try a caustic granular type which contains a high percentage of caustic soda or potash that will dissolve grease or hair. Most caustic cleaners cannot be used in garbage disposers.

For the bathroom drain, where hair may have caused the clog, use a caustic liquid. If it fails, try caustic granules.

Follow directions carefully and with caution. Caustic cleaners can ruin cabinet tops, aluminum trim, walls and floors, and they can burn body tissue. For a sluggish drain, try using ½ pound washing soda to 2 cups boiling water.

Toilet bowl cleaners often have an acid base for removing discoloration in the vitreous china bowl. These are toxic and should be used with caution. For a safer way, scrub the toilet bowl with ¼ cup detergent.

Abrasives clean by friction. Scouring powders and pads, sandpaper, meshes of metal, plastic or nylon, steel wool, pumice and whiting are common abrasives.

Harsh abrasives, such as scouring powder, will gradually cause damage by scratching the glossy finish on painted surfaces, porcelain enamel or plastics. Once the surface is dull, it will soil faster and stain.

Use the mildest or finest abrasive possible to avoid marring the surface to be cleaned.

Feel the abrasive between your fingers to judge its harshness. Plastic or nylon mesh, cream silver polish and whiting are examples of mild abrasives.

Make your own porcelain cleaner by using 4 parts whiting and 1 part soap jelly.

To make soap jelly, shave 1 cup bar soap; dissolve it in 1 quart boiling water. When cool, store in a jar. Use as a multi-purpose soap cleaner.

Chlorine bleach is an alkali and will damage many surfaces if used without dilution with water. It is an effective sanitizer if used according to directions. Some products claim to "disinfect or sanitize" that do not really kill bacteria.

Used according to directions, chlorine bleach, pine oil, phenolic or quaternary disinfectants will kill harmful bacteria.

Chlorine bleach reacts with ammonia and with acid cleaners such as toilet bowl cleaners and rust removers to form a dangerous and irritating gas. Never mix chlorine bleach or a product containing it with other cleaners.

You can clean all floors, except cork and wood, with water. If badly soiled or if wax has built up, mop with a mild detergent solution or a wax remover diluted according to directions.

Use water base wax on rubber and asphalt tile floors.

For vinyl floors that require wax; linoleum, terrazzo and concrete floors,

---

AUTHOR *Doris M. Myers* is a state home management specialist, Texas Agricultural Extension Service, Texas A&M University, College Station.

use a water base or a solvent cleaning and polishing wax.

Wood and cork floors should be cleaned with solvent cleaning and polishing wax. Paste wax offers the best protection.

Rub heel marks and streaks with a small amount of the appropriate wax on a nylon scrub pad or very fine steel wool.

Spray waxes may be used on furniture where a shine is desired. Liquid cleaning wax used periodically protects some furniture. For antique or very fine furniture, use paste wax or lemon oil.

A homemade cleaner for wood is: 1 part gum turpentine and 3 parts boiled linseed oil.

To clean and shine surfaces such as countertops, ceramic tile, cabinets and appliances, use a creamy cleaning wax.

When choosing tools for cleaning, only two types are necessary: one to soften and remove moist soil which has hardened on washable surfaces and one to loosen and remove dirt and dust.

Basic tools needed for washable surfaces include a wet mop, sponges or cloths, containers for water and toilet-bowl brush.

Wet mops are made of cotton or cellulose sponge. Shop for a lightweight, smooth handle that is comfortable to hold. The handle should attach firmly to the mophead. A string mop should have lintless, long staple cotton in four or more ply yarns. A sponge mop should be refillable.

Look for a mop on which the wooden or metal base of the mophead is recessed, rounded or padded to prevent scarring baseboards and furniture. Some mops have a device for squeezing out the water.

Another house cleaning tool is the sponge. Select one that fits your hand, yet holds enough moisture to cover a fairly large area.

A lintless cloth is very satisfactory for cleaning. Paper cloths, cheesecloth, worn diapers or cotton undershirts can be used. Chamois is excellent for washing windows because it cleans and polishes at the same time.

Two containers for water are desirable—one for a cleaning solution and one for rinsing. Durable plastic buckets are easier to handle than aluminum or galvanized iron.

Circular or ball-shaped toilet-bowl brushes are made of stiff animal, plant or synthetic bristles and fibers twisted in a rustless wire. Those fastened around a wood ball are more difficult to keep sanitary as the wood absorbs water. Bristle brushes do not drip after the water is shaken out.

You may choose to buy an electrical appliance to scrub floors that dispenses the cleaning solution then picks it back up. Or you may choose the electric floor machine that can scrub, refinish or polish floors. You may also want an appliance designed for shampooing rugs and carpets. This appliance dispenses dry foam over the pile and down between the fibers without soaking the carpet fabric.

When choosing an electrical appliance that uses water be sure that both the appliance and the cord have the Underwriters Laboratories (UL) seal of approval.

Basic tools to lift and remove loose dry dirt and dust may be as simple as a vacuum cleaner and attachments.

There are three basic types of vacuum cleaners. When deciding on a vacuum cleaner know what you expect to clean. Then choose the one best suited to your needs.

The canister/tank type cleans from suction produced by a motor driven fan. The suction pulls the litter and dust into the dust bag. This type cleaner is lightweight and good for general floor care, as well as above-the-floor cleaning.

The upright vacuum cleaner has both agitation and suction. The suction lifts the rug against the nozzle. The brushes and/or beater bars vibrate the dirt and litter loose from the rug where the air flow can carry it into the dust bag.

For cleaning carpets and rugs, an upright cleaner does a superior job. Most upright cleaners have attachments for cleaning above the floor. When using the attachments, insert the hose into the machine to divert the suction to the tool used.

The combination vacuum cleaner takes the suction of the canister/tank and the powered agitator head of the upright, and combines them. This is done by adding a powered rug nozzle to the canister/tank models.

If you want a dual approach to cleaning, you will need both a canister/tank and an upright or a combination.

Other makes and models of vacuum cleaners include the small hand or portable model for small jobs, the stick broom for general floor care, and the built-in system.

The built-in system consists of a power unit with a dirt-collecting container located outside the living area. The container is connected to dirt-carrying tubes which open into various walls in the home. A long, flexible hose with numerous attachments can be plugged into the covered outlets to silently and efficiently clean all areas of the home. The central system is the most expensive vacuum cleaning equipment and has the advantage of no recirculation of dirt, no machine to pull around, and little equipment to store.

Another type of cleaner filters collected dust and dirt through water, which is automatically flushed down a drain. It can also be used as a wet pick-up device, as well as for regular dry vacuum cleaning.

A vacuum cleaner may seem expensive in comparison to other cleaning tools which may be used to replace it. However, the vacuum cleaner does a superior job of cleaning.

Be sure to read the vacuum cleaner guarantee. Make sure the manufacturer has a reputation for making reliable products.

Manual tools that clean are the carpet sweeper, dust mop, dustcloth, broom and dustpan.

If you have rugs and no vacuum cleaner, a carpet sweeper does a good job of removing surface litter and dust. It cannot remove dirt between the fibers. It is an effective quick pick-up to use in combination with a vacuum cleaner for rug cleaning.

When selecting a dust mop look for one that will pick up and hold dust. Choose one that has a removable, washable mophead and lint-free fibers. If oil or wax-treated mops are chosen, store the mophead in an air-tight metal container to avoid a fire hazard.

Dustcloths must be absorbent, clean and lint-free. You can purchase treated dustcloths or make one from a soft cloth.

Spread a few drops of furniture oil or wax in a tin container or jar. Insert a cloth and cover tightly overnight. The cloth will absorb enough oil or wax to remove dust and polish at the same time. (For dusting waxed surfaces, do not use oil because it softens the finish).

Brooms come in a variety of sizes, weights and fibers. Choose a broom that is lightweight with a smooth, long handle. Look for a mixture of curly and rough fibers stitched together at the top. The fibers should have short, split ends.

Push brooms scatter less dust than a regular broom. Those made of horse hair are excellent for use on floors. Fiber bristles are more effective for sweeping large areas, such as garages and walks.

Before purchasing new tools, consider questions such as:

- Would it be used enough to justify the cost?
- How many kinds of jobs will it do?
- Is it easy to operate, carry and store?
- Would it save more time than another piece of equipment?
- Is it safe to operate?

Tools You Need for Repair Jobs

MATCH YOUR HOUSEHOLD repair and maintenance tools with your ability, interest, budget, and tool storage area. Keep your most used tools, a common 3/16th inch flat slot screwdriver and a 7 inch slip joint pliers, in a convenient place.

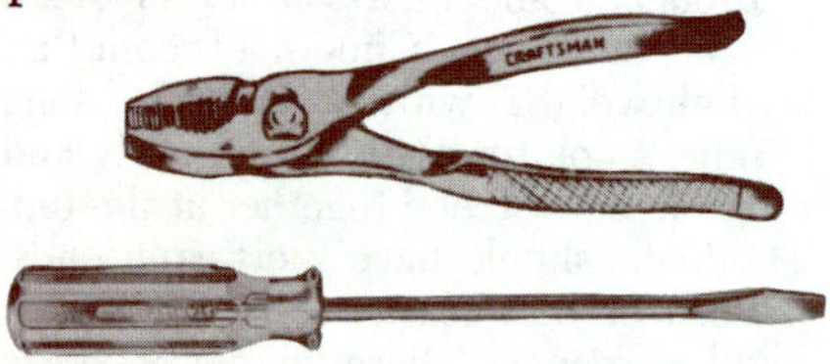

Keep less frequently used tools in the work and storage area. A basement or garage, or one of your closets, might serve as a tool center.

After the screwdriver and pliers already mentioned, your next most frequently needed tools will probably include additional screwdrivers, sheet metal screws, a hammer, nails, a stone or file for sharpening knives, a drill, square, level, a toilet and drain plunger, faucet repair tools, painting supplies, and glazing or window glass replacement equipment.

Two flat slot screwdrivers, one with a ¼″ blade, the other with a 5/16″ blade, and a #1 (small) and a #2 (medium) Phillips head screwdriver, round out a set of screwdrivers that will meet most household needs.

Select a good quality 12 or 13 ounce, curved claw hammer. Good quality hammers have thinner and stronger claws than the bargain bin version.

Now for a good nail collection. Get a small box of each: ¾″, 1″, and 1¼″ wire brads (small heads), and a box of each of the same size wire nails (flat heads), plus a pound box of six penny finishing nails.

If you need shorter nails, you can cut the pointed end off the ¾″ brad or nail with a pair of nippers, side cutting pliers or a hack saw.

A nail with the head cut off makes a low cost workable drill bit for use in either a hand drill or an electric drill. It works well for drilling in plaster or drilling pilot nail holes in wood to prevent wood splitting and nail bending.

For pilot holes in wood, use a nail bit slightly smaller in diameter than the nail to be driven, or else drill a shallow hole so the tip of the nail will be securely anchored in the wood.

A light duty ¼″ electric drill, on a sale special, can be purchased for just a little more than a good quality hand drill. Before buying, examine to see that the chuck will close tight enough so it will hold a ¾″ headless wire brad as a drill bit.

The ¼″ electric drill with a five to seven piece set of high speed steel drill bits will drill holes in metal up to ¼″ in diameter. The lower priced carbon-steel drills are recommended for use in wood only.

Wood boring bits with ¼″ shanks are available in sets of five to six pieces up to 1″ in diameter. Larger sizes are also available. Use the large bits carefully to avoid stripping gears in the light duty drill.

An extension cord may be desirable for use with the electric drill. It should

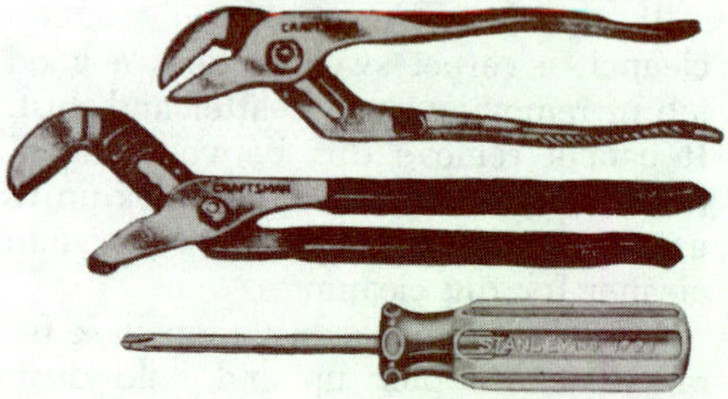

AUTHOR *Glenn Barquest* is an Extension Agricultural Engineer at the University of Wisconsin-Madison, Madison.

be at least #16 gauge wire (#14 is larger than #16). If you purchased a drill with an insulated housing and a two prong connector, a two wire cord will be satisfactory. If the drill has a three wire electric connector, a three wire grounding type cord is needed for protection from electrical shock.

A 1½″ by 9″ general purpose flat tapered sharpening stone, or 6″ to 8″ mill file, can be used to sharpen household knives and scissors as well as lawn and garden tools.

A 6″ to 12″ level is desirable for occasional use in leveling appliances and pictures. You may purchase the level as an item, or purchase a steel combination square with a level as part of the head or handle. If you purchase them separately, a 6″ to 12″ level and an 8″ by 12″ steel utility square make a good pair.

A push-pull type steel tape, or a folding rule, is a convenience for additional measuring. A yardstick or tape measure may be used as a substitute. However, the tape measure may be inaccurate.

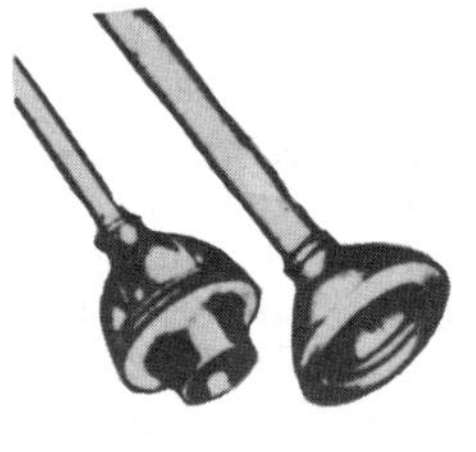

In most homes a toilet and drain rubber plunger, or force cup, is a necessity. The lower cost bell shaped plunger is workable but the more expensive hornet nest shaped 2-way plunger is more effective, especially in toilets.

Most people force the handle of both types of plungers down too far so the rubber doubles back on itself. Try pushing the handle down about one inch, then pulling it back up in rhythmic strokes to get the water surging back and forth. The extended bottom of the 2-way plunger can be tucked in at the bottom for use in sinks.

A flexible coiled spring steel "snake" —called a closet or drain and trap auger—will receive less use than the plunger, but it may save an expensive

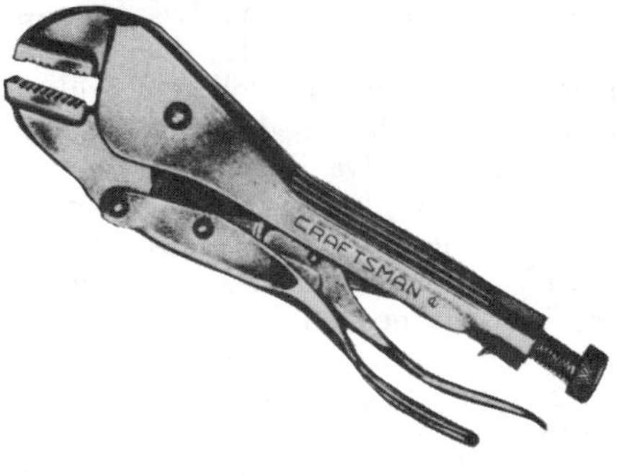

trip by the plumber. The "snake" should have a handle to provide rotary motion.

The screwdrivers mentioned earlier will meet the needs for faucet washer replacement, but a 10″ or larger adjustable open end wrench is needed for the faucet nuts. Mechanics pliers or arc joint pliers may serve as a substitute, but the jaws may mar the finish on the faucet nuts unless they are taped or wrapped with cloth.

If you plan to do interior painting and varnishing, you need equipment for both latex (water-base) and oil-base materials. A 5′ or 6′ stepladder is needed for wall and ceiling painting.

For wall or ceiling painting with latex paint, it's desirable to have a 7″ roller and tray set, and a nylon bristle brush 1″ to 2″ wide to get into the corners. A plastic cloth to cover the floor is convenient, but you can use old newspapers instead. Some people are enthusiastic about the 4″ x 6″ foam brush pads instead of the roller and others are disappointed with their use. I prefer the roller and brush, but you have to decide for yourself.

A nylon bristle brush works best for applying latex enamel. However, a roller with a short nap cover may be desirable for large areas such as the ceiling, because the latex enamel dries so fast it is difficult to keep the lap joints wet when using the slower brush method.

High quality animal bristle brushes are best for applying oil-base enamel, varnish, and varnish-like finishes, but high quality nylon bristle brushes will work.

Plaster patching compounds are

available at paint and hardware stores for holes and small cracks. A crack repair kit consisting of a roll of fiberglass cloth netting about 4″ wide and a binder or adhesive is available for repairing wide plaster cracks. A putty knife is desirable for applying the patching compound and a special wide applicator is needed for the fiberglass material.

The putty knife is needed if you replace glass in a wooden sash. Glazier points with a driver and hammer, and putty and glazing compounds are other needs. To protect yourself from cuts, wear gloves when handling and removing broken glass.

A glass cutter is required for cutting glass, but it may be better to have the cutting done at a store.

Placing glass in aluminum sash is a special process. Have it done in a shop or store where special equipment is available.

Lubrication materials, tape, glue, sandpaper, hex wrenches, locking plier-wrench, c-clamps, wood screws, woodworking and metal working tools are next on the list.

A can of light machine or household oil is suitable for lubricating electric motors, door hinges, etc. A tube of dry graphite lubricating powder or dry white lubricating powder is ideal for lubricating door latches and locks.

Some masking tape, black cloth friction tape and black electrician's plastic tape, as well as white polyvinyl glue, will receive monthly use in most family situations. The white glue is not waterproof, so resorcinol or epoxy adhesive should be used on items which will get wet or be used outdoors.

You will need screws, saws, sandpaper, and wood smoothing or forming tools if you plan to build or repair items made from wood. An assortment of flat head and round head woodscrews is desirable. A five to six piece set of woodscrew pilot hole bits for drilling pilot holes and countersinking is a real convenience. If such a set is not available, twist drills and a countersink bit can be used instead.

A cross cut hand saw, 20″ to 22″ long with 10 to 12 teeth points per inch is ideal, but a 26″ saw with 8 to 10 points is satisfactory. For more accurate cuts, clamp another piece of lumber as a guide block along the pencil mark and rub the side of the saw against the guide while sawing.

Avoid a low cost wooden miter box, unless the saw guide notches are narrow. Most of them are made with notches ⅛″ wide or wider. The wide notch allows the saw to wobble, which results in poor cuts.

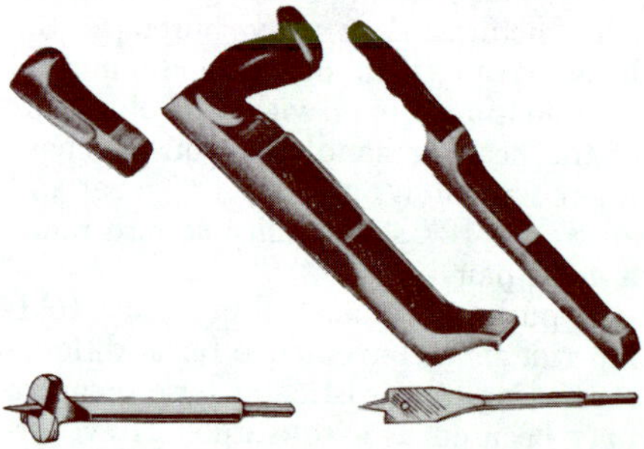

A flat multi-blade wood forming tool can be used in place of a wood plane for smoothing and removing small amounts of wood. The wood forming tool has a replaceable blade, which eliminates the task of plane iron or blade sharpening. The tool is available with either a plane type or file type handle. Wood forming tools are also available in round, half-round and other special shapes.

Use sandpaper for final smoothing. Garnet or aluminum oxide is the best as it is sharper, and will cut faster than the cheaper flintpaper. Flintpaper works most satisfactorily on soft wood.

If you do much work with wood, get a set of four or five wood chisels ranging from ¼″ to 1″ in width. A 2″ x 5″ or larger combination sharpening stone is needed to keep them sharp.

A hacksaw, ⅜″ x 4″ center punch, a small pin punch or lineup punch, and a set of box or open end wrenches complete the list.

GARDENING

Buying Seeds—Pellets, Tapes and Blankets

MENTION SEEDS and most people think of seed catalogs, those colorful harbingers of spring that signal the first after-Christmas mail each year. Today they may not be as flamboyant as in the past, but they do raise hopes anew that "this will be the year."

Or maybe seeds mean to you the pleasures of choosing from the colorful seed packets in a store rack. The corner wishing well, as it were.

Both seed catalogs and seed racks are still much in evidence, and they provide one of the most inexpensive ways to get into gardening. Even the new super hybrids (listed as F_1), hand produced slowly and patiently and thus many times more costly, are still in the pennies class, not dollars as you might think.

Many ingenious but different ways to buy seeds are now being offered, for flowers, vegetables and lawns.

These include pre-seeded peat pellets that you merely drop into water until they swell to make "soil" and "pot." Later, after the seeds have sprouted and the young seedling developed enough, you plant "pot and all" in the garden. You have avoided the need to hunt for suitable seeding soil. There's no mess of sterilizing the soil, and no risking quick loss of tender seedlings in contaminated soil. There's no clay pot to break, or plastic pot to buy and discard. And you are sure that the seeds are at the right depth in the soil.

Even the youngest child can have success with a variety of plants that otherwise require finger dexterity he hasn't yet developed.

Seed tapes have long intrigued gardeners. The idea is that you merely unroll a long tape where you want the pre-spaced seeds to grow. For the past dozen or more years there have been tapes in the stores. And every year they get better.

Early tapes frustrated users by failing to stay in tight contact with the soil. The seeds never got moist enough to sprout, or the new seedlings died from thirst because the tape was up a bit from the moist soil which they needed to stay alive and grow.

Even today you must use tapes carefully. Follow the maker's directions to the letter.

Seed blankets are in effect an all-in-one series of seed tapes. You plant the garden as if rolling out a carpet. The same precautions as in using seed tapes must be followed.

Seed blankets do serve to establish a garden, say of wild-flowers, on a slope where otherwise seeds would wash away before they could sprout and the seedlings become firmly rooted into the soil.

Pelleted seeds are widely used today. The coatings vary. They may be just enough to make all the seeds exactly the same size and shape—and color—for easier handling to achieve individual spacing as you plant, by hand or machine. Or they may be elaborate multi-coatings of fertilizers, fungus retardants, growth regulators, or pesticides, added layer by layer like a "12 hour cold tablet" (and as sizable!).

Home gardeners like pelleted seeds for the ease in spacing in hand sowing. With the sophistication of modern pill making equipment, we can look forward to pelleting seed into half-inch "balls" —environmental cells—that permit the seed to sprout and the seedling to grow, all before the roots venture out into what may be less than ideal soil environment. And it is this exposure before the seedling is strong that kills so many so quickly during conventional seeding.

"Sized" seeds are the latest improve-

AUTHOR *Joseph E. Howland* is Professor of Horticulture at the University of Nevada and at the DuPage Horticulture School, West Chicago, Ill.

ment in seed itself. Research had shown that removing the smaller seeds eliminated weaker seedlings that would succumb later to diseases. The separations have been mechanical, literally screening out through sieves the unwanted little seeds.

More recent research, however, indicates that it's not just the small and immature seeds you want to avoid planting. Today there is reason to believe that the chemistry in some seeds keeps them slow sprouting, slow growing seedlings, low producing plants—as much as 10 percent less than other seeds of exactly the same size and weight.

Tomorrow you will undoubtedly be able to order "super seeds." Even a 100 percent premium in their price would make them a bargain, for the cost of seed is always by far the smallest cost in gardening.

Lawn seed is unique in your seed buying. Unlike flowers and vegetables, lawn seed usually is sold by area coverage rather than by weight, although by law the weight must also be included somewhere on the label. Also by law, the blend (percentage of the different grasses—and weeds!) must be printed in easy to read type sizes on the label.

Unfortunately, the weed content is by weight: 99.9 percent pure can mean 1,000 weeds in every pound of lawn seed you buy. And that's as pure as you can buy, so just know that when you spread lawn seed you invariably spread weed seeds too.

Reputable companies see to it that there are no weeds a simple weedkiller won't eliminate quickly if the first few mowings of the new grass don't do it without further attention by you.

Note that *no* lawn seed is likely to include crabgrass seeds. Crabgrass doesn't go to seed until many weeks after lawn seed is harvested. So don't be taken in by package claims on cheap grass seed—"guaranteed 100 percent crabgrass free." Anybody can make that claim without any risk.

One of the large grass seed growers, processing many millions of pounds each year, reports finding only 14 crabgrass seeds in more than 20 years of searching.

Bedding Plants

Starting with seeds isn't for everyone, of course. Maybe your soil is too rough, or too sticky, or too slow to dry in the spring, for easy success. Or maybe you lack time, either to baby your sprouting seeds and tender seedlings through the first critical weeks, or because you started too late to think about a flower or vegetable garden this year.

Garden centers now feature started plants—called "bedding plants" by the professionals. All the hard work has been done for you. You buy sturdy, well-rooted plants, ready to grow in just about any soil.

Bedding plants are sold in many ways:

- Single plants in pots, often peat pots that you plant "pot and all," avoiding any risk of disturbance to the roots or slowdown in growth of the plants.
- "Cell packs," where each plant is in its own little rooting "cell," readily slipped out for planting.
- Paper or wood fiber trays—"market packs"—of six to 12 plants that you must separate for planting.

What to Look For

Whether you buy seed by mail, or from a neighborhood seed rack, start with good seeds. The law requires that the seed be fresh: look for the date that must be on the packet. Seeds do have a respectable life—as much as five to seven years for many kinds—but only if they are properly stored, meaning kept dry and cool. Sitting around from one year to the next in a hot storeroom obviously is bad for seeds.

Reputable seed companies guarantee varietal purity, that you will get what you think you are buying, and that there will be no chaff or weed seeds in the packet.

Are the seeds in the packet alive and ready to grow? Look for a printed statement of the germination as tested. It notes the *most* seedlings you can expect, under ideal laboratory conditions. Expect maybe half as many if you are seeding outdoors exposed to the vagaries of spring weather.

All seeds need moisture, fresh air, and some warmth to start the germination process. A few need light. None should be "buried." The old rule of not more than two or three times the thickness of the seed is about right. Exceptions will be noted in the directions on the seed packet.

Seedlings Guide: Grow Your Own or Buy Them

ANNUAL flowers and vegetables offer a great opportunity to display your creative talents and satisfy your curiosity about nature, and they provide a form of therapy for both mind and body.

There are several ways to produce these plants for your gardening pleasure. All of them, if properly done, will result in a garden filled with color—as well as food for your table.

If you are a do-it-yourselfer, buy your own seeds, germinate them, and then plant the seedlings in your garden. This is the least expensive way to garden, but requires work and knowledge to be successful.

If you are looking for instant color, or you want to harvest the first vegetables in your neighborhood, you can purchase started seedlings or plants, available as bedding plants in pots or flats from your local garden center. All you need do is buy them, take them home, and plant them in your yard. These plants will cost more than seeds, but require a great deal less work and demand little knowledge from you of seeds, germination or seedling care.

AUTHOR *William H. Carlson* is Associate Professor and Extension Specialist in Horticulture at Michigan State University, East Lansing. He also serves as Executive Secretary of Bedding Plants, Inc., a non-profit trade association.

Sowing Your Own Seed

The most inexpensive way to start your garden is to sow your own seed. Seeds can be purchased at your local garden store, supermarket, or from many mail order seed suppliers. Instructions for sowing the seeds are usually on the back of the seed packet.

Many people will prepare seed beds in their yard by raking the soil in the garden area very level and to a fine texture. They then sow the seeds in rows.

While this method is the easiest, results are usually the poorest. Seeds need proper temperature and moisture to germinate, and these factors are difficult to control outdoors. To control these factors, many gardeners start their seeds indoors and then transplant the seedlings into their garden.

One of the best places for the average homeowner to germinate seed is on a window sill in small plastic flats, or in bread, pie or foil pans. Be sure to punch a few holes in the bottom of the pan for proper drainage.

One of the most important factors in germination is a good soil mix (media). This media should be free from insects, disease organisms, weed seeds and harmful chemicals. It should be well-drained and contain a relatively low amount of nutrients. For this reason *you cannot use garden soil only.* A good mix might consist of one part garden soil, one part peat moss, and one part perlite or vermiculite.

The best and easiest method of providing correct soil conditions for seed germination is to obtain a peat-lite mix from your garden center, or make your own.

Fill your container with this mixture and moisten the medium thoroughly. Then sow the seeds according to directions on the package. Next, place the entire container inside a plastic bag (such as a large sandwich bag or a polyethylene clothes wrapper used by cleaners to cover garments). Blow up the bag as you would a balloon and tie the end closed.

Formula for Peat-lite Mix

Ingredients	To Make 2 Bushels
Shredded Sphagnum peat moss	1 bushel
Horticultural vermiculite No. 2, 3, or 4	1 bushel
Ground limestone	10 T*
Superphosphate 20%, powdered	5 T
5–10–5 fertilizer	15 T
Iron (chelated such as NaFe, 138 or 330)	1 level teaspoonful
Non-ionic surfactant (A detergent like Tide or Dreft)	1 level teaspoonful**

*level tablespoon amounts
**mix with one gallon of water, and water medium with this solution once before planting.

Place the container at room conditions, preferably 70° F. There should be an abundance of light, but not direct sunlight. Do not open the bag until the seeds have germinated. Once the seeds germinate, remove the bag and water as needed.

Seeds need moisture and proper temperature to germinate. The following list indicates the optimum soil temperature for germination of popular annuals and vegetable plants, their need for light and darkness to germinate, as well as the usual time needed for germination.

You will note from the table that most annual seeds require light to germinate. There are, however, a few exceptions. The seeds of Calendula, Centaurea, Annual Phlox, Verbena and Vinca should be germinated in total darkness for best results.

Most annuals germinate between 55° F and 75° F. Therefore, if temperature, moisture, and light and dark conditions are met, seed germination will be no problem.

Many gardeners find that when seeds are germinated on window sills, the results vary from poor to excellent. This variability usually occurs because of temperature. On a bright, sunny day temperatures sometimes rise above the optimum soil temperatures needed for germination, thus delaying or inhibiting germination by drying out the soil mix or by actually dehydrating the seed.

On other days, when it is cloudy and cool, soil temperatures fall below the optimum level. The media thus remains too wet and temperatures are so low that germination is retarded or inhibited. To avoid these problems, the gardener may build a starting environment or home propagation unit.

To start seedlings of most vegetable and bedding plants after germination, a minimum of 500 foot candles of cool white fluorescent light is required. That level can be obtained at about 6″ from new 40-watt fluorescent lamps spaced 6″ apart. There are commercial growing carts available, or a unit can be built on a table or bench in your basement.

Usually ½″ of a coarse, sterilized gravel is placed on the bench or tray to help retain moisture and increase humidity around the flats.

Proper watering of seed flats is important. The soil should be thoroughly moistened before sowing seeds.

If the flat is covered, more water will not usually be required until after germination.

Seedlings should be carefully watered so the soil is thoroughly moistened each time and so that 10 percent of that water runs through the bottom of the flat. Water along the edge of the flats or at soil level with a watering can to avoid getting moisture on the tiny plants. Moisture retained on seedling plants themselves for long periods of time will lead to plant diseases.

Poor germination usually results from one of the following reasons:

- Improper temperature
- Improper moisture
- Lack of light (except for those few seeds which require darkness)

- High salt level (too much fertilizer in the soil or too much added in the form of liquid soluble fertilizer)

Buying Seedlings

In order to purchase seedling plants that will perform, you need to understand what quality means in seedlings. Seedlings should be husky, uniform, compact plants. They should be dark green, and the roots white. The plants should also be free from insects and diseases. Avoid wilted plants or those with damaged leaves. Torn and broken leaves indicate crowding somewhere. Remember, bruised areas or cuts are prime entryways for rots, diseases and insects.

Look for plants that are labeled. This will indicate the name of the variety, and many labels also provide care instructions that help you in spacing and planning your garden.

Unlabeled plants, especially vegetable seedlings, may lead to disastrous results. Cabbage looks like broccoli. One tomato looks like another. Only the label will indicate the difference.

Seedlings are packaged in many different types of containers which vary greatly in size, shape, number of plants and size of plants.

There are two basic types of containers: community packs and individual pots or packs.

Community packs are those with more than one plant per container. Disadvantage of this type is that the plants have to be divided and their roots cut apart before they are planted in your yard. Often this will cause a check in plant growth for the first week to 10 days until the roots become reestablished. Also, greater care must be taken with plants from community containers to provide ample water so plants do not become stressed and dry.

Individual or unit pots or packs are those with one plant per pot, pack or cell. These plants can be taken from the containers and planted directly in your yard without disturbing the root system. There is no check or stress in transplanting, and the plants will continue to grow unchecked.

There are also individual containers made of peat, or cubes made of peatlite mix, that can be directly planted into the garden. These perhaps are the most desirable, since there is no waste to dispose of and the container will decompose in the soil.

Remember that one pack may not be equal to another. When you observe a price per pack that is different from another price per pack, check to see if the number of plants, size of container, and quality are the same.

The flat or master container can hold 6, 8, 10, 12, or 15 packs. Each pack may have 3 plants or 4, 6, 9, or 12 plants. The total number of plants may vary from 24 to 96 per flat.

A large number of plants per flat usually indicates smaller soil volume per plant; thus smaller, less-developed seedlings. Flats with fewer plants usually contain more soil volume per plant and are bushier and larger (more developed plants).

You as the consumer must make the decision: many smaller plants or fewer more-developed plants.

For the beginner, fewer more-developed plants per flat will usually be the safest route with less loss, no transplant shock, and plants which are able to withstand more abuse.

For advanced gardeners, or those who will spend the time and effort in good cultural practices, the higher number of plants per flat (if the price is less) will be the most economical buy and will provide excellent results.

To assure the maximum in growth and potential, bedding plants should be purchased as seedlings which are not full flower. If transplanted to the garden at this stage they will quickly become established, there will be no transplant shock and they will develop into the best possible plants.

But practically speaking, most gardeners are impulse buyers and want to see what the flowers look like before they buy and plant them. Ninety percent of annuals, therefore, are sold in flower. A gardener can be successful with flowering plants by following good cultural practices, but the plants will never reach the full potential that can be realized by earlier transplanting. However, the differences in many cases are not significant.

Recent research developments on seedlings allow the commercial grower, or you as a consumer, to do prescription growing. This means that if you provide the proper temperature, growing media, moisture and light in the amount prescribed, plants can be flowered in the shortest possible time with the highest quality material possible.

For example, with prescription growing, USDA researchers are able to flower a petunia in 28 days. Commercially, anywhere from 70 to 84 days not uncommon, and 50 days would be an average crop time.

Seedlings are grown commercially under several different regimes. In one method the seeds are germinated at warm temperatures, 70° F for most species in the greenhouses. They are held from three to four weeks at this temperature, then transplanted and grown at 60° F night temperature until they are about to flower (four to six weeks), at which time the temperatures are dropped to 50° F night times until flowering (two more weeks).

This produces a hardened seedling that is able to withstand adverse conditions at the retail outlet or adverse conditions on the part of the consumer.

In a second method, temperatures are maintained at 70° F during the entire growing cycle, and the plants flower faster.

These plants will perform well in the garden if handled properly, but will not withstand adverse conditions such as drought or cold temperatures as well as hardened seedlings.

In recent years seedlings have been grown in accelerated environments, germinated at 70° F to 80° F with lights (either fluorescent or high intensity) in environments enriched with carbon dioxide, and then transplanted in two weeks. The plants are kept at 70° F after transplanting and in some cases still kept under these lights with carbon dioxide added. With this system petunia plants can be flowered commercially in 40 to 45 days.

If plants grown this way are given adequate care by the retail outlet and handled properly by the consumer, they will provide the best display in the garden. The plants will withstand adverse conditions less well, however, than those from the first two systems.

The trend is to produce seedlings commercially in a shorter period of time, and thus a slight movement toward the accelerated environments has occurred. If retail handling is improved, and if you, as the consumer, provide adequate care, this type of plant will give the most value for your money.

If you purchase seedlings and are unable to plant them immediately place them in a location with plenty of light, but no direct sunlight. Be sure they are well watered and kept at temperatures between 50° and 70° F. Avoid cold drafts, freezing temperatures and drying out. Certain annuals can withstand light frosts: pansies, snapdragons and petunias, for example.

Plant annuals as soon as possible in a prescribed location: sunny annuals in a sunny spot with at least four hours of direct sun per day; shady annuals in an area with no more than four hours of direct sun per day.

If you have grown your own seedlings, plan to have them ready for transplanting after the danger of frost is past. When you have to hold them for a period of time, place them outside during the day—if temperatures are above freezing—and then put them in a protected area such as the garage or in the house at night until the weather is warm enough for planting.

Planting Care

Garden soil must be properly prepared to insure good growth of annuals. In the spring just before planting add a 1″ to 2″ layer of peat moss to the garden. If your soil is a heavy clay, use twice this amount of peat moss, as well as 1″ to 2″ of sand. By adding peat and sand to your soil you will eventu-

Guidelines for germination of selected annuals and vegetables indicating optimum soil temperature, need for light or darkness, and usual time required for germination

	Optimum Temperature	Light or Dark*	Usual number of days required for germination
Ageratum	70	L	5
Alyssum	70	DL	5
Amaranthus	70	DL	10
Aster	70	DL	8
Balsam	70	DL	8
Begonias (Fibrous)	70	L	15
Begonias (Tuberous)	65	L	15
Browallia	70	L	15
Calceolaria	70	L	15
Calendula	70	D	10
Campanula	70	DL	20
Candytuft	70	DL	8
Carnation	70	DL	20
Celosia	70	DL	10
Centaurea	65	D	10
Clarkia	70	L	10
Coleus	65	L	10
Cosmos	70	DL	5
Cynoglossum	60	D	5
Dahlia	70	DL	5
Dianthus	70	DL	5
Dimorphotheca	70	DL	10
Gaillardia	70	DL	20
Gazania	60	D	8
Gomphrena	65	D	15
Gypsophila	70	DL	10
Heliotrope	70	DL	25
Hollyhock	60	DL	10
Impatiens	70	L	15
Kochia	70	DL	15
Larkspur	55	D	20
Lobelia	70	DL	20
Lupine	55	DL	20
Marigold	70	DL	5
Mesembryanthemum	65	D	15
Morning Glory	65	D	15
Nasturtium	65	D	8
Nemesia	65	D	5
Nicotiana	70	L	20
Nierembergia	70	DL	15
Pansy	65	D	10
Petunia	70	L	10
Phlox	65	D	10
Poppy	70	D	10

	Optimum Temperature	Light or Dark*	Usual number of days required for germination
Portulaca	70	D	10
Rudbeckia	70	DL	15
Salpiglossis	70	D	15
Salvia	70	L	15
Scabiosa	70	DL	10
Schizanthus	60	D	20
Snapdragon	65	L	10
Statice	70	DL	15
Stock	70	DL	10
Sweetpea	55	D	15
Thunbergia	70	DL	10
Torenia	70	DL	15
Verbena	65	D	20
Viola	65	D	20
Vinca	70	D	15
Zinnia	70	DL	5
VEGETABLES			
Cabbage	70	L	7
Cauliflower	70	L	14
Celery	65	L	28
Cucumber	80	L	seed in pots 3 to 6 weeks before planting in garden
Eggplant	80	L	21
Lettuce	65	L	7
Muskmelon	80	L	seed in pots 4 to 6 weeks before planting in garden
Onion	65	L	seed in flat 8 to 10 weeks before planting in garden
Pepper	75	L	21
Summer Squash	75	L	seed in pots 4 to 6 weeks before planting in garden
Watermelon	75	L	seed in pots 4 to 6 weeks before planting in garden
Tomato	70	L	14

*L indicates that seeds require light to germinate; D indicates that seeds germinate best in the dark; DL indicates that seeds germinate under either condition.

ally improve even your poor subsoil to make a good garden.

A complete fertilizer should also be added at this time: about 2 pounds of a 5-10-5 to every 100 square feet of soil. If your soil is acid, lime may also be needed.

A soil test sent to your State Agricultural University or to any private soil testing service will indicate the soil pH and the amount of lime to apply. Annuals thrive at a soil pH of 5.5 to 7.0. Be certain your soil is in this range, then turn the soil over and rake to a smooth surface. After raking, the soil will be ready for seeding or planting with seedlings.

Annuals vary in their light requirements. Some perform best in shade, while others perform best in full sunlight. Some annuals do well in either sun or shade. See the table for the amount of light that each plant will require.

Do not rely on natural rainfall to take care of all the water needs of your annual plants. In some years rainfall will be sufficient to produce fine annuals. Most years, however, plants require watering at various times to supplement the rain.

Do not use a sprinkler and do not water the tops on annuals. Splashing water damages flowers on many of the annuals, especially petunias and geraniums.

Water the plants at soil level to get as little moisture as possible on the foliage. This can be done easily with a watering wand that is available from most garden centers, or you can place a soaker type hose or plastic watering system in the flower beds.

These systems give water to the roots of the plant while the foliage remains dry. Many diseases start when moisture remains on the foliage more than 48 hours. It is true that rain will create this condition, and it usually takes a few days for the annuals to recover from heavy rain.

Plants should be watered thoroughly and less often, rather than lightly and often. This builds deep roots that will produce stronger plants.

When the flower bed is initially prepared, 2 pounds of the 5-10-5 or 10-10-10 fertilizer should be applied per 100 square feet of flower bed. This should be incorporated into the soil and worked in with the peat moss to make the flower bed acceptable for annuals. Then plant the annuals at the proper spacing according to the listed table, and allow them to grow for about six to eight weeks before adding more fertilizer.

The amount of fertilizer depends on the amount of rainfall or water applied to the plants. In general, the more water applied, the more frequent the fertilization needed. When more fertilizer is needed, apply a 5-10-5 or 10-10-10 at the rate of one pinch (the amount of fertilizer you can hold in your thumb and first index finger) to each plant.

Make sure the fertilizer is not in contact with the foliage or on the crown of the plant. If fertilizer comes in direct contact with the plant, it may burn the foliage. Place it between 1 to 2 inches from the stem of the plant. It takes only a small amount of fertilizer to make plants grow, and if you apply too much the plants will wilt, even when wet, and finally die.

Overwintering Annuals

Annuals listed in the table are not winter hardy in most areas. All will die when exposed to a few heavy frosts, so you will have to grow new plants from seed or buy new plants each year. It is rarely worthwhile to save seeds or annuals from one year to another, or to collect your own seeds. Frequently these saved seeds will not grow true to type.

However, if you wish to save seeds, choose them from healthy plants where the flowers have been left to set seed and to grow to maturity during the summer. As soon as the pods are brown, place them in a cool, airy place. When they are completely dry, remove the seeds and store them in small paper bags.

Many annuals can be overwintered

Characteristics of popular annuals and plants treated as annuals

	Color	Height, Inches	Exposure	Plant Spacing, Inches	Use
Ageratum	blue or white	6 to 18	part or full sun	10	border plant
Alyssum	purple or white	2 to 4	sun	10	good border plant
Amaranthus	red colored foliage	24 to 36	sun	24	good background plant
Aster	blue-purple	12 to 24	sun or partial shade	12	good for cut flowers
Balsam	red, pink, white, purple	6 to 36	sun	12–18	background plant
Begonia	white, pink, red	12 to 18	shade	12	good for formal beds, hanging baskets, requires little maintenance
Browallia	white, blue	12 to 24	sun or partial shade	12	good for hanging baskets or planters
Calendula	white, yellow, orange, red	6 to 12	sun	12	good for window boxes or hanging baskets
Campanula	white, pink, blue	24 to 36	sun	12–18	beds, cut flowers
Candytuft	white, pink, blue	6 to 12	sun to partial shade	8–10	good for cut flowers
Carnation	white, yellow, pink, red	6 to 24	sun	12	good as cut flowers
Celosia	yellow, orange, pink, rose, red	6 to 24	sun	12	good as cut flowers, dried flowers and hanging baskets
Centaurea	white foliage	18 to 24	sun	12	excellent foliage annual used in combination baskets
Clarkia	white, pink, red, blue	18 to 24	sun or partial shade	12	good cut flower
Coleus	blue flower, colored foliage	12 to 24	shade	12	good for window boxes and planters
Cosmos	white, pink, rose, red	36	sun or partial shade	18–24	good for cut flowers, hedge or screen
Cynoglossum	blue flower, colored foliage	12 to 24	partial shade, sun	12	good for cut flowers, dried flowers and climbing vines
Dahlia	red, yellow, pink, multi-color	6 to 36	sun	18–24	good as cut flower

Characteristics of popular annuals and plants treated as annuals

	Color	Height, Inches	Exposure	Plant Spacing, Inches	Use
Dianthus	white, pink, red	6 to 12	sun	12	good as cut flower
Dimorphotheca	white, yellow, orange, pink	6 to 12	sun	12	beds
Gaillardia	yellow, orange, red	12 to 24	sun	12	good for cut flowers and window boxes, planters
Gazania	yellow, orange, pink, rose, red	6 to 12	sun	12	beds
Gomphrena	white, yellow, orange, pink, rose, blue, purple	6 to 24	sun	12	dried arrangements, window boxes
Gypsophila	white, pink	12 to 24	sun	12–18	cut flower
Heliotrope	white, purple	12–24	sun	12	cut flower, fragrant
Hollyhock	white, yellow, pink, red	36	sun	24	hedges, screen
Impatiens	white, yellow, pink, rose, red purple	6 to 24	shade	12	formal beds, hanging baskets, window boxes, planters
Kochia	green foliage	24 to 36	sun	12–18	hedges, screens
Larkspur	white, blue, pink, rose, purple	24 to 48	sun	18–24	cut flower, background plant
Lobelia	white, red, purple	6 to 12	sun	12	edging plant, window boxes, planters, hanging baskets
Lupine	white, yellow, orange, pink, blue	12 to 36	sun, partial shade	12–18	cut flower
Marigold	yellow-orange, red	6 to 36	sun	8–24	flower beds, window boxes, planters
Mesembryanthemum	white, yellow, orange, pink, rose, red	6–12	sun	8–12	planters, window boxes, beds
Morning glory	white, pink, red, blue	36	sun	18–24	climbing vine, hedge or screen
Nasturtium	orange	24–36	sun	18–24	climbing vine
Nemesia	white, yellow, orange, red, blue, purple	6–12	sun	8–12	planters, cut flowers
Nicotiana	white, yellow-orange, pink-rose, red	12–24	partial shade, sun	12–18	cut flower, fragrant

Characteristics of popular annuals and plants treated as annuals

	Color	Height, Inches	Exposure	Plant Spacing, Inches	Use
Nierembergia	blue-purple	6–12	partial shade, sun	8	window box, planter
Pansy	white, yellow, rose, blue, purple	6–12	partial shade, sun	12	fragrant, cut flowers, beds, window boxes
Petunia	white, yellow, pink, rose, red, blue, purple	6–12	sun	12	hanging baskets, flower beds, window boxes, planters
Phlox	white, yellow, pink, rose, red, blue	6–24	partial shade, sun		planters, bed, window boxes
Poppy	white, yellow, pink, red	12–24	sun	12	cut flower, fragrant
Portulaca	white, yellow, orange, pink, rose, red	24–36	sun	12	beds, window boxes, planters
Rudbeckia	yellow, orange	24–36	partial shade, sun	12–18	cut flowers
Salpiglossis	yellow, orange, pink, rose, blue, red	24–36	sun	12–18	cut flowers
Salvia	white, pink, rose, red, blue	6–36	partial shade, sun	8–18	beds, planters
Scabiosa	white, pink, rose, red, blue	12–36	sun	12	cut flower, fragrant
Schizanthus	white, yellow, pink, red, blue	6–24	partial shade, sun	12	hanging baskets, cut flower, window boxes, planters
Snapdragon	white, yellow, pink, red, purple	6–36	sun	8–18	fragrant, cut flower, beds,
Statice	white, pink, blue, purple	6–12	sun	12	cut flower, dried arrangement
Stock	white, yellow, pink, red, blue	6–24	sun	8–18	cut flower, fragrant, beds
Sweetpea	white, yellow, pink, red, blue	6–36	sun	12	cut flower, climbing vine, fragrant
Thunbergia	orange	36	partial shade, sun	18	climbing vine, window boxes, hanging baskets
Torenia	white, yellow, blue	6–12	shade	12	hanging baskets, window boxes, planters

Characteristics of popular annuals and plants treated as annuals

	Color	Height, Inches	Exposure	Plant Spacing, Inches	Use
Verbena	white, pink, red, purple	6–12	sun	8–12	window boxes, hanging boxes, fragrant
Viola	blue, white	6–12	partial shade, sun	8–12	beds, window boxes, planters
Vinca	blue	6–12	partial shade, sun	8–12	beds, window boxes, planters
Zinnia	white, yellow, orange, pink, purple	6–36	sun	8–18	beds, cut flowers, planters

by taking terminal cuttings from plants just before frost. Coleus, geraniums, wax begonias, impatiens and ageratum can be successfully propagated by taking 2″ to 3″ of terminal stem with leaves, stripping the lower leaves off, leaving one or two sets of leaves on the top, then placing the cut end into a medium of sand or of peat and vermiculite.

Cover the container with medium and the cuttings with a plastic bag, making sure the medium is moist at all times. Usually a period of 2 to 3 weeks will be required for rooting. Then pot in a 3″ or 4″ pot and place in a sunny window. Water and fertilize just as you do your other house plants.

In spring when the frost danger is over, replant in your garden. This procedure will work well if the annuals receive enough light indoors, but it will not work if they are placed in a dark area in your home.

Vegetable transplants require about the same cultural requirements as annuals. The table indicates the proper garden spacing and location for these plants. A small vegetable garden will provide food for your table and the satisfaction of producing your own food. If you don't have such a garden, consider planting these vegetables in with your flowers, thus mixing food and beauty together.

Your imagination is the limiting factor in using annuals in your home and

Garden planting guide of popular bedding plant vegetables

Species	Garden Spacing	Location
Cabbage	3′ x 12″–24″	Sun
Cauliflower	3½′ x 16″–20″	Sun
Celery	3′ x 4″	Sun
Cucumber	5′ x 3′	Sun
Eggplant	3′ x 3′	Sun
Lettuce	1½′ x 1′	Sun
Muskmelon	6′ x 4′	Sun
Onion	1½′ x 3′	Sun
Pepper	3′ x 1½′	Sun
Summer Squash	5′ x 3′	Sun
Watermelon	7′ x 6′	Sun
Tomato	4′ x 2′	Sun

landscape. They can be used in many interesting ways, such as in wood dividers, planted in chain link fences, in old shoes made into planters, in old bathtubs, sinks, etc. The more conventional ways, of course, are in flower beds, urns, patio boxes, window boxes and in rock gardens. They can also be trained to grow like small trees or shrubs.

It is usually desirable to plant many of the same type of annual and the same color of annual in one area, instead of using one or two plants of each type. Examples of nice flower beds would be a center of red geraniums with a border of blue ageratum, or a center of pink petunias with a border of white alyssum. Use the colors and heights wisely, and you will add a new dimension to gardening in your home, apartment and landscape—"instant color."

Buying and Caring for Cut Flowers; Arrangements

THIS IS A wonderful age for consumers to decorate homes and offices inexpensively and to brighten the lives of friends with cut flowers. Flowers are attractively priced today by traditional retail florists and mass outlets. One can choose the services desired and know that there is a wide selection of cut flowers available throughout the year.

Just a few flowers in the living room or on a desk will turn a dull, dreary day into one filled with warmth and sunshine. There is truly something magic in just a single rose or carnation, a bouquet of mixed flowers, or a beautiful floral arrangement.

A number of cut flowers are available in a variety of colors throughout the year. Roses, carnations, and spray and standard chrysanthemums are produced by the specialists who provide quality flowers.

Surprisingly, the exotic anthurium commonly seen in Hawaii and the Bird of Paradise are available throughout the year. Featuring excellent lasting life, they are bound to capture attention.

Colorful daisies can be found in prepackaged bouquets at almost any time of the year. Whether in combination with other flowers or just in a bud vase, they radiate warmth and cheerfulness sure to brighten the hearts and souls of all ages.

Midwinter and early spring is a good time to look for heather, iris, stock, freesia, tulips and daffodils. Freesia reminds one of the daylily as its buds open over a period of time.

Buying Cut Flowers

Retail florists offer a variety of services that range from cash and carry sales to arrangements personally designed, delivered to the recipient, and charged to the buyer. The consumer has a wide range of choices today in terms of both product and services when patronizing retail flower shops.

Pre-packaged cut flowers, priced below $2.50 and at times as low as $1, now appear in many retail flower shops. This merchandise receives the special care of the retailer and represents an excellent buy for the consumer. Consumers save money in terms of the costs normally associated with the time of a designer, special wrapping, delivering, and then charging for the merchandise.

A growing number of shoppers now make it a point to regularly visit retailers offering this service to purchase a small bouquet for themselves or a friend.

Consumers often have the opportunity of saving money in terms of taking loose or arranged flowers home, direct to the office, or to a hospital. The merchandise can be charged in

---

AUTHOR *Lou Berninger* is Extension Horticulturist (Floriculture), University of Wisconsin, Madison.

normal fashion. Consumers and retailers both save with the elimination of delivery charges.

Retail florists employ talented designers capable of creating beautiful arrangements and decorating rooms for special occasions. Cost of this unique service is naturally built into the final price for a product or bid for handling all aspects of a special party. It is impossible to compare the full services of professional florists with a cash and carry operation or one offering standard arrangements.

A variety of outlets such as supermarkets and discount stores now market cut flowers and occasionally provide some services associated with a traditional retail florist. The services offered are generally limited in scope and rarely include delivery and opportunity to charge the order.

A growing number of firms recognize that flowers are highly perishable and that quality merchandise is essential to insure customer satisfaction and repeat business.

These firms offer a quality product at reasonable prices.

Consumers can quickly learn to distinguish good from questionable merchandise. Here are some tips:

- Cut flowers displayed in discolored water and water that has a slimy feeling will probably have a short life span in the home.
- Wide open flowers indicate age and should be avoided by those interested in enjoying the blooms for more than a couple of days.
- Limp foliage suggests that the base of stems have been plugged and little, if any, water has been reaching leaves and petals.
- Crowding of flowers in a small cooler can result in severe bruising of leaves and petals.

A neat display suggests that someone has carefully handled this product.

Caring for Cut Flowers

Cut flowers provide a riot of color as they unfurl their petals from a bud stage to fully mature flowers. Some flowers like the chrysanthemum can be depended upon to grace our lives for a week and longer, while others may show their full beauty for a shorter period. One of the most important factors determining life span, however, is the care you provide the flowers.

Cut roses have been known to wilt and their "necks" bend or droop soon after arrival in the home. The beautiful rose should provide days of enjoyment as the petals unfurl to show their full beauty.

Leaves and thorns are frequently removed from the lower portion of the rose stem. Peeling back some of the stem tissue when removing thorns and leaves actually destroys part of the absorption system. Stems must be recut just above the injured area to reestablish the flow of water to the petals.

Some roses may be cut in a tight bud stage, First, cut at least one inch off from the base of the stem. Then, plunge the stems in a deep container of warm or bath temperature water (110° F), and allow them to remain for several hours. You can place polyethylene film over the buds to reduce air circulation and increase humidity in the immediate vicinity of the petals.

Warm water should contain a floral "preservative" to control bacteria and provide sugar or food for the developing blooms. Bacteria usually accumulate due to the breakdown of leaves and stems below the water surface. Retail florists and outlets offering floral supplies sell a variety of cut-flower "foods".

Untreated water should be changed daily and stems recut to insure water reaching leaves and petals. This usually is not convenient when one has constructed an arrangement. Try a floral "preservative" and your cut flowers will respond with extra days of life.

Floral containers should be washed thoroughly before and after each use. Bacteria may be present and multiply on the inner walls.

Placing the stem on a wooden board and cutting down can crush the stem tissue. This stem injury restricts water uptake and shortens the life of flowers. Try holding the stem in your left hand and using a sharp knife in your right hand. Make a clean, slanting cut away from your body and remove approximately one inch of the stem base.

Floral "foams" sold by retail florists, and those handling floral supplies, aid designers in constructing simple and attractive arrangements. A key to success involves thorough moistening of the block before insertion of stems.

The moistened foam block can be easily shaped to fit most containers. Floral tape or similar material can be employed to keep the foam in position. Some containers have ridges or projections on the inside walls to anchor the foam in place.

Carefully insert each flower to its correct position and avoid partial withdrawal of a stem. An air pocket might form just below the base of the stem and result in little or no water being available to the petals.

Some stems like the dahlia and poinsettia exude a milky fluid when cut. Sometimes these flowers seem to wilt rapidly and have a short life span. To offset this, one technique calls for immersion of the base of the stem in boiling water for a few seconds. Protect the blooms from the heat. In another technique you take a lighted match and singe the basal area.

These treatments are to coagulate the milky substance and minimize plugging of the water-conducting vessels.

Recutting the stem requires that you repeat the treatment. Some report success in treating these flowers in exactly the same fashion as all other blooms.

Warm and drafty locations can lead to rapid decline of cut flowers. You can insure some extra days of life by placing a bouquet or arrangement in a cool location at night, and avoid locating flowers near heat outlets. A bright location also is desirable in terms of extending the life of most flowers.

Tulips and daffodils bring a real warmth into our lives from midwinter through spring. The secret to having tulips last a week or longer lies simply in cutting them when they are still in tight bud.

A red cultivar (variety) should be selected when there is just a small amount of color showing and the petals are virtually green. Most cultivars in this stage will last from seven to ten days in a moderate environment. Lasting life drops to approximately five days when the bud is all red, and even less when the petals have started to open.

Daffodils should be purchased when the petals are tight and the bud is straight up or in a goose-neck position. Selecting this flower when the petals have unfurled reduces lasting life to just a couple of days.

Tulips and daffodil buds should be conditioned in cold water (60° F) for several hours. It is wise to use separate containers as daffodils exude a toxic substance that reduces the life of tulips. You can combine the blooms into an interesting arrangement after a few hours of the conditioning treatment.

Select flowers that are in bud stage or just reaching their peak of maturity. Carefully remove some of the lower leaves, and slice one inch from the base of the stem. Use a sharp knife and cut on a slant to avoid crushing the basal area. Place stems in a deep container of warm water (tulips, daffodils in cold water), and allow to stand for several hours.

Arranging Flowers

Flower arrangements and bouquets can be constructed with just a few flowers. Pre-packaged flowers are ideal for simple bouquets to grace living and dining rooms and for an office desk. Often they contain sufficient material for a simple arrangement.

An arrangement features a readily identifiable form such as a triangle, "S" curve, crescent, round, oval or vertical design. A bouquet can be formed by spreading out and staggering the length of stems to form an attractive display. The emphasis is really on the colorful flowers and not on the overall design.

Selection of the right container represents an important element in creating an attractive bouquet or arrangement. A tall, narrow vase, a low bowl, and a medium sized container permit one to construct all types of designs. Your basic collection should focus attention on simplicity and green or plain colors.

The initial step in constructing an arrangement involves forming a picture of the design in your mind. Then select the container that will complement and support the design.

Flower selection often is the key to success. Most designs feature a definite form that can be developed with two or three line flowers. Delphinium, larkspur, Bells of Ireland, forsythia shoots and almost anything that has a vertical profile will serve as a line. A triangle can be constructed with three lines and a crescent or "S" curve with two.

Foliage materials and clusters of small flowers such as Gypsophila can be used as filler material. Their prime purpose is to fill in spaces and hide the rim of containers. This material is inserted at the last stage.

Round flowers predominate in the flower border. Carnations, roses, marigolds and zinnias are placed at the center of interest and toward the base of the arrangement.

The following will help you create a simple and attractive arrangement:

-develop the outline of the arrangement with your line material

-insert the center of interest or focal flower located low and in the center of the arrangement

-place a round flower in front of and almost touching each main line halfway between the top and base of the line

-complete the arrangement with round and filler material

A wide variety of flowers are available throughout the year and priced inexpensively by retail florists and a growing number of mass outlets. Selecting flowers in or near the bud stage, conditioning them, and using a floral "preservative" will help to extend their life. The beauty and warmth of a single flower, bouquet or arrangement will brighten every day of the year.

Potted Plants to Brighten Your Life

BLOOMING POT PLANTS bring beauty, life and color to more people now than ever before. A huge pot plant industry has grown up, sending blooming plants to supermarkets, flower shops, garden stores and discount outlets across the country at all seasons. The idea of a living, growing plant in bloom—complete with pot and roots—has a unique appeal. By buying a potted plant you know you have something more durable than cut flowers kept in a vase for a few days and then thrown out.

Thanks to the many horticultural advances, you now have an abundance of kinds from which to choose. Most of them are longer lasting, and more tolerant and vigorous, than their counterparts of a few years ago. If you use normal good judgment in selecting, you get your money's worth from almost any potted flower that takes your eye. Some offer more than others, however, in such attributes as duration of bloom, compatibility as house plants, and possibilities for repeat bloom in the future.

The best place to buy a pot plant, but probably the most expensive, is from the greenhouse florist who grew it.

There you know the plant probably has had proper care. Garden stores and boutiques are also usually reliable sources.

The riskiest place to buy a pot plant is the produce department of a supermarket or discount store. On the other hand, if you know what to look for, you may find a good bargain there, because high volume means low prices. These stores now sell plants in amazing variety and numbers.

The care of living plants at such places is haphazard, and the rush of heavy traffic exposes plants to breakage and destructive temperatures. Inspect carefully before making a selection, feel the soil or heft the pot to be sure the soil has not dried out. Check buds and reject any with tell-tale brown edges showing they are about to fall or abort. Select specimens with plenty of unopened flower buds to prolong their beauty.

The best time to buy from mass market outlets is within a day or two after the shipment arrives, before damage or neglect can happen.

Often plants come with a decorative foil or plastic pot wrap. This causes trouble if it catches and holds water. Pierce the wrapping on the bottom beneath the pot drain hole so moisture can run through, then set the plant on a saucer to prevent water stains on furniture.

As you take a new pot plant home, remember that it is undergoing great changes from conditions it had before. From the sheltered security of a controlled greenhouse, the plant is shifting to the fluctuating temperatures, extremes of moisture and humidity, and dubious lighting of your house.

Do what you can to ease the transition. Attend carefully to watering.

- Always use water of room temperature or warmer
- Use a hand mister occasionally to lift humidity
- And keep temperatures cool to moderate.

The following plant-by-plant discussion describes 11 main kinds found today during the year throughout the country, with hints for selecting, care, and handling if you wish to have them bloom in future years.

Poinsettias rank high for cheerful color in midwinter, durability and ease of care. As a symbol of Christmas they are uniquely American, having originated in Mexico and come to their present perfection with U.S. breeders.

Modern poinsettias were carefully bred for good behavior in pots, and pollution tolerance for city conditions. They remain low and compact, produce large showy "blooms" (bracts, to be technically exact), with longevity twice that of old kinds. They come in beautiful clean tones of pink, cream-white and coral, in addition to red.

You can keep a poinsettia from year to year with a little special care. While it blooms in winter, water it daily with tepid water. Keep it away from cold drafts in a sunny window, at 68° to 70° F. After blooms fade, reduce watering to rest the plant. It may drop some leaves, the colored bracts and true small flowers. At this time, cut off stems 6″ above the soil, leaving three or four bud points on each.

Water sparingly again, and soon new shoots will grow. Shift the poinsettia now to a larger pot with fresh soil; feed it monthly with a liquid balanced plant food. In July, cut it back again six inches above previous cuts, to keep the plant from becoming too tall.

To bring bloom again, start October 1 to give the plant 14 hours of complete darkness every night. Set it in a closet, or put a light-proof box over it. As soon as blooms are set and bract color shows, restore its schedule to match your own for full enjoyment through Christmas.

Azaleas blooming in pots have become popular gift plants for Thanksgiving, Christmas, Valentine's Day, Easter, and other winter-spring occasions. They are unequalled for their glowing crimson, pink, coral and white colors.

These varieties were chosen especially for one-time pot bloom, and not for subsequent uses. In the mild winter areas, however, you might keep them to plant outdoors. It is also possible, but difficult, to keep them in pots year round and have them bloom again.

Keep the brown peat medium moist by daily watering, or even by submerging the pot occasionally. The cooler and more humid your home, the longer the blooms last. Temperatures of 65° to 68° F daytimes, and 60° at night are ideal.

After azalea blossoms fall, foliage growth begins. Keep up daily watering,

---

AUTHOR *Rachel Snyder* is editor of *Flower and Garden Magazine* and author of *The Complete Book for Gardeners.*

misting, and feeding every two months with balanced liquid house plant food.

Place the plant in a bright window for winter but in shade outdoors for summer. Leave it out as days cool in autumn, but bring it in before hard frost.

If the azalea's cooling requirements have been met, it should soon set buds again and bloom, although perhaps not at the same time as before.

In quantity, CHRYSANTHEMUMS are probably the all-around top pot plant in America. As a result of horticultural wizardry they are sold in flower at all seasons, and not just in autumn. Growers use varieties that are willing to grow crowded in a pot, and to open blooms in accord with the greenhouseman's system of blackouts by which he tricks it into unseasonal bloom. To enjoy this plant best, keep it well watered, cool, and in a sunny place.

A chrysanthemum is not intended for a permanent house plant. You might add a mum experimentally to your outdoor garden, although it may not be hardy in your winters, or able to bloom early enough to escape frosts. Trying it is the best way to know. So after blooms fade, cut off the tops, keep soil slightly moist, and when frosts end set the separated plants out in a prepared place.

RIEGER BEGONIAS, hybrids from Germany, are showy, long-lasting pot plants highly popular in Europe and increasingly used in the United States. They usually have wide, single or semi-double flowers with a small yellow eye.

Called Rieger-elatior, and sometimes Schwabenland or Aphrodite, these are available in more than a dozen different varieties and colors from pink through orange to brilliant red.

They resemble tuberous begonias, but have no true tuber, growing from a dense fibrous root system. Apparently they need no dormancy, and bloom almost the year round if groomed of old flowers and fed occasionally with a liquid house plant fertilizer.

Give them a bright cool window (daytimes under 70° F, cooler at night), and water whenever the soil feels dry. Summer them outdoors in high shade.

JERUSALEM OR CHRISTMAS CHERRY, *Solanum pseudo-capsicum,* a potato relative, is often marketed in late fall as a Christmas plant. Its bright orange-red, marble-size fruits are its main attraction. The plant probably grew from seeds started the previous spring in a moist greenhouse. The greater warmth and dryness of your house may cause it to yellow and drop leaves.

To enjoy it as long as possible, place it in a sunny but cool window and provide extra humidity. Water whenever the soil feels dry.

Fruits naturally shed in spring; usually at this time the plants are discarded. There are two other options, however: You can cut the top back halfway and repot, to grow and bloom again the following summer. Or you can dry seeds and sow them to produce your own new plants. Do not eat the fruits—they are toxic.

WHITE TRUMPET LILIES blooming in pots at Easter are probably a strain of *Lilium longiflorum* such as 'Ace' or 'Nellie White.' 'Croft' was once the

Opposite top, chrysanthemums are probably the all-around top pot plants in America. Above top, Fragrant Easter lilies have a short useful life indoors, but could bloom again in your garden. Above, in a cool, bright place, cyclamen holds its beauty well.

commonest Easter lily but it has been largely supplanted by new easier kinds that are more compact.

Lilies grow from bulbs brought to bloom by careful temperature regulation in greenhouses. In your home, keep them well watered and cool, so all buds open successfully. It is impractical to try preserving them as house plants. The bulb is fairly hardy, and could live on in your outdoor garden unless your winters are extremely severe.

With this in mind, keep watering even after petals fall, and when the outdoor garden soil is warm, remove the pot and sink the plant four inches deeper than it grew before. The top should remain to mature naturally. Usually such bulbs will come up and bloom the next spring, about when roses bloom.

CHRISTMAS PEPPER (*Capsicum* species) is handled the same as the Jerusalem or Christmas cherry. Its colorful fruits are not poisonous, although they are usually blistering hot. Seeds may be started as late as April or May, for colorful plants by winter.

CYCLAMEN, long popular in Europe, is increasingly seen here. Now that homes are kept cooler, it may become more promising as a winter-blooming pot plant kept from year to year. It demands cool temperatures, and in the over 70° F warmth formerly found in most houses, it had a short bloom expectancy.

Place a cyclamen in a cool, bright window, preferably below 68° F in daytime and down to 55° at night. Keep it moist but not soggy, and the humidity as high as you can manage by misting occasionally or standing it on a tray of wet pebbles. After flowering, reduce but do not stop watering as long as foliage lasts.

Summer the pot in cool shade outdoors. If leaves disappear, turn the pot on its side and stop watering, to avoid rotting the resting corm. Most cyclamens are lost over hot summers. As days cool in autumn, new growth should appear, and soon, bloom buds. Then resume watering, feed with mild plant food, and return the plant to the best cool, bright, humid location you have.

The succulent KALANCHOE may be the most adaptable and long lasting of all the flowering pot plants. Florists grow kalanchoes from seeds, and sell most of them from November through February. They bloom naturally when days are short. Even out of bloom, the foliage is attractive.

Normal house temperatures suit kalanchoe, and it does not demand high humidity. Keep it in sun. In summer, set the pot outdoors in light shade where you will remember to water it. Remove dead flower spikes, and shape plants by pinching over-long shoots. Water when the soil feels dry. Two or three times a year, feed it with a mild house plant fertilizer.

To get bloom the following winter, keep kalanchoe at a bright window in a room unused at night, where no artificial light reaches it.

From late winter to Memorial Day you can buy HYDRANGEAS blooming in pots—pink through rose to tones of blue, and sometimes white—huge trusses of crisp flat flowers atop compact green foliage. Unless you live in a mild-winter climate, it is best to accept your pot hydrangea as a beautiful but short-lived product of the florist's skill.

Keep it as long as possible by copious watering (twice daily) and setting it in a cool bright place. The florist created the plant from stem cuttings rooted the year before, artificially "wintered" in storage, and forced into bloom in a warm greenhouse.

If you have garden space in the shade outdoors, set the plant out there, removed from the pot, to enjoy its handsome foliage the rest of summer.

Where winters are mild, the plant might succeed in your outdoor garden. Set it in high shade, in humusy soil. Allow at least one square yard of garden space for hydrangea.

Specialty flower shops increasingly offer potted and blooming ORCHIDS. This trend will grow as more people learn how easy and durable many orchids are. New propagating methods have increased the supply. A phalaenopsis hybrid or miniature cymbidium is a pot plant of lasting value. It will come already potted in suitable porous medium such as fir bark, and should need no reworking for at least two years.

Give it a bright, cool window but not intense sun. Since blooming may be triggered by day length, its place should be unlighted at night.

Provide extra humidity, as by misting occasionally or standing the pot on a tray of wet pebbles. Take care to avoid overwatering, the greatest cause of orchid mortality. Once a week is usually ample.

When the plant is obviously growing, feed it monthly with mild liquid plant food.

FOR FURTHER READING:

Snyder, Rachel. *The Complete Book for Gardeners,* D. Van Nostrand Co., Inc., Princeton, N.J. 08540, 1964.

Those Fascinating Cacti, and Other Succulent Plants

CACTI and other succulent plants originate in areas where water is only occasionally available, and are therefore conditioned to deal with long periods of drought. They possess structural modifications enabling them to store moisture for use in times of scarcity.

Such adaptations may be similar in both groups (note that all cacti are succulents, but not all succulents are cacti). Storage areas include thickened leaves, stems and corms. Leaves, which transpire precious moisture, may be eliminated altogether (with the stem taking over the process of photosynthesis), or the moisture in the leaves may be protected from evaporation by a leathery surface, or covered with wiry or velvety hairs, thick spines or even with a powdery coating.

The very shape of many succulents provides the same protection; globular and columnar forms offer the least exposed area to the drying effects of sun and wind.

Many times there are "look-alikes" in the two groups. Certain cacti coming from the New World closely resemble counterparts in the Euphorbias of Africa.

Courtesy of Better Homes and Gardens

A sedum for indoors.

How do we then differentiate between cacti and other succulents? It is not always easy. Presence or absence of leaves can be helpful; size and brilliance of flowers also, but the real test comes by learning to recognize the areole.

The areole is possessed by cacti alone, and consists of cushion-like modification on the body of the cactus from which arise spines, hairs (and the barbed hairs or spines of *Opuntia*), flowers, fruit, and often the new growth.

The flowers of cacti are usually more conspicuous and most often appear from areoles near the top of the plant. In other succulents they are inclined to be less showy and more likely to emerge from between the leaves or from the base.

In addition, with a very minor possible exception (a form of *Rhipsalis*), all cacti are native to the Western Hemisphere. It is sometimes hard to believe this because of the vast areas of escaped cactus in many parts of the world today.

The majority of other succulents (excluding *Agave, Echeveria, Sedum, Sempervivum* and a few others) are indigenous to Africa and a few scattered areas in the Eastern Hemisphere.

Both cacti and other succulents are excellent subjects for the outdoor garden, greenhouse or window-sill as they can put up with a minimum of care, provided they have a requisite amount of sunlight and their condition of hardiness is respected.

Cacti for the outdoor garden in areas incurring frost are more or less limited to the genus *Opuntia,* but *Pediocactus, Coryphantha* and a few species of *Echinocereus* can also withstand frost in well-drained sandy soils, and in May and June will reward the grower with large satiny shimmering flowers of incomparable beauty.

If one is so lucky as to enjoy frost-free conditions such as those provided in parts of Florida, the southwestern United States and California, then there are literally several hundred genera and thousands of species to choose from for an ornamental garden.

Colorful lawns can be created by the use of members of the ice-plant family (Aizoaceae); charming borders can be fashioned of *Echeveria, Sedum, Sempervivum,* etc., all of which produce masses of flower.

Pin-cushion plants (*Mammillaria*) can be combined with white-haired columnar cacti (*Cephalocereus*) and golden-barrels (*Echinocactus grusonii*) to design a delightful desert garden filled with interesting and bizarre shapes.

Take care to provide the best exposure to the sun, a soil which is one-half sharp sand and one-half rich loam or leaf mold, and occasional water. It is

---

AUTHOR *Helen B. Fogg* of Merion Station, Pa., is an active member of the Cactus and Succulent Society of America.

CO-AUTHOR *John M. Fogg, Jr.* is Director of the Arboretum of the Barnes Foundation, at Merion Station.

not true that these desert plants want no water at all or that they enjoy impoverished soil. They merely put up with poor conditions, but do their best blooming with more charitable treatment.

Although most of us are not privileged to grow tender plants out of doors, we still can make gardens of cacti in summer by sinking the pots in the ground to produce attractive effects, and at the same time give the plants a summer vacation in the fresh air.

For indoors the choice is almost limitless. One may, according to one's fancy, have cacti with such intriguing names as "Sand dollar" (*Astrophytum asterias*), "Bishop's cap" (*A. myriostigma*), "Old man" (*Cephalocereus senilis*), "Old lady" *(Mammillaria hahniana),* "Powder puff" (*M. bocasana*), "Peanut-cactus" (*Chamaecereus sylvestri*), "Rainbow cactus" (*Echinocereus dasyacanthus*), "Boxing-glove" (*Opuntia mamillata*), "Bird's-nest" (*Mammillaria camptotricha*), "Rat-tail" (*Aporocactus*), "Silver-torch" (*Cleistocactus straussii*), and so forth.

The common names of succulents other than cacti can also engage our fancy and as fully live up to the image created. For example, there is the "Plush-plant" (*Kalanchoe tomentosa*), "Adam's needle" (*Yucca filamentosa*), "Airplant" (*Kalanchoe pinnata*), "Baby's-toes" (*Fenestraria rhopalophylla*), "Tiger-jaws" (*Faucaria*), and many other names which summon up the image of the plant.

One can make a really fanciful and diverse collection.

To grow these plants into healthy specimens and make them flower—any grower's supreme ambition—it is necessary to give them optimum conditions.

Never make dish-gardens using both cacti and other succulents, for their moisture requirements are not the same. Cacti, except for the "leafy" types (*Epiphyllum, Rhipsalis* and others originating in the jungle), demand far less water than other succulents which are happier with a twice-a-week wetting.

Either clay or plastic pots are usable. Clay pots, which allow transpiration, require more watering. They are perhaps more attractive, but harder to keep clean and heavier to handle.

To the previously mentioned soil mixture (sand, rotted leaf-mold, loam) many growers add a little bone meal, a small amount of superphosphate and a small amount of cow manure (these are optional).

A few camphor crystals tend to discourage the root mealy-bug. The pot should have a drainage hole which is covered by broken crock.

Most succulents and many cacti can be propagated from cuttings or offsets. Cacti should be allowed to dry about 48 hours and succulents for half that time or until a callous has formed. Dip the calloused end in a rooting hormone and stand on the surface of a damp sandy mixture, propped up with toothpicks or other suitable support until rooting has taken place. Cover the top of the soil with a quarter inch of sand. Do not water for at least a week.

When and if mealy bugs are evident, remove them with a fine camel's-hair brush dipped in rubbing alcohol.

Red spiders attack many succulents. An effective cure is a forceful spray of cold water or a weak solution of Volck Oil Spray.

It is well to know the place of origin of your plants, as most of them require resting periods. Those from South Africa, for instance, rest during the summer and require little water at that time. Cacti, on the other hand, need a long dry resting period and should receive no water from mid-October to mid-March. During these months they welcome a temperature down to 40° to 45° F, but still prefer full sun. An exception should be made to this treatment in the case of cacti originating in the jungle, the so-called "leafy" cacti such as *Epiphyllum, Rhipsalis,* and *Zygocactus.*

In this connection a hint as to the flowering of "Christmas Cactus" is perhaps in order. Actually, there are two different genera going by this name.

Zygocactus truncatus blooms about Thanksgiving Day and its leaves are flat joints characterized by claw-like projections. *Schlumbergera bridgesii* blooms about Christmas time and its joints are more rounded at the tips and possess no claws.

They both bloom best if left outdoors in summer under slightly filtered light until there is danger of frost, then brought in to a sunny windowsill but where there is no artificial light at night.

Water should be withheld during October, but otherwise these flat "leafy" cacti of jungle origin need water regularly, up to several times a week—that is, far more than the globular or columnar shapes will tolerate.

With correct treatment they will produce, at their chosen time, two-inch irregularly-shaped flowers in shades of fuchsia-pink, salmon-red, or pale pinkish-white at the tip of the final joint of each stem.

Where does the beginner find plants for his starting collection? Today succulents of all kinds are readily available in most five-and-ten cent stores and in commercial greenhouses everywhere. Most experienced collectors of cacti and succulents find it more satisfactory, however, to order direct from growers, notably those of Arizona, Texas and California. Mention will be made of only a few of these, though they abound in number and are to be found advertised in succulent plant journals.

Hardy outdoor plants may be ordered from Karr Kactus, 1822 Poplar, Lincoln Park, Box 87, Route 7, Canon City Col. 81212. For the more tender type may be recommended: Abbey Garden, 1593 Las Canoas Road, Santa Barbara, Ca. 93105. Kirkpatrick's, 17785 de Anza St., Barstow, Ca. 93311. Grigsby Cactus, 2354 Bella Vista Dr., Vista, Ca.

This list could be multiplied many times, did space permit. The advantage of ordering from these extremely reputable sources lies in knowing that your plant will almost certainly arrive in good condition and properly named.

Reference has been made to journals devoted to the subject of succulents. One such, published monthly ($7.50 a year) is the *Cactus and Succulent Journal,* the organ of the American Cactus and Succulent Society.

Books on cacti and other succulents are legion. The beginner will find, especially for house plants, much information in a series of four volumes by Edger and Brian Lamb, Blandford Press, London. There is also a *Pocket Encyclopedia of Cactus* by the same authors. All their books are abundantly illustrated and contain culture hints.

To be recommended highly—*Cacti and Their Cultivation* by Martin, Chapman and Auger, Winchester Press, New York, and *Cacti and Succulents* by Walther Haage, E.P. Dutton & Co., New York.

For all succulents other than cacti, the most complete coverage is found in *A Handbook of Succulent Plants* by Herman Jacobsen, 3 volumes, Blandford Press, 16 West Central St., London, W.C.I.

The above books and a number of others may be obtained from the Abbey Press, Box 167, Reseda, Ca. 91335.

Seeds may be purchased from most commercial nurseries.

Joining Societies

One may learn much by joining one of our many cactus and succulent societies, which meet in various large cities to exchange plants and information, arrange shows of succulent plants, and give the members the chance to show off their blooming plants.

For under proper conditions these plants do bloom! The blossoms of many cacti compare favorably with orchids. While the flowers of most other succulents are smaller and less conspicuous, they make up in mass effect, and have the advantage of blooming in winter.

The beginner is advised to supply himself with those plants that bloom most readily, for example such genera as *Rebutia, Gymnocalycium, Echinopsis, Crassula,* and *Kalanchoe.*

Even if the windowsill cactus proves to be a shy bloomer, the interesting form, texture, covering and color will make it an outstanding asset.

Tips on Interior Landscaping

PLANTS AND FLOWERS can be directly associated with contentment and happiness. Direct contact with nature and plants can develop a mental wholeness necessary to man's overall well being.

An excellent example is the office landscaping concept, which some eight or ten years ago was initiated in West Germany as "Burolandschaft". The concept consists of various arrangements of office furniture, using a few screens, and many live indoor plants and trees, all judiciously placed with the complete absence of partitions. In other words, the traditional office cubicle is gone.

Interior landscaping today basically consists of three general areas: homes, offices, and the more intricate and expanded commercial designs. Ideas for each are unlimited and may be as simple or elaborate as space and conditions permit.

The private homeowner often has the most freedom with his interior gardens. These may range from a few plants on a windowsill to a lean-to-greenhouse, to an entire solarium room, depending upon:

- The amount of light intensity.
- How much time and care can be allotted to maintenance
- The amount of space available for proper placement as related to design elements

Types of plants and trees to be used also depend on available light and humidity. Most tropical plants are grown in Florida or California.

Recently home owners are turning to house trees in preference to house plants. A house tree is a plant large enough to have developed its own individual character. Sizes can range from 5′ to 8′ tall (sometimes up to 15′ to 20′) and are preferably not pinched, sheared or trained, but rather grown as nature intended.

A house tree can be thought of as an architectural element, or a "living sculpture." It can serve as a very functional part of a decor, creating interest, color, texture, and form to complement the simplicity or richness of almost any residential interior.

Special attention should be given to the color and texture of leaves, stem or trunk structure, and overall height and span as related to textures, weaves, colors and patterns existing in draperies, slipcovers, floor coverings, wall finishes, and upholstery.

For example, a home designed with an Oriental influence might utilize several varieties of trees, such as the Bamboo Palm (*Chamaedorea erumpens*) or the Chinese Aralia (Ming Tree). A more Victorian decor might employ a Kentia Palm (*Howeia forsteriana*) or a Giant Dumb Cane (*Dieffenbachia amoena*).

Interior foliage can grace almost any room in the home.

The office landscaping concept described earlier is more limited in the species and size range desired. As a rule the plants and trees used serve a very functional purpose, as well as a decorative one.

At the ends of partitioning screens, plants ranging from 4′ to 8′ may be placed with an overall spread of 18″ to 26″, depending upon available space and the desired overall effect intended. Usually a designer or architect will specify placement areas with many variations in mind.

A very lush effect may be specified which would utilize twice as many plants for a more dense but effective design. Generally, open offices have good interior lighting available, ranging from 125 to 150 foot candles, often supplemented with natural lighting in window areas.

Special areas such as cafeterias,

AUTHOR *Everett Conklin* is president of Everett Conklin and Co., Inc., interior landscape contractors, Montvale, N.J.

Above, a hotel lobby. Above top, a foundation's interior garden. Right, an office planting.

lounges, reception areas, and elevator lobbies may receive unusual treatments with a wider range in height and overall spread. Outstanding specimen trees may be used for creating interesting effects.

Intricate and expanded commercial designs may include the largest variety of interior foliage imaginable.

Hotel and bank lobbies have been turned into massive and exciting interior gardens using waterfalls, fountains, and streams to make the plantings as natural and refreshing as possible. To create a well designed and unified effect within the planting, sizes ranging from 40′ trees to tiny ground cover creepers are often specified.

An enclosed shopping mall can be made more attractive by the addition of tropical plants and trees. Use of skylighting facilitates the existence of large trees to turn the public area into a year-round seasonal park situation.

Selection of planting material available is virtually unlimited. One of the largest problems, however, concerns the quality of the material.

As I mentioned before, most of the tropical plants used in interior plantings originate in Florida or in California. There they are grown in full sunlight of 10,000 foot candles with a relative humidity of 80 to 90 percent and natural rainfall, with supplementary irrigation constantly available.

When placed in our interior environment, these same plants and trees are expected to live in conditions of opposite intensity. Lighting is reduced to 150 foot candles, humidity drops to 15 percent or less, and watering usually occurs every 7 days.

Naturally, one would expect very poor results from this massive shock to the plant's system. Leaves turn yellow and drop, foliage and branch dieback occur, and the natural resistance to disease is weakened.

What is the solution? Each plant and tree must be subjected to gradual conditioning or acclimatizing before it is ready to be used in an interior area. The conditioning must include an adjustment period for the plants, where they can be exposed to increasingly less light, water and humidity over a period of time.

Heavily shaded greenhouses and cloth houses are used at the present time, but even these cannot produce the desired results. Humidity and sunlight are hard to regulate as they depend on the elements (sunny days vs. rainy or cloudy days). Hopefully in the near future we will begin to see a more perfected means of acclimating in order that "interior shock" can be eliminated completely.

Plant sources today are rapidly expanding. Plants in small amounts are available in retail plant specialty shops, supermarkets, variety stores, and flower shops. Garden centers supply a wider selection in varieties and sizes. Often a complete reference area is available to enable you to do research. It is most important to know your plants, realize their growing conditions, and employ proper maintenance precautions.

Large scale plantings are usually purchased from the more specialized interior landscaping firms that facilitate acclimating in their own greenhouses, and have the space and volume to deal with the quantities needed for office landscaping and complex commercial jobs. These larger specialized firms can offer more expert advice, individual maintenance programs, and rental or leasing plans.

Professional maintenance programs involve complete plant servicing including watering, feeding, cleaning, and spraying. Rental plans are especially effective for flower shows, display areas, temporary plant placement, or general convenience.

Selection of plants as related to the available environmental conditions is a topic of extreme importance. Generally, tropical plants can be placed in three categories based on necessary light intensity: low, medium, and high light levels.

Low light plant varieties are usually the hardiest species, requiring light ranging from 50 to 75 foot candles. Medium light plant varieties are more sensitive to drafts and available humidity, and need between 75 and 200 foot candles. High light plant varieties require 200 or more foot candles and are most sensitive to a correct maintenance program.

The dracaena family and the philodendron family include perhaps the hardiest plant varieties commonly used for interior foliage plantings. Light specifications can range from 25 to 150 foot candles, with higher light naturally determining better growth and strength. These families can take the most abuse and lack of watering, and so are classed among the favorites for interior uses of all types.

Here are some general notes on plant care:

Do not overwater. This is by far the most frequent cause of plant failure. It is far better to have a dryness present than to have the plant virtually soaked and standing in water. The roots will begin to rot and will destroy the plant's general health.

The amount of water used should depend on the type of pot (clay or plastic—clay tends to absorb and evaporate more water as it is a porous substance) and the size of the pot as related to the root system.

Allow for proper drainage within the pot. For house plants, put a layer of crushed stone or pebbles beneath the planting medium. For larger plants and trees which are often placed in individual planters, two systems of drainage are recommended: a layer of crushed stone at the base of the outer planter and also at the base of the inner plant pot. It is advisable to mix porous substances such as perlite and peat moss within the actual planting medium.

Do not over-fertilize. Basic nutrients are found within good planting media; however, they do occasionally need to be supplemented. Two or three times a year is usually more than sufficient, otherwise a buildup of mineral salts occurs and may impair plant growth.

Remember to spray plants occasionally as a disease preventative measure. Research common pests and diseases to which your plant varieties are susceptible. It is far better to take the necessary precautions than to risk the plant's health. Be sure to carefully follow the manufacturer's directions.

Plants also need to be cleaned and dusted, once a week if possible. To maintain the esthetically pleasing natural gloss of leaves, "mist" the leaf surfaces occasionally with water or with a weak solution of mild soap and water, or a leaf shining product available in most garden centers. Again, follow instructions.

Trees and Shrubs for the Landscape

Trees and shrubs form a significant part of most landscape plantings. Many kinds are available, and because of their diverse characteristics they can be used to develop many interesting and functional landscape compositions. The possibilities are almost unlimited.

The most effective landscape plantings are groupings of plants arranged in a pleasing or functional manner. Solitary plants, haphazardly arranged, are seldom effective. Consequently, a well thought out basic landscape scheme is necessary before plant selections are made.

Basic planning should include determining the location and shape of the planting beds; the need for decoration, shade, screen or windbreak; and the consideration of other home and garden activities. Once the basic plan has been determined, then selection of plants can proceed.

Selecting trees and shrubs for landscape use is similar to selecting other items for the home and garden. The more you know about the product you intend to buy, in this case trees and shrubs, the more likely you will be satisfied with the end results. Information should include not only desirable characteristics but also those features that might have an influence on the performance and suitability of the plant as it develops and matures.

Sources of this information should be varied. Numerous garden books are available. A partial listing of useful books is given at the end of this chapter. Additional information is often available through cooperative extension offices and is especially helpful in providing information on the local performance of specific trees and shrubs.

Where possible, I recommend that every effort be made to see the living plant before final selection is made. This means visits to a garden center or local nursery, a botanic garden or arboretum, or, in some cases, to a neighbor who has the plant growing in his landscape plantings.

All sorts of information should be assembled about trees and shrubs before final selections are made. Most of the rest of this chapter is devoted to the things to look for.

Winter hardiness potential is of special significance for woody plants in most sections of the United States. Trees and shrubs differ in their ability to tolerate the cold of winter, and hardiness ratings have been established for most kinds. However, this information for newer introductions may be lacking.

Most books give a winter hardiness rating for each plant covered. This should be carefully noted for each kind of plant considered for landscape use.

Landscaping of a home in the Washington (D.C.) Area.

Plants used in key locations in the planting should be completely winter hardy. Less hardy kinds can be used but they should be restricted to smaller numbers and more protected locations.

The mature size of trees and shrubs is an important consideration. Several sizes are available for landscape use. Selection of the proper size will avoid overcrowding, excessive shading, or other undesirable results.

Trees can be selected that are large (60′+), medium (30′ to 50′), or small (15′ to 30′) in size at maturity. On most properties, large trees should be used sparingly and located carefully for maximum efficiency in shading. Small trees are useful for small properties and many have outstanding seasonal interests.

Shrubs also are available in three sizes, large (8′ to 15′+), medium (4′ to 5′), and small (1′ to 3′). Large shrubs are best in border or screen plantings. Medium and small kinds can be used effectively in foundation plantings near the home, where even at maturity they can be expected to remain in scale with minimum maintenance requirements.

AUTHOR *Robert G. Mower* is Associate Professor, Department of Floriculture and Ornamental Horticulture, Cornell University, Ithaca, N.Y.

Shape (outline of the plant) and branching habit (arrangement of branches within the outline) vary considerably among trees and shrubs. These characteristics can add distinctive features to a landscape planting.

Different shapes available include round, oval, ovate (broadest below the middle), obovate (broadest above the middle), broader than high, conical, columnar, and irregular. Branching habits include upright-narrow to spreading, upright-arching, horizontal, pendulous, and irregular.

Plant density is important when selections are being made for screening or barrier purposes. Dense-compact plants are particularly suited for this purpose and a number of kinds, both trees and shrubs, are available with these characteristics. On the other hand, if plants with a loose-open characteristic are needed, these kinds are available also.

Foliage characteristics include duration, color, and texture. Both trees and shrubs have kinds that are evergreen (foliage persists more than one year) and others that are deciduous (foliage drops at the end of the growing season). Evergreen kinds may be either broadleaved or narrowleaved and they are particularly suited for screening purposes.

Variation in foliage color is available in both evergreen and deciduous trees and shrubs.

For the most part, green or shades of green should make up the bulk of foliage color in a landscape planting. However, other foliage colors can create a feeling of more space, brighten a dark corner, or serve as the accent feature of a specimen plant. Colors available include reddish-purple, blue, gray-green, yellow, and various combinations of yellow, white, and green in variegated forms.

Texture (variation in leaf size) can also be used for interesting landscape effects. Those kinds with coarse texture (large leaves) and fine texture (small leaves) are particularly distinctive.

Most trees and shrubs are selected for landscape plantings on the basis of their seasonal interests of flower, fruit, and fall color. While these characteristics are very important, they should be considered in the context of the other plant characteristics discussed previously and with the total landscape setting in mind. In this way, a balanced and effective garden setting can be developed.

A wide array of shrubs and small trees with showy flowers are available for landscape use. Colors range from white to yellow, red, orange, blue, and purple. While most bloom in the spring, it is possible to select kinds that flower at different times. These will provide nearly continuous bloom throughout the growing season.

All trees and shrubs are not showy when in bloom, so some care in selection is important if showy flowers are desired.

Attractive fruits are also an important and useful seasonal interest of trees and shrubs. They are usually most prominent in late summer and early fall, but some kinds persist well into winter and are very effective when other interests may be somewhat limiting.

Certain types of fruit are particularly attractive to birds and are useful additions to a border planting, while others can be counted on to remain on the plants for garden color and interest.

Selection of trees and shrubs for fruiting characteristics should be done carefully in order to select the best kinds and to avoid undesirable features that many have.

Some kinds of trees and shrubs have excellent fall color while others have little or no interest at this season. Colors are mostly yellow, orange, or red but a few kinds are reddish-purple. Evergreen trees and shrubs with green foliage can be used effectively to accent the fall coloration of other plants, and in addition will continue to be effective during winter.

Only a few kinds of trees and shrubs have showy flowers, fruits, and fall color as part of the same plant. Because of this it is usually necessary to select a combination of several kinds of trees and shrubs in order to have all seasonal interests represented in a landscape planting. However, this does provide an opportunity to introduce a wide variety of plants into the garden or to develop a garden emphasizing a specific seasonal interest (fruit garden, flower garden, spring garden, fall garden, etc.).

Plantings at Reston, VA.

In the areas where deciduous plants predominate, selection considerations should include winter features as well. Characteristics such as bark color and character, branching habit and texture, and twig color can be significant contributors to the winter garden scene. A number of trees and shrubs have excellent winter characteristics and they should be used where appropriate.

Besides determining the many desirable characters that trees and shrubs have, you should find out any undesirable features that may limit their effectiveness in a landscape planting.

Nearly all plants have problems that may limit their usefulness. Some kinds are particularly susceptible to damage by insects and diseases. While the problem can often be controlled, certain plants are best avoided due to their very common pest problems.

Other plants have weak wood, have undesirable fruits, develop exceptional amounts of litter, or produce hazards (such as thorns) that limit their usefulness.

Other kinds are hard to transplant or

require special soil conditions if they are to grow properly.

Information on potential plant problems is often more difficult to obtain yet it should be a major factor in plant selection.

When all the information is assembled for each plant, including both the good and bad features, then the best selections to meet each kind of planting situation can be made.

Planting Maintenance

Once final selections have been made, the ultimate success of the new plantings will be determined by proper planting and maintenance techniques. Some things to consider are:

Soil should be well prepared with particular attention towards adequate soil drainage.

Planting holes should be of sufficient size to accommodate the root system without crowding. The plants should be set at the proper level and the soil firmed in place.

Watering should be thorough and continued periodically until the root system is well established. Trees may benefit from wrapping and staking and the removal of a portion of the lateral branches (not the leader).

Once plants are established, maintenance practices may include periodic fertilization and watering. If the plants are not being used as hedge material, pruning should be restricted to removal of interfering or crossing branches, dead or dying branches, or the occasional branch that is not in keeping with normal growth characteristics of the plant. Excessive pruning is neither necessary nor desirable.

Many kinds of trees and shrubs are available for landscape planting. Selection based on as much information as possible will lead to wise decisions and a more effective and satisfying garden scene. The choices are up to you!

The Cooperative Extension Offices throughout the country usually have circulars, leaflets, or information bulletins on the various aspects of plant selection and maintenance. Many are free or available at a nominal charge. Consult your local Cooperative Extension Office for what is available in your area.

FOR FURTHER READING:

Robinette, Gary O. *Plants/People/Environmental Quality,* 139 pp., for sale by Superintendent of Documents, Washington, D.C. 20402, 1972.

Sunset Books, Lane Books. *Pruning Handbook,* 96 pp., Menlo Park, Ca. 94025, 1972.

———. *Landscaping Book,* 159 pp., Menlo Park, Ca. 94025, 1971.

———. *Western Garden Book,* 448 pp., Menlo Park, Ca. 94025, 1967.

Bush-Brown, James and Louise, *America's Garden Book,* 752 pp., Charles Scribner's Sons, New York, N.Y., 1958.

Flemer III, William. *Nature's Guide to Successful Gardening and Landscaping,* 331 pp., Thomas Y. Crowell Company, New York, N.Y., 1972.

Johnson, Hugh. *The International Book of Trees,* 288 pp., Simon and Schuster, Inc., New York, N.Y., 1973.

Nelson Jr., William R. *Landscaping Your Home,* 151 pp., University of Illinois Cooperative Extension Service, Cir. 858, Urbana, Ill. 61801, 1963.

A Rose Is a Rose, But Roses Come by the Thousands

OFTEN SAID to be the most popular flower in America today, the rose may be readily grown in the home garden. There is relatively little investment, and the time and materials used give great return in prolific and beautiful blooms over a long season. Proper location and care are the main factors for success.

Roses are representative of the earliest flowers native to our country. In Oregon and Colorado fossil remains of rose blooms date back at least 35 million years.

Of course, it is only the wild or species forms of roses which occurred prehistorically. It has been just in the past century or two that the continuously flowering types of good color, shape and size have evolved.

The work of hybridizers, cross-pollinating various roses and growing them from seed, has accounted for many thousands of different roses. The book *Modern Roses VII* by the American Rose Society has about 10,000 names of varieties (cultivars) of roses.

Roses today are mostly field propagated in nurseries. Bushes are produced by budding each of the many varieties on a relatively few different kinds of rootstocks, known also as understocks.

Annual production of field-grown rose bushes in the United States is nearly 45 million bushes, principally in California, Texas, Arizona, Pennsylvania, Ohio, and Oregon. Soil and climate are the main factors restricting field propagation to certain areas in these states. Bushes produced in one state may be just as good as those grown in another. Acclimatization really is unimportant with roses.

At harvest, bushes are called 2-year plants because the rootstocks are about that age at digging time. However, the canes, or tops, develop in the second year, and so this portion would be less than one year old.

Grading of bushes is, according to the American Standard for Nursery Stock (ANSI Z60.1–1973), with the No. 1, or best grade, having three or more good, heavy canes. (These national standards are sponsored by the American Association of Nurserymen, Inc., and approved by the American National Standards Institute, Inc.). Each bush should have a well-spread root system. Quality of bushes depends on size and maturity when dug for storage or marketing.

Confusing at first are the many classes, all representing growth habits. The wild or species roses mentioned earlier bloom only once a year, if from America, and are not so decorative as kinds grown in most gardens.

But fortunately, through hybridizing over many decades, the roses of today range from tiny miniatures to shrubs and climbers, with continuous or recurrent blooming, mostly on strong, upright stems. Blooms come in many different shades, sizes and petalages with conformations varying from single to cluster flowering. Fragrance ranges from slight to intense, in about the same proportion now as a century ago.

Roses with exceptional fragrance—and many of these are new—include, to name but a few: Mister Lincoln, Crimson Glory, Chrysler Imperial, and Avon (red hybrid teas); Pink Peace, Perfume Delight, Tiffany (pink hybrid teas); Fragrant Cloud (orange red hybrid tea); Sutter's Gold (yellow blend hybrid tea); Granada (red-yellow blend grandiflora); Sterling Silver (lavender or mauve hybrid tea); Angel Face (lavender floribunda); Apricot Nectar (apricot blend grandiflora); White Beauty (white hybrid tea).

Classes of roses for the garden are based mainly on growth and flower characteristics. The hybrid teas vary from short to tall, from about 2′ to 5′. Blooms generally are large and one to a stem, but if multiple, not usually over three. The hybrid tea is the largest class according to number of bushes grown, being the most popular for cut flowers. (Peace, Tropicana, Eclipse, Christian Dior, Royal Highness).

The grandifloras are similar to the hybrid teas, but have somewhat smaller blooms, with a tendency to cluster. Each stem is suitable for a cut flower. (Queen Elizabeth, Montezuma, Scarlet Knight, Golden Girl).

Floribundas are prolific blooming, with cluster flowering, mostly short stemmed individually. They are useful particularly for borders—and some for cut flowers. (Europeana, Summer Snow, Pinocchio, Goldilocks, Fashion).

Polyanthas produce many clusters of small flowers on plants of short stature. (China Doll, Gloria Mundi, Margo Koster, The Fairy).

AUTHOR *Eldon W. Lyle* is Plant Pathologist, Texas Rose Research Foundation, Inc., at Tyler, and Past President of the American Rose Society.

Miniatures are diminutive in both size of plants and blooms. Full-grown, they are seldom over a foot tall, with blooms that usually are much less than an inch across. This is one class that may be grown in small pots. Most miniatures are surprisingly winter hardy. (Starina, Tom Thumb, Toy Clown, Red Imp, Cinderella).

Climbers are tall, and have either pillar or vine-like growth, needing trellises or other support. These roses vary from climbing minatures to climbing hybrid teas, pillars and regular climbers, with flowers from small to large, few petals to very double. (Don Juan, Golden Showers, Blaze, Joseph's Coat, Rhonda, Marechal Niel).

Shrub roses are usually round-formed bushes, planted singly, although they may be planted in hedges or groups. (Agnes, Golden Wings, Empress Josephine).

Old garden roses represent an overlapping class, mainly of antiquity in bush and flower traits. They often are in the shrub class. (Baronne Prevost, Cardinal de Richelieu, Frau Karl Druschki).

Tree (standard) roses really is not a class but a form of growth, with any of the above classes budded on special stocks at levels from 1′ to 6′ or more above ground.

Beauty of roses in gardens depends much on the selection of kinds and colors available. Some people want an outdoor display, others cut flowers for arrangements or bouquets. A few desire one-stemmed specimens for exhibition.

Information about habit, size and color of more than 1,000 varieties is contained in *1974 Handbook for Selecting Roses,* available at 10¢ a copy from the American Rose Society, P.O. Box 30,000, Shreveport, La. 71130.

Varieties having highest ratings as exhibition roses in the United States today include the following partial list from an American Rose Society report.

Hybrid Teas are: First Prize (pink blend), Pascali (white), Peace (yellow blend), Royal Highness (pink), Garden Party (white blend), Swarthmore (pink blend), Mister Lincoln (red), and Miss All-American Beauty (medium pink).

Grandifloras are: Granada (red blend), Aquarius (pink blend), Pink Parfait (pink), Queen Elizabeth (pink), Montezuma (orange red), Mount Shasta (white), Camelot (coral pink), and Apricot Nectar (apricot blend).

Floribundas are: Europeana (red), Little Darling (yellow blend), Gene Boerner (pink), Ivory Fashion (white), Fire King (orange red), Iceberg (white), Redgold (yellow blend), and Vogue (pink blend).

Nineteen of these 24 varieties have rated as winners of All-America Rose Selections awards. This is a result of two years of trial from some 24 gardens over the United States prior to commercial introduction in the states. Nearly all have been patented; however, a patent is not a guarantee of quality or hardiness, but does give credit for being unique and new. It provides royalty for at least part of the cost of developing and introduction. Patent tenure is for 17 years.

The best time to plant is about four weeks ahead of the average last frost date in the spring, but in moderate climates the planting may be anytime in the winter. In places that may have frozen soil, spring planting is preferable. In either case, the site should be where the sun can reach the bushes during the growing season for at least half the day—not under trees or next to hedges.

Areas previously in lawn usually are suitable. Grass should be removed for the width of the bed (from 3′ to 4′ for two rows of bushes). Leave a walkway about 4′ or 5′ wide between beds.

One of the main requisites is to have raised beds, about 4″ or more above the surrounding lawn area. Along the Gulf Coast, a 12″ to 16″ elevation is desirable.

Organic matter—such as ground pine bark, peat, rotted manure, or composted leaves—may be mixed with good, weed-free top soil, and enough should be prepared so that settling still will leave at least 4″ of raised bed.

A good soil mixture will stay friable (easily crumbled) and yet be moisture-retentive without being overwet.

Edging the beds with special kinds of boards, cement blocks or poured cement, or other materials should keep the soil-fill in place. The edging must not trap water in the beds. Drainage holes may be fitted or cut into the edging, if necessary to prevent this.

Hybrid teas and grandifloras should be spaced at least 18″ apart in each row, while floribundas and polyanthas should be closer because of smaller size bushes. Climbers should be set along borders of the garden, usually, and in a single row. A raised bed is advocated, as for other roses.

Bare-Root Often Best

Whether to buy bare-root, root-wrapped, or container-grown rose bushes depends on the time of year and availability of the varieties. Each kind can give good garden results.

Bare-root roses that have been suitably stored to retain good maturity, without breaking dormancy, often will prove most satisfactory.

Those which are root-wrapped and treated to prevent drying out usually are more readily available, often at a lower price. They give good results provided they are suitably mature when packaged, and drying of the canes and roots has not occurred prior to planting.

In either case, buds on the canes should be plump and yet without much forcing.

Bare-root bushes ordinarily come from the nursery, and the packaged ones from a store or by mail order.

Both the bushes obtained bare-root and those received in root-wrapped condition need to have damaged or broken canes or roots removed by pruning. Also it is suggested that you trim the canes to about 8″ in length and the roots to approximately 12″ prior to planting. Soaking the roots in water for about an hour before planting is another recommendation.

It is important to have the bud union, which is the knob or swelling just above the roots and where the branches originate, set just above the level of the top of the bed when planting is completed. This applies in northern climates as well as southern.

In most places it is well to bring soil or mulch up around the canes for a few inches until chance of possible drying or freezing is past. This protection is to be removed from around the canes soon after new shoots appear.

Immediately after planting, water should be hosed in around the roots, removing air pockets and settling the plants. This watering also makes sure the roots have direct contact with moisture. Such procedure is less damaging to the roots than tamping.

The container-grown rose already has foliage, and possibly blooms, when purchased. It usually is more expensive than bare-root or root-wrapped roses, but permits extending the planting season as well as having flowers quickly.

No pruning is needed before planting, but take care not to loosen soil material in the pot when the bush is removed and placed in the rose bed. Planting level in the bed should be slightly above normal to allow for settling, with canes and bud union above the surface of the bed before mulching.

Suckers may develop from below the bud union with new growth arising from the understock. This growth should be removed as soon as it appears, to avoid vegetative growth and flowering of the undesirable understock.

Care of the rose bed includes use of a good mulch. Many materials serve well on the surface of the rose bed to aid in weed control, conserve moisture, and provide cooling of the soil in warm climates. Some are ground pine bark, pine needles, shredded oak bark, sugar cane residue, and calcined clay.

Cultivation is not needed or desirable with a good mulch, with the amount equal to a depth that still will permit water penetration and good aeration.

After planting and mulching, it is important to start immediately a once a week spraying with a good fungicide.

Although roses are quite hardy and may survive a long time without pesticides, spraying will make the bushes more vigorous and prolific with blooms.

Prevention of foliage diseases such as black spot, powdery mildew, and rust is easy if care is given early, rather than trying to control them after damage already is evident. Loss of leaves, or leaf damage, cause stunting of the bushes and a decrease in number, color, and fragance of the blooms. In locations of continuously cool weather, the problem is reduced, and regularity of fungicide care may be lessened.

Some of the recommended fungicides include benomyl, folpet, maneb, and Daconil. Spray until there is dripping from the foliage, and do not use concentrations stronger than advised.

Use insecticides only as needed, after the first evidence of insects. Too frequent treatment with insecticides tends to kill beneficial insects which normally might handle the problem.

Some of the preferred insecticides include dimethoate, carbaryl, malathion, diazinon, Isotox, and Fundal. Perhaps only three or four applications a year will control the insects, and a general rule is to apply the least that will accomplish this.

On established bushes, use of fungicides should begin early and regularly, as in the case of newly planted bushes, until disease control is assured. And in the case of insect troubles, wait for the insects to show before treatment.

Pruning out dead wood may be done any time, but general pruning back is best carried out in late winter, about four weeks ahead of the average last frost date.

The extent of cutting back depends on the landscape effect desired. For bushes to reach 4′ to 8′ high, pruning back to about 20″ is advised. If shorter, more compact growth is wanted, pruning should be more drastic, even as low as 8″. The main thing is to make the cuts smooth and flush with joints. Do not leave stubs.

Freezes may kill the canes and justify pruning back to the bud unions. Even then, vigorous new growth may result, especially if preventive care against diseases has been effective the previous year.

Climbing roses, which bloom only once a year, should be pruned back only immediately after the spring bloom is over. Otherwise the old wood from which the blooms originate will be removed or limited.

In fertilizing roses, commercial concentrates are very worthwhile if the right kind. A balanced, pelleted, mostly-soluble, complete fertilizer is advised.

Wait to fertilize until after new growth occurs in the spring. Begin with one level tablespoon around each bush, and repeat with the same amount about six weeks later. Avoid getting any fertilizer on the leaves, or fertilizing in the summer or fall, and never apply fertilizer at the same time as planting.

While some fertilizers may be diluted and then be safe on rose foliage, these are less effective than pelleted fertilizers applied to the soil.

Ample watering is a must. Watering may be done entirely with lawn sprinklers if regular weekly spraying is done to prevent disease. The main thing is to assure that about an inch of water is available to the roots each week during the growing season, whether it comes from rainfall or supplemental watering, on the ground or from overhead.

In cutting rose blooms, only a short portion of the stem should be taken during the first bloom period, especially with new plants. Often it is best to take just the flower without leaves, floating it in a tray as a partially open bloom. Once the bush is of good size, longer stems may be taken without any devitalizing effect. The cuts should be with a sharp tool and close above a joint (node).

Mounding, with soil or mulch, around the canes in early winter is a means of winter protection where severe freezes are anticipated. A 10″ mound will give a lot of protection. The main thing is to protect against damage to the bud union.

Actually, only a little labor is needed for growing good roses. Regular care is the problem and will continue to be until more resistance is bred into roses, and until spray materials are available that will give a longer lasting effect. However, it has been demonstrated that a bed of 100 bushes may be kept in excellent condition and yet require only 30 minutes a week spent in maintenance during the growing season.

Ground Covers and the Vines

DURING RECENT decades we have come to understand how we can improve our landscape plantings vastly with short and spreading plants used in massed groups. Plants that perform for us in this way are called ground covers.

As we use plants of an appropriate color, texture and height to form a carpet-like appearance, we attain both esthetic and functional achievements. Ground covers do much to complete the needed semblance of balance and form through directing more emphasis to the surface plane. Uniformity and simplicity must receive consideration if our home landscaping is to appear restful and attractive.

Ground covers perform for us in a number of useful ways. Being plants which naturally dwell in the lower level of our landscape, the floor area, they offer innumerable rewards in landscaping our homesites.

Some of the rewards are reduction of glare, conservation of moisture, less maintenance, and erosion control. In addition, ground covers help to entrap pollutants, delineate traffic circulation, and provide a better scale relationship in the overall landscape design.

Then, of equal importance, we are able to create appropriate texture and color variation, direct attention, and tie together the key landscape elements.

In our humble way, we try to improve on nature in today's landscaping, and do it in a way that will accent and highlight the garden areas to our satisfaction. Ground covers are our landscape carpeting tools. Since there are so many plants which serve satisfactorily as carpeting tools, we can be very discriminating in choosing those which will best serve for the intended effect.

Cost is a factor, so there is economic significance in selecting plants which will do the job correctly and economically within the bounds of hardiness and ease of maintenance. There is no point in adding to our home management problems, if garden care becomes a chore instead of a pleasure. As a general rule, however, ground covers—once established—lessen overall landscape maintenance.

With installation cost and future care as major factors, we must seriously consider the site and just why carpeting plants are appropriate and where they should go. We often hear recommendations made for using ground covers only in problem spots, those places where grass has been tried and failed. These positions usually are in deep shade, lack moisture, and otherwise do not have conditions suitable to grow shallow rooted plants readily. This is expecting too much, even of ground covers, though sometimes there is a degree of success despite these conditions.

Using ground covers only in problem areas is of secondary importance; their real worth relates to the creation of a fastidious and harmonious carpet. The carpet-like effect is obtained when we use plants either as underplanting or to tie together those strong, accenting features of the landscape, but chiefly in areas where cultural conditions assure reasonable success.

We must select covers having the best chance of doing well. If positions are shady, use shade-loving plants like, for example, Ivy and Pachysandra. If

---

AUTHOR *W. E. Cunningham* is president of Cunningham Gardens Inc., Waldron, Ind.

Ground Covers for Special Locations

Botanical Name	Common Name
Sunny	
Antennaria neodioica **(1, 6)**	Pussytoes
Arctostaphylas uva-ursi **(1, 2, 3, 6)**	Bearberry
Cotoneaster dammeri & cultivars **(1)**	Bearberry Cotoneaster
Cotoneaster apiculata **(1)**	Cranberry Cotoneaster
Euonymus colorata **(3, 4, 6)**	Purpleleaf Wintercreeper
Juniperus horizontalis & cultivars **(6)**	Creeping Juniper
Juniperus procumbens nana **(4, 6)**	Japanese Juniper
Lonicera japonica halliana **(3, 4, 6)**	Hall's Honeysuckle
Pachistima canbyi **(1, 2, 6)**	Pachistima
Potentilla tridentata **(1, 2, 6)**	Wineleaf Cinquefoil
Potentilla verna nana **(1, 5)**	Cinquefoil
Sedum species **(5, 6)**	Stonecrop
Waldsteinia ternata **(1, 3, 6)**	Barren Strawberry
Shady	
Ajuga reptans & cultivars **(3, 4)**	Carpet Bugle
Convallaria majalis **(4, 5)**	Lily-of-the-Valley
Euonymus fortunei varieties **(3, 4, 6)**	Wintercreeper
Hedera helix & cultivars **(4, 6)**	English Ivy
Hosta species **(5)**	Plantain Lily
Liriope spicata **(6)**	Lily Turf
Pachysandra terminalis **(2, 6)**	Japanese Spurge
Vinca minor & cultivars **(3, 6)**	Periwinkle or myrtle

1. Requires well-drained soil
2. Requires acid soil
3. Good in sun or shade
4. Confine, may grow out-of-bounds
5. Herbaceous
6. Foliage retention in winter

Pachysandra terminalis *provides a year-round carpet.*

positions are hot and dry, open and sunny, use plants such as Cotoneaster and Euonymus. When the space is large, perhaps sloping, there are plants, too, which are well suited to these demands.

Though we must try to match the plant to its tenable ecology, there usually is enough flexibility in most ground covers to allow some deviation. Even so, we must not neglect in any way good site preparation, for here lies the basic difficulty often experienced in easily and quickly establishing plant material.

By devoting a little more than the usual effort to site preparation—particularly by incorporating very deeply and thoroughly liberal quantities of humus materials such as peat moss, composts or rotted manure, plus the required chemical elements—we take a big step toward ultimate success.

Good preparation does pay off, and handsomely, with faster growth, more rapid maturing cover, and better winter hardiness.

Perhaps the most common error in planting ground covers is that of spacing. If spacing is too far apart, the intended effect is not produced for a long time and in the interim weeding becomes burdensome. Though relatively close spacing is more costly, the effect is NOW. There really is no economy in wide spacing; maintenance is increased and the landscape enhancement is negligible.

Proper care of ground covers is of primary importance.

Fertilization, irrigation and pruning is required if there is to be retention of vigor, drought tolerance, and tidy appearance.

One of our most versatile ground covers, *Euonymus colorata* (Purpleleaf Wintercreeper), has a tendency to ascend, and even climb trees and structures. To maintain an even-topped appearance, clipping is required and this is easily accomplished with a rotary mower set high.

Periodic fertilization and summer irrigation of *Vinca minor* (Periwinkle) and *Pachysandra terminalis* (Japanese Spurge), are particularly noteworthy recommendations.

Another of our especially useful carpeting plants, *Hedera helix* (English Ivy), and its hardy cultivars, requires pruning on occasion, though mostly at the bed edges and in places where there is a tendency to climb walls or sprawl into shrubs or evergreens.

Vines Play Big Role

Vines are a part of the plant kingdom that can play an important role in landscaping. The effect of climbing plants, however, is an extension of the garden in a vertical direction, wherein the straight line of the horizontal planting is broken.

Clematis (pronounced clem-a-tis) is perhaps the finest, most admirable of all the flowering vines. Once a strong vine develops and flowering occurs, there is eye-catching attention and enviable admiration.

To assure trouble-free success with clematis, pay special attention to choice of site and to soil preparation. For the permanent location, choose a spot offering sun at least half the day, a place which promises to be just as good years hence—since clematis will thrive for many years if growing conditions are right at the start and are kept right.

Too much emphasis cannot be placed on the importance of planting clematis where some shade will be cast

VINES FOR SPECIAL USES

Botanical Name	*Common Name*
Akebia quinata **(1, 2, 3, 4)**	Five-leaf Akebia
Clematis species & hybrids **(1, 2, 3, 4)**	Virgin's Bower
Euonymus fortunei **(2, 3)**	Wintercreeper
Hedera helix & cultivars **(2)**	English Ivy
Hydrangea petiolaris **(1, 2)**	Climbing Hydrangea
Parthenocissus tricuspidata **(2)**	Boston Ivy
Wisteria floribunda **(1, 2, 3, 4)**	Japanese Wisteria

1. Flowering
2. Wall Cover
3. Screening
4. Trellis

over the root area, and on furnishing a porous, heavy mulch to keep the growing space cool and moist.

Most difficulties experienced in establishing clematis are due to exposing or subjecting plants to extremes of temperature and to moisture stress. Prepare soils very deeply, and thoroughly, as recommended for the planting of ground covers.

In the garden, clematis will entwine and hold to shrubs, evergreens, trellis, fencing, or any prepared facility.

For special effect, though, some assistance is required. In many varieties a succession of bloom will occur if clematis vines are pruned heavily early in March, then slightly after each flush of bloom. Do not permit seed heads to develop—unless you desire the masses of feathery, silky heads for your enjoyment. Also, to assure recurrent bloom throughout the summer, fertility and moisture must be kept adequate for new shoot growth.

A most common difficulty experienced with establishing clematis is caused by a disease called "dieback", indicated by sudden wilting and collapse of vine growth. Sanitation and aeration at the soil surface are requisites to success.

The "dieback" disease in clematis comes from a localized infection. In most cases the fungus originates at ground level, but it can infect the leaves and then provide a basis for further infection.

Along with the mulches and well-prepared soils, periodic fungicide sprays should be applied while plants are in the juvenile stage. Sprays should be directed heavily at the stems near the soil surface and to foliage as well.

Fungicides which are designed for control of foliage diseases of roses will work very well in controlling foliar and stem infection of clematis, if applied regularly during the moist and humid periods of the spring season.

Of course there are other fine vines, among them *Wisteria floribunda* (Japanese Wisteria) and *Parthenocissus tricuspidata* (Boston Ivy). The Japanese Wisteria requires strong, sturdy support for twining and also some assistance in training. Boston Ivy adheres to wall surfaces with its own appendages. Many of the climbing plants are of special interest and beauty, for they can provide a screen and help to cover wall surfaces.

Japanese Wisteria provides a spectacular bloom display in late May, and Boston Ivy offers lustrous green foliage in summer which changes to a brilliant scarlet in fall.

Another exceptionally fine climber for wall areas is *Hydrangea petiolaris* (Climbing Hydrangea). Large, white flowers are freely produced in June, and contrast well with its large deciduous dark green leaves.

Some of our vines serve a dual purpose, both as ground cover and wall cover. English ivy and euonymus are good examples. As with all vines, when grown on walls only a little growing space is required. The chief interest is upward, at eye level or above.

The what to plant and the when to plant in the way of ground covers and vines presents important decisions for the home landscaper. Landscape material originally came from many and varied climatic zones. Your choice of site should fit as closely as possible the environmental requirement of the plants to be used. Microclimates even occur within one's own homesite.

Fortunately, many of the most dependable ground covers and vines are very hardy and withstand the severest wintry conditions.

In developing plans for home landscaping it is recommended that you make first-hand observation in your immediate community and that you consult with your local nurseryman, garden center horticulturist, or with your landscape architect. Mail-order catalogs also contain a wealth of horticultural information.

Seeing how plants are used in actual growing conditions, discerning their appeal, and seeking advice from the horticulture professional in your neighborhood will certainly help to get you off to a good start on your planting.

Climbing plants add interest and beauty.

ARBORETUMS & BOTANICAL GARDENS FOR STUDY OF VINES AND GROUND COVERS

Beal-Garfield Botanic Garden
Michigan State University
East Lansing, Mich.

Strybing Arboretum
Golden Gate Park
San Francisco, Calif.

Arnold Arboretum
Case Estates
Weston, Mass.

Brooklyn Botanic Gardens
Brooklyn, N.Y.

Longwood Gardens
Kennett Square, Pa.

Missouri Botanical Gardens
St. Louis, Mo.

Morton Arboretum
Lisle, Ill.

National Arboretum
Washington, D.C.

Our arboretums and botanical gardens contribute immeasurably to the advancement and dissemination of horticultural knowledge; they exhibit the best plants for ornamental and functional use under local conditions. Fortunately many of these institutions are located within easy daytime, week-end or holiday travel distance for most, thus permitting great pleasure in the pursuit of horticultural information.

The opportunity to see and study ornamentals in well-designed and cared-for landscaped settings aids greatly in learning how ground covers and vines are used, why they are used, and in determining the potential value and adaptability these special purpose plants will have in your own home landscape improvement program.

FOR FURTHER READING:

U.S. Department of Agriculture. *Growing Ground Covers,* G 175, Office of Communication, Washington, D.C. 20250.

The Morton Arboretum Quarterly. *Gardening with Ground Cover Plants,* Vol. 5, No. 1, Lisle, Ill. 60532, 50 cents, 1969.

University of Illinois. *Ground Covers and Their Uses,* Vocational Agriculture Service, College of Agriculture, 434 Mumford Hall, Urbana, Ill. 61801.

Ohio State University. *Ground Covers in the Landscape,* Ext. Spec. Landscape Horticulture, 2001 Fyffe Court, Columbus, Ohio 43210.

Nursery Stock—What to Buy and What to Expect

SALES OF trees, shrubs, vines and other plants purchased at nurseries and other retail establishments offering nursery stock in 1973 are estimated at $2.3 billion. In recent years, with the heavy emphasis on ecology and environmental improvement, the number of plant purchasers has increased markedly, particularly among the younger age groups in their late teens and twenties.

It is not at all unusual today to find "plant boutiques" and other retail plant specialty shops in the major metropolitan areas where young people live and shop. This market is in addition to the garden centers, retail nurseries, hardware stores, department stores, produce departments, roadside markets, and other nursery plant outlets well known to the older age groups.

In addition, local retail outlets, mail order nursery catalogs, magazine advertisements, and newspaper ads continue to furnish information on sources of nursery-produced plants.

As is the case in just about any other field, the nursery industry has its own jargon. Purpose of this chapter is to review some of these terms, as well as give some information on where and how to buy nursery-produced plants.

Within the nursery industry, nurseries specializing in the production of plants—or growing nurseries—are referred to as *wholesale nurseries.* Many of the wholesale nurseries choose not to sell to individuals, but only to retail nurseries and other retail outlets selling to the general public, to government agencies such as parks departments, departments of streets and highways, and other commercial users of plants.

On a year-round basis *garden centers* and *retail nurseries* offer plants as well as garden tools, mulches, soil conditioners, fertilizers, and other supplies and equipment used in gardening. It is not at all unusual to find that these establishments have a landscape department which will prepare a design plan as well as make actual plantings for the customer.

Some *landscape firms* do not have a retail sales department and only provide design, planting and landscape maintenance services.

Many other types of retail establishments offer plants and garden supplies only during the peak of the spring and fall planting seasons. These include many *department stores, multi-outlet retail stores, hardware stores, grocery stores, roadside markets,* and others.

Generally speaking, those retail nurseries, garden centers, and other retail establishments with year-round garden or nursery departments are most apt to have sales personnel with professional or "on the job" horticulture training. Thus they are better prepared to offer sound horticultural suggestions to the purchaser.

Many *mail order nurseries* offer a wide selection of shade trees, flowering trees, conifers, flowering shrubs, broad leaf evergreens, vines, fruit trees, small fruits, and other plants of interest to both the homeowner and the apartment dweller.

Citizens associations, garden clubs, and other local groups often arrange with a local garden center or retail nursery for special plant sales such as spring bulbs, azaleas, roses, bedding plants, or other landscape plants.

At one time practically all nursery plants, especially those which lose their leaves (deciduous plants), were offered for sale *"bare root."*

This means that plants were grown in the nursery row or field and after they had shed their leaves in the fall were dug and held dormant in special nursery storages over winter. During

---

AUTHOR *Ray Brush* is administrator of the American Association of Nurserymen, Washington, D.C.

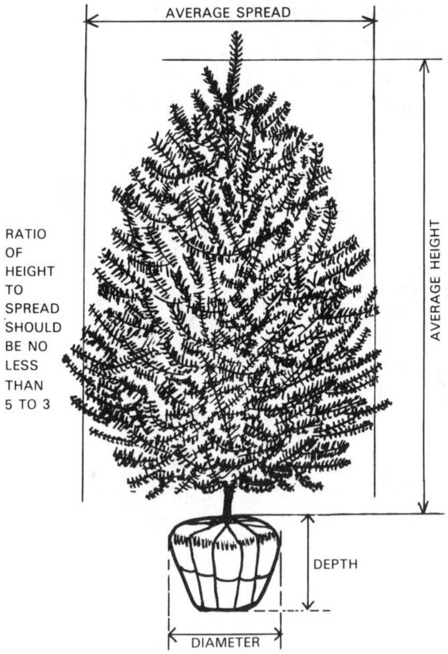

Conifer evergreens are sized by height. "Average spread" is secondary. The ratio of height to spread will vary with the type of conifer. Pyramidal conifers should have a ratio of height to spread of not less than 5 to 3.

the winter months these were sorted, labeled, and inspected for freedom from insects and disease damage.

With the advent of polyethlene and other plastics following World War II, the roots of these plants frequently are wrapped in plastic or placed in a plastic bag with a moisture holding material such as sphagnum moss, or "shingle toe," to keep the roots moist and healthy during transportation and display at the retail outlet.

Mail order nurseries usually ship dormant, deciduous nursery stock in cartoons or packages lined with plastic or waterproof paper.

Needle evergreens (conifers) and broadleaf evergreens are plants which do not lose all their leaves at the same time. Such plants are never completely dormant, that is, their leaves are continuing to function although at a reduced rate even at temperatures below 40° F.

Customarily these evergreens are sold as "balled and burlapped." This means the plants are dug from the nursery row with the ball of earth about the roots intact. Burlap wrapped around the ball of earth and roots is fastened with pinning nails or twine to keep the ball intact, avoiding injury to the fine feeding roots and rootlets.

Care should always be taken when handling B & B nursery plants by picking the plant up by the ball. Rough handling or picking them up by the stem or trunk is very apt to result in root injury. One of the advantages of B & B stock is that large size, even mature shrubs and trees, can be moved in this fashion.

Container grown plants are plants grown in the container in which they are sold. To be considered container grown, the plants should have been transplanted into the container and grown there sufficiently long for new fibrous roots to have developed so the root mass will retain its shape and hold together when removed from the container. On removal from the container only the fine or fibrous roots should be evident.

It is currently estimated that over 30 percent of the annual U.S. production of nursery plants sold at retail is container grown.

As the nursery industry continued to develop and specialize in production of different plants in various regions of the country, a standardized system of sizing and describing plants became necessary. Since 1921 the American Association of Nurserymen (AAN) has maintained an active committee on standards.

Standards have been periodically revised, and the current edition of *American Standard for Nursery Stock ANSI Z60.1–1973* was authorized on Feb. 1, 1973, by the American National Standards Institute, Inc.

In addition to the AAN's Standards Committee, 15 national and regional societies, associations, and governmental agencies reviewed and endorsed the latest revisions.

These technical standards describe

COMPARISONS IN THE VARIOUS TYPES OF DECIDUOUS SHRUBS

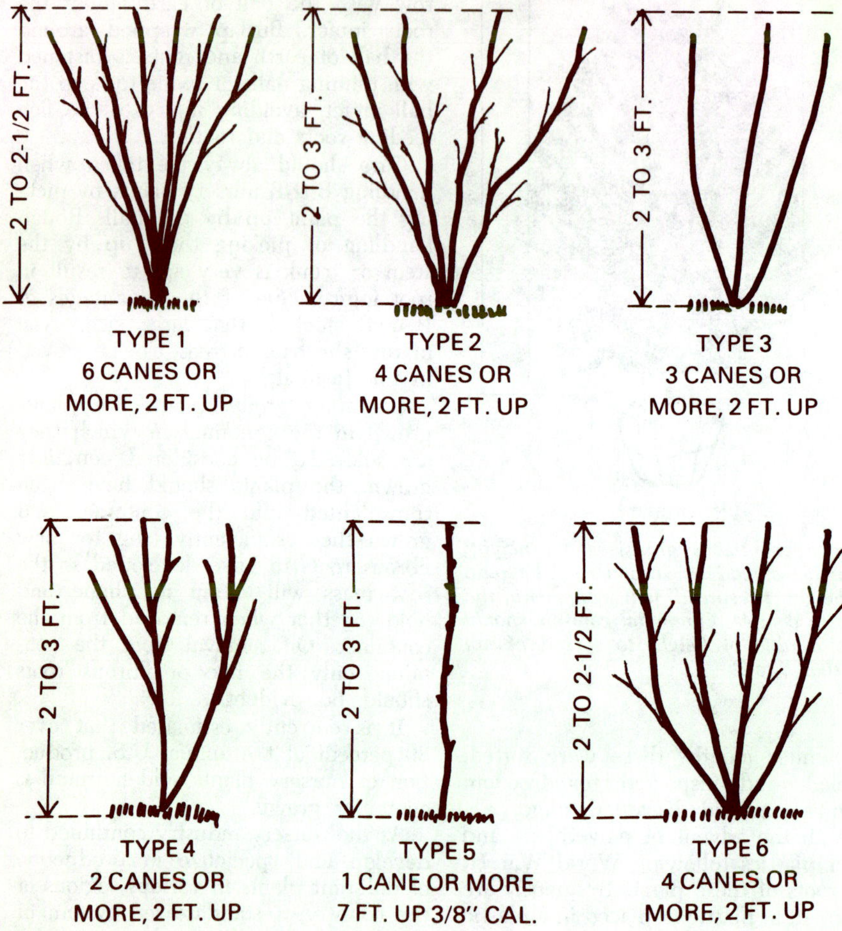

Deciduous shrubs are graded by size and number of canes. Typical examples of each type are:

Type 1—'Crimson Pigmy' barberry
'Anthony Waterer' spiraea

Type 2—Deciduous azaleas
Redosier dogwood

Type 3—Forsythia
Spiraea (tall growing varieties)
Weigela

Type 4—Buckthorn
Lilac

Type 5—Shining Sumac

Type 6—Barberry

the system for sizing various kinds of nursery plants as well as indicating numbers of branches, height of branching, numbers of canes, minimum root ball sizes and grades for roses and small fruits.

Where to Buy

Depending on the type of nursery stock one wants to purchase, there are alternatives. For example: if one is seeking small plants at a minimum cost realizing that they will have to be cared for over several years before they mature, one should look for special advertisements in horticultural magazines and special sections in the mail order catalogs devoted to lists of liner or seedling stock.

For a consumer who wishes a little larger stock which has already begun to branch and develop into its natural shape, mail order catalogs as well as local garden centers and other retail establishments are good sources. Fruit trees , small fruit plants, bare-root shrubs, and small shade trees as well as perennials may be purchased by mail order or at local retail nurseries.

Catalogs and advertisements in magazines and newspapers should indicate the regions of the country where the plants are adapted, or restrict their advertising to only those regions.

Consumers wishing landscape size plants will usually find it to their advantage to purchase such plants locally at garden centers and retail nursery outlets. In this case one has the advantage of examining the plants to select those characteristics most desired, before purchasing.

Some customers prefer to purchase from garden centers or nurseries with a landscape department which provides planting services. When the planting is done by the firm a more favorable customer guarantee will usually be offered.

Because digging, transporting, displaying, and transplanting result in a shock to the plant, it should be carefully transplanted and tended during the recuperative—or establishment—period. Good mail order nurseries furnish specific planting and care instructions. Local garden center and landscape firms are able to supplement the written planting instructions with added verbal explanation.

Each firm is responsible for its own guarantee, which should be clearly stated in the advertising copy and the sales slip.

These and other points are covered in the *Amended Trade Practice Rules for the Nursery Industry,* promulgated by the Federal Trade Commission after extensive public hearings held at the request of the nursery industry.

To assist the consumer in analyzing

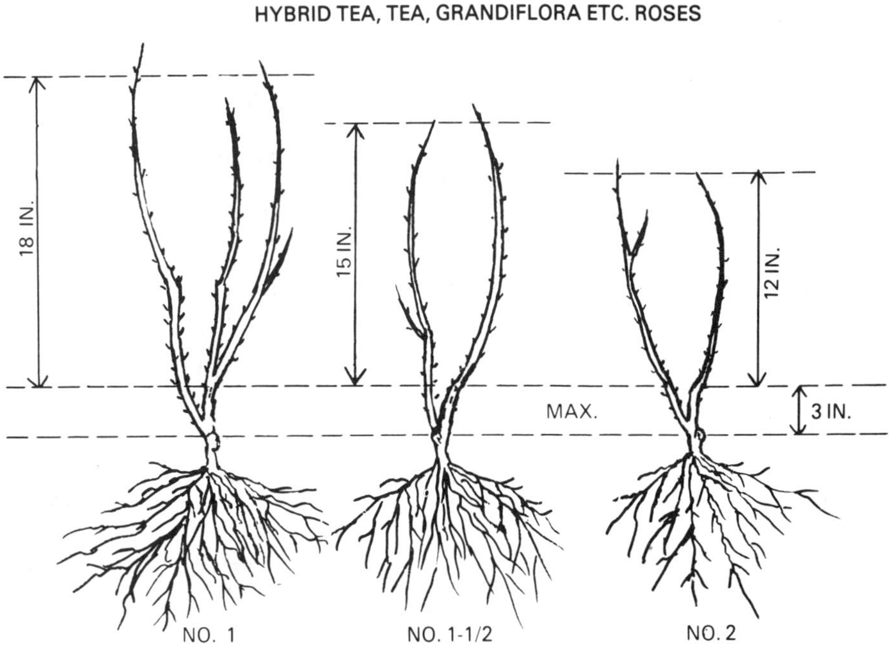

Grades for two year field grown roses.

advertising and sales claims on nursery stock, the American Association of Nurserymen in cooperation with the Council for Better Business Bureaus has recommended standards which include:

• When a plant has a well recognized common name it should be used. If an advertiser coins a new name, the common name or the complete botanical name should be included.

• A guarantee should be limited to obligations the seller can and will fulfill. It should clearly and conspicuously disclose the nature and extent of the guarantee, the manner in which the guarantor will perform, and the identity of the guarantor.

• No reference to "nursery" or "nurseries" should be made for trees or shrubs collected from the wild state and sold without cultivation in a nursery. "Nursery stock" is that which is grown under cultivation, or transplanted from the wild and grown under cultivation for at least one full growing season.

There are many sources of information on the characteristics and description of plants as well as information on the planting and care of various kinds of plants. Horticultural and gardening magazines are valuable for this purpose, as are the public libraries.

Most metropolitan newspapers carry good gardening columns with the writers adapting the recommendations to local climate and soil conditions.

Many plant societies maintain libraries, have membership publications, and hold educational meetings. Among these are the American Boxwood Society, American Rose Society, the Holly Society of America, Inc., the American Camellia Society, American Horticultural Society, Men's Garden Clubs of America, Garden Club of America, National Council of State Garden Clubs, Inc., and the Women's National Farm and Garden Association, Inc.

For information on addresses of these as well as other organizations consult your local library. Or you may wish to purchase the *Directory of American Horticulture*, available from the American Horticultural Society, Inc., Mount Vernon, Va. 22121.

Another valuable source of information adapted to a local area is the Cooperative Agricultural Extension Service Office in each county of the United States. For the phone number look under your county government listing in the phone directory.

In the United States there are over 100 major arboretums and botanic gardens maintaining outstanding plant collections and display gardens, and providing horticultural information.

Retail garden centers and landscape firms often answer questions and work with garden clubs, service clubs, chambers of commerce, or municipal agencies in community environmental improvement projects.

Home Gardening With Small Fruits

You as a home gardener may have overlooked the possibility of growing small fruits when space is limited. Yet space used to grow strawberries, blackberries, raspberries, blueberries, grapes, currants, and gooseberries pays big dividends in tasty, nutritious fruit, even though the space may be small.

There's a thrill to harvesting juicy, flavorful strawberries and in munching crisp, delicately flavored blueberries right from the plants. And it's a bit of a challenge, requiring some ingenuity, to grow the plants well.

On well grown mature plants the quantities of fruits produced are about as follows: 50 strawberry plants yield 25 pounds; 5 blackberry plants give 25 pounds; 10 raspberry plants yield 20 pounds; 5 blueberry plants yield 25 pounds; 5 grape plants give 50 pounds; 5 currant plants give 10 pounds; and 5 gooseberry plants yield 20 pounds.

Strawberry plants will bear a full

crop a year after planting, but all the other kinds will bear only light crops until the plants are 2 to 3 years old.

Space needed by the various plants differs. Space strawberry plants 1′ apart in the row and cut off all runner plants so that only the original plants produce fruit. Blackberries need 4′ to 6′ spacing in the row. Plant red raspberries 2′ apart in the row and purple and black raspberries 4′ to 5′ apart. Blueberries in time fill the row when spaced 5′ apart. Grapes must have 8′ to 10′ in the row. Currants need 3′ in the row and gooseberries 4′.

The rows need to be 6′ to 7′ apart for all crops except strawberries, where 1′ suffices.

Growing the different small fruit crops requires some specialized knowledge. Detailed information on planting, cultivation, fertilizing, pruning, and pest control is available in bulletins published by the Office of Communication, U.S. Department of Agriculture, Washington, D.C. 20250 and by the State agriculture experiment stations. Your County Extension office is another good source of help.

Certain requirements must be met, but generally the same practices used for growing vegetables and landscape plants are satisfactory.

All plants need some pruning each year.

Points to consider first are soils, planting sites, climatic conditions, and what kinds of crops can be grown in a particular area.

Well drained silt loam soils are ideal for all the berry crops, but plants can be grown on clay loams, if well drained, or on sandy loams, if irrigated during dry periods. Blueberry plants require an acid soil with a pH of 4.5 to 5.5, and the plants benefit from a mulch of peat moss, wood shavings or chopped leaves.

Since most home gardeners are restricted in their choice of planting sites, keep two points in mind: 1) The plants will occupy the site for several years so they should be planted along one edge of the garden, and 2) most of the crops require full sun, although late afternoon shade may be tolerated.

If late spring frosts occur, strawberries probably will be flowering and the plants should be covered on cold nights since the blossoms are near the ground where the air is the coldest.

Don't try to grow a crop that isn't adapted to your area. Currants and gooseberries grow well in the northern United States, but are worthless in the South. Some varieties may be banned in certain northern areas where white pines are grown as landscape plants and as timber trees, since currants and gooseberries are an alternate host for white pine blister rust. Check with your State Department of Agriculture.

Raspberry is another crop that grows well in the North but is intolerant of prolonged high summer temperatures and, therefore, usually is not satisfactory in the South. Southland and Dormanred can be grown farther south than any other raspberries.

Plant black raspberries only if you are reasonably sure that the purple and red raspberries you are growing are vigorous and healthy. Use essentially virus-free plants whenever possible with raspberries and strawberries.

Two types of cultivated blueberries are grown: The highbush in central and northern areas of the United States, and rabbiteye in the Gulf Coast region and northward to southern Arkansas and southern North Carolina.

Blackberry varieties differ greatly in winter hardiness and in their chilling requirements, so check carefully on the variety before buying plants. Use thornless varieties in the areas where they are recommended.

AUTHOR *D. H. Scott* is Research Horticulturist with the Fruit Laboratory, Agricultural Research Service.

Grapes can be grown almost universally, but not the same type in all regions. American bunch grapes, such as Concord, are grown in central and northern regions, muscadines (Scuppernong and Hunt are examples) in the South, and European—such as Thompson Seedless—mostly in California and Arizona. The hardiest European can be grown in protected areas of the Great Lakes and Pacific Northwest, but they are not so reliable as the American bunch grapes.

Strawberries are a universal crop but, for greatest satisfaction and best quality, grow the varieties recommended for your locality.

What varieties should you plant? They are legion. Selection of the proper varieties is one of the most critical decisions that a gardener must make for all the berry crops.

Most varieties have a limited area where they grow best, and they may not be satisfactory at all in another locality. For example, Surecrop strawberry is productive and has good quality in the northeastern States, but is unproductive in the upper north-central region.

Descriptions given in nursery catalogs are for the performance of varieties where they are best adapted, but that may not be your area. So check the recommended list of varieties before ordering plants.

Choose disease-resistant varieties to reduce losses from disease. Some diseases such as red stele root rot of strawberries and cane canker of blueberries can be controlled only by use of disease-resistant varieties.

Consult your local or State agricultural experiment stations or U. S. Department of Agriculture publications for a list of varieties recommended for your conditions. Here are some general recommendations:

Currants—Itasca and Red Lake.

Gooseberries—Pixwell, Poorman, and Oregon Champion.

Highbush blueberries—for the North: Bluecrop, Blueray, Berkeley, Collins, Coville, Darrow, Herbert, and Jersey (plant two or more varieties for cross pollination). For the South: Croatan, Morrow, Murphy, Wolcott.

Rabbiteye blueberries—for the South: Briteblue, Delite, Southland, Tifblue, Woodard (plant two or more varieties for cross pollination).

Blackberries—for the North: Darrow. For the central States: Darrow, Smoothstem, Thornfree. For the South: Brazos, Oklawaha, Boysen, Georgia Thornless. For the West: Aurora, Boysen, Marion, Olallie, Thornless Evergreen, Thornless Logan.

Raspberries—for the North: Chief, Heritage, Fallred, Latham, September, Taylor. For the upper south: Dormanred, Southland. For the West: Canby, Meeker, Puyallup, Willamette.

Grapes—American Bunch for fresh: Buffalo, Concord, Fredonia, Niagara, Steuben; for juice: Aurore, Baco Noir, Catawba, Chelois, Concord, Delaware, De Chaunac, Landot 4511, Seyval Blanc, Cayuga White. Muscadines: Cowart, Dearing, Magoon, Magnolia, Roanoke. European for fresh: Cardinal, Perlette, Thompson Seedless; for juice: Alicante Bouschet, Carignane, Cabernet Sauvignon, Palomino, Petite Sirah, Pinot Noir, Rubired, Ruby Cabernet.

Strawberries—for notheast and north central: Catskill, Gem, Guardian, Holiday, Fletcher, Midway, Raritan, Redchief, Sparkle, Surecrop. For Northern Plains States: Dunlap, Ogallala, Stop-

light, Trumpeter. For south Atlantic and south central: Apollo, Atlas, Albritton, Blakemore, Pocahontas, Sunrise, Tennessee Beauty, Titan. For Gulf Coast and deep south: Dabreak, Florida 90, Headliner, Tioga. For western: Fresno, Hood, Northwest, Sequoia, Shuksan, Tioga, Tufts.

What is so good as strawberries and cream—it could be a blueberry pie made from garden fresh berries! Not only can most of the berry crops be eaten fresh, but they can be converted into most delectable cooked products.

Delicious jams, jellies, juices, wines, pies, preserves, tarts, and muffins made from the fruits start the taste buds salivating just to think of them.

Strawberries, raspberries, blackberries, and blueberries are easily processed by freezing, to be used later in pies, jams, and jellies at the cook's leisure.

Grapes are often used to make wines. Homemade grape wines can range in quality from worse than mediocre to excellent, depending to a considerable extent upon the varieties of grapes used. Again be guided by the recommendations of specialists at your State experiment station.

All home gardeners should grow some, if not all, of the berry crops. The space dividends are high. The taste treats are unexcelled. And the satisfaction from growing bounteous crops is unsurpassable.

FOR FURTHER READING:

U.S. Department of Agriculture. *Growing Blackberries,* F 2160, Office of Communication, Washington, D.C. 20250.

———. *Growing American Bunch Grapes,* F 2123, Office of Communication, Washington, D.C. 20250.

———. *Control of Grape Diseases and Insects in the Eastern United States,* F 1893, Office of Communication, Washington, D.C. 20250.

———. *Controlling Diseases of Raspberries and Blackberries,* F 2208, Office of Communication, Washington, D.C. 20250.

———. *Strawberry Varieties in the United States,* F 1043, for sale by Superintendent of Documents, Washington, D.C. 20402.

Apples, Cherries Pears, Plums and Other Fruit Trees

MANY KINDS of tree fruits can be grown in the backyard of both urban and rural homes. This can be turned into a family project to be enjoyed by all. The growing of fruit trees is relatively easy, but controlling diseases and insects to assure good quality fruit is more difficult. This fact should not discourage the average family from growing their own fruits and enjoying some of the labor involved and the taste of the fruit produced.

Since fruit pests can and should be controlled, the backyard enthusiast should be familiar with control measures, as well as tree management practices, before planting many of these trees.

Apples are the easiest to grow. The trees respond readily to pruning, training, and fertilizer. The only apple trees to grow in the backyard are the dwarf ones. The desired variety should be budded on one of the following rootstocks: Malling 9, M.26 or M.7. When these rootstocks are used, the trees are smaller at maturity and more easily cared for, in addition to fruiting earlier and more regularly than trees on standard rootstocks.

Many favorite apple varieties grafted on dwarfing rootstocks are listed, described, and handled by nurseries dealing with fruit trees.

Here are a few varieties suitable for the home garden which are most likely to be available: 'Delicious' (spur types or strains of 'Delicious' are preferred because they are slightly dwarfing and usually more productive), Yellow (Golden) Delicious, McIntosh (spur type), Jonathan, Spartan, Cortland, Idared, Prima, Macoun, Gravenstein, Jerseymac*, Paulared*, Red Tydeman*,

Lodi*, and Quinte*. (An asterisk indicates early apples).

Apricot trees are not as hardy or long-lived as apple trees, but can be grown in more protected areas of the backyard. The fruit is excellent for eating out-of-hand and for home canning. Available varieties are 'Goldcot', 'Tilton', 'Curtis', and 'Early Orange'. These are not dwarf, but can be kept within 10 feet in spread and height by annual pruning.

Both sweet and tart cherries should be included in the home orchard. Sweet cherries are delicious to eat in June and July. Tart cherries are easily canned or frozen for year-round use.

The most popular tart cherry varieties are Montmorency, which has a light juice, and English Morrello, a dark juice cherry. Both varieties are usually listed and available from local nurseries. Although both sweet and tart cherries can have problems, they may be grown successfully by following the recommendations outlined in pest control bulletins.

Sweet cherries come in various fruit colors: black, red, deep red, yellow, and shades in between. Fruit of early varieties begin to ripen in June and late maturing varieties in July. Here are a few varieties in order of maturity: Vista (b), Vega (y), Napoleon (y), Emperor Francis (y), Hedelfingen (b), Vic (b), and Hudson (b). (b indicates black fruit color; y indicates yellow).

Most of the stone fruits—cherries, peaches, plums, and nectarines—are subject to brown rot disease, with nectarines the most susceptible. A sanitation practice of pruning out brown rot branch cankers and careful spraying at regular intervals should result in excellent fruit.

Although similar to peaches, nectarines are quality fruits for eating out-of-hand. A few of the most readily available nectarine varieties are: Independence, Mericrest, Flavortop, Stark Sunglow, and Fantasia.

AUTHOR *R. F. Carlson* is Professor, Department of Horticulture, Michigan State University, East Lansing.

The peach is truly a dual purpose fruit for the home dweller because it is good to eat fresh and frozen or out of the can. There are many varieties to choose from. Peaches can be grown in the backyard from Florida to Michigan, but before ordering trees it is best to find out which varieties will be best for your area. Local nurseries usually list varieties adapted to their areas, and those are the ones to consider.

A few of the best available peach varieties are: Garnet Beauty, Sunhaven, Redhaven, Velvet, Sunhigh, Madison, Cresthaven, Redskin, Jersey Queen, and Rio-Oso-Gem. Descriptions of these as to color, firmness and maturity are included in most catalogs. While the early ripening sorts are good to eat out-of-hand, the mid-season to late maturing varieties are the best for home canning and freezing.

Pear varieties grafted on dwarfing quince rootstocks are available from some nurseries. Standard trees of pear will live longer because they are hardier and, although vigorous, can be held small by pruning.

Bartlett is the pear variety usually grown and should be considered as one of two or more varieties to plant. Other varieties suitable to plant in the backyard are: Bosc, Anjou, Moonglow, and Seckel.

Spartlet, a new variety which matures 10 days after Bartlett, is larger, keeps longer, and is good both fresh and canned.

The plum is another dual purpose fruit which is excellent eaten fresh at harvest time, and also as a canned product. Plums require about the same care as peaches. For eating fresh, the Japanese types are favorities, among them Formosa, Frontier, Santa Rosa, and Burbank. European type plums are good for both canning and fresh, and some of these are Stanley, Bluefre, Seneca, and President.

Although most peach and tart cherry trees are self-fertile and do not need pollen from another variety, most other fruit varieties need cross pollination. Therefore, to insure good fruit set, at least two varieties of each fruit should be planted. For example, for good fruit set, plant two sweet cherry varieties such as Vega and Emperor Francis; for plums Abundance and Methley; and for apples Macspur and Cortland. Since certain varieties are not good pollen sources, you should check into this matter carefully.

For best results and success in growing tree fruits, the soil should be a well drained sandy loam. Heavy clay and muck soils are to be avoided. Spring is the usual time for planting trees. However, if trees are available, they can be planted in the fall, especially in the southern temperate zone.

A large hole should be dug, one that will allow for spreading of the roots in all directions. Place the top soil to one side when digging the hole, then use this soil around the roots. It is best to water the tree from the top after planting rather than to mix water with the soil during planting. Fertilizers should never be placed in the hole.

If fruit is wanted a year or two after planting, order older trees from nurseries which have 2-year-old trees available. Older trees cost more, but they often are more rewarding when only a few trees are needed. One-year-old trees are more plentiful, cost less, and when on dwarfing rootstock will fruit in the second year—especially apple trees. To insure getting the desired variety and rootstock, trees should be ordered from the nursery at least six months before planting.

Because of root competition and shading, fruit trees should not be planted near large shade trees or ornamental border plants or shrubs. They need sunshine for quality and colorful fruit. For best results the trees should be spaced at least 6′ from each other, or if planted in rows 8′ between trees and 12′ between rows. Apple trees should be grouped in one section and stone fruits in another section of the garden.

Each fruit crop and variety needs special care in training and pruning. Generally, pruning consists of selecting strong main branches which are spaced on the central leader so that they point in different directions. For example, a 5-year-old apple tree should have four to six main branches. Upright growing varieties such as 'Delicious' need to have their branches spread outward away from the central leader.

The information service of most agricultural experiment stations and extension service offices can provide information and descriptions on how to plant, prune, and care for fruit trees and how to fertilize and spray, and harvest the fruit. Furthermore, most recognized fruit tree nurseries have excellent catalogs describing varieties, ripening dates, cost, and so on.

FOR FURTHER READING:

U.S. Department of Agriculture. *Establishing and Managing Young Apple Orchards,* F 1897, Office of Communication, Washington, D.C. 20250, 1971.

———. *Why Fruit Trees Fail to Bear,* L 172, Office of Communication, Washington, D.C. 20250, 1971.

The "Spartlet" Pear. Fruit Varieties Journal, Vol. 27, No. 3, pp. 60–62, 1973.

Handbook on Fruit Trees and Shrubs. Brooklyn Botanical Garden Record Plants and Gardens, Vol. 27, No. 3, 1971.

Michigan State University. *Developing Dwarf Apple Trees,* Research Report No. 17, Agricultural Experiment Station, East Lansing, Mich. 48823, 1971.

———. *Pest Control Program for Home Grown Fruit,* E 608, Agricultural Experiment Station, East Lansing, Mich. 48823, 1971.

———. *Pear Culture in Michigan,* E 519, Agricultural Experiment Station, East Lansing, Mich. 48823, 1971.

———. *Jonathan Apple—Quality and Storage Life,* E 627, Agricultural Experiment Station, East Lansing, Mich. 48823, 1968.

———. *Peach Culture in Michigan,* E 509, Agricultural Experiment Station, East Lansing, Mich. 48823, 1971.

Subtropical Fruits For Warm Climates Or Tub Growing

If you have retired recently or changed jobs and moved to one of the favored regions where warm-climate plants can be grown, then a new world of gardening excitement is literally at your doorstep. If, however, you've spent much of your life in such an area you may already be aware of the rich store of benefits that come from amateur fruit growing, and chances are that you haven't tired of such pursuits.

Origins of many warm-region crops such as the mango are lost in antiquity. But others are comparatively new to cultivation and systematic research on most is still in its youth. This means you can engage in home garden experimentation to the degree that your pocketbook and inclination will permit. At the same time, enough knowledge is now on tap to allow you to plant a good many subtropical species outdoors in much of the Southern and Western States with confidence of being successful.

Most subtropical fruit plants make excellent landscape items that lend a characteristic "tropical" flavor to your surroundings. For this reason you can include many in your home planting as dual-purpose ornamentals or shade trees that regularly add vitamin-rich delicious fresh fruit to the family's menu.

Guava jelly and paste, mango chutney, calamondin marmalade, loquat pie, and passionfruit jelly and wine join a nearly endless list of gourmet foods that become practical possibilities once you grow the most important raw materials in your own yard.

AUTHOR *Robert J. Knight, Jr.* is Research Fruit Horticulturist at the Subtropical Horticulture Research Unit, Agriculture Research Service, in Miami, Fla.

An effort to place each warm-climate fruit crop into a "tropical," "subtropical," or "warm-temperate" pigeon-hole over-simplifies matters. This is because our cultivated fruits, collected from many parts of the world, come from a variety of climates.

An important group that requires near-equatorial growing conditions and grows outdoors in the United States only in Hawaii and Puerto Rico includes the mangosteen *(Garcinia mangostana)*, the durian *(Durio zibethinus)*, rambutan *(Nephelium lappaceum)*, and pili nut *(Canarium ovatum)*.

A group that requires warm subtropical conditions includes the mango, Antillean (West Indian) avocado cultivars, the guava, and the most tender citrus fruits such as the Key or Mexican lime. More than half a million homeowners now live in parts of southern Florida where these fruits can be grown. This group occupies the first section of the accompanying table as "Fruits Suited to the Warmest Parts of the United States."

Zones of cultural adaptation are important because you spend your money for plants that you expect to survive the normal extremes of winter cold and summer heat, and to yield satisfactory crops in your area.

Individual plant species (and groups within some species) vary widely in their range of climatic suitability. The USDA Plant Hardiness Zone Map, Misc. Pub. No. 814, affords the most practical means for you to determine beforehand whether a given fruit is likely to succeed in a particular locality.

Several cities in the zones covered by this chapter are listed at the bottom of the table. In addition, zones where a species is expected to grow well are included under "cultural information."

This means that a mango or Key lime, which you'd normally expect to grow and fruit well only in zone 10b, may occasionally fruit in sheltered spots within zone 10a through a combination of good luck and special protective measures taken during cold spells. So

10a is placed on the table, but in parenthesis. Of course your chances of success in zone 10a will be greater if instead of the mango you plant hardier fruits such as the loquat and Mexican and Mexican-Guatemalan hybrid avocados (listed in the second section of the table, under "Moderately Hardy Fruits").

A select group of warm-temperate plants that withstand more winter cold than those listed includes the carob *(Ceratonia siliqua)*, fig *(Ficus carica)*, Japan persimmon *(Diospyros kaki)*, kiwi *(Actinidia chinensis)*, olive *(Olea europea)*, and pomegranate *(Punica granatum)*. None of these thrive in the warmest parts of zone 10, but you may want to try them if you live in cooler parts of the area we are discussing and if locally experienced gardeners have succeeded with them.

One plant adapted to warmest conditions but omitted from the list is the papaya *(Carica papaya)* which is difficult to grow because of its susceptibility to diseases and the papaya fruit fly. Another excellent tree for zone 10b is the tamarind *(Tamarindus indica)*, but it grows too large for any except king-sized yards.

Special information is included in the table where appropriate. For example, many fruiting plants are admirably suited to pot or tub culture in patios or on porches in the Northeast and Midwest where summer weather suits them (and they can be sheltered inside during winter), and this is noted under "Cultural information."

Guavas and loquats produce well in zone 10 but in common with other soft fruits they can be ruined by infestation with Caribbean fruitfly *(Anastrepha suspensa)* larvae. Therefore where this pest is abundant, as it is at present in much of peninsular Florida, you may want to defer planting susceptible fruits until adequate control measures are developed. For your information, particularly susceptible species are identified by the letters "CF."

Trees and shrubs of outstanding value as landscape plants are marked by "LDSCP." Avocado cultivars more successful in California's Mediterranean climate than in the Gulf States are identified by a "W", and others more successful in the East are marked by an "E". All the fruits listed in the table are evergreen in growth habit.

If you are moving into a new home and your landscape architect is sympathetic to the idea, you can start from scratch with outstanding ornamental plants that double as fruit-producers: loquat, carissa, cattley guava, sea grape, lychee, longan, and many citrus species are examples. If on the other hand your basic planting has already been made, you can add or delete as conditions and your inspiration dictate.

Many subtropical plants are container-grown for sale. These offer advantages over bare-root stock, since from containers the shock of transplanting is minimized and your planting season is not confined to those times when plant growth is at low ebb.

Sizes of container plants will seem small if you are used to growth rates of trees and shrubs in the Northeast and Midwestern States. But unless immediate effect is important, you may find that a small but vigorous lime or avocado tree is a better investment for a congenial site than a larger, more expensive specimen.

Where to get the young trees and vines for your home planting is a question whose answer depends on your own

Carambola fruit.

FRUITS FOR HOME PLANTING IN WARM CLIMATES
Fruits Suited to the Warmest Parts of the United States

Fruit: cultivars	*Uses of fruit*	*Cultural Information*
Acerola (*Malpighia glabra*): Florida Sweet, B 17, others	Bright red ade drinks and ices of sprightly flavor. Rich in Vitamin C.	Zone 10b (10a). Shrub or small tree with glossy dark foliage. CF.
Avocado (*Persea americana*) West Indian and hybrid: Ruehle, Simmonds, Fairchild, others	Salads, guacamole spread, sandwiches, puree to add to soup; a rich pie filling, milk shakes.	Zone 10b. Medium-sized to large tree. A rich soil is very desirable, and *perfect drainage is absolutely essential.*
Banana (*Musa* spp.): Apple, Cavendish, Orinoco, many others	Fresh and in puddings, cakes and custards, and ice cream. Fruit is delicious fried or baked.	Patios, large tubs (Cavendish); Zone 10b (10a). Giant herb which gives a tropical "jungle" effect. LDSCP.
Black sapote (*Diospyros digyna*): Seedlings	Blend pulp with cream or brandy and spices to substitute for chocolate pudding, mousse or pie filling. Richer in Vitamin C than Citrus.	Zone 10b. Handsome medium-sized tree with glossy deep-green leaves and dark-colored bark. LDSCP.
Carambola (*Averrhoa carambola*): Golden Star, Robert Newcomb, Mih Tao, Tean Ma, others.	Float star-shaped slices on punch or add to salads. Juice is rich in Vitamin C and has a tea-rose scent.	Zone 10b (10a). Small or medium-sized tree that bears waxy orange or yellow fruit at least twice a year.
Coconut (*Cocos nucifera*): Malay Golden	Milk and pulp used in cakes, pies, beverages and puddings.	Zone 10b. Malay Golden resists lethal yellows disease. LDSCP.
Grumichama (*Eugenia dombeyi*): seedlings	Eat fresh; similar to northern cherry, black with a single stone.	Tub for patios. 10b (10a). Large shrub with glossy leaves and white flowers like pear blossoms. CF. LDSCP.
Guava (*Psidium guajava*): Indian Red, many others	Jelly, paste, preserved shells, punch. Rich in Vitamin C.	Zone 10. Medium-sized tree with ribbed leaves. CF.
Jaboticaba (*Myrciaria cauliflora*): Sabara, others, seedlings	Used as grapes are: fresh, or for juice, jelly, or wine.	Tub for patios. 10b (10a). Large shrub or small tree bearing white flowers and black grape-like fruit on trunk. Grows slowly. CF. LDSCP.
Limes (*Citrus aurantifolia*): Key (Mexican), *C. latifolia:* Tahiti (Bearss)	Essential component of many drinks, sherbet, and one of the world's great pies, a gourmet dessert.	Zone 10b (10a). Straggly, shrubby trees that need frequent pruning to shape them properly. Thorny.
Longan (*Dimocarpus longan*): Kohala, Shek Kip, Chom Poo, others	Eat fresh; peel, pit and can like cherries. Stew for an ice cream topping, quick-freeze whole or dry in the traditional way.	10b (10a). Vigorous, excellent shade tree. Bears erratically; in "off" years branches may be girdled to induce fruit. LDSCP.
Lychee (*Litchi chinensis*): Brewster, Mauritius, Sweetcliff, Bengal, others.	A superior fruit to eat fresh, canned, frozen, or dried (the traditional method). Fresh fruit resembles a strawberry with a thin, rigid skin and a grapelike flavor.	10b (10a). Umbrella-shaped tree that needs rich acid soil, good drainage and a dependable moisture supply. Brewster and Bengal may crop erratically. LDSCP.

FRUITS FOR HOME PLANTING IN WARM CLIMATES (Cont.)

Fruits Suited to the Warmest Parts of tahe United States

Fruit: cultivars	*Uses of fruit*	*Cultural Information*
Mango (*Mangifera indica*): Florigon, Irwin, Keitt, many others	Popular everywhere. Eat fresh, juiced, and in or on ice cream. Immature fruit, an essential ingredient of chutney recipes, makes an excellent pie.	10b (10a). Medium to large tree of graceful habit, it thrives on most soils. Don't plant near air conditioner inlet or bedroom windows because flowers are allergenic. CF (occasional).
Passionfruit (*Passiflora edulis*, purple; *P. edulis* f. *flavicarpa*, yellow): seedlings of purple and yellow forms	Fresh in salads, as a richly aromatic juice in ades and sherbets, or a fine-flavored jelly, also pie and cake fillings. Makes an aromatic wine suggestive of sherry.	Zone 10a (purple), 10b (yellow). Vigorous vines that need support and late-winter pruning to remove old wood. Plant more than one yellow seedling for pollination.
Pineapple (*Ananas comosus*): Abachi, Red Spanish, Cayenne, others	Eat fresh, candied, in pies, sherbets and as juice. Fruit ripened on your own plant is superior to shipped. Harvest when it "smells ripe".	10b (10a). Patios, planters. Large leafy perennial, a favorite house plant. Cut-off tops of fruit from stores often root to make healthy plants that may fruit after two years.
Sapodilla (*Manilkara zapota*): Prolific, Brown Sugar, others	Eat fresh; latex from trunk, chicle, was formerly the chief ingredient of chewing gum.	Zone 10b. Medium-sized to large shade tree, resistant to high winds. LDSCP. CF.
Seagrape (*Coccolobis uvifera*): seedlings, selected cuttings.	Large-seeded fruit makes a mild-flavored jelly.	10b (10a). Highly ornamental tree resists salt. LDSCP.

Moderately Hardy Fruits for Warm Regions

Avocado (*Persea americana*) Guatemalan and hybrid: Choquette (E), Fuerte (W), Hass (W), Winter Mexican (E), Yon (E) Mexican race: Bacon (E-W), Brogden (E), Duke (E-W), Gainesville (E), Mexicola (E-W), others	Fresh in salads, guacamole spread; pureed in soups, as pie filling and in milk shakes. Eaten alone with salt and/or lime juice as a vegetable. Halves of 'Mexicola', unpeeled, make excellent canape containers for shrimp spread and such foods.	Guatemalan and hybrid cultivars, Zone 10 (9b); Mexicans, 9b (9a). Attractive spreading or tall trees that prefer rich soil and demand perfect drainage.
Calamondin (*Citrus blancoi*)	Aromatic juice is excellent in drinks. Fruit makes a superb marmalade.	Patios, pot culture. Zone 9b (9a). An upright tree which bears colorful mini-oranges. LDSCP. CF.
Carissa (*Carissa grandiflora*): Fancy, Alles, Atlas	Makes a beautiful jelly resembling red currant jelly; also jam; eat fresh when fully ripe.	Zone 9b–10. Patios. Fancy is upright, Alles low and spreading, Atlas moderately upright and nearly thornless. CF. LDSCP. Thorny.
Cattley guava (*Psidium cattleianum*): seedlings of red and yellow-fruited forms.	Eat fresh; makes an excellent jelly and a good "butter" or marmalade.	Zones 9b–10. Shrub or small tree of outstanding ornamental value with smooth, vari-colored trunk. CF. LDSCP.

FRUITS FOR HOME PLANTING IN WARM CLIMATES (Cont.)
Moderately Hardy Fruits for Warm Regions

Fruit: cultivars	*Uses of fruit*	*Cultural Information*
Feijoa (*Feijoa sellowiana*): Coolidge, Pineapple Gem, others.	Eat fresh; juice jells easily because it is high in pectin. Flowers are edible.	Zones 8b–10. Attractive shrubs with dark, glaucous foliage. CF. LDSCP.
Kumquat (*Fortunella japonica*): Nagami, Marumi, Meiwa	Fresh fruit is unique with sweet peel, tart flesh. Whole spiced preserved kumquats are a gourmet treat, as is kumquat marmalade.	Patios, pots. Zones 9–10. Small citrus tree of unsurpassed ornamental value. CF. LDSCP.
Limequat (*Citrus aurantifolia* x *Fortunella japonica*): Eustis, Lakeland	Hybrid for same uses as lime: acid juice for drinks; used as condiment and in confectionery.	Patios, pots. Zones 9b(a)–10. Hardier than the Key lime which it resembles. LDSCP. Thorny.
Loquat (*Eriobotrya japonica*): Champagne, Thales (Gold Nugget), Wolfe, others	Eat fresh; can, preserve; use in pies.	Zones 8b–10. Small tree of elegant aspect with ribbed, glaucous green leaves. Fire blight disease can be serious. CF. LDSCP.
Macadamia nut (*Macadamia intergrifolia* and hybrids): Keauhou, Beaumont, others.	Fine quality nut, usually borne in a very hard shell, is roasted and salted or used in confectionery.	Zone 9b(9a)–10. Beautiful oak-like tree of moderate size; plant more than one for cross-pollination.
Rose-apple (*Syzygium jambos*): seedlings	Children like the crisp fresh fruit which can be brandied like peaches.	Zone 9b–10. Moderately large shade tree with pointed leaves and creamy colored mimosa-like flowers.
Surinam-cherry (*Eugenia uniflora*)	Eat ribbed red or black fruit fresh, drink juice, or use in ices.	Zones 9b–10. Compact shrub with glossy green leaves. CF. LDSCP.
Tangelo (*Citrus reticulata* x *C. paradisi*): Minneola, others	Fresh dessert fruit, easily peeled; juice is comparable to orange juice but brighter colored.	Citrus tree, handsome at all seasons. LDSCP.

Cities in Zone 9a: Charleston, Savannah, Jacksonville, Baton Rouge, San Antonio, Corpus Christi and San Bernardino; *in Zone 9b:* Daytona Beach, Orlando, McAllen, Sacramento; *in Zone 10a:* Melbourne, Tampa-St. Petersburg, Brownsville, San Diego to Santa Barbara (S. Calif. Coast), San Francisco Bay cities; *in Zone 10b:* Palm Beach, Ft. Lauderdale, Miami, Naples and Key West.
CF: this designates soft fruits prone to infestation by Caribbean fruitfly larvae.
LDSCP: indicates trees or shrubs outstandingly attractive and useful for landscape planting.

Golden brown fruit of the Longan.

situation and desires. Nurseries, Garden Centers, and Feed-and-Seed stores are excellent sources of locally adapted planting stock in many places.

Once you get the plants, information on cultural requirements is essential. Experienced salespeople in these stores, when you are fortunate enough to meet them, can supply valuable information.

More generally, reliable information is available from your County Agricultural Extension or Farm Agent. You can usually find necessary addresses and numbers listed under the county heading in the white pages of your local telephone directory.

Nursery items are frequently advertised in garden magazines and other agricultural publications. Regional mail-order nursery catalogs are interesting and fun to absorb at leisure but they are not as prominent in the warmest parts of the country as elsewhere, so you are not likely to find them a rich source of subtropical material.

Garden clubs and organizations of people interested in fruit growing can be enormously helpful as sources of cultural information and sometimes of the plants themselves, when both are scarce.

You may find it rewarding to join one or more of these groups, depending on their geographic accessibility and your interests. Most of them welcome new members, and the more knowledgable of the older members can often supply practical information that you can't readily find elsewhere.

ORGANIZATIONS OF INTEREST:

Rare Fruit Council International, Inc., P.O. Box 601, Miami, Fla. 33143 (one branch meets in Miami, another in West Palm Beach.)

Rio Grande Valley Horticultural Society, P.O. Box 107, Weslaco, Tex. 78596.

California Rare Fruit Growers, Northern Section, 3370 Princeton Ct., Santa Clara, Cal. 95051, or Southern Section, Star Route P, Bonsall, Cal. 95051.

Florida Mango Forum, 18710 S.W. 288 St., Homestead, Fla. 33030.

FOR FURTHER READING:

U.S. Department of Agriculture. *Plant Hardiness Zone Map,* MP 814, for sale by Superintendent of Documents, Washington, D.C. 20402.

Lane Magazine & Book Co. *Sunset Western Garden Book,* Menlo Park, Cal., 1967.

Chandler, William H. *Evergreen Orchards,* Lea and Febiger, Philadelphia, Pa., 1950.

Sturrock, David. *Fruits for Southern Florida,* Horticultural Books, Inc., 219 Martin Ave., Stuart, Fla. 33494, 1972 (reprint 1959 ed.).

Florida Department of Agriculture and Consumer Service. *Florida Market Bulletin,* published semi-monthly, 407 S. Calhoun St., Tallahassee, Fla. 32304.

The Why and How Of Garden Design

WHEN WE THINK of a garden we imagine many things...A place for flowers...or where we can sit and look at greenery and sky...perhaps a place perfectly situated so one can watch the sunrise or sunset...or a spot where just vegetables grow.

No matter how each of us interprets a garden, we almost invariably associate it with a restful, serene area—maybe even mysterious and secluded—or where we can go to be warm or cool.

Gardens do touch our deeper senses. They represent privacy and shelter, comfort and relaxation. Simultaneously, we can witness nature's brilliant mixture of colors and textures emerge into full glory during many seasons. It could be said that a garden is truly where variety is the spice of life...and that is why good garden design becomes such a challenge.

But how do these wonderful gardens grow? And is your garden exactly what you've always thought it should be? Gardens begin with a pen and paper, a tape measure and time, and above all, interest and imagination. Because a garden is a very personal, individual expression, designing your own garden, with help and consultation, is one of the most rewarding experiences.

There are basic steps in planning and/or planting a garden. If you are successful with them, the goals which you can achieve will be order, unity, beauty and creativity.

- Examine your site carefully. Write down interesting spots, clumps of trees, things you may not be able to identify, how your house is situated, and what you would like to put where.
- Determine the ecological idiosyncrasies of your environment, its advantages and disadvantages. You must be aware of the basic ecology: soil, vegetation,

moisture and pollution . . . amounts of sunlight, and where it is during certain times of the day.

Are you in a hot climate or cold? All weather patterns plus soil conditions must be studied carefully before planting can begin. As you discover things concerning your area, you will learn about indigenous plants and trees that can be used effectively and beautifully. So where you live is a vital element in planning your garden.

• Take into consideration your family needs and priorities, both present and future. Are you going to have children, and will the garden accommodate your family activities? Think about play areas, patios, swimming pool, picnic area.

You must analyze all aspects of a garden and how it can realistically be executed and still retain its aura of mystery, excitement and pleasure.

• Keep in mind that unity is imperative. Everything must relate. A garden does not mean just a small patch of space in the backyard . . . quite to the contrary, a garden means the whole of your property. It should include the front entrance, driveway, landscape, utility area, swimming pool, patio, play area—all in proportion to your house and its size and style.

Therefore, in the early stages of planning the garden should be divided into main activity or "use zones": a semi-public front entrance area, the private garden area, and separate places for service and storage.

Traffic patterns between these zones can be arranged, and the main zones further broken down. For example: the main garden area could naturally divide into a patio zone for outdoor living which might include utility and recreation play areas. The entrance could be treated as two places—a strong entry way with a secondary zone of shrubs, flowers and trees.

There are many ways to divide your site and keep the unity, the family requirements, and type of total garden landscaping exactly the way you want. Perhaps a vegetable garden in one spot would be good; or a bluestone patio to set out those sun-starved house plants; maybe a compost heap or a greenhouse. And maybe you'd like a place to just let things grow wild—a natural place that would attract small animals and birds, not to mention the beautiful, native wildflowers.

Another interesting and important point is that residential architectural changes have allowed us to expand our home living areas which enable us to bring the outside in. This can be done with sliding glass doors or panels, plexiglass skylights, or any other transparent wall.

It is a whole new dimension that compels us, when planning, to consider the garden as a permanent point of interest, one that will be part of our inside decor . . . something that will let us commune with nature from indoors at any given point of the day . . . so we can watch things happening, understand our surroundings to their fullest, and draw nearer to the ultimate goal—that of beauty and its power of expression.

Now we come to a few of the practical problems of contemporary garden design.

First, there's the problem of water drainage. If your land slopes, water is going to drain somewhere. If drainage water flows to a low spot with no way out, you could very well find it in your basement. Or, if your soil has no natural porosity, the result could introduce adverse conditions for plant growth. And if water drains too fast it could erode your precious topsoil.

Therefore, the land should be properly graded so excess water will not prove damaging. Which brings us to the matter of soil analysis.

A proper analysis will tell you if there is any impervious clay or hard pan layer below the surface, and whether the soil is sandy or loamy, acid or sweet, wet or dry. These conditions will decisively determine whether the plant you choose will be successful.

AUTHOR *A. E. Bye* is Principal and CO-AUTHOR *Armistead W. Browning is* Designer, A. E. Bye Associates, landscape architects, Cos Cob, Conn.

Above, patio surrounded by plants selected for low maintenance, and for seasonal color qualities. Top, plants add to feeling of intimacy and naturalness of pool setting. Left, boulders and native plants frame entrance.

The next step is deciding on what plants, trees, shrubs, vines, flowers, etc. you want and the ones that will grow effectively. Attention must be paid to their basic structure, rate of growth, final size and shape.

Think of the characteristics of each plant: color, foliage, flowers, bark, fruit, or fragrant blossoms.

Work out the climatic tolerances, the light and shade, water requirements and susceptibility to pests and disease.

In selecting your plants think in terms of composition. Single plants and plant groupings can be interesting and effective. They should, however, relate to each other in terms of scale, textural contrasts and proportion.

Are your plants placed too close together? That's quite a common mistake. Harmony is essential, but keep groupings simple, so each plant has room to grow and breathe.

Think seriously about the powerful environmental effects that trees can accomplish. They reduce air temperature, heat, glare, wind, sound. And, they filter atmospheric dust and pollutants, as well as raise the oxygen level in the immediate area.

Visually, trees are a definite art form. Each has its own, distinct characteristics, be it leaf color or shape, or bark. Trees are indispensable for complementing or being the highlight of your total garden landscape concept.

To work well, the garden landscape must also include other requirements such as Surface Materials (or ground cover). This means making a choice between grass and grass substitutes. Surfacing is ground, what you will be walking on (or part of it), and what will be surrounding your plants and trees.

The decision is between pachysandra, myrtle, juniper or mulches such as bark, as a plant type cover. A harder surface could include such things as gravel, brick, tile, wood, slate and bluestone.

Naturally, there is always grass. It is usually considered the perfect ground cover—it is rich, verdant and quite beautiful. However, proper lawn care can be costly and time consuming. Lawns require constant maintenance. On the positive side, grass is durable under foot, soft, reasonably resistant to insects and drought, and when mowed emits a fresh smell that is incomparable. Ground cover is, again, a matter of climate, soil, and water drainage.

Ground covers can be as imaginative and ecologically useful as you want. The natural meadow, for instance, complete with wildflowers, could be a totally wonderful garden-landscaping experience. In this natural meadow, various grasses (bluegrass, fescues, nurse crops, clovers, etc.) would be mixed and sown, and, in the growing season, clipped with a cutter bar every four to six weeks when it reaches a height of four to eight inches.

This is a marvelous way to let nature take its course with limited human control. A natural meadow is fun to watch —new things happen every day. There is no set pattern. And it is relatively maintenance-free.

Pachysandra, another good, sturdy ground cover, is common in many parts of the country. It is an excellent base for trees, flowerbeds and as a mulching agent. Pachysandra is hearty and will flourish with little or no sunlight. It can be the ideal solution to covering bare spots on your lawn where grass or something else will not grow. Pachysandra is also a lovely, natural border around a patio, tree, front walk or driveway.

The idea of Enclosure is another factor when planning your garden landscape. Again, it should relate to the total picture of your site. Some people prefer structural devices such as grape stakes, picket fences, panels, lattices, or one of the many wood fences (slat, louvered, basket weave). Enclosure is primarily to create privacy in one area of the garden.

Other enclosures can be plants and trees, which provide excellent screening. This type of enclosure can include dense evergreen hedges, such as juniper and yew, or deciduous hedges or barberry. The selection of plant and/or tree enclosures will again depend on height and shape, and a coordination of their growth rates.

Another consideration in garden design is Ceiling. The obvious one is the sky. But some people like a canopy feeling overhead. This can be achieved by using lattice work covered with vines. It can be an awning. But to be more of a challenge, the enclosure could be the

The fewer plant varieties used, the better.

selection of proper trees which will grow to the right height, and perhaps bend to create a natural arch.

We speak again of trees: nothing else can lend itself to such a variety of uses. And, in relation to a "ceiling", what could be more beautiful than looking up and seeing the delicate foliage silhouetted against the sky. In winter, the breathtaking sight of frosted limbs traced against a moonlit sky is worth all your efforts.

As you can see, garden landscaping on the total scale is an enormous project. You must be organized in your thinking. When in doubt, don't hesitate to ask. But whom do you ask? Should you call a landscape architect or contractor? Then there is always the question of money—it's so expensive! What should you do?

This is not an uncommon dilemma. But to all homeowners, the first question you must ask yourself is: What advantages do I have in seeking professional assistance, versus a trial and error do-it-myself job?

The answer is simply this: an accurate landscape plan, prepared by a licensed landscape architect, will give you a condensation of years of experience, and techniques for good, tight design using economic construction methods and less expensive materials.

The landscape architect will be able to translate your ideas, advise you on technical matters, and guide you in your selection of plants. He will help supervise, and can be depended upon to answer questions you'll have regarding pruning, seeding and general care.

Unlike a commercial establishment, where emphasis is more on profit and turnover, the landscape architect can offer not only knowledge, but creativity and design-sense that really has no price. In terms of cost, your architect may seem expensive, but will ultimately save you a considerable amount of "experiment" money, time and frustration.

Most homeowners have little or no experience with contractors. They must be advised on setting up bids and contracts and ultimately deciding on the right contractor—not necessarily the cheapest. Supervision of the work, a thorough follow-up, is an important phase and this is where the landscape architect can be invaluable.

To get a general idea of cost, and length of time required to complete the job, simply look at your list and/or diagrams of things you want. Then, work out a projected time sequence.

If you choose to retain a landscape architect, automatically add 15 to 20 percent to your costs. A professional landscape architect will draw detailed plans, which ultimately will be approved by you, and followed by the contractor.

Should budgeting be required, you and the landscape architect can work out a program spread out over several years. The payment structure can be done in the same manner. It is always a good practice to draw up a contract which clearly states the terms and services to be rendered.

If, after carefully weighing all of your objectives, you still decide that this garden design will be the product of your own plan and two hands, then it should be so. However, it will be time consuming in terms of research, learning, correctly analyzing and considering all of the other things I have mentioned.

Designing your garden and/or total landscape is a big project, perhaps bigger than you imagine. You can do it—it's possible—but only if you are prepared to devote much of your energies and be constantly aware of all the elements with which you will be dealing.

What, then, will make your garden landscape design special, and why? The answer is that garden and landscape designing is just as unique and one-of-a-kind as you are. It is a means of identifying and translating your ideas through other forms of expression.

Also, it is a love of wanting to build something you've always dreamed of, using natural materials. Your garden can be everything and anything you want it to be.

Remember, gardens have always held a fascinating, alluring and intriguing spot in the minds of men, perhaps ever since the Garden of Eden.

Botanic Gardens And Arboretums

A GREEN OASIS awaits you in nearly every population center in this country. These oases of green, of beauty and of plant learning are our botanical gardens and arboretums. They may be a big help to you in solving your gardening problems.

The botanic gardens and aboretums should not be confused with parks for pleasure or active recreation. They are educational and research institutions concerned with accumulating and disseminating knowledge about plants.

The botanic garden evolved from the medicinal gardens of Europe into scientific and educational institutions concerned primarily with botany. Gradually they have expanded their concern to include the practical application of botanical principles to horticulture, gardening and ecology.

By definition, the botanic garden grows all kinds of plants and the arboretum only woody plants. However, the distinction between the two is often blurred and some of our better known gardens such as Longwood Gardens do not include botanic garden or arboretum in their name.

The important distinction that should be made is whether the plant collections and programs of a park or garden meet the minimum qualifications to be designated as a botanic garden or arboretum. The bona fide botanic garden or arboretum should as a minimum contain authenticated and labeled plant collections and conduct educational programs with plants. Research is highly desirable but not necessary.

Many parks and gardens cannot qualify as botanic gardens or arboretums under this definition but are important horticulturally because they contain outstanding and historically important plants.

The changing image of botanic gardens and arboretums has made them more appealing as places to visit because many of their plantings and programs are designed to help homeowners with their gardening problems.

In demonstration gardens designed for spaces that approximate the areas available to the average homeowner, the visitors can learn the names of plants that are adapted to his region, how they can be arranged in various styles of gardening, and how such construction materials as rocks, fencing, railroad ties, etc. can be used effectively in landscaping. Most gardens now display turf plots, and trial gardens of annuals and perennials.

Workshop and lecture programs are regularly scheduled for children and adults in a wide range of gardening subjects, such as propagating plants, care of the lawn, pruning, fertilizing, and caring for house plants. Painting and photographic displays featuring plants are often on exhibit.

Annual flower shows of plant societies and special meetings of ecology and conservation groups are frequently scheduled at botanic gardens and arboretums. Libraries of these institutions are a rich resource for information on plants and are being used by the general public, educational and research institutions, and industry.

In the hope that you will find time to visit your local garden or a garden in another area of the country, a partial list of botanic gardens and arboretums is published with this chapter. The exclusion of gardens from the list does not imply they are not worth visiting.

The location of small and specialized gardens can be determined by visiting or writing to the major gardens within a state or geographical area. Take advantage of most gardens' willingness to respond to requests for an informational leaflet on their own garden, and suggestions on other horticultural points of interest in their area.

AUTHOR *Francis de Vos* is Director, Botanic Garden of the Chicago Horticultural Society, Glencoe, Ill.

The simple act of writing ahead for information and planning your visit can save you the frustration of having passed an interesting place along the road, having gotten lost and arriving after the gates are closed, or having missed a special flower show or exhibit by a day.

If you have a choice, plan your visit for a weekday. Weekends are usually crowded and only a skeleton staff is available to answer questions. On hot days plan your visit for the morning tours after the dew is off the grass and before the temperature reaches the 90's. For your own sake, as well as that of the staff at the garden you are visiting, don't show up 15 minutes before closing time.

The special features and plant collections listed for each garden represent a small part of what there is to see. For additional information write to the garden that you plan to visit, or purchase a copy of the *Directory of American Horticulture* from the American Horticulture Society, Mount Vernon, Va. 22121, or *The Arboretums and Botanical Gardens of North America* published by the Arnold Arboretum of Harvard University, Jamaica Plain, Mass. 02130, or *American Gardens—A Traveler's Guide,* $1.50, Brooklyn Botanic Garden, 1000 Washington Ave., Brooklyn, N.Y. 11225.

BOTANICAL GARDENS, ARBORETUMS, AND PLACES OF HORTICULTURAL INTEREST

Northeast

Arnold Arboretum
Jamaica Plain, Mass. 02130

This outstanding institution is over 100 years old and contains many outstanding specimens of trees and shrubs. Collections of special interest are the forsythias, cherries, magnolias, crabapples, azaleas, rhododendrons and lilacs. A special hedge collection and a collection of Bonsai (dwarf potted trees) are open to the public. The arboretum testing ground known as the Case Estates in Weston, Mass., is also open to the public.

Brooklyn Botanic Garden
1000 Washington Avenue,
Brooklyn, N. Y. 11225

Besides its contribution to scientific botany, Brooklyn has provided outstanding educational programs for children and adults in all facets of botany, horticulture and gardening. Plantings of special interest are the Japanese gardens, Royanji Stone Garden, fragrance garden for the blind, waterlilies, and tropical plants in the conservatories.

Highland and Durand-Eastman
Park Arboretum
375 Westfall Road,
Rochester, N. Y. 14620

Highland Park is noted for its outstanding collection of approximately 500 varieties of lilacs. There are also noteworthy collections of peonies, azaleas, crabapples, rhododendrons and roses. The conservatory at Highland Park has seasonal shows at Thanksgiving, Christmas and Easter.

Longwood Gardens
Kennett Square, Pa. 19348

Longwood Gardens was developed by the late Pierre Samuel DuPont and is considered by many to be this country's finest display garden. The extensive conservatories contain thousands of tropical species from throughout the world. The extensive and highly maintained grounds have such outstanding features as an Italian Water Garden, rock garden, display of waterlilies and many outstanding specimens of trees and shrubs. The system of electric fountains is among the most intricate and beautiful to be found anywhere in the world.

New York Botanical Garden
Bronx Park,
New York City, N. Y. 10458

The most complete botanical garden in this country. Most aspects of botany and horticulture are included in the extensive scientific and applied programs. The conservatories house a wide variety of tropical plants. Other outstanding features are the rock garden, naturalistic plantings, the conifer collection and the museum exhibits.

National Arboretum
Washington, D. C. 20002

The National Arboretum is best known to the public for its extensive collection of azaleas. The mass planting of 70,000 azaleas is usually at its peak of bloom during the last week of April. The arboretum's dwarf conifer collection is the best in the country. The collections of holly, magnolia, firethorn, viburnum, crepe myrtles, and camellias are outstanding.

Also, Arthur Hoyt Scott Horticultural Foundation, Swarthmore College, Pa.; Bayard Cutting Arboretum, Islip, Long Island, N. Y.; Bowman Hill Wild Flower Preserve, Washington Crossing, Pa.; New Jersey Agriculture Experiment Station Arboretum, Rutgers University, New Brunswick; Morris Arboretum, Philadelphia, Pa.; Phipps Conservatory, Pittsburgh, Pa.; John J. Tyler Arboretum, Lima, Pa.; Planting Fields, Oyster Bay, Long Island, N. Y.; Winterthur, at Winterthur, Dela.

Home landscape center at Botanic Garden of the Chicago Horticultural Society.

Southeast

Callaway Gardens
Pine Mountain, Ga. 31822

Callaway Gardens is a remarkable exception to the idea that serious horticulture and recreation can not be combined in one institution. In this oasis of beauty, swimming, boating, fishing and golfing are carried out in a setting of natural beauty and colorful horticultural plantings of azaleas, hollies, magnolias, camellias, rhododendrons and seasonal plantings of bulbs and annuals. A wide range of tropical plants are on display in the greenhouses.

Fairchild Tropical Garden
10901 Old Cutler Road
Miami, Fla. 33156

This beautifully designed garden represents one of the best examples of how the talents of a landscape architect can provide the botanist and horticulturist with an outstanding setting in which to display plants for educational and research purposes. The palm collection is among the finest in the world. There are also outstanding collections of vines, orchids, and bromeliads.

Norfolk Botanical Garden
Airport Road
Norfolk, Va. 23518

Locally the Norfolk Botanical Garden is referred to as the "Gardens-by-the-Sea." The garden has outstanding collections of camellias, azaleas, and other broadleaved evergreens in a setting of loblolly pines and quiet lakes. The demonstration gardens illustrate different styles of landscaping, planting combinations, and solutions to special landscaping problems.

Also, Brookgreen Gardens, Georgetown, S. C.; Bellingrath Gardens, Mobile, Ala.; Biltmore House and Gardens, Asheville, N. C.; Magnolia Gardens, Charleston, S. C.; Memphis Botanical Gardens, Memphis, Tenn.; Tennessee Botanical Gardens and Art Center,

Nashville; Sarah P. Duke Memorial Gardens, Duke University, Durham, N. C.

Midwest

Alfred L. Boerner Botanical Garden
5879 S. 92nd Street
Hales Corner, Wis. 53130

Horticultural excellence characterizes Boerner Botanical Garden. This compact garden is in Whitnall Park located on the outskirts of Milwaukee. Outstanding among its diversified plantings are the perennial border, peony collection, rose garden, herb garden, rock garden and the field trials of annuals.

Botanic Garden of
the Chicago Horticultural Society
Box 90, Glencoe, Ill. 60022

This major botanic garden is still under development but open to the public. The 300-acre site is composed of 240 acres of rolling land and 60 acres of water with nine islands. Major features for the public at this time are the Home Landscape Center with its demonstration gardens planted with the best trees and shrubs for the Chicago area and highlighted with spring bulbs and annuals, and a nature trail with Braille labels.

Holden Arboretum
Sperry Road
Mentor, Ohio 44060

This slowly evolving arboretum is located on over 2,000 acres of rolling land east of Cleveland. Some of its outstanding features are Stebbin Gulch, a gorge which reveals the geologic past of the area and provides a site for subarctic plant life left by the retreating glaciers, and ever increasing plant collections of lilacs; ornamental fruit trees, conifers, nut trees, rhododendrons and azaleas.

Kingswood Center
Box 1186, Mansfield, Ohio 44903

Kingswood is a cultural and garden center that excels in horticulture. The specimen trees and shrubs form a background for superb plantings of spring bulbs, wildflowers, iris, peonies, summer annuals, daylilies, gladiolus, dahlias and chrysanthemums.

Morton Arboretum
Lisle, Ill. 60532

The Morton Arboretum was established by Joy Morton, whose father—J. Sterling Morton—founded Arbor Day. This extensive arboretum of over 1,200 acres contains outstanding collections of a wide variety of trees and shrubs that have been arranged for maximum landscape effect. The arboretum has a number of fine nature trails and an excellent hedge collection.

Missouri Botanical Garden
2315 Tower Grove Road,
St. Louis, Mo. 63110

Founded in 1859, this is the oldest botanical garden in existence in this country. The garden is well known to the scientific community throughout the world and to local citizens. It gained national prominence with the building of the Climatron, a geodesic dome made of aluminum and plexiglass, for the display of tropical plants. The garden has excellent collections of orchids and waterlilies, and wide selections of trees and shrubs.

Also, Beal-Garfield Botanic Garden, Michigan State University, East Lansing; Dawes Arboretum, Newark, Ohio; Garfield and Lincoln Park Conservatories, Chicago; Mt. Airy Arboretum and Stanley M. Rowe Arboretum, Cincinnati, Ohio; University of Michigan Arboretum, Ann Arbor; University of Minnesota Landscape Arboretum, St. Paul; University of Wisconsin Arboretum, Madison.

Rocky Mountains, Southwest and West Coast

Denver Botanical Garden
909 York Street,
Denver, Colo. 80206

This relatively new garden is rapidly developing into a major botanic garden. The huge conservatory houses a wide variety of tropical plants. Outdoor plantings contain a wide variety of perennials and there is an extensive collection of iris.

Desert Botanical Garden of Arizona
Tempe, Ariz. 85281

Chief function of this botanical garden is to grow, display and study desert plants from all the world's deserts. The garden has a display greenhouse and good collections of agave, cactus and yuccas.

Huntington Botanical Gardens
San Marino, Cal. 91108

The botanic garden provides a setting for the Huntington Library and for the Art Gallery that houses Gainsborough's famous "Blue Boy." The planting of cacti and succulents is especially outstanding. There is also a Shakespeare Garden, a Japanese Garden, and an extensive collection of camellias.

Los Angeles State and County Arboretum
301 North Baldwin Avenue,
Arcadia, Cal. 91006

Since its beginning in 1948, this arboretum has distinguished itself in developing plantings and programs to relate botany and horticulture to the people of this large metropolitan area. It is rich in plants native to the Mediterranean region and Australia. The demonstration gardens show how plants, landscape construction materials, and outdoor furniture can be combined in practical and pleasing combinations.

Santa Barbara Botanic Garden
1212 Mission Canyon Road,
Santa Barbara, Cal. 93105

This is an excellent place to see native California plants. These plants are grown in landscape settings for display and for experimentation to determine their adaptation to ornamental use.

Strybing Arboretum and Botanic Garden
Golden Gate State Park,
San Francisco, Cal. 94118

Plants from all over the world are grouped according to the region of origin. Other plantings include demonstration gardens, a garden of fragrance, rhododendron test area, a rock garden featuring dwarf conifers, and a five-acre area devoted to 300 species of native California plants.

University of Washington Arboretum
Seattle, Wash. 98105

The favorable climate of this area makes it possible to grow a very wide range of plants. The arboretum plantings are especially rich in broadleaved evergreens, and particularly rhododendrons, camellias and hollies. Other well represented plant groups are the maples and pines. The excellent Japanese garden is very rich in plant species.

Also, Boyce Thompson Southwest Arboretum, Superior, Ariz.; Fort Worth Botanic Garden, Fort Worth, Tex.; Descanso Gardens, La Canada, Calif.; Hoyt Arboretum, Portland, Ore.; Rancho Santa Ana Botanic Garden, Claremont, Calif.; University of California Botanical Garden, Berkeley.

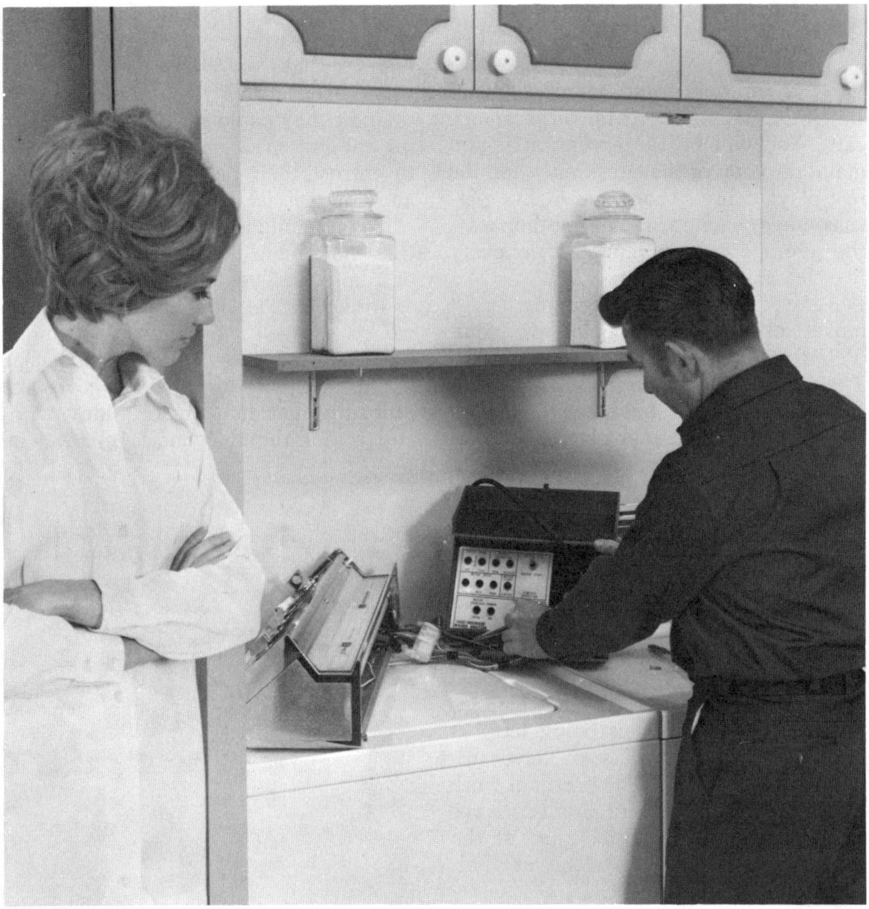

SERVICES

When You Move— Do's and Don'ts

YOU ARE GOING to move! That statement will ring true for most Americans. You will be the exception if you maintain your present residence for the rest of your life. About one in five persons moves each year. Put another way, the average person moves once every five years.

Again, dealing in averages, most moves of household goods are completed without difficulty. Some are not. The moving experience can be uneventful, but it should be recognized that many of the factors involved can lead to frustrations, uncertainties, and expected courses of action that suddenly must be changed.

Most moves involve fulfillment of a positive development. A promotion has come through. Perhaps an opportunity to move to a better climate. Maybe the long-sought chance to be closer to the home folks, or the grandchildren.

On the other side of the coin, a familiar neighborhood is being left behind. Old friends will soon have distance between them. The personal work that must be put into a move can leave family members exhausted, just at the time when they need to be at their sharpest.

Key to a successful move is preparation. The preparation must include the best information available that suits one's particular needs.

Needs vary considerably, from requirements for the free-spirited nomad who refuses to be burdened by personal possessions—to the large family suddenly confronted by the need to move the accumulations of a lifetime in a bulging household that must be shifted halfway across the country, or the world. In the latter situation, the family can take some tips from the lifestyle of the nomad: move only what is considered necessary, be flexible, leave all options open.

Do it yourself? Although commercial movers have been around for thousands of years, existing even in the days of man's earliest societies, there have always been heads of households who thought they could do the job better or for one reason or another preferred not to entrust their personal belongings to any commercial operation.

Today, millions of Americans move their household goods, using their own or a borrowed vehicle or renting a truck or trailer for the job. This operation can work very well if one has the strength, facilities, and knowledge to do the job —plus adequate insurance to cover any difficulty that may arise. Many truck and trailer rental agencies provide instructions for the do-it-yourselfer. The guidelines for such an operation are relatively few:

- Plan the move well in advance
- Insure that the required vehicle will be available at the time needed and that it is in good and safe working order and properly licensed
- Obtain proper packing materials and rent pads for furniture protection
- Line up necessary assistance for the day of the move

Professional movers on the job.

THIS CHAPTER was prepared by the Interstate Commerce Commission.

• Buy adequate insurance for protection of household goods and the vehicle used

• Keep flexible for changes in the weather and other surprises

• Don't expect the entire operation to be a snap. The professional who makes the job look easy has experience and capabilities the average person lacks

These words of precaution should not discourage one who has adequate competence and the right set of circumstances from doing the job himself. It can be fun and relatively inexpensive. And it has an attribute that no commercial mover can match: The householder's belongings are never out of his possession and no one can match the prudent care he can give them.

Hire a mover? While those who use commercial or for-hire carriers reflect vastly different lifestyles and family compositions, the types of moves involved fall into only three categories:

- Local—within a city or county
- Intrastate—within a single state
- Interstate or foreign

There are widely different guidelines for each type of move.

Local moves, the transfer of household goods within a single metropolitan area or county, can be the easiest type of move. Minor distances are involved. The time in which the household goods are in transit usually is short enough that the pickup, movement and delivery can take place within a single day. Costs are relatively low, and often are negotiable. Because of the time and distance involved, furniture and other objects do not have to be packed as securely as for long-distance moves.

The carrier performing the service is a local businessman who intends to remain in the community. He must maintain the goodwill of his patrons in order to stay in business. He is aware that his reputation is his best advertisement.

While local moves can be the easiest, the degree of protection for the consumer often is minimal. The mover may or may not be licensed beyond the license plate on his truck. He may not be under any prescribed rules for the rates that he charges or the services he provides, or even his degree of responsibility or liability.

The degree of his obligation to the consumer may be only as prescribed by the contract between consumer and mover. Often the contract is not even in writing. At times it may only be an implied contract.

Inquiry to local consumer assistance offices, better business bureaus, and neighbors who have utilized the services of the moving company in question is a first step. The last step before moving is to make certain that the contract between mover and consumer is fully understood by both parties.

Transfer of household goods within a single state is similar to a local move, except longer distances and greater times will generally prevail. At the same time, state governments usually are better organized for the licensing or certification of household goods movers.

The state's public utility commission, public service commission, or state corporation commission often can provide guidelines for the consumer to consider before he engages a mover. Most states also have consumer information offices that can provide pertinent information.

The same precautions apply here as for local moves: consumers should fully understand the contractual relationship which they are entering and they should have a precise understanding of the obligation and liability the carrier is assuming.

Because of the time and distance involved, movement of household goods across state lines represents the most complex type of transfer of personal property. At the same time, this type of move is backed by the most precise set of requirements and rules for protection of the consumer.

If household goods are going to be transported across state lines by a for-hire carrier, the movement comes under jurisdiction of the Interstate Commerce Commission (ICC).

Household goods carriers who perform this service must be certified by the ICC. They must possess the required amount of insurance to protect the public. Their routes and their rates are regulated by the ICC. They must adhere to a strict set of rules which clearly spell out the obligations of the carrier, as well as the responsibilities of the shipper.

Information on these rules may be obtained from the Interstate Commerce Commission (Consumer Information), Washington, D.C. 20423, or from any of the 78 ICC Field Offices located at principal transportation points throughout the country.

The information which follows relates to interstate moves performed by for-hire carriers under jurisdiction of the Interstate Commerce Commission. Although local moves and those which do not cross state lines may not be subject to such strict regulations, the following guidelines can be useful in planning any move.

Success in moving one's household depends upon recognition of the unfolding events in three time periods:

- Before the move
- During the move
- After the move

Before the move—plan to be flexible. Try to avoid moving during peak periods—the summer season and those days preceding the first of the month when many households are being shifted.

Send for helpful information that is available without charge from the Interstate Commerce Commission (Consumer Information Office), Washington, D.C. 20423. Ask for:

Public Advisory No. 1—*Householders' Guide to Accurate Weights.* Tips on preventing being charged for the wrong weight of your shipment.

Public Advisory No. 2—*Arranging Transportation for Small Shipments.* This publication is useful if you decide to ship some of your goods, rather than have them transported by a mover.

Public Advisory No. 3—*People on the Move.* This contains general guidance and a form which you can use to advise the ICC of any comments concerning your move.

Public Advisory No. 4—*Lost or Damaged Household Goods.* Preventing, correcting and resolving shipping problems.

Another useful publication compiled by the ICC is *Summary of Information for Shippers of Household Goods,* (Form BOp 103), Stock No. 2600–00966. It is for sale by Superintendent of Documents, U.S. Government Printing Office, Washington, D.C. 20402. Or you can ask for a copy from any for-hire household goods carrier certificated by the ICC.

Decide what you intend to move, which material (such as fragile and unusually valuable possessions) you will transport yourself, which articles you will pack, which articles you wish to have packed (for a fee), and the time span available for the move.

Select moving companies with good reputations in the community and ask for estimates (without charge). Make certain that estimators are aware of everything that must be moved. Remember that the charge for interstate moves will be based on weight and distance according to tariffs on file with the ICC. The actual weight and not the estimated weight will determine the cost that must be paid—no more and no less.

Ask for a written estimate. You still must pay a cost based on the actual weight, but the written estimate can have an effect on the amount of cash necessary for delivery of your shipment.

Determine what degree of legal protection is needed for the safety of your household goods. From acceptance to delivery of your goods, the carrier is responsible for your shipment. Responsibility is not the same as liability, though; meaning that a carrier will not automatically pay the shipper the fair market value of lost or damaged goods. Carrier negligence may have to be proven before any reimbursement takes place. Perhaps an act of God, rather than negligence, was the cause of the loss. In such situations the carrier may have no liability.

A good starting point here is to recognize the difference between insurance and carrier liability. Carriers do not sell household goods insurance. This must be purchased through your insurance agency. You must determine if it is worthwhile.

As to liability of an interstate carrier, this can be as little as 60 cents per pound if you ship your goods at the lowest (limited liability) rate. Consumers can pay a somewhat higher rate and receive a higher value on the carrier's liability. Movers are not liable for the full value of lost or damaged goods *unless* you pay an additional charge for such protection.

Your best bet is to obtain copies of Public Advisory No. 4 and BOp 103 described earlier. And remember—liability is not the same as insurance!

Continuing with things to do before a move: Be sure that agreements between you and the carrier are in writing and on the Order for Service and the Bill of Lading which the carrier will provide.

The Order for Service, to be signed by both parties, will include the time period or the actual dates for pickup and delivery of household goods. If the carrier cannot meet these committments he must notify you, at his expense, and provide alternatives. The carrier is expected to exercise reasonable diligence in attempting to meet the commitments described in the Order for Service.

Upon request, the mover will provide expedited service, giving a definite date on or before which your shipment will be delivered. There is an additional fee for this service if the date is met, but no such charge to you or penalty against the carrier if it is not.

Decide which of your belongings you wish the mover to pack (for a fee) and what you intend to pack yourself. Agree on the time when the packers will do their work. Give them space to operate and provide a table on which to pack things.

Household goods shipments are similar to C.O.D. actions, with payment made by cash or certified check. Actual charges must be paid before delivery, unless they exceed the estimate by 10 percent. In that case, the mover must unload your shipment if you pay the estimate plus 10 percent, and you will have 15 business days in which to pay the balance.

If you are not prepared to pay for the move when the carrier arrives at your new residence within the designated time period, be prepared for a refusal to unload the vehicle. Your household possessions may wind up in storage, at your expense. Carriers are permitted to extend credit but are not required to do so. Such arrangements must be handled in advance, not at the time and point of delivery.

During the move. When the driver arrives, and before loading begins, insist on exchanging information necessary for the transaction to run smoothly. Obtain his name, home office location and telephone number of the carrier, vehicle license and equipment numbers, location of the scale he will use to weigh your shipment, his route, expected arrival time and where he can be reached en route, let him know your plans, and provide an address and a telephone number where he can contact you.

An inventory will be made of your goods, and their condition. Have someone accompany the mover's representative who writes up the inventory. If there is disagreement over the described condition of an article, note this in writing before signing off after completion of the inventory.

The mover will issue you a bill of lading, which serves as a receipt and represents the contract of carriage. Examine it carefully. Be certain you understand the portion setting forth the liability of the mover for any loss or damage to your goods.

Verify that the tare weight is listed. This represents the weight of the vehicle before your goods were loaded. The difference between the loaded and tare weights will establish the weight of your shipment.

You have the right to go with the driver to the scales to observe weighing of the loaded vehicle. Make sure that the driver is the only person aboard the vehicle when it is weighed. Three 200-pound helpers would add 600 pounds to the weight for which you will be charged.

ICC's Public Advisory No. 1 provides helpful guidance in assuring that you pay only for the proper weight of your goods.

If you are unable or choose not to observe the weighing of the loaded vehicle and later question whether the designated weight is correct, you may obtain a reweighing, at a reasonable charge to you. The reweighing of the truck with your shipment and then without your shipment can be observed by you.

The lower of the two shipment weights, either the initial weighing or the reweighing, determine the transportation charges you pay. If the reweigh net weight is more than 120 pounds below the billed net weight, you do not have to pay for the reweighing procedure. Nor if the billed net weight exceeds by at least 25 percent the estimated net weight on the Estimate of Charges for Transportation given you.

Plan to be at the delivery site on or before the agreed delivery time. Movers need wait only three hours for you to accept your goods, and less time if the move is under 200 miles. The driver, however, cannot show up for an early delivery without your consent.

Remember, if the mover has met all his obligations but delivery cannot be made because of your inability to pay the lawful charges or accept delivery within the free waiting period, your household goods could wind up in storage—at your expense. Redelivery costs will add to the bill.

Upon delivery have a family member check each article against the inventory and examine for any damage. Before signing the delivery receipt or the inventory, make sure they include written notations of loss or damage, and be specific.

After the move. If you obtained a copy of Public Advisory No. 3, earlier described, you may use the questionnaire provided to let the ICC know your views of the manner in which the move was performed. The publication also lists local ICC offices that can provide assistance and advice.

Although most movement of household goods is conducted without the householder encountering serious problems, the ICC's analysis of thousands of transactions indicates that complaints often stem from two principal areas: estimates (discussed earlier) and handling of loss and damage claims.

Proper settlement of loss and damage actions begins with your written notations on the inventory. Without these the burden may be on you to show that the receipt was incorrect and items actually were lost or damaged. To file a claim, notify the destination agent or mover and request a company claim form. (Public Advisory No. 4 describes the filing procedure).

Movers are required by ICC rules to acknowledge claims in 30 days and to act on them in the following 120 days or report the reason for the inaction. Only the courts have authority to adjudicate loss and damage claims, but the ICC will try to assist you in understanding your rights and obligations.

While this information has been structured to assist the householder who will be making an interstate move under jurisdiction of the Interstate Commerce Commission, the principles should prove helpful in any type of move.

Where You Shop Is as Important as What You Buy

IN TODAY'S crowded marketplace all kinds of sellers are jostling for your attention and your money by offering different prices, services and quality of goods. There are so many kinds of stores and so many different deals that it's hard to keep them straight and—easy to get stung.

To get the best bargain you need to carefully weigh the advantages and disadvantages of each kind of outlet before making your final selection.

Not all the many varieties may be available to you but chances are most of them are if you live in or near a big city. Remember, too, that retailing is a highly competitive business and the distinctions between stores can easily blur. The differences aren't always as sharp as we describe them.

Retailers come in a diversity of sizes and modes of operation. There are specialty shops, variety stores, department stores, and discount merchandisers of several kinds.

Some outlets are franchises, some are independents run by the owner, while others are parts of local, regional or national chains.

The chains may be operated by a single company or they may be a voluntary association that is bound together for group buying and advertising.

A specialty shop by definition handles a limited type of goods—say major appliances, audio equipment, clothing, furniture, or health and beauty aids. But usually the selection within the specialty is wide and you can count on getting personal attention from well-trained sales people. Prices might be higher than at stores that handle a diversity of products.

A variety store, such as S.S. Kresge and F.W. Woolworth, generally handles a good selection of many different kinds of small and inexpensive items through large self-service outlets. The prices may be low in variety stores but you may sacrifice a lot in service and the availability of skilled salespeople.

A department store sells an assortment of goods in many price ranges. And it offers you a wide selection of services such as several kinds of credit plans, specialty areas within the store, and liberal return policies.

You can get just about anything at a department store including clothing, furniture, major appliances, sporting and hobby goods, home improvement needs, auto equipment and service, toys, garden and workshop tools, health and beauty aids, and perhaps even food.

Many department stores that started out as independent operations are now part of chains. Yet even today certain cities are closely identified with the great merchandisers operating in them: Filene's in Boston; Gimbels and Macy's in New York City; Wanamaker of Philadelphia; Marshall Field and Carson Pirie Scott of Chicago; Hudson's in Detroit; and Nieman-Marcus of Dallas. Stores like these generally pride themselves on selling top-quality goods and providing a full range of services in a fine-store setting.

AUTHOR *Alan Cleveland* is an associate editor of *Changing Times,* The Kiplinger Magazine, Washington, D.C.

Probably even more familiar to most people, though not identified with any one city, are the big department store chains such as Sears (the world's largest retailer), Montgomery Ward and J.C. Penney, each with hundreds of outlets in cities and towns all over the country as well as huge catalog operations that let people shop via the mail from anywhere.

Most of the items they have will carry the store name though the firms also sell well-known name-brand goods such as Fisher Price toys and Kodak photo equipment and supplies.

Some of the store-brand products are made by big-name manufacturers while others come from factories you never heard of that specialize in making private-label merchandise—and these firms, incidentally, might also make things for the name-brand companies as well.

The chain might maintain a great deal of control over some of the products it sells, even to the point of setting specifications and running tough quality control checks on important items such as clothing, home improvement supplies like paints, major appliances like kitchen and laundry equipment, TVs and audio equipment. These products can rival or exceed many name brand products in value and quality.

In a few instances the retail chain may own or have a large financial interest in its suppliers. Sears is a prime example. It holds stock in Whirlpool, the major appliance maker; Roper, which supplies Sears with kitchen ranges; Kellwood, a source of camping and hunting equipment and home furnishings; Armstrong Tire and Rubber Company; Warwick Electronics, maker of TVs and audio equipment; and Desoto, which provides Sears with paint, wallpaper and home furnishings. While a good deal of the output from these firms goes to Sears, it doesn't rely on them for all its needs in these lines.

Of course, the chains don't set specs on all the items they purchase and the amount of specification setting varies from firm to firm. In some cases a company simply buys part of a factory's out-

put and slaps its name on the product. Quality control on these items by the retailer might not be as rigid as on major items, either.

However, even with big products the retailer can't make many substantial changes in factory assembly-line procedures or reject too many items through quality standards without adding to the final cost. The stores must fight a constant battle between production costs and getting good quality goods; to keep expenses down the trade-off might be against quality.

Yet the big national chains often can keep their prices lower or offer more services than the name-brand producers on items from the same factory because they don't have the higher start-up costs of inventing, developing and advertising new items. They also buy and sell in large volumes and have relatively more efficient methods of distribution. Sometimes a company can save simply by buying lower quality goods.

Remember, the simple reason a store sells goods with its own name on them is that the company generally makes

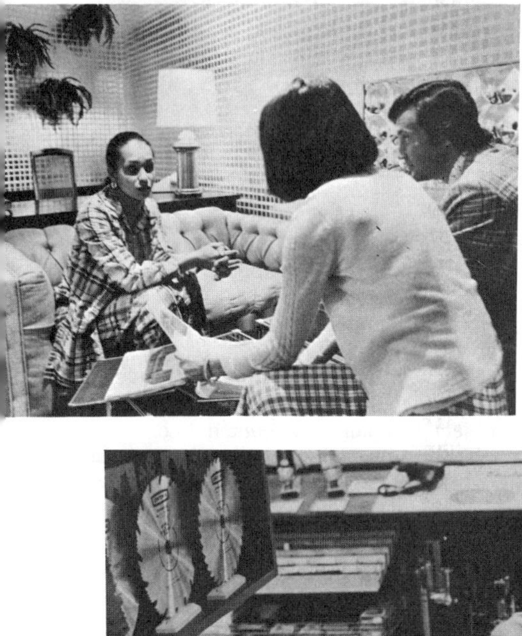

Scenes at a big department store chain.

higher profits than it would selling name-brands.

While the national department stores have been around a long time, the discounters are of relatively more recent vintage.

Discounters aren't so much a separate kind of store as a different way of doing business. Like other retailers they may be independents or chains and they can be specialty, variety or department stores. They may operate out of stripped-down warehouse-like buildings selling merchandise in factory cartons—or they may run posh showrooms with carpeted aisles, sparkling showcases, indirect lighting and piped-in music. They may sell only well-known name-brand goods or they may feature their own private-label products.

However they do business, the point is to offer you lower prices than ordinary outlets—or at least appear to.

They have many ways of doing this. One way is to keep overhead expenses low by providing few services, or by locating in low-rent districts off the beaten track, or by keeping personnel costs down by hiring fewer clerks who aren't as highly trained or well-paid as those who staff specialty shops. They may even depend heavily on part-time help.

Discounters might also handle fewer items, singling out ones that sell fast at a good mark-up. Another way to keep costs down is to sell lower quality name-brand products or knock-offs that have a higher profit margin. Knock-offs are items that look like popular name-brand goods but often are cheaply made, typically by an overseas company that specializes in this business.

The store may also push certain items as loss leaders, taking a very small profit on each unit while boosting the prices and making more profit on other goods.

The discounter may give the appearance of offering good deals by printing his prices alongside the considerably higher suggested retail tag of the manufacturer. And finally, a store may simply use the word "discount" without really cutting its prices—offering the illusion of savings instead of the fact.

One of the newer kinds of discounter is the catalog showroom. A lot of these outfits started out as wholesalers open only to a select few, such as company purchasing agents, who had to have a courtesy card to get in. Now they are mailing their catalogs to tens of thousands of people.

Usually they don't advertise extensively (which spells higher operating costs) but a few are using TV, radio, newspaper and magazine ads to reach more customers.

Generally they handle only a few lines such as jewelry, timepieces, small appliances, photo equipment, or silver. Mixed in with the name-brands are off-brands.

The aim of the catalog-showroom is to combine the quick service and surroundings of a fine department store with the savings you'd expect at a discount house.

The catalogs show two prices: the factory-suggested price in plain dollars and cents and the showroom price (which you pay) in an easy-to-unscramble code. The coded cost is always way below the factory-suggested list, but not necessarily much below what regular outlets sell the same item for. Reputable discounters try to stick to their printed prices but all have a warning in the catalog that prices are subject to change without notice.

To buy from them you pick the item out of the catalog (or from the showroom display), fill out an order form, and plunk down your money. In a few minutes your purchase, probably still in its carton, is delivered to you from backroom inventory. You can also order by mail but shipping charges and insurance are extra.

Buying clubs or groups are another kind of outlet offering bargain deals. They may be commercial setups or non-profit operations run by a union, professional association, co-operative, or whatever. Generally they deal in big ticket articles like cars, furniture, appliances, and expensive furs or jewelry.

The buying organization acts as a go-between the shopper and the seller, delivering large numbers of customers to the sellers and getting discounts for the buyers and—in the case of commercial outfits—collecting fees for itself. The fees, which are relatively small, are paid by the shopper or in some cases by the seller.

A few so-called "buying clubs" are really rackets run by sharpies out to make a fast buck at the expense of bargain hunters. These phonies promise huge savings, maybe as much as $10,000 over 10 years, and they charge "members" initiation fees and dues as high as $300, $400 or more.

They'll urge you to sign up quick or lose the golden opportunity of guaranteed bargains. Actually the paper they have you sign is a promissory note that will be quickly sold to a finance company. By the time you get wise the operators may have skipped town to set up shop elsewhere, but you will still be paying on that note and at high interest rates.

Even if they don't operate in this hit-and-run way they really won't sell you things any cheaper than you could purchase them on your own by shopping carefully. All you get for your membership is the right to buy through them at inflated prices.

Okay, now that you know something about the way sellers operate, how do you sort through the facts and turn them to your advantage? How do you shop for the best deal?

First, decide exactly what you want to purchase. If possible, narrow the field to a specific model (and get the model number) or brand. Get a good fix on the features you want. Make up your mind early what you can afford to spend and what you demand in the way of quality.

How much time you devote to this early decision-making and information-gathering depends, of course, on how much time you have and what it is you are buying.

But do remember that you can save yourself a lot of traipsing about by using ads, catalogs and the telephone to gather facts before you start visiting stores. You can also combine shopping for several items at a time.

A good place to start your browsing is in a specialty shop that handles a good selection of the merchandise you want. These places usually have the most knowledgeable and helpful clerks. The smaller outfits may be operated by the owner, and he's the one to dicker with about price. Specialty stores may charge a little more than other retailers but often they throw in a lot of extra services at no extra cost.

For example, a couple in the Washington, D.C. area recently discovered that an owner-operated appliance shop charged about $3 more for a washing machine than did a big volume discount appliance store, but didn't tack on $10 for delivery and installation or $7.50 to haul the old washer away as the big volume dealer did.

The owner-operator also gave better terms on the warranty, and his own skilled crew is on call for repairs all week and week-ends too.

What about services? You have to consider them as well as the price. Check such things as delivery and installation, store location, convenient parking, repair services, warranties and guarantees, credit, check cashing policies, return policies, alterations, shopping hours, gift wrapping, fashion and decorator advice, and ordering by mail or telephone.

Generally the more services a store provides the higher its prices will be relative to stores that don't offer them. An outfit that sells appliances in cartons out of a warehouse may keep prices down partly by not making deliveries or installation (or by charging extra for them), or because it doesn't have credit arrangements but accepts cash or certified checks only. If lots of services aren't important you may have found yourself a bargain.

What about the quality of goods? Does the store sell only top quality name- or store-brand products? Often items are inexpensive because they are low in quality or lacking in important features. A discount appliance outlet may be selling you last year's goods even if they are still in the factory package. That doesn't necessarily detract from them, of course, but you should know what you are getting.

Watch out for merchandise advertised at very low prices. It can be bait to get you into the store so a smooth-talking salesman can switch you to more expensive goods.

How knowledgeable are the salespeople? In a lot of stores, all the way from fine department stores through discount houses, the clerks are mere order takers and you can't really count on what they say. In some cases they are well-informed but they may be paid partly in "spiffs" of "PMs". These are bonuses from manufacturers or the retail store.

If this week the sales people are pushing item A it might be because the commission is better. Next week they'll tell you item B is clearly superior because they'll be getting a better spiff from company B. This sort of thing goes on in mattresses, audio equipment, photo supplies, and appliances.

If you find what looks like a good bargain don't be stampeded into making a quick and possibly costly decision. Take the time to check further for the same item at lower prices—or with more services at no extra charge—through other outlets. Also consider buying seconds, irregulars, seasonal closeouts or floor models, often at much reduced prices.

The many varieties of retail outlets give you more places to hunt for good deals, but you can't count on any of them for a guarantee in bargains. There is nothing automatic about saving money when you shop. You still have to work at it.

The Steps to Take When a Purchase Doesn't Satisfy

When a purchase doesn't live up to its billing . . . doesn't last as long as it should . . . gives you service and maintenance problems . . . or tastes terrible, you perform a public service by telling the manufacturer and the retailer exactly what you think of it and why.

Strangely enough, surveys have shown that only one out of four consumers bothers to complain about unsatisfactory merchandise, possibly because most people

- Don't know where to write
- Aren't sure how to describe the problem
- Aren't sure complaining is worth the effort

With the growth of the consumer movement over the last ten years or so, this negative attitude is changing. More consumers are stating their problems loud and clear. With this chapter I hope to help you complain effectively.

Reputable retailers and manufacturers, as well as consumers, are equally interested in consumer satisfaction. Hearing about your reaction to problems with a product will help concerned and responsible business and industry to improve their products.

There has been a noticeable response to the active consumer movement from business in the establishment of specialized departments which handle consumer complaints and provide consumer information.

Of course, sometimes the consumer service departments in business don't measure up to our expectations, and sometimes consumer information is inadequate. Again, this is a reasonable basis for complaints by consumers, individually and collectively.

The consumer's first line of defense is information. Before you buy any product—especially before you make a major purchase of any kind—get all the information you can about various styles and models, degrees of difference between products, and the manufacturer's guarantee or warranty provisions.

Check the reputation of the local dealer with your Better Business Bureau. If Merchant X has a file full of unresolved complaints, protect yourself by taking your purchasing power elsewhere.

Advance preparation for major and even minor investments can save you a lot of time, money and trouble.

Once you've decided on the kind of product you want, and which retailer to buy from, think further about the model that's best for you.

If you're in the market for a new washer, the shocking pink superwasher with seven temperature selections and four forward speeds may be just what you're after. Then again, perhaps it isn't, and you would prefer the simpler model.

Once your decision is made, *stay with it.* Don't let an aggressive salesman talk you out of the simple washer and into the superwasher.

Don't wait until the product needs service to find out how good the guarantee or warranty (interchangeable terms) may be. The time to ask questions about the warranty and service is *before* you buy the product. If the salesman cannot answer your questions satisfactorily, ask to speak to someone who can.

Remember, a guarantee is a statement by the manufacturer or vendor that he stands behind his product or service. Guarantees and warranties usually have limitations or conditions, so be sure you know what *isn't* covered under what circumstances as well as what *is* covered.

I suggest immediate suspicion of so-called "unconditional" guarantees. Conditions are almost inevitable, so get all promises in writing. Any businessman who is unwilling to put his promises in writing is not the one to deal with.

Before you buy any product or service covered by a guarantee or warranty, make sure you resolve these questions:

-What, exactly, is covered? The entire product? Only certain parts? How about labor costs?

-Whom should you call when you need repairs under the warranty? The manufacturer? The retailer? A service agency?

-Must repairs be made at the factory or by an "authorized service representative" to keep the warranty in effect? If so, *where is the nearest service representative?* He'd better be close by for good service!

-Who pays for parts, for labor, for shipping charges?

-How long does the warranty last on the entire product? On parts and assemblies?

-If pro-rata reimbursement is provided, what is the basis for it? Length of ownership? Usage? Original cost?

-If the warranty provides for reimbursement, is it in cash or credit towards a replacement?

Before you use the product, be sure to read the owner's manual or instruction sheet. Follow the operating instructions and make sure that any routine maintenance or service is completed as suggested or required by the manufacturer. Otherwise you may find you've cancelled your warranty.

Keep the warranty and sales receipt for future reference.

A great place to keep them is in a recipe file. Write down the date of purchase and date of installation. Register appliances with the card provided for that purpose by the manufacturer. And it's a good idea to record any service or repair work done after purchase.

If you have a complaint about merchandise that has not lived up to your expectations, the first place to register your complaint is with the store where it was purchased. Many complaints can be settled as simply as that.

If you can't return the merchandise, if your problem can't be solved at the retail level, or if the problem seems to drag on for an unreasonable length of time, write to the manufacturer. If you don't have his address, your local Better Business Bureau or Chamber of Commerce may be able to secure it for you.

Or you may wish to invest 50 cents in a booklet called *Information for Consumers* which lists the names, addresses and phone numbers of key executives of major U.S. manufacturers

---

AUTHOR *Bette Clemens* is director of consumer affairs for the Council of Better Business Bureaus, with headquarters in Washington, D.C.

and retailers. Order it from *Everybody's Money,* Dept. SS, Box 431, Madison, Wis. 53701, and keep it on file with your warranties.

Before you write your letter, put the facts in order so that your communication will be clear, concise and to the point. Be sure to include:

—Your full name and address (You'd be amazed at the number of people whose letters can't be answered because their addresses are illegible or incomplete!)

—What you bought. Include the model number, serial number, etc., to assist the manufacturer's identification of the product.

—Where you bought it.

—Date of purchase and amount you paid.

—The problem—the appliance doesn't work, the carpet shows wear, the jeans came apart in the wash, or non-delivery of ordered merchandise.

—Warranty dates, if applicable.

—Your preferred resolution of the problem: adequate repair, refund, replacement, or whatever.

—Keep a copy of your letter for future reference.

If you don't have an answer to your original letter at the end of three weeks, write again, enclosing a copy of the original letter.

If there's still no answer after a reasonable period of time, report your experience to the local Better Business Bureau, state or county Consumer Protection Agency, to the local newspaper's Action Line, to the appropriate federal regulatory agency (for their records), or to one of the recently-developed Consumer Action Panels.

In response to consumer complaints about products, service and warranties, complaint-handling mechanisms have been set up by four major industries. They are called Consumer Action Panels (CAPS) and they constitute a major step forward for consumers and for the industries as well. They 1) receive comments and complaints from consumers, 2) study industry practices, 3) advise the respective manufacturers of ways to improve their consumer services, and 4) provide consumer information materials.

Their names and addresses are:

Carpet and Rug Industry Consumer Action Panel (CRICAP)
Box 1568
Dalton, Ga., 30720

Furniture Industry Consumer Action Panel (FICAP)
Box 951
High Point, N.C. 27261

Major Appliance Consumer Action Panel (MACAP)
20 North Wacker Drive
Chicago, Ill. 60606

These three CAPS maintain central offices to which complaints and inquiries can be referred. The fourth, AutoCAP, uses local and state panels organized under auspices of the National Automobile Dealers Association. As of February 1974, pilot panels have been established in Colorado, the District of

Charles Kemp of the Washington-based Council of Better Business Bureaus takes consumer information out where the consumers are.

Columbia, Florida, Idaho, Kentucky, Ohio, Oklahoma, Oregon, Pennsylvania, Utah, and Washington.

For complete information on AutoCAPS and their locations, write to the National Automobile Dealers Association, 2000 K Street N.W., Washington, D.C. 20006.

As of February 1974, some 44 states have enacted the so-called "Little FTC Act" to prevent deceptive and unfair trade practices. At that time, the states without such laws were Alabama, Georgia, Mississippi, Nebraska, Tennessee and West Virginia.

Consumer protection in 40 states is the responsibility of the State Attorney General. In the remaining states, consumer protection agencies have been set up within the governor's office or within a designated state department—such as agriculture, commerce, or labor.

If a State Consumer Protection Bureau is not listed in your local telephone book, contact the Office of the Attorney General in your state capitol for information on your state's consumer protection services.

Other sources for assistance with your complaints are city and county consumer offices. Responsibilities and powers of these agencies vary. Consumers are well advised to keep themselves informed on the status and functions of local agencies.

Although federal agencies do not act upon individual consumer complaints, such complaints are valuable background information for regulatory agencies as well as for the President's Office of Consumer Affairs.

Their addresses and functions are:

Federal Trade Commission (FTC)
Washington, D.C. 20580

FTC has jurisdiction over restraint of trade and unfair business practices, false and deceptive advertising, product labeling, and flammable fabrics.

Food and Drug Administration (FDA)
5600 Fishers Lane
Rockville, Md. 20852

FDA is responsible for overseeing the marketing of food, drugs, cosmetics, and medical devices.

Consumer complaints concerning these areas should be directed to this agency. Though FDA does not attempt to resolve individual complaints, such communications will help keep the agency informed of current problem areas.

U.S. Postal Inspection Service
Washington, D.C. 20260

This is the oldest, least known law enforcement agency in the United States. The Chief Inspector's Office processes more than 100,000 complaints of fraudulent use of the mails each year, and conducts more than 10,000 full field investigations annually. It maintains liaison with other federal agencies, and with state and municipal authorities.

Consumer Product Safety Commission (CPSC)
1750 K Street N. W.
Washington, D. C. 20036

This agency is relatively new. It has power to:

- -Set safety standards for all common household and recreational products
- -Seize and bar hazardous products from the marketplace
- -Ban from the market any product that presents an unreasonable risk of injury
- -Order manufacturers, distributors, or retailers to notify purchasers about hazardous products and to repair, replace or refund the cost of such products

CPSC maintains a toll-free hotline for consumer questions and complaints. The number to call with questions concerning possibly hazardous products is 800-638-2666 for residents of the continental United States. In Maryland only, call 800-492-2937. You may also report suspected product safety defects on this line.

Obviously, there are more sources for consumer assistance than can reasonably be summarized in a single chapter. Books can be and have been written on this subject. What's most important to remember is: *Complaining is a public service.*

Consumers should be able to make their voices heard in the marketplace. Your voice counts.

Ways to Shop the Educational Marketplace

SHOPPING FOR educational services can become a complex and confusing problem because there are so many options. Yet the variety of choices from nursery school through post-graduate college programs and the countless opportunities for specialized training make it possible to secure suitable educational services much more easily than even ten years ago.

And this shopping is just like any other kind. It involves:

1) The needs and desires of the individual seeking the service.
2) The kind and quality of the product.
3) The means available to purchase it.

In other words, you need first to outline your present situation and your goal in seeking additional education.

Are you a junior or senior high school student planning for vocational training, or seeking good general education until you decide on your future?

Are you at college level seeking professional post graduate specialization or an alternative educational program?

Are you a member of the work force seeking to expand your occupational knowledge for purpose of advancement?

Are you any citizen seeking to learn something for its own sake and your personal satisfaction?

The combinations of goals and desires are almost as numerous as the population. But in each individual case, deciding on *your* goal is the first step in shopping for an educational service.

The obvious next step, of course, is to select the best educational service to accomplish your purpose. Although time and cost factors are inevitably tied to this selection, they will be discussed separately.

To find out what services are available, start in your own community.

Many public libraries contain numerous reference works describing career and college programs, facilities available, and requirements for admission. Your local school and college guidance counselors are also a good source of information and advice. Some business concerns, even if they do not underwrite their own training programs, may provide practical and up-to-date suggestions.

If you are interested in some particular school, write for a catalog.

There are many other sources of general and specific information on both college and vocational options. The list with this chapter gives you some idea of the types of organizations that may be helpful.

To assist you in making a wise selection when you become aware of the various possibilities, you may wish to apply the following general criteria:

> Does the school have a program and adequate faculty in your area of interest?
> Is the school accredited?
> What is its general reputation?
> What is its organization plan?
> Does it offer a summer placement program?
> Are its facilities (library, laboratories, classrooms) adequate?
> Does it offer a strong, supportive, student personnel program?

Note that there is no official ranking of schools or colleges in the United States. Academic standing is controlled by accreditation, the recognition given to an educational institution that has been evaluated and has met or exceeded certain required standards established by a competent agency.

All the institutions that an accrediting agency has approved meet at least a minimum level of quality, but the agency does not rate one institution as being of higher or lower quality than another.

Accreditation of public school programs is customarily conducted by state departments of education, with each state setting its own educational standards.

Public and private schools, colleges and universities may voluntarily seek accreditation by a regional accrediting association.

Accreditation may also operate through an association of practitioners in a given profession; an association of specialized professional schools or colleges; or a council composed of professional schools, practitioners, and a state licensing or certificating agency.

Many vocational schools and home study programs are also accredited.

In addition to these general considerations you will need to think about your own personal requirements:

> Is it vital that the school be nearby?
> Do you prefer to attend a large or small school?
> Does religious orientation in a school make a difference?
> Is more than one level of training or education available?
> Are there both day and evening programs? A summer program?
> Would you prefer independent study to a structured program?
> Is a school available in your area of interest?

Having determined your educational goal and the best way of achieving it, you need to look at possible obstacles and ways of coping with them.

Surveys indicate that the cost of higher education, both vocational and professional, is rising steeply. If your funds are limited you may wish to consider the advantages of a public college or university vs. a private one; the practicality of a two-year community college program vs. a four-year state university program.

With the development of technology the requirement for some education beyond the high school level has also grown, but for entry into many occupations a two-year program is quite satisfactory.

You might also consider whether a combination of high school courses and

---

AUTHORS *Dave Darland* and *Mary Heath* are Instruction and Professional Development Staff Members, National Education Association, Washington, D.C.

a community college training program would be as useful as private vocational school training.

In recent years the concept of the community college has been radically changed. Traditionally these were "junior colleges" which simply provided two years of college training with the expectation that students would transfer to four-year institutions when they graduated. Now there are over 1,000 two-year public colleges in the United States. They offer advantages not nearly so available in conventional four-year institutions, advantages well worth your consideration.

Not every school offers every advantage, but many offer both academic and career programs. Others give credit for courses taken on television, operate on an "open door" policy, hold early and late classes at a variety of sites for the convenience of students, encourage work-study programs on both a continuing and inter-term basis, and form consortiums with other two-year colleges and four-year institutions where cross registration is permitted.

Financing the purchase of educational services is often a large stumbling block. A survey made in 1969–70 showed that parents contributed the largest single share (an average of 44 percent) of yearly income of the students surveyed. However, there were wide variations according to race and sex of the student, the type of school attended, and whether the student commuted or lived at school.

This same survey indicated that relatively few students had obtained scholarships or grants which involved no debt for the student.

The group surveyed were second-year students.

Individual colleges and universities administer grants, scholarships and most student loans for their schools, including federal grants under the Educational Opportunity program and student loans under the National Defense Student Loan program.

Information concerning these programs can be secured from the financial aid office of the college.

General information concerning possible eligibility for loans and scholarships can be obtained by writing the College Scholarship Service, Princeton, N. J. 08540.

Another common source of funds is part-time employment during the school year and full-time vacation employment. Savings, of course, can be a great help in financing school expense.

A number of constructive approaches can reduce costs materially. One is to plan ahead and then take courses at the high school level or in your community continuing education program where the cost is nominal. This will help you develop the skills or knowledge to gain advanced placement or pursue an accelerated program.

Another way to save money—and time—is to take the College Level Examination Program (CLEP) tests. They are not easy, but many people pass them successfully and secure college credit on that basis. If you wish to follow this plan, contact the college you wish to attend.

There are 5 general and 34 subject matter tests available. Individual colleges and universities use different combinations of them. Scores acceptable at one college may not be recognized by another. However, over 500 colleges and universities do give some credit under this program.

Descriptive booklets with sample questions may be obtained free of charge by writing to the College Entrance Examination Board, Box 593, Princeton, N. J. 08540.

Many colleges and universities require scores from other College Entrance Examination Board tests (SAT and subject matter tests) which are routinely made available in many high schools throughout the country. Taking the trial version, the Preliminary Scholastic Aptitude Test, will give you practice and may help you in your own decision making.

Other colleges and universities may require scores from the American College Testing program battery (ACT) which is also available at the high school level. Some institutions discount the value of these standardized tests and use other criteria for admission.

Many of these same principles and strictures apply to advanced degree programs. Aptitude and subject-matter test battery scores may be required. Costs generally increase. But given the greater maturity of the student, better jobs at better pay may be found, along with more scholarships, fellowships, and grants.

But perhaps you are not interested in the conventional programs outlined above. We have all been hearing of "Schools Without Walls," "Open Universities," independent study programs, and free universities. These programs are so highly individualized that they may only be analyzed in relation to your own needs and goals. To assist you in this direction a brief bibliography is included at the end of this chapter.

Many educational institutions have recognized a community desire for specialized courses ranging from "Investments" to "Pre-Columbian Art." Although most courses designed to fill these needs do not carry degree credit, they are useful and often exciting. Public continuing education programs also make a contribution in this area, including in many cities courses designed to help students pass the High School Equivalency examination.

For career training there are other options. The armed services have a wide variety of training programs, and in many cases the skills developed can easily be adapted to civilian jobs. Private industry has also recognized the need for career development. Some firms conduct their own training programs during work hours. Other firms use outside facilities, sometimes sending groups of employees to specially designed classes and at other times paying tuition for a single employee.

Technological growth and the acceleration of change in the United States indicate that it may well become quite usual for any individual to have three career changes in a lifetime, not just to another job, but to a different line of work. In addition, there is an obvious trend toward a shorter work week.

Fortunately the abundance of educational services and the many options available to fit them into an individual's life-style make the educational marketplace a most worthwhile place to shop.

MISCELLANEOUS SOURCES OF INFORMATION:

American Artists Reprints. *1973 American Artist Art School Directory,* 24 p., New York, N.Y., 1973.

American Association for Health, Physical Education and Recreation. *Dance Directory: Programs of Professional Preparation in American Colleges and Universities, 80 pages,* 1971; *Directory of Professional Preparation Programs in Recreation, Parks, and Related Areas,* 111 p., 1973; 1201 16th St., N.W., Washington, D.C. 20036.

Barron's Educational Series, Inc. *Barron's Guide to the Two-Year Colleges, Volumes 1 and 2;* Volume 1—304 p., 1974; Volume 2—112 p., 1975; Woodbury, N.Y.

Barron's Educational Series, Inc. *Barron's Profiles of American Colleges, Volumes 1 and 2;* Volume 1—1024 p., 1974; Volume 2—264 p., 1973; Woodbury, N.Y.

College Entrance Examination Board. *A Chance to Go to College: A Directory of 800 Colleges That Have Special Help for Students from Minorities and Low-Income Families.* 248 p., Princeton, N.J., 1971.

J. G. Ferguson Publishing Company. *Ferguson Guide to Two-Year College Programs for Technicians and Specialists,* 390 p., Chicago, Ill., 1971.

National Association of Broadcasters. *Radio-Television Programs in American Colleges and Universities,* 120 p., Washington, D.C., 1972.

National University Extension Association. *Guide to Independent Study Through Correspondence Instruction,* 40 p., Washington, D.C., 1973.

Office of Education, U.S. Department of Health, Education and Welfare. *Fact Sheet on Financial Assistance for Higher Education,* Washington, D.C. 20202.

READINGS ON ALTERNATIVES IN HIGHER EDUCATION:

Benoit, Richard P. *Alternative Programs for Higher Education: External and Special Degrees.* Intellect 101: 422–25, April 1973.

Boyer, Ernest L., and Keller, George C. *Big Move to Non-Campus Colleges,* Saturday Review 54: 46–49, 58: July 17, 1971.

Brooks, Dennis. *The First Year's Experience at the Open University,* College Management 7: 28–29; March 1972.

Innovations, Part III: Students Enroll in Without Walls U., College Management 6: 26, 28; October 1971.

Lichtman, Jane. *FUD: Free University Directory,* American Association for Higher Education, Room 780, One Dupont Circle, N.W., Washington, D.C. 20036, $1.50.

Gould, Samuel B., and Cross, K. Patricia, editors. *Explorations in Non-Traditional Study,* Jossey-Bass, Inc., San Francisco, Cal., 1972.

Lester, Richard I. *Britain's University of the Second Chance,* American Education 7: 7–11; August–September 1971.

London, Herbert. *University Without Walls: Reform or Rip-Off?* Saturday Review 55: 62–65; September 16, 1972.

Read, Gerald H. *Open University in Britain,* Phi Delta Kappan 53: 230–33; December 1971.

Smith, Peter J. *Britain's Open University: Everyman's Classroom,* Saturday Review 55: 40–50; April 29, 1972.

The Chronicle of Higher Education, Vol. VI, No. 10, November 29, 1971.

The Federal-State Food Programs—A Helping Hand

FOOD AND NUTRITION go together. America's outstanding agricultural production has created food supplies abundant enough to nourish all the American people. But not all Americans have access to—or, in some cases, the means to—acquire the foods needed for adequate nutrition. Federal-State food programs help correct this imbalance by providing school children and needy families the opportunity to obtain adequate food and therefore an improved nutritional status.

These food programs serve people in two primary ways—children in group situations, mainly in schools; and needy people, mainly in families. About 25 million children are eating lunches in schools, and 15 million persons are receiving the means to obtain adequate diets through the family program.

Following is a guide to the USDA's Food and Nutrition Service programs: how they work, whom they serve, and what you can do to help fight malnutrition in your community.

Federal-State food programs are national in scope, but local in orientation and application. Food assistance is provided to recipients through direct funding, technical assistance, nutritious foods and a dedicated cadre of Federal, State, and local workers—both paid and volunteer.

The goal of all child nutrition programs is to safeguard the health and well-being of the Nation's children. The programs provide Federal cash and donated-food assistance for meal service for children in group settings away from home.

Backbone of the programs for children is the National School Lunch Program. Since 1946, this program has made it possible for public and private nonprofit schools of high school grade and under throughout the Nation to serve wholesome low-cost lunches to children each school day. These lunches make an important contribution to the good nutrition so vital to children's mental and physical development.

Lunches served must contain specified minimum quantities (which may be adjusted based on age considerations) of milk, meat or meat alternates, vegetables and/or fruits, bread, and butter or margarine. This pattern was designed to meet about one-third of the National Research Council's recommended daily dietary allowances for boys and girls.

A second, newer and smaller program—the School Breakfast Program—is designed to help children who come to school hungry. A hungry child simply cannot stay alert and learn. The Breakfast Program can help children to be better students by providing them with nutritious breakfasts before the start of classes.

The program is important in improv-

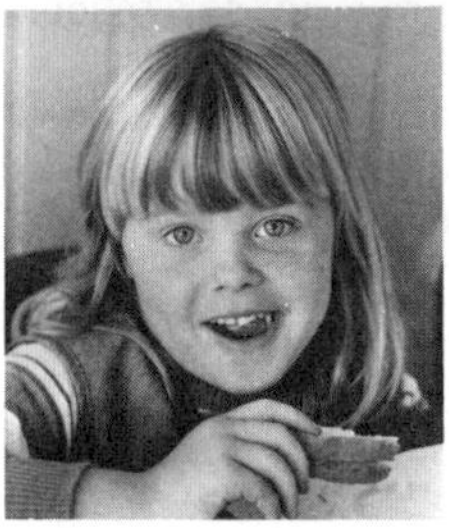

Top left and right, school lunch participants. Above, kids have school lunch in a one-room schoolhouse on a Louisiana island in the Mississippi river. Right, school breakfast program scene.

ing the nutrition and dietary practices of children eating breakfast at school. A school must meet certain standards in its breakfasts; these must include fruit or juice, milk, bread or cereal, with a meat or meat alternate served as often as possible.

Additional Federal assistance is provided to help schools reach needy children through the School Lunch and Breakfast Programs. Needy children must be served meals *free* when their family's income falls below minimum national income eligibility standards. States and local schools may set more liberal eligibility standards for free meals, up to certain limits; and even higher limits for reduced-price meals, if they choose to offer meals at reduced prices.

Local officials determine (from parents' signed statements of family size and income) which children in schools are eligible for free or reduced-price meals. These children then receive the meals at a reduced cost or at no cost to them, with the Federal Government providing additional cash reimbursement to the schools for each lunch or breakfast served a needy child.

The Special Milk Program encourages children to drink more milk by reimbursing schools, child-care centers, and camps for part of the cost of the milk over and above the milk served as part of other child nutrition programs. These payments made by the Federal Government make it possible for schools and child-care institutions to provide additional milk for children at a reduced cost.

AUTHOR *Orval Kerchner* is Assistant Deputy Administrator, Food and Nutrition Service.

The Special Food Service Program for children offers Federal help to States and local communities to assist in improving the nutritional status of both preschool and school age children. It is available to public and nonprofit private institutions providing nonresidential care to children from low income areas and areas with many working mothers, and also to handicapped children.

It operates in two phases: A year-round program in child-care centers, primarily for preschool children; and a Special Summer Program in recreation activities in parks, playgrounds and recreation centers primarily for school-age children.

Meals served under the Special Food Service Program may include breakfast, a lunch or supper, or between-meal snacks—which might include a milk, fruit or vegetable juice, and bread or cereal. All meals must meet certain minimum nutritional standards.

Child nutrition programs are now available to about 85 percent of the Nation's school children. In an effort endorsed by the National Advisory Council on Child Nutrition, the U.S. Department of Agriculture and the States are working toward the goal of making food service programs available in all schools.

Some schools which offer food service choose not to participate in these Federal-State programs. Others do not offer food service at all for various reasons —such as local attitudes, a belief children should go home for lunch, and so forth.

In some areas, local resources are not available to equip the schools for food service. In such cases, the nonfood assistance program is available to provide cash grants for acquiring equipment to schools which need help to equip a kitchen.

Federal nonfood assistance funds help schools and service institutions in needy areas that have no equipment or inadequate equipment. Half the yearly funds are reserved for schools with no food programs.

Primary source of food assistance to individual needy families and households is the Food Stamp Program, which is now mandated by law to operate on a nationwide basis. Through this program, households with limited means to buy food receive enough additional purchasing power to enable them to obtain nutritionally adequate diets by shopping in retail food stores.

To receive food coupons, a household must meet national uniform standards of eligibility based on income and resources. They must also comply with a work registration requirement.

Eligible households pay a certain amount, called a "purchase requirement," in return for a larger amount of food coupons, known as a "coupon allotment." The amount a household pays for its coupons is based on its size and net income, and may not exceed 30 percent of the household's net income.

Households with net income less than $30 a month receive their coupons free.

The coupon allotment a household receives is based on the cost of a nutritionally adequate diet for the size of the household. Allotments are adjusted every six months according to changes in the price of food. In July, 1974, a four-person household received $150 in coupons each month.

This difference between a household's purchase requirement and the coupon allotment it receives represents "bonus coupons." And that's the food purchasing power the household otherwise would not have enjoyed.

The Food Stamp Program is administered cooperatively by the Federal and State Governments. States accept the responsibility for certifying people as eligible to participate in the program, and for issuing coupons.

To apply for participation in the program, a person should contact his local welfare office which will determine whether the household's income and resources meet the national uniform standards of eligibility.

An applicant for the program must, therefore, give certain financial information to the welfare office. For example, he must report all income received by each member of his household. This

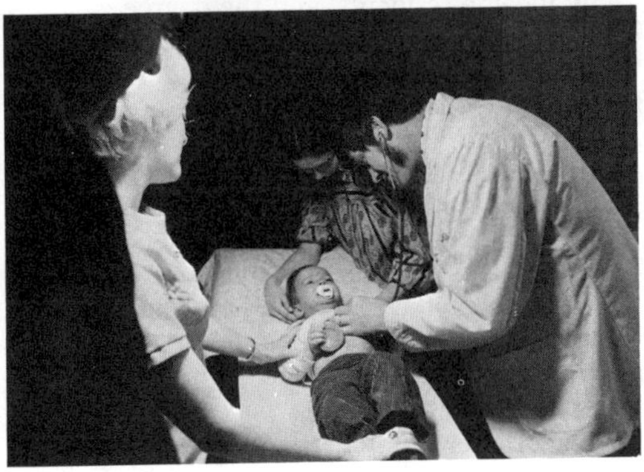

Top above, mother and child are certified for WIC program. Above, child receives medical evaluation. Right, the mother gets nutritional advice on her first trip to the supermarket under the program.

includes income from salary, self-employment, social security payments, welfare assistance and income from any other source.

The person must also tell the welfare office about any resources such as bank accounts which household members have, and must answer questions about certain expenses.

The welfare office will then calculate the household's net income by subtracting certain "deductible" expenses from the household's total countable income.

"Deductible" expenses include items such as taxes, union dues, certain educational and medical expenses, shelter costs which are determined to be excessive, and a number of other expenses which reduce the household's ability to meet normal expenses of daily living.

Besides meeting resource and income eligibility standards, most households must have cooking facilities, and most able-bodied adults between the ages of 18 and 65 must register for employment.

If an applicant does not agree with the determination of the welfare office concerning eligibility or the purchase requirement which the household is required to pay, he may request a review of the determination. Such a review is called a "fair hearing."

If a household qualifies for the program, it will receive a card authorizing it to purchase coupons, which are sold by various agents, such as banks, post offices, or offices set up to issue coupons.

Coupons are issued at least twice each month and each household has the option of purchasing its full monthly allotment or a quarter, a half, or three-quarters of the allotment.

Food stamp recipients may take their coupons to retail food stores authorized by the Federal Government to participate in the program, and purchase any food for home consumption. They may also use coupons to purchase garden seeds or plants intended to produce food for the personal consumption of the household.

Food coupons may not be used to buy nonfood items or tobacco or alcoholic beverages.

Coupons accepted by retail food stores are redeemed through authorized wholesalers or banks.

The Food Stamp law also provides for a number of special uses of coupons to meet particular needs of the elderly, drug addicts and alcoholics, and certain Alaskans.

Specifically, elderly persons who meet the income and resource eligibility standards may receive and use coupons to purchase communally-served meals; or, if the recipients are disabled, to purchase home delivered meals from authorized meal services.

Drug addicts and alcoholics who are regularly participating in rehabilitation programs may receive and use coupons to purchase meals served by authorized meal services.

Persons living in remote areas of Alaska may use coupons to purchase hunting and fishing equipment for use in procuring food.

The Agriculture Department is conducting an evaluation of a feeding program for specific vulnerable groups. This Special Supplemental Food Program for Women, Infants and Children (WIC) is designed to reach pregnant women and women who are nursing, and infants and children under 4 years of age.

Persons in this group are eligible for the WIC Program if they reside in an approved project area, are eligible for free or reduced-price medical care, and are determined by a competent professional in the local agency to need supplemental foods.

Participants in the WIC Program receive food assistance from designated local agencies. These local agencies may directly dispense food, or issue vouchers redeemable for food at local grocery stores.

The food package for infants provides iron-fortified infant formula, infant cereal fortified with iron, and fruit juice.

The package for children and pregnant or lactating women provides whole fluid milk, cereal with iron fortification, fruit or vegetable juice and eggs. Evaporated milk, skim or low fat milk, or nonfat dry milk or cheese may be substituted for the whole fluid milk.

This program operates through the State Health Department, the Indian Health Service Area office, or Indian tribes. The State agency, through grants from the Department of Agriculture, then supervises local agencies providing health care to the target population.

Local health agencies submit applications to take part in the program. These applications are reviewed to determine the type of medical facilities and staffing available, the percentage of low income residents, and the degree of "nutritional risk" in the project area.

Nutritional risk data include incidence of nutritional anemia, premature births, infant mortality, and other health indicators.

The roles for volunteers are as many and varied as the food programs, but "outreach" is one important area where volunteers serve a real function. Outreach is needed to increase participation in the programs and to make everyone aware of the importance of good nutrition, not only with regard to food assistance programs but also in terms of the well-being of all Americans.

Making door-to-door canvasses in low-income neighborhoods, conducting meetings for interested groups, generating community support for school food service programs, preparing posters, operating information booths, and encouraging nutrition education are some of the ways to carry on outreach efforts.

Direct help—such as providing transportation, baby-sitting, clerical assistance in certification offices, or assistance in school cafeterias—is another way that volunteers can help. Other volunteer activities include monetary support, educational programs, and promoting community understanding of programs.

Towns, cities, counties and public and private nonprofit schools interested in participating in the food programs should contact their State Department of Public Welfare for the Food Stamp Program, or their State Department of Education for the Child Nutrition Programs.

Inquiries to the U.S. Department of Agriculture about the food programs should be directed to the Food and Nutrition Service in Washington, or to any of its local or Regional Offices.

Toward a Network Of Services for Older Americans

IF YOU ARE one of the 30 million people 60 or older, you could expect to need some kind of service at one time or another and not be able to find it, at least at a price you could afford. Even if you are younger, you may know someone who has had it happen.

But last year the Administration on Aging, a Federal agency created to help older people, began to spearhead an effort to change this situation.

Under its direction, State agencies on aging in every State are establishing sub-State agencies. These area agencies on aging are charged with planning for a full range of services to meet the needs of older Americans in the areas for which they are responsible. They will tap local resources and, where necessary, use Older Americans Act funds to expand existing services or fill gaps in the service network.

Each agency is charged with seeing that information on services is available to all older persons in its area and that they are referred to services to meet their needs. There will also be efforts to find the older people who need services (outreach efforts) and who do not know about them, and special transportation to help them get to services.

As yet not every area in the country has an area agency on aging or an information and referral service. A total of about 600 area agencies are needed to cover all of the 50 States, the District of Columbia, Puerto Rico, the Virgin Islands, and Guam. But areas where large numbers of older people live were the first to be covered, and they will be the first in which service networks will operate.

Initial emphasis in creating these networks is on services to help older people stay in their own homes and out of institutions.

Institutions are necessary for people who are really sick. But some authorities estimate that almost a third of the older people now in nursing homes, for example, need never have entered them if home health care, homemaker services, home-delivered meals, and transportation had been available to them.

As it is, only about 5 percent of the people 65 and over are in institutions, at any one time.

Under current legislation, the following services are among those that can be funded in an area:

-Counseling to help older Americans use health and social services and cope with personal problems
-Health screening and evaluation
-Friendly visiting to those who are socially and geographically isolated
-Telephone reassurance to determine if older individuals who live alone are safe and well
-Protective services to assist older people who are no longer able to manage their own affairs
-Assistance to help them obtain adequate housing or improve their present living arrangements
-Services to provide employment information to older persons
-Legal services
-Recreation and continuing education

One of the most important preventive health measures—nutrition—is being provided through the Nutrition Program for the Elderly, administered by AoA under a separate title of the Older Americans Act. Nutrition projects

---

AUTHOR *Olivia W. Coulter*, Chief of the Public Information Staff, Administration on Aging, was Editor of the periodical *Aging* for 11 years.

funded under this program are among the resources which area agencies on aging will use in creating their service networks.

A nutrition project serves a nutritious hot meal once a day five days a week to groups of older people, usually at several sites.

Many of the projects also provide home-delivered meals, but their major aim is to get older people out and into a social setting where they can enjoy the companionship of others and where they can receive some of the services they may need. For this reason, meal sites are chosen which will be as accessible as possible to a number of older people, although transportation may also be provided for those who need it.

People 60 years of age or older and their spouses are eligible for the meals. There is no charge and no means test for participants, but people may pay what they feel they can afford if they wish. The law requires that each State's nutrition projects serve minority persons in proportion to their numbers in the State.

The U.S. Department of Agriculture's food assistance programs can also help supplement the food-buying power of older people with limited budgets. Those receiving Supplementary Security Income from the Social Security Administration can qualify in most States for the Food Stamp Program administered by the U.S. Department of Agriculture through local welfare departments. USDA donated foods are also available to senior centers and other non-profit groups for meal programs.

Thus, even if your community does not yet have an area agency on aging, it may provide a number of services to help you. State agencies on aging are using a percentage of their allotments under the Older Americans Act to fund projects for older people in areas without area agencies. In addition, other Federal, State, and private agencies also are providing services.

There are more than 2,000 senior centers in the United States, some of them originally funded under the Older

Volunteers assist in service programs.

Americans Act, and many centers provide services such as information, referral, and counseling or assistance in finding employment, as well as companionship, recreation, and continuing education.

Welfare departments make services available to Supplemental Security Income recipients or those who could become recipients in the future. They also administer the Medicaid Program to help the medically needy.

The U.S. Department of Labor has funded a number of projects which provide employment for older low-income people. Congress appropriated $10 million in January 1974 for an Older American Community Service Program designed to convert these projects into permanent, ongoing national programs.

Labor's Senior Aides Program, administered by the National Council of Senior Citizens, offers part-time employment in community service agencies in 33 urban and rural areas.

The Senior Community Service Project, conducted by the National Council on the Aging, employs older people to work part-time in community services in 18 areas.

And the Senior Community Aides Program, sponsored by the National Retired Teachers Association and the American Association of Retired Persons, recruits, trains, and finds part-time work for older people in a variety of semi-skilled and unskilled jobs in 31 cities.

The U.S. Department of Agriculture's Forest Service offers part-time employment in conservation and beautification projects in 21 States.

The National Farmers Union operates the Green Thumb Program, funded by the Department of Labor, in 24 States. It provides part-time employment to workers with rural or farming backgrounds in conservation, beautification, and community improvement projects or in existing community service agencies providing outreach services to aid the aged, handicapped, and shut-ins.

The Foster Grandparent Program, administered by the Federal ACTION agency, employs about 10,500 older people working part-time and providing love and companionship to disadvantaged children. Eventually a new ACTION program—Senior Companions—may employ as many to help adults, including the elderly.

Older people also serve in ACTION's Peace Corps and Volunteers in Service to America (VISTA), and as part-time interviewers for the Bureau of the Census.

The Veterans Administration has been using older volunteers in its hospitals for many years.

ACTION also operates two large programs using the services of older volunteers. Under the Retired Senior

Volunteer Program (RSVP), which pays out-of-pocket expenses, nearly 100,000 older people are serving in a great variety of community service programs.

Between 4,500 and 5,000 retired executives enrolled in the Senior Corps of Retired Executives (SCORE) are helping owners or managers of small business and community organizations in need of management counseling. On request, they also may be paid out-of-pocket expenses.

Last year when Project SSI Alert was conducted to find people eligible for the Supplemental Security Income Program, groups called consortia—composed of members of national organizations of older people—were instrumental in seeking out older people and establishing their eligibility.

These older members of national organizations and other older Americans like them are increasingly making an outstanding contribution to their peers and to their country. Half the members of the advisory committees to State and area agencies on aging which are establishing policies on service networks are older Americans. And, under the law, older people who apply to work in AoA's nutrition projects are considered for jobs before other applicants.

With the limited number of service personnel now available, this Nation cannot afford to put its older people on the shelf. And one of the things older people often need is a sense of involvement in community life . . . a legitimate role to play in society. For many, the best role of all consists of helping people, whether it is other older people, younger people, or the whole community.

If you or someone you know needs a service or wants to help in a program, contact your area agency on aging or its information and referral service. If you cannot find these listed in your local telephone directory, write to your State agency on aging in the State capital or to the Administration on Aging, Office of Human Development, U.S. Department of Health, Education, and Welfare, Washington, D.C. 20201.

Shopping for Credit Can Save You Cash

You shop for credit the way you shop for anything else. It's best to shop at more than one place. And it's best to know what to look for. A typical household with a good credit rating can save enough for an annual vacation by shopping for the money it "rents" in order to buy now and pay later.

Here are some pointers to help you shop for money for installment buying through contracts and through credit cards and other kinds of revolving charge plans. This chapter will not deal with financing a home or other real property.

Compare Costs

Credit can cost you pennies or dollars. It depends on your character, your capital and your capability to repay, the money market, and other economic factors.

Two choices you frequently have are closed-end and revolving transactions. Under the closed-end plans you ordinarily sign a promissory note, if you are borrowing cash, or a retail installment contract, if you are using sales credit. You agree in advance on the specific amount to borrow, the number and size of weekly or monthly payments, and a due date.

On the other hand, the revolving charge plan is open-ended. A top limit is agreed upon, but purchases are added as they are made and finance charges are figured on the unpaid balance each month.

A monthly interest rate is quoted—usually 1 or 1½ percent a month, which is a 12 or 18 annual percentage rate.

Revolving charge comes in many forms. There are credit cards from stores, gas and other companies for charging at company branches. Bank credit cards and those issued by travel and entertainment groups allow you to arrange a line of credit and to charge at many participating retailers, or even to borrow cash.

Banks and some credit unions also offer books of special checks or drafts indicating preapproved loans. As you spend the redi-checks or drafts, interest begins. A check credit plan at some banks allows you to overdraw your checking account and pay interest on the overdrawn amount.

What you pay for credit depends a good deal on whether you use closed-end or revolving charge plans and where you arrange for them. In buying a car, for instance, what you would pay for the use of $2,000 for two years might vary from $127 to $684, which is from a 4 (available on some insurance loans) to a 30 annual percentage rate, depending on where you financed it and the plan you used.

The kind of security the lender or dealer requires from you also affects the cost. Sometimes the word collateral is used instead of security. Both words mean "something having money value." The more security you can offer, the lower the cost of credit as a general rule. A cosigner or comaker may lower the cost for you.

Annual percentage rate, which is the unit pricing of money, is the key to cutting your cost of credit. It's a rather new approach made possible by the Truth in Lending law, officially titled the Federal Consumer Credit Protection Act of 1969. Here is how you use the annual percentage rate approach in shopping for closed-end credit.

All merchants and lenders are required under the Truth in Lending law to show the unit price for money on all consumer credit contracts. They do this by stating the cost in terms of the *Annual Percentage Rate*, the cost of buying an item or service on time, expressed as a percentage figured on the unpaid balance.

Just as consumer sense has taught you to shop for the lowest cost per pound on grocery items, economy dictates that you shop for money by looking for the lowest annual percentage rate.

Here's how it works in closed-end credit shopping. Often each lender you approach offers you a different loan amount, for a different time period, with a different sized payment.

For his special package, he works out the finance charge. This is the dollar cost including interest and other charges for extending the credit. He converts the finance charge into the annual percentage rate he can offer for his transaction.

You can quickly tell which deal offers you the most credit for the money. It's the one with the lowest annual percentage rate. Meanwhile you compare total dollar cost through the finance charge.

On the telephone, and across the desk, be sure to ask the lender specifically for "annual percentage rate." Some lenders might make loan rates sound lower by quoting some other rate.

With regard to revolving charge, you simply look for the lowest annual percentage rate to compare cost. To save the most when using revolving credit, join the one-third of all consumers who pay within the 25 or 30 days allowed without any finance charges. This gives you the convenience at the same cost as paying cash.

It helps if you have a general image of where you can "rent" money the cheapest.

The following table of maximum rates allowed in the State of California in 1974 should help you formulate such an image. It was developed by Constance Burgess, Extension Consumer Education Specialist with the University of California. Remember that state laws vary and lenders do not always charge the maximum.

You may have other borrowing options. Does your life insurance policy have a loan clause? If you have paid-up insurance, can you risk short-changing

---

AUTHORS *Jeannette M. Lynch* and *Eleanor M. Kelly* are Consumer Education Specialists, Division of Consumer Education, Federal Trade Commission.

MAXIMUM CREDIT CHARGES ALLOWED IN CALIFORNIA

1. Credit Charged for a Year, Figured on the Starting Balance. Repaid in Monthly Installments.

Type and Source of Credit	Annual Percentage Rate
• Retail Installment Sales	
First $1,000	18.0%
Over $1,000	14.5%
• Auto Installment Sales	21.5%
• Bank Loans (rate varies with bank)	
Typical unsecured loan	18.0%
Typical secured loan	10.9%

2. Credit Charged Per Month, Figured on the Reduced Balance Owed. Repaid in Monthly Installments.

• Retail Credit	
Revolving Accounts	
First $1,000	18%
Over $1,000	12%
• Cash Loans	
Credit Unions:	
Unsecured	12%
Secured by new auto	10%
Secured by Credit Union shares (Debt often secured by life insurance at no extra cost.)	9%
Savings & Loan. Secured by pass book. Rate established by the association—usually 1% above current interest rate on savings.	
Finance Companies:	
Personal property brokers	
First $200	30%
$200 to $500	24%
$500 to $1,500	18%
$1,500 to $10,000	12%
Industrial loan companies	
First $700	24%
$700 to $10,000	12%
Small loan companies	
First $100	30%
$100 to $300	24%
Pawnbrokers	
Small loans, up to 90 days	160–240%
$200 to $5,000	30–12%

your protection? If so some insurance loans run at a 4 to 6 percent annual rate.

Another option might be borrowing on passbook savings you have at a savings and loan association.

Compare Other Terms

There are things to consider other than cost in shopping for closed-end credit. When you buy on credit you make many promises. If you cannot meet your payments, you may have to give back the merchandise, pay damages, and continue to make the payments you owe. And you may even have to forfeit personal belongings right down to your silverware.

Closed-end contracts vary a good deal from one lender to another.

Let's say you want to buy a $300 stereo. You've found just the right one. You know that you do not have to finance it through the dealer and that closed-end credit may be less expensive than letting the salesperson charge it on your revolving account or your bank credit card.

You must know the size of payment each week or month which you can handle without risking disaster.

Let's say that you have talked to three lenders and found the deal with the lowest annual percentage rate. But the payment was too high, so you have just about decided to borrow so that you can pay less each time by stretching out the payments for a longer period. You recognize that credit will cost you more this way, but there is less risk that you will be unable to meet the payments.

Before you sign the contract it's important to weigh the other risks.

This **checklist** should help you:

__________*Downpayment*

A larger downpayment can help you cut the cost of the credit. Beware of borrowing the downpayment from a second lender. This means two payments instead of one.

______ *Size of payments*

Are they all the same? Watch out for a larger final payment or "balloon clause." Even if you make all but the balloon payment you may lose everything.

______ *Your home as a security*

Is it included? If so the seller should give you a cancellation form. The Truth in Lending law allows you three days to change your mind and rescind.

______ *Repayment in advance*

Is there any refund of the finance charge?

______ *Missing a payment*

What happens? Penalty charges? Entire debt due? Immediately?

______ *Default*

What if you just can't pay—and you have to default? Collection charges? Storage or court costs? Can you reclaim the item? If it's sold but doesn't cover your debt, must you pay the difference?

______ *Faulty work or merchandise*

Is there a time limit for your complaints? To whom should you complain? Your installment contract probably will be sold to another company. Will the new creditor stand behind your purchase?

______ *Moving the merchandise*

Can you remove it from the state?

______ *Insurance*

Is it involved? On the item? On you, to assume full payment of the debt in case of accident, illness, death? Who collects? Can you get cheaper coverage from your own insurance company?

______ *Waiving your rights*

Must you sign away other rights? Avoid signing a statement that work has been completed or an item received when it hasn't been.

______ *Add-on contract*

Think twice before you add an item to a contract you already have with a store. A missed payment can mean you lose all the items even though you've paid for the first ones.

If there are contract terms you do not want, ask the lender to strike them out. If he agrees, you and he both must initial the modifications on his copy and on yours. It's only the written agreement that counts, not oral promises.

If you cannot understand the contract, ask for a blank copy. Compare terms other than cost, and discuss it with a friend who can help you. But avoid signing any statement or contract that is not completely filled out. Such action allows the lender to fill in amounts and terms that you did not agree to in conversation.

The checklist is useful primarily for closed-end credit but can be used for revolving plans. Here are more pointers on revolving credit.

Notice how much you are paying each month. Total all the *finance charges* from your bills for a typical month. Multiply by 12 for the yearly cost. Is the credit worth it?

When amounts outstanding become sizable, would you do better to pay them off by arranging a closed-end credit deal? Or by arranging a less expensive revolving plan? Some credit unions offer annual percentage rates lower than 18 percent on their "draft" preapproved loans. Some banks offer less than 18 percent on their check credit plans.

In considering which system might be less costly, keep in mind these variations among revolving plans: Some require an initial or annual fee. Some do not. Some allow more time than others between date of purchase and due date. And some have a way of figuring the finance charge so that their credit costs you less than others.

A word about revolving charge arrangements with the door-to-door salesman. If you make a small weekly payment and add items from time to time, ask the salesman what annual percentage rate he charges. Even if he says "None," remember that the price tags have to be high enough to cover the cost of the credit. You may save by using department store or bank credit. Have you tried to get it?

It's important to take advantage of your credit worthiness. What you pay for credit, to a considerable degree, depends on the image the lender has of you as a credit risk. Occasionally his image is inaccurate because a credit reporting agency has no report on you or has an inaccurate one.

What is your image of yourself? Have you met past payments? Are you honest? Reliable? Willing to pay? Are you able to pay? What is your financial future? Is your paycheck completely uncommitted?

If you have been refused credit, you have the right under the Fair Credit Reporting Act of 1971 to learn from the credit reporting agency what is in your file, at little or no cost.

If you've never used credit before, you might arrange a small loan at a bank and pay it off to establish a credit rating.

In using credit and in shopping for money the skill lies in understanding your needs and wants, and balancing them against the cost and the risks involved in having things now and paying later.

FOR FURTHER READING:

Burgess, Constance. *Maximum Credit Charges Allowed in California, Credit Do's and Don'ts,* Cooperative Extension, University of California, Berkeley, Cal., 1973.

Federal Trade Commission. *Teaching How to Use Truth in Lending* and *A Money Saving Offer,* 6th St. and Pennsylvania Ave. N.W., Washington, D.C. 20580.

Household Finance Corporation. *It's Your Credit—Manage it Wisely,* Money Management Institute, Prudential Plaza, Chicago, Ill. 60601, 1970.

National Foundation for Consumer Credit. *Using Our Credit Intelligently,* 1819 H St. N.W., Washington, D.C. 20006, 1970.

Having Appliances Repaired for a Minimum Cost

American families own an average of five major appliances and many small appliances. We depend on our appliances, and when one fails to perform its task, our routine schedules are upset and we are unhappy. We want the appliance repaired quickly and at minimum cost.

Simple repairs can be done at home by the handyman or woman, but many of our appliances now are so complex that special skills and tools are needed to repair them.

Appliance failures fall into two categories: the appliance does not function, or it functions but the results are not satisfactory.

If an oven does not heat, a washer does not agitate, or a refrigerator motor does not run, it is obvious that the appliance is not working, and it is relatively easy to describe the observed condition to the service technician.

On the other hand, if the complaint is that the cake is not baked properly, that the clothes are not getting clean, or that fresh vegetables sometimes freeze in a refrigerator, it may be much more difficult to pinpoint the problem.

Improper performance of an appliance can be detected by comparison with its past performance, the performance of other similar appliances, or expectations based on statements in the manufacturer's literature including the use and care manual.

Before calling for service, consult the instruction manual to make sure you are using the appliance properly and check the instructions for additional suggestions to avoid an unnecessary service call. Finally, if you cannot correct the situation yourself, contact a service agency.

If the appliance is still under warranty, call the dealer or the servicing agency recommended by the dealer. If the warranty has expired, you may have more choices for repair service.

When requesting service, report the type of appliance, brand name and model number. Sometimes the serial number also is needed. Describe the problem as accurately as possible. The call taker may ask for additional information to identify the problem more precisely.

After describing the problem, seek information on the cost of the repair, whether the bill must be paid at the time of service or can be charged, and the time that the service can be performed.

Some service agencies base their service charge on actual time spent. The time may include that required to travel to the consumer's home, make the diagnosis, repair the appliance, and instruct the consumer in proper use of the appliance.

Other companies use job charges based on the average time required to accomplish a particular repair. When job charges are used, the consumer seems to be paying a high hourly rate for a fast worker but a low rate for a slow one.

A definite appointment should be made, if necessary, to be sure that some responsible person is at home when the service technician arrives. If it seems likely that replacement parts will be required, ask whether they are on hand. If they must be ordered, determine when they can be expected.

When a major appliance fails, the question of whether to repair or replace the appliance is often raised. Usually the decision depends, at least in part, on cost of the needed repair, present value of the appliance, and cost to replace the appliance. An older appliance, needing major repair, is likely to be replaced rather than repaired.

Many small appliances, such as irons and toasters, are replaced rather than repaired because of the low cost to replace compared to the repair cost.

To make a rational decision about repair or replacement, you must know the cost of the service before the service is attempted. Most reliable service agencies, after diagnosing the problem, can give accurate estimates of service costs.

Non-monetary considerations are also important. For example, if you want features not on the present appliance (a self-cleaning oven, a larger freezer section on a refrigerator-freezer), you may choose to replace rather than repair. Other considerations, such as plans for remodeling or a desire to keep an appliance you are familiar with, may also influence your decision.

If an accessory such as the clock on a range or the rotisserie in the oven stops working, you may decide that the feature is not worth the cost of repair. You may neither repair nor replace but continue to use the appliance without those features.

Appliances vary from simple devices that rarely need repair to highly complex ones that seem to need more frequent service. Because complex appliances depend on many parts to function, it is not surprising that they sometimes require service.

Heat producing appliances that are not temperature controlled and have no function other than heating are among the least complicated and require the least service. On temperature controlled devices such as ovens, thermostats sometimes need to be recalibrated and adjusted; less frequently thermostats may need to be replaced. Heating elements themselves rarely become defective or need to be replaced.

Oven users sometimes report that the oven does not heat. In many cases the problem is that the controls are set for automatic turn-on at a set time rather than manual turn-on. Pilot flames that have gone out cause service problems for gas ranges. Controls on self-cleaning

---

AUTHOR *Mary E. Purchase* is a Professor in the Department of Design and Environmental Analysis, New York State College of Human Ecology, Cornell University, Ithaca, N.Y.

ovens have also caused some service problems.

An important part of a refrigerator, freezer or air conditioner is the motor/compressor. When it stops running, the appliance no longer cools. If the refrigerant leaks out, the motor will run but insufficient or no cooling occurs.

Other parts that are most likely to require servicing include: The temperature regulator and the fan that cools the condenser on a refrigerator, freezer or air conditioner; timers and switches used in self-defrosting refrigerators; and fans used to circulate air within a frost-free refrigerator or freezer. In addition, gaskets on refrigerators and freezers deteriorate over time and must be replaced.

Automatic washers probably have a higher frequency of repair than any other major appliance. This is because of the complexity of the appliance and the high humidity to which the functioning parts are exposed.

Parts most likely to require service include the timer that controls cycling of the washer, the pump for circulating water and emptying the washer, the transmission, and the motor.

Practically all new appliances are covered by a warranty or guarantee when they are sold. In common use the words warranty and guarantee mean the same, but warranty is becoming the preferred word.

The warranty is the manufacturer's promise. It protects you from the risk of defective materials and workmanship, but it is not a promise that appliance parts will not wear out.

Because the warranty is part of the sales agreement, its value is included in the price of the appliance. To be binding, warranties must be in writing; oral commitments have no legal standing. Be sure to read and understand the warranty before buying the appliance.

Warranties differ in their coverage with regard to the length of time that the warranty is in force, and the parts and/or labor covered. A common length of time for a warranty is one year from time of purchase, but the warranty may be for a longer or a shorter time.

Cleaning and adjusting a blender.

Some warranties cover the entire appliance for one period of time and cover selected parts—such as the transmission in a washer or the sealed refrigeration system in a refrigerator—for a longer time. For replacement of some parts, such as the tank in a water heater, you may be required to pay a prorated fee that increases with the age of the appliance.

Many appliance warranties cover parts; warranties may also cover service labor. Parts and labor may not be covered for the same length of time.

When labor is covered, the manufacturer may reimburse the servicing agency, or the dealer may be responsible for cost of the labor. When service labor is the responsibility of the dealer and you move out of the dealer's locality, you may be required to pay for service from another agency.

Even though parts and labor may be covered in a warranty, travel costs to reach your home or shipping charges for the parts may not be.

For protection after the warranty expires, a service contract can be purchased. A service contract, like health insurance, is most worthwhile when there is a chance of a large expense. It is useful also because it spreads the cost of repairs over many consumers and allows you to budget for repairs. Furthermore, if your past experience indicates that your appliances need frequent servicing, a service contract may save you money.

The extent of coverage differs from one contract to another. For example, the contract might cover parts, labor, and travel to the home, or it might cover parts only.

Some contracts do not cover nuisance calls (to plug in the appliance) or calls for education only. Other contracts might have a minimum fixed fee for each service call, beyond which the contract covers the costs; this would be similar to auto insurance with a deductible clause.

You can expect cost of the contract to vary with extent of the coverage.

Service contracts may be available at any point in the appliance's life. Because the chance that service may be required is likely to increase with the age of the appliance, the cost of service contracts may also increase with its age.

Only relatively large dealers or dealers with strong connections with the manufacturer are likely to be able to offer service contracts. Beware of contracts with dealers who might go out of business before the contract expires.

Consumers frequently complain about the cost of servicing appliances. The repair bill may be broken down to show details of the charges, or the cost of parts may be separated out and all other charges combined into a labor charge.

Sometimes consumers assume that the entire charge for labor goes to the serviceman. In reality the labor charge must cover not only the cost of the serviceman's time in the home but also his travel time, the expenses of the truck, the inventory of parts, training the serviceman, and maintaining the office. To cover all costs, the charge for the serviceman's time should be two and a half to three times the wages paid to the repairman.

Although most servicing is done well and charges are fair, sometimes consumers are not satisfied with results of repair work or with the charges. If dissatisfied, you may choose one of many ways to handle your complaint.

First, discuss the problem with the servicing agency. Describe the complaint fully but in as concise a way as possible. If you cannot resolve the problem locally, write to the manufacturer giving details of the service problem and all other information needed to understand the complaint.

If you choose to handle your complaint locally, contact your Better Business Bureau.

If you feel that a law suit against the servicing agency is in order, check on use of small claims court. Such courts have been established in many states. A small fee is required to register your case but a lawyer is not needed.

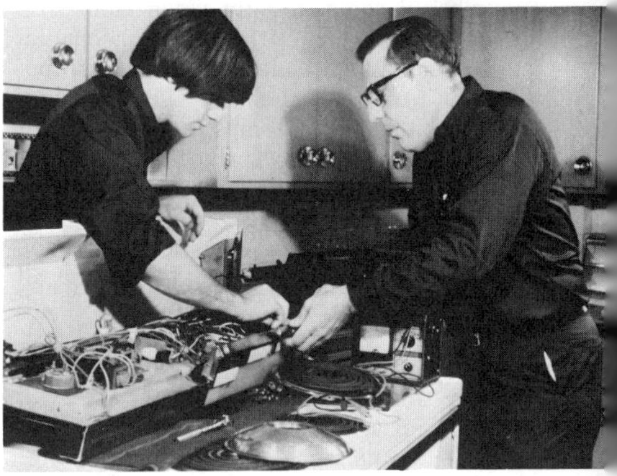

Complaints may also be registered with the Federal Trade Commission and the President's Office of Consumer Affairs.

The appliance industry has established a mechanism for handling complaints about major appliances. If you have reported your problem to the manufacturer and are not satisfied with the action, write to the Major Appliance Consumer Action Panel (MACAP), 20 N. Wacker Drive, Chicago, Ill. 60606. Report details of the problem, including actions previously taken. MACAP will study the problem and recommend a solution. More than 90 percent of the complaints handled by MACAP have been resolved to the consumer's satisfaction.

Servicing Your Car Without Anguish

UNTIL America puts an end to the energy crunch, the nation's private car owners will find the problems of owning an automobile compounded by rising gasoline prices, uncertainties of fuel availability, and attendant motoring inconveniences. All this means that today's driver has more reason than ever to get the most for his dollar when it comes to auto repair work.

The vast majority of auto mechanics are honest and most are fairly competent. Still, tales of shoddy workmanship, exorbitant service bills, and downright fraud continue to surface.

On the plus side, though, is the fact that the 1970s have also brought more opportunities than ever before for the car owner to be better informed on all aspects of vehicle ownership.

This happy turn of events makes it far easier for the average person to follow the two unalterable rules that will get him a lot farther down the road to safe, economical and carefree driving: Proper vehicle maintenance and the selection of an expert and reputable serviceman. That old analogy about personal well-being—preventive medicine in the form of good health habits, and choosing the right doctor—prevails as strongly as ever.

The importance of regular inspection and routine maintenance for your car can't be stressed enough. And the "bible" for this vital task is your owners manual. It contains service recommendations designed for your particular model of car.

Read your owners manual thoroughly if you haven't yet, and keep it handy in your car's glove compartment. Always follow it to the letter on such matters as tune-up specifications, recommended tire pressure, correct motor oil, and so forth.

To avoid costly repairs, have a maintenance inspection made periodically. Persons who drive an average of 10,000 miles a year should check the following items at the beginning of each month when the first tank of gasoline is purchased:

- All lights (for burned out bulbs)
- Oil level in crankcase
- Transmission fluid
- Battery electrolyte condition, level, and cleanliness of terminals
- Brake pedal to be sure of firmness and high pedal
- Level of brake fluid in master cylinder
- Windshield washer fluid level; condition of wipers
- Water level in radiator
- Fluid level in power steering
- Air filter cleanliness
- Condition and strength of coolant
- Condition of tires (cuts, imbedded foreign articles)
- Tire tread depth and pressure
- Condition of hoses and belts

Most of these items can be checked visually. Others require simple tools.

In addition to the above list, the following tasks should be performed every spring and fall: Engine tune-up, tire rotation, and a check of anti-freeze and shock absorbers.

While all these maintenance checks are vital, never leave inspection of a vehicle's electrical system to the last.

Also, the "safety belt starter interlock" system on late model cars makes it impossible to start the engine unless front seat occupants are belted in when they are seated. While the safety value of such combination lap and shoulder belts has been clearly demonstrated, some motorists will be tempted to tamper with the interlock system.

This practice could lead to unnecessary repair bills, since it threatens damage to other parts of the car's electrical system, to which it is linked.

When you are looking for the right service station, don't let your fingers do the shopping! Instead, get the names of three or four facilities from friends

---

AUTHOR *Bonnie Aikman* is news editor in the Public Relations Department of the American Automobile Association, with headquarters at Falls Church, Va.

who already patronize them. Then do some comparison shopping. Once you've found a reliable service station facility, continue to patronize it.

It's generally a good rule of thumb to take your car to a dealer that services your make of car, since his mechanics will be skilled on how to handle any problems that may occur. Many service stations do, however, perform the same range of repairs that dealer outlets do, except of course for warranty work.

For major engine overhauls and automatic transmission repairs, you will probably need to take your car to a locally owned independent garage or repair shop that specializes in either job, or to a dealer who services your make of car.

The serviceman who works on your car must have a high level of competency too. With creation of the new National Institute for Automotive Service Excellence, there are promising signs on this front.

Through this non-profit, independent organization, any mechanic in the country can volunteer for a series of tests on automotive diagnosis and repair.

If a mechanic passes one or more of these tests, he is awarded a special certificate and can be identified by an orange and blue shoulder patch. As of January, 1974, some 26,000 mechanics had been certified, and the Institute feels the numbers will increase measurably as the tests continue.

A directory of employers of certified mechanics was scheduled to be published in 1974. Car owners who would like a copy (a nominal fee will be charged) should write to the Institute at 1825 K Street N.W., Washington, D.C. 20006.

To lessen the threat of faulty repair work or repair frauds, there are a number of constructive steps you can take. While these measures can't offer full protection, they are wise insurance against dented pocketbooks and time schedules.

First, never wait until a small problem becomes a big and costly one. Always take your car in for a check at the first sign of trouble.

But before you take the car in, make a list of all problems and "symptoms" so you will be prepared to describe the nature of the trouble as accurately and specifically as possible.

Don't just ask to have the car put in "working order." That kind of general statement can lead directly to unnecessary work. But do avoid trying to explain in detail exactly what *you* think should be done.

On your initial visit, make certain you get a copy of the work authorization that you sign, or a general estimate of the total cost of the repairs. Don't leave until you do.

Ask the repair garage to telephone you when the exact work to be done is determined. When you receive the call, say you now want to return to the station to obtain another work order itemizing the cost of each repair to be made.

Usually, a good garage will have no objection to this. If you are told that expensive repair work is needed, get confirmation from a second garage.

You also might consider taking the car to a diagnostic center. Generally, such a step is a worthwhile precaution. Fees charged by diagnostic centers are fairly low, ranging from $6 to $20 and averaging about $10.

Just as when hunting for a good service station, be selective! Have a diagnostic center recommended by someone who can testify to its thoroughness and dependability. Or call your local American Automobile Association (AAA) or other auto club, which may be able to give you a selection of two or three good ones to choose from.

If at all possible, pick a diagnostic center that is not associated with a repair garage.

Should you suspect that your service facility is charging you for parts that haven't actually been replaced, ask for the old parts back. Have the service station manager explain any charges you don't understand, and be certain you are not charged for repairs that are covered under your warranty. If your warranty does cover some repairs, have them made at your new car dealership.

Never accept inferior work or price gouging. If you have a complaint, discuss the matter with the dealer or owner of the service facility. It may be the trouble is simply the result of a misunderstanding that can easily be resolved.

If you find you are getting nowhere with a complaint, take action.

When a dealer outlet is involved, send a letter to the nearest zone office of the auto-maker.

Make certain the complaint and the specific action to be taken are thoroughly detailed. Include your name, address, telephone number, make and model of the car, the dealer's name and location, and the car's age and mileage.

If the problem is especially frustrating, do not make accusations or threats. A far more constructive approach would be to send a copy of the letter to the central consumer office of the manufacturer, and, if the complaint is safety-related, to the National Highway Traffic Safety Administration, Department of Transportation, Washington, D.C. 20590.

If another type of service facility is involved, you can get in touch with your local chapter of the Better Business Bureau, contact a community consumer complaint office, or have an attorney write a letter to the service manager.

Perhaps, as more and more people do today, you may want to handle certain car repairs yourself. Experts say even the simplest maintenance jobs can save a car owner up to $100 a year.

Also, if you know how to change a tire or replace a burned-out fuse, you won't always have to resort to emergency road repairs. During the winter months, this could save you waiting the extra amount of time such service often requires because of a heavy overflow of calls from motorists.

Besides the tasks already noted, the most basic maintenance jobs requiring simple tools include giving your car a tune-up (changing or cleaning spark plugs and points, changing condenser and air filters, changing oil and oil filters), cleaning the battery terminals, and flushing the cooling system.

Before beginning any such venture, however, make certain to re-read your owners manual *thoroughly* for specific pointers.

To learn the ABC's of car repair, you can attend courses in automotive maintenance offered by community colleges, local civic groups, and some AAA clubs. Such courses vary widely. Some simply stick to classroom instruction in basic repairs, some require an abundance of technical study, and some even afford students a "greasy gloves" experience by arranging for them to actually work on cars.

Also, recognizing that Americans are showing increasing interest in doing their own minor tinkering, most automakers are offering "do-it-yourself" booklets on various makes of autos, free to new car buyers. This is especially true of the sub-compact models, since they are frequently bought by people with economy in mind.

Those who already have a car can usually obtain these booklets from their dealers. Lists of parts and tools needed are generally included.

For the most ambitious troubleshooter, "shop" or service manuals are issued every year for each new model of automobile. Including far more technical detail than the do-it-yourself booklets, they are generously illustrated with diagrams and individual drawings of each part. In effect, they offer instructions on how to handle the most complicated repair job—even an engine overhaul.

The manuals may be ordered at prices ranging from about $2 to $8 by writing to the headquarters office of the auto-maker. Delivery usually takes a few weeks.

One note of caution! Complicated repairs should be undertaken *only* if you're certain you know what you're doing. A faulty wire connection or an improper adjustment could cost you much more than you set out to save, and more important, threaten your safety.

As already noted, cars that are properly maintained usually don't become disabled.

However, the wise motorist is always prepared for emergency situations, especially during long distance drives on freeways or remote roads.

Earlier it was noted that you can avoid having to call for emergency help if you have the know-how to make minor repairs. Whatever the case, always equip your car with emergency equipment. Some of the most useful items (besides that ever-present owners manual) are:

A flashlight (with extra batteries)
Minor repair tools (pliers, adjustable wrench, screwdriver, two feet of wire, all purpose tape)
First aid kit
White handkerchief or cloth
Wiping cloth
Tire gauge
Jumper cables
Ice scraper
Lug wrench
Jack with flat board for soft surfaces
Flares or reflectors
Extra fan belt
Blanket
Fire extinguisher
Replacement fuse of the correct rating for your car's electrical system
Pencil, notebook

If you can't correct a problem, and you are on a limited access highway, pull well off the roadway onto the shoulder. Signal for help by raising the hood and tying a white handkerchief to your radio antenna or door handle, or place the handkerchief in the left front window.

Also, turn on your emergency flasher. Then stay in the car to wait for the police or emergency repair vehicle.

If you're stranded on other roads, move off the street as far as possible and try to find a level piece of ground to park on. Then, if you are a member, telephone your local AAA or other motor club for help.

If you're not a member of any motor club, contact a local garage that provides towing service. But try to avoid unscrupulous towing operators. Make certain the car *needs* to be towed.

Reputable towing operators carry a booster battery, as well as spare cans of gasoline.

Never, of course, carry extra fuel in your own car. The practice is extremely dangerous. Those who carry extra fuel are endangering not only themselves, but others on the road, especially in the event of a domino-type accident.

Find out exactly where a tow truck is going to take you, how many miles are involved, and exactly what the fee will be. Also determine whether towing is covered under your insurance policy, and if there are limits on the service.

Still another vital reason for a sound program of regular car maintenance is protection of your warranty. Simple neglect is sufficient reason for a warranty to be voided. If it's determined, for instance, that your engine has failed because you didn't change the oil and filter within the recommended intervals specified in your owners manual, you may be refused an important repair free of charge.

Your warranty is a valuable document. It is a joint statement to you from the dealer and auto-maker that the vehicle will perform in the manner for which it is designed, and that any part which does not work or fails—if there's a design, construction, or assembly fault —will be repaired or replaced by the dealer. Always be certain to read your warranty carefully as soon as possible.

Just what is covered by a warranty, and for how long, depends on when the car was made. Most auto warranties cover defects in the manufacture of parts, and defects in assemblies that make up the car, for a full year or 12,000 miles, whichever comes first. Also, most warranties state that the auto-maker will repair the defect, or at his option replace the part with a rebuilt or new part.

Generally, most U.S. auto warranties cover every moving and stationary component in the engine, transmission, drive-shaft, axle assemblies and all other parts of the car except tires and batteries, which have their own warranties.

There are a number of other expendable items not covered that normally wear out, such as oil filters, points, and spark plugs.

Remember, too, that *within 90 days* of the delivery of a new car, most dealers will make a number of adjustments in the vehicle free of charge, such as correcting headlight aim, tightening belts and bolts, and other assembly line oversights.

On 1972 or later model year cars, most warranties also cover certain additional features, including heating and air-conditioning systems, radios, power steering, brakes, seats, windows, and *defects* in paint and interior trim, as well as vinyl tops, if factory-installed.

Certain pre-1971 cars have a five-year, 50,000-mile warranty on the engine, transmission and rear axle, including the drive-shaft.

Putting Your Finger On Green Thumb Garden Helpers

TRYING to find the right person or business firm to take the proper care of your home grounds is probably as difficult as catching a will o' the wisp.

In most sections of the United States it boils down to almost a "catch-as-catch-can" deal. You keep hiring and firing until you find the one that comes nearest to satisfying your wishes.

The more highly organized and better trained services are available where gardening is a year-round business. In those parts of the country where the growing season is short, gardening services on a professional basis practically disappear.

The best solution, of course, is to do as much of it as you can by yourself. Hire the professional for the rest.

With rapid changes in our habits of living, more and more home gardeners realize they need some sort of outside help in caring for their grounds.

The "old-time professional gardener" is now almost a museum piece and in his place you have the following to choose from:

-Lawn Specialists (local franchises of a national parent organization). They will agree to build, rebuild or maintain your lawn area.

With perhaps a slight variation between companies and perhaps in different parts of the country, the basic agreements call for fertilizing, seeding, liming, and aerating; weed, disease and insect control; and in some cases, patch-up work.

This service is accomplished in a

very short time due to ingenious modern, mechanized machinery.

-New Lawn Specialists. They will either make your lawn from beginning to end and seed it, or they will prepare your lawn area and then sod it. They will also do parts of each if the situation calls for it.

In most parts of the country, sodding is now considered to be competitive with seeding. Sodding will cost you more per square foot than seeding, but you must remember you can start using the lawn almost immediately.

A long period of waiting is necessary on a seeded lawn. Erosion and weeds are also a problem in the seeded lawn.

-Professional Garden Maintenance. These firms usually will cut the lawn, feed, trim, prune, remove leaves, edge, weed, and trim hedges. Add to this, disease and weed control work, and even sometimes snow removal.

-Professional Landscape Maintenance. Same as the preceding item except that many of the firms will also do small landscape plantings. This also includes the planting of annuals, perennials, bulbs and ground covers.

-Professional Lawn Maintenance. Some firms will do nothing except cut your grass, trim the edges and sweep your walks. Others will do the above plus spread lime and fertilizer and clip hedges.

-Landscape Contractor-Maintenance Outfits. They do all that's mentioned in the last three items plus the actual planting of a landscape job. In addition, they do construction work such as build walls, steps and paths, as well as seeding and sodding lawn areas. This is perhaps the most all-inclusive type of operation.

-Youngsters and Retired Personnel (sometimes with practically no previous experience). This usually means an individual working for himself.

Youngsters can be found either through word-of-mouth or by going through the various youth employment agencies. The older person is usually filling in for some extra money after retirement. These people may have to be shown how to do even the most basic jobs.

The youngster usually has pep, vim and vigor. That's his strong point. The oldster has a steady pace and experience, as a rule.

Both of them usually come a little cheaper than the previously mentioned operations. They usually don't do much more than cut the grass, trim the edges, and maybe rake up the debris.

Should you get a good one from this group you can train him also to spread your lime and fertilizer. If you have the time and know-how you can even train him to apply insect and disease sprays.

-Specialties. Now and then you find people who specialize in certain kinds of gardening chores. As examples, some will do nothing but plow a garden area (flowers, fruit or vegetables). Others do nothing but lay sod. Then there are the hedge trimmers, the tree surgeons, the stump removers and the wood splitters.

If you go to the yellow pages for assistance you will be absolutely overcome with confusion. Don't give up. The trick is to mark down a few of those ads that *seem* to come closest to what you want. Then arrange for a personal visit to your property, and discuss the problem with the advertisers.

Any time you may spend in these meetings will be well worth it. Many headaches and disappointments can be avoided. A few of the *key* words to look for in the ads are maintenance, landscape contractors, tree experts, landscape nurserymen, and gardening services.

Like anything else, no matter what the charges may be you will always think they are too high. If you are fortunate enough to find a satisfactory person that does the work the way you want it when you want it, he is worth as much as any plumber, electrician, or carpenter. In most instances, however, you will find his fees to be about only

---

AUTHOR *Raymond P. Korbobo* is Extension Specialist in Landscape Design at Rutgers University, The State University of New Jersey, in New Brunswick.

a third to a half as much as for those other tradespeople.

Like any inept professional, if his results are substandard then anything you pay him is too much.

Many maintenance firms will make an annual contract or agreement with you. Most of them use a monthly charge as the basis for the arrangement. This takes care of the areas where gardens are, so to speak, "put to sleep" for the winter.

Once in a great while you can still get a man who will charge you an hourly rate. This is better, of course, in case of prolonged dry spells when the lawns do not need cutting. You will then only be paying for work actually performed.

Some firms have two sets of prices based upon who supplies the equipment. If you provide the power tools and all the gardening equipment and they furnish just the labor, naturally it would be less out of your pocket.

In any event, it is wise to have insurance coverage for any personal injuries or property damage incurred while they are working on your property. The larger and more professional firms usually carry their own coverage. It is very important to discuss these fine points before you sign any contract.

Besides trying the yellow pages and employment services, you may want to double check with someone from the Cooperative Extension Service in your county or state. Contact your County Agricultural Agent, whose offices are listed under "County Offices." They are usually located in the county seat.

If the agent can't answer your problem, he will get the assistance of the state specialist in that particular field, such as Landscape Design, Diseases, Insects, etc. These Cooperative Extension people can very often help put you on the best path to the type help you desire.

If you are an able-bodied person, my suggestion is to do as much as possible of the gardening yourself. It is not only good physical exercise but also great therapy for the mind. In addition, you will be doing the job the way you want it done.

In general, go to the professional when it involves transplanting large plants, sodding, seeding or cutting large lawn areas, grading the property, trimming large hedges or installing drainage systems.

Any time spent reading literature on how to do various gardening chores will be a very profitable investment of your time.

By reading such information you will learn the general "garden calendar" and become familiar with tasks which should be done at precise times. This is important to know even though you do hire professional helpers. Don't ever think they know all the answers!

Since "taking them to court" for a job poorly done usually would cost more than the job itself is worth, perhaps the best bit of advice would be to be careful whom you hire in the first place.

Take your time in selecting the person you will sign the contract with, and then hope for satisfactory work. Treat him with respect and you will find that usually he will be anxious to please you even to the point of doing some work over again at your request.

You will find, however, that many of the people you hire are very insistent on doing things "their way." This is probably the most disheartening thing in the entire garden maintenance world. Therefore, try to make them understand that occasionally you may ask them to do something "your way" which may not agree with their way. Settle this bone of contention before you sign them on.

RECREATION

Vacation Planning, With Tips for Trips To Save Your Gas

BUDGET considerations and family preferences normally influence the selection of a vacation plan. In recent years challenge and adventure have also become important factors.

However, future restraints on automotive travel imposed by the energy situation may limit your vacation options to sites close to home or reasonably accessible by public transportation.

The following vacation plans avoid excessive use of personal vehicles in seeking outdoor recreation opportunities. Frequently the choices described are accessible by train, bus or other public transportation.

Specific information on location, accessibility, facilities, and fees is given in a wide variety of vacation and camping directories and travel atlases available at most large newsstands and bookstores.

Here's a listing of vacation options:

National Forests

The 187 million acre National Forest System, administered by the Forest Service, U.S. Department of Agriculture (Washington, D.C. 20250), extends from coast to coast. The 154 National Forests include lands adjacent to metropolitan areas as well as more remote attractions. Thousands of developed camping, picnicking, swimming, and boating sites are offered in an environment of your choice—along a seashore or river, in an alpine meadow, or in tall timber.

AUTHOR *Roy W. Feuchter* is Assistant Director of Recreation for the Forest Service.

Recreational maps are available for individual forests. Facilities range from primitive to those with all the amenities.

A special attraction to hardy outdoors people is the over 11 million acres of designated Wilderness, in which no motorized equipment is permitted.

The National Forest System offers over 90,000 miles of trails for backpackers.

Fees, if charged, vary according to the amount of site development; however, the majority of sites are free. Average fee at charge sites is less than $2 per night per family.

Interpretive facilities and programs often are provided, but electrical and sewer hookups for recreation vehicles seldom are available.

For beginners, and especially those with small children, several short visits to more highly developed sites is recommended for a start, since many modern conveniences are not present in the average National Forest recreation facility.

National Parks

The 35 National Parks in the National Parks System, administered by

Scenes on the National Forests.

the National Park Service, U.S. Department of the Interior (Washington, D.C. 20240), generally require an entrance fee. In some cases, user fees are also appropriate. The Golden Eagle Passport will cover the entrance fee on an annual basis.

National Parks are situated in areas that have outstanding natural attractions, historical significance, or special recreational opportunities.

The principal features are included in the free interpretive programs.

Lodges and dining facilities cater to the public in the larger parks.

Although camping is permitted in designated areas, camping activity is considered secondary to the opportunity to enjoy the attractions which the park is established to protect. Hunting is not allowed.

Neophytes will generally find a short visit to a National Park a good introduction to this fine national heritage, prior to making more extended camp-outs. Reservations may be required at some places.

Public Domain

The Bureau of Land Management, also in the Department of Interior, has a number of camping and picnic sites in the Western States, generally of a more rustic nature.

Seashores

These units of the National Forest and National Park Systems put special emphasis on recreation.

Facilities are usually more highly developed than in the average National "area," but otherwise the previous discussion applies.

State Parks

Almost all of the States provide excellent recreation facilities in attractive State Parks, with a wide range in number and quality. The respective Departments of Parks, c/o The State Capitol, can furnish detailed directories.

Reservations often are required and fees usually are collected. Generally, supplies including firewood can be purchased.

On the average, sites are usually closer to population centers than the National Areas, and more highly developed. Often these parks offer a good introduction to camping and picnicking, prior to embarking on tours to the more remote parts of the National Areas.

Corps of Engineers Installations

The ten million acres of land and water included in water impoundments constructed by the U.S. Army Corps of Engineers (Washington, D.C. 20314) for flood control or navigation purposes frequently have been developed to provide marinas, picnic sites, and camping facilities.

Currently 390 Corps lake projects have heavy recreation use.

Directories can be obtained from the Corps of Engineers or from local Chambers of Commerce.

Roughly two-thirds of Corps lakes having recreation use are located within a 50-mile radius of metropolitan areas having a population of 50,000 or more.

Fees are sometimes required for the more highly developed facilities.

Activities at Corps of Engineers installations.

Recreation opportunities are generally water-oriented, and most visitors are attracted by the appeal of water sports. Rental boats are generally available at the marinas but instruction in boating and skiing normally is not provided.

Facilities for recreation vehicles are usually furnished, as are attractive picnic and camping sites.

Power Company Impoundments

Many of the private utility companies that furnish hydro-electric power have developed the shore areas of their reservoirs intensively to provide a wide variety of attractive recreational facilities. Included are marinas, picnic sites, campgrounds, golf courses, and tennis courts. Facilities are open to the public; fees are often collected.

Full facility hookups for recreation vehicles often are available. Information on location and facilities can be obtained through local Chambers of Commerce in the geographical area of your choice or through the power companies.

The Tennessee Valley Authority and similar organizations likewise have constructed water impoundments whose shorelines have been developed for public use.

Privately Owned Campgrounds

Booming interest in camping and the overcrowding of public recreation sites have stimulated commercial development of privately owned campgrounds, many of them with excellent facilities. Fees are charged.

Over 50 separate companies now provide more than 8,000 family units. Some firms have a national chain system.

Two kinds of development are found:

1. Those that offer rental sites available for picnicking or camping, on a first-come, first-served basis, or by reservation.

2. Those that offer a tract of land which can be purchased individually or cooperatively as a permanent personal campsite. House trailers, mobile homes, or recreactional vehicles can either be rented or purchased privately for use on these lots, seasonally or otherwise. The lots essentially are second-home sites or sylvan condominiums.

Both types of area usually offer central laundry, store, swimming, playground equipment, gameroom, and other facilities for the pleasure of the tenants. In addition to the Camping Directories, the Family Camping Federation (Bradford Woods, Martinsville, Ind. 46151) has information.

Some private timber companies have campsites and picnic areas on their forest lands, open for public use. Facilities tend to be primitive. Most are free but numbers are still rather limited.

Contact timber companies directly or the American Forest Institute, 1619 Massachusetts Avenue N.W., Washington, D.C.

Farm Vacations

You can join old McDonald on his farm and spend anywhere from a few days to several weeks being one of the family.

The kids can see live farm animals and eat wholesome food. The parents can help do chores, if they wish, or simply take it easy.

Cost is modest and varies with your choice. The rural environment is educational, peaceful, and satisfying and provides an outstanding opportunity for families to identify with nature in easy steps.

A farm vacation is recommended for young families and those making their first "escape" from the urban environment. Information on location can be obtained through local Chambers of Commerce or Travel Services in the geographical area of your choice, or through Conservation Districts or County Agents.

Dude Ranches

These are variations of the farm vacation, but without the work angles.

You stay at a ranch house in rural or mountainous settings amidst scenic attractions, and participate in trail rides, hiking, swimming, and games.

Dining and dancing are an added attraction not available with most outdoor vacations.

The ranches usually are near National Forests or National Parks. Some offer the opportunity to watch a working ranch and cowboys in action, though these are liable to be a more rustic experience best reserved for a second trip.

Contact the Dude Ranchers Association, 2822 Third Avenue North, Billings, Mont. 59101.

Resorts

A wide variety of private resorts ranging from fairly rustic tent camps to modern full facility spas are available in most vacation regions.

Prices vary with location and facilities provided, but resorts are surprisingly inexpensive and offer wonderful opportunities to "rough it" in a gentle fashion.

Evening entertainment and special facilities for children are often available.

Guided trail excursions are another source of vacation fun.

You can obtain further information from: National Forest Recreation Association, 22841-A Media Lane, Cupertino, Calif. 95014. Also, from the Conference of National Park Concessioners, 1003 Abby Way, McLean, Va. 22101.

Condominiums, Second Homes

Almost 5 percent of American households now own a second home, mostly

for recreation or vacation use. Many condominiums can be rented, and offer a good opportunity for a change of scenery with little loss of convenience or comforts. Arrangements must be made through local realtors for the area of your choice, or with the owner.

Costs are generally higher, since most rentals are found in the more popular recreation areas where values may be on the rise. However, the opportunity to reduce food costs by doing your own cooking is significant, and many recreation activities are usually at hand nearby, including golf, horseback riding and cycling.

Wilderness Trail Excursions

The American Forestry Association, the Wilderness Society, Sierra Club and similar organizations based in Washington, D.C., sponsor completely equipped and supervised excursions into back country and roadless areas of outstanding scenic attraction. Many of these trips penetrate units of the National Wilderness Preservation System.

Guide service is furnished. Transportation is generally by horseback, though some hiking trips are also offered with pack stock to transport the equipment and supplies. All you need bring is yourself and suitable clothing.

Trips range in length from several days to two weeks. They are not so rugged as to exclude small children but are still not recommended for a first experience in camping or hiking, since modern facilities are non-existent and medical aid is limited.

Fishing Ponds

Thousands of fishing ponds constructed by farmers for conservation purposes or personal use are sometimes available for limited public use, under restrictions. They offer an inexpensive outing close to home.

Many of the larger cities are fringed with commercial fishing ponds. Here you can rent fishing gear or use your own. You pay for what you catch, by the pound, and you may be guaranteed a catch.

See your local Fish and Game Commission or County Agent for addresses.

Float Trips

Floating down many of the major rivers of the West and South is similar to a wilderness trail excursion, except the transportation is by boat or raft.

"White Water" trips should be reserved for a second venture since excitement and challenge are their specialty. Calm water trips are fun for all ages and abilities.

Information is available from several organizations such as the American Canoe Association, 4200 East Evan Street, Denver, Colo.

National Forests and National Parks frequently provide the locale for such trips. Reservations are usually necessary.

Houseboating

You can rent a completely furnished houseboat and head upstream, downstream, or across a lake, berthing each

night at a different spot along friendly shores, or you can stay moored in one place.

Rental services that supply these accommodations limit houseboat availability to relatively large bodies of water, but a wide variety of experiences are available. The necessary nautical savvy for most rental adventures can be acquired easily at the site.

For families the experience is generally relaxing and slow tempo, with fishing and swimming in abundance. Contact the Chamber of Commerce or Tourist Bureau in the area of your choice.

Skiing

Winter vacations are becoming increasingly popular. Although somewhat more difficult to fit into work and school schedules, the popularity of this form of outdoor recreation is increasing rapidly, since it combines desirable features of several of the summer recreation opportunities.

Skiing can be a family experience which brings you close to nature at an exciting time of year, provides physical activity at whatever level is individually appropriate, and offers opportunity for evening entertainment if desired.

Downhill skiing on lift-served hills is available at a wide variety of resorts with centers of activity in New England, the Lake States, the Rocky Mountains, and the Sierra and Cascade Mountains from California to Washington. Commercial airlines serve these centers.

Some 200 of the popular skiing areas are provided on National Forests by concessionaires operating under Forest Service guidelines.

Detailed information can be obtained from the U.S. Department of Agriculture or from the National Ski Areas Association, 61 South Main Street, West Hartford, Conn.

Cross-country skiing or ski touring offers challenges wherever there is good snow. Popularity of the sport is booming due to the low costs and sheer adventure. Enthusiasts feel this is the ultimate back to nature experience for pure enjoyment of nature's beauty.

Detailed information can be obtained from the U.S. Department of Agriculture, or the U.S. Ski Association, 1726 Champa Street, Denver, Colo.

Instructions on survival technique and first aid should be obtained before starting out in both types of skiing.

Travel Services

It's possible to travel by train or other public transportation to another city or area and then rent a car or take a bus to reach a recreational attraction such as the Disneylands, skiing areas, etc. Commercial airlines offer many attractive "package" excursions.

Travel clubs organized for mutual benefits can obtain special charter rates or even operate their own buses or aircraft. The Civil Aeronautics Board requires that you must have been a member of a travel club for at least six months before you can join an affinity charter flight.

Many Federal agencies have their own travel clubs, some of which include ski trips in their itineraries.

In the Washington, D.C., area a service called Auto-Train transports automobiles and their passengers to Florida via railroad, thus saving both highway travel and precious fuel. This type of service is expanding.

Bus Tours

Both Greyhound and Continental Trailways offer "See-America" Tours that provide a 30-day low cost trip on which you can stop over locally as you like for a stay at many desirable spots.

A car can be rented, if you wish to take a side trip. Meals and other costs are your own.

Chartered package tours for special attractions such as Fall colors are quite popular. Many of the bus routes go through National Forests or National Parks.

From the Horse's Mouth—How Not To Ride for a Fall

WITH THE INCREASE in leisure and recreational time, more and more people are turning to activities involving the use of horses. The energy situation has placed emphasis on local recreational activities, which most likely will spur the demand for renting or buying horses. Today, over six million horses occupy pastures or stables in the United States, mostly in suburban areas.

Horses benefit the community in that they can develop in children a strong sense of responsibility, and thus prepare them to become better citizens. Riding fulfills the psychological needs of many people to escape the tensions of today's fast pace, in addition to providing physical exercise for a people who so desperately need it. It's a sport in which the entire family can take part.

A novice rider will experience ups and downs, thrills and spills, aches and pains, as he takes to the bridle trails, fields and parks in the spring. Horseback riding is seldom boring, sometimes painful, and different each day you ride.

Horses are widely used in sports just about everywhere. Horse racing is a valuable source of tax revenue in many States. Horse shows and rodeos have become competitive sport attractions.

Polo is an increasing sports draw in the East as its popularity grows and the competition becomes keener. Jousting events are held annually near the Washington Monument in the Nation's capital. Steeplechases, barrel races, endurance rides, hunt meets, roundups, and organized trail rides continue to give riders a variety of activities.

Already many cities and municipalities have had an increase in requests for established bridle trails and use of horse-drawn vehicles. The natural affinity of people for horses has propelled the horse into a significant role, particularly in youth development programs.

Programs designed to rehabilitate physically handicapped and emotionally disturbed youths have become widespread throughout the United States. The youths are learning respect, discipline and a feeling of security by riding horses and finding that they can accomplish control and authority over these large animals. The psychological therapy in horsemanship is encouraging them to keep trying and fighting to overcome their handicaps.

As more and more people take to horseback riding, many ask, "Should I rent or buy?" To help you decide which method is best for you, let's look at the options.

If you rent, you do not have to be concerned with the care and upkeep involved in owning a horse. The tack (riding equipment) is usually furnished with the rented horse. Most commercial stables have the horse cleaned and tacked when you arrive and all you do is get on and ride.

You may be limited to the estab-

AUTHOR *Larry L. Finks* is a Lieutenant with the U.S. Park Police, stationed in Washington, D.C.

lished trails that connect with the stable. This means that you usually ride the same trails each time you rent.

A well run stable will have dependable horses which are accustomed to even the most inexperienced riders. This does not mean that some horses may not have become trail sour. That is to say, they respond slowly to commands of the rider and often will respond only with a slow walk.

Some stables require that you have previous riding experience or riding lessons before you will be allowed to rent a horse for trail rides.

Rates for renting will vary with each locale, but an average rate in several cities surveyed ranged from about $4 to $5 per hour on weekdays and $4.50 to $5.50 on weekends. Lessons for the beginner ranged from $6.00 per half hour and up for private lessons, and $5 and up per hour for group lessons.

Call the local public stable nearest you for its rates. Rates vary according to the upkeep and conditions of the stables and horses.

If you buy, you must have facilities to stable and ride the horse.

Are there ordinances or regulations prohibiting stabling or riding in your community? Many municipalities prohibit riding horses except on established trails. Check with your local authorities before purchasing a horse.

You must consider such expenses as feed bills, veterinarian fees, tack and equipment, blacksmith fees, and methods of disposing of manure. Someone has to be available to clean the stalls and feed and water the horse twice daily.

If you are thinking of owning a horse, you should be willing to spend at least an hour a day riding him.

Owning your own horse offers many advantages. You can ride at your convenience. You always ride the same horse. You will have greater satisfaction because eventually you become attached to your horse and take pride in your riding.

Horses come in different shapes, sizes, colors and breeds. Which particular horse you select depends on your personal preference. In picking a horse, emphasize the quality and disposition of the horse and not the particular breed or color. Soundness or good health is essential.

Absence of vicious habits such as biting, kicking or striking with the forefeet is important. The horse should not object to being saddled or groomed, nor should he balk, rear, shy, or be hard to catch when turned out. You should be aware of stable vices such as cribbing, halter pulling, tail rubbing, weaving, and bolting. Many of these habits may lead to more serious problems.

Analyze your own needs to determine the type of horse you buy. Most horses are bred for different kinds of work and pleasure. To help you decide which breed is best for you, contact your local veterinarian or perhaps your county agent.

The horse should never be too spirited or unmanageable for the rider's skill. Your horsemanship will be reflected in the control you exhibit and not on how spirited the horse is.

The horse's size should match the size and weight of the rider (A small horse or pony for children; a larger horse for an adult).

A small person may fit a large horse, but a large person shouldn't be paired with a small horse. This applies either to a person's weight or height.

A suitable horse usually can be purchased for several hundred dollars and maintained for $30 to $50 a month at home. Boarding will usually cost $40 and up depending on type of stall, facility, and locality.

When selecting a horse, look him over carefully for any deformities, sores, scars or injuries.

Examine the horse from a distance. Are his legs straight? Does he move freely and smoothly? Does he carry himself proudly? Is he like a picture? Then inspect him close up.

If you decide this is the horse you like, insist that he be examined by a veterinarian of your own choosing before you buy.

Unless you are a professional horse

Horses can be rented by the hour or day.

buyer, avoid purchasing your horse at a public auction.

Equipment Needed

To care for the horse, you will need such items as a body brush, a hair brush, a mane and tail comb, a hoof pick, sweat scraper, water bucket, feed bins, straw fork, broom and shovel.

For the horse, you will need a halter, a bridle, saddle, saddle pad, and a blanket if the weather gets cold in your area. These are the minimum needs, but many other accessories are available for stable management and riding activities.

Saddles can be purchased for as little as $100. The price depends on the quality of the leather and the added accessories, which may amount to hundreds of dollars if you so desire and can afford it.

Used saddles generally can be purchased at most horse auctions, or you may find tack shops that carry used riding equipment.

If you live in an area without convenient trails, you may need a horse trailer. The most popular are the two-horse trailers which can be purchased for $1,200 and up. Many people prefer a two-horse type because it can be towed by most medium size cars if properly equipped. With this type trailer, you can always take along a friend and his horse.

A trailer with an escape door, a three section tail gate, and electric brakes is recommended for safety reasons. The size, shape, color, and price range depend on your individual preference.

Clothing will vary with the individual, the type of riding he is doing, and the locality. Boots are recommended for all riders. Whether they be English style or Western depends upon the riding apparel you wear.

Riding breeches are designed for those wearing English boots. However, when breeches are not available, a pair of heavy jeans should be worn to protect the legs, especially if you ride cross country on brushy trails. Optional riding apparel such as gloves, hard hats, spurs, and coats may also be worn to fit the occasion.

Wearing loose or bulky clothing should be avoided because it is apt to inhibit the rider's freedom or become entangled in brush, tree limbs, or other obstacles which could lead to serious injury.

An old cowboy once said, "There is something about the outside of a horse that is good for the inside of a man."

Wheeling Along With a Bicycle

BIKOMANIA, a highly contagious fever, is sweeping the country from coast to coast. The only known cure is to ride a bike. Nearly 100 million happy victims, including Mom, Pop and the kids, now are taking this delightful treatment and pedaling their two-wheelers into an exciting new world of fun and adventure.

America's love affair with the bike has spawned some startling statistics. In 1973 this new life-style in transportation stimulated the sale of more than 15 million of the pedal-propelled vehicles, over half of which were bought by adults. Sales in 1974 are outpacing those of 1973. At that rate bike sales will soon outstrip the car sales records set at its peak by the automobile industry.

Why buy a bike? Partly because riding a bike benefits both you and your environment. A bike doesn't foul up the air, makes no noise, keeps you in top physical shape, takes up little room on the road, and is easy to park in a small space. With appropriate accessories—such as saddle bags, luggage racks, or baskets—a bike can be used on shopping missions, picnic excursions, or bicycle tours.

What kind of bike should you get? Bewildered by the tantalizing display of racing models with 10-speed gearshifts and lots of fancy gimmicks, you're apt to plunge for something you really don't need. Best advice: buy the simplest model that meets your transportation requirements. You need not invest in dropped handlebars, multigear ratios and special frames that may be too complicated for your purposes.

Total investment in a bike for an average person with average transportation requirements should not exceed $100. After you're genuinely hooked, you can turn professional and become addicted to one of the super models that sell in price ranges up to $500 or more.

Try renting a bike before you buy one. Spend a couple of weekends pedaling various makes over typical terrain in your area; this tryout will answer many of your questions. Names of rental agencies are listed in the yellow pages of telephone directories or can be obtained from cycle shops. If you rent, try several no-shift models as well as geared models.

Find a reliable dealer with an established reputation and a service outlet. Rely upon his good judgment. With plenty of models to choose from, he can give you frank and honest advice. You can compare different models in the sales room and judge their relative qualities.

Used bikes aren't always a bargain. A good one will sell for about 75 percent of the price of a new one. Be careful in buying a used bike from an individual. If it's too cheap, the bike probably has been stolen. Used bikes

---

AUTHOR *Albert Arnst* is with the Forest Service. He prepared this chapter from material furnished by the Bicycle Institute of America.

generally have no guarantee, so select a reliable dealer.

Where do you live? If your riding locale is flat or gently sloping country and you intend to use the bike mostly on weekend commuter trips for relaxation and simple errands, a three-speed commuter model should be satisfactory.

This type bike usually has upright handlebars, fender guards (great for wet weather), a comfortable conventional saddle seat, and a reliable "old-fashioned" coaster brake. The coaster brake has several plus features: It's simple, requires little maintenance, and works well in wet weather.

If you live or work in hilly country, a three-speed job won't have enough gear ratio to push you over the humps in comfort. To climb the steeper grades without tiring yourself too much, you will need a bike equipped with a 5 or 10 speed system; such a unit usually costs more than $100.

You will have to give up the coaster brake, because the multiple-gear rigging prevents any brake installation on the rear wheel. Dual wheel caliper brakes operated by hand from the handlebars are standard equipment. In wet weather caliper brakes must be used cautiously. Apply them intermittently to keep the brake pads squeezed free of water and partially dry.

A cycling neophyte using his bike in hilly country could compromise on a five-speed job with a convenient gear shift device on the handlebar grip. The simpler models will give the newcomer a chance to acquire confidence. As his interest develops, he can grow into a sportier dropped-handlebar model, lighter in weight, with more gear ratios for cross-country trekking.

The bike frame must fit your body—you can't grow into it. Children should not use bikes that are too big.

A simple test will determine how tall you are in the saddle. Stand astride the frame, feet on the ground, with the seat elevated about two inches. You should be able to touch the ground with the ball of one foot, while the other foot is on an upraised pedal. There should be an inch or so of clearance between the frame and your crotch.

Bike frames are important. Lighter frames cost more. Cheaper bikes have welded frames; they aren't as strong

MIDDLEWEIGHT

HIGH-RISE

LIGHTWEIGHT

as lugged frames. The latter are brazed so that the steel or alloy tubing can be thinner than the heavy steel requirement for welding. Alloy frames are light but expensive. The average biker can settle for a good lugged straight steel frame.

Women, older men, or families should consider a girl's frame style. It's easier to mount and can be adjusted readily to fit people of different sizes.

A wide variety of bike frame and handlebar styles is available for all age groups. These include the small 16-inch sidewalk bikes with coaster brakes and training wheels. The jet set among the young folks will go for the high rise handlebars, "banana" type seat, sissy bars, floral design saddles, chrome plated fenders, and other deluxe features. Similar deluxe adornments also are available for adult size bikes with the 26-inch wheels.

Pedal style influences peddling ease. Experts advise against using plastic ones—they are too slippery. Three-speed bikes usually have rubber pedals, which are satisfactory. Multi-gear bikes generally use rat-trap pedals, made of light, strong metal, with a serrated surface for foot grip. For cross-country cycling, experts recommend rat-trap pedals with a "cage" to capture the upward thrust of your leg.

Checking over the equipment on a 10-speed hi-rise bike. Note reflectors.

Bikes are also popular with people who don't own one; they steal over 400,000 yearly. Protect your bike by registering the serial number with the local police department.

Buy a good lock. Get a case-hardened steel, plastic covered cable to go with it. Don't use combination locks—hammers will open them. Kryptonite locks are almost steal-proof. Fasten the bike to a parking meter or a solid post or bicycle rack. Loop the cable through the wheel and around the frame.

Insure your bike separately if it isn't covered in your standard homeowners policy.

Bike riders must observe all traffic laws. Local regulations specify the lighting equipment required for night riding. A white beam light is required in front and adequate red reflectors in the back. Amber reflectors fastened to wheel spokes, bicycle frame or pedals increase rider visibility.

Like skiing, you'll find that better cycling opportunities are located in rural areas. You can transport your bikes to a distant site by installing a bike rack at the rear of your car. Models for one or more bikes are available at modest cost.

You can do much of the simple bicycle maintenance once you buy an inexpensive basic wrench set. Ask your dealer to show you how to use it. For the fussier jobs, take the bike to a reliable service outlet, preferably at your dealer.

Keep abreast of cycling activities and helpful workshops in your area. Become an active member of a local club or join the Bicycle Institute of America in New York City, which publishes many helpful booklets. Other national groups with effective educational materials include the 4-H Clubs in the Extension Service, and the National Safety Council in Chicago.

Municipalities, counties, States, and the Federal Government are concerned with building bikeways for the exclusive use of cyclists.

"Instant" bikeways are created by closing off access roads in metropolitan parks to automobile traffic. Scenic or historic bikeways take advantage of unusual attractions. Urban bikeways provide pleasant excursions in the quieter sections of metropolitan areas.

Several bikeways have been developed by the Federal Government and others have been added to the National Park System.

The Federal Highway Act of 1973 allotted $120 million for bikeways over the next three years and establishes an educational program for bike rider safety.

FOR FURTHER READING:

Bicycle Institute of America and Amateur Bicycle League of America. *How to Improve Your Cycling,* Athletic Institute, Chicago, Ill.

Leete, Harley M., ed. *The Best of Bicycling!,* Trident Press, New York, N.Y., 1970.

Sloane, Eugene A. *The Complete Book of Bicycling,* Trident Press, New York, N.Y., 1970.

Sommer, Robert and Lott, Dale F. *Bikeways in Action: The Davis Experience,* University of California, Davis, Calif., 1970.

American Youth Hostels. *North American Bicycle Atlas,* 20 W. 17th St., New York, N.Y. 10011, $1.95.

National Technical Information Service. *Bicycling and Bicycle Trails* (a bibliography), 5285 Port Royal Rd., Springfield, Va. 22151, $3.00.

Park Maintenance. *Bicycles: How Parks are Meeting the Demand for Facilities,* June, 1967.

Backpacking Gear: Shoes and Packs To Sleeping Bags

BACKPACKING RANKS 18th in popularity among outdoor sports and it is rapidly gaining in popularity. Within the past three years some half dozen new backpacking and wilderness type camping magazines have hit the newsstands. The number of stores that cater to the backpackers' needs have increased greatly.

Suppose that you have an adventuresome spirit and that you are young in years . . . anywhere from 10 to 70, and want to take up backpacking.

Oh, you think 70 is a bit too old? Perish the thought! The legendary Grandma Gatewood took up the gentle pastime of backpacking at age 65 and hiked the 2,000-mile Appalachian Trail. She did it again at age 67 . . . and again in her early 70's.

So let's suppose you have accepted an invitation to participate in a three-day backpacking trip. There is one little problem. You have no equipment. What should you buy and how much should you spend?

I know of one man who, in three nights of intensive shopping, purchased $1,000 of backpacking equipment for himself and two very young sons. That's one extreme.

Grandma Gatewood's cash outlay for equipment was the price of a pair of Ked basketball shoes plus the cost of one yard of blue denim cloth which she fashioned into a bag with a drawstring at one end. That's the other extreme.

Hopefully your tastes and your pocketbook will put you somewhere between these two extremes.

Where do you buy backpacking equipment? If you live in a metropolitan area, look in the yellow pages of the phone book under Camping Equipment. You will know you're in the right place if you see yellow page ads that feature backpacks with names like Kelty, Camp Trails, or Jansport; hiking shoes with names like Vasque, Lowa or Fabiano; sleeping bags with names like Camp Seven, Sierra Design, or North Face.

If you do not have access to an outdoor store you must resort to catalogs. Check outdoor type magazines at your local library or newsstand and send for catalogs.

Some nationally known outdoor merchandisers via catalogs are L. L. Bean of Freeport, Maine; Holubars of Boulder, Col.; and the well-known cooperative of Seattle, Wash., Recreational Equipment, Inc. ("REI").

And in considering catalogs, don't overlook those old American standbys, Montgomery Ward and Sears and Roebuck. Each of these mail order houses has recognized the growing popularity of backpacking. Each has included in its catalogs a small assortment of the backpackers' basic needs . . . shoes, packs, sleeping bags and tents.

Now for some basic advice on your shopping procedure and then we will proceed to a discussion of what things you should buy and the price you should pay.

DO NOT let a salesman, a magazine advertisement, or even a fellow hiker convince you that you MUST buy the XYZ backpack, Model 3J; or the ABC sleeping bag, Model 12W. Don't believe it!

Since 1971 I have been affiliated with a small chain of outdoor stores in the Virginia, Maryland, and North Carolina area. This permits me to see and examine new products coming into the market. I also get feedback from both store employees and customers who use the products.

Competition is keen in the manufacture and distribution of backpacking gear, and a variety of competing makes and models are available that will fulfill your needs. Your decision should be based on the advice of the salesman and fellow hikers, your own appraisal of the article being purchased, and that very important consideration . . . how much you wish to spend.

If you are dealing with a salesman, and if you are green as grass in knowledge of backpacking gear, inform the salesman of that fact. And if you have a definite limit on how much you can spend for a certain item, inform the salesman of that fact also. Any salesman worth his salt will be appreciative of both situations.

AUTHOR *Edward B. Garvey* is affiliated with Appalachian Outfitters of Oakton, Va. His book *Appalachian Hiker* describes his 1970 hike of the entire Appalachian Trail.

Nutritional food buying emphasizes the "Basic Four." Backpacking also has its basic four, these being in order of importance: 1) hiking shoes, 2) the backpack, 3) sleeping gear, and 4) shelter.

Selection of hiking shoes should be your first concern. Even a one-day hike can be misery without comfortable, good fitting, well broken-in shoes.

If your hike is to begin tomorrow or the next day, don't buy your shoes today. It's too late! But, assuming you have the time to break in your shoes properly, what should you look for?

Today's hikers prefer a shoe that is six inches high, is made of leather, and has thick sturdy composition soles. Within this framework you could purchase shoes that weighed from 2½ lbs per pair to over 5 lbs per pair (for a size 10 shoe). The cost could range from $20 to $50 (1974 prices).

If you are just getting into backpacking, I would suggest (using size 10 as an indicator again) a pair of shoes that weigh in the 3 to 4 lb range and that would cost somewhere between $28 and $34.

Take plenty of time in getting your shoes fitted. Wear the type of socks (usually a thin inner pair and a thick outer pair) that you will wear while hiking. Insist on a roomy fit to allow for the swelling that comes from carrying a 30 to 40 lb pack hour after hour. Break the shoes in thoroughly on short walks before going on any extended hike.

In purchasing a backpack you will find an almost bewildering array of makes, styles, and materials to choose from.

Over the past 20 years, the backpacking fraternity has come to prefer a combination aluminum frame to which is attached a pack of heavy duty nylon taffeta or cordura nylon with various side pockets and compartments to permit quick access to any desired article. The backpacking frame must have both shoulder straps and a waist strap, the latter strap being of such design as to permit much of the weight of the pack to rest on the sturdy hip bones rather than on the more fragile shoulder bones.

Backpacks that meet these general requirements can be purchased at costs ranging from $25 to $70. Cubic inch capacity may range from 1,500 to 6,000.

For growing youngsters and for adults who feel they may make only occasional use of their packs, I would recommend a pack and frame combination costing in the $25 to $30 range and having a cubic inch capacity of perhaps 2,000 to 2,500.

If you've already had your initiation into backpacking and know that it's going to be your thing, then I would suggest a pack and frame combination in the $45 to $60 range with a capacity from 2,500 to 4,000 cubic inches.

Two other items to consider are waterproofing and padded hip belts. There are waterproof backpacks and those made with no waterproofing. You can get valid arguments either way.

If you buy a non-waterproof bag and you are hiking in wet weather areas you will wish to buy a waterproof cover of some type for your pack.

A padded hip belt is a belt approximately one-half inch thick and four inches wide that distributes the weight of your pack more comfortably over a wider area of your hips than does the conventional inch-wide belt. It adds $6 to $8 to the cost of your backpack.

The sleeping bag and its two accessories (ground cloth and mattress) are next on the list of basics.

A sleeping bag can be made or bought in a variety of fabrics and with a variety of filler material.

You can make a simple sleeping bag from a single blanket by sewing it so that it is closed on three sides. The bags that you buy at an outdoor store, however, are generally made with nylon ripstop or taffeta cloth and filled with either goose down, duck down, or a synthetic material such as Dacron II.

Goose down is generally considered the warmest ounce for ounce, and duck down is rated as 85 percent as effective as goose down.

A backpacking couple takes a break.

Synthetic fills such as Dacron II do not enjoy wide popularity but a small and growing segment of the backpacking fraternity thinks the synthetic fills are superior to anything on the market. For one thing they generally are cheaper than goose and duck down.

The synthetics are also bulkier and firmer . . . the firmness being an asset in that you need less protection between you and the ground than when the highly compressible down filling is used. Bags with synthetic fill are also easier to clean.

EQUIPMENT RENTALS

Many outdoor stores will rent backpacks, sleeping bags, and tents. You can rent all three for as little as $10 to $12 a weekend. You may wish to try the rental route until you are sure that backpacking is for you.

When you backpack into isolated areas, it's important to register.

In considering how warm a sleeping bag to buy and how much to pay, you first must decide in what months of the year you plan to use it. Perhaps 80 percent of all sleeping bag use in the United States occurs between April 1 and Oct. 31.

If you anticipate that all of your backpacking will be done in temperatures above 20° F you can purchase a lighter weight, less expensive bag than you would need if you were a cold weather enthusiast who planned to backpack in the snow and ice of winter months.

Presuming you are one of the 80 percent hiking in the warmer months, a bag with 2 lbs of goose down or its equivalent should be more than sufficient. Such a bag may cost from $40 to $80. Things which make for increased cost are better materials, better workmanship, and extra design features which result in additional labor cost.

If you are buying a bag at an outdoor store, ask to try it on for size. A bag that is two inches too short is MUCH too short!

There are mummy type bags, barrel type bags, and full rectangular bags. The mummy type bag is tapered to fit the body, is the lightest to carry, and the easiest to keep warm. Some people find the mummy type bag too confining.

If you're in doubt, by all means try the bag on for size. If the store has no facilities or the salesman tries to brush off your request as unreasonable, merely excuse yourself and go somewhere else.

When buying a bag costing from $40 to $100 you have every right to try it on for size.

Two accessories to the sleeping bag are the ground cloth and mattress. The ground cloth can be an inexpensive piece of clear plastic (costing, say, 80¢) about 6 ft by 8 ft in size. Or you can buy a piece of waterproof nylon—easier to handle but more expensive—for about $11. A few backpackers require no mattress whatever, but most of us want some type of protection between the sleeping bag and the ground (in addition to the razor thin groundcloth).

Veteran backpackers have progressed from air mattresses to foam pads to the present-day preference for either Valera or Ensolite (trade names of two types of closed cell insulation). Of the two I prefer the Ensolite as it is softer and easier to roll up into a small bundle . . . even as protection for a rolled up sleeping bag.

The Ensolite does not absorb water and it provides excellent protection against cold. It comes in various thicknesses and sizes. For warm weather camping I use a piece 20 in x 40 in that is a fourth of an inch thick (cost, $3). For temperatures that are below 30° F, I would use a piece approximately 21 in x 56 in and three-eighths of an inch thick, costing $6.

This brings us to the fourth and last of our basic four . . . the tent or other emergency shelter.

A very inexpensive type shelter is the plastic tube tent. A tube tent for one person costs $1.50. Next on the list of inexpensive shelters is an 8 ft x 10 ft waterproof nylon tarp with grommets which cost $17. This can be used as a tent or a ground cloth or partially as both.

From here we move into bona fide tents, those ingenious little homes on your back that are made from colorful ripstop or taffeta nylon, with sewn-in floors, and mosquito netting. One- and two-man tents weighing from 3 to 5 lbs can be purchased for as low as $25, and they range up to $150.

Space does not permit detailed descriptions of the other items you will need for backpacking.

But I have prepared a price chart showing at 1974 prices what you might expect to pay.

Start slowly and shop carefully. That's

BACKPACKING PRICE CHART

(1974 Prices)

ITEM	GOOD *(Inexpensive or Make Do)*	BETTER	BEST
HIKING SHOES	$0–$15	$30	$50
BACKPACK	$25	$40	$50–$70
SLEEPING GEAR	$30	$60	$100
SHELTER OR TENT	$2–$15	$23–$60	$90–$140
STOVE	$0–$2	$12–$15	$12–$15
COOKING AND EATING GEAR	$0–$2	$7–$10	$18–$25
RAIN GEAR	$1–$2	$8–$15	$23–$30
HIKING CLOTHES	$0–$15	$30–$50	$70–$150
MISCELLANEOUS First Aid Kit, Cord, Flashlight, Matches, Compass, Toilet Articles	$6–$8	$14–$16	$20–$25
ROUGH TOTAL	$92	$262	$520

Insert your own figures for such "Not Necessary But Nice" articles as

Camera	________	________	________
Binoculars	________	________	________
Tiny Radio	________	________	________
Books	________	________	________
Thermometer	________	________	________

half the fun! And hopefully, one day you will have completed all your purchasing, and your hiking shoes will have been thoroughly broken–in and waterproofed. You and your friends will reach the trailhead where the hike is to begin. You square your shoulders, take a final cinch on the waistband of your pack, and you're on your way.

Good hiking!

FOR FURTHER READING:

Garvey, Edward B. *Appalachian Hiker,* Appalachian Books, Oakton, Va. 22124, 1971.

Fletcher, Colin. *The Complete Walker,* Alfred A. Knopf, New York, N.Y., 1971.

Keeping Afloat With a Boat

AMERICA'S water-oriented recreation activities have surged upwards as more people head for their favorite rivers, lakes, bays and coastal areas to enjoy boating. This trend will continue as new kinds of boats and boating equipment are developed.

In the Bureau of Outdoor Recreation's economic analysis in 1973, boating was projected to be the third fastest growing outdoor recreation activity. In 1972 approximately 18 million activity days were spent in canoeing, 32 million in sailing, and 126 million in other types of boating.

With the energy crisis now a reality, interest in boating will take new directions, with emphasis on boats that don't use gasoline or diesel fuels. As an example, river running on fresh water streams may climb in popularity, as will the use of rowboats, canoes, and other muscle-powered watercraft and sailboats.

Because of the new directions in boating, let's talk mainly about the non-motorized kind of boat.

There are several factors in deciding on the type of boat or boating experience you want to buy. Perhaps most important is the type of water where you will use it the most. For example, a canvas-covered wood canoe is great for open lakes, but not very satisfactory in white-water rivers. The type of boat will change when used for salt water versus fresh water—large lakes and the ocean will call for a much sturdier boat than needed in calm bays, small lakes, and farm ponds. Be sure to talk to experienced people for the type of water experience you are planning.

There are dozens of types of boats and many categories under each type. Only major varieties of the small family type boat without a motor, for daytime use, will be considered in this chapter.

Sailboats are the fastest growing type of boats, and probably the most popular of these is the cartop sailboat. This is a small boat, 11 to 12 feet long, normally with a single hull and single sail. Most will have less than 100 square feet of sail.

The smaller and cheaper cartop sailboats are relatively flat on top, which is where you lie or sit. But most of these sailboats will have a recessed area so that you can put your feet inside. The recessed type tends to be more comfortable.

While most sailboats have a single hull, many modern boats have two hulls, called a catamaran, or three hulls, which is a trimaran. Fiberglass is the most popular material, but many of the smaller boats are made of polystyrene, some with a hard surface covering.

These cartoppers are "fun boats" but as with any boat, skill in operation is important. It is strongly recommended that you wear a life preserver while sailing.

Sailing of any sort requires special skills. Any person planning to sail should take instructions, and then practice in lower wind velocities before venturing into higher winds and larger bodies of water.

Resting after sailing on a blue water lake.

Catamarans are probably the fastest sailing craft afloat, with double floats spaced some distance apart, and a good sized sail. Sails vary from about 90 square feet on a 12-foot boat to around 200 square feet on an 18-footer. There is little water resistance. Usually with a rudder on each float, catamarans are highly maneuverable.

Trimarans generally are larger boats and even more stable than catamarans. Since they are substantially bigger and more expensive, it is recommended that a family try smaller boats before getting a trimaran.

Probably most persons start out with rowboats. They are safe, maneuverable, durable, hold a small family comfortably, are easily transported on a cartop or in a station wagon, and may even be operated with a small outboard motor. They are also available for rent at most parks and boat rental agencies.

Rowboats are stable for fishing and general family use. Aluminum is the most common material, but some are now being made with fiberglass.

Canoes are the oldest type of boats in America, having been used by the Indians. They are light, maneuverable, readily operated by one or more persons, easy to portage around rapids or from one lake to another, an efficient way of moving over the water, and generally more fun than a rowboat.

While generally used for paddling in rivers and lakes, they also are used quite often in white water canoeing over rapids and in fast water, for floating down a river, and even for sailing. Canoes are more sensitive in operation than a rowboat and require more skill and care.

Kayaks are small, one-man canoe type boats, very light, very maneuverable, and fast.

Easily upset and righted again, a kayak usually has a canvas with a drawstring to fasten around the person to keep water out of the boat.

Kayaks generally are made of canvas over a framework. Some are made of rubberized inflatable material, and a few kayaks are aluminum.

AUTHOR *Karl Munson* is a recreation specialist in the Extension Service.

CO-AUTHOR *Ralph Patterson* is an agricultural engineer in the Extension Service.

There are a great number of rubberized inflatable craft for many uses. A small one-man raft is carried on some airplanes and boats for emergency use.

Rubberized craft are popular for duck hunting.

Sizes range from the one person type to big ones carrying 12 persons for large river floating. Probably the most common size is the four-man type.

Rubberized craft are made with compartments so that if one section is damaged and loses air the other units can keep the craft afloat. They are lightweight and ride on the surface of the water. Thus, wind can carry them over the water and make maneuvering difficult.

Some inflatable boats are in the shape of kayaks, canoes, and even rowboats. Rubberized canvas material is superior to vinyl or plastic in most cases. Some of the larger units have a provision for mounting outboard motors.

Heavy duty units are great for river floats and can even go through rough water. However, great caution must be observed to keep from hitting sharp rocks and other objects. Extreme care must be exercised during inflation of rubberized boats to guard against excess pressure and avoid opening seams.

Dinghies are very small light boats normally used in conjunction with a larger boat for emergency use or to get from the dock to the larger boat. They come in aluminum, fiberglass, polystyrene, and other materials. Probably the most common material is fiberglass. Some can be equipped with sails, but most have oars or paddles.

A few types of boats are available that can be folded for transport on cartops or in station wagons. They take considerable time for assembling. In purchasing this type boat, check very carefully to be sure you are saving time and the boat is what you want to meet your needs.

A john boat is essentially the same as a rowboat, except it is square at both ends. It is very stable and frequently used for fishing and hunting. It is usually transported on a cartop or in a station wagon.

Before buying a boat, try to attend a boat show where boats may be seen, analyzed, and compared. And if you can, take a ride in the type boat you decide to buy prior to signing on the dotted line.

Package Trips and Rentals

Different types of package trips can give you a great chance to see what kind of boating experience you like best. Package trips run from part of a day to several weeks. Generally a professional guide plans for the equipment and supplies needed.

Float trips can be found all over the U.S. Guide fees average around $25 per guide per day. The total package with food and other supplies varies greatly by the type of trip and comfort desired. An average might be $35 per 24 hours per person.

The best way to find out about these trips is to write the public authority for the area you want to visit. An example would be Grand Canyon National Park Headquarters. Some of the more popular trips require reservations six months in advance. So plan early and know what is furnished and what you must furnish.

There are whitewater schools in Colorado, California, and Canada that supply all the equipment and teaching for $130 a week and up. These schools generally last two weeks. Look for the special schools in sailing and navigating, often provided by the Coast Guard Auxiliary.

Boat Materials

Many types of materials are used in boats. Information from a reliable dealer for the type boat you are considering is highly desirable.

Generally speaking, aluminum for the smaller boats is light in weight, will bend rather than break or tear, is normally riveted but may be welded, and is easily maintained. Aluminum varies in thickness and in quality, primarily in heat treatment which increases strength and resistance to bending.

Fiberglass is a very popular material for boats. It is heavier than aluminum, is tough, can generally be very smooth on the surface, is easily maintained and corrosion-resistant, comes in many colors and color combinations, and is easily repaired. If color fades on fiberglass, it can be treated with a rubbing compound and waxed.

A.B.S., a new type material used primarily in canoes and light craft, is a high impact type plastic. In canoes it sometimes is used as one skin on the inside and outside, giving a glasslike appearance, with three layers of inner foam for flotation.

Corlite is a polystyrene with a plastic type covering. It is light and yet resists damage. Polystyrene is a foam type material which is very light, but easily damaged unless protected with a tougher coating. Some small sailboats are made of polystyrene.

PVC is a polyvinyl chloride material used with rubberized type rafts and boats. It is more durable and more flexible than rubber and will not rot as fast.

Hypalon is a very heavy, durable nylon type material. It is practically puncture-proof and is thus used for river rafts and inflatable boats. It is more expensive but worth the extra cost.

Canvas over wood is used as a covering for many small boats and canoes. It is lightweight and rather durable, but unless protected can be easily punctured and damaged.

In purchasing any boat be sure to check the various types of materials available in that particular boat, and select the one most suitable for your needs and the conditions under which you will be boating.

As a beginner, rent or arrange some tryout for any kind of boat you think you would like. Remember that skill is needed for real enjoyment.

Start with simple equipment, and trade for more advanced equipment as your skill and enthusiasm increases. A lot of people have bought expensive equipment, had a bad experience, and then found themselves taking a much lower price in order to sell.

Often money can be saved by purchasing good used equipment. Many camps and resorts use equipment for one year and then sell. You can try out the exact boat you might want to buy.

Dealers often have good used bargains, too.

Basic Equipment For Fishermen

If fishing were a man, he would be a man for all seasons. No other sport offers such breadth of year-round satisfaction or such a gamut of challenges to both mind and hand.

It provides compensations to the most vigorous who seek the stimulation and rewards of fishing the remote mountain lakes and creeks reached only after arduous back-packing excursions, or of deep-sea expeditions after giant marlin and tuna. But it also serves the more contemplative who seek the quiet repose of still fishing from an anchored skiff, or who gain fulfillment from the artful practice of fly tying.

As a start let's consider the various species of fish you might wish to catch. We shall divide fish into three broad categories; panfish, gamefish, and sea fish.

Generally most of us start fishing for panfish. This group includes the sunfish family, yellow perch, and catfish. All these fish take readily and willingly to a wide variety of lures or baits, and they are delicious when served in or directly from the pan.

Panfish can be enticed by fishermen with the simplest of equipment and the most elementary technique. A cane pole, a length of line, a float, a hook, and a worm will suffice for any of the panfish. Once caught they can be prepared for the pan by scaling and gutting or alternatively they may be skinned and filleted.

Once the panfish angler achieves his initial goal of demonstrating his or her ability to catch panfish repetitively, he may strive to enhance the quality of his fishing experience. In so doing the first step is to upgrade his equipment so that the available range of lures, line weights, distances, etc., is substantially increased. Usually a spinning reel and rod are selected as the next phase in advancement.

The spinning reel consists of a stationary spool carrying a length of monofilament line, a bail or pickup device to direct the line onto the reel and a crank which rotates the pickup device restoring the line to the spool.

In operation the lure, attached to the monofilament line and dangling several inches beyond the rod tip, is cast by swinging the rod from a position slightly behind the shoulder through a forward arc to a position in front at approximately eye level. Proper timing of finger pressure on the line as it leaves the reel combined with the rod acceleration controls the distance the lure will travel.

Spinning gear will provide the family with a very versatile fishing tool. Lures as light as a sixteenth of an ounce with two-pound test monofilament line will provide enjoyable sport with any of the panfish. Heavier lures and lines will more than adequately subdue far larger fish.

Lures are available in a near infinite range of weights, sizes, shapes, and colors and include such items as spoons, spinners, jigs, plugs, and bugs as well as natural baits.

With adequate spinning gear, anyone is prepared to pursue the fascinating and challenging game fish. This category includes the world famous and aristocratic salmon, the trout, the chars, the grayling, the basses, and the pike family.

Salmon fishing is quite specialized, essentially restricted to the more northerly coastal states, and tends to be the province of the relatively affluent angler. However, the Kokanee and Coho salmon offer reasonable angling opportunities in many cold water lakes.

Pursuit of the trout in free-running streams or cold water lakes satisfies the needs of many persons for physical as well as intellectual involvement. Although many trout annually are taken with spinning gear employing artificial lures as well as natural baits of a wide variety, the prime quality experience accrues to those who meet the gamefish with a fly fishing rig.

Perhaps the most sought after gamefish are the trout and chars. These fish —such as the brown, rainbow, and brook trout—not only provide an abundance of pleasurable and uncounted hours to fishermen but also support an enormous tackle and hatchery industry as well. Trout can be found in commercial ponds, in cold water lakes, and in free-running clear and cold streams.

At commercial ponds, equipment is usually readily available or one may choose to try out personal fishing gear with an assured probability of success. However, most fishermen find the easily repetitive success of the commercial ponds totally lacking in intellectual stimulation and seek the trout on more even sporting terms.

In fly fishing the angler casts a minute, lightweight lure, the fly, to either a spot where he has detected a fish rising to the surface or where he thinks there might be one lurking.

Because of the lightness of the fly it is not possible to cast it directly, employing its mass to drag line off a reel as is the case in spin or bait casting. Instead, a length of the heavier fly line is stripped off the reel. Using the fly rod, you flip the line into the air overhead and behind and then follow through with a forward power stroke accelerating the line so that it travels toward the selected stream spot. The weightier fly line in its forward mo-

---

AUTHOR *Thomas L. Kimball* is Executive Vice President, National Wildlife Federation, Washington, D.C.

Top, simple fishing gear for a youngster. Above, lucky fisherman holds a trout.

mentum carries the leader and the fly with it.

In this manner by casting the fly line instead of the lure, it is possible to deliver an ultra-lightweight fly to a specific fish with delicacy and accuracy.

Longer flyrods, 8½ to 9 feet, provide matched sport for the larger gamefish such as the salmon and salt water species as well as possessing the necessary strength and stiffness to deliver larger bug lures for the bass family. More probably, however, the bass fisherman will want to select either spin fishing, spin-casting or bait casting equipment.

Spin-casting gear is quite similar to spin fishing in that a closed-face, fixed spool reel is employed. Because the line spool is enclosed, direct finger pressure cannot be used and instead a thumb key is provided to control the flow of the line. Due to the greater confinement of the line, higher friction loads are developed. Thus, spin-casting reels won't function with lures as lightweight as those usable in spinning.

Bait-casting rigs employ a free running spool and are used to deliver lures and baits similar in size to the spin-casting gear. Both of these units are often applied to trolling for pickerel, pike, and muskellunge as well as for large– and smallmouth bass and a wide variety of other pan– and gamefish.

Of necessity, highly–specialized fishing activities demand the appropriate furnishings.

For example, backpacking fishing expeditions favor the use of lightweight reels and combination spin and fly rods which dismount into four or more short sections.

When ice covers many of the lakes and ponds, different fishing techniques come into play. Holes chopped through the ice cover let the fisherman present his lure, which is usually a live minnow, to the fish below.

The remaining category of fish, namely seafish, share many of the characteristics of the other classes and hence quite similar equipment is used. There are, however, two major environmental differences which deserve specific consideration:

1. The corrosive nature of salt water puts a premium on equipment able to withstand its effects.

2. The generally larger size of the fish and the surging nature of the surf tend to favor substantially heavier gear whether it be flyrods, spin, spin-casting, or bait-casting in nature.

Frequently, worrisome choices are faced in selecting the first set of fishing gear for the family. For the very youngest a bamboo pole with line, bobber, hook, and worms will suffice. For those with better coordination, spinning gear is the suggested choice to cover a very broad range of fishing needs.

In selecting equipment for women, lighter weight tackle will prove to be doubly satisfying from the criteria of handling ease and fishing pleasure.

If the very best is desired, split bamboo rods or the newest boron or high modulus graphite fiber rods deserve attention.

For the ultimate in an enjoyable, peak quality experience, try fly fishing with barbless hooks which allow injury-free release of the fish in accord with the highest principles of conservation.

Bring It All Back Alive, On Film

THE GREAT MOUNTAIN with its everlasting glaciers reflected the pink alpine glow of a midsummer sunset over a Western National Forest. In the foreground, a pair of mountaineer tents, one yellow and one orange, nestled in the high-country meadow as the family of four huddled over a flickering campfire.

"Wow, Dad, it's just like being there again," exclaimed a young voice from the darkness.

The living room lights came on to break the magic on the screen, and the smiling father switched off the projector, silently congratulating himself again for taking the effort to carry those extra few pounds of photographic gear on the family backpacking trip the previous summer.

It was well worth that effort, for the record of priceless experiences shared by the family will be relived time and time again, thanks to the medium of photography. Like countless thousands of people, the family had left only footsteps, and taken only pictures. The footsteps would disappear; the pictures would live on to recall carefree days on the trail.

The father-photographer had planned well, choosing carefully from the broad array of photographic equipment available. He had decided that color slides would best serve his needs, but he wanted the capability of photographing everything from a dewdrop on the delicate petal of a wildflower, to the wide panorama of a glaciated valley, to a full-frame closeup of a deer feeding at the edge of the meadow.

This man is my friend. Unlike me, photography does not help provide his living, but it is something he wants to do well, and does do well.

Photography, like most things in life, represents a lot of compromise. In some 20 years of taking pictures, I've never yet found the exact combination of cameras, lenses, and film to do everything. I don't think any other photographer has either, or ever will. But there are nearly perfect combinations for many if not most photographic needs.

Getting back to my friend, he talked a lot to me and other photographers and to photo dealers before deciding on some major photographic purchases. He based his purchase decisions on his particular needs and what he could afford.

My friend is an outdoorsman in a medium income bracket. He and his family do a lot of backpacking in the National Forests. The photo equipment he chose and the rationale behind his decisions may be of interest to others with similar likes.

AUTHOR *Jim Hughes* is a photographer-writer with the Forest Service's information office in Portland, Oreg.

For his basic camera, he opted for a 35 mm single lens reflex (SLR) with a standard 50 mm lens. (A single lens reflex, for the benefit of those just venturing into photography, has the valuable feature of allowing you to focus and frame on your subject through the same lens that will take the picture. In other words, you see what the film will see and record.)

The SLR would provide my friend with the versatility he needs to take many kinds of pictures. Versatility, translated, means he could use a wide range of interchangeable lenses, from extreme wide-angle to far-reaching telephoto. The through-the-lens feature allows him to frame on his subject with exactness, and this is very important in making that closeup picture of the dewdrop or honey bee on a flower petal.

There are many, many SLR cameras on the market—most of them good, and some of them superb. Brand names are familiar, like Nikon, Canon, Pentax, Minolta, Topcon, Mamiya, Konica, Olympus, Yashica, Miranda, and the Rolls Royce of the bunch, Leicaflex. You can pay anything from around $200 to well over $500.

My friend, who is not rich, looked them all over, and finally found one that really felt good to him. He could focus easily and quickly (and he wears glasses), and all the controls seemed to be in the right place.

The camera was in a bracket he could afford. It was also a brand that's apt to be around for a long time. No "photographic Edsels" for him.

His new camera featured built-in light metering, as do most if not all SLR's on the market today. Some are even so sophisticated that the process is entirely automatic—you just point the camera, focus, and shoot. Other SLR's haven't gone quite that far, and the photographer still has to set the exposure by manually positioning a needle visible in the viewfinder.

My friend couldn't begin to afford all the interchangeable lenses available for his camera, nor would he even want them all. But he did buy two lenses besides the standard 50 mm lens that came with his camera. He decided on a 35 mm wide-angle for around $150, and a 100 mm telephoto for $175. With the three lenses, he could cover most photo situations.

The whole outfit set him back around $700, quite a lot of money, but it represented part of his income tax refund,

Taken with a medium telephoto lens.

and credit unions do loan money for such purchases. Later there will be other acquisitions, like a super wide-angle lens and maybe a 200 mm telephoto, or a macro lens capable of focusing extremely close.

With his initial purchases, my friend was actually starting on the acquisition of a photographic system that can be broadened as far as his interest and resources dictate. Many people start only with the basic camera and lens, and it might be years before they add the wide-angle or telephoto.

My friend could have saved money by buying used lenses. Real bargains are available, provided care is exercised in making the choice.

A worn-out lens is just that, however, and usually they can be spotted by assorted scratches, gouges, and dents in the mount, perhaps scratches on the lens elements, and looseness in the focusing mechanism. Be wary of such "bargains" at any price.

Another route might be to choose from the wide selection of lenses made for the camera, but by different manufacturers. Usually they are much less expensive, although the quality varies greatly. Ask to see some test evidence of lens quality before you invest in one.

Used cameras also can be found at bargain prices, but here again the buyer should be wary. The best rule is to buy from reputable dealers, who may even be willing to let you try out the equipment for a short time, during which you can consult with a trusted camera repairman.

Back to my photographer friend, he bought a few other necessities for his trail trip. He was going to shoot only color transparency film, so he purchased a skylight filter for each lens.

My own perhaps overly simple theory about filters is that they probably will help the pictures, and will harm them only very rarely.

I use skylight filters for all outdoor color photography, and medium yellow filters for outdoor black and white pictures. Skylight filters provide a slight corrective influence over outdoor color

A single lens reflex camera enables you to focus closely and compose carefully for subjects such as this wildrose.

film in most cases, and the yellow filters help bring out clouds and make the sky darker for black and white photography.

An added advantage, of course, is that filters offer fairly cheap insurance against surface damage to the front optics of those precious lenses. That's reason enough for using filters when you're working in the outdoors.

My friend also bought a lightweight tripod to give him the camera steadiness so necessary for making sharp pictures at slow shutter speeds, say at 1/60th of a second or less.

He has discovered, as have lots of other photographers, that some of the best pictures are made when light conditions aren't exactly bright, especially that magic time just before, during, and after sunup, and just before, during, and after sundown. The colors seem to take on a whole new aura that is sometimes breathtaking. But to take such pictures, one must use a steady tripod. Added weight for the pack, but well worth it.

A tripod-mounted camera can, for instance, record the poetic, flowing motion of a mountain stream dashing over mossy rocks in a mountain glen. Try it sometime, when the light is dim

Backpackers who carry their camera in a ready position are always prepared.

enough to dictate slow shutter speeds and the required tripod.

On most modern cameras, there's another device which can be put to good use. My friend used it when he took the picture of sundown on the mountain, with him and his wife and two children around the campfire. The device, of course, is the self-timer. With the camera mounted on a tripod, he set the timer and had ample seconds to join the family group and get himself into the picture before the shutter tripped.

My friend's total outfit weighs around five pounds. When hiking, he carries the camera slung in front of him from the frame of his backpack. The accessory lenses, in their cylinder-like leather carrying cases, are also slung from the pack within easy reach. Film, tripod, and other accessories are close at hand too in side pockets of the pack.

On other than hiking trips, the whole outfit can be compactly packed in a leather gadget bag.

Opposite page, hikers find ample use for medium telephoto lens, such as for this view of aptly named Solitude Lake in The Enchantment area of Wenatchee National Forest, Washington.

My friend's penchant for keeping his photo outfit small and compact is being shared by more and more photographers, even those who aren't hikers or bikers. With cars becoming smaller, with less and less trunk space for carrying anything, and with more and more people relying on public transportation, the advantages of simplifying one's photo gear are obvious.

There are other ways to simplify that should not be overlooked. Consider, for instance, the marvelous zoom lenses which are gaining increasing acceptance from professional and amateur photographers alike.

One of my colleagues used a 43 to 86 mm zoom lens on a trip through Germany and relied on it completely. He was especially appreciative of the fact that he could get semi-wide-angle views and medium telephoto shots, and everything in between, without having to carry extra lenses.

"I was taking pictures while others in the party were fiddling around, trying to choose the right lens for the view, or wishing they had the right lens," my colleague said.

Another space and weight saving photographic option worthy of consideration involves the compact little rangefinder cameras which have really come of age as a serious photographic instrument.

The better ones have the feature of operating either completely automatically—point, focus, and shoot—or their exposures can be set manually.

The cameras are small. A typical one measures only 2¾ inches high by 4¼ inches wide, and less than 2 inches thick—a true pocket or purse sized camera. It uses standard 35 mm film, and provides a full size 35 mm negative.

Most of the compact rangefinder cameras sell, at this writing, in the $100 to $150 price range. Considering the quality of the cameras and the pictures they can produce, the compacts appear to be the photographic bargain of the present era.

There are, of course, many other camera options to consider, like the instant loading models with their drop-in film cartridges, the sub-miniatures, and the bigger cameras that use 120 roll film.

It all comes down to what best fits your photographic needs.

To help you make the choice, excellent photographic publications—monthly magazines, directories, photo annuals—are available, helping you to answer the "what shall I buy and how much must I expect to pay" questions peculiar to each individual. Photo store clerks also stand ready for consultation, and always there are people like me to talk with.

The ultimate rewards in photography come in responses such as that from the young son of my hiking photographer friend:

"Wow, Dad, it's just like being there again."

Don't Rush Out For a Ski Outfit: Make Sure It's Your Snowflake

WHEN THAT DAY comes, with snow hanging in the trees, with billions of sparkling diamonds at your ski tips, with the wind in your face as you plunge down a steep hill through untracked snow, when everything is just right, you will realize why you joined millions of others in taking up skiing.

Although new equipment and teaching methods have made skiing less of a struggle to learn, you will still put forth effort and spend money. This is not to imply that skiing is only a rich man's sport. But if you're serious about skiing, you will find it to be your prime outdoor interest. You will save for skiing and be glad you did.

Cross-country is the fastest growing and the most economical phase of skiing. For the basics, you'll spend about $100—on skis, bindings, poles and boots.

Another $15 or $20 will pay for a few lessons and you'll be on your own to ramble along through the mountains and the valleys. You need no lift tickets, only leg and lung power.

But it is the downhill, the alpine skiing, that provides the real thrills and challenges. Alpine can be compared to cross-country as a sprint runner might contrast his sport with hiking.

The cross-country skier appreciates the solitude of the forests and fields as he glides on his way. The alpine skier appreciates these things; but he gets more kick from his plunge down a steep trail or a moguled face, showing his technique by mastering whatever springs up in his path.

The first big question is to find out if you really *are* a potential skier. The

Chair lift takes skiers to jumping off site.

most economical solution is to rent equipment the first time around. Best bet is to sign up for one of the short courses of lessons, perhaps four or five weekends of them ($25 to $75). You'll be in a class of six to 12, all beginners.

Be sure to rent *good* equipment for the class periods. Junky or poor-fitted equipment will discourage you easily.

If you happen to enroll in a GLM (Graduated Length Method) class of instruction, and most beginners learn by this method now, your equipment is set up for you. You gradually progress to longer lengths of skis as your instructor decides your proficiency has reached that point.

From a reputable ski shop you can usually rent skis, boots and poles for a month or so, at a package price. Some shops have a lease-purchase plan where you can apply at least a portion of your rental fee toward a later purchase.

AUTHOR *Bill Keil,* of Portland, Oreg., a skier for more than 30 years, is a freelance writer and photographer specializing in skiing, forestry and other outdoor subjects.

At first, don't worry about ski clothes which can take a big bite from your budget. Be sure you're serious, first.

Nearly everyone in the cold country has some sort of parka. You can wear jeans or other rough outdoor clothing, though you'll want a pair of warmup pants ($15 to $20) to wear over them.

You need a good warm cap, preferably wool, at $5 to $7.50. Wool is the best cold weather clothing. Even when wet, it provides good insulation.

Dark glasses and sunburn preventive are other musts. Even on cloudy days, you can singe your skin. Generally, you ski at higher elevations where there is less atmosphere to screen out the sun's burning rays. You not only get sun from above, but the rays are reflected back from the snow surface to provide a double dose.

Costs of equipment and lifts are rising, along with everything else in the inflationary economy. Lift tickets can cost from $7 to $11, where a few years ago a $3 to $5 tab was the rule. But the lifts are more sophisticated, longer and faster, and the slopes are maintained much better for more pleasurable skiing.

A seat-mate on a chairlift not long ago confessed that he had never skied in deep snow. He had always been on tractor-packed slopes.

And this is all part of the current trend toward quite short skis, easier to handle for beginners, easy to turn, and perfectly adequate on packed slopes.

However, in deep snow and at faster speeds for more advanced skiers, longer lengths are probably more appropriate.

Skiers are starting on skis as short as 140 to 150 centimeters, gradually working upward toward 200 centimeters or slightly longer lengths.

Ski equipment is in the vanguard of the gradual U.S. conversion to the metric system. Skiers are in the habit, perhaps because nearly all the higher quality models of skis once came from Europe, where metrication is standard.

After you're hooked on skiing is the time to think about buying equipment. You can take some advice from your instructor who is familiar with your skiing and your potential. He can tell you the quality and length of skis you need.

It's best to stick with a reputable ski shop. After you become intimately familiar with equipment, you can consider the cut rate and discount outlets. Often you can get good buys from bankrupt stocks and abandoned lines from the cut-raters, but you have to know your way around. I bought my first pair of skis from one of those places, paying a fast-talking salesman twice what they were worth.

Most ski shops have good money-saving sales in September or October and in February.

Of the four major equipment items, boots are probably the most important. Then come the skis and bindings. Poles ($7 to $30) have the lowest priority on the money scale.

Get Plastic Boots

There is no reason to consider anything other than plastic boots these days. They provide the nuance of control you need with the present high performance skis and skiing methods. Rely on a good boot salesman to get a good fit. And the boots *must fit*. Plastic boots do not "break in" to any great extent, although small adjustments can be made.

The boots will cost you from around $50 to $200.

There is no need to go into the various styles and components of skis here, other than the fact that the all-wood ski is nearly gone, although wood is a component of nearly every ski—both metal and plastic. Rely on your instructor and the salesman for advice. Skis will cost you from $75 to $200.

Dozens of binding models are produced with the general principle that the binding will release your boot from the ski should stresses build up which might be strong enough to injure you.

Here, again, rely upon professional advice.

Bindings must be adjusted tight enough so they will not release during the normal stresses of skiing. You can get hurt should a ski release while you are skiing normally, just as you can be injured in a fall if the binding does not release.

Insist that your binding settings be checked on a machine, of which several are available. Your ski shop has tables to correctly set the bindings for your size and ability. Insist that a proper non-friction device be installed on the ski surface so your boot will slide out of the binding with minimum friction, when necessary.

Once you've made the large investment in ski equipment, you will certainly want to protect it. Put some kind of inconspicuous personal mark on your skis so you can identify them, if stolen. Probably you will want your name engraved on them, and you will record the serial number stamped on the skis. Poles are more difficult to identify so mark them, too.

You wouldn't leave a $250 camera lying in the snow while you went into the lodge for coffee; but skiers do this all the time with their skis.

Coin-in-the-slot locking ski racks are available in most ski areas. The dime or quarter is cheap insurance.

Now, perhaps, you will want a pair of regular ski pants ($30 to $50), although you'll find that the warmup pants will generally serve well.

In any case, you want only the over-the-boot type pants, or knickers, with your new plastic boots. The high tight-fitting boots will prove quite uncomfortable if you put them on over the old conventional ski pants with an elasticized loop under the instep.

Either layered ($15) or fishnet ($8) underwear will help keep you warm on colder days as will a good fitting sweater.

So much for the equipment. Of course, there are ski racks, ski and boot-carrying bags (a good idea if you travel much by airplane or bus), and gobs of other items, some useful, some gimcracks.

In this day of growing transportation problems, you might consider joining a ski club known for its travels. More clubs are chartering buses for trips, even to their local ski areas, as well as for longer trips. You can take advantage of group rates. This applies to lodging as well.

Often you can save on your budget by patronizing small hotels or motels a short distance from the ski resort.

Cross-country skiing can naturally extend into winter camping. For a reasonably healthy outdoorsman, winter camping is not much more strenuous than summer camping.

A good warm down sleeping bag ($60 to $100), a two-man lightweight tent ($40 to $100), a miniature lightweight stove ($12 to $20) are the only real essentials. These are the general run of prices in my part of the country.

Of course, you will want the usual back-packing essentials, food, and a good backpack ($35 to $75). If you plan to do much downhill skiing on your camping trips you might want a heavy-duty rucksack, where the weight will be carried lower than in a regular frame backpack.

You lose heat fast if you're wet, so get a good lightweight rain and wind parka and rain pants ($15 to $20). Your warmup pants can do double-duty here.

But you must be familiar with the basics of winter survival, map and compass work, and travel in a group for safety with definite word left with a responsible person as to your location.

You might want to winter-camp from your car, although there are problems. Many campgrounds are closed in the winter. At times there are even problems of finding a safe place to park your car when you go off on the trail. The car can't be left in the way of snowplows.

For on-the-road camping, such things as catalytic heaters make life easier. They are not much of a fire hazard, except during startup when they flare for a bit before settling down to a warm glow.

They burn oxygen, and adequate ventilation is necessary to replace the oxygen and to dispense the water vapor given off.

A tent or camper-truck can become saturated, with the cold walls providing condensation surfaces. Moisture from cooking and even your breath collects, too, so you can bring down a rainstorm when you brush against the wall or ceiling.

Perhaps it's all a throwback to America's frontier heritage—finding comfort in a little discomfort, and recreation in a little adversity.

But with today's equipment, you have to work to find either discomfort or adversity.

Bow and Arrow Hunting Gear

BOWHUNTING is America's First Sport, starting with the Indians, and it's growing everyday. Millions of Americans have added a new dimension to the sport of hunting—the challenge of hunting game, fish and varmints with bow and arrow. Most States offer a special season, during which hunters can try their hand at this age-old sport.

Like any other sport, it's important to have proper equipment to obtain the maximum enjoyment. Let's look at the equipment aspect of this all-American adventure sport.

Archery itself is quite simple, requiring only a bow, a few arrows, an arm guard, and a glove or tab. A few bales of hay will provide a safe target. Bowhunting requires a better grade of equipment, special arrows, and a host of minor items of importance to the hunting archer.

The best source of information about bowhunting is an archery club or hunting club with active bowhunters. Lacking this, perhaps the next best thing is to see a competent archery dealer. If you can find a sports shop or store that specializes in archery, ask the store's advice on getting outfitted.

Archery tackle may look alike but much of it is unique and an archery pro shop, indoor archery lane operator, or a willing bowman is the best way to get off on the right foot.

Advice is what you are seeking, so listen to the pro. Your tackle depends much on the game that you will be hunting: An Alaska moose hunter requires different bows and arrows than does a Texas rabbit hunter.

Deer are the most popular target for bowhunters, and are hunted in all 50 States, even in Hawaii. For deer the lightest weight bow a man should use would be a 45 lb draw weight bow. Ladies and youths may use a 40 lb bow; check your State laws, because some States have a minimum weight. An adult male can use a 50 lb bow, which with a little practice will take deer, black bear, antelope and similar game.

Bows come in three basic types: (1) A straight bow, (2) a recurve with the tips drawn against the curve, and (3) the modern compound bow with a pair of wheels, a pair of pulleys and a pair of cables.

A hunting bow will cost anywhere from $35 on up to what one would pay for a fine rifle or shotgun. Average price for a good recurve hunting bow runs about $50 to $75, and compound bows run from $100 to $255. Bowhunters take pride in their equipment; with proper care a bow can last a lifetime.

Arrows are the most important part of the bowhunter's equipment. This is the part of the tackle most often overlooked by the novice hunter. Arrows must be matched to each other, to the bow being used, and to the hunter's draw length.

If the arrows do not match one another, they will never shoot in a consistent manner, regardless of the marksmanship of the archer or the quality of the archer's bow. When purchasing arrows, make sure the box states they are for a "50 lb to 55 lb Bow." An arrow made for a 40 to 45 lb bow will not shoot correctly from a 55 lb bow.

Likewise it's very important that all the arrows match in size, length, feather,

Above, practice makes perfect. Note new compound bow. Top, a hunting bow.

etc. Mixed arrows will not fly in a group. You may use your "odd" arrows for small game or practice, but for your big hunt, use the very best arrows you can get.

Modern arrows are wood, made from Port Orford Cedar, or hollow fiberglass, or alloy aluminum which also is hollow. Wood is the least expensive and best for novices. Fiberglass is the toughest, and stands abuse better. Aluminum is the most accurate and can be restraightened when bent.

Veteran bowhunters favor aluminum while the tyro starts with glass or wood.

Most important part of the hunting arrow is the tip. Big game hunters use a broadhead, an arrowhead with steel blades with 2, 3, 4, or 6 cutting edges.

Only a few heads that use actual injector blades are sharp enough to hunt with, and all must be sharpened before being used for hunting. A suitable test is to see if the arrow will shave hair off your forearm. If it won't, it's not sharp enough to hunt with.

Flat mill bastard files, oil stones, and carbon steel kitchen knife sharpeners will sharpen a broadhead to shaving sharpness.

Some heads use real razorblades which insert into the head; they are great time-savers.

Small game hunters may use a blunt tip arrow for rabbits, squirrels, and birds. These kill by the stunning, shocking action of the blow.

Rough fish are popular targets. The

AUTHOR *Tink Nathan* is Contributing Editor of *Bowhunter Magazine* and has hunted big game with bow and arrow the world over. He lives in McLean, Va.

bowfisherman uses a solid glass arrow with a harpoon tip called a fish point with a heavy 100 lb test line for taking carp, gar, rays, skates, shark, turtles and other water-based game. Check with your game warden for local laws and regulations. Here any bow is suitable; even a child's solid glass target bow will work on rough fish.

A bowfishing outfit with reel runs from $5 to $9, not including the bow. Most bowhunters use a bow quiver which protects the fine edges the hunter has worked to apply to his broadhead hunting arrows. This bow quiver, which fits on the bow, must have a shield to protect the hunter from the deadly tips. A good bow quiver costs from $10 to $20 and may hold from 4 to 18 arrows.

Hunting bows run heavier in draw weight than lighter target and field archery bows, and a glove is preferred to protect the fingers from the string. A good glove costs about $4 and an arm guard about $5.

Modern bowhunters often use a sight. A simple sight with 4 pins (set at 5, 15, 25, and 35 yards) will cost under $7.

Bowhunters should carry a spare string or two with them. Most wear camouflage clothing to match the terrain they hunt in. A camo hat, jacket and pants can be made from an old pair of army fatigues or khaki and dye and shoe polish, or can be purchased for under $15.

Bowhunting is a family sport, one that Mom and Junior can share with Dad and Grandpa. It need not be expensive and it yields more enjoyment per dollar and hours invested than any other sport I know. During the few off months, magazines and books on bowhunting sharpen one's skills and provide additional hours of recreation.

Once a family starts bowhunting, hunters can make their own equipment. With a simple set of tools the home craftsman can make the finest hunting arrows his heart desires with his own crest and feather colors.

If you're handy with power tools and possess some patience, you might buy semi-finished bow kits or kits with which to build bows. Savings up to 80 percent are possible. Many industrial arts teachers instruct in bow building at high schools and some fine looking bows are produced as a result.

For good reading on bowhunting try "Bowhunting for Deer", published by the National Field Archery Assn., Rt. #2, Box 514, Redlands, Calif.; the "Archer's Digest" and "The Archer's Bible" by Fred Bear. The only national magazine devoted solely to bowhunting is *Bowhunter Magazine,* P.O. Box 5377, Fort Wayne, Ind. 46804.

Bow clubs thrive across the nation; you may find one near you. Since getting off to the proper start requires accurate information, it pays to check on these clubs.

Another source of information is your local game warden, who might tell you where area bowhunters meet. Outdoor writers on newspapers may be able to guide you to the club or group in your area.

Many large archery manufacturers will send free catalogs. Some contain valuable shooting information and instructions. Another source of information is the American Archery Council, 618 Chalmers Street, Flint, Mich.

Each year many people become bowhunting enthuiasts through archery. Likewise, many people enjoy the fun of archery through bowhunting.

Now that archery is an Olympic sport, and especially since Americans won both Gold medals in 1972 at Munich, more and more of us are becoming well aware of these two sister sports. That's why both sports gain new fans each year. In 1973 Pennsylvania alone sold 190,000 archery hunting licenses!

Last year close to 2 million people used a bow for hunting. The romance of the bow is here to stay, and it's just a matter of time before the bow will be as common a sight as a tennis racket or golf club. It's been said that archery is the King of Sports, and that Bowhunting, America's First Sport, is also "The sport of man since time began."

Good Hunting!

SOURCES OF PHOTOGRAPHY

THE PUBLISHER gratefully acknowledges the kindness of all organizations for permission to reprint their photographs, sketches, and diagrams. While most of the photographs in this publication were prepared by the photographers from the U.S. Department of Agriculture (USDA), contributions have been made by other federal agencies, the state land grant universities and colleges, magazines, authors, associations, and industry. Photo credits follow, with page numbers indicated; USDA photographs are listed only where the photographer's name is known.

Molly Adams for Alice R. Ireys, landscape architect, 263 (bottom right)
American Standard, 172 (top left)
Mary Ann Bader, American Automobile Association, 307
Don Baldwin (USDA), 319
Designed by Armand Benedek, landscape architect, 263 (top)
Charles L. Benn, Iowa State University, 137, 140 (all photos), 141 (all photos)
Murray M. Berman (USDA), 29

Illustrations courtesy *Better Homes and Gardens*: 152 © Meredith Corporation, 1970, 9, 20, 227, © Meredith Corporation, 1973.

Bicycle Institute of America, Inc., 324, 326
Brick Institute of America, 95 (all photos), 97 (all photos)
A. E. Bye Associates, 264
Chicago Horticultural Society, 268
Everett Conklin and Company, Inc., 231 (all photos)
Council of Better Business Bureaus, 284, 285
W. E. Cunningham, 242, 245
Duane D. Davis (USDA), 315 (top right)
Robert J. DeWitz (USDA), 330
Fiat Corp., 172 (bottom right)
Food and Drug Administration, 64
Frigidaire Division—General Motors Corp., 271
Chuck Herron (USDA), title page, 1
Hoard's Dairyman, 163
Jim Hughes (USDA), 313, 339, 340, 341, 342, 343
Starr Jenkins (USDA), 318 (both photos)
Charles Johnston, Arkansas Cooperative Extension Service, 193 (all photos)
Louis Joyner, *Southern Living*, 89
Kohler Co., 171, 172 (top right)
Murray Lemmon (USDA), 185, 186, 234, 235, 352
Larry L. Lundquist, Kansas State University, 177 (both photos)
Bluford W. Muir (USDA), 323 (top), 329, 333, 337 (top)
Elaine Myers, Texas Agricultural Extension Service, 201
National Live Stock & Meat Board chart, 79
National Swimming Pool Institute, 123 (all photos)
New York State College of Agriculture and Life Sciences at Cornell University, 224, 225 (both photos)
R. J. Obyc (USDA), 338
Portland Cement Association, 90, 91
Lee Prater (USDA), 337 (bottom)
Larry Rana (USDA), 2
Rival Manufacturing Co., 167
George Robinson (USDA), 304
Edwin C. Rockwell (USDA), 345
Jack S. Schneider (USDA), 291 (top left, bottom right)
Sears, Roebuck and Co., 279 (all photos)
Lester Shepard (USDA), 55
Ray T. Steiger (USDA), 315 (bottom left)
Dan Todd (USDA), 314, 320
U. S. Army Corps of Engineers, 316 (all photos)
Harold Walter (USDA), 315 (top left)
Fred S. Witte (USDA), 3, 291 (top right), 323 (bottom)

INDEX

AAN Standards Committee, 247
Abrasives, 198–199
ABS plastic pipe, 132
Acclimating house plants, 232–233
Acerola, 258
Acid water, 130
Acoustical and Insulating Materials Association, 115
Acoustical tile, 114
Acrylonitrile-Butadiene-Styrene, 131
Actinidia chinensis, 257
Adam's needle, 228
Administration on Aging, 295, 298
Agave, 227
Ageratum, 212, 215, 218
Aikman, Bonnie, 306–310
Air conditioners, 164
Aizoaceae, 227
Allen, Marcile, 44–50
All Weather Comfort Standard, 135-136
Aluminum filters, 166
Alyssum, 212, 215
Amaranthus, 212, 215
American Archery Council, 350
American Association of Nurserymen, Inc., 237
American Boxwood Society, 250
American College Testing, 288
American Gas Association, 164, 178
American Hardwood Association, 115
American Horticultural Society, Inc., 250
American National Standards Institute, Inc., 237
American Rose Society, 250
American Society for Testing and Material, 98
Ananas comosus, 259
Anderson, Jacqueline, 164–168
Annual flowers and vegetables, 208–219
Anodization, 142
Antillian avocado, 256
Aphrodite begonias, 224
Aporocactus, 228
Apples, 8, 253–255
Appliance repairs, 302–305
Apricots, 254
Arboretums, 245, 266–271
Archery, 348–350
Arnold Arboretum, 245
Arnst, Albert, 324–327
Asbestos Insulation, 127; shingles, 113; vinyl, 119
Ascorbic acid, 3
Asparagus, 8
Asphalt tile, 119
Association of Home Appliance Manufacturers, 164, 165
Aster, 212, 215
Atrium, 198
Astrophytum, 228
Attic fans, 160–161
Automatic defrost freezer, 166
Automatic washers, 168
Automobile diagnostic center, 308
Automobile transmission repairs, 307
Averrhoa carambola, 258
Awning, 264–265
Azaleas, 223–224, 268

Baby foods, 67
Baby's toes, 228
Backpacking: belt, 329; catalogs, 328; expense, 327, 329; frame, 328–329; gear, 327–332; magazines, 327; packs, 327; shoes, 327, 328, 332; sleeping bags, 327, 329–331; socks, 328; storage bag, 329; tent, 331
Bakery products, 20
Balconies, 195
Balsam, 212, 215
Bamboo Palm, 230
Banana, 258
Barbecue, 94
Bare root, 237, 239, 246, 257
Barquest, Glenn, 202–204
Batcher, Olive M., 21–26
Bath mats, 174
Bathroom exhaust systems, 173
Bathroom, 170–175; fixtures, 130; gadgets, 174
Bathtubs, 171–173
Batts, 133
Beal-Garfield Botanic Gardens, 245
Begonias: fibrous, tuberous, 212, 215
Bells of Ireland, 222
Beans, 8, 20
Beaverboard, 112
Beck, Sara, 87–88
Beef, 78–80; freezing, 44–50
Bellis, Tom, 55–62
Bengal, 258
Berninger, Lou, 219–222
Berry, Jane, 195–198
Better Business Bureau, 282
Bellingrath Gardens, 268
Bicycle: 3, 5, and 10 speed, 325; baskets, 324; bikeways, 327; brake pads, 325; coaster brake, 325; cycling activities, 326; dropped - handlebar model, 325; dual wheel caliper brakes, 325; educational program, 327; fender guards, 325; handlebars, 325; Kryptonite lock, 326; luggage racks, 324; main-

tenance, 326; multiple gear, 325; pedal style, 326; racing models, 324; rat trap pedals, 326; renting, 324; rubber pedals, 326; saddle bags, 324; safety, 326; safety from theft, 326; sales, 324; styles, 324–325; test for size, 325; tours, 324; training wheels, 326; used, 324–325; workshops, 326
Bidets, 173
Biotin, 3
Bird of Paradise, 219
Bird's Nest cactus, 228
Bishop's cap, 228
Blackberry, 250–253
Black sapote, 258
Blankets, 206–208
Bleaches, 170
Blueberry, 250, 252
Bluefre plums, 254
Bluegrass, 264
Bluestone, 264
Board selection, 102–108
Boating: A.B.S., 335; aluminum, 334; canoes, 333; catamarans, 333; Corlite, 335; dinghies, 334; fiberglass, 334; folding boats, 334; Hypalon, 335; john boat, 334; kayaks, 333–334; materials, 334; oars, 334; outboard motors, 334; package trips, 334; paddles, 334; plastic, 334; polystyrene, 334; polyvinyl chloride, 335; rentals, 334; rowboats, 333; rubberized boats, 334; rubberized canvas, 334; sailboats, 332–333; trimarans, 333; vinyl, 334; whitewater schools, 334
Body enegry, 8
Body tissues, 9
Border roses, 237
Bosc pear, 254
Boston ivy, 244
Botanic gardens, 245, 266–271
Boxing glove cactus, 228
Bowhunting, 348–350
Bows and Arrows: American Archery Council, 350; catalogs, 350; equipment, 348; fishing, 348, 349; hunting, 348; information, 348; publications, 350; targets, 349
Bracket lighting, 182
Bradshaw, Patricia Anne, 195–198
Bread, 7, 9
Brevik, Theodore J., 115–118
Brick, 93–98, 264; barbecue, 94; dividers, 95; edgings, 94–96; enclosures, 95–96; fences, 95; fireplace, 94, 96; flooring, 96; planting boxes, 94–97; sizes, 94; texture, 96; veneer, 98; walls, 94–97
British Thermal Units, 177
Broccoli, 8
Brooklyn Botanic Gardens, 245
Brooms, 201
Browallia, 212, 215
Browning, Armistead W., 261–265
Brown-outs, 164–165
Brush, Ray, 246–250
Brushes, 203
Brussels sprouts, 8
Buckthorn, 248
Budget, 18–21
Building: carports, 149–153; codes, 152; ceiling insulation, 135; cement flooring, 122; chimneys, 175–176; closets, 174; concrete, 90–102; doors, 137–142, 153; electrical wiring, 125–129; garages, 149–153; home improvements, 90–102; insulation, 133–136; lumber, 102–108; nails, 111–113; paneling, 108–115; plywood, 108–114; remodeling, 174–175; roofs, 142–143, 153; ventilation, 115–118; windows, 137; wood flooring, 118
Building Officials and Code Administration International, Inc., 131
Bulbs, 246
Burgener, Maurice L., 90–93
Burolandschaft, 230
Butter, 83
Bye, A. E., 261–265
Buying: cut flowers, 219–222; food, 21–27; a horse, 322–323; seedlings, 208–218; seeds, 207–208; small appliances, 166

Cabbage, 8, 213, 218
Cabinets, 183
Cacti, 226–229
Calamondin, 256
Calceolaria, 212
Calcium, 3, 6, 27, 63
Calendula, 209, 212, 215
Callahan, Kevin D., 98–102
Cameras, 339–344
Campanula, 212, 215
Canarium ovatum, 256
Candytuft, 212, 215
Canners, 41–44
Canning, 41–44; fruits, 59; meats, 41–44; vegetables, 41, 59
Canoes, 333
Cantaloupes, 8
Carambola, 258
Caribbean fruit fly, 260
Carica papaya, 257
Caring for cut flowers, 219–222
Carissa, 257
Carlson, Jean K., 168–170
Carlson, R. F., 253–255
Carlson, William H., 208–219
Carnation, 212, 215, 219
Carob, 257
Carpet, 118, 197
Carpet and Rug Industry Consumer Action Panel, 284
Carports, 149–153
Carrots, 8, 34
Car servicing, 306–307
Casein, 3
Cast iron pipe, 132
Catamaran, 333
Cattley guava, 257
Cauliflower, 213, 218
Caustic liquids, 199
Ceiling insulation, 135; light fixture, 180; tile, 112; plywood, 112–113
Celery, 8, 213, 218
Cellulose fiber, 133
Celosia, 212, 215
Celotex, 112
Cement flooring, 122
Centaurea, 209, 212, 215
Central heating, 154
Cephalocereus, 227
Cephalocereus senilis, 228
Ceramic tile, 118; floors, 119; walls, 148
Ceratonia siliqua, 257
Cereals, 7–8, 20
Chain department stores, 278–280
Chamaecereus sylvestri, 228
Chamaedorea erumpeus, 230
Chandelier, 180
Charcoal filters, 166
Chassy, Judy P., 27–40
Cheese, 6, 83–84
Cherries, 253–255
Chest freezers, 166
Chicken, 21
Child nutrition, 292
Chimneys, 175–176
Chlorinated Polyvinyl Chloride, 131
Cholesterol, 64
Christensen, Edith A., 84–86
Christmas cherry, 224
Christmas pepper, 225
Chrome chandeliers, 180
Chrysanthemums, 219
Chutney, 256
Citrus, 257; *aurantifolia*, 258; *blancoi*, 259
Clarkia, 212, 215
Clay tile, 118, 122
Cleaning materials, 198–201
Cleistocactus, 228
Clematis, 243
Clemens, Bette, 282–286
Cleveland, Alan, 277–282
Climbing hydrangea, 244
Closets, 174, 183–186
Clostridium botulinum, 42–43
Clothes for riding horses, 323
Clover, 264
Coccolobis uviferas, 259
Coal and wood burning stoves, 176
Coconut, 258
Cocos nucifera, 258
Coffee, 21
Cold water pipe, 131
Coleus, 212, 215, 218
Collector plates, 154
College Entrance Examination Board, 288
College Level Examination Program, 288
College Scholarship Service, 288
Combining foods, 5–18
Committee on Food and Nutrition, 2
Concrete, 90–102; barbecue, 94; blocks, 98–102; casting flagstones, 92; finishing, 92; fireplace, 94; home improvements, 90–102; mixing, 90–92; mortar, 101; patio, 94; paving, 94; shadowall block, 101; steel reinforced, 90; texture, 100–101; types, 94; units, 101; weep holes, 95; workmanship, 101
Concrete Block, 98–102; designs, 98–102; size, 98; texture, 100
Conduction, 133
Conklin, Everett, 230–233
Consumer Action Panels, 284
Consumer Product Safety Commission, 286
Consumer Report Buying Guide, 166
Consumer service, 282
Container grown plants, 247
Container plant growth, 257
Convection, 133, 157
Cooling, 133–136
Cooling systems, 154–162
Copper, 3
Copper pipe, 132
Cords, appliance, 127; asbestos insulated, 126–127; coil, 127; color coded, 127; dryer, 127; range, 127; telephone, 127
Cork tile, 120
Corn, 43; products, 85–86
Cornice lighting, 182
Corps of Engineers installations camping, 316
Corrosion resistant pipe, 132
Coryphantha, 227
Cosmos, 212, 215
Cottage cheese, 6
Coulter, Olivia W., 295–298
Counseling for older people, 295
Cove lighting, 182
Crandall, Mardel L., 44–50
Crassula, 229
Cream cheese, 6
Credit shopping, 298–302
Creosote, 177–178
Crimson Pigmy barberry, 248
Cromwell, Cynthia, 18–21
Cucumber, 213, 218
Cultivars, 257, 260

Cunningham, W. E., 241–245
Currant, 250–253
Curtains, 186–190
Cut flowers, 219–222
Cutting flowers, 220
Cyclamen, 225
Cynoglossum, 212, 215

Dahlia, 212, 215
Daily Dietary Requirements, 2–5
Damper, 178
Darland, Dave, 286–290
Dash, Kenneth S., 146–147
Dawes Arboretum, 269
Deciduous plants, 246
deHoll, J. C., 68
Delphinium, 222
Design for gardens, 261–270
Desserts, 84
Detergents, 170; 198–199
Detty, G. William, 93–98
de Vos, Francis, 266–270
Dianthus, 212, 216
Diet, 20–21
Diffused lighting, 179, 181
Dimmer switches, 183
Dimocarpus, 258
Dimorphotheca, 212, 216
Diospuros kaki, 257
Direct lighting, 179
Directory of American Horticulture, 250
Dishwasher, 165
Dogwood, 248
Dollar stretching, 27–41
Door openers, 153
Doors, bi-fold, 141; exterior, 137; factory finished, 141–142; glass, 140; hollow core, 137; interior, 137–142; metal, 142; plastic, 141; refrigerator, 140; screen, 137; solid core, 137; steel 140; unfinished, 141; vinyl-covered, 140; width, 141–142; wood, 140
Doors, garage, 153; automatic, 153; pedestrian, 153; remote controlled, 153
Dracaena, 232
Drain pipe, 132
Drapes, 186–190
Dried foods, 5
Drill Bits, 202–203
Dryers, 168–170
Ducts, 154
Dude ranches, 317
Dunning, H. Neal, 62–70
Durian, 256
Durio zibethinus, 256
Dwarfing fruit trees, 253–254
DWV pipe, 132

Earthquake construction, 175–176
Easter lily, 224–225
Echeveria, 227
Echinocactus grusonii, 227
Echinocereus, 227
Echinocereus dasyacanthus, 228
Echinopsis, 229
Education planning, 286
Eggplant, 213, 218
Eggs, 20, 29, 56; grade standards, 56; labeling, 56
Electric: casserole, 167; cords, 126–127; drill, 202; dryers, 169; fireplace, 178; grooming aids, 174; motors, 125–126; outlets, 174; range units, 167–168; wattage, 126; wiring, 125–129
Electrical maintenance: amperage, 125; asbestos insulation, 127; bulbs, 129; circuit breaker, 125; cords, 126–127; fluorescent tubes, 129; fuses, 125; fustats, 125–126; Krypton gas, 129; repair, 125; rheostat, 127; switches, 127–128; volts, 126
Electrolysis, 131
Electrostatic air cleaner, 154–156
Ellithorpe, Vera E., 175–178
Emergency automobile aids, 309
Emperor cherries, 254
Encyclopedia of cactus, 229
Energy, body, 8; efficiency ratio, 164; foods, 10; heating, cooling, 133
English ivy, 243
English Morello cherries, 254
Environmental effects, 263–264
Epiphyllum, 228
Epoxy, 118
Eriobotrya japonica, 260
Eugenia dombeyi, 258
Eugenia uniflora, 260
Euonymus, 244
Euonymus colorata, 243
Extension cords, 174, 202–203

Fabricated foods, 5
Factory built fireplaces, 176
Facts about freezing, 44–51
Fair Credit Reporting Act of 1971, 302
Fantasia nectarine, 254
Farm vacations, 317
Fast, M. T., 108–111
Fats, 10
Faucets, 173
Faucharia, 228
Federal Food Standards, 55–62
Federal-State food programs, 290
Federal Trade Commission, 285
Fences: basket weave, louvered, slat, 264
Fenestraria rhopalophylla, 228
Fernemetal, 144
Ferris, Eleanor, 51–54
Fertilizers, 70, 214, 246, 255
Fescue, 264
Feuchter, Roy W., 314–321
Feijoa, 260
Fiber, 8
Fiberboard, 112
Fiberglass filters, 166; shower, 172
Fig, 257
Filters, 166
Finks, Larry L., 321–323
Fireboxes, 175
Firebrick, 176
Fireplaces, 94–96, 175–178; chimneys, 175–176; damper, 178; Earthquake construction, 175–176; electric fireplace, 178; factory built, 176; fireboxes, 175; firebrick, 176; firescreen, 178; flue, 176; Franklin Stove, 176–177; gas logs, 178; hearth, 176; masonry fireplace, 176; metal, 176; modified, 176; non-combustible heat-resistant material, 176; prefabricated, 176; spark arresters, 178; ventilation, 178; wall-hung chimney, 176
Fiscus carica, 257
Fish, 9, 20–21
Fishing: bait casting, 337–338; bamboo pole, 338; barbless hooks, 338; boron rods, 338; bugs, 336; cane pole and equipment, 335–336; fly fishing, 336–337; flyrods, 337; high modulus graphite fiber rods, 338; ice fishing, 338; jigs, 336; natural baits, 336; plugs, 336; ponds, 319; spin casting, 337; spinners, 336; spinning gear, 336; spoons, 336
Flagstones, 92–94
Flat roof, 176
Float trips, 319
Floor, asphalt tile, 119; brick, 96; carpet, 118; cement, 122; ceramic tile, 118; clay tile, 118, 122; cork tile, 120; drains, 153; epoxy, 118; furnace, 154; insulation, 135; latex, 118; linoleum, 118; mosaic tile, 122; quarry tile, 122; resinous matrixes, 122; rubber tile, 118, 119; sheet vinyl, 119; stone, 120; terrazzo, 120; vinyl, 119; vinyl-asbestos, 119; wood, 118
Floribunda roses, 237
Florida Mango Forum, 261
Flower arranging, 221–222
Flue, 176
Fluorescent lighting, 179; tubes, 129
Fogg, Helen B., 226–229
Fogg, John M., Jr., 226–229
Folacin, 3
Folding boats, 334
Foliage characteristics, 234
Food and Drug Administration, 285
Food and Nutrition Board, 2
Food: barbecue, 94; beans, 26, 29, 56, 60; beef, 78–80; budget, 18–21; butter, 83; calcium, 6, 27, 63; calories, 5; canned, 5, 26, 41–44; carrots, 29–34; cereals, 26, 56, 60; cheese, 27, 51, 56, 60, 83–84; cherries, 59; chicken, 21, 27–28, 51, 53, 56–57, 60, 68; cholesterol, 64; cleaning, 88; color quality, 59; corn, 43; corn products, 85–86; costs, 18–21; desserts, 84; dried, 5, 26, 29; eggs, 29, 53, 56, 60; energy, 8–17; fabricated, 5; fats, 10; fish, 27, 51, 60; fortified, 5; frankfurters, 59; freezing, 87; fresh, 5, 26; frozen, 26, 60; fruit flavored, 5; fruits, 26, 29, 41, 48, 51, 53–54, 56, 60; grades, 51–54; handling, 88; health foods, 71–73; ice cream, 27, 60, 62; jams, 43; jellies, 26, 43; labels, 55–58; lamb, 52; leftovers, 26; marmalade, 43; meat, 27, 41, 46–47, 51, 57–58, 60, 68, 78–81; mellorine, 62; menu suggestions, 12–16; milk, 6, 27, 51, 53–56, 60, 65, 81–83; niacin, 63; nutrients, 3, 5, 48; nutrition, 62–70; Nutritional Quality Guidelines, 69; oat products, 86; oleomargarine, 62; orange juice, 34–36; organic, 70–73; pasteurization, 43; peas, 29; pickles, 43; planning, 18–21; pork, 80; potatoes, 26; poultry, 27, 51, 53, 56–58, 60, 68; preparation, 5; preservation, 41–44; preserves, 43, 53, 56, 60–61; processed, 72; protein, 9, 29–40, 63; quantity guide, 21–26; refrigeration, 87; relishes, 43; riboflavin, 63; rice, 26, 56, 60; rice products, 86; safety, 87–88 servings, 21–26; spinach, 26; stamps, 18; standards, 55–59, 62–70; sugar, 43; tomatoes, 41; turkey, 27–28, 51, 53, 56, 60, 68; unit pricing, 76; utensils, 87–88; vegetables, 26, 29, 41, 46–48, 51, 60; vitamins, 5–17; warming trays, 167; waste, 26; yogurt, 27
Food dollars, 21–26
Food Stamp Program, 292
Forsythia, 222, 248
Fortified foods, 5
Fortunella japonica, 260
Foster Grandparent Program, 297

Fountain, Sarah F., 147-149
Frankfurter, 59
Franklin Stove, 176-177
Free universities, 289
Freezers, 44-50, 164, 166
Freezing fruits, 253
Fresh foods, 5
Frost-free freezer, 166
Frozen foods, 5
Fruit flavored foods, 5
Fruits, 6-17, 250-253; blackberry, 250, 253; blueberry, 250, 253; canned, 26, 54; currant, 250-253; fresh, 54; frozen, 26, 54; gooseberry, 250-253; grades, 54; grape, 250-253; Home Freezing, 47; *How to Buy Fresh*, 47; raspberry, 250-253; strawberry, 250, 252-253; trees, 253-255
Fuel, 154-162; coal, 156; electricity, 156; gas, 156; natural gas, 160; oil, 156; wood, 156
Fulton, Lois H., 21-26
Fungicides, 244
Furniture: 185; aluminum, 195; bedding, 194; cast iron, 196; cushions, 191; drawers, 193-194; fabrics, 191; fiberglass, 196; finishes, 192; glass, 196; investment, 190-195; molded, 196; outdoor, 195; steel, 195; upholstering, 191; value, 190-195; wrought iron, 195-196
Furniture Industry Consumer Action Panel, 284
Fuses, 125
Fustats, 125-126

Gaillardia, 212, 216
Galvanized iron pipe, 132
Garages, 149-153
Garcinia mangostana, 256
Garden centers, 246; Garden, 261-265; drainage, 262; maintenance firms, 312
Garden Club of America, 250
Gardening, 205-219
Garnet beauty peach, 254
Garvey, Edward B., 327-332
Gas logs, 178
Gazania, 212, 216
General diffused lighting, 181
Geraniums, 218
Gilman, Francis E., 149-153
Glare-free light, 182
Glue, 110, 204
Godbey, Luther C., 154-162
Gomphrena, 212, 216
Gooseberry, 250-253
Gottschalk, Anna Marie, 195-198
Grab bars, 174
Grades: canned fruits, 54; canned vegetables, 54; dairy products, 53; eggs, 53; frozen fruits, 54; frozen vegetables, 54; lumber, 103-108; meats, 51-52; plywood, 109-111; poultry, 53
Grading roses, 237
Grain products, 84-86; flour, 84; macaroni, 85; spaghetti, 85; wheat cereals, 85
Grandifloras, 237
Grape, 250-253
Grapefruit, 8
Grass, 264
Gravel, 264
Grease traps, 166-167
Green Thumbers, 206-270, 297, 310-312
Ground covers, 241-245
Ground-Fault Interrupter, 129;
Growing seedlings, 208-218; small fruits, 250-253
Grumichama, 258
Guacamole, 258
Guava, 8, 256, 257
Guide to Federal Consumer Services, 285
Gymnocalycium, 229
Gypsophila, 212, 216, 222
Gypsum Association, 115

Hacksaw, 202
Hale, E. B., 130-132
Hammer, 202
Hanging light fixture, 181
Hard temper copper pipe, 132
Harding, Virginia L., 137-142
Hardwood Plywood Manufacturers, 115
Health foods, 71-73
Hearth, 176
Heat control, 167
Heaters, 175-178
Heath, Mary, 286-290
Heating, 133-136, 167, 175-178; systems, 154-162, 175-178
Heavy duty tubing, 130
Hedelfingen cherries, 254
Hedera helix, 243
Heliotrope, 212, 216
Hemoglobin, 9
High School Equivalency examination, 289
Hill, Mary M., 5-17
Hill, Walter H., 118-122
Hollyhock, 212, 216
Holly Society of America, Inc., 250
Homasote, 112
Home-delivered meals, 296
Home: freezers, 44-50; gardening, 250-253; heating, 164; improvements, 90-93; laundry appliances, 168-170
Home construction: asbestos insulation, 127; asbestos shingles, 113; brick flooring, 96; brick walls, 94-97; building codes, 152; carports, 149-153; ceiling insulation, 135; ceiling tile, 112; cement flooring, 122; central heating, 154; chimneys, 175-176; closets, 174; concrete, 90-102; cooling systems, 154-162; doors, 137-142, 153; electrical wiring, 125-129; floor drains, 153; garages, 149-153; heating systems, 154-162, 175-178; home improvements, 90-102; insulation, 133-136; lumber, 102-108; nails, 111-113; paint, 148; paneling, 108-115; plywood, 108-114; plywood ceilings, 112-113; remodeling, 174-175; roofs, 142-143, 153; ventilation, 115-118; windows, 137; wood flooring, 118
Home Ventilating Institute, 116, 164
Horses: buying a horse, 322-323; clothing for riding, 323; equipment, 323; novice riding, 321; polo, 321; renting a horse, 321-322; saddles, 323; trailer, 323
Horticulture training, 246
Hot air gravity heating, 154
Houseboating, 319
Household equipment, 164-170; goods shipment, 276
House remodeling, 183-186
Housing for older Americans, 295
Howland, Joseph E., 206-208
Hub type joint, 132
Hudson cherries, 254
Hughes, Jim, 339-344
Human food requirements, 3, 5
Humidifier, 156
Humidistat, 156
Hunt grapes, 252
Hunting with bow and arrow, 348-350
Hybrids, 206
Hybrid tea roses, 237
Hydrangea, 226
Hydrangea petiolaris, 244
Hydrogen, 70

Ice: cream, 6, 27; dams, 145; fishing, 338; milk, 6
Impatiens, 212, 216, 218
Incandescent lighting, 179
Independence nectarine, 254
Indian Health Service, 294
Indirect lighting, 179
Indoor lights, 182
Information for Consumers, 283
Inorganic, 70-73
Insecticides, 240
Insulation: batts, 133; ceiling, 135; cellulose fiber, 133; conduction, 133; convection, 133; cooling, 133-136; effects of moisture, 136; fire resistant, 136; floor, 135; heating, 133-136; mineral wool, 133; neoprene, 126; polyurethane, 133; radiation, 133; ratings, 134; reflective, 133; rigid, 134; standards, 135-136; structural requirements, 136; values, 134-136; ventilation, 136; vermiculite, 133; vermin resistance, 136; wall, 135
Insulation board, 113
Insulators, 133
Insulite, 112
Interior landscaping, 230-233
Iodine, 3
Iodized salt, 69
Iron, 5, 9

Jaboticaba, 258
Jams, 43, 61
Japanese persimmon, 257
Japanese spurge, 243
Japanese Wisteria, 244
Jellies, 26, 43, 56
Jerusalem cherry, 224
John boat, 334
Johnson, Ogden C., 62-70
Juices, 8
Junior foods, 67
Juniper, 264

Kalanchoe, 225; *tomentosa*, *K. pinnata*, 228
Kayaks, 333-334
Keauhou, 260
Keil, Bill, 344-348
Keller, Patsy, 190-195
Kelly, Eleanor M., 298-302
Kerchner, Orval, 290-295
Kerr, Richard, 18-21
Key lime, 256
Kilocalories, 3
Kimball, Thomas L., 335-338
Kira, Alexander, 170-175
Kitchen appliances, 164; cabinets, 184; light fixtures, 179; test, 57
Kiwi, 257
Knight, Robert J., Jr., 256-261
Kochia, 212, 216
Kohala, 258
Korbobo, Raymond P., 310-312
Krypton gas, 129
Kumquat, 260

Labeling, 55-70, 62-70, 73-75; standards, 55-62; artificial color, 59; beef, 57; milk, 55; pork, 58; poultry, 57
Labor's Senior Aides Program, 297
Lactating females, 3
Lamb, 9, 52

Lamp shades, 182
Lanais, 195
Landscape architect, 265
Landscape Contractor Maintenance, 311
Larkspur, 212, 216, 222
Latex tile, 118
Lattices, 264
Laundry equipment, 164–166, 168–170
Lavatories, 173
Lavender hybrid tea rose, 237
Lawn seed, 207; specialists, 310
Lead pipe, 132
Leaf texture, 234
Leftovers, 26
Legal Services for Older Americans, 295
Legumes, 8, 20
Lemons, 8
Lettuce, 213, 218
Leverton, Ruth M., 70–73
Lighting: bathroom, 174; bracket, 182; ceiling fixture, 180; chrome chandelier, 180; cornice, 182; cove, 182; diffused, 179, 181; dimmer switches, 185; direct, 179; equipment, 179; fixtures, 179; fluorescent, 179; general diffused, 181; glare-free, 182; hanging fixture, 181; incandescent, 179; indirect, 179; indoor, 182; kitchen fixture, 169, 179; lampshades, 182; outdoor, 182, 197; pendant, 181; permanent fixture, 180; permanent outdoor, 182; portable, 182; portable fixture, 180; recessed fixture, 180; sidewalk, 182; specific, 182; standards, 164; switches, 127–128; table lamps, 182; three-way, 182; timers, 183; tungsten filament, 179; wall mounted, 181; weatherproof outlets, 182
Lilac, 248
Lilium longiflorum, 224
Limes, 256, 258
Lines to sewers, 132
Linoleum, 118
Litanium dioxide, 148
Loans, 298–300
Lobelia, 212, 216
Local plumbing contractor, 132
Logs: artificial, 177; gas, 178
Longan, 257
Longwood Gardens, 245
Loquat, 256, 257
Low acid foods, 41
Lumber, 102–108; American Lumber Standards Committee, 106; American Softwood Lumber Standard, 106–108; beams, 107; boards, 103–106; California redwood, 108; common, 103; dimension, 103–106; dressed, 106; factory and shop, 103; framing members, 108; furring strips, 108; grades, 103–108; headers, 106; joists, 106; light framing, 106; marks, 103–107; National Grading Rule, 107; paneling, 108; pressure-treated, 107; rafters, 106; rough, 106; select, 103; selection, 102–108; sills, 107; sizes, 103–106; sleepers, 107; softwood, 102; span tables, 107; structural joints and planks, 106; structural light framing, 103, 106; stud, 106; tidewater red cypress, 108; timbers, 103–106; types, 103; Western red cedar, 108; worked, 106
Lupine, 212, 216
Lychee, 257
Lyle, Eldon W., 236–241
Lynch, Jeannette M., 298–302

Macadamia nut, 260
Magnesium, 3
Mail order nurseries, 246, 249
Major Appliance Consumer Action Panel, 165, 284
Major engine overhauls, 307
Mammillaria, 227; bocasana, 228; *hahniana*, 228
Mangifera, 259
Mango, 8, 256
Mangosteen, 256
Manual defrost freezer, 166
Manufacturer's guarantee, 282
Marigold, 212, 216, 222
Markert, William P., 122–125
Marmalade, 43
Masking tape, 204
Masonite, 112
Masonry: fireplace, 176; flue, 176; patterns, 101; veneers, 101
Master bath, 171
Meat, 20, 78–81; alternates, 9; Beef, 78–80; canning, 41–44; cookery, 81; cuts of, 78–81; *Home Freezing*, 47; *How to Buy For Your Freezer*, 47; Lamb, 81; Pork, 80; products, 78; terms, 79–81
Medicaid Program, 297
Mellorine, 62
Melons, 8
Men's Garden Clubs of America, 250
Menu suggestions, 12–16
Mericrest nectarine, 254
Mesembryanthemum, 212, 216
Metal fireplace, 176
Mexican lime, 256
Mexicola, 259
Microwave range, 165
Milk, 6, 81–83; canned, 82; cream, 82; cultured, 82; dry, 82–83; freezing, 48; products, 6; terms, 81
Mineral wool, 133
Miniature roses, 238
Minimum Daily Requirement (MDR), 62–70
Minimum Property Standards, 136
Missouri Botanical Gardens, 245
Modern Roses VII, 237
Modified fireplace, 176
Modular shower, 172
Montmorency cherry, 254
Morning Glory, 212, 216
Morton Arboretum, 245
Mosaic tile, 122
Moving: foreign, local, interstate, intrastate, 274–275; furniture, 272–277; planning a move, 272–277
Mower, Robert G., 233–236
Mulches, 238, 246, 264
Munson, Karl, 332–335
Musa, 258
Muscadine grapes, 252
Muskmelon, 213, 218
Mussman, Harry C., 55–62
Myers, Doris M., 198–201
Myrciaria cauliflora, 258
Myrtle, 264

Nails, 202; aluminum, 111; annular-grooved, 113; hot dip galvanized, 111; nonstaining, 111; shingle, 111
Napoleon cherries, 254
Nasturtium, 212, 216
Nathan, Tink, 348–350
National Academy of Sciences, 2
National Arboretum, 245
National Automobile Dealers Association, 284
National Council of State Garden Clubs, Inc., 250
National Defense Student Loan, 288
National Electric Code, 129
National Forest Products, 107
National forests, 314
National Marine Fisheries Service, 56
National parks, 314–315
National Particleboard Association, 115
National Research Council, 2
National Retired Teachers Association, 297
National Sanitation Foundation, 132
National School Lunch Program, 290
Nectarines, 254
Nemesia, 212, 216
Neoprene insulation, 126
Nephelium lappaceum, 256
New lawn specialists, 311
Newman, Jerry O., 142–145
Newspaper logs, 177
Niacin, 9–17, 63
Nichols, Jennie B., 27–40
Nickerson, Anne, 149–153
Nicotiana, 212
Nierembergia, 212, 217
Noise Control, 113, 114
Non-combustible heat-resistant material, 176
Non-resilient flooring, 120
Non-skid decals, 174
Novice horse riding, 321
Nurseries: catalogues, 246, 249, 254, 255; mail order, 246, 247, 249, 255; retail, 246, 247, 249, 255; stock, 246, 248, 249, 250, 253; wholesale, 246, 255
Nutrients, 5, 20, 48, 62–70
Nutrition, 20, 62–70
Nutrition Program for the Elderly, 295, 298
Nutritional Quality Guidelines, 69

Oat products, 86
Older American Aid, 295–298
Older Americans Act, 295
Older Americans Community Service Program, 297
Old lady cactus, 228
Old man cactus, 228
Oleomargarine, 62
Olive, 257
Olsson, Charlene, 55–62
Opuntia, 227; *O. mamillata*, 228
Onion, 213, 218
Open Dating, 76–77
Open universities, 289
Orange juice, 34–35
Oranges, 8
Organic, 70–73
Outboard motors, 334
Outdoor: lighting, 182; living, 195–198

Pachysandra, 264; *P. terminalis*, 243
Packing to move, 272
Paint: equipment, 148, 203; flat, 148; high gloss, 148; latex, 148; oil-based, 148; semi-gloss, 148; water based, 148
Paneling: chipboard, 112; chipcore, 112; flakeboard, 112; gypsum board, 112; hardboard, 112; insulation board, 111–113; paperboard, 112; plywood, 108–111; products, 112–115; shavings board, 112; sheathing, 111, 113; sizes, 112
Pansy, 212, 217
Pantothenic acid, 3
Papaya, 8, 257
Paperboard, 112
Paraffin, 43

Parevine, 62
Parthenocissus tricuspidata, 244
Passionfruit, 256, 259
Pasteurization, 43
Patios, 195
Patterson, Ralph, 332–335
Peaches, 254
Peanut butter, 20
Peanut-cactus, 228
Pears, 253–255
Peas, 8, 20
Pediocactus, 227
Pellets, 206
Pendant light fixture, 181
Peppers, 8, 213, 218
Periwinkle, 243
Perlins, 145
Peterkin, Betty, 73–75
Peterson, William H., 125–129
Petunia, 212, 217
pH, 41
Phlox, 209, 212, 217
Phosphorous, 3, 71
Photography: cameras, 340, 341, 343, 344; directories, 344; film, 343–344; filters, 341; gadget bag, 343; lenses, 340, 341, 343; light meter, 340; photo annuals, 344; range-finder, 344; self timer, 343; tripod, 341–343; zoom lens, 343
Picket fence, 264
Pickles, 43
Pifer, Glenda, 183–186
Pili nut, 256
Pineapple, 8, 259
Pipe: ABS plastic, 132; cast iron, 132; cold water, 131; copper, 132; corrosion resistant, 132; deposits, 130; drain, 132; DWV, 132; for chemically active material, 132; galvanized iron, 132; hard temper copper, 132; lead, 132; plastic, 132; plastic DWV, 132; polyethelene, 131; PVC plastic, 132; smooth interior, 132; steel, 132; underground drain, 132; vent, 132; waste, 132; wrought iron, 132
Pitched roof, 176
Plant flats, 210
Plant Hardiness Zone Map, 256
Planters, 94–97
Planting roses, 239
Plants and humidity, 232
Pliers, 202
Plumbing supply outlet, 132
Plums, 8, 253–255
Plush plant, 228
Plywood, beviled siding, 110; built-ins, 109; cabinets, 108; ceilings, 109; doors, 109; edges, 110–111; exterior siding, 109, 111; fencing, 108; flooring, 110, 114; furniture, 109; Glued Floor System, 110; Identification Index, 109; insulation, 112; lap, 110; Medium Density Overload, 109; outdoor, 108; panels, 108, 109; patio decking, 108; processing, 108; resin-treated fiber, 109; roof sheathing, 111; sealed, 109; shelving, 108; Single Wall System, 110; species classification, 109–111; textured, 110; types, 109; unsanded, 109–110; varnished, 109; veneers, 108–111; water-repellent preservative, 110; waxed, 109; wind screens, 108
Poinsettias, 223
Polyantha roses, 237
Polybutalene, 131
Polyethylene, 131
Polyunsaturated, 63–64
Polyurethane, 133
Polyvinyl chloride, 148
Polyvinyl glue, 204
Pomegranate, 257
Pool: cleaning, 124; cost, 122; equipment, 123–124; installation, 122; selection, 123; site, 123; types, 124; upkeep, 123–125
Poppy, 212, 217
Pork, 9
Portable: dryers, 169; heaters, 178; lamps, 182; light fixture, 180; washers, 168
Portulaca, 213, 217
Potable water, 130
Potatoes, 26
Potted plants: Adam's needle, 228; *Agave,* 227; *Aizoceae,* 227; aphrodite begonias, 224; *Aporocactus,* 228; Astrophylum, 228; *A. myriostigma,* 228; Azaleas, 223–224; Baby's toes, 228; Bird's Nest Cactus, 228; Bishop's Cap, 228; Boxing glove cactus, 228; Cacti, 226–229; care of, 222–226; *Cephalocereus,* 227; *Cephalocereus senilis,* 228; *Chamaecereus sylvestri,* 228; Christmas Cherry, 224; Christmas pepper, 225; chrysanthemums, 224; *Cleistocactus,* 228; *Coryphantha,* 227; crassula, 229; cyclamen, 225; Dracaena, 232; Easter lily, 224; *Echeveria,* 227; *Echinocactus grusonii,* 227; *Echinocereus,* 227; *E. dasyacanthus,* 228; *Echinopsis,* 229; *Epiphyllum,* 228; *Faucharia,* 228; *Fenestraria rhopalophylla,* 228; *Gymnocalycum,* 229; Hydrangea, 226; *Kalanchoe,* 225; *K. pinnata,* 228; *K. tomentosa,* 228; *Mammillaria,* 227; M. bocasana, 228; M. hahniana, 228; Old Man cactus, 228; Old Lady cactus, 228; *Opuntia,* 227; O. mamillata, 228; Peanut-cactus, 228; *Pediocactus,* 227; Plush plant, 228; Poinsettias, 223; Powder Puff cactus, 228; rainbow cactus, 228; Rat tail cactus, 228; *Rebutia,* 229; *Rhipsalis,* 227; Rieger begonia, 224; sand dollar, 228; Schwabenland begonias, 224; *Sempervivum,* 227; Silver torch cactus, 228; *Sola pseudo-capsicum,* 224; succulents, 226–229; Tiger jaws, 228; White Trumpet Lily, 224; *Yucca filamentosa,* 228; Zygocactus, 228–229
Poultry, 20–21
Powder puff cactus, 228
Prange, Gerald F., 102–108
Prefabricated fireplace, 176
Pregnant females, 3, 6
Preliminary Scholastic Aptitude Test, 288
Preserves, 43
President's Office of Consumer Affairs, 305
Pressure canners, 41; Pressure cooker, 41–44; Pressure rating, 132; Pressure treated posts, 153
Pritchard, Iola, 41–44
Privately owned camp grounds, 317
Probe thermostat, 167
Processed food, 72
Professional garden maintenance, 311; landscape maintenance, 311; lawn maintenance, 311
Protective services for older Americans, 295
Protein, 3, 9, 29–40, 63
Protein Efficiency Ratio (PER), 3, 66
Pruning roses, 239
Psidium cattleianum, 259
Public domain vacation, 315
Punica granatum, 257
Purchase complaints, 282–286
Purchase, Mary E., 302–305
Purpleleaf Wintercreeper, 243
Puttying, 204
PVC plastic pipe, 132

Quarry tile, 122

Racks, 174
Radiation, 133
Radiators, 157–159
Rainbow cactus, 228
Rambutan, 256
Range hoods, 164; fans, 164
Rare Fruit Council International, Inc., 261
Raspberry, 250–253
Rat tail cactus, 228
RDA, 2–5
Rebutia, 229
Recessed light fixture, 180
Recommended Daily Allowance, 62–70
Redosier dogwood, 248
Reflective insulation, 133
Refrigerators, 164
Refrigerator-Freezer, 44–50
Refurbishing furniture, 185
Relishes, 43
Remodeling tips, 174–175
Renting a horse, 321–322
Repair jobs, 202–204
Repair services, 281
Resinous matrix flooring, 122
Resorts, 318
Retired garden help, 311
Retired Senior Volunteer Program, 297–298
Rheostats, 127
Rhipsalis, 227
Riboflavin, 3, 6, 9–17, 63
Rice, 26; products, 86
Ridge roof, 176
Rieger begonias, 224
Rodgers, Ava D., 190–195
Roofing: aluminum, 142; asbestos, 143; asphalt, 143; coatings, 142; copper, 143; flint, 143; gable, 153; gambrel, 153; shingle, 143; single-sloped shed, 153; slate, 143; weather-resistant, 142
Rootstocks, 237
Rose-apple, 260
Roses, 219, 236–241; border roses, 237; culture, 238–240; grading, 237; Polyantha, 237; floribunda, 237; hybrid tea roses, 237; miniatures, 238; planting roses, 239; pruning roses, 239; shrub roses, 238; tree roses, 238; vine roses, 238
Roth, Fred W., 137–142
Rowboats, 333
Rubber tile, 118, 119
Rubberized boats, 334
Rubis, Joseph A., 81–84
Rudbeckia, 213, 217
Rules for canning, 41–44

Saddles, 323
Safety aids, 174
Sailboats, 332–333
Salpiglossis, 213, 217
Salvia, 213, 217
Sand dollar, 228
Sanding machine, 204
Sandpaper, 204
Sanitizers, 198
Sapodilla, 259
Saturated, 64
Sauna, 170
Saw, 204
Scabiosa, 213, 217

Schizanthus, 213, 217
Schwabenland begonias, 224
Scissors, 203
School Breakfast Program, 290
Schools Without Walls, 289
Scott, D. H., 250–253
Screwdrivers, 202
Scuppernong grapes, 252
Seashore, 316
Seckel pear, 254
Second homes, 318
Sedum, 227
Seedlings: care, 209, 211–219; guide, 208–218
Seeds, 206–210
Sempervivum, 227
Senior Corps of Retired Executives, 298
Service contract, 304–305
Service and repair agencies, 303
Services for older Americans, 295
Shade-loving plants, 241–242
Shadowall, 101
Shank, Sandra Westall, 179–183
Sharpening stone, 203
Sheet vinyl, 119
Shelves, 174
Shingles: asbestos, 144–145; asphalt, 145; slate, 144–145; wood, 144
Shopper help for food buying, 51–55
Shopper language, 78–87
Shopping hints, 277–286
Shower heads, 174
Shrub roses, 238
Shrubs, 233–236, 263
Shutters, 186–190
Silver torch cactus, 228
Sinks, 173
Skiing: camping, 347–348; clothing, 347; equipment, 344–348; lease-purchase plan, 345; lessons, 345; lifts, 346; racks, 347; rentals, 345; safety, 347; shops, 345–346; sleeping bags, 347
Slate, 264
Small fruit by geographical excellence, 252–253
Smooth interior pipe, 132
Smyth, Julia M., 170–175
Snapdragon, 213, 217
Snyder, Rachel, 222–226
Soffits, 111
Softwood flooring, 120
Soft temper tubing, 130
Sola pseudo-capsicum, 224
Solder-type copper fittings, 131
Souders, Helen J., 2–5
Spark arrester, 178
Spartlet pear, 254
Special dietary foods, 67
Special Food Service Program, 292
Special Milk Program, 291
Special Supplemental Food Program for Women, Infants, Children, 294
Specific lighting, 182
Sphagnum moss, 247
Spinach, 26
Spinner washers, 168
Spiraea, 248
Standard tubing, 130
Standards: artificial color, 59; beef, 57; eggs, 56; fish, 55; milk, 55; nutrition, 62–70; pork, 58; poultry, 55
Stanford Research Institute, 164
State parks, 316
Statice, 213, 217
Stebbin Gulch, 269
Steel pipe, 132
Stepladder, 203
Stepping stones, 92
Stock, 213, 217
Stone flooring, 120
Storage, 149–153, 173–175; expandable shed, 153; gable roof, 153; gambrel-roofed, 153; portable, 153; prefabricated, 153; single-sloped shed roof, 153
Strawberries, 8, 250, 252–253
Strybing Arboretum, 245
Subtropical fruits, 256–261
Succulents, 226–229
Sugar, 21, 43
Sumac, 248
Summer squash, 213, 218
Sunhaven peach, 254
Supplementary Security Income, 296
Surinam-cherry, 260
Sweetpea, 213, 217
Switches, 165
Syzygium jambos, 260

Table lamps, 182
Tamarind, 257
Tamarindus indica, 257
Tangelo, 260
Tangerines, 8
Tapes, 206–208
Taylor, Eileen F., 76–77
Telephone shopping, 281
Terrace, 195
Terrazzo, 120
Thermostatically controlled: appliances, 167; electric heating units, 178
Thiamin, 3, 9–17
Thin walled tubing, 130
Thompson seedless grapes, 252
Three-way lighting, 182
Thunbergin, 213, 217
Tiger-jaws, 228
Tile floor covering, 118–122
Timers, 183
Toilet, 173
Toilet plunger, 200, 203
Tomatoes, 8, 41, 213, 218
Tools, 202–204
Torenia, 213, 217
Travel services, 320–321
Three roses, 238
Trees, 233–236, 263, 265
Trimaran, 333
Tropical fruit, 256
Tub growing, 256–261
Tubing: types L (standard), K (heavy duty), M (thin walled), 130
Tungsten filament, 179
Tyler, W. Edmund, 78–81

Underground drain pipe, 132
Underwriters' Laboratories, 164, 176
Unit pricing, 76
Upright freezer, 166
U.S. Postal Inspection Service, 285
Utilizing space, 183

Vacation planning, 314–321
Vacation sites: Corps of Engineers Installations, 316; dude ranches, 317; farm vacations, 317; fishing ponds, 319; float trips, 319; houseboating, 319; National Forests, 314; National Parks, 314–315; power company impoundments, 317; privately owned campgrounds, 317; public domain, 315; resorts, 318; seashores, 316; second homes, 318; skiing, 320; state parks, 316; wilderness trail excursions, 319
Vacuum cleaners, 201
Valves, insulation, 134–136
Vega cherries, 254
Vegetables, 6–17, 41–44
Vegetarian diet, 8, 17
Veneers, brick, 96; concrete, 99, 101; masonry, 101; plywood, 108–115
Vent pipe, 132
Ventilation, 115–118, 136–142; air movement, 116; bathroom, 116–118; building codes, 118; control, 118; crawl space, 115–116; doors, 116–117; ducts, 118; exhaust fan, 116–118; laundry, 116–118; range hood, 116; wall fans, 118
Verbena, 209, 213, 218
Vermiculite, 133
Vinca, 209, 213, 218, 243
Vine roses, 238
Vines, 241–245, 263
Vinyl: chloride resin, 148; flooring, 119; wall paper, 147; walls, 148
Viola, 213, 218
Vista cherries, 254
Vitamins, 5–17

Wall covering, 147–148, 173
Wall-hung chimney, 176
Wall insulation, 135
Wall materials: aluminum, 146; brick, 146; cedar, 146; ceramic tile, 147; concrete block, 146; cork, 147; fabrics, 147; fireproof, 146; gypsum board, 148; hardboard, 146; lap siding, 146; leather, 147; linoleum, 147; plastic materials, 147; plywood, 146; pressed wood, 148; redwood, 146; sheetrock, 147; stone, 146; stucco, 147; termite-proof, 146; vinyl, 146; wallpapers, 147
Wall-mounted light fixtures, 181
Wallpaper, 147–148
Wallpapering equipment, 148
Walls: exterior, 146; interior, 147
Warm-temperature fruit, 256–257
Warranties, 165, 281, 304–305
Warwick, Mary Ann, 108–111
Washing machine, 165–166, 168–170
Waste pipe, 132
Water: flavor, 130; hammer, 131; heating, 164
Watermelon, 213, 218
Wax, 199–200
Wax begonias, 218
Weatherproof outlets, 182
Weber, Jaunita, 186–190
Weep holes, 95
Weigla, 248
Werren, Fred, 112–115
Wheary, Cecil D., 133–136
White Trumpet Lily, 224–225
Whitewater boating schools, 334
Wholesale nurseries, 246, 249
Wilder, Russell M., 2
Wilderness trail excursions, 319
Windows: covering, 189; draperies, 190; fixed, 137; frames, 188; planning, 142; screens, 186; shades, 187; shutters, 187; sliding, 137; swinging, 137
Wiring, 154–162
Wisteria floribunda, 244
Women's National Farm and Garden Association, Inc., 250
Wood: flooring, 118, 120; plane, 204
Wrenches, 204
Wringer washers, 168

Yardstick, 203
Yogurt, 27
Youngsters for yard work, 311
Yucca zilamentosa, 228

Zinc, 3
Zinnia, 213, 218, 222
Zygocactus, 228–229